ENCYCLOPEDIA
OF THE
STATELESS NATIONS

ENCYCLOPEDIA OF THE STATELESS NATIONS

Ethnic and National Groups
Around the World

VOLUME IV
S–Z

James Minahan

GREENWOOD PRESS
Westport, Connecticut • London

Library of Congress Cataloging-in-Publication Data

Minahan, James.
    Encyclopedia of the stateless nations : ethnic and national groups around the world /
James Minahan.
      p. cm.
    Includes index.
    ISBN 0–313–31617–1 (set : alk. paper)—ISBN 0–313–32109–4 (v. 1 :
alk. paper)—ISBN 0–313–32110–8 (v. 2 : alk. paper)—ISBN 0–313–32111–6 (v. 3 :
alk. paper)—ISBN 0–313–32384–4 (v. 4 : alk. paper)
    1. World politics—1989—Dictionaries. 2. Nationalism—History—20th century—
Dictionaries. 3. Ethnic conflict—History—20th century—Dictionaries. 4. Stateless-
ness—Dictionaries. I. Minahan, James. Nations without states. II. Title.
D860.M56 2002
909.82'9'03—dc21   2001033691

British Library Cataloguing in Publication Data is available.

Library of Congress Catalog Card Number: 2001033691
ISBN: 0–313–31617–1 (set)
      0–313–32109–4 (Vol. I)
      0–313–32110–8 (Vol. II)
      0–313–32111–6 (Vol. III)
      0–313–32384–4 (Vol. IV)

First published in 2002

Greenwood Press, 88 Post Road West, Westport, CT 06881
An imprint of Greenwood Publishing Group, Inc.
www.greenwood.com

Printed in the United States of America

The paper used in this book complies with the
Permanent Paper Standard issued by the National
Information Standards Organization (Z39.48–1984).

10 9 8 7 6 5 4 3 2 1

CONTENTS

Contents

Contents

PREFACE

This volume is an updated and greatly expanded sequel to the award-winning *Nations without States: A Historical Dictionary of Contemporary National Movements*, which was published in 1996 and contained information on over 200 national groups and their homelands. Since that time, many new national groups have emerged as part of the nationalist revival that began with the end of the Cold War a decade ago. The purpose of this encyclopedia is to provide readers with an easy-to-use, accurate, up-to-date guide to the many national groups in the contemporary world. It is being published at a time when national identity, ethnic relations, regional conflicts, and immigration are increasingly important factors in national, regional, and international affairs.

Encyclopedia of the Stateless Nations: Ethnic and National Groups Around the World follows the development of over 300 national groups from the earliest periods of their histories to the present. That collection of national surveys is an essential guide to the many emerging groups and the national groups that the world ignored or suppressed during the decades of the Cold War, the longest and most stable peace in the history of the modern world. The Cold War did give the world relative peace and stability, but it was a fragile peace and a stability imposed by force. When reading the descriptions of national groups and the analyses of their histories, it is important to keep in mind the broader context—the growing role of national identity worldwide. This encyclopedia, like its 1996 predecessor, addresses the post–Cold War nationalist resurgence, by focusing on the most basic element of any nationalism, the nation itself.

This encyclopedia contains 350 national surveys, short articles highlighting the historical, political, social, religious, and economic evolution of the many national groups that are now emerging to claim roles in the post–Cold War world order. The worth of this encyclopedia in part derives from its up-to-date information on the often virtually unknown national groups that are currently making news and on those that will produce future headlines, controversies, and conflicts.

In this book I have followed the same general approach taken in the previous book for choosing which national groups to cover. Selecting the national surveys to be included in the encyclopedia again presented numerous problems, not the least of which was the difficulty of applying a uniform criteria that could accommodate language, religion, common history, occupational specialization, regional localization, common culture, self-identification, and identification by others. In general, strict adherence to official government lists of ethnic groups has been avoided, as the compilation of such lists is often driven by political considerations. If government criteria were followed, national groups in such states as Turkey or Japan would not be included, because of government claims that there are no national minorities within their borders.

The national groups chosen for inclusion represent a perplexing diversity that share just one characteristic—they identify themselves as separate nations. The arduous task of researching this diversity has been made more complicated by the lack of a consensus on what constitutes a "nation" or "nation-state." There is no universally accepted definition of "nation," "country," or "state." The subject continues to generate endless debate and numerous conflicts.

An attempt to apply the criteria used to distinguish independent states foundered on the numerous anomalies encountered. Size is definitely not a criterion. Over 40 states recognize a building in Rome, covering just 108.7 acres, as an independent state. Nor is United Nations membership the measure of independence; Ukraine and Belarus (Byelorussia) were founding members of the United Nations in 1945 yet became independent only in 1991. Membership in such international organizations as the International Olympic Committee (IOC) or the Organization of African Unity (OAU) does not necessarily signify political independence. Antarctica issues postage stamps but has no citizens; Palestine has citizens and embassies in dozens of countries but is not in practice an independent state; and so on.

Webster's Unabridged Dictionary defines the word *nation* as "a body of people, associated with a particular territory, that is sufficiently conscious of its unity to seek or possess a government particularly its own." On the basis of this definition, the criteria for selecting nations for inclusion was narrowed to just three important factors, modified by the diversity of the nations themselves. The three factors are self-identity as a distinctive group, the display of the outward trappings of national consciousness (particularly the adoption of a flag, a very important and very emotional part of any nationalism), and the formation of a specifically nationalist organization or political grouping that reflects its claim to self-determination. Many stateless nations were eliminated from the encyclopedia when one of these three factors could not be found during the exhaustive research process. National identity is often difficult to define and is very tricky to measure. For that reason this definitive volume of twenty-first-century nationalism contains a number of national groups whose identity is disputed but that met the criteria.

In any compilation, the selection process for choosing which material to include is a complex evolution of subtractions and additions. Estimates of the number of national groups in the world run as high as 9,000, making the selection process truly a process of elimination. The nations included in these volumes therefore represent only a fraction of the world's stateless nations.

Each national survey is divided into several parts or headings: the name and alternative names of the group; population statistics, incorporating the total national population and its geographical distribution; the homeland, including location, size, population, capital cities, and major cultural centers; the people and culture; the language and religion; a brief sketch of the national group's history and present situation; the national flag or other pertinent flags; and a map that places the national homeland in a local geographic setting.

Most of the nations included in this encyclopedia played little or no role in international politics before the end of the Cold War. Some of the national groups will be familiar, historically or more recently as news items, but the majority are virtually unknown and do not have standardized names or spellings in English. Familiar names often were, or are, the colonial or imposed names that in themselves represented a particularly harsh form of cultural suppression. That situation is now being reversed, with scholars, cartographers, and geographers attempting to settle on the definitive forms of the names of national groups, territories, and languages. Until that process is completed, many of the names used in these volumes will not only be unfamiliar but will not appear in even the most comprehensive reference sources.

The population figures are the author's estimates for the year 2002. The figures are designated by the abbreviation "(2002e)" before the appropriate statistics. The figures were gleaned from a vast number of sources, both official and unofficial, representing the latest censuses, official estimates, and—where no other sources were available—nationalist claims. Where important disparities over group size exist, both the official and the claimed population figures are included. Official rates of population growth, urban expansion, and other variables were applied to the figures to arrive at the statistics included in the encyclopedia. Since very few of the world's national groups are confined to one territory, the population statistics also includes information on geographic distribution.

Information on the homeland of each national group includes the geographic location and general features of the territory. Most of the national groups are concentrated in defined national territories—a state, province, region or historical region, department, etc. The corresponding features are included in this section, even though most territorial claims are based on historical association, not modern ethnic demographic patterns, provincial boundaries, or international borders. The geographic information incorporates the size of the territory, in both square miles (sq. mi.) and square kilometers (sq. km). The population figures for the larger cities cover the populations within city limits, and where appropriate, populations of surrounding urban or metropolitan areas. The two figures are included in an effort to reconcile the vastly different methods of enumerating urban populations used by the various governments and international agencies. A list of the principal statistical sources is provided at the end of this section.

Current political events have graphically demonstrated that the overall numbers are much less important than the level of national sentiment and political mobilization. A brief sketch of the people and their culture accompanies each entry, highlighting the cultural and national influences that have shaped the primary national group. A related section covers the linguistic and religious affiliations of each national group.

Each of the stateless nations has its own particular history, the events and conflicts that have shaped its national characteristics and level of mobilization. The largest part of each national survey is therefore devoted to the national history, the historical development of the national group. The national history survey follows the evolution and consolidation of the nation from its earliest history to the present. Although meticulous attention has been paid to the content and objectivity of each national survey, the polemic nature of the subject and, in many cases, the lack of official information have made it impossible to eliminate all unsubstantiated material. The author apologizes for the unintentional inclusion of controversial, dubious, or distorted information gathered from myriad and often unsatisfactory sources.

The national flags and other flags intimately associated with national groups are images of the actual flags; however, due to the informal use of these flags and a lack of information on actual size, all are presented in the same format. In many cases more than one flag is presented, particularly when a national flag has not been adopted or when other flags are equally important. The maps are the author's own, provided to complement the text. They are simple line drawings provided to aid the reader and as supplements to a comprehensive atlas.

The two appendices will allow the reader to develop a better understanding of the historical evolution of national sentiment over the past century and of the rapid proliferation of national organizations that has attended the post–Cold War wave of nationalism. Appendix A sets the numerous declarations of independence in a historical and chronological context, explicitly illustrating the waves of nationalism that have paralleled or accompanied the momentous trends and events of contemporary history. Appendix B provides a geographic listing, by region and nation, of the ever-expanding number of national organizations that herald the mobilization of national sentiment. The number of groups that exist within each national movement graphically illustrates the range of nationalist opinion, although little is known or published about the ideologies, aims, or methods of the majority of these national organizations.

Very few of the stateless nations developed in isolation; they were shaped by their relations with various governments and neighboring peoples. Accordingly, nations mentioned in the various entries that are themselves the subjects of separate entries appear with an asterisk (*). An extensive subject index is provided at the end of the last volume. Each encyclopedia entry also includes a short bibliographic list of sources.

This historical encyclopedia was compiled to provide a guide to the nations in the forefront of the post–Cold War nationalist resurgence, a political process all too often considered synonymous with the more extreme and violent aspects of nationalism. This work is not presented as an assertion that a multitude of new states are about to appear, even though political self-rule is the ultimate goal of many the national groups included in the survey. This encyclopedia is presented as a unique reference source to the nonstate nations that are spearheading one of the most powerful and enduring political movements in modern history, the pursuit of democracy's basic tenet—self-determination.

PRINCIPAL STATISTICAL SOURCES

1. National Censuses 1998–2001
2. *World Population Chart*, 2000 (United Nations)
3. *Populations and Vital Statistics*, 2000 (United Nations)
4. *World Tables*, 2000 (World Bank)
5. *World Demographic Estimates and Projections*, 1950–2025, 1988 (United Nations)
6. *UNESCO Statistical Annual*, 2000
7. *World Bank Atlas*, 1998
8. The Economist Intelligence Unit (Country Report series 2000)
9. *World Population Prospects* (United Nations)
10. *Europa Yearbook*, 2000
11. U.S. Department of State publications
12. *CIA World Factbook*
13. *United Nations Statistical Yearbook*, 2000
14. *United Nations Demographic Yearbook*, 2000
15. *The Statesman's Yearbook*, 2000
16. *Encyclopedia Britannica*
17. *Encyclopedia Americana*
18. Bureau of the Census, U.S. Department of Commerce 2001
19. National Geographic Society

20. Royal Geographical Society
21. *Webster's New Geographical Dictionary*, 1988
22. *Political Handbook of the World*
23. The Urban Foundation
24. *The Blue Plan*
25. Eurostat, the European Union Statistical Office
26. Indigenous Minorities Research Council
27. The Minority Rights Group
28. Cultural Survival
29. World Council of Indigenous Peoples
30. Survival International
31. *China Statistical Yearbook* (State Statistical Bureau of the People's Republic of China)
32. Arab Information Center
33. CIEMEN, Escarré's International Centre for Ethnical Minorities and Nations, Barcelona
34. International Monetary Fund
35. American Geographic Society

INTRODUCTION

The human race has never been a uniform whole, composed of rigorously identical individuals. There are a certain number of characteristics common to all human beings, and other attributes belonging to each individual. Besides the division of the human race by sex, age groups, and class divisions of economic origin, there is another very important separation, which is of a linguistic, ethnic, religious, or territorial type: the division into discernible national groups. Just as social classes are defined by economic criteria, even though they include global human realities and not just economic parameters, national groups are characterized not simply by linguistic or ethnic realities but also by global human realities, such as oppression or other forces of history.

The emphasis on the rights of states rather than the rights of the individuals and nations within them has long dictated international attitudes toward nationalism, attitudes buttressed by ignorance and failure to understand the "nation" versus the "nation-state." The use of condemnatory labels—separatist, secessionist, rebel, splittist, etc.—has been a powerful state weapon against those who seek different state structures on behalf of their nations. The rapid spread of national sentiment, affecting even nations long considered assimilated or quiescent, is attracting considerable attention, but the focus of this attention is invariably on its impact on established governments and its effect on international relations. As the Cold War withered away, it was replaced by a bewildering number and variety of nationalisms that in turn spawned a global movement toward the breakdown of the existing system of nation-states.

Current trends toward decentralization of government and empowerment of local groups inadvertently fragment society into often contending and mutually unintelligible cultures and subcultures. Even within a single society, people are segmenting into many self-contained communities and contending interest groups, entities that often take on the tone and aims of national groups.

The human race was divided into national groups long before the division of labor and, consequently, well before the existence of a class system. A class is defined by its situation in relation to production or consumption, and it is a universal social category. Each individual belongs to a horizontally limited human group (the economic class) and to a vertically limited group (the nation or national group). People have had identities deriving from religion, birthplace, language, or local authority for as long as humans have had cultures. They began to see themselves as members of national groups, opposed to other such groups, however, only during the modern period of colonization and state building.

An offshoot of the eighteenth-century doctrine of popular sovereignty, nationalism became a driving force in the nineteenth century, shaped and invigorated by the principles of the American and French revolutions. It was the Europeans, with their vast colonial possessions, who first declared that each and every person has a national identity that determined his or her place within the state structure. Around the world colonial and postcolonial states created new social groups and identified them by ethnic, religious, economic, or regional categories. Far from reflecting ancient ethnic or tribal loyalties, national cohesion and action are products of the modern state's demand that people make themselves heard as groups or risk severe disadvantages. Around the world, various movements and insurgencies, each with its own history and motivations, have typically—and erroneously—been lumped together as examples of the evils of nationalism.

Over the last century, perhaps no other subject has inspired the passions that surround nationalism and national sentiment. We can distinguish two primary kinds of nationalism, often opposed: unifying or assimilative nationalism; and separatist nationalism, which seeks to separate to some degree from the nationalism of the nation-state. Unifying nationalism shades off gradually into assimilation and imperialism, which reached its apex in the nineteenth century and continues to the present. Nationalism, in its most virulent forms, has provoked wars, massacres, terrorism, and genocide, but the roots of nationalist violence lie not in primordial ethnic and religious differences but in modern attempts to rally populations around nationalist ideas. Nationalism is often a learned and frequently manipulated set of ideas rather than a primordial sentiment. Violent nationalism in political life is a product of modern conflicts over power and resources, not an ancient impediment to political modernity.

The question of what a nation is has gained new significance with the recent increase in the number of claims to self-determination. The legitimacy of these claims rests upon the acceptance of a group in question as a nation, something more than just a random collection of people. The international community primarily regards nations as territorially based, and the consolidation of nations within specific territories has lent legitimacy to self-determination struggles in many areas. Yet this limited definition can give both undue influence to territorially consolidated groups seeking full sovereignty and independence, as well as undermine equally legitimate claims for self-determination among nonterritorial groups that do not aim for statehood but aim, rather, at greater control over their own lives.

National identity becomes nationalism when it includes aspirations to some variety of self-government. The majority of the world's stateless nations have embraced nationalism, but even though nationalists often include militant factions seeking full independence, most nationalists would probably settle for the right to practice their own languages and religions and to control their own territories and resources. Although the nationalist resurgence has spawned numerous conflicts, nationalism is not automatically a divisive force; it provides citizens with an identity and a sense of responsibility and involvement.

The first wave of modern nationalism culminated in the disintegration of Europe's multinational empires after World War I. The second wave began during World War II and continued as the very politicized decolonization process that engulfed the remaining colonial empires, as a theater of the Cold War after 1945. The removal of Cold War factionalism has now released a third wave of nationalism, of a scale and diffusion unprecedented in modern history. In the decade since the end of the Cold War, regionalist movements across the globe have taken on the tone and ideology of nationalist movements. The new national awakening, at the beginning of the twenty-first century, in many respects resembles the phenomenon of the turn of the twentieth century. Ethnicity, language, culture, religion, geography, and even economic condition—but not nationality—are becoming the touchstones of national identity.

Nationalism is often associated with separatism, which can be an offshoot of nationalism, but the majority of the world's national movements normally mobilize in favor of greater autonomy; separatism and separatist factions usually evolve from a frustrated desire for the basic tenet of democracy, self-determination. The conflicts resulting from this latest nationalist upsurge have reinforced the erroneous beliefs that nationalism is synonymous with extremism and that separatism is confined to the historical "hot spots" in Europe and Asia. One of the basic premises of this encyclopedia is that the nationalist resurgence at the end of the twentieth century is spreading to all corners of the world and is likely to mold the world's political agenda for decades to come. Academics too often define nationalism in terms of its excesses, so that its very definition condemns it.

The post–Cold War revival of nationalism is not limited to any one continent, nor is it a product of any particular ideology, geographic area, religion, or combination of political or historical factors. The latest wave of nationalism affects rich and poor, large and small, developed and developing, indigenous and nonindigenous peoples. National diversity is often associated with political instability and the likelihood of violence, but some of the world's most diverse states, though not without internal nationalisms, have suffered relatively little violence between national groups, while countries with relatively little cultural or linguistic diversity, including Yugoslavia, Somalia, and Rwanda, have had the bloodiest of such conflicts.

Nationalism has become an ascendant ideology, one that is increasingly challenging the nineteenth-century definition of the unitary nation-state. The worldwide nationalist revival is an amplified global echo of the nationalism that swept Europe's stateless nations in the late nineteenth and early twentieth centuries, now including the indigenous-rights movements that are major moral, political, and legal issues in many states, and a growing number of groups based on religious distinction that have taken on the characteristics of national groups.

The United Nations estimates that only 3% of the world's 6,000 national groups have achieved statehood. Although the last decade has seen the emergence of an unprecedented number of new states, the existing world order remains conservative in the recognition of new states. There is no perfect justice in dealing with nationalist aspirations; each case should be viewed as separate and distinct. Joining the club of independent states remains a privilege of few of the world's national groups.

The failure to understand national identity and nationalism is often reinforced by the view that nationalism represents a tribal, waning stage of history. The world's insistence that national structures conform to existing international borders for the sake of world peace was one of the first casualties of the revolution brought on by the world's new enthusiasm for democracy and self-determination. Between the end of World War II and the end of the Cold War, nationalism spawned only three new states—Iceland, Singapore, and Bangladesh—while the decolonization process created many more. However, between 1991 and 2001 nationalism accounted for the splintering of the Soviet Union and Yugoslavia, and the partitions of Czechoslovakia and Ethiopia, leading to the emergence of twenty-two new states. The belief that political and economic security could be guaranteed only by the existing political order faded as quickly as the ideological and political divisions set in place after World War II.

The world is in the midst of an extended post–Cold War transition that will last well into the present century. The community of democratic states is expanding, but this era of transition remains complex and dangerous. In much of the world there remains a potentially explosive mix of social, demographic, economic, and political conditions that run counter to the global trends toward democracy and economic reforms. The transition has taken the lid off long-simmering ethnic, religious, territorial, and economic disputes and has stimulated the growth of national identities on a scale unimaginable just a decade ago.

The definition of a "nation" remains controversial and undecided. The nineteenth-century French scholar Ernest Renan stated that a nation is a community of people who have endured common suffering as a people. National identity and nationalism are highly complicated and variable phenomena that resist simple diagnoses of any kind. The most basic premise remains that nations are self-defining. In a broad sense, a nation may be defined as any group of people that perceives itself to be a nation.

The growth of national sentiment can be based on a common origin, language, history, culture, territorial claims, geographical location, religion, economics, ethnicity, racial background, opposition to another group, or opposition to bad or oppressive government. The mobilization of national sentiment is most often a complicated mixture of some or all of these components. No one of these factors is essential; however, some must be present if group cohesion is to be strong enough to evolve a self-identifying nationalism. None of the world's national groups is a hermetically sealed entity. All are influenced by, and in turn influence, other national groups. Nor is any national group changeless, invariant, or static. All national groups are in states of constant flux, driven by both internal and external forces. These forces may be accommodating, harmonious, benign, and based on voluntary actions, or they may be involuntary, resulting from violent conflict, force, or domination.

Democracy, although widely accepted as the only system that is able to provide the basis of humane political and economic activity, can be a subversive force. Multiparty democracy often generates chaos and instability as centrifugal forces, inherent parts of a free political system, are set loose. The post–Cold War restoration of political pluralism and democratic process has given rise to a rebirth of ethnicity and politicized national identity, while the collapse of communism in much of the world has shattered the political equilibrium that had prevailed for over four decades. The Cold War blocs had mostly succeeded in suppressing or controlling the regional nationalisms in their respective spheres, nationalisms that now have begun to reignite old national desires and ethnic rivalries. Around the globe, numerous national groups, their identities and aspirations long buried under decades of Cold War tensions, are emerging to claim for themselves the basic principle of democracy, self-determination. The centrifugal forces held in check by the Cold War have emerged to challenge accepted definitions of a nation and its rights. The doctrine of statism is slowly being superseded by a post–Cold War internationalism that is reshaping the world's view of the unitary nation-state and, what is more important, the world's view of who or what constitutes a nation.

Two main trends are vying to shape the post–Cold War world. One is the movement to form continental or regional economic-political groupings that would allow smaller political units as members. The other is the emergence of smaller and smaller national units as older states are broken up. The two trends are not mutually exclusive. The nation-state, with its absolute sovereignty, is fading and giving way to historical trends—the nation rather than the nation-state in one direction, and supranational bodies, such as the United Nations, the European Union, and even

NAFTA, in the other. The rapidly changing political and economic realities have swept aside the old arguments that population size, geographic location, and economic viability are deterrents to national self-determination. The revival of nationalism is converging with the emergence of continental political and economic units theoretically able to accommodate ever smaller national units within overarching political, economic, and security frameworks.

The third wave of modern nationalism, with its emphasis on human rights and democratic self-determination, is set to top the international agenda for decades to come. The nationalist revival, global in scope, has strengthened submerged national, ethnic, and regional identities and has shattered the conviction that assimilation would eventually homogenize the existing nation-states. The nationalist revival is now feeding on itself, as the freedom won by many historically stateless nations has emboldened other national groups to demand greater control of their own destinies.

A unique feature of this current wave of nationalism is the growing mutual cooperation and support among and between the stateless nations, both nationally and internationally. A number of national groups in countries such as Russia, China, and Myanmar have joined together to work for common goals. Many of the nations selected for inclusion in the encyclopedia are members, or aspiring members, of two organizations that for the first time provide legitimate forums in which to gain strength through numbers and to publicize causes without recourse to violence. The larger of the organizations, the Unrepresented Nations and Peoples Organization (UNPO), was formed in 1991 by six stateless nations, four of which have since been recognized as independent states. The organization, its membership now swollen by the representatives of dozens of stateless nations, is already referred to as an alternative United Nations, representing over 100 million people. The second group, the Free Europe Alliance, is less global in scale but, like the UNPO, is inundated by membership applications.

The political and cultural renaissance spreading through the world's national groups is inexorably moving global politics away from the present system of sovereign states, each jealously defending its authority, to a new world order more closely resembling the world's true national and historical geography. A world community dominated by democracy must inevitably recognize the rights of the world's stateless nations, including the right of each to choose its own future. The twin issues of national identity and self-determination will remain at the forefront of international relations. The diffusion and force of contemporary national movements make it imperative that the nationalist phenomenon be studied and understood. One of the most urgent concerns of our time is to fashion a principled and effective policy toward all national groups.

ENCYCLOPEDIA
OF THE
STATELESS NATIONS

Sahrawis

Western Saharans; Saharawis; Saharawus

POPULATION: Approximately (2002e) 320,000 Sahrawis in northwestern Africa, concentrated in the Western Sahara region, under Moroccan control. Over 165,000 remain in refugee camps in adjacent areas of Algeria. Other large communities, numbering over 100,000, live in Europe, mostly in France and Spain, and in other parts of Algeria.

THE SAHRAWI HOMELAND: The Sahrawi homeland occupies a largely arid desert region in northwestern Africa, lying on the Atlantic Ocean between Morocco and Mauritania. Western Sahara, the Sahrawi Arab Democratic Republic, is recognized diplomatically by over 70 countries and the Organization of African Unity; however, most of the region is under Moroccan military occupation. The territorial conflict is to be decided by an

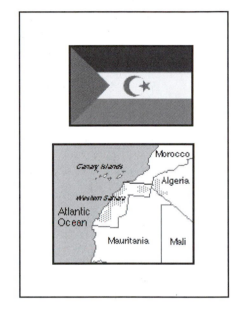

often-postponed United Nations referendum. *Territory of Western Sahara (Sahrawi Arab Democratic Republic)*: 97,344 sq. mi.—252,120 sq. km, (2002e) 333,000—Moroccans 65%, Sahrawis 35%. The Sahrawi capital and major cultural center is Laâyoune, called Aiun by the Sahrawis, (2002e) 189,000.

FLAG: The Sahrawi national flag, the official flag of the republic, is a horizontal tricolor of black, white, and green bearing a red triangle at the hoist and charged with a centered red crescent moon and five-pointed star.

PEOPLE AND CULTURE: The Sahrawis are a North African tribal people of mixed Berber and Arab background. They are descended from the Sanhaja Berbers, Bedouin Arabs known as the Beni Hassan, and black African slaves. Divided into 22 tribes and numerous clans, the Sahrawi are united by history, religion, and language. Sahrawi society is divided, however, by a rigid caste system. Disputes over the population estimates have become one of the major stumbling blocks to the proposed UN plebiscite. The Moroccan government claims the Sahrawi number as few as 175,000, while nationalists assert that there is a Sahrawi national population of up to a million. An estimated fifth of the Sahrawi population in the region remains nomadic and regularly move across the international borders. The government settlement plan has moved hundreds of thousands of Moroccans into the territory, turning the Sahrawis into a minority.

LANGUAGE AND RELIGION: The Sahrawis speak a distinct dialect called Hassinya or Sahrawi. combining both Berber and Arabic influences. The language, classified as a south Arabic dialect, is not intelligible to speakers of other Arabic dialects, including Moroccan Arabic, now the official language of the region. Many of the forms and vocabulary are of Berber origin or derive from archaic Arabic brought to the region with the early Arab conquerors.

The Saharawis are overwhelmingly Sunni Muslims, although their system of beliefs retains many traditions and customs that predate Islam. The urbanized Sahrawis adhere to the more orthodox practices of Islam, but the nomadic groups continue to believe in spirits and shamanistic practices.

NATIONAL HISTORY: The western reaches of the Sahara Desert, populated by Berber tribes, possibly of Celtic origin, had little to interest potential invaders, though the region was claimed by several ancient states. The Berbers, divided into a number of autonomous tribal groups, lived an isolated existence until the Arab invasion of the eighth century. Converted to Islam, the nomadic tribes adopted the social and religious structures of the Arab conquerors but remained nominally independent.

The Arab state of Morocco, to the north, claimed the region in the tenth century; traditionally, Morocco's eleventh- and twelfth-century Almoravid dynasty originated in the area. The dynasty began with Abdullah ibn Yasin, who converted some of the Saharan tribes to his own reform version of Islam and led them north to conquer Morocco. The western reaches of the Sahara Desert again came under nominal Moroccan rule in the sixteenth century. Although claimed as subjects of the sultan, the Saharan tribes had little contact with the Moroccan authorities.

In the middle of the eighteenth century, Europeans explored the coast and made contact with the coastal tribes. In 1860 the Moroccan sultan granted Spain rights in the region. In 1884 the Spanish government established a protectorate comprising two territories, Saguia El Hama in the north and Rio de Oro in the south. The Spanish colonial administration, confined to the coast and several oases, was extended to the interior only in 1934. The extension of Spanish authority to the interior was possible only with the assistance of soldiers from neighboring French Morocco.

Sheikh Ma el Amin, a widely revered religious leader, from 1900 to 1910 led the Sahrawi resistance to Spanish rule in the northwestern part of the territory. The sheikh was in direct contact as an ally of the sultan of Morocco, enabling the rebels to purchase arms from German and Spanish traders. This campaign later passed to his son, and the movement he began became the basis of the nationalist movement formed in the 1950s.

The Tekna and Regueibat tribes rebelled in 1957 and drove out the Spanish authorities and soldiers. The Spanish, aided by the French, returned in 1958 and inflicted severe punishment on the rebel tribes. The rebellion resumed, supported by most of the population, spread across the desert, and effectively restricted Spanish authority to a few garrison towns.

The Moroccan kingdom, independent from France in 1956, laid claim to the region on historical grounds, claiming that the tribes had traditionally paid tribute to the Moroccan sultans. Neighboring Mauritania to the south, independent in 1960, citing clan and family ties between the Sahrawi and its northern tribes, also put forward a claim. The claims were rejected by the Spanish colonial authorities, and in 1958 the Spanish government changed the region's status to that of an overseas province. Spanish and French troops defeated a Moroccan attempt to take the region by force in 1959. One of the world's richest phosphate deposits, discovered at Bu Craa in 1963, gave the conflicting claims to the province economic as well as political importance.

In 1966, the Spanish government promised the United Nations that it would eventually allow self-determination in the territory, but the promise was never kept. This resulted in the nationalist mobilization of the Sahrawis. Rebellious tribal leaders formed the Popular Front for the Liberation of Saguia el Hama and Rio de Oro (Polisario) in 1973. Drawing recruits from the thousands of refugees from Spanish rule living in camps across the Algerian border, the rebels overran all but the main towns by early 1975.

In the mid-1970s, King Hassan II of Morocco reiterated his claim to the region and made its incorporation into Morocco a national issue. Pressured by world opinion, the Spanish government finally signed an agreement with the Polisario leaders allowing for the orderly withdrawal of Spanish troops as a prelude to Sahrawi independence. The UN General Assembly passed a resolution endorsing the Sahrawis' right to independence.

King Hassan rejected the pact and on 6 November 1975 launched the so-called Green Revolution, an organized march of 350,000 Moroccan civilians into Western Sahara. The king hoped to use the issue to stabilize his rule in Morocco, which had been shaken by several attempted military coups in recent years. The Moroccans also wanted access to the region's phosphates, fishing, oil, and iron resources. Over 200,000 civilians had crossed the border when the Spanish authorities abruptly began to abandon the province on 14 November 1975. The last Spanish troops left Western Sahara in February 1976. In December 1975 the International Court of Justice ruled on the conflict, favoring independence for Western Sahara.

At UN urging the Moroccans agreed to evacuate the civilian marchers, but in December the Moroccan government again changed its position and reached an accord with Mauritania for a partition of the region. On 26 February 1976 Morocco formally annexed the northern districts, and Mauritania annexed the southern third of the territory. The Polisario leaders rejected the partition as illegal and appealed to the UN to enforce its earlier endorsement of Sahrawi independence. On 27 February 1976 the rebel leaders declared the independence of the Sahrawi Arab Democratic Republic and launched a guerrilla war against the Moroccan and Mauritanian occupation forces. In 1978, following Polisario guerrilla attacks well inside their country, the government of Mauritania renounced its claim to the southern districts, which the Moroccans promptly occupied and annexed.

The Moroccan government, to protect the important phosphate mining operations and the growing number of Moroccan colonists, built a 400-mile wall of sand and rock, topped with sensors and explosive mines, around the government-held lands. The Moroccans later extended the wall by another 800 miles. Attacks by Moroccan jets on towns and villages sent thousands of Sahrawi civilians into refugee camps in Algeria.

The conflict quickly involved states far beyond North Africa. In October 1979 the United States government announced that it would aid the Moroccans with advanced weapons, though it refused to recognize Morocco's claim to the territory. The French government also supplied arms and assistance to the Moroccans. The Moroccan government withdrew from the Organization of African Unity in 1985 due to its recognition of Western Sahara as a member state.

In the late 1980s battles continued, but the Moroccan wall effectively blocked Polisario operations. Increasing international pressure for a negotiated settlement prompted both sides, each of which believed that it would win, to accept a proposed UN-supervised referendum. In 1987 the UN sent a mission to the region to prepare a cease-fire and referendum on the future status of the Western Sahara. Both sides agreed in principle to a 1988 UN peace plan calling for a cease-fire, an exchange of prisoners, and a referendum on independence or integration into the Moroccan kingdom.

The Moroccan government wanted the referendum to include only the 74,000 Sahrawis counted in the 1974 Spanish census; that position was rejected by the Sahrawis, who claim that many more had fled oppressive Spanish rule and were not counted. In August 1991 King Hassan called on the UN to delay the referendum, which was planned for January 1992, for four months due to the dispute over the voting lists. The referendum has since been repeatedly postponed. In July 1993 the first direct talks were held between Polisario leaders and the Moroccan government, but little was accomplished. The UN force began registering voters in the territory in August 1994 but was blocked by the Polisario in January 1995 to protest Moroccan actions in the region. Registration resumed, but the controversy over the legitimacy of about 120,000 people added to the rolls by the Moroccan government remained a major stumbling block to the holding of the referendum.

The UN group continues to attempt to implement the referendum, knowing that if it leaves, the Polisario would probably return to war, which could draw in the Algerians. The UN presence legitimizes the Moroccan presence without officially accepting its sovereignty, but it also gives the Moroccan government time to move more thousands of Moroccan settlers into the region. By 1995 over 100,000 Moroccan nationals had been settled in the territory.

The former American secretary of state, James Baker, was appointed as special UN envoy in 1996 in the hope that he could break the deadlock. In June 1997, for the first time, Moroccan officials met with leaders of the Polisario, but little of value came from the meeting. The Moroccan government rejected a compromise that would have given the Sahrawis limited autonomy. Baker announced that referendum negotiations would resume in June 1997, and he later announced that an agreement had been reached over the issue of the identification process of eligible voters. In early 1998, the stalled talks were restarted, although reports of Moroccan intransigence continued.

The two sides agreed in September 1998 to rules for the upcoming referendum. They also agreed to accept the outcome regardless of the results. The voter list drawn up by the UN was published in January 2000; the Moroccans lodged 135,000 appeals, mostly on behalf of people who had been disqualified from voting. The appeal process is projected to last until 2002 or beyond. The president of the Sahrawi Arab Democratic Republic, Mohamed Abdelaziz, stated that if the referendum is once again delayed that the UN should declare its mission a failure and withdraw. The cease-fire, observed on the basis of a referendum being organized, would then become irrelevant, and Polisario would resume their independence war.

The Secretary-General of the United Nations, Kofi Annan, spent 10 days in the region in November 1999 trying to resolve the census conflict that has led to the repeated postponement of the promised referendum, but with little cooperation from Moroccan authorities, no headway was made. The government refused to accept a new deadline, December 1999, for a vote on independence. The referendum was again delayed until July 2000, then it was to be held by the end of 2000, but then was postponed indefinitely. As an alternative the UN began promoting limited autonomy for the Sahrawis, although they have always insisted that a referendum was the only acceptable solution.

The continuing conflict and the never-ending negotiations have been denounced by the Sahrawis, several UN officials, and human rights groups internationally. The refugees that languish in camps in Algeria have mostly been ignored during the long years of negotiations and UN intervention. The territory remained under the military occupation of 100,000 Moroccan troops, the refugees remained stuck in the Algerian desert, the negotiations continued sporadically, and dates for the referendum came and went, constantly postponed over the disagreement as to who is Sahrawi and who can vote.

The death of King Hassan II opened the way for limited reforms in Morocco. The new king, Mohamed VI, announced a new commission for Saharan affairs and tried to placate the Sahrawis with promises of jobs, better housing, and other social improvements as part of what he calls a "new approach." However, the situation in the territory is worsening. Conscription of young Sahrawis aged 18–25 began. Of the 400 undergoing training in northern Morocco, 33 needed hospitalization, and two died. The government is also reportedly moving more settlers into the region; settlers already reportedly formed about 70% of the population of the territory in early 2000. The Sahrawis claim the continuing government-sponsored migration is ethnic cleansing rather than participatory democracy and conclude that the Moroccan government wants a referendum only if it can be sure of winning.

An autonomy plan approved by the UN was accepted by Morocco in June 2001, but was rejected by the Sahrawis. The plan, which would give Morocco complete control for 4 years leading to a new referendum, in which all residents of the region would vote, including the Moroccan settlers and soldiers that moved into the territory after 1975. The accord was seen as grossly unfair by many human rights groups who support Sahrawi self-determination. The UN, after 10 years and half a billion dollars, has failed to organize the promised referendum and seemed to accept its failure.

The Moroccan government considers the region pacified, but to commemorate the anniversary of the Moroccan invasion of Western Sahara on 31 October 1975, tracts were distributed by night in the major cities in October 2001. They denounce the colonial occupation and call for "the intensification of the struggle to expel the invader." Recent deals between the Moroccan government and French and American oil companies for exploration of the Sahrawi coastal waters have also been protested as illegal.

In November 2001 a visit to the disputed region by Mohamed VI prompted protests by Sahrawi leaders. They called the visit an affront and a flagrant violation of UN resolutions. The Sahrawis reported that most of the people who acclaimed the king in the streets were Moroccans; people who work as civil servants were forced to be present as well as the poor who survive on government aid.

SELECTED BIBLIOGRAPHY:

Ball, David W. *Empires of Sand.* 1999.
Firebrace, James. *Exiles of the Sahara: The Sahrawi Refugees Shape Their Future.* 1997.
Gretton, John. *Western Sahara: The Fight for Self-Determination.* 1993.
Pazzanita, Anthony G., and Tony Hodges. *Historical Dictionary of Western Sahara.* 1994.

Sakhas

Sakhalars; Sahas; Yakuts; Tungus; Jekos; Urungkhay Sakhas

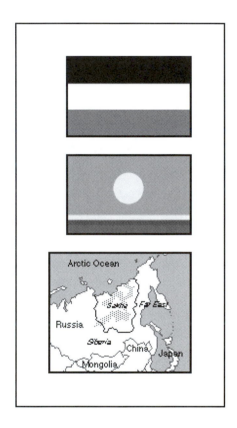

POPULATION: Approximately (2002e) 520,000 Sakhas in northeastern Russia, concentrated in the Sakha Republic and neighboring regions in the Russian Far East.

THE SAKHA HOMELAND: The Sakha homeland, called Sakha Omuk, occupies a vast area of mountains and plateaus in northeastern Siberia around the basin of the Lena River. The region, about twice as large as Alaska, is mountainous in the east and south; about 40% of the territory lies within the Arctic Circle, including several islands in the Arctic Ocean and over 600,000 lakes. Sakha Omuk, called the Sakha Republic, forms a member state of the Russian Federation. *Sakha Republic (Saha Réspublikata/Sakha Omuk)*: 1,198,146 sq. mi.—3,103,198 sq. km, (2002e) 945,000—Sakhas 42%, Russians 41%, Ukrainians 5%, Evenks* 2%, Tatars* 2%, Evens 1%, others 8%. The Sakha capital and major cultural center is Yakutsk, called Kalar by the Sakhas, (2002e) 194,000.

FLAG: The Sakha national flag, the flag of the national movement, is a horizontal tricolor of black, white, and red. The official flag of the republic is a pale blue field charged with a centered white disc and bearing narrow horizontal stripes of white, red, and green at the bottom.

PEOPLE AND CULTURE: The Sakhas, called Yakuts by the Russians, are considered the largest group of the Altaic branch of the Turkic peoples and the largest indigenous group in the Russian Far East. They emerged as a distinct ethnic group in the fourteenth century. The Sakhas are divided into two primary groups, based on economics and geography—the northern group, seminomadic hunters, fishermen, and reindeer breeders; and the southern group, horse and cattle herders and farmers. They are considered a Turkic people but are actually of mixed Turkic, Mongol, and

Paleo-Siberian background. The Sakha population displays two distinct physical types, Mongol and Turkic, a division that reflects their mixed ancestry. Unlike the other nations of northern Siberia, who keep herds of reindeer, the Sakhas are traditionally herders of cattle and horses although they have diversified since the 1920s. The Sakhas are known for their oral epics, the *toyons*, which tell of the ancient leaders.

LANGUAGE AND RELIGION: The Sakha language, Saha Tyla, without dialects and with few regional differences, is distantly related to the Turkic languages of Central Asia. The language, of which the roots are about a third Turkic, a third Mongol, and a third unknown, and was probably adopted from the earlier Paleo-Asiatic peoples, became a literary language in the nineteenth century, when political exiles created a local alphabet. Saha Tyla is geographically the most remote of the Turkic languages. The number of Sakhas speaking it as their first language rose from 95% in 1989 to over 97% in 1995. The language was a lingua franca for a huge area of Siberia until the mid-twentieth century and remains the means of intergroup communication among the Sakhas' reindeer-herding neighbors. The Sakha language has been written in the Cyrillic alphabet since 1938. It is spoken as a second language by some Russians, Evenks, and others living in the region, while most Sakhas are bilingual in Russian. In January 2000, the Sakha Republic's president, Mikhail Nikolayev, published a decree making English a mandatory language to be taught in schools and one of the working languages of the republic.

The majority of the Sakha are Orthodox Christian, with a minority retaining the traditional shamanistic beliefs, mostly in the more remote parts of the huge Sakha homeland. Their shamanistic beliefs have been revived since the early 1990s, and shamans remain active, using numerous traditional techniques for curing and leadership. Shamans are believed to have the ability to act as intermediaries with the world of the spirits. They are at once doctors, priests, social workers, and mystics. The core of traditional beliefs is a cult of heaven, based on worship of the "white creator," called Er Toyen.

NATIONAL HISTORY: The Sakhas probably migrated to northeastern Siberia in the Middle Ages, pushed north by Buryat Mongol invaders during the turbulent times following the collapse of the Mongol Empire. Sakha legend traces their national origin to a Tatar hero and a Buryat maiden living on the shores of Lake Baikal in Buryatia.

A Turkic people, the Sakha fled the region around the lake to escape the thirteenth-century Mongol invasion. By the fifteenth century the Sakha had occupied the basin of the Lena River in the cold country far to the northeast. They first settled along the river lowlands of the middle Lena, the lower Vilui, and Aldan Rivers, where they found grass for grazing and protection from the extremes of the northern winter.

Herdsmen and horsemen, the Sakhas adapted to the harsh conditions of their new homeland with remarkable flexibility. The Sakhas absorbed or pushed farther north the nomadic Evens, Evenks, and Yukagirs. From the indigenous groups they learned to adapt their culture to the hunting, fishing, and reindeer breeding that meant survival in the harsh climate. Unlike their Turkic relatives in Central Asia, the Sakha were never affected by the Islamic religion but kept their ancient shamanistic beliefs. Traditional Sakha society was dominated by the *tonjon* or tribal chiefs and remained divided, although the Khangala tribe came to prominence.

Russian explorers and traders moved into the area in the sixteenth century, trading tobacco for valuable furs to sell in European Russia. In 1632 Cossacks founded a fort at Yakutsk, which became an important military center during the war to subdue the Sakhas in 1634–42. The Russians called the people Yakuts and their homeland Yakutia. By 1710 thousands of Slavic colonists had occupied the more productive lands in the southern river valleys. Several Sakha rebellions followed the colonization and the imposition of the *yasak*, the Russian tax on the Sakha trappers. The Sakhas, heirs to a Turkic tradition of mounted raids, fiercely resisted Russian domination but were finally subdued after a brutal campaign by Cossack troops.

Russian Orthodox missionaries began effort to convert the Sakhas in the late 1600s. Many Sakhas converted not because of an affinity to Christianity but mainly because Christians were exempted from paying the *yasak*. In practice, the Sakhas mixed their shamanistic and Christian beliefs in a unique belief system.

In the 1700s, many Sakhas migrated from their traditional territories under Russian political pressure and because of the depletion of the natural environment, particularly the furs demanded as taxes and tribute. The new Sakha territories in the north and east were soon annexed to Russia, and Cossacks moved into the regions to establish Russian authority. In 1782 the Russian authorities established administrative units in the region, often using the local chiefs to govern the new tribal territories.

Yakutsk became the center of Slavic colonization in the region. The Slavic influx, limited to the southern districts, had little effect on the Sakha majority in the huge region until the arrival of political and criminal deportees at labor camps established after 1773. Many of the Poles and Russians exiled to Yakutia were highly educated scholars and scientists who devoted themselves to the study of the Sakha culture and language. The exiles from Europe opened a Yakut museum in 1891, and a political exile compiled the first dictionary of the Sakha language.

Gold deposits were found in the region in 1846, bringing a new influx of Slav settlers. The Slav migration was aided by the construction of the Siberian railroad in the 1880s and 1890s.

Primary schools opened by political deportees and the Russian Orthodox Church aided the development of a Sakha literary language and the emergence of a university-educated minority before World War I. Revolutionary ideas espoused by the exiles, freedom and self-determination, found fertile ground in the region, where poverty and malnutrition were endemic. The Yakut Union (Soyuz Yakutov), formed by nationalists in 1906, demanded the complete rejuvenation of the Sakha homeland and the return of all Russian-confiscated wealth. The tsarist authorities reacted by arresting the organization's leaders, which only encouraged the growth of nationalism.

The Sakhas, as a non-European minority, were exempted from military service when war began in 1914, but desperate for manpower the tsarist government began to conscript Sakhas for labor battalions in 1916. Resistance to the conscription aroused antigovernment feelings and strengthened the Sakha national movement. The nationalists mobilized following the overthrow of the tsar in February 1917 and in alliance with liberal Russian political parties took control when the breakdown of civil administration left the region without a government.

The Bolshevik coup in October 1917 pushed the majority of the Sakhas to form an alliance with the anti–Bolshevik White forces. In alliance with the forces of Gen. Wasili Pepelayev the Sakhas created the Autonomous Government of the Yakut Region, turning their homeland into an anticommunist bastion. Over White opposition, the Sakha national leaders declared the region independent on 22 February 1918, calling the new state Sakha Omuk. A minority joined the Bolsheviks, believing the promises of independence in a federation of socialist states. Far from the Russian heartland, the state escaped the devastation of the Russian Civil War, but in 1920 it fell to the advancing Red Army. On 27 April 1922 the Soviet government established the Yakut Autonomous Soviet Socialist Republic.

The Soviet attempts to settle the 240,000 Sakhas on collectives provoked a widespread rebellion in November 1921. The last rebels and counterrevolutionary groups were finally eliminated in 1923. To avoid further violence the Soviet authorities accepted the necessity of a seminomadic way of life as guardians of their collectivized herds. In spite of continuing unrest and a renewed rebellion in 1928, the Sakhas benefited from Soviet educational and cultural policies.

The period of collectivization, which was fiercely resisted in the 1930s, began a long decline in the Sakha population. Thousands of shamans and other leaders, targets of Stalinist repression, were eliminated or disappeared into the forced labor camps established in the region after 1931. Sakha organizations, schools, and publications were banned, particularly anything connected with the destroyed *tonjon* class.

The Sakha territory was greatly changed by the large number of deported Poles sent to the region after the Soviet invasion of eastern Poland in 1939. The Poles became the main component of the Gulag, the string of forced labor camps. They were mostly set to forest clearing and road building. Later, German war prisoners and others who were viewed as enemies of the state were sent to the region.

After World War II the Sakha intelligentsia abandoned their traditional way of life and moved into the professions. The region's enormous gold, diamond, and coal deposits and Soviet industrialization drew in a large Slavic population in the 1950s and 1960s. Pollution from the poorly controlled mining and industrial concerns scarred the region and left behind dead rivers and ruined grazing lands.

The Sakha percentage of the population dropped from 80% of the total in 1946 to less than 50% in 1965 and just 33% in 1989. Growing resentment of the Slav workers who came to the mines for a few years and then left, having accumulated by Soviet standards considerable wealth, fanned a resurgence of Sakha nationalism and demands for local control of the important mining industry. As the only form of protest possible against Soviet rule, the Sakhas fiercely resisted giving up their language.

Severe ethnic disturbances swept the autonomous republic between 1979 and 1986, indicating a revival of the Sakha nation. Sakha national sentiment increased dramatically with the Soviet liberalization of the late 1980s. The first Sakha demand in the more relaxed atmosphere, that they be allowed to de-Russify family names, opened a torrent of grievances and discussion of past abuses and oppression. Nationalists demanded that control of the lucrative mines be moved from ministries in Moscow to the local government. Militants called for the expulsion of many of the Slav workers who had settled in the region since World War II.

The regional government declared the autonomous republic a sovereign state in October 1990, and in the wake of the disintegration of the Soviet Union it unilaterally declared the renamed Sakha Republic a full member state of the Russian Federation. The Sakhas' moves toward economic and political autonomy were denounced as secessionist and needlessly provocative, but the Sakhas claimed they are only taking control of their own future. In 1992, the republican authorities denied rumors that the republican government was following a secessionist course. In April 1994, Russia's president, Boris Yeltsin, issued a decree denouncing the persecution of ethnic Sakhas during the Stalin era.

The collapse of the Soviet Union in 1991 began a strong outward migration. Thousands of the Slavs who had settled in the region during the Soviet era began to leave as government economic subsidies disappeared. The number of Russians in the region fell from about half the population in 1989 to about 40% in 2000, and Ukrainians dropped from 7% to less than 5%. The Slavic outflow increased the overall percentage of the Sakhas and helped them win control of local governments and the republic's natural resources, which include 100% of Russia's antimony, 99% of its diamonds, 24% of its gold, and 33% of the silver. The Sakha diamond industry is the main source of Russia's foreign currency earnings.

The Sakha renaissance of the 1990s had its roots in the nationalist movement of the early part of the twentieth century and in the fact that although their homeland was rich in natural resources, the republic's non-Slav population was among the poorest in the Russian Federation. A 1997 survey showed that Yakutsk was the most expensive city in the Russian Federation, while the Sakha Republic ranked in the 10 poorest regions in the Russian Federation. The republic's Sakha leaders took control of the region's resources and began to sell raw materials on the world market and to establish cash reserves outside the control of the Russian central bank. In January 1995, the Sakha government banned recruitment of its citizens into the Russian military, on the grounds that draftees would be sent to fight the rebel Chechens.* The takeover of the republican government by ethnic Sakhas did much to dampen nationalist militance.

Economic problems added to the unrest in the late 1990s. Ignoring central government agreements, the Sakha government signed economic agreements with Belarus and North Korea in an effort to stimulate the local economy. In late 1997, in response to the Russian government's inability to pay wages on time, the republican government began to issue a new type of security, known as commercial coupons.

Russian president Vladimir Putin signed a decree in May 2000 creating seven federal districts in Russia, including the Far East Federal District, which includes the Sakha Republic. The move was an attempt to curb the independence of the regions. Relations between the Yakuts and the central government, which improved following concessions made by Boris Yeltsin, again deteriorated following the loss of some autonomous rights.

Sakha nationalist demands for independence have widespread support, but moves toward secession have been tempered by the prospect that the Slav-dominated mining region would stay with Russia should the Sakhas eventually secede from the federation. Although the enormous ecological damage done by the uncoordinated extraction of the region's raw materials is one of the major themes of the nationalist movement, the loss of part of their homeland would be an even greater disaster.

SELECTED BIBLIOGRAPHY:

Kempton, Daniel R. *The Republic of Sakha-Yakutia: The Evolution of Centre-Periphery Relations in the Russian Federation.* 1996.

Kotkin, Stephen, and David Wolff, eds. *Rediscovering Russia in Asia: Siberia and the Russian Far East.* 1995.

Tishkov, Valery. *The Principal Problems and Prospects of the Development of National-Territorial Entities in the Russian Federation.* 1992.

Ushakov, Nikolai. *Yakutia: Frozen Gem of the USSR.* 1978.

Samis

Sámi; Samme; Saami; Sabme; Lapps; Laps; Laplanders; Finns; Fenns

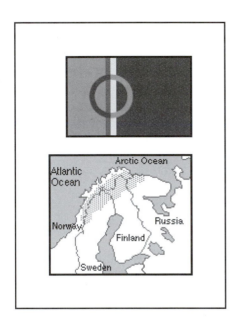

POPULATION: Approximately (2002e) 105,000 Samis in northwestern Europe, concentrated in the far north, with 70,000 in Norway, 22,000 in Sweden, 8,000 in Finland, and another 3,000 in the Kola Peninsula region of northwestern Russia.

THE SAMI HOMELAND: The Sami homeland, Sápmi, occupies a vast region of northern Europe, largely within the Arctic Circle. Much of the region is frozen tundra, which provides space for the Sami reindeer herds. The homeland has no official political status in any of the Scandinavian countries or Russia. The region includes Finnmark and parts of Tromsø and Nordland Provinces of Norway, the eastern districts of Norrbotten and Vasterbotten Provinces of Sweden, the northern districts of Finland's Lappi Province, and most of the Kola Peninsula of the Russian Federation. Lapland (Samiland/Sápmi) has an area of about 150,000 sq. mi.—388,500 sq. km, (2002e) 200,000—Samis 51%, Norwegians, Swedes, Finns, and Russians 49%. The unofficial capital of the European Samis is Kautokeino, called Guovdageaidnu by the Samis, (2002e) 3,000, located in Norwegian territory close to the Finnish and Swedish borders. Other important Sami cultural centers are Lakselv (Leavdnja) and Karasjok (Kárásjohka) in Norway, Kiruna (Giron) and Kvikkjokk (Huhttán) in Sweden, Sodankylä (Soadegilli) and Ivalo (Avvil) in Finland, and Lovozero (Lujávri) in Russia.

FLAG: The Sami national flag, recognized by all Sami groups, is a blue field with a broad red stripe at the hoist divided from the blue by narrow vertical stripes of green and yellow, and bears a circle divided vertically blue near the hoist and red on the fly.

PEOPLE AND CULTURE: The Samis are a Finnic people, a distinct nation living in far northern Europe, in the Scandinavian and Kola Peninsulas. Although popularly called Laps or Lapps, the Samis consider the name to be derogatory. The Samis are divided into five regional-cultural groups—the Coast Samis, Forest Samis, Mountain Samis, River Samis, and the Skolt and Kola Samis. About a third of the Samis are nomadic, living during the winter in the interior and during the summer along the coast. This Sami minority, numbering about 30,000, have not settled in permanent homes and represent the last nomads in Europe; they are often counted as the only ethnic Samis, with the settled populations counted as of the majority nations. Most Samis now live permanently in scattered settlements on the coasts and fjords, and many are established in villages at the heads of valleys or on well-stocked lakes. The largest Sami population is in Norway, where they are commonly called Finns. The total Sami population is a matter of conflict, as census figures often leave settled Sami populations out of the calculations. The definition of a Sami is still a matter of dispute; unofficial census figures gathered by Sami experts are much higher than the official government figures. Extensive intermingling has nearly erased the Sami's Asian origins, and although Samis are generally short and muscular, they are otherwise now nearly indistinguishable from their Scandinavian neighbors. The distinctive clothing and headgear, combining the bright blues, reds, yellows, and greens, are still worn in many areas and proclaim the Sami's home regions. Only 10% of the Sami population still engage in reindeer herding, but that minority represents a continuation of traditional Sami culture.

LANGUAGE AND RELIGION: The language of the Samis is a group of languages of the Finnic branch of the Finno-Ugric language group; it is related to Finnish and other Finnic languages of northern Europe. Spoken in three major dialectical groups, North, South, and East, and over 50 dialects and subdialects, the Sami language has great regional variety; the dialects are not mutually intelligible. Many scholars consider the nine major dialects as separate languages. The number of Sami speakers has been declining since the 1950s as the language gives way to the various national languages. The first Sami-Russian dictionary was published in 1985. There are six literary languages in use—Southern Sami in Norway, Lule Sami in Sweden, Inari and Skolt Sami in Finland, Kildin Sami in Russia, and North Sami, spoken in Norway, Sweden, and Finland by about two-thirds of all Sami speakers. The standard literary language is based on North Sami and has a literary tradition that began with the publication of the Bible and other religious works in Sweden in the seventeenth century. Nearly all Samis are bilingual, speaking one of the Sami dialects and a national language. In Russia there is a movement to replace the Russian Cyrillic alphabet with the Latin alphabet used by the Scandinavian Samis.

The majority of the Samis, like the other Scandinavian nations, are Lutheran; a small Orthodox minority is mostly made up of Sami refugees from the former Soviet Union. The Samis of the Kola Peninsula were baptized into Russian Orthodoxy in the sixteenth century. The first Lutheran missions were established among the western Sami groups in the seventeenth century. Many of the Samis' pre-Christian traditions, particularly those associated with reindeer herding, weather, and the seasons, have been incorporated into their Christian beliefs.

NATIONAL HISTORY: Little is known of the ancient history of the Samis, a people of early Mongol origins thought to have migrated west from Central Asia in prehistoric times. Mentioned as a separate tribal people living north of the Germanic tribes in Europe by the Roman historian Tacitus in A.D. 98, the Samis nearly 2,000 years ago were driven north into the barren Arctic by successive waves of Slavic, Finnic, and Gothic peoples. The Samis believe that they adopted their Finnic language from the newcomers in the last millennium B.C.

The nomadic tribes pursued fishing, hunting, whaling, and, in the lands warmed by the Gulf Stream, farming. The main activity of the Sami tribes revolved around the vast herds of reindeer. Traditionally the Samis followed their reindeer herds, wintering in the lowlands and summering in the western mountains. On skis, a Sami invention, herders traveled great distances with their herds, which provided the resources for survival in the north and became their measure of wealth.

Norwegian and Swedish Vikings conquered the western Sami tribes in the early Middle Ages, beginning in the ninth century, but mostly left the Samis to their traditional way of life as nomadic herdsmen and fishermen. The Samis were taxed by the Norwegians in the ninth century and by the Karels* in the thirteenth century. After that time they continually retreated northward under pressure from their southern neighbors. The Kola Peninsula came under Russian influence in the thirteenth century. Between the thirteenth and eighteenth centuries, Norwegians, Swedes, and Russians vied for authority in the Sami regions, with the Sami tribes often paying tribute to more than one of their more powerful neighbors.

The frigid environment of the Arctic tundra prevented a large influx of settlers until the Swedish king began directing Swedish and Finnish settlement from 1673. In the East the Sami tribes of the Kola Peninsula came under the rule of the expanding Russian state in 1721. Long resistance to Christianity, finally overcome by Lutheran and Orthodox missionaries, meant that the last Sami tribes were not converted until the eighteenth century.

Scandinavian and Russian colonization of the Sami homeland accelerated in the seventeenth and eighteenth centuries. The settlers concentrated on the most productive lands and mainly farmed, forcing the Samis to move to even less habitable lands farther north. Hunting by the settlers brought beaver to the brink of extinction. Farms and cattle herds disrupted traditional nomadic patterns, and the economic foundation of the Sami culture gradually collapsed.

The boundaries of the Sami homelands were not demarcated until the mid-eighteenth century. The frontier between Sweden and Norway was agreed to in 1751, and that between Norwegian and Russian territory was finally delimited in 1826. The official agreements on international boundaries effectively separated the various Sami tribes between several national states. The massive Russian colonization of the Kola Peninsula began in 1868.

A change of official attitudes brought the end of active Sami resistance in 1851–52. Administrative reforms were introduced, particularly in Norway, starting with the area's schools. At the end of the nineteenth century, however, teachers were instructed to restrict the use of the Sami language. In Norway after 1902 it was forbidden to sell land to anyone unable to speak Norwegian. Land-use practices such as clear cutting, mining, and water diversion for hydroelectric power were embarked upon without regard to Sami land claims. Across the region, many Sami children were sent to boarding schools, where the history, culture, and religion of their ancestors were ignored, further eroding the Sami cultural identity.

In the twentieth century, Norway, which split from Sweden in 1905, counted the largest number of Samis within its national territory. The second-largest population, in the Kola Peninsula of northwestern Russia, came under Soviet rule in 1920. The Kola Samis, their herds collectivized and cross-border contacts with their kin forbidden, suffered discrimination and hardship under Soviet rule. All publications and texts written in the Sami dialects were burned by the Soviet authorities in 1937. During the Russo-Finnish War in 1940, thousands of Samis fled Soviet territory for refuge in the West. By 1941 only about 2,000 of the 1939 Soviet Sami population of 15,000 remained in the Soviet Union.

The contemporary world intruded into the Scandinavian Sami homelands in northern Europe, particularly Norway, during World War II. The conflict brought bombs, tanks, and destruction to a people whose language has no word for war. Germany's scorched early policy in northern Norway in 1944 left virtually every building in Finnmark burned and the Sami herds slaughtered.

The experience of war profoundly affected the peaceful Sami, raising the first demands for greater control of events that concerned their small and threatened nation. The postwar increase of the Arctic region's non-Sami population began to curtail the traditional Sami way of life in the 1950s and 1960s, though more liberal laws were applied in Norway, Sweden, and Finland. New mining towns were created, and roads, power stations, dams, and national parks crowded in on the Sami grazing lands. Tourism and rural depopulation became serious problems for the Sami nation. The Nordic Sami Council was founded in 1956 and is still consulted by all three Nordic governments on matters of interest to the Sami.

Confused by the differing national policies of Norway, Sweden, Finland, and the Soviet Union, Sami activists formed the Nordic Saami Institute in 1973. The organization's aim was to press for Sami political and land rights. Later renamed the Sami Council, the organization was recognized by the governments of Norway, Sweden, and Finland as the legitimate representative of Sami interests at local and international levels. Sami parliaments were established in Finland in 1972, in Norway in 1989, and in Sweden in 1993.

The Russian Sami remained isolated under communist rule until delegates were allowed to attend the twelfth Conference of Nordic Sami in 1983 in Finland. After that time the Sami language, spoken by only 45% of the Russian Sami, experienced a revival, along with the culture. Renewed contact between all the Sami groups in the 1980s aided the broad national revival. The Kola Sami Association was founded in Russia in 1989, and joined the Sami Council in 1992. Pressed by environmental issues, Sami nationalism grew rapidly during the 1970s and in 1983, Sami leaders from across the region declared the collective sovereignty of the divided Sami nation.

In 1986, the Chernobyl nuclear disaster spread radiation across the Sami homeland. The Sami reindeer herds were found to be contaminated by the released radiation, leading to the slaughter of most of them. Two years later, in 1988, when the herds had begun to recover, national leaders demanded the creation of a regional Sami parliament that would have influence over planning and development. In 1992, the Sami language was given equal status with Norwegian in Norway.

The integration of Europe began to impact on the Sami in the 1990s. The Samis overwhelmingly voted against European Union (EU) membership; the entry of Sweden and Finland into the EU on 1 January 1995 provoked a serious debate on the future of the Sami nation. Sami leaders began a campaign to join the European Union as a separate nation—not Norwegian, Swedish, Russian, or Finnish but Sami. Without full participation in the union as a separate nation, these Samis felt, they would have to meet regulations not of their making, that took no account of the unique conditions of life in the European Arctic. They also feared that the membership of Nordic countries in the EU would eventually lead to loss of control over their land.

Norway's king, Harald V, made an official apology in 1997 for the government's past treatment of the Samis. A government minister in Stockholm apologized to the Samis for past oppression in Sweden in August 1998. The Scandinavian governments have attempted to support Sami culture and their traditional way of life, but in many areas they are still under threat from tourism, land pressure, and assimilation. In January 2000 the Norwegian government announced yet another step to compensate the Sami for damage done to their culture over more than 200 years. The government established a $9.3 million dollar fund to compensate the Samis for the country's policy of forced assimilation, also known as Norwegianization.

The Samis today have equal rights and status in both law and practice in Norway, Sweden, and Finland. The major conflict with the governments is over the continued use of traditional lands, both public and private, and the degradation of the Sami environment.

SELECTED BIBLIOGRAPHY:

Gaski, Harald. *Sami Culture in a New Era: The Norwegian Sami Experience.* 1998.

James, Alan. *Lapps: Reindeer Herders of Lapland.* 1989.

Valkeapaa, Nils-Aslak. *Greetings from Lappland: The Sami—Europe's Forgotten People.* 1983.

Vitebsky, Piers. *The Saami of Lapland.* 1994.

Sanjakis

Sanjaki Muslims; Sandzhakis; Bosniaks; Bosniacs

POPULATION: Approximately (2002e) 525,000 Sanjakis in Yugoslavia, concentrated in the Sanjak (Sandzhak) region, which straddles the border between Serbia and Montenegro.

THE SANJAKI HOMELAND: The Sanjaki homeland lies in the center of the Balkan Peninsula in southwestern Yugoslavia, forming the border region between Serbia, Montenegro, and Bosnia and Herzegovina. The mountainous region includes the Sanjak Plateau, which straddles the border between Serbia and Montenegro. The population is concentrated in the valleys of the Lim and Raska Rivers and their tributaries, with six Sanjaki municipalities in Serbia and five in Montenegro. The Sanjak region has no official status. The historical Sanjak region formed the Turkish Sanjak of Novibazar and now forms the Sandzhak regions of the Yugoslav republics of Montenegro and Serbia. *Region of Sandzhak (Sanjak)*: 3,354 sq. mi.—8,687 sq. km, (2002e) 714,000—Sanjakis 67%, Serbs and Montenegrins* 28%, Albanians 3%, other Yugoslavs 2%. The Sanjaki capital and major cultural center is Novi Pazar, called Novibazar by the Sanjakis, (2002e) 62,000. Other important Sanjaki cultural centers are Pljevla, called Tasildza by the Sanjakis, (2002e) 22,000, and Ivangrad (Andrijevica), (2002e) 20,000, in Montenegro, and Priboj (Pribol), (2002e) 18,000, in Serbia.

FLAG: The Sanjaki national flag, the flag of the national movement, is a white field charged with a centered shield divided diagonally green over blue, separated by a white diagonal stripe, the green bearing three white crescent moons and the blue bearing three gold fleur-de-lys.

PEOPLE AND CULTURE: The Sanjakis, also called Sanjak Muslims, are a South Slav nation related to the Bosnians. Although ethnically related to the neighboring Serbs and Montenegrins, their conversion to Islam during the centuries of Turkish rule set them apart both religiously and culturally. The Sanjaki culture is a Slavic culture that contains many

Turkish traditions and customs and is closely tied to their Muslim religion. The descendents of early Slavs and a later Turkish military aristocracy, the Sanjakis are often called Turks, a derogatory term in the Balkans. The Serbs claim that the Sanjakis are not Slavs but the descendents of Muslims settled in the region by the Turkish authorities in the seventeenth and eighteenth centuries. Many Sanjakis call themselves "Bosniacs," a term that was adopted by several Sanjaki political parties and national societies in 1996.

LANGUAGE AND RELIGION: The Sanjakis speak a dialect of Serbian that is written, like Serbian, in the Cyrillic alphabet. The dialect, called Sanjaki, is a western dialect of Serbian that has incorporated many borrowings from Turkish and Albanian, which is spoken in neighboring Kosovo. At the beginning of the 1990s the Serbian government launched a campaign to eradicate words of Turkish origin from the local dialect.

The Sanjakis are a Sunni Muslim people, as a result of the conquest of the Balkans by the Muslim Turks in the fourteenth century. Religious and social differences kept the Sanjakis from intermarrying with neighboring Slav groups in large numbers. Polygamy, part of the Muslim religion, is prohibited by state law. The Yugoslav communist government established after World War II tolerated Muslim religious observances and institutions, including Islamic schools, but in the early 1990s this toleration ended.

NATIONAL HISTORY: Migrating South Slav tribes, probably from an original homeland in eastern Poland and Ukraine, settled the Lim River valley and the surrounding mountains in the seventh century A.D. The Slavs accepted the authority of the Byzantine Empire, which controlled the region, and by the ninth century the majority of the tribes had adopted the Christian religion of the Byzantines.

In the tenth century, the tribes living in the southern Dinaric Alps embraced a new faith brought to the region by travelers. The faith, a dualistic creed attributed to Bogomil, a Bulgarian priest, taught that every action has two sides—good and evil, life and death, light and dark, etc. The creed, intensely nationalistic and political as well as religious, opposed Slavic serfdom, the authority and wealth of the church, and Byzantine cultural domination. The Slav believers in the region, called Bogomils, were branded heretics by church authorities and were subjected to severe persecution; nonetheless, the Bogomil sect flourished from the tenth to the fifteenth centuries.

In the twelfth century a powerful Serb state emerged in the region with its capital at Raska, near the site of present Novi Pazar. The Orthodox faith of the Serb majority became an integral part of the Serb state culture. The Serbians gradually extended their authority into the isolated Bogomil valleys. Thousands of Bogomils died in massacres and heretic hunts from the twelfth to the fourteenth centuries. The persecuted Bogomils looked to the Turks of the expanding Ottoman Empire for protection from Christian violence. In 1389, just to the south of the Bogomil homeland, at Kosovo Polje, the Field of Blackbirds, a coalition of Christian forces met defeat in one of medieval Europe's largest battles. The defeat opened the way for the expansion of the Turkish Ottoman Empire in the Balkan Peninsula. In 1456 the advancing Turks occupied the Bogomil heartland in the Lim Valley.

The Bogomils, hated and persecuted by both Orthodox and Roman Catholics, were offered protection by the Turks and largely converted to their Islamic religion. As Muslims they became a favored minority; with the Turkish military aristocracy settled on the lands of the annihilated Serb nobility, formed a ruling class that controlled large estates, worked by Christian and Muslim serfs. From the mid-fourteenth century, the Slav Muslims of the region enjoyed full cultural and limited political autonomy.

The region prospered under Turkish rule, and the city of Novibazar gained importance as a regional trading center. The area around the Lim Valley, administered as a separate Turkish province or *sanjak*, called the Sanjak of Novibazar, separated Orthodox Serbia on the east from Orthodox Montenegro to the west. Surrounded by Orthodox majority territories, the region suffered sporadic Christian uprisings during the seventeenth and eighteenth centuries. In 1718 the Austrians occupied the province but made no changes to the existing social structure before withdrawing in 1739.

A widespread uprising in Turkish territory, in 1875, brought Austrian and Russian military intervention and ultimately the Austrian occupation of Bosnia, Herzegovina, and Sanjak in 1878 as part of the Treaty of San Stefano. In 1908, in partial compensation to the Ottomans for the Austrian annexation of Bosnia and Herzegovina, the Austrian authorities returned the Muslim-majority Sanjak of Novibazar to Ottoman Turkish rule.

At the height of the First Balkan War, in October 1912, Serbian and Montenegrin armies overran the Turkish troops defending the Sanjak region. The demarcation line between the two armies became the partition line and eventually the border between Serbia and Montenegro. The Balkan wars left unresolved territorial conflicts that were partly to blame for the outbreak of World War I in 1914. The Serbs and Montenegrins, at war with the Austrians in 1914, were unable to impose changes, and the medieval social organization of the Sanjak remained intact.

An emigration of the Sanjaki population began in 1912–13 and continued after the establishment of the Kingdom of the Serbs, Croats, and Slovenes in 1917. Hundreds of Sanjaki villages were pillaged, and nearly 15,000 Sanjakis were killed in ethnic and religious violence. Sanjaki emigration was encouraged by the Yugoslav and Turkish governments. At the end of the First World War in 1918 the Muslim landlords were ousted and serfdom was outlawed. The Sanjakis, formerly the landed gentry of the region, became a despised, landless Muslim minority in an intensely nationalistic and Christian state. Between the two world wars, they were denied official recognition and suffered official discrimination and periodic, often violent, persecution. Only the Communist Party of Yugoslavia, in 1937, recognized the Sanjakis as a separate ethnic group.

In 1941 Yugoslavia fell to the invading Fascist forces of Germany and Italy. The Sanjak region became the focus of ethnic fighting, reprisals, and widespread atrocities perpetuated by all sides. The Sanjaki leaders declared the region autonomous in 1943, but following the withdrawal of German troops in 1944, thousands of Sanjakis fled as Tito's communist partisans took control and systematically eliminated all opposition. Tito's postwar division of Yugoslavia into six ethnic republics brought Sanjaki demands for the unification of the Muslim majority territories in Serbia and Montenegro and for the creation of a separate Sanjak republic within the Yugoslav federation. The neighboring Montenegrins, with approximately the same national population, were given their own republic, but Tito refused to consider the demands of the Muslim Sanjakis.

Up to World War II the Sanjakis identified themselves only by their religion, or as Muslim Serbs or Montenegrins; in the decades after the war there evolved a separate national identity. In the 1948 census, the Sanjakis were listed as Muslims, and in 1953 they were counted as "undetermined Yugoslavs." Though recognized, along with the neighboring Bosnians, as a separate Muslim nationality in 1969, they were again counted as simply Muslims in the Yugoslav census of 1981. According to the Council of Migrant Affairs, over 200,000 Sanjakis emigrated from Sanjak, Kosovo, and Macedonia from the end of World War II to 1960.

The death of Tito in 1980 began a slow unraveling of the federation he had held together. The collapse of communism in 1989 accelerated the growth of nationalism across the Balkans and stirred the long-dormant Sanjaki national identity. In late 1989 and early 1990 large demonstrations demanded national rights and protested growing Serb oppression. The disintegration of the Yugoslav federation in 1990–91 stimulated a Sanjaki campaign to follow the other Yugoslav national groups to independence; however, their lack of arms and the threat of the powerful Yugoslav National Army dampened pro–independence fervor, but not demands for cultural and political autonomy. Serb paramilitary groups formed and engaged in violent harassment of the Sanjaki Muslims.

Serbian president Slobodan Milosevic in March 1991 mobilized Serbian police regiments against alleged separatist unrest in the region. In late October 1991, 70.2% of the regional population took part in a referendum on autonomy; 98.9% voted in favor in defiance of the Serb authorities. Just hours after the polls opened Serb police moved in to forcibly close them, but the voting continued in secret. The Serbian government declared the referendum illegal and rejected demands for autonomy. As part of a campaign to remove Turkish elements from the language, the region, popularly known as Sanjak, was renamed the Raska Region.

The Sanjakis boycotted a 1992 referendum that affirmed the truncated Yugoslav federation of Serbia and Montenegro. In late 1993, violent incidents broke out between Sanjaki demonstrators and radical Serb nationalists but were quickly brought under control, as the Serbs feared a violent confrontation within their own borders while their armed forces were fighting in Croatia and in Bosnia and Herzegovina. In 1994, 24 Sanjaki nationalist leaders were arrested and put on trial, charged with plotting the secession of the Sanjak from Yugoslavia. The trial fueled Sanjaki nationalism but raised new fear among the Sanjakis that the repression suffered by the neighboring Kosovars could easily be inflicted on them by the Serbian authorities. Regional health-care centers were closed, and Sanjaki Muslims were expelled from local police forces and schools.

During the Bosnian war, the Sanjak was used by Serbian troops and militias as a hinterland to which they could withdrew from the fighting. The Sanjaki Muslims were terrorized by the Serbian radicals, and about 80,00 fled, seeking shelter in other parts of the country or abroad. Around 70,000 Sanjakis were forcibly expelled from villages close to the Bosnian border or in other militarily sensitive regions. Bomb attacks against mosques, houses, and stores continued into the late 1990s. The spokesmen of the leading national organization, the Muslim National Council of Sanjak (MNCS), in 1994 described Serbian allegations that the Sanjakis wished to unite with the Bosnians as pure imagination.

Several international human rights organizations and the U.S. government reported on the increasing human rights violations and ethnic cleansing in the region in 1995–96. This included official intimidation, tolerance of violent activities by Serbian paramilitary groups, political arrests, and the arrest and conviction of Sanjaki activists. In August 1995, the Serbian government began settling Serbian refugees from Bosnia and Croatia in the Sanjak region. Nationalists accused the Serbian government of trying to alter the region's ethnic composition. Thousands of Sanjakis fled to Muslim regions of neighboring Bosnia or Montenegro. In 1996, the Montenegrin government recognized the Sanjakis as a separate ethnic group within the Republic of Montenegro.

In 1997, Dr. Sulejman Ugljanin, a member of the federal parliament of Yugoslavia and president of the MNCS, was tried, as part of a crackdown on Sanjaki nationalism that began in 1993, for advocating secession. The trial was accompanied by a wave of violence and arrests of Sanjaki leaders. Many Sanjakis were prevented from voting in local and parliamentary elections throughout the 1990s, but particularly in the municipal and federal elections in 1996. In July 1997, the government of Slobodan Milosevic dismissed the Muslim-led local government in Novi Pazar and replaced it with members of Milosevic's own Socialist Party and his wife's Yugoslav United Left.

The overthrow of Milosevic brought a new Serbian government to power, although still dominated by Serbian nationalists little disposed to allow Muslim autonomy within the republic. The Sanjakis were cautiously optimistic that international pressure would bring democratic changes and end the oppression they had endured for over a decade. They hoped for an end of the Serbian government policy of official and unofficial harassment, including ethnic cleansing, which would allow the estimated 200,000 Sanjakis who left the region between 1989 and early 2000 to return to their homeland. Should a new democratic Yugoslavia emerge from the change of government, the Sanjakis will again press for cultural, religious, and economic autonomy.

In early October 2000, several Sanjaki groups demanded special ties to the Muslims of Bosnia, like the special relationship of the Serbs of Bosnia and Herzegovina with Serbia.

Nationalists in November 2000 put forward a proposal for a Sanjak republic with equal status with the partners of the Yugoslav Federation, Serbia and Montenegro. Moves by the Montenegrins to separate from Yugoslavia, including a referendum scheduled for early 2002, led to calls for the Sanjakis to follow. In October 2001 Sanjakis in Montenegro appealed to the government to support Sanjaki plans for the reunification and self-determination of Sanjak.

SELECTED BIBLIOGRAPHY:

Kaplan, Robert D. *Balkan Ghosts.* 1993.

Kappeler, Andreas, ed. *Muslim Communities Reemerge: Historical Perspectives on Nationality, Politics, and Opposition in the Former Soviet Union and Yugoslavia.* 1994.

Murvar, Vatro. *Nationalism and Religion in Central Europe and the Western Balkans.* Vol. 1. *The Muslims in Bosnia, Hercegovina and Sandzak: A Sociological Analysis.* 1990.

Silber, Laura, and Allan Little. *Yugoslavia: Death of a Nation.* 1997.

Santhals

Santals; Adivasis; Sandals; Sangtals; Santhalis; Sentalis; Santhalas; Hor; Har; Satars

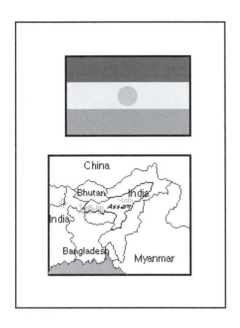

POPULATION: Approximately (2002e) 890,000 Santhals in northeastern India and neighboring countries, concentrated in the state of Assam, but with sizable communities in the neighboring districts of the states Meghalaya and Tripura, and in Bangladesh and Nepal.

THE SANTHAL HOMELAND: The Santhal homeland lies in northeastern India, in the western districts of Kokrajhar, Bongaigaon, Dhubri, and Nalbari of the state of Assam. Much of the region is given over to the cultivation of tea. The tea plantations, locally called tea gardens, provide employment to the majority of the Santhals. Santhal nationalists demand the creation of a separate state to be called Adivasiland, but their territorial claims remain fluid and undeveloped. The Santhal capital and major cultural center is Kokrajhar, (2002e) 33,000.

FLAG: The Santhal national flag, the flag of the national movement, is a horizontal tricolor of green, white, and red, bearing a centered gold disk on the white stripe.

PEOPLE AND CULTURE: The Santhals are a tribal people originally from the Chota Nagpur Plateau now in the states of Jharkhand, Orissa, Madya Pradesh, and West Bengal. Traditional festivals, such as Karem, a celebration of coming of age involving 9 days of fasting by young, unmarried girls, are very popular among the Santhal population. The festivals usually include singing, dance competitions, and sports events such as football matches.

LANGUAGE AND RELIGION: The Santhal language is an Austric language belonging to the Munda language group. The language, spoken by over 5 million people spread over Bihar, Orissa, West Bengal, Tripura, and Assam, is made up of a number of regional dialects. The dialects spoken by the Santhals of northeastern India, in Assam and Tripura, is often called the tea dialects. The language does not have a script but is written, in the northeast, in the Bengali or Roman scripts. The language has incorporated considerable borrowings from the neighboring Indo-European languages, Assamese and Bengali. English words have often been adopted for items or activities brought to the region during colonial times. A bible was written the Santhal language in 1914, and was finally published in 1994 in the Bengali script.

The Santhals are divided religiously, with Hindu, Christian, and animist communities. The basis of traditional Santhal religion is the belief that they are totally surrounded by *bongas*, spirits, and are frequently visited by deceased ancestors. About 15% belong to various Christian sects, primarily Baptist.

NATIONAL HISTORY: Munda peoples, believed to have originated in central or southeastern Asia, inhabited large tracts of northern India before the Dravidian occupation pushed them into the least productive jungle highlands. Isolated from the plains, the tribes developed distinctive cultures. They adopted many Dravidian cultural traits, but retained their indigenous cultures.

The Santhals, the largest of the Munda tribes, survived the Aryan invasions that swept northern India between 1700 and 1200 B.C. from the Iranian Plateau. The Aryans, lighter skinned and more warlike, drove the Dravidians into southern India, but mostly ignored the inaccessible jungles of the Chota Nagpur Plateau. Under successive Aryan kingdoms the Santhals maintained semi-independent status under local chiefs and rulers.

In the twelfth century, the plateau was overrun by Muslim invaders and in 1497 was annexed to the Muslim-dominated Delhi Sultanate. Efforts to convert the pagan and Hindu Santhals to Islam was partially successful, although Muslim rituals and beliefs were added to the animist and Hindu mixture that developed as the Santhal religion.

The British gained control of the Chota Nagpur Plateau in 1765. They added the plateau region to the huge province of Bengal. In 1826, the British took control of Assam in the northwest, which was also added to Bengal. Rapid development of the rich agricultural areas of Assam became official colonial policy. Government incentives were offered to European entrepreneurs to establish plantations for the production of rubber, hemp, jute, and most importantly, tea. Since the indigenous peoples of Assam refused plantation work, the British recruited impoverished Santhals and other tribal peoples from southern Bihar, western Bengal, and Orissa. By the turn of the century more than one-half million of these "coolies" were employed on over 700 plantations producing 145 million pounds of tea annually.

Many Santhals were converted to Christianity by British and American missionaries in the nineteenth century. Conversion to Christianity was often embraced as a way of escaping the rigid Hindu caste system that relegated the Santhals to the lowest rungs of society. Western-style education began a process of change among the poor and oppressed tea workers. New leaders, educated at mission schools, soon challenged the traditional hold on the Santhals that amounted to virtual slavery.

The imported tea workers ultimately settled down and successive generations intermingled and assimilated much of the Assamese culture to develop a lifestyle of their own in close rapport with the tea plant. In spite of hardships and deprivations, the tribal workers, taking the name of the largest of the groups, the Santhals, developed a distinct culture, including a unique musical tradition, dances refined in their new homeland in Assam, and the production of tea, which formed a central part of the Santhal culture. In the 1920s and 1930s, some Santhals began to leave the tea plantations to take work in the growing towns and cities.

Considered outsiders by the indigenous Assam tribal peoples, the Santhals were often the target of ethnic violence. Their largest population centers were located in the western foothills and plains of the Brahmaputra River basin, a region populated by the Bodos* and other Tibeto-Burman peoples. In the 1930s and 1940s, there were a number of violent confrontations between Bodos and Santhals. The Santhals and Bodos who cohabited areas without any animosity for years began to view each other with a sense of fear and distrust.

During World War II, when Assam was the object of a Japanese thrust into India, the Santhals were at first courted as Japanese allies, but their refusal to join the anti-British forces led most to join the British forces fighting the Japanese. After World War II, the British prepared to grant independence to the subcontinent, but rejected numerous demands for separate statehood and finally agreed to the partition of British India into two large states, India, a secular state dominated by Hindus, and Pakistan for the Muslims.

The state of Assam, which included many non-Assamese tribal groups, remained a center of nationalist tensions. Regional cultures and variations were too distinct to remain within a single political administration. New tribal states were carved out of Assamese territory, Nagaland in 1963, followed by Meghalaya and Mizoram in 1971, and Arunchal Pradesh in 1972. The creation of these states spurred numerous separatist movements among the remaining tribal groups in Assam, including the increasingly militant Santhals.

The Bodos, claiming a majority in the western districts of Assam, demanded an autonomous state in the mid-1980s. Young Bodo militants turned on the large Santhal population in an effort to drive them from the region. Conflict between the two peoples became a serious threat, the only restraint being the lack of arms.

In the 1980s, young Adivasis, weary of government inaction and a lack of protection against attacks by Bodos and other tribal peoples, formed the Adivasi Cobra Force (ACF). Militants of the ACF, often trained by other militant groups operating in Assam, concentrated in retaliation attacks against Bodo aggression. The violence between the two peoples spread across a large part of western Assam.

The creation of an autonomous Bodo homeland in 1995 in western Assam was opposed by the large Santhal population. Santhal activists claimed that the Bodos were not the majority group in the Bodo Autonomous Council and that there were more Santhals in Assam than Bodos. The Santhals, not accepted as a scheduled tribe, were unable to block the Bodos, who secured election to the autonomous assembly and the parliamentary seats reserved for the scheduled tribes. Santhal leaders demanded that all areas dominated by Santhal communities should be excluded from the autonomous council area.

The Assamese government responded to Santhal concerns by stating that it would not discriminate in providing rations, medical, and other facilities to the Bodos and Santhals. State government spokesmen also added that the government had no intention of further dividing the state.

Violations of human rights became rampant in Assam State. Abductions, ransom, extortion by militant groups, and the atrocities unleashed by state and federal security forces made life very difficult for the Santhals, still considered outsiders by most Assamese groups. Unprecedented levels of violence and the emergence of a number of insurgent groups and militant organizations further complicated the ethnic conflict.

The Bodo Accord, signed in 1992, envisaged the creation of an autonomous council for the Bodos, but was signed without finalizing the boundaries and jurisdiction of the council. Disputes over the inclusion of villages and areas with over 50% Bodo population, as stipulated by a clause inserted later, led militants to espouse the idea of driving non-Bodos from disputed areas to achieve a Bodo majority, setting the scene for one of Asia's bloodiest conflicts.

In 1993 and 1996, ethnic rioting swept the region, pitting the Santhals against the Bodos. Hundreds were killed and up to 40,000 Santhals were driven from their homes in areas claimed by Bodo nationalists. The Birsa Command Force (BCF) began to operate after the ethnic riots to protect the Santhals. The BCF and ACF activists served notice to all communities irrespective of any profession or ethnic affiliation that attacks on Santhals would be revenged.

The ethnic conflict disrupted the vital tea industry. Executives and managers of tea plantations employing Santhals also became the targets of Bodo militants. Although the Assamese government stood to loose considerable revenue from the disruption, little was done to end the conflict.

Santhal leaders chalked out a plan to form a separate Santhal homeland in Assam by force. The proposed homeland, called Adivasiland, stretched from the Sankoch River in Kokrajhar District to the Panch River and the

Indo-Bhutanese border to the southern railway line north of the Brahmaputra River.

Bodo militants, armed with bows and arrows, axes, and machetes, attacked a number of Santhal villages in September 1998, driving several thousand Santhals into already overcrowded refugee camps in Kokrajhar District. With over 200,000 people in the camps by early 2000, the problem became one of South Asia's biggest refugee crises. By January 2000, 30 inmates of the Bhaoraguri refugee camp in Bongaigaon District died of starvation. The camps, stalked by hunger and violence, fed the growing militancy of the Santhal population. Many view the creation of a separate Santhal state, within India or not, as the only protection they will ever have from Bodo ethnic cleansing.

Santhal militants stepped up their activities in Kokrajhar and Bongaigaon districts in 2000, collecting funds from sympathizers to buy arms and finance the increasingly violent struggle for self-determination and a Santhal homeland. Extortion was also used against non-Santhals, particularly Bengalis and Assamese businessmen. The number of Santal organizations and group, both moderate and militant, proliferated.

Between 1996 and 2002, over 5,000 people died in the conflict and over 250,000, mostly Santhals, were driven from their homes. Santhal militants, from camps inside Bhutan near Kokjahar District, which borders West Bengal, became more aggressive as the conflict worsened. Where the Santhals were mostly victims in the late 1990s, but early 2000 militants were retaliating against the Bodos for every attack on the Santhals.

In early 2001, Christian leaders of both the Santhals and Bodos attempted to mediate the conflict to end the violence. Catholic and Lutheran workers were also the major aid providers in the refugee camps, subsidizing government food supplies. Missionaries have opened schools inside the camps, besides providing medical help. Although the Christians try to create an atmosphere of peace between the two groups, the ethnic war goes on.

A government minister, in March 2001, proposed that the Santhals living in Assam prior to Indian independence in 1947 should be accorded the status of scheduled caste, with the facilities and benefits enjoyed by other similarly placed communities. While the proposal was accepted by some Santhal leaders, the militant groups rejected it.

A ten-member delegation representing the All Adivasi Students' Association of Assam (AASAA) traveled to New Delhi in August 2001 to meet the Indian prime minister and officials of the home ministry. The AASAA representatives pressed their three main demands, scheduled tribal status for all the Santhals of Assam, provision of proper relief and rehabilitation of riot victims and refugees from the 1993, 1996, and 1998 ethnic fighting, and a permanent solution of the problems of the non-Bodos in the Bodo Autonomous Council of Assam.

SELECTED BIBLIOGRAPHY:

Baruah, Sanjib. *Assam and the Politics of Nationality.* 1999.

Chhabra, K.M.L. *Assam Challenge.* 1992.

Gokhale, Nitin A. *The Hot Brew: The Assam Tea Industry's Most Turbulent Decade, 1987–1997.* 1997.

Sen, Sipra. *Tribes and Castes of Assam.* 1999.

Sanussis

Senussis; Sanusis; Sanusiyya; Cyrenaicans

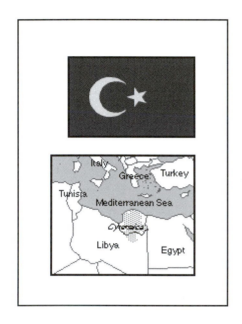

POPULATION: Approximately (2002e) 1,485,000 Sanussis in Libya, concentrated in the eastern region of Cyrenaica.

THE SANUSSI HOMELAND: The Sanussi homeland, Cyrenaica, lies in northern Africa, consisting of a coastal plain that gives way gradually to fertile highlands, the Jabal Akhdar or Green Mountain, which suggests Mediterranean Europe, and still farther south is the vast Sahara Desert, a barren wasteland of sand. To the west the desert region called the Sirtica separates the Maghrib, western North Africa including Tripolitania, from the Mashriq, the part of North Africa oriented to the Arab Middle Eastern countries. The historic region of Cyrenaica forms the provinces of Ajdabiyah, Banghazi, Darnah, Al- Jabal al Akhdar, al-Kufra, and Tubruq. *Region of Cyrenaica (Barqah)*: 330,258 sq. mi.—855,368 sq. km, (2002e) 1,703,000—Sanussis 78%, other Libyans 22%. The Sanussi capital and major cultural center is Benghazi, called Banghazi in the local dialect, (2002e) 714,000, metropolitan area 1,066,000. Other important cultural centers are Ajdabiyah, (2002e) 121,000, al-Bayda, called Beida locally, (2002e) 130,000, Darnah, (2002e) 119,000, al-Marj, (2002e) 157,000, and Tubruq, (2002e) 145,000.

FLAG: The Sanussi national flag, the traditional flag of the Sanussi movement and the flag of independent Cyrenaica, is a black field charged with a white crescent moon and five-pointed white star.

PEOPLE AND CULTURE: The Sanussis are an ethnoreligious group influenced by their ancient Greek past, the traditional nomadic lifestyle of the Bedouins, and the religious teachings of a prophet, Sayyid Muhammad ibn 'Ali as-Sanussi. Many Sanussis have fair skin and light eyes, traits attributed to their Greek ancestors. They are renowned as warriors, and the *qabilah*, or tribe, remains the basic unit of their social structure. The Sanussi are divided into two social classes, the seminomadic shepherds along the edge of the desert, and people who have embraced settled farming in the fertile coastal strip. As in most Bedouin societies, the women form the labor force, while the men protect and plan for the group. Although the Sanussis once considered it degrading to do manual labor, this has changed somewhat in recent years, particularly among the increasingly urbanized population. Marriage outside the group is rare, although increasing among the urban Sanussis.

LANGUAGE AND RELIGION: The language of the Sanussis is a dialect of Badawi or Bedouin Arabic, unlike the dialects of Tripolitania and Fezzan, which belong to the Maghribi group spoken throughout northwestern Africa. The Cyrenaican dialect, called Eastern Libyan Arabic, more closely resembles those of Egypt and the Middle East than the dialect spoken in the Libyan capital, Tripoli, 620 miles (1,000 km) to the west. Urban and coastal dialects differ somewhat from those of the desert hinterland. Despite an Arabization process during the 1970s, English occupies an increasingly important place as the second language of the region. In 1986 Muammar Qadhafi announced a policy of eliminating the teaching of English in favor of instruction in Russian at all levels, but with the collapse of the Soviet Union the English language became the second language of the urban and professional Sanussi population.

The Sanussis are Sunni Muslims of the Malikite school. They follow the teachings of Sayyid Muhammad ibn 'Ali as-Sanussi, a nineteenth-century Muslim prophet who sought to revive the early purity of Islam. The Sanussi movement is a religious movement adapted to desert life, and it remains strong in Cyrenaica, where it gives the disparate tribes a religious attachment and a feeling of unity and purpose. Their particular Muslim beliefs have made the Sanussis one of the more gentle of the North African peoples, less attracted to radical movements or Islamic fundamentalism.

NATIONAL HISTORY: Greek colonists settled the northern half of ancient Cyrenaica in the seventh century B.C. The region, lying just 186 miles (300 km) south of Crete, was known as Pentapolis, for five major cities the Greek colonists established. The city of Cyrene, the mother city and the cultural and trade center of the Pentapolis, eventually gave its name to the entire region. Cordial relations between the Greeks and the indigenous tribes resulted in much intermarriage. The last Greek ruler of Cyrenaica, Ptolemy Apion, bequeathed the region to Rome on his death.

Successive waves of Arabs, beginning with the Arab conquest in A.D. 642, imposed Islam and the Arabic language along with political domination of the mixed inhabitants of Cyrenaica. Conversion to Islam was largely accomplished by 1300 A.D., but Arabic replaced the indigenous Berber dialects more slowly. Geography was the principal determinant in the separate historical development of Cyrenaica, which was cut off from neighboring regions by formidable deserts.

In the eleventh century, other Bedouin tribes, the Bani Hilal and the

Bani Salim, invaded Cyrenaica and imposed their nomadic way of life. This influx of Bedouins disrupted Berber settlement patterns, and in many areas tribal life was introduced or strengthened.

The Bedouins of Cyrenaica remained fiercely independent, although Egyptians or Turks often claimed the region they exercised little more than nominal control. In the fifteenth century, merchants from Tripoli revived the markets in some areas, but the main source of income for centuries was from the pilgrims and caravans passing between the Maghrib and Egypt who needed to buy protection from the Bedouin tribes. Early in the eighteenth century Cyrenaica became a Turkish possession, eventually known as Bengasi.

The founder of the Sanussi religious order, Muhammad ibn 'Ali as-Sanussi, was a religious scholar and holy man. Early in his religious life he had come under the influence of the Sufis, religious mystics who inspired an Islamic revival in northern Africa in the eighteenth and nineteenth centuries. Born near Oran in Algeria in 1787, he traveled widely, studying and teaching. His reputation spread, and in 1830 he was honored as the Grand Sanussi, the Sanussi al-Kabir. Disturbed by divisions and dissension within Islam, the Grand Sanussi believed that only a return to the purity of early Islam and austerity in faith and morals could restore the faith to its rightful grandeur. Concerned with both the perceived weakening of Islamic political power and the decline of Islamic thought, he organized a religious order near Mecca in 1837, but threats from the Turkish authorities forced him to return to North Africa. His original intention, to settle in Algeria, was impossible due to the expansion of French authority in his homeland, so he settled in Cyrenaica, where Turkish rule was only tenuous. The tribesmen of the Green Mountains were particularly receptive to his ideas, and in 1843 he founded the first Cyrenaican association, at al-Bayda.

The Grand Sanussi refused to tolerate fanaticism and forbade the use of stimulants. The practice of voluntary poverty was encouraged, and members were to eat and dress within the limits of religious law. Unlike in other religious orders, members were to earn their living through work instead of depending on alms. The Bedouins of Cyrenaica had shown no interest in the ecstatic practices of the Sufi orders, which were gaining popularity in the towns, but they were attracted in great numbers to the Sanussi teachings. The austerity of the Sanussi message was especially suited to the character of the Cyrenaican Bedouins, whose way of life had not changed markedly in the centuries since the Arabs overran North Africa in the seventh century.

The leaders of the Sanussi movement encouraged the Bedouins to render homage that verged on veneration of the Grand Sanussi as a Muslim saint, an act forbidden in orthodox Islamic teachings. The Cyrenaican tribesmen regarded him as a *marabout*, or spiritual leader, but he won their allegiance as both a religious and secular leader. The order eventually added a network of lodges throughout Cyrenaica that bound together the disparate tribal systems of the region. Before his death in 1859, the Grand Sanussi established the order's center at al-Jaghbub, at the intersection of the pilgrimage route to Mecca and the main trade route from the Mediterranean coast and the Sudan. The Grand Sanussi's son, Muhammad, succeeded him as the leader of the order. Under his rule, the Sanussis reached the peak of their influence; Muhammad was recognized as their *mahdi*, spiritual and political leader.

The Sanussi order ultimately allowed its leaders to transform themselves into a potent political force capable of holding together a growing national movement against the expansion of French influence in North Africa. Although the order had never used force in its missionary activities, the Mahdi proclaimed a *jihad* or holy war to resist French encroachments, bringing the Sanussis for the first time into confrontation with a European colonial power. Upon the Mahdi's death in 1902 he was succeeded by his young cousin, Muhammad Idris as-Sanussi. The call to political activism was concentrated in North Africa, where the Sanussi warriors fought French expansion from 1902 to 1913; in 1911, following the Italian invasion of Cyrenaica, they concentrated there.

For many Sanussis, Ottoman Turkey's defeat by the Italians in the Italo-Turkish War of 1911–12 was a betrayal of Muslim interests to infidels. The 1912 Treaty of Lausanne formally granted independence to Tripolitania and Cyrenaica, and the Italians simultaneously announced the formal annexation of the former Turkish territories. The treaty was meaningless to the Sanussi tribesmen, who continued to fight against Italian domination. Fighting in Cyrenaica was conducted by Sanussi units led by Ahmad ash Sharif, acting as regent for the young Idris as-Sanussi, whose determined resistance prevented Italian consolidation.

The Sanussi tribesmen's purpose in fighting the colonial power was defending Islam and the free life they had always followed in their tribal territories. In 1914 the Sanussis attacked into Fezzan, quickly wiping out recent Italian gains there. By early 1915 captured rifles, artillery, and munitions allowed them to attack into Tripolitania, but the success of the Sanussi campaign was compromised by the traditional hostility that existed between the Cyrenaican tribes and the Tripolitanians.

When Italy entered World War I as an allied power in 1915, the war in Cyrenaica became part of the wider conflict. Germany and Turkey sent arms and advisers to the Sanussi leaders, who aligned the tribes with the Central Powers with the objective of tying down Italian and British troops in North Africa. In 1916, Turkish officers led the Sanussis on a campaign into Egypt, where they were defeated by British troops. Ahmad ash Sharif fled aboard a German submarine, leaving the young Idris to open negotiations with the victorious allies on behalf of Cyrenaica in 1917. Pro-

British Idris obtained a truce rather than a conclusive peace treaty, for neither the Italians nor the Sanussis fully surrendered their claims to Cyrenaica. Italy and the United Kingdom recognized Idris as the emir of interior Cyrenaica on the condition that Sanussi attacks on coastal towns and into Egyptian territory cease. Further consideration of Cyrenaica's political status was deferred until after the termination of the war.

Italy's claim to the territories of Tripolitania, Fezzan, and Cyrenaica were recognized by the allies at the end of the war, but Italian authority was still confined to the coastal enclaves, sometimes under conditions of virtual siege. On 31 October 1919, the Italian government granted autonomy to Cyrenaica and recognized Idris al-Sanussi as emir, but with limited authority. The provinces of Tripolitania and Cyrenaica were administered as separate colonies, and southern Fezzan was organized as a military territory. In 1920 an accord was reached between the Italian authorities and the Sanussi leaders that confirmed Idris as emir of Cyrenaica and recognized the virtual independence of an immense area that encompassed much of the Libyan Desert and the principal oases.

The Italians easily controlled neighboring Tripolitania, which lacked the leadership and organizational structure of the Sanussis in Cyrenaica. The aims of the Tripolitanian nationalists and the largely Bedouin Sanussis were fundamentally opposed, the Tripolitanians being concerned with a united, centralized Libyan republic, while the Sanussis were interested in creating an independent tribal state in Cyrenaica. In 1919 and 1920, Tripolitanian leaders negotiated with the Italians for autonomy, but the talks failed when the Tripolitanians claimed to represent the Cyrenaicans. In 1922, the Tripolitanians met with the Sanussi leaders of Cyrenaica and offered to support Idris as emir of both Cyrenaica and Tripolitania. Idris eventually accepted, bringing renewed fighting with the Italian forces; Idris was forced into exile in Egypt.

The second Italo-Sanussi war began early in 1923 with the Italian occupation of territory around Benghazi. The Sanussi order was officially abolished in 1930, and al-Kufrah, the last Sanussi stronghold, fell to the Italians in 1931. In 1934 the Italian government merged the colonies of Cyrenaica and Tripoli into the colony of Italian North Africa or Libya. By 1940 some 50,000 Italian peasant colonists had converted fertile northern Cyrenaica into an Italian province, producing cereals, fruits, and wines for export to Italy.

Nationalists in Cyrenaica saw their best hope for liberation from the colonial regime in Italy's defeat following the outbreak of war in Europe in September 1939. Idris was accepted as leader of the Nationalist cause by Tripolitanians as well as the Sanussis, with the proviso that he designate an advisory committee with representatives from both regions. Differences between the two groups proved too profound for the committee to work well. When Italy entered the war as an ally of Germany in June 1940, the leaders of Cyrenaica immediately declared their support of the Allies, but the Tripolitanians vacillated until arrangements for cooperation with the British were initiated. Five Libyan battalions, largely with veterans of the Italo-Sanussi wars, were organized by the British. The Libyan Arab Force, popularly called the Sanussi Army, served with distinction throughout the desert campaigns that ended with the liberation of Cyrenaica. Cyrenaica changed hands three times and was largely destroyed before British troops finally occupied the region in 1942 and allowed the last Italian colonists to be evacuated. Cyrenaica in 1945 was 98% Muslim and Arabic-speaking and had largely reverted to pastoralism. Many Sanussis were not enthusiastic about Libyan unity and pressed for a separate, British-supported Sanussi government in Cyrenaica.

Italy by 1947 had relinquished all claims to Libya, and two years later a United Nations General Assembly resolution approved the independence of Libya as a federal state of Cyrenaica, Fezzan, and Tripolitania. Emir Idris, with British backing, unilaterally proclaimed Cyrenaica an independent emirate on 1 March 1949. In 1951 the United Kingdom of Libya was proclaimed, with Emir Idris enthroned as Idris I. A national assembly was formed, consisting of delegates from the three regions. In February 1952 the first national elections were held. The Sanussis demonstrated their determination to retain their regional autonomy even after Libyan unification and independence, and they pressed for the formation of a loose federation with a weak central government that would permit major autonomy under Idris.

In the countryside traditional Arab life, including traditional forms of dress, persisted into the 1950s. The oil boom of the 1960s transformed the Libyan kingdom, creating great prosperity and raising the Libyan living standards from among the lowest in the world to a level that began to accommodate substantial reforms. Employment opportunities grew rapidly and plans were set in motion for improved housing, health care, and education. In 1963 Cyrenaica was abolished as a province of the United Kingdom of Libya as the government increasingly centralized its authority.

In September 1969 a revolution bought Muammar al Qadhafi to power in Libya, transferring power from the Sanussi elite to the tribesmen of the Fezzan interior and the urban population of Tripoli. The one-party state imposed by Qadhafi made the first real attempt to unify Libya's diverse peoples and to create a distinct Libyan identity. Financed by oil revenues, the Qadhafi regime aspired to leadership in Arab and world affairs, while imposing a strict authoritarian rule on Cyrenaica and other reluctant regions. A significant degree of government direction, much of it dictated by Qadhafi himself, organized national life and stifled dissent in whatever form. The name Cyrenaica was changed to Eastern Libya; however, the older name remained intimately associated with its distinct history and people.

The Sanussi movement was virtually banned, but in the 1980s and 1990s Sanussi resistance to the Qadhafi regime continued despite harsh repression. Although the government denied that any problems existed, scorched hills and other damage were often attributed to rumored fighting in the region in 1996. Despite official denials of unrest in the region, hundreds of foreigners were expelled from the region after September 1996. Rumors of a serious rebellion in the Green Mountain region were strenuously denied by the Libyan government.

Under Qadhafi's rule the three regions, in spite of efforts at unity, have retained their separate identities. Tripolitania, the dominant region, has retained its cultural ties with the Maghrib to the west, with which it shares culture, geography, and a common history. Its traditional capital, Tripoli, now the Libyan national capital, has become the only important city in the country, while Cyrenaica's capital, Benghazi, has languished. In contrast to Tripolitania, the Sanussis of Cyrenaica have remained oriented toward Egypt and the Middle East. The degree of separateness of the Libyan regions is still sufficiently pronounced to represent a significant obstacle to the government's efforts to create a unified Libyan state.

The region remains the center of resistance to the Qadhafi government in 2001–02. The government's security forces maintain checkpoints every 12 miles (20 km) or so along Cyrenaica's main roads. Although the pragmatic Sanussis now concentrate on economic matters, Sanussi rebels called Jihadis remain hidden in caves and strongholds in the Green Mountains. From their hideouts they continue to harass Libyan patrols and to disrupt government attempts to gain full control of the fertile region. Since the lifting of the seven-year-old United Nations air embargo in early 2000, the Sanussis have hoped for greater contact with the outside world, particularly neighboring Egypt.

SELECTED BIBLIOGRAPHY:

Collins, Robert O., ed. *Africa's Thirty Years War: Libya, Chad, and the Sudan 1963–1993.* 1999.
Evans-Pritchard, E.E. *The Sanusi of Cyrenaica.* 1963.
Ovendale, Ritchie. *The Longman Campanion to the Middle East since 1914.* 1992.
Vikor, Knut. *Sufi and Scholar on the Desert Edge: Muhammad bin 'Ali al-Sanusi and His Brotherhood.* 1995.

Sards

Sardinians; Sardu

POPULATION: Approximately (2002e) 1,952,000 Sards in Italy, 1,335,000 in Sardinia, with large Sard populations in other regions of Italy and in France, Switzerland, and Germany. Outside Europe there are Sard communities in the United States, Australia, and South America.

THE SARD HOMELAND: The Sard homeland is an island, the second largest in the Mediterranean after Sicily. Mountainous Sardinia lies in the western Mediterranean Sea some 100 miles west of the Italian mainland and just south of the French island of Corsica, which is separated from Sardinia by the Strait of Bonifacio, just seven miles wide at its narrowest point. The region of Sardinia has long been the poorest of Italy's regions. Sardinia, called Sardigna in the Sard language and Sardegna in Italian, has formed a semi–autonomous region of the Italian republic since 1948. *Region of Sardinia (Sardigna)*: 9,302 sq. mi.—24,098 sq. km, (2002e) 1,668,000—Sards 80%, other Italians 15%, Corsicans* 2%, others 3%. The Sardinian capital and major cultural center is Cagliari, called Calaris in the Sard language, (2002e) 164,000, metropolitan area 332,000. The other important cultural center is Sassari, called Tàttari in Sard, (2002e) 120,000.

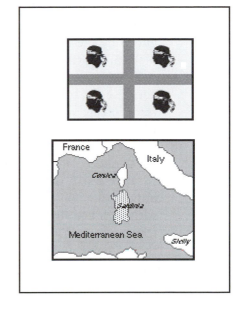

FLAG: The Sardinian national flag, the official flag of the region, is a white field divided by a centered red cross, each white rectangle charged with a black Moor's head with a white headband in profile.

PEOPLE AND CULTURE: The Sards are a distinct Romance people, the descendents of early Latins and the island's many later conquerors. The Sards have the most distinct culture and language of all the Italian peoples, except the German-speaking Tyroleans,* and they have a tradition of resistance to foreign influence that extends from Roman rule to the present. Traditionally the Sards are more soft-spoken and reserved than the other Italian peoples, but at the same time they are very proud and have often engaged in violent vendettas over points of honor. A small minority, around the city of Algero, has preserved much of the culture and language brought to the island by the Catalans.* The differences in dialects, local traditions, and historical rivalries sharply divide the Sard regions and communities; however, hospitality to strangers and loyalty characterize the Sard code of honor. The traditional isolation of the island has preserved many traditions.

LANGUAGE AND RELIGION: The Sards speak a distinct Romance language called Sardu. The language is the most similar of all the Romance languages to Vulgar Latin and is spoken in four major dialects—Campidanese in the south; Gallurese, influenced by the Tuscan and Corsican dialects, in the northeast; Logurdese in the center; and Sassarese, influenced by the dialect of the Ligurians,* in the northeast. Each of the four dialects is further divided into regional subdialects, none of which has been selected as the standard language. The dialectical differences led to the adoption of standard Italian as a lingua franca. The Logurdorian dialect traditionally provided the basis for a conventionalized literary language that has been used mainly for folk-based verse. The Sard dialects are as close to ancient Latin as to modern Italian; some of the dialects are transition dialects to Spanish or Catalan. The language sounds more like Spanish or Catalan than standard Italian. An estimated 8% of the Sards speak only Sardu, while around 80% are bilingual in Sardu and standard Italian. Although the first documents in the Sard language—*condaghi*, legal contracts—date from approximately 1080, there is virtually no literature in the language, not even a newspaper, although satirical journals appear from time to time.

The majority of the Sards are devoutly Roman Catholic, although church influence has decreased since World War II. Traditionally church authority extended to many areas of island life, particularly where secular authority was weak. The liturgical calendar still dictates the rhythm of life for much of the rural population.

NATIONAL HISTORY: The origins of the Sards is mostly unknown. The island of Sardinia was a very early center of Mediterranean culture; hundreds of *nuraghi*, truncated conic structures built of huge blocks of basalt, were constructed. The Bronze Age Nuraghic civilization flourished from about 1800 B.C. Sardinia was mentioned in Egyptian chronicles of the thirteenth century B.C. as a distinct Mediterranean culture. About 800 B.C., Phoenicians established trading colonies on the island; however, according to Greek legends the island was first settled by Carthaginians led by a sailor named Sardo about 500 B.C. The Greek name for the island, derived from Sardo, was adopted by other Mediterranean cultures. Between 500 and 400 B.C. the Carthaginians established colonies that became the present Sardinian cities.

A brutal Roman occupation began in 238 B.C. and lasted for 700 years. The Romans gradually imposed their Latin culture on the Semitic Carthaginians and the Greek colonies on the coast. The Sards of the interior adopted Roman culture more slowly, although by the first century A.D. they spoke Latin and generally lived as Romans. Roman power collapsed in the fifth century, leaving the island without defenses. Goths and Vandals from the mainland overran Sardinia but were expelled in 533 by the Byzantines of the Eastern Roman Empire. The Byzantines held the island until the eleventh century, but little material or cultural progress was made. Muslim Arabs from North Africa, called Saracens, conquered the island from the Byzantines but held it only briefly before being expelled by forces from the Italian mainland. The Saracens continued to raid and harass the Sardinian coastal regions from the eighth through the eleventh centuries, pushing most of the population to the interior, where it remains to the present.

The island was nominally independent from 1016, but in the eleventh and twelfth centuries the maritime republics of Pisa and Genoa fought for control of the island. In 1294 the Genoese took control of the northern districts and the Pisans took the south, but three years later Pope Boniface VIII bestowed the island on the Catalan kingdom of Aragon. The Catalans ruled the island as part of their extensive Mediterranean empire until the unification of Spain in 1469. Spanish administrators took control of the island from the Catalans, bringing yet another Romance language and culture to the island. The Pisans, Genoans, Catalans, and Spaniards all influenced the evolution of the Sards' culture and language.

Spain ceded the island to the Austrians in 1713, but in 1717 a Spanish force again occupied the island. A settlement of 1720 gave Sardinia to Victor Amadeus II of Savoy, who took the title of king of Sardinia. In exchange he gave Sicily to the Holy Roman Emperor, Charles VI. The kings of Sardinia resided in Turin, the capital of the kingdom, but maintained a royal residence at Cagliari on Sardinia. The House of Savoy ruled an area that included not only Sardinia but Piedmont, Savoy, Aosta, Liguria, Nice, and Menton on the Italian mainland. The island was a neglected appendage where feudal privileges prevailed; most Sards remained poverty-stricken, bandit ridden, and backward.

In the early nineteenth century the Sardinian kingdom's administrators tried to establish some degree of order on the island and finally abolished the nobility's feudal rights in 1835. In 1847 the island's administrative autonomy was abolished, which again strengthened the hold of a handful of local nobles. The house of Savoy held the crown of Sardinia until 1861, when it became the Italian royal house and the Savoyard kings became kings of united Italy.

The adoption of a Tuscan dialect as the official language of united Italy was accompanied by the banning of regional dialects in education, publishing, and official use. The new language laws, in effect from 1870, relegated the Sard dialects to the peasantry in the countryside, while the larger towns and cities increasingly became Italian in language and culture.

In the late nineteenth century the Sards remained a basically peasant nation ruled by a small nobility that adhered to the Italian culture and language. The island's feudal conditions spawned a culture of violence and blood feuds; banditry became a way of life for the disadvantaged Sards. In these years, however, the first stirring of the later autonomy movement began, with the establishment of cultural organizations and Sard political groups.

Feudal conditions continued well into the twentieth century; vendettas and lawlessness remained widespread. The island remained virtually unchanged by the wars that swept across Europe in the first half of the twentieth century. Only in the post–World War II period did change begin to come to the island, mostly in the form of a growing tourist industry along the coast.

The arrival of mainland Italian culture in the 1950s and 1960s, including television, galvanized a generation of Sards. Young Sards began to take a new interest in their language and culture in the 1960s. The Sard language became a rallying point of the growing national movement, its use a matter of pride for the young nationalists. In 1968 Sard nationalists attempted to stir up a separatist uprising on the island, but the movement collapsed following arrests and the arrival of Italian troops. More moderate nationalist organizations used threats of separatism to pressure the Italian government for more autonomy and for the development for the economically backward and bandit-infested island.

Economic hardship drove between 500,000 and 700,000 Sards to emigrate between the 1950s and the 1970s. The emigrants, seeking economic opportunities, settled mostly in the industrial northern regions of Italy, with smaller numbers settling in other European countries. After 1962, the Italian government invested heavily in the island's industrial development, but the factories were largely controlled by mainland Italian companies and did not create as many jobs as originally planned. Sard nationalists claimed that government industrialization was just another form of colonization.

Sard nationalism revived in the late 1970s and increased dramatically thereafter; the majority of the islanders supported moderate nationalist demands for direct and autonomous management of resources to meet Sardinian needs. Long neglected by the Italian government, the island's agrarian sector was still characterized by large estates, and throughout the island work was scarce, utilities primitive, and the schools inferior. The island's neglect created fertile ground for nationalist calls for independence from the inefficient and increasingly polarized Italian state.

The language issue assumed great importance in the 1980s as Europe increasingly integrated. Sard leaders called for separate Sard membership in the European Economic Community (EEC), later the European Union (EU). In 1985 Pope John Paul II visited Sardinia and urged the Sards to overcome the traditional culture of violence, rooted in ancient tradition, vendetta, ransom, destruction of property, degradation, and kidnapping.

The Sardinian Action Party (PSA) pursued greater Sard autonomy within the conventional political process in the 1970s and 1980s. In the 1970s the autonomists attracted only about 3% of the popular vote, but by 1985 the PSA had increased its share to nearly 14% and had become the key political party in the island's coalition government. In the mid-1980s, the regional council proclaimed Sardinia to be bilingual, pending eventual approval from the Italian government.

Young Sards, unable to find work on the island but refusing the island's traditional outlet, emigration, turned to violence to publicize the island's plight in the 1980s. The campaign of violence escalated in the late 1980s and early 1990s. In 1991–92 over 200 bombings rocked the island. Militant Sard nationalists particularly targeted state-owned industries and Italian government offices.

In the 1990s growing numbers of Sards looked to the EU as the island's economic salvation, hoping the union would deliver the needed aid the Italian government has long promised but has not delivered. Bills providing economic aid for the island chronically fail to pass the Italian parliament.

Pressed by the growth of nationalism in several regions, the Italian government officially recognized minority languages for use in education, administration, and commerce in November 1991. The legalization of the Sard language ended a ban on the language that had been in effect since Italian unification. To the Sard nationalists seeking recognition as a separate European people, however, the legalization of the language was only a first step to the realization of the Sards' national rights.

The Italian government sent 5,000 troops in 1992 to the island to improve government control in remote areas dominated by local gangs. Some Sards saw the troops as an occupying force. A 1993 nationalist rally accused the Italian government of illegally installing gates and barriers on footpaths and public land next to beaches, denying access to local people. In the late twentieth century the familiar problems still plagued the Sards—underdevelopment, banditry, kidnappings, and poverty. Sard unity remained difficult due to the differences in dialect, local traditions, and the historical rivalries that sharply divided the Sard nation.

Italian deputies in June 1998 approved a draft law to protect and promote linguistic and cultural minorities in Italy by allowing their languages to be officially used in courts and by permitting ethnic names that had been Italianized to revert back to their original forms. Although the measure stopped short of recognizing the non-Italian culture of Sardinia, moderate nationalists welcomed the move as a step toward eventual cultural and linguistic autonomy.

SELECTED BIBLIOGRAPHY:

Altman, Jack, ed. *Sardinia*. 1996.
Gravette, Andrew. *Sardinia*. 1992.
Lima, Robert. *Sardinia: Sardegna*. 2000.
Waite, Virginia. *Sard*. 1977.

Savoyards

Savoisians; Savoisiens; Harpeitains; Arpitanians; Mountain Occitans; Valdotains; Valdostans; Valdostanos

POPULATION: Approximately (2002e) 1,115,000 Savoyards in Europe, 910,000 concentrated in the Savoy region of France, 75,000 in the Valle d'Aosta region of Italy, and 40,000 in the Valais canton of Switzerland. Outside the region there are Savoyard communities in other regions of France, particularly in Paris, and in North America.

THE SAVOYARD HOMELAND: The Savoyard homeland occupies a mountainous region in eastern France, northwestern Italy, and southwestern Switzerland. Lying in the Savoy, Graian, and Pennine Alps, the region commands many important passes that connect France, Italy, and Switzerland, and it is the site of the highest of the Alpine peaks, Mont Blanc. Savoy has no official status and is divided between three European states—France, Italy, and Switzerland. French Savoy is divided into the departments of Haute-Savoie and Savoie, Italian Savoy comprises the region of Valle d'Aosta, and Swiss Savoy embraces the southwestern districts of the canton of Valais. *Region of Savoy (Savoie)*: 4,026 sq. mi.—10,428 sq. km, (2002e) 1,023,000—Savoyards 77%, Occitans* 8%, other French 15%. *Region of Valle d'Aosta (Val d'Outa)*: 1,260 sq. mi.—3,262 sq. km, (2002e) 122,000—Savoyards (Valdostans) 61%, French 2%, other Italians 37%. The Savoyard cultural centers include Chambéry, (2002e) 56,000, the historical capital of Savoy; Annecy, (2002e) 50,000, in French Savoy; Aosta, called Outa in the Savoyard language, (2002e) 34,000, the

capital of Aosta region in Italy; and Martigny, (2002e) 14,000, the largest town of Swiss Savoy.

FLAG: The Savoyard national flag is a red field charged with a centered white cross. The flag of the Savoyard national movement, the Movement Haripitanya, is a red field divided by a white cross bearing a vertical black stripe charged with three white five-pointed stars on the hoist. The flag of the Valdaostan national movement is a vertical bicolor of black and red. The national flag of the Valdaostans is a horizontal bicolor of black and red divided by a centered white cross.

PEOPLE AND CULTURE: The Savoyards, are a distinct Gallo-Romanic nation that evolved from the Romanized alpine tribes of the first century A.D. In Italian Savoy the inhabitants are popularly called Valdaostans or Valdsostains. The unique Savoyard culture is an alpine culture that incorporates borrowings from the French, Occitans, and Piedmontese.* The Savoyards have shown an unconquerable resilience and have survived in their alpine homeland since before the Roman conquest of the region. The relative isolation of the region has allowed to survive in the high valleys many traditions and customs that have long since disappeared in the lowland areas.

LANGUAGE AND RELIGION: The Savoyards speak various dialects of Franco-Provençal, a hybrid language that evolved from the mixing of forms and words from Occitan and French. The language, also called Harpeitanya, is spoken in a number of regional dialects, the most important being Savoyard in France, Patoé Valdoten or Valdaostan in Italy, and Valaisien in Switzerland. Franco-Provençal historically has shared most vowel developments with the languages spoken to the south but many consonant changes with the languages spoken to the north. Some scholars have labeled the language as a French patois or a variant of Occitan, but it is a distinct language, structurally separate from the neighboring language groups—Occitan, including Provençal, French, Piedmontese, and Lombard. The growing influence of French is threatening the survival of the language in France, which remains the most culturally and linguistically centralized state in Western Europe.

The majority of the Savoyards are Roman Catholic, with a small, important Protestant minority, mostly in the high alpine valleys of French Savoy. During the Protestant Reformation many of the inhabitants embraced the new teachings but were later brought back to Catholicism by St. Francis de Sales, the region's patron saint.

NATIONAL HISTORY: The alpine region was the stronghold of the Allobroges and the Salassi, Celtic tribes that came under nominal Roman rule in 121 B.C. Between 25 and 15 B.C., the Emperor Augustus ordered several military campaigns against the tribes holding the alpine territories that effectively divided Roman Italy from Gaul and the Roman territories to the north. Some of the Celtic alpine tribes were decimated during the campaigns, while members of others were sold as slaves and deported to far-flung corners of the empire.

The ensuing period of peace and the newly established unity of the empire allowed the construction of Roman roads through the passes in the high Alps. At the highest point, on the summit of La Turbie, the "Trophy of the Alps" was constructed in honor of Augustus; it bore the names of the 44 regional tribes defeated by the Roman legions. Roman influence became predominant in the culture and language of the region, and the native Celts adopted Latin norms. Many of the region's present cities and towns began as Roman trading posts or forts. Christianity was introduced to the Romanized region in A.D. 380.

The Roman Empire began to disintegrate after three centuries of relative stability, and the alpine tribes found themselves resisting successive invasions of Germanic tribes from beyond the empire's borders. The Burgundians* invaded in 437, finally overrunning the region's last Roman defenses about 460. They conquered the lowlands to the west in 480. The combined territories were joined in the Christianized Burgundian kingdom.

The Franks conquered the Burgundian kingdom in 534, and the conquered territories, including the highland region in the east, were incorporated into the Frankish kingdom. In the tenth century the region was included in the kingdom of Arles, which was ceded to the Holy Roman Empire in the eleventh century. The region was politically divided; the counts of Genevois held Annecy and the north, while the house of Savoy gained control of the south. A powerful feudal lord of Arles, Count Humbert the White-Handed, consolidated his small holdings in Savoy and gained control of various fiefs in Piedmont by marriage. In 1232 Humbert acquired Chambéry, which he made the capital of his expanding domain. From that point on the history of the region was closely linked to the house of Savoy. His successors secured additional territories that are today in France, Italy, and Switzerland.

The population of the region expanded rapidly from the tenth to the twelfth centuries, assisted by a period of glacial retreat that raised the vegetation limits by as much as 6,561 feet (2,000 m), allowing more extensive colonization of the valleys and easier transit of the high passes. The increased contact between the peoples of the high alpine valleys stimulated the development of the distinct Savoyard culture and dialects.

The expanding bilingual Savoyard state emerged as the most powerful in the region. Haute-Savoy became part of the Savoyard territories in 1401. In the early fifteenth century, under Amadeus VIII, Savoy was an extensive, increasingly powerful state; it was raised to the status of a duchy in 1416. By the beginning of the sixteenth century the rule of the Savoyard dukes had grown weak, and Savoy came under French and Swiss dominance. Savoy lost its Swiss territories—Vaud, Valais, and Geneva—between 1475 and 1536. The region was again divided during the Protestant Reformation; monastic institutions and the seat of the bishop of Geneva were expelled from Protestant Geneva but restored in Annecy. St. Francis de Sales, bishop from 1602 to 1622, is now considered the patron saint of the Savoyards.

In the sixteenth century the center of the Savoyard state shifted from Savoy to Piedmont, in Italy. In 1559 Emmanuel Philibert moved the state's capital from highland Chambéry, which was too exposed to the French military threat, to Turin, in his Italian territories. However, the language and tone of the court remained French until the eighteenth century. The French language became the second language of the state, the Savoyard dialects remained the language of daily life in the western districts, and Piedmontese was the most widely spoken language in the eastern districts.

French troops, to control the alpine passes, occupied Savoy three times during the seventeenth century, greatly weakening the political cohesion of the Savoyard territories. In the War of the Spanish Succession, 1703–13, Victor Amadeus II at first sided with the French but later switched sides and joined the forces of the Holy Roman Emperor led by his cousin, Eugene of Savoy. At the Peace of Utrecht in 1714, Savoy gained control of Sicily and in 1720 exchanged the island for the Austrian ruled island of Sardinia. Duke Victor Amadeus of Savoy assumed the title "king of Sardinia," applying the name of the island to his territories in Savoy, Nice, Menton, Piedmont.

In 1792 the region was occupied by the French under Napoleon, ostensibly to bring freedom to the oppressed Savoyards. A new French department, Mont Blanc, was organized, with Chambéry as its capital. Anti-French sentiment remained strong, small groups fought the French troops from strongholds high in the mountains. A French effort to raise an army of 300,000 from the region was dashed when only 33 young men presented themselves for conscription. The French occupation lasted for 23 years, leaving a lasting hatred of the centralized French government. In 1815 the house of Savoy was restored as the ruling house of the Kingdom of Sardinia, and the territories of Genoa and Liguria were added to the kingdom's Italian holdings.

Italian Savoy was a center of the Risorgimento, the movement for Italian unification, which the house of Savoy led. On 23 January 1859, the secret Treaty of Plombières was signed, exchanging alpine Savoy for the military assistance of 200,000 French soldiers in the unification of Italy under the House of Savoy. The treaty remained a state secret until it was finally made public in 1928.

The Risorgimento, finally achieved with French aid in 1860, left only Rome and the Papal States outside the domains of the House of Savoy. Emperor Louis Napoleon of France, for his aid in the Italian unification, received the French-speaking parts of the kingdom, Savoy, Nice, and Menton. Savoy was annexed to the French state on 24 March 1860, with only the French-speaking Aosta Valley of the former Savoyard duchy remaining part of Italy. The annexation agreement set up a unique neutral zone on the Swiss border and provided for the creation of a free trade zone in the border region of France, Italy, and Switzerland.

Relations between the Savoyards and the highly centralized French government worsened following France's defeat in the Franco-Prussian War of 1870. A popular nationalist movement, the Republican Committee, appeared in northern Savoy, denouncing the 1860 annexation and conquest and demanding a referendum. The movement was crushed when the French authorities sent in 10,000 troops. The centralized French and Italian kingdoms banned the official use of the Savoyard dialects and pressed assimilation, but the culture and dialects survived in the high mountain valleys. By the turn of the twentieth century the cities and towns of Savoy had become French-speaking, and in Aosta a sizable Italian-speaking minority had settled in the towns; however, in the rural areas and the alpine valleys the Franco-Provençal dialects remained the language of daily life.

In the years after World War I, centralized governments increasingly intruded in the isolated region. In 1919 the French government suppressed the Savoyard neutral zone and the free trade zone. The Fascist Italian regime, in power from 1922, posed the first major threat to Savoyard culture in Italy. In the 1930s the Fascist authorities banned both French and Franco-Provençal and ordered all names, even family names, changed to Italian forms. Cultural repression increased during World War II but merely strengthened Savoyard resolve. In the latter years of the war, both French Savoy and the Valle d'Aosta were centers of dissent against fascism and the Nazi occupation.

The House of Savoy, held partially responsible for Italy's World War II defeat, was deposed in a 1946 referendum. As the new republican government of Italy began drafting a postwar constitution, Savoyard nationalists in the Aosta Valley demanded secession from Italy and reunification with Savoy and part of the Swiss canton of Valais, in an independent *État Montagne*. The movement gained considerable support in Savoy, but separatist sentiment died down after the Italian government separated the Aosta Valley from Piedmont and granted a degree of political autonomy in 1948.

The opening of several tunnels in the 1960s eliminated the seasonal restrictions on the accessibility of the region and brought an influx of outsiders. The tunnels turned the region into a major commercial route between France, Italy, and Switzerland, raising levels of traffic congestion, noise, and pollution. The scale of the growth of tourism necessitated a vast expansion of local services and an imported workforce to staff them; the majority of these workers originated in areas of different cultures and languages. The rapid expansion of tourist facilities and holiday homes sparked the first calls for linguistic and cultural autonomy across the region. In 1965 several regionalist movements were created, and in 1978 nationalists formed the National Savoyard Front to work for the reunification and autonomy of Savoy within an integrated Europe.

The rapid changes brought to the region by alpine tourism and industrialization between the 1960s and 1970s raised standards of living dramatically but also posed a serious threat to the Savoyard culture as the percentage of the indigenous population decreased and intermarriage increased. The language and traditions of the region were being lost. The Savoyards, after centuries of resistance, were threatened no longer by armed invasion but by rural depopulation and the cultural and environmental impact of mass tourism.

The Savoyard sense of identity remained strong. In the 1990s there was a growing awareness that the limited autonomous powers allowed by the French and Italian governments had done little to prevent the increasing loss of their unique culture or the destruction of their fragile alpine environment.

Valdaostan nationalists on 3 September 1991 set in motion the procedures for a referendum on secession from Italy, seen as a first step toward a reconstituted Savoyard state within a united European federation. In May 1993 the Valdaostan nationalists took 37.3% of the vote in local elections, the highest in their history. Radical separatists, vowing to secede and reunite with neighboring Savoy, took a surprisingly high 5% of the vote. The militancy of the nationalists in Italian Savoy fueled a strong regionalist and environmental movement in the alpine regions of Italy, France, and Switzerland. In spite of the declining use of the local dialects, the sense of identity was still very strong in all three areas, which the Savoyards consider the heart of Europe.

The Savoy League, launched as an openly separatist organization in 1994, published a platform for an independent Savoyard state that would embrace the traditional territories that formed part of historical Savoy, in a decentralized democracy based on the Swiss Federation model. Nationalists organized the first Savoyard national day in Aix-les-Bains on 19 February 1997; hundreds of supporters, including the mayors of several local towns, pledged support for a sovereign Savoyard state and announced the nullification of the 1860 annexation of western Savoy to the French state. In 1998 French regional elections over 5% of the electorate supported the pro-independence groups, slightly more than in 1993.

In a poll taken in late 1998, 28% of the regional population supported Savoyard sovereignty in a united Europe. The growing integration of Europe is paralleled in Savoy as the three regions, divided between France, Italy, and Switzerland, renew their historical ties.

Pro-European sentiment is strong in all three regions, with the Savoyards in Switzerland consistently voting in favor of closer ties to the European Union in 1992 and 2000. Political organizations across the region have adopted a pro-European stance and espouse Savoyard sovereignty as part of a reorganized European Union.

SELECTED BIBLIOGRAPHY:

Brustein, William. *The Social Origins of Political Regionalism: France, 1849–1981.* 1982.

Cox, Eugene L. *The Eagles of Savoy: The House of Savoy in Thirteenth Century Europe.* 1983.

De Pingon, Jean. *French Savoy: History of an Annexed Country.* 1996.

Jochnowitz, George. *Dialect Boundaries and the Question of Franco-Provençal.* 1995.

Saxons

Sachsens; Saxonians; Old Saxons

POPULATION: Approximately (2002e) 7,775,000 Saxons in Germany, concentrated in the states of Saxony, Saxony-Anhalt, and Thuringia. Outside the region there are Saxon communities in Berlin, other parts of Germany, in the Czech Republic, Romania, and in North and South America.

THE SAXON HOMELAND: The Saxon homeland occupies a region of flat, fertile lowlands in southeastern Germany, mostly in the valleys of the River Elbe and its tributaries, the Saale and the Spree, and the Neisse River, which forms the boundary between Saxony and Poland. In the south the land rises to a mountainous highland, the so-called Saxon Switzerland in the Erzgebirge (the Ore Mountains) and the Thüringer Wald (the Thuringian Forest). Formerly forming part of the German Democratic Republic, the region is heavily industrialized, but also heavily polluted, mostly due to the mining of brown coal and uranium. The historical region of Saxony as a geographic area has changed greatly in the course of its history. The region presently inhabited by Saxons includes the German states of Saxony, Thuringia, and the Halle region of the state of Saxony-Anhalt. *Free State of Saxony (Freistaat Sachsen)*: 7,078 sq. mi.—18,337 sq. km, (2002e) 4,399,000—Saxons 88%, Sorbs* and other Germans 12%. *Free State of Thuringia (Freistaat Thüringen)*: 6,275 sq. mi.—16,252 sq. km, (2002e) 2,414,000—Thuringian Saxons 79%, other Germans 21%. *State of Saxony-Anhalt (Staat Sachen-Anhalt)*: 7,956 sq. mi.—20,606 sq. km—(2002e) 2,602,000—Saxons 55%, other Germans 45%. The Saxon capital and major cultural center is Dresden, (2002e) 421,000 (metropolitan area 1,031,000), on the River Elbe. The other important cultural center is Leipzig, (2002e) 417,000 (Leipzig-Halle metropolitan area 1,429,000). Other important Saxon cultural centers include Halle, (2002e) 248,000, in the Saxon region of southern Saxony-Anhalt; and Erfurt in Thuringia, (2002e) 197,000.

FLAG: The Saxon national flag, the traditional flag of the Saxon regions, is a horizontal bicolor of white over green. The flag of the state of Saxony is the same bicolor of white over green with the traditional state arms centered. The flag of the state of Thuringia is a horizontal bicolor of white over red with the state arms centered. The flag of the state of Saxony-Anhalt is a horizontal bicolor of yellow over black bearing the state arms centered.

PEOPLE AND CULTURE: The Saxons are an eastern German people, the descendents of early Germanic tribes and Germanized Slavs. The traditions and culture of the Saxons reflects their long association with the neighboring Slavs, as do their distinctive dialects and worldview. Formerly the Saxons were often referred to as the "Old Saxons," to distinguish them from the Saxon tribes that participated in the occupation of Britain between the fifth and seventh centuries A.D. In spite of centuries of disunity, the Saxons have retained a sense of identity that even decades of communist rule failed to destroy. The major Saxon groups are the Saxons of Saxony state, the Thuringian Saxons in the west, and the Anhalt Saxons in the north.

LANGUAGE AND RELIGION: The Saxon dialect of High German, Saxonian or Upper Saxon, is actually a group of nine dialects, four of them spoken only in Thuringia; it is the language of daily life in the region. The nine dialects, considerably different from standard German, incorporate extensive Slavic borrowings, and since German unification in 1990 they have been giving way to standard German. Cultural groups in the region have begun efforts to save the unique Saxon dialects from extinction. The Saxons can be distinguished readily by their characteristic pronunciation of standard German. Martin Luther's writings, which began the Protestant Reformation, were in the Saxon dialect.

The majority of the Saxons are Lutherans, with a small Roman Catholic minority and a substantial number professing no religious beliefs. Since the overthrow of communism and the reunification of Germany, evangelical Protestant sects from western Germany have made inroads.

NATIONAL HISTORY: The Saxons are believed to have originated in the area of modern Schleswig and along the northern Baltic coast. The Saxon tribes were first mentioned in the second century A.D. as inhabiting the area around the mouth of the River Elbe and the nearby islands in northwestern Germany. From their original territory, the Saxons extended their territory southward across the Weser River.

The era of Roman decline in Central Europe was marked by Saxon attacks and piracy. During the early part of the fifth century the Saxons spread through northern Germany and along the coasts of Roman Gaul. The expanding Saxon tribes split, some joining the Angles and Jutes in the invasion and conquest of Angoland (England). Other Saxon tribes followed the Elbe south to conquer Thuringia in 531. Compelled to pay tribute by the Franks in 566, the Saxons were forcibly Christianized in the seventh century.

In the eighth century the Saxons were brought under the control of Charlemagne's Frankish empire after a war that lasted 32 years. The Saxons established a duchy in the ninth century, one of the original duchies of the Holy Roman Empire. Duke Henry I, called Henry the Fowler, was elected king of the Holy Roman Empire in 919. His son, Otto I, bestowed Saxony on a Saxon nobleman, Hermann Billung, whose descendents held the duchy until the extinction of the male line in 1106. During this period the Saxons expanded eastward, conquering and absorbing the new territory's Slav populations. Saxon culture adopted many Slavic linguistic characteristics and cultural traditions.

The Saxon's Wettin dynasty, established as the ruling house of the increasingly powerful margravate of Meissen in 1100, extended its authority to control eventually a large part of the Holy Roman Empire. In 1423 Margrave Frederick the Warlike gained control of Electoral Saxony, and in 1425 he became Elector Frederick I. In 1485 the Wettin lands were partitioned between the two sons of Elector Frederick. The division became permanent, with the Ernestine line taking control of the territories in the west, and the Albertine branch retained the ducal title in eastern Saxony. From the fifteenth century the Ernestine line divided Thuringia into a number of small states, known as the Saxon duchies.

In 1517 a dissident Catholic priest, Martin Luther, pinned to a church door in Wittenberg a tract making the case for free choice in religion. Luther's action began the momentous Protestant Reformation. The great popularity of Luther's works, written in a Saxon dialect, helped to standardize the Saxon dialects as a literary language. A Protestant stronghold during the wars of religion, in the seventeenth century Saxony emerged as one of the two most powerful of the Protestant German states, beginning a long and bitter rivalry with Brandenburg-Prussia.

The political and economic rivalry between the Saxons and the Prussians to the north was a decisive factor in the history of the Saxon nation. The election of Augustus II, who took the name Frederick Augustus I as elector of Saxony, to the throne of Poland pulled the Saxons eastward but diminished their prestige. The death of August III in 1763 ended the union with Poland, a period marked by economic and social decay but also by a great flowering of Saxon culture and art, which was shared by the Saxon duchies of Thuringia. Weimar, the capital of the duchy of Saxe-Weimar-Eisenach, had become an intellectual center of Europe. August II and August III were patrons of art and learning and had greatly beautified their capital, Dresden. Leipzig, with its famous university, led the rise of German literature and music in the eighteenth and nineteenth centuries.

The military rise of France following the French Revolution pushed Saxony into an anti–French alliance with its antagonistic Prussian neighbor. In 1806, during the Napoleonic Wars, Saxony switched sides. Napoleon raised the Saxon elector to the status of king of Saxony, but the new king's failure to abandon his French ally before Napoleon's fall cost him the northern half of his kingdom. In 1815 the victorious Prussians annexed the northern districts of Saxony. Passionately anti-Prussian and determined to recover the lost provinces, the Saxons mostly sided with the Austrians during the Austro-Prussian War of 1866. Defeated by superior Prussian forces, the kingdom and the defeated Saxon duchies were forced to pay large indemnities and to join the Prussian-dominated North German Confederation. In 1871 Saxony and the Saxon duchies, under Prussian pressure, joined the German Empire. Saxony's abundant mineral wealth stimulated rapid industrialization in the late nineteenth century.

Saxony's industrial zones, important to Germany's war effort, became centers of radical political movements, many supporting a 1917 movement for Saxon secession from Germany and separate peace with the allies. In early November of 1918 King Frederick Augustus III, along with the Wettin rulers of the small Saxon duchies and principalities in Thuringia, abdicated as revolution swept defeated Germany. On 19 November, inspired by the Russian Revolution, workers and soldiers councils took control of Saxony and declared the independence of the Soviet Republic of Saxony. The new government announced sweeping nationalization and expropriations. During the months that followed violent clashes and running battles between communists, Saxon nationalists, and pan-German groups left thousands dead or injured.

The Saxon states joined the Weimar Republic, but in April 1919 the government of Saxony severed all remaining ties to the German federal government. The action provoked an invasion of federal troops and the overthrow of Saxony's communist government, called Red Saxony, in March 1920. There were an estimated 250,000 registered communists and many more who supported them. In March 1921, a new armed revolt broke out, supported by the communist Hungarian government of Bela Kun, and in 1922 the communists again supported the separation of Saxony from Germany. The German government again dispatched troops to put down the separatists; in 1923 the Saxon government was dissolved and the Saxon militia was disbanded.

The Saxon regions remained centers of communist and socialist activities until the dissidents were driven underground by armed Nazis in 1933.

The communists and socialists of the region formed worker defense units, called Hundreds, to secure the Saxon lands from Nazi domination. In 1933, after Hitler became chancellor of Germany, the German government dispatched SS and SA troops to Saxony and the other Saxon states on the pretext that the Saxon authorities were unable to maintain order. The Saxon states lost all their former autonomy.

The mayor of Leipzig from 1930 to 1937, Carl Frederick Goerder, was the leader of the Saxon resistance to Nazism during World War II. He was arrested and executed in 1944 but was recognized as a Saxon national hero only in 1991. Dresden was severely damaged by British and American bombing in February 1945. Many of the city's famed art and architectural treasures disappeared in the firestorm generated by the bombing. The art that was saved was later stolen by the Soviets.

The Saxon homeland fell to advancing American troops in 1945. The Americans later traded control of the region to the Soviets in exchange for Western control of six boroughs of Berlin, ignoring the pleas and petitions of Saxon leaders. The states of Saxony, Thuringia, and Saxony-Anhalt were reconstituted under Soviet military rule in 1947. Finding themselves in the communist German state created in 1949, many Saxons fled to West Germany, which was closely integrated into the Western alliance. As part of the official program of opposition to regionalist sentiment, the Saxon states were abolished in 1952 and replaced with administrative units.

Saxon resistance to Soviet domination remained strong, though communism and socialism had long histories in the region. Economic hardship and suppression of all opposition stiffened resistance in the early 1950s; serious anti-Soviet rioting broke out in the major Saxon cities in 1953 but was brutally suppressed. Relative economic success in the 1960s and 1970s was accompanied by certain accomplishments of the communist government, including an impressive educational system, social welfare services, and job security, but oppressive government policies continued to be met by passive resistance or attempts to escape to West Germany. The presence of Soviet troops was a reminder of dependence on the Soviet Union. By the 1970s resistance had coalesced around the peace movement, led by Lutheran clergymen, but arrests and detentions drove the dissidents underground. The church, however, remained a refuge for antinuclear groups during the years of the Cold War. In 1978, the Lutheran Church received concessions allowing limited freedoms.

Local communist authorities, faced with severe shortages and the desire of many Saxons to leave for the West, appealed to German nationalism and the past glories of the Saxons. In 1984 the East German government finally had to arrange for the transmission of West German television into the Dresden area to alleviate absenteeism among workers who had been leaving "Blind Dresden" to watch television in areas where reception was possible. In September 1988, demonstrations in Leipzig and other large cities were staged by Saxons demanding the right to leave for West Germany. The demonstrations underscored growing Saxon dissatisfaction with the ruling Communist Party.

Saxon cultural identity, having survived over fifty years of communist rule, resurfaced in 1989 with demands for the partition of East Germany into Saxon and Prussian states. The rediscovered Saxon nationalism was put aside in the euphoria that accompanied the collapse of East Germany and the rush to German unification in October 1990. Disillusionment with reunification, which was followed by mass unemployment and economic hardship, spurred a nationalist resurgence. A poll in October 1993 demonstrated the growing despair: 25% saw themselves as the losers in unification, 15% were so disillusioned that they wanted a return to communist rule, and 20% felt that independence for the Saxons would be a better alternative.

In the late 1990s, in spite of massive government investment and economic reforms, the Saxons remained relatively poor in comparison to the western German states. The continuing economic disparities between the former East and West Germans fueled the growth of regionalist feelings in the Saxon regions. Some aspects of Saxon life improved markedly after 1990, but other parts remained grim. Unemployment remained over 15%, and productivity remained at only 60% of the level of western Germany. The civil services of the Saxon states remained bloated and inefficient.

The Saxons are frustrated and humiliated by the need for financial aid, which will have to continue for many more years if they are to reach the living levels of the western German peoples. Estimates in 1999 of another 30 years of grudging financial handouts from the west were met with outrage.

The post-unification economic boom began to slow in 1997 and by 2001 economic problems were again a serious impediment to full Saxon integration in united Germany. Socially and economically the Saxons chafe under administration and business leaders imported from western Germany. Many Saxons, disillusioned with the long process of integration, have left the region for the greater opportunities of the western German states.

SELECTED BIBLIOGRAPHY:

Lapp, Benjamin. *Revolution from the Right: Politics, Class and the Rise of Nazism in Saxony, 1919–1933.* 1997.

Retallack, James. *Saxony in German History: Culture, Society, and Politics 1830–1933.* 2000.

Shlaes, Amity. *Germany: The Empire Within.* 1993.

Szejnmann, Claus-Christian W. *Nazism in Central Germany: The Brownshirts in "Red" Saxony.* 1999.

Scanians

Skånes; Skanelanders; Skanska

POPULATION: Approximately (2002e) 1,645,000 Scanians in Scandinavia, concentrated in the historical Scania region of southern Sweden, the Danish island of Bornholm and the smaller islands surrounding it, and in neighboring regions of Denmark on the other side of the narrow body of water called the Øresund. Outside the region there are Scanian communities in Stockholm, Copenhagen, and other areas of Scandinavia.

THE SCANIAN HOMELAND: The Scanian homeland lies just south of the Smaland Plateau in southern Sweden, but it also includes the Danish island of Bornholm, 40 miles southeast of the Scanian mainland. The region, traditionally known as the "granary of Sweden," is surrounded by the Baltic Sea, the Øresund, and the Kattegatt; it mostly consists of open plains in the south, with wooded hills along the northern border. Bornholm Island is a generally hilly, rocky plain. Scania includes the official region of Scania, formed from Malmöhaus and Kristianstad Provinces in 1997, and the provinces of Blekinge (Blëgen) and Halland (Hällen) in Sweden, and the island county of Bornholm, Baornehålm in the Scanian language, which belongs to neighboring Denmark. *Region of Scania (Skåneland)*: 7,660 sq. mi.—19,839 sq. km, (2002e) 1,556,000— Scanians 91%, other Swedes and other Danes 9%. Bornholm, or Danish Scania, has a population of (2002e) 44,000. The Scanian capital and major cultural center is Malmö, called Målme by the Scanians, (2002e) 244,000 (metropolitan area 608,000, which forms part of the Copenhagen-Malmö metropolitan area, (2002e) 2,314,000). Other important Scanian cultural centers include Lund, called Long, (2002e) 73,000, and Helsingborg, called Haelsengbår. The most important town on the island of Bornholm is Rønne, (2002e) 14,000, the capital of the Danish county of Bornholm.

FLAG: "Den Skånska," the Scanian national flag, the flag of the national movement, is a red field charged with a yellow Scandinavian cross. The flag of Bornholm is identical, except that the cross is pale green. The official flag of Scania region, adopted in 1999, is a blue field bearing a yellow griffin head.

PEOPLE AND CULTURE: The Scanians are a Scandinavian people of mixed Danish and Swedish descent, their culture and language incorporating customs and influences from both, alongside many unique traits. In spite of centuries of Swedish cultural and linguistic pressure, the Scanians have retained a strong sense of identity and consider themselves a separate Scandinavian nation. Their distinct history remains almost a secret or oral history; although it is researched and written about by local historians, no Scanian history is taught in the schools of Scania or Sweden. The history of the Scanian nation has been traced back to the fourth century A.D.

LANGUAGE AND RELIGION: The Scanian dialect, widely spoken in the region and claimed by nationalists as a separate Scandinavian language, is in some ways closer to Danish than to Swedish. The existence of a separate Scanian language is denied by the Swedish government, which regards the language as a Swedish dialect, but the distinct Scanian language remains the language of daily life in the region. A closely related Danish dialect, called Eastern Danish, is spoken on Bornholm and the smaller islands of the group.

The Scanians mostly belong to the Lutheran faith, which forms an integral part of their culture. The ecclesiastical center at Lund remains one of the most important centers of Scandinavian Lutheranism and a renowned center of learning. The Lutheran faith, shared with both the Danes and Swedes, has a very local character in Scania due to the continuing importance of Lund.

NATIONAL HISTORY: Germanic tribes occupied the region in ancient times but remained disunited and often warred among themselves. Remains of the ancient inhabitants include numerous dolmens and tumuli in the region. During the Bronze Age, close ties were established between the inhabitants of present-day Scania and the inhabitants of present-day Denmark. In A.D. 380 a tribal chieftain, Alaric, was the first to claim the title "Rex Scaniae," king of Scania. Between 380 and 770 fifteen known kings ruled the region. In 770 a Scanian king, Ivar Vidfamne, began to extend Scanian power, becoming the first empire builder in the Scandinavian region.

The Scanians of the overpopulated coastal regions, unable to sustain the growing population, participated in the great Viking expansion during the eighth and ninth centuries, which included the colonization of the island of Bornholm. Scanian Vikings, searching for land and plunder, raided Britain, Ireland, and northern Europe. The great king of the Danes, Canute, in 811 united Denmark and Scania under the Danish crown. Canute eventually controlled Denmark, Scania, England, and Norway under his rule, which lasted until 1035. Growing rivalry between the Danes and Swedes led to the division of the island of Bornholm between Denmark and Sweden in 1149. Canute's line ruled the region until 1047, when Sven Estridsin, a Scanian, became king of Denmark. Denmark's medieval power was largely based on Danish control of the Baltic–North Sea waterway. Sven Estridsin and his sons held the Danish throne until 1330. From 1330 to 1360 Scania was under the rule of Count Johan of Holstein; although Canute's empire disappeared, Scania remained the heartland of the Danish kingdom.

The Nordic union of Sweden, Finland, Norway, and Scania under King Magnus Eriksson Smek from 1331 to 1360 was a forerunner of the later Nordic Union. King Magnus, based in Scania, used the title Rex Scaniae. Danish rule of the rich Scanian provinces, in the thirteenth century, was increasingly challenged by the emerging Swedish power to the north.

The Nordic area seceded from the archdiocese of Hamburg-Bremen in 1104 in order to establish a separate bishopric at Lund, the ecclesiastical center of Scandinavia. Lund became the center of Scandinavian Christianity not only for the Danes but also the Swedes and Norwegians. The Scania region, the crossroads of northern Europe, became a prosperous center of religious life and commerce. From 1327 to 1522 the archbishop ruled the island of Bornholm.

The Union of Kalmar united Scandinavia with the crowns of Denmark, Norway, and Sweden in 1397. Because the kingship was elective in all three countries, the union could not be maintained by inheritance; it was dissolved in 1523. At the dissolution of the union the Danes retained control of Scania and Norway. The religious divide in Europe greatly affected the region, which was the ecclesiastical center of Scandinavia. The Protestant Reformation, accepted by the Danes in 1534, was embraced by the Scanians two years later, ending a serious religious rift between the Scanians and the Danes.

Denmark's military control of both sides of the Øresund, the narrow strait between Denmark and the Scandinavian Peninsula, allowed the kingdom to halt trade and military traffic between the Baltic and North seas during the frequent European wars. The Danes' control of Scania and the narrow Øresund allowed them to control shipping and compete with the powerful Hanseatic League, which controlled Bornholm, for Baltic trade. Sweden's hostile relations with the Danish kingdom centered on a desire to annex Scania to attain a natural coastal frontier and to end Danish control of the Kattegat, the entrance to the Baltic Sea. Control of Scania, the so-called Skåne Question, dominated northern European politics in the late sixteenth and early seventeenth centuries.

The Danes and Swedes remained at war nearly continuously in the mid-seventeenth century. A Danish defeat resulted in the loss of Halland to Sweden in 1645, and renewed hostilities led to the Swedish conquest of the remaining Scanian provinces in 1658. War again broke out in 1660; invading Danes were aided by an ultimately futile Scanian uprising against Swedish rule. The Danes, however, gained control of the island of Bornholm. The Scanians again rose when the war resumed in 1675, welcoming the Danes as liberators from the hated Swedes. The Danish victory in the Scanian War did not result in the return of Scania to Danish rule, however, as this was vetoed by the powerful French kingdom. Reprisals marked the return of the Swedish authorities to Scania when the Danes withdrew and peace was negotiated in 1679.

The Scanians suffered for their active resistance to Swedish rule and from the repressive policies of the Swedish government. Through economic, political, and cultural pressure, the Swedish authorities gradually diminished Danish influence in the region, described as "a domestic but foreign territory." The policy, instead of making the Scanians into Swedes, led to the evolution of a unique Scanian culture and language, incorporating both Danish and Swedish influences. The emergence of a distinctive Scanian culture led to a decline of pro-Danish sentiment. When the Danes again invaded the region in 1709, the majority of the Scanians remained loyal to the Swedish kingdom or adopted a neutral stance.

Devastated by the long series of Danish-Swedish wars, Scania began to recover only in the mid–eighteenth century. The Swedish government divided the historical region into three provinces—Scania, Blekinge, and Halland—in 1809. To forestall Scanian unrest, the Swedish government relaxed cultural and linguistic restrictions in the nineteenth century. Sweden and Denmark lost their position as leading European powers, and the Skåne Question disappeared from regional politics.

A cultural revival took hold in Scania in the 1870s and 1880s, reversing over two centuries of gradual assimilation. Unlike many European minorities, the Scanian revival did not evolve a strong nationalist sentiment. The revival, more cultural than most parallel European movements, focused on the modernization of the Scanian language and a renewal of interest in Scania's folklore, crafts, and traditions. The Scanians' red and yellow flag, adopted during the cultural revival, became popular across the historical Scania region as the symbol of the rebirth of the Scanian nation.

Historical researchers at Lund led the reculturation by unearthing material in the great ecclesiastical and university libraries in the city. Historical research combined with the nationalism sweeping late-nineteenth-century Europe to create a strong national-cultural movement that embraced all of southern Sweden and Bornholm. The concept of a politically united Scania grew from the cultural revival. The old Skåne Question had reappeared in a new form.

The Scanians cooperated with the Danes to save nearly all of Denmark's Jewish population during World War II. Sympathy for the Danish plight and cooperation with the Danish resistance to the Nazi occupation led to closer ties to the Danes during and after the war. The Swedish government's murky relationship with Nazi Germany is still a controversial issue in Scania.

In the decades after World War II, Sweden attained one of Europe's highest standards of living under liberal, democratic governments. The first modern Scanian national day, celebrated on 16 July 1967, was widely condemned in Sweden as treason or separatism. The organizers were investigated by the SÅPO, the Swedish special police. The flying of the Scanian flag was also seen as an affront to the Swedish state. A small national movement in the 1970s began a campaign for a separate Scanian state in a Nordic confederation, arguing that if Scania were to become the sixth Scandinavian state, it would give the Scandinavians another voice in international forums such as the United Nations and the Council of Europe.

The assassination of Sweden's prime minister, Olof Palme, in 1986, followed by a series of government scandals and a sharp economic decline, politicized the formerly complacent Scanians. A resurgent national movement began to question the benefits and the social costs of Sweden's welfare state. In 1988 the first openly separatist political party, the Skånepartier, formed in Scania as the debate over membership in the European Community galvanized the population. A regionalist cultural organization, Skansk Framtid, was founded in 1989 with the goal of a fully autonomous Scania.

Sweden's entry into the European Union (EU), strongly supported in Scania, raised the question of sovereignty within a united Europe. The Scanian national movement in February 1994 accused the Swedish government of betrayal when the government dropped Scania from an aid blueprint during negotiations on EU membership. The fervently pro–European Scanian nationalists gained support for a sovereign Scania with close ties to both Denmark and Sweden in a united European federation.

In 1995 Scanian officials protested Swedish government attempts to divide the area among several regions under the policies of the EU. Skansk Framtid, now the largest nationalist organization, set up branches in most cities and towns in the region. The organization was allied to a separate Scanian organization on the Danish island of Bornholm. Other nationalist organizations formed on the bases of ideology, geographic region, or ultimate aims. The more militant groups sought independence within a Nordic association within the European Union.

In 1997 the Swedish government, pressured by the Scanian national movement, joined the two provinces of Malmöhaus and Kristianstad in a new region of Scania. The Scania region, Regionen Skåne, headed by an elected regional assembly, began to operate on 1 January 1999. The regional assembly adopted heraldic arms and an official flag, but in a controversial decision it chose to fly the official flag alongside the better-known red and yellow national flag, the symbol of the unity of the historical region.

The 10-mile (16 km) bridge joining Copenhagen and Malmö that opened in 2000 created a metropolitan region, Copenhagen-Malmö, with a mixed Danish-Scanian population of over 2.3 million. The bridge, linking the Danish capital and Scania's largest city, is seen as strengthening the already strong ties between the Danes and the Scanians. Although many predicted that the Danes and Scanians are too different to work efficiently together, both admit that their immediate neighbors are easier to work with than the people from northern Sweden, particularly Stockholm.

The autonomy of the new region of Scania is still very limited, leaving the nationalists unsatisfied with the amount of self-government and with the Swedish government's refusal to extend the boundaries of the new region to include all of Scania. Other nationalists continue to demand the creation of a new European region based on the historical Scanian homeland to include Scania, Blekinge, Halland, and Danish Bornholm.

SELECTED BIBLIOGRAPHY:

Gibbons, Eric. *Scania*. 1994.
Kjrgaard, Thorkild, ed. *The Danish Revolution, 1500–1800: An Ecohistorical Interpretation*. 1994.
Loiit, Aleksander. *National Movements in the Baltic Countries during the Nineteenth Century*. 1985.
Pred, Allan. *Place, Practice and Structure: Social and Spatial Transformation in Southern Sweden, 1750–1850*. 1986.

Scots

Albans; Scotians

POPULATION: Approximately (2002e) 5,765,000 Scots in the United Kingdom, concentrated in Scotland, the northern half of the island of Great Britain. Other large Scottish communities live in Canada, the United States, Australia, and New Zealand.

THE SCOTTISH HOMELAND: The Scottish homeland occupies the northern third of the island of Great Britain, which its shares with England and Wales. Scotland is separated from England by the Tweed River, the Cheviot Hills, the Liddell River, and Solway Firth. The terrain of Scotland is predominantly mountainous but is roughly divided into three distinct regions—the Highlands in the north, the Central Lowlands, and the Southern Uplands. Over half of Scotland's total area lies in the Highlands, the most sparsely populated region and the most rugged area on the island of Great Britain. To the south of the Highlands lies the Central Lowlands, a narrow belt constituting about a tenth of Scottish territory but containing the majority of the population. The coastline is highly indented by fjordlike indentations called "lochs." Scotland forms a political division of the United Kingdom of Great Britain and Northern Ireland. *Scotland (Alba)*: 30,414 sq. mi.—78,772 sq. km, (2002e) 5,069,000—Scots 96%, English 2%, Irish, Indians, and Pakistanis 2%. The Scottish capital and major cultural center is Edinburgh, called Embro in Lallans and Dùn Éidaenn in Eise, (2002e) 382,000 (metropolitan area 688,00). The other major cultural center is Glasgow, Glesga in Lallans and Galschu in Eise, (2002e) 610,000 (metropolitan area 1,927,000), Scotland's largest city.

FLAG: The Scottish national flag, the official flag of Scotland, is a blue field charged with a white saltire, the cross of St. Andrew. The traditional Scottish flag, the flag of the former kingdom, is a yellow field charged with a centered red rampant lion and bearing two thin red stripes near the perimeter decorated with spaced red pike heads.

PEOPLE AND CULTURE: The Scots are a people of mixed ancestry, descended from the earliest inhabitants (the Picts), later Celtic migrants from Ireland, and Norsemen, who controlled parts of Scotland for centuries. The Scottish culture, Celtic in origin, has been influenced by centuries of contact with the English but retains such symbols as the tartan, the bagpipe, and the cross of St. Andrew, the patron saint of Scotland. Celtic Scottish culture, although influencing the wider Scottish culture, remains most traditional in the Scottish Highlands, which are separated from the Lowlands by the Grampian Mountains. Clans, the traditional keystones of Scottish society, are no longer powerful, except in the Highlands. Originally, the clan, a grouping of an entire family with one head, or laird, was also important as a fighting unit. The solidarity associated with clan membership has been expanded into a strong national pride.

LANGUAGE AND RELIGION: The Scots are now an English-speaking nation but retain a distinctive Scots dialect, Lallans or Lowlands Scottish, that developed between the fifteenth and seventeenth centuries from medieval Northumbrian, a northern English language, but without the Norman French influence of the standard English spoken by the neighboring Northumbrians.* Compilation of the first Lallans dictionary began in May 1996 and was published in early 2001. Lallans, formerly called Scots English, first known though the songs of the eighteenth-century Scottish poet Robert Burns, differs considerably from standard English in pronunciation and for the number of words of Scandinavian origin. Some argue that Lallans is not a dialect but a language in its own right, with records dating back to the sixth century. There are several distinct Lallans dialects. In the Highlands and the northwestern islands the inhabitants still use the Scots original Celtic language, called Gàidhlig or Eise; it is spoken by over 80,000 peoples. In bilingual areas, Eise is usually the first language of education. A form of Gaelic was brought to Scotland by Irish invaders in the fifth century, replacing an older Brythonic language. By the fifteenth century, with the accretion of Norse and English loanwords, the Scottish branch differed significantly enough from the Irish to warrant definition as a separate language. Scottish Gaelic exists in two main dialects, Northern and Southern, roughly geographically determined by a line up the Firth of Lorne to the town of Ballachulish and then across to the Grampian Mountains. The Southern dialect is more akin to Irish Gaelic than is the Northern.

The Highland Scots have remained largely Roman Catholic, while the majority of the Scots are Protestant, mostly belonging to the national church, the Church of Scotland The Puritan zeal of Scottish Presbyterianism, which is traceable to John Knox, the sixteenth-century Scottish religious reformer and statesman, retains a strong hold on the Scottish culture. The Roman Catholic minority, mostly in the Highlands, used to fear independence as liable to result in a Protestant hegemony, but recent polls show that a higher proportion of Catholics (39%) support independence than did the Protestant majority (32%)

NATIONAL HISTORY: A fierce warrior people, the Picts, inhabited the northern part of the island of Britannia in prehistoric times. They defeated repeated Roman attempts to penetrate their homeland in the first century A.D. The Romans finally constructed a series of fortifications across the island to divide Roman Britain from the wild tribal lands, which they called Caledonia, to the north, but even the Roman fortifications proved inadequate against the Pict and Celtic tribes.

In the fifth century, a century and a half after the Roman evacuation, missionaries, particularly St. Ninian and his disciples, introduced the Roman religion, Christianity. St. Columba, who came from Ireland in 563, spread the new creed through much of the region. Celtic Christianity was firmly established by clergy coming with the Scots settlers from Ireland.

The area was divided into four small, warring kingdoms—that of the Picts in the north; that of the Scots, who came from Ireland and founded Dalriada in the southwest; that of the Northumbrians, founded by the Angles and largely settled by Germanic migrants from the European mainland; and that of the Britons in Strathclyde. Between the eighth and eleventh centuries, after the decline of Northumbrian power in the region, the kingdoms became the object of raids by Norse Vikings. The Norsemen established colonies in the region, probably owing largely to the overpopulation of the west coast of Norway.

The union of the Picts and Scots under Kenneth mac Alpin in 843 is considered the origin of the Scottish kingdom, the Kingdom of Alba. Known as Kenneth I, mac Alpin established his rule over nearly all the territory north of the Firth of Forth. His descendents extended their rule into Northumbria. In 1018 the Scottish king extended his authority to the formerly independent Strathclyde kingdom and ruled all of Scotland except northern Pictland and the islands under Norse rule.

The English king, in 1189, recognized Scotland's independence, but the ambiguous terms in which he did so opened a long and bitter struggle between the two neighboring kingdoms. Edward I of England laid claim to Scotland in 1294, provoking a war that continued until his death in 1307. His son, Edward II, gathered the largest force ever raised on the island, and in 1314, 100,000 English troops moved north into Scotland, intent on conquest. Some 30,000 Scots, led by Robert Bruce, finally defeated the English at the Battle of Bannockburn, which secured the independence of the Scottish kingdom, but not a cessation of English interference or the gradual Anglicization of the Lowland Scots. For more than 200 years after Robert Bruce's death in 1329 and the accession of his infant son as Scotland's king, there was almost continuous strife among the Scottish nobility. The feudal anarchy was especially pronounced because of the prevalence of the clan system in the Highlands and various other areas. Close personal relations existed among the clan members and their leaders, who were powerful and contemptuous of royal authority. The period was also marked by almost uninterrupted warfare with the English.

In the fifteenth century, the Lallans dialect diverged sharply from Northumbrian, acquiring many forms and words unknown south of the border. The language became the language of dissent, both religious and political.

In the sixteenth century the Protestant Reformation, led by the religious reformer John Knox, swept Scotland except for the Highlands, which remained resolutely Roman Catholic and Gaelic speaking. The growth of Protestantism in Scotland led to opposition to the Scots traditional alliance with the Roman Catholic French. The general hostility to the pro-French monarchy was deepened by the marriage in April 1558 of Mary of Scotland to the dauphin of France. In 1560 the Scottish parliament abolished the jurisdiction of the Roman Catholic Church, and the Church of Scotland became the official church of the kingdom.

The long conflict with England, which was complicated by religious questions, ended in 1603 when the Scottish king James VI succeeded to the English throne and combined the two kingdoms in an uneasy dynastic union. A disastrous and expensive colonial adventure forced the Scots to choose between independence and poverty or prosperity in union with England. In 1707 the Scots voluntarily gave up their separate parliament and crown and joined the United Kingdom. Only the political and economic systems were united; the Scots retained their separate legal system, educational structure, national church, culinary traditions, national sports, and popular culture.

The union with England was opposed by many, particularly the Highland clans, who rose in support of the Stuarts in the Jacobite rebellions of 1708, 1715, and 1745–46. Following the defeat of the 1745–46 rebellion, the British government broke up the clan system. After the Scottish defeat the British government pressed assimilation of the Scots into English culture and banned the Scots' Gaelic language. The Roman Catholic minority, mostly in the Scottish Highlands, often suffered discrimination.

At the same time that the Highlanders were in rebellion, Edinburgh, the home of the "Scottish Enlightenment," was becoming one of Europe's most important cultural centers. Scottish thinkers in economics and philosophy won fame across Europe, and literary figures writing in English, such as Robert Burns and, somewhat later, Sir Walter Scott, became known throughout Europe and North America. The Scottish revival was based on the English of London, while their own Lallans was dismissed as coarse and lower class. The dialect survived among the less-educated lower classes and in rural areas.

The Scottish participation in the expansion of the British Empire included emigration to many parts of the world. The empire brought industrialization and prosperity, and the evolution of a large middle class, which necessitated reforms of the country's outmoded social institutions. In the eighteenth century a specifically Scottish renaissance developed; such names as Hume, Adam Smith, Burns, and Scott became known throughout the world. In the nineteenth century, the Clyde region became one of world's great shipbuilding centers.

The influence of the English culture and language became an issue in the early nineteenth century, as the industrialized lowlands became an urbanized, largely English–speaking region. In the 1840s, Scots resistance to English influence grew into a nascent national movement. Nationalists formed the Society for the Vindication of Scottish Rights, the forerunner of the modern national movement. In 1872 the compulsory teaching of standard English threatened the Gaelic and the Lallans dialect spoken by the majority of the Scots. In an effort to win wider support for the government among the Scots, a ministry for Scotland was created in 1885, and its top official was given cabinet status in 1926.

Many thousands of young Scots fought for Great Britain in the world wars, while munitions manufacturing brought the Scots unprecedented wealth. In the post–World War I era, however, a declining economy encouraged support for a nascent national movement. In 1928 Scottish nationalists formed the Scottish National Party to work for greater independence for the Scots. World War II again saw thousands of Scottish soldiers fighting in many areas of the world. Scottish industries supplied Britain with much of its war material, but the Scottish cities, unlike those in England, were not heavily bombed. The nationalist controversy was briefly put aside during the Second World War but resumed in 1945. Many prominent Scots signed the Scottish Covenant in 1949, binding its signatories to work for Scottish home rule.

The Scottish National Party (SNP) remained a fringe party until the discovery of oil off Scotland's coast in 1971. Claiming the oil wealth for Scotland, nationalists led a campaign for control of natural resources and the restoration of the Scottish parliament, the first step toward recovering Scotland's independence. Under the slogan "Rich Scots or Poor Britons," the nationalists campaigned for a referendum on autonomy. A 1979 referendum on home rule was narrowly defeated by the Scottish voters, partly due to nationalist opposition to its continuing restrictions.

Growing economic problems and progress toward a united Europe spurred a nationalist resurgence in the 1980s. The centralization of the British government under Margaret Thatcher stimulated widespread support for some sort of devolution, a granting of wider regional powers to local authorities in Scotland. In the late 1980s the old-style Scottish nationalism of the 1960s and 1970s, with its heady mixture of Gaelic culture and left-wing rhetoric, quickly gave way to a more businesslike approach.

Though the Scots are most pro-European of the British peoples, support for independence within a united Europe continued to win only minority backing, while devolution, home rule, and a separate Scottish parliament maintained widespread support. Polling of public opinion in 1990 showed 36% favored full independence. A similar poll in January 1992, however, revealed that separatist sentiment had risen to 50%, with only 15% favoring the status quo. Another poll showed that 69% of Scottish voters considered themselves "Scottish not British" or "more Scottish than British" and that only 21% considered themselves both Scottish *and* British.

The Stone of Scone, also called the Stone of Destiny or the Coronation Stone, taken from Scotland by the English king Edward I in 1296, was finally returned to Scotland in 1996, seven centuries after it was carried off by the English invaders. The stone, symbolic of the Scots nation, had been incorporated into the English throne, and many English kings and queens had been crowned on it. (The stone had actually returned to Scotland during the Christmas season in 1950, when it was stolen from Westminster Abbey by a number of Scottish students; it was later recovered and returned to England.)

In July 1997 the government minister for Scotland unveiled a proposal to devolve power from the British parliament to a 129-member legislature in Edinburgh. On 11 September 1997, the Scots voted to approve the initiative. The first elections took place in May 1999, and the legislature met in early 2000. Scots representatives now also make up part of all British delegations to the European Union (EU) and other international organizations.

The union between Scotland and England was formed as a partnership between nations, but Scotland has relentlessly lost ground to British centralization. The rebirth of Scotland as a nation came about through committees of lawyers, clergymen, and accountants rather than through the acts of radical nationalists. The Scots are proud that they have achieved so much without spilling a drop of blood, even if they have still not achieved full nationhood. To the Scots, devolution is not just decentralization of the government of the United Kingdom but the shape of the future relations between Scotland and England. In 1999, the SNP began to change its attacks on British institutions, now seeking not immediate independence but greater autonomy within Britain, which many Scots continue to believe gives their nation net benefits. Nonetheless, to the Scottish nationalists, devolution is only the first step toward genuine autonomy and the eventual independence of Scotland. Scottish nationalist political parties have vowed, should they be voted into power in Edinburgh, to hold a referendum on independence.

Political devolution has taken the sting from the independence debate. The SNP is the second largest political party in the Scottish parliament. In polls taken in 2001 support for immediate independence has gone down, but support for the devolved Scottish parliament and demands for greater autonomy has increased dramatically.

SELECTED BIBLIOGRAPHY:

Davidson, Neil. *The Origins of Scottish Nationhood*. 2000.
Harvie, Christopher. *Scotland and Nationalism: Scottish Society and Politics 1707–Present*. 1999.
Hutchinson, I.G.C. *Scottish Politics in the 20th Century*. 2000.
Traquair, Peter. *Freedom's Sword: The Scottish Wars of Independence*. 1998.

Seborgans

Seborghinis; Saborgans

POPULATION: Approximately (2002e) 2,000 Seborgans in Italy, concentrated in and around the village of Seborga in northwestern Italy. Nationalists claim that the Seborgan nation comprises a regional population of over 19,000.

THE SEBORGAN HOMELAND: The Seborgan homeland, slightly larger than nearby Monaco, lies at the foot of the Ligurian Alps surrounded by Italian territory in northeastern Italy close to the French border. The region is located in the mountain foothills overlooking a lush valley and the distant coastline of the Ligurian Riviera. The majority of the Seborgans are involved in the flower trade, cultivating and exporting flowers all over the world. Seborga is a self-proclaimed independent principality. *Principality of Seborga (Principato de Seborga)*: 5.4 sq. mi.—14 sq. km, (2002e) 19,000—Seborgans 11%, other Italians 89%. The Seborgan capital and major cultural center is Seborga, (2002e) 400.

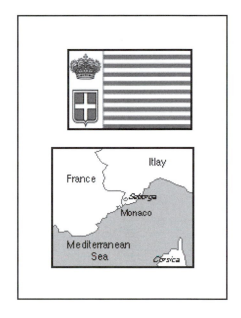

FLAG: The Seborgan national flag, the official flag of the principality, has eighteen white and blue stripes with a wide vertical white stripe at the hoist bearing the coat of arms, a white cross on a blue background, surmounted by a gold and red crown.

PEOPLE AND CULTURE: The Seborgans are an Italian people of mixed Ligurian and Occitan background. Their culture is basically the same as that of the surrounding Ligurians,* a Mediterranean culture based on that of the ancient Romans overlaid with influences from the region's many invaders and conquerors.

LANGUAGE AND RELIGION: The Seborgans, like the neighboring peoples, speak a dialect of Ligurian, an Italian language with considerable Occitan and French admixtures. The Seborgans also speak standard Italian, which is based on a Tuscan dialect, but the language of daily life remains their own Ligurian dialect.

The ecclesiastical history of the region, including its close association with St. Bernard, has ingrained religion in the local culture. Roman Catholic festivals, particularly 20 August, the annual celebration of their patron saint, remain extremely important.

NATIONAL HISTORY: The town of Seborga was founded as a Roman settlement called Castrum Sepulcri. The decline of Roman power brought invasions by Germanic tribes from outside the empire. Eventually Seborga came under the rule of the Burgundians,* then the Frankish empire of Charlemagne. The ancient name Castrum Sepulcri was later changed to Sepulcri Burgum, then to Serporca, and ultimately to the modern name of Seborga.

In the Middle Ages, the region formed part of the feudal holdings of the counts of Ventimiglia. The town was an important base for the Cathari sect that opposed the materialistic Catholic church. The Cathars, who lived lives of poverty in comparison to the opulent lifestyle of the Catholic hierarchy, were often persecuted by Catholic forces. The counts were finally deprived of their power to collect taxes for their support of the Cathars. In 954, most the region was handed over to the Benedictine monks of Santo Onorato of Lerins. The monastery's abbot also became prince of Seborga. The small principality of Seborga, under the rule of the prince-abbots, was recognized as independent by the Holy Roman Empire and formed one of the hundreds of city-states of Italy. The Cathars obstructed the possession of the Benedictine monks who decided to transform the church of San Michele in Ventimiglia into a monastery where the prior held feudal power over the region although he was unable to extend his authority to the Seborgan territory.

The territory was not included in the principality of Ventimiglia created by the Holy Roman Emperor in 1079, but was again recognized as an independent state, a principality within the Holy Roman Empire. Saint Bernard of Chiaravalle visited Seborga in 1117. He restored the chapel of Santa Petronilla and took possession of the town. In 1118, the prince-abbot of Seborga ordained the first nine templars, known as the Knights of St. Bernard, and Seborga became the first and only sovereign Cisterician state in history.

The French crusades against the Cathars overwhelmed the region in 1150, with over 300 men, women, and children burned alive in their stronghold near Seborga. In 1158, the prince of Ventimiglia returned from the Crusades to dedicate Seborga to Saint Bernard, who died on 20 August 1153.

The Templars, feudal knights who fought the Muslims in the Holy Land, returned from Jerusalem established an association in Seborga called the Confraria, an assembly of Seborgans to exercise their right of self-government. St. Bernard ordained Huges de Payns as the first Grand Master of the Knights of St. Bernard. The Confraria, during the thirteenth century, was extended to the neighboring towns that were claimed as part of the Seborgan state. The Templar principality of Seborga was recognized as an independent state.

The Seborgans created a mint in 1666 under Prince Abbot Edward. The currency it minted, the Luigino, was valued at a quarter of a French Louis. The silver and gold coins bore the image of St. Bernard, the patron saint of the principality.

The Genoese republic claimed the region in the fourteenth century, taking control of part of Seborga's territory, including the towns of Vallebona and San Remo. The Seborgans retained a precarious independence until 1697, when the duke of Savoy bought the entire territory with the approval of the pope and the king of France. The sale was opposed by the Genoese, but a document from the pope in Avignon authorized the sale of Seborga.

Seborga remained a Cistercian state until 20 January 1729, when the principality was sold to Vittorio Amedeo II of Savoy, prince of Piedmont and king of Sardinia. The Treaty of Aquisgrana in 1748, which recognized the sale of territory in Liguria, but the Principality of Seborga was not listed among the transferred territories. The change in Seborga's status was never registered with the Sardinian kingdom nor with the House of Savoy. Forty years after the sale to the Kingdom of Sardinia of most of Liguria, the Austrian Empire still recognized the sovereign Principality of Seborga.

The French Revolution, in 1789, reverberated in the neighboring territories, including Seborga. Overrun by French troops, the remaining territories of the Republic of Genoa became part of the Kingdom of Sardinia, but again the principality of Seborga was not listed. At the Congress of Vienna, convened in 1815 to reorganize post-Napoleonic Europe, Seborga was ignored and its claims to independence were summarily dismissed although it technically remained a sovereign state. The unification of Italy in 1861 also ignored the small principality, which was not mentioned among the numerous territories in the Act of Unification.

The Seborgans benefited from the prosperity of northern Italy in the late nineteenth century, their claim to independence ignored and forgotten. They carried Italian passports, used Italian currency, and participated fully in the civil life of the region. The rise of fascism in Italy after 1922 was met with passive resistance and a stubborn claim to independent status. None of the fascist decrees bothered to mention tiny Seborga, and in 1934 even Mussolini specifically waved it off as "not Italian" during a speech in 1934.

The end of the Savoy dynasty at the end of World War II in 1946, again raised the question of the tiny states within Italian territory, San Marino, the Vatican, and Seborga, but the postwar economic prosperity again dictated participation in the modernization. Legally tiny Seborga did not form part of the modern Italian republic.

In the late 1950s, Giorgio Carbone happened upon the ancient town charter. He discovered that Seborga was actually an independent state with a history far longer than Italy's. Regardless of the complacency of the nineteenth-century Seborgans, their small homeland had never been officially annexed by the new Italian state. The Seborgans began to press their case for independence. As they had never formally surrendered their sovereignty they proposed to create an independent ministate modeled on nearby Monaco. In 1963 the people of Seborga elected as monarch Giorgio Carbone, a commoner, as Giorgio I, prince of Seborga. Carbone is one of the leaders of the national movement formed in the early 1960s.

Giorgio I was reelected as prince of Seborga in 1993 for another 8-year term. On 23 April 1995, the Seborgans of the village of Seborga voted for a general statute with 304 against 4 voters supporting independence for the ancient principality. The following day the tiny principality adopted its own currency, the Luigino. On 20 August 1996, on the feast of St. Bernard, Prince Giorgio reaffirmed the territorial sovereignty and jurisdiction of the principality. The Seborgans claimed the territory of the medieval Templar state, which includes neighboring towns and a total population of 19,000.

The Italian government has refused to recognize Seborgan claims to sovereignty even though San Marino, also situated within Italian territory, was the first to recognize Seborgan sovereignty. The African state of Burkina Faso recognized Seborga as an independent state and exchanged ambassadors in 1998, followed by many other African states. The Seborgans take their sovereignty very seriously and intend to join San Marino, Monaco, and Andorra as one of Europe's mini-states.

The claims to sovereignty by the Seborgans have created a tourist boom. Upwards of 100,000 tourists a year visit the tiny principality. The region's restaurants and souvenir shops selling Seborgan flags, stamps, and other souvenirs are increasingly prosperous. Seborga's brass-colored currency, the Luigino, is traded in the shops at about $7.50, up from just $6.00 in 1998. The tourist trade, based on the region's claim to independence, is one of the most powerful reasons for the Seborgans to continue their fight for recognition as a sovereign European mini-state. The Seborgans have received envoys from Russia, Libya, Luxembourg, Sri Lanka, and Andorra and now maintain 3 consulates in France, 6 in Italy, and 1 each in Bulgaria, Brazil, Scotland, and Chile. In early 2000, the Seborgans formally applied for membership in the United Nations (UN).

SELECTED BIBLIOGRAPHY:

Cox, Eugene L. *The Eagles of Savoy: The House of Savoy in Thirteenth Century Europe.* 1983.
Facaros, Dana. *Northwest Italy.* 1991.
Lambert, Malcomb. *The Cathars.* 1998.
Monteverde, Franco. *The Ligurians: An Italian and Mediterranean People.* 1994.

Shans

Tayoks; Dai; Dtai; Tai Yàan (Great Tai); Tai Shan; Ngios; Ngiows; Sams

POPULATION: Approximately (2002e) 6,350,000 Shans in southeast Asia, concentrated in Shan State of Myanmar, where most of the country's 4,445,000 million Shans live, with smaller communities in adjacent areas of China, with a Shan population of 1,150,000, and about one million in Laos and Thailand.

THE SHAN HOMELAND: The Shan homeland, often called Shanland, occupies the broad Shan Plateau on both sides of the Salween River valley in northeastern Myanmar, southern Yunnan in China, and adjacent areas of Laos and Thailand. Most of the region consists of river valleys and flat highlands between mountains covered with tropical rain forests. The Shans mostly inhabit the valleys and plains, while smaller national groups inhabit the foothills and mountains. The Shan heartland in Myanmar forms a state of the Federation of Myanmar. *Shan State (United Shan States)*: 60,155 sq. mi.—155,801 sq. km, (2002e) 5,544,000—Shans 48%, Burmans 20%, Karennis* 10%, Wa* 9%, Kachins* 5%, Chinese (Kokangs) 4%, Pa-O,* Lahu,* Pa-laungs,* and other Burmese 4%. The Shan capital and major cultural center is Taunggi, (2002e) 157,000. The other important cultural center is Lashio, (2002e) 128,000. The major Shan center in China is Luxi, called Mangshi in Shan, (2002e) 42,000.

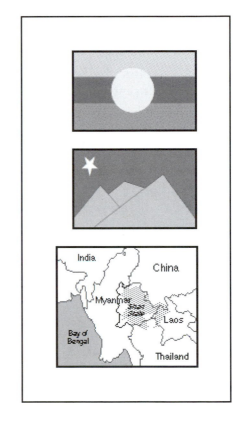

FLAG: The Shan national flag, the flag of the national movement, is a horizontal tricolor of yellow, green, and red bearing a white disc centered on the green. The flag of the largest national organization, the Shan State Progressive Party, is a red field charged with three crossed yellow arrows surrounded by a yellow cog within a wreath of yellow plant leaves. The Shan war flag, the flag used by several Shan organizations, is a pale blue field bearing three yellow mountains at the bottom and a five-pointed star on the upper hoist.

PEOPLE AND CULTURE: The Shans, called Tayok or Dai in China, call themselves Tai yàan, which translates as "big Tai." "Shan" is a corruption of Siam or Syam, the name given them by the Burmans. They form one of the three main divisions of the Thai peoples and comprise seven divisions separated by international boundaries in four countries. Originally the name Shan was synonymous with "mountaineer" and was used to describe several highland peoples. With lighter skin than the Thai or the Burmans, the Shans are thought to have mixed with early non-Thai peoples; the mixture is evident in their culture and language. Although ethnically and linguistically the Shans are related to the Thais of Thailand, culturally they are more closely related to the Burmans. The Shan are extremely conscious of their national identity and consider themselves the older, wiser brothers of the Thais and Laos. Descent is traced through the male line; children are given the surnames of their fathers. Traditionally Shan society was divided into two classes, aristocracy and commoners, based on blood origins. The Shan minority in Thailand is being assimilated, although the arrival of thousands of illegal refugees from Myanmar has stimulated a cultural revival among the Thai Shans.

LANGUAGE AND RELIGION: The Shan language is a Tai language of the Sino-Tai language group. Shan, spoken in two major dialects, is related to Thai and Lao but is not mutually intelligible with them. In China children are taught to write their native language in Buddhist temples, a fact that has created tension between state schools and teachers working in the temples. The Shan language has been a core issue of the national movement. In the 1960s the government collected all Shan textbooks and replaced them with texts in the Burman language. Many Shans are bilingual in Burman, and the more educated often speak English.

The Shans are a Buddhist people, practicing their own form of Theravada Buddhism. This sect emphasizes Buddha as a historical figure, the virtues of religious life, and the authority of the *Tripitika*, or the Three Baskets, referring to self-discipline, preaching, and discussing doctrine. The Buddhist religion dominates Shan society both religiously and politically. For this reason, the Buddhist tenets have for centuries played an important role in both informal social control and in the training of children. Many Shans have retained belief in spirits, some of which are helpful, while others are considered wicked or harmful. Extravagant Buddhist festivals are an integral part of Shan culture; Shans faithfully follow magic rituals, horoscopes, and dreams. Most Shan boys join the Buddhist priesthood for a year or two when they are about 10 years old.

NATIONAL HISTORY: Tai peoples began to migrate southeast along the rivers from their original home in China, possibly as early as the first century A.D. In the seventh century, Thai tribes occupied the fertile upper valleys of the Salaween, Irrawaddy, and Chindwin Rivers, absorbing or displacing the earlier inhabitants. The Mongol invasion of the Burman kingdom of Pagan in 1238 created a power vacuum that the Shans moved south to fill. They extended their authority to the lowlands of the Irrawaddy Basin, using soldiers recruited from the Northern Tai* fleeing the Mongol conquest of the state of Nan Chao, now in China.

The resurgent Burmans drove the Shans from the Irrawaddy Delta in the fifteenth century and in 1604 took control of all but the Shan Plateau. Forced to retreat to their highland homeland, the Shans created there 34 *muongs*, or principalities. The princes, the *saohpas*, exercised hereditary and absolute rule over a small aristocratic elite and the mass of commoners. The still powerful Shans defeated a Chinese invasion in 1766–70, losing only some small eastern districts, but exhausted by the struggle, they declined as a power. By the nineteenth century the principalities had become tributaries of the Burman kings.

Shan expansion to the east was halted by the Thais near Chiang Mai in 1869. The Chinese conquered the eastern Shan territories in a bloody campaign in 1873. Shan pleas for Burman military assistance were ignored, and the Chinese held on to their conquests in the eastern districts. The princes renounced their allegiance to the Burman king in the late 1870s, plunging northern Burma into chaos. The turbulence gave the British a pretext for intervention.

British and American missionaries arrived in the 1890s. The first Christian religious texts were published in 1892. Although the missionaries won a few converts among the commoners, their impact was most felt among the aristocracy, who sent their sons to mission schools for education. By the early twentieth century an educated elite, able to deal with the British authorities, had moved into positions of authority.

The British annexed what they called the Shan States in 1886, leaving the princes to rule under British supervision, their succession subject to confirmation by the colonial authorities. Not included in British Burma, each of the Shan States maintained direct treaty relations with the British from 1887. In 1922 the states united to form the Federated Shan States but retained their separate relations with the colonial administration. For the first time the Shans united in a governing body common to all the principalities in the Federated Shan States' Council. The council comprised all the ruling princes and the British governor in Rangoon.

Partly because of their separate administrative status, the Shans were never affected by the prewar nationalist movement in Burma. The colonial authority was also tenuous in the Shan States. The British presence was confined to a chief commissioner in the administrative center at Taunggi, and a few political officers were assigned to the courts of the most important states. For the Shans, the colonial period was one of peace and stability, but also a period of economic and political stagnation. The British ignored the region's natural resources, developing only the lowland agricultural lands to produce rice and exports for India.

Overrun by Japanese and Thai forces during World War II, many Shans collaborated, believing Japanese promises of independence. Neighboring Thailand, allied to Japan, annexed two of the largest Shan states, Kentung and Mong Pan, in 1942. Shan nationalists declared the remaining Shan states of the federation independent on 3 October 1942. The Japanese created a nominally independent Burma on 25 September 1943, and to placate their Burman allies the Japanese dissolved the nationalist Shan government in December. Placed under direct Burman rule for the first time in their long history, the Shans rebelled. The Shan revolt continued until the return of British rule in March 1945.

The British announced their intention to grant Burma independence at the end of World War II. Insisting on their treaty rights, the Shans demanded separate independence for the Federated Shan States. Under pressure from the British authorities and promised autonomy by the majority Burman government, the Shans finally agreed to inclusion in the Union of Burma. Burma's constitution allowed for Shan secession after 10 years if the Shans felt that continued association harmed their interests. Within months of Burma's independence in 1948 the new Burmese government abrogated the independence constitution and attempted to impose direct rule on the Shan federation.

Led by rival princes, the Shans produced a bewildering array of rebel forces, the groups often fighting among themselves. The Shan princes in 1958 notified the Burmese government of their intention to secede under the terms of the 1948 independence constitution. Refusing to honor the agreement, the government retaliated by stripping the hereditary princes of their titles and privileges in 1959. This affront to national dignity united most of the Shan rebel groups in a war against the Burmese government. In 1962 the Burmese government abolished the union constitution and militarily occupied the Shan federation.

The Shan insurgency was complicated by their traditional connection with the production of opium and the massive influx of defeated Kuomintang armies escaping the victorious communist forces in China. To finance the continuing separatist war, several Shan groups turned to the opium trade. Called the "Shan passport to independence," the drug trade nevertheless drew in groups and organizations with little interest in the nationalist cause, including many high-ranking Chinese generals.

The nationalists joined rebel Karens* and Mons* in 1969 to coordinate the insurgency against the hated Burman-dominated military government. The group later expanded to include many of the other ethnic groups fighting the Burmese military. The combined group drew up a plan to replace the military government with a loose federation of independent states in Burma. A new constitution adopted by the Burmese military government in 1974 abolished all local autonomy. The combined group supported the prodemocracy movement that swept the country in 1988 but returned to insurgency following the crushing of the democracy movement by the military and the overthrow of the results of a democratic election.

U Khun Sa, the so-called king of opium and chief of the Mong Tai Army, a private force of over 20,000 soldiers, offered in July 1994 to end opium poppy cultivation in Shanland in return for a withdrawal of the Burmese military troops. He later offered to surrender in return for Burma's recognition of Shan independence. The legitimate nationalist organizations disavowed his offer but endorsed the call for the withdrawal of the Burmese military and the end of the drug trade, which has damaged the Shan nationalists' attempts to win international support in their fight for independence. By 1990, an estimated half the heroin flooding the United States originated from the poppy fields of the Golden Triangle. Khun Sa was indicted by a U.S. court in early 1990 for heroin trafficking. The government of Myanmar refused to extradite Kun Sa to the United States. On 13 December 1993, Khun Sa declared an independent Shan state with himself as president, but his declaration was rejected by senior Shan leaders.

In 1991 the State Law and Order Restoration Council, the ruling military junta, legalized certain Shan insurgent groups in an effort to divide further the factionalized Shan national movement. In 1995, Khun Sa's Mong Tai Army split over concerns that Sa's drug trafficking was taking precedence over Shan nationalist aspirations. A new council was formed by a breakaway faction that favored full Shan autonomy in a reconstituted democratic Myanmar federation. In December 1995, Khun Sa signed a cease-fire agreement with the government. Government troops took over Khun Sa's stronghold in eastern Shan State in January 1996.

The SLORC signed cease-fire agreements with other Shan groups between 1994 and 1996. Groups that signed were allowed to increase their earnings through unhindered opium and heroin production. After Khun Sa's agreement in 1995, the military offensive against the Shans intensified as the government attempted to wipe out the remaining Shan resistance. Many government officials became engaged in the lucrative drug trade in the "Golden Triangle."

Several Shan organizations announced they were ready to hold talks with the Myanmar government, suggesting that representatives of other countries (China, Thailand, and Laos) with large Shan populations also be invited. The offer was ignored, and in March 1996, in order to end support for Shan separatists, government authorities ordered massive retaliation against the Shan civilian population. Over 300,000 Shans were forced to flee their homes by government forces between 1996 and 1998. Many fled into Thailand, but others were pursued into the jungle highlands. Others were rounded up and forced to work as porters for the army or on roads, dams, and railway construction. Those forced into slave labor were often beaten and deprived of food. By late 1998 much of southern Shan State had been depopulated, and many ethnic Burmans, sponsored by the government, were moving into the region.

Journalists and human rights organizations were denied access to the region, so the full scale of the tragedy was difficult to gauge. What is clear is that in the late 1990s the Shans were being targeted solely because of their ethnic origins or their perceived support for antigovernment groups. By 1998 an estimated half-million Shans had fled into Thailand, where they were not recognized as refugees but had to work as illegal laborers. In 1997 there were reports of special Burmese death squads targeting the civilian population. In 1998 human rights groups accused the government of using the abduction and rape of increasing numbers of Shan women and young girls as a tool of war. In May 1999 a government offensive in northern Shan State left thousands dead or homeless and forced many to flee into Thailand, where they joined the Shans already living in 16 squalid camps just inside the border. An alliance of three armed Shan resistance groups in 1996 formed the Shan Democratic Union, which functioned as the foreign ministry of the Shan federation. The name of the federation was changed to United Shan States in 1997.

The continuing factionalism of the Shan national movement is a major hindrance to coordinated resistance to the Burmese military government. There is also an active debate on the subject of independence versus autonomy in a federal union. Most Shans feel that the Burmans cannot be trusted and that only independence will ensure the survival of the Shan nation, although the possibility of Shan participation in a reconstituted Burmese union is not ruled out.

At a conference held in September 2000 constituent delegates voted in favor of a constitution for the people of Shan state. It was discussed whether the state should be a federal state, a unitary state, or a member state in a proposed "Federal Union of Burma." The concensus favored a independent, federal republic made up of a number of autonomous states.

Representatives of the Myanmar and China governments met in December 2001 following Chinese accusations that the Myanmar government was not doing enough to stop the flow of drugs into China. The discussions also dealt with the ongoing Shan insurgency, which is closely tied to the drug trade.

SELECTED BIBLIOGRAPHY:

Cochrane, Wilbur W. *The Shans*. 1988.
Gravers, Mikael. *Nationalism as Political Paranoia in Burma*. 1998.
Lintner, Bertil. *Land of Jade: A Journey through Insurgent Burma*. 1990.
Yawnghwe, Chao Tzang. *The Shan of Burma: Memories of a Shan Exile*. 1988.

Shetlanders

Islanders; Zetlanders; Shetland Islanders; Shelties

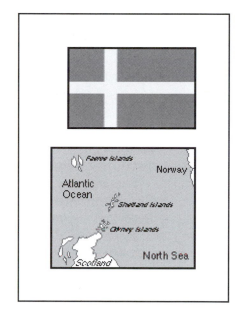

POPULATION: Approximately (2002e) 35,000 Shetlanders in the United Kingdom, mostly in the Shetland Islands north of the Scottish mainland, but with small communities in other parts of Scotland, in England, and in Canada, the United States, Australia, and New Zealand.

THE SHETLANDER HOMELAND: The name "Zetland" (Anglicized as "Shetland") stems from Old Norse and is thought to mean "high land." The Shetlander homeland, the most northerly territory of the United Kingdom, comprises a long archipelago 130 miles (210 km) north of the mainland of Scotland and 250 miles (400 km) west of Bergen in Norway. The Shetland Islands include about 100 islands and islets, of which only 19 are inhabited. The major islands, most with Scandinavian names, are Unst, Fettar, Whalsay, Foula, Papa Stour, Yell, and Mainland. Unst is the most northerly point of Britain. The majority of the population, around 18,000, lives on the largest of the islands, Mainland. The islands are generally low-lying and treeless. The Shetland Islands form an administrative region, the Shetland Islands Area, of Scotland in the United Kingdom. *County of Shetland (Zetland)*: 553 sq. mi.— 1,433 sq. km, (2002e) 23,000—Shetlanders 94%, other Scots* 6%. The Shetlander capital and major cultural center is Lerwick, (2002e) 8,000.

FLAG: The Shetlander national flag, the flag of the national movement, is a dark blue field charged with a white Scandinavian cross.

PEOPLE AND CULTURE: The Shetlanders, popularly called "Shelties," are a distinct island nation, a mixture of early Viking settlers and later Celtic Scots. Ethnically the Shetlanders are more closely related to the Icelanders and Faeroese* than to the other peoples of the British Isles. Due to the relative isolation of their islands, the Shetlanders have retained their traditional island culture, which combines Norse and Celtic customs and traditions. The modern Shetlanders remain more Scandinavian than Scots, and marked traces of Norse speech and culture survive among them.

The annual Up-Helly-Aa, the Fire Festival, is held at the end of January; a full-scale Viking longship is dragged through Lerwick in a torchlight procession, then burned on the beach. Shetland is so different from Scotland that the Scottish national symbols, the Gaelic language and tartans, are virtually unknown in the islands. Traditionally the Shetlanders were crofters, subsistence farmers, but also fishermen, initially to supplement food supplies and later for trade.

LANGUAGE AND RELIGION: The Shetland dialect, claimed by nationalists as a separate language, is virtually unintelligible to mainland Scots. The dialect combines the former Scandinavian language of the islands, Norn, based on Old Norse, with Celtic words and phrases, and later English, Dutch, and German influences. Radio broadcasts since the 1970s have been made in the local dialects. Island children until the 1970s were rebuked for speaking the dialect in school, but the dialect has now taken on a new authenticity. Younger Shetlanders now speak the dialect as a matter of pride, and it is now taught in some schools and in private academies. The Shetlanders speak standard English, the language of administration and education, but continue to use the Shetlander dialect at home.

The majority of the Shetlanders are Presbyterians, belonging to the Church of Scotland. Many pre-Christian traditions and festivals have survived and become part of the Shetlander culture. Many of the Christian customs more closely resemble the Christianity of Norway and the Faeroe Islands than that of the Scottish mainland.

NATIONAL HISTORY: Shetland has been inhabited for at least 6,000 years. The islands were originally settled by Picts from the Scottish mainland. Their Bronze Age remains, especially round towers called *broachs*, are still found throughout the archipelago. In the seventh and eighth centuries, the conversion of the island population to Christianity was begun by missionaries from the Scottish mainland. A distinct culture developed in the isolation of the North Sea.

In the eighth century the islands were invaded by Vikings as part of the Norse expansion that spread Viking culture to Iceland, Greenland, the Faeroe Islands, and nearby Orkney. By the ninth century Scandinavian colonists had settled many of the islands, absorbing the indigenous Picts. Annexed by Harold Fairhair, the first king of Norway, the islands were organized as a separate earldom in 875. The Norse conquest and settlement are recounted by the *Orkneyinga Saga*, a Norse epic about the colonization of Shetland and Orkney.

The islands, called Zetland in the Norse language, remained a Norwegian dependency until the Norwegian kingdom, with its possessions and dependencies, passed to Denmark in 1397. The Danish king, Christian I, in 1468 pledged the islands to James III of Scotland as security for the dowry of Margaret of Norway on her marriage to the Scottish king. King

James, when the dowry was not delivered, annexed the islands to his king-dom in 1472.

In 1540, James V of Scotland visited the islands and proclaimed Shetland a county of the Scottish kingdom. Several Scottish nobels were granted entensive land grants in the islands. To ensure the loyalty of the islands, Scottish colonists from the mainland were settled in the islands. They slowly mixed with the Norse population to form the distinctive Shetland culture.

Traditionally the Shetlanders were crofters, farming small plots of family land. The lack of good farmland forced most Shetlanders to engage in other occupations, mostly fishing, to supplement their farming income. Later fishing became commercially viable, and a majority of the population gave up farming to join the large fishing fleet. The fleet often smuggled goods from Norway or the Netherlands, bypassing British customs.

Scotland's union with England in 1707 began a long campaign in the islands for separation from Scotland and for a distinct legal status within the United Kingdom. The islanders demanded the political and economic autonomy that would recognize their distinct culture and history, a status similar to the autonomy granted the Manx,* Guernseians,* and Jerseians.* Relative isolation and a small population facilitated the efforts to preserve the unique island culture and dialect, even though the English language spread to the isolated islands in the eighteenth and nineteenth centuries. A lack of industry and high unemployment caused the islands' population to decline from 1871 onward.

The Shetland Islands developed as the United Kingdom's major fishing region, while excess population left for the mainland, keeping the population nearly constant during the early decades of the twentieth century. The relative prosperity of the region renewed the island campaign to win separate legal status within the United Kingdom. Fishing and the manu-facture of woolens from the famous Shetland sheep remained the major occupations.

The islands became important to the British fleet during both world wars. In November 1939 the islands were the target of the first German air raids on the United Kingdom. Fishing, particularly herring fishing, became important as food scarcity became a serious problem during the war. The population of the islands began to drop after World War II, with the postwar decline of the fishing industry. The islanders, forced to leave in search of work, loudly denounced the lack of development in their is-lands.

Shetland's population continued to decline through the 1950s and 1960s. The discovery of the Brent and Ninian oil fields in the North Sea, northeast of Shetland, in 1970 reversed the trend. The islands became a center of the North Sea oil industry; oil workers from many parts of the world were brought in by the British and international oil companies. The most advanced technology entered Shetland's traditional way of life when a large oil terminal was built at Sullom Voe, in the north of Mainland. Pipes were extended from the North Sea fields to the tanker depot, which is in a sheltered, deep water.

The idea of home rule for the islands north of the Scottish mainland emerged in 1962 after a local delegation visited the Faeroese homeland. The vigor of the autonomous government of the Faeroe Islands stimulated local nationalism in Shetland. Their culture and way of life threatened by the massive influx of oil workers and companies, the islanders began to mobilize during the 1970s. Nationalist organizations demanded autonomy and separate legal status to protect their unique culture and to give them local control over the oil companies' activities that were causing ecological damage.

In 1979 the islanders threatened secession, as their pristine islands were being practically overrun by the oil companies going after the rich oil deposits in the North Sea. Local groups, particularly the Shetland Movement, led the campaign for greater autonomy. The national movement, with support from the large Shetlander population living on the British mainland, led a peaceful campaign for home rule and protection of the island culture.

The region's oil wealth, which stimulated Scottish nationalist demands that the British government leave the control of the booming industry to the Scots, also roused Shetlander demands that the Scots keep their hands off Shetland's oil. The nationalist program, with growing support for local control of development and the offshore oil fields, included demands for a fairer share of the oil revenue; it added another element to the dispute between Scotland and the government of the United Kingdom over control of natural resources.

Scottish desire for independence within a united Europe stimulated Shetlander sentiment for separation from Scotland in the 1980s and 1990s. The islanders expressed in numerous polls their preference for separate legal status within the United Kingdom; a large minority favored eventual independence within a European federation; pro-Scottish opinion was a distant third. In the 1990s pro–European sentiment gained support due to the realization that future European regulations and funding would be more important to the islands than decisions made in either Edinburgh or London. On 21 February 1994, the islanders in Shetland called for a referendum on independence from the rest of Scotland. The islanders were worried that their culture and way of life would be damaged under Scotland's home rule government.

In an effort to lessen reliance on oil revenue, fishing was upgraded and aquaculture introduced. By the early 1990s, salmon farms contributed nearly as much to the local economy as the traditional fishing sector. The boom North Sea oil years had passed, and the Shetlanders looked to traditional industries to sustain their economy.

The Shetlanders, part of Scotland through a quirk of history, mostly oppose Scottish nationalism; if loose ties to the United Kingdom are not possible, they look with some confidence to independence. An independent Shetland within a European framework, controlling the North Sea oil production in the eastern Shetland Basin territorial waters, valued at around $18 million a day, would be a viable, even wealthy, sovereign state.

The devolution of government to a new Scottish parliament in 1999 began a new phase of Shetlander efforts to create a self-governing state within the United Kingdom. Though the islands have been a part of Scotland for over 500 years, the attachment has been a loose and fragile one. The Shetlanders still resent the Scottish lords who originally appropriated the best lands and subjugated the Shetlanders to centuries of "foreign" rule.

New oil discoveries west of the islands in June 2002 raised hopes for the return of the prosperity of the 1980s, but without the ecological degradation that accompanied the first oil boom. Activists insist that any expansion of oil production to previous levels must be controlled by the Shetlanders themselves.

SELECTED BIBLIOGRAPHY:

Crumley, Jim. *Shetland: Land of the Ocean*. 1996.
Newton, Norman. *Shetland*. 1995.
Ritchie, Anna. *Shetland*. 1998.
Schei, Liv Kjørsvik, and Gunnie Moberg. *The Story of Shetland*. 1988.

Siberians

Siberiaks; Siberyaks; Sibirs; Sibirhs; Asian Russians

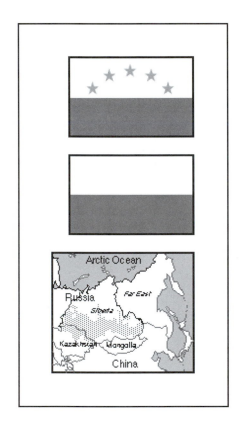

POPULATION: Approximately (2002e) 20,500,000 Siberians in the Russian Federation, concentrated in the southern provinces and republics of central Siberia. Outside the region there are large Siberian communities in European Russia, the Russian Far East, and in the former Soviet states of Central Asia, particularly in adjacent areas of Kazakhstan.

THE SIBERIAN HOMELAND: The Siberian homeland occupies a huge area in the central Russian Federation, lying between European Russia and the Russian Far East. The vast territory, extending from above the Arctic Circle to the borders of Kazakhstan and Mongolia on the south, is roughly divided into two regions, the lowlands of the West Siberian Plain and the highlands of the Central Siberian Plateau. The Siberian region is vastly underpopulated. Siberia has no political status. Administratively the region is divided into the West Siberian Region and the East Siberian Region, further divided into the *oblasts* (provinces) of Chita, Irkutsk, Kemerovo, Kurgan, Krasnoyarsk, Novosibirsk, Omsk, Tomsk, and Tyumen; the Territory of Altay; and the Republics of Altai, Buryat, Khakass, and Tuva. *Region of Siberia (Sibirh)*: 2,600,042 sq. mi.—6,734,077 sq. km, (2002e) 22,818,000—Siberians 73%, Ukrainians 7%, Volga Germans* 1%, Buryats* 1%, Sakhas* 1%, other Russians 17%. The Siberian capital and major cultural center is Novosibirsk, (2002e) 1,397,000. Other important cultural centers are Omsk, (2002e) 1,143,000, Krasnoyarsk (2002e) 872,000, Irkutsk (2002e) 594,000, and Barnaul, (2002e), 577,000.

FLAG: The Siberian national flag, the traditional flag of the region, is a horizontal bicolor of white over green. The flag of the national movement, representing a proposed United States of North Asia, is the Siberian bicolor with the addition of an arc of five pale blue stars on the white stripe.

PEOPLE AND CULTURE: The Siberians, calling themselves Siberiaks or Siberyaks, are the descendents of Slavic settlers, deportees, and exiles, with admixtures of the region's 70 different ethnic groups. The Siberian culture, developed by the harsh conditions and frontier history, is a mixture of archaic Russian traditions and cultural traits borrowed from the region's indigenous peoples. The historical separation of the Siberians from European Russia is demonstrated by the Siberian custom of referring to the Russian heartland as the "mainland," as if Siberia were an island. About three-quarters of the Siberians live in urban areas, particularly the large cities in the southern areas of the territory. While more than 70 national groups of varying sizes live in Siberia, including 30 groups officially recognized by the Russian government, Siberians of Russian or Ukrainian origin form the vast majority.

LANGUAGE AND RELIGION: A number of regional dialects are collectively called Siberian, a language as different from standard Russian as Ukrainian, and claimed as a separate Eastern Slav language by nationalists. The dialects, which have borrowed heavily from the languages of the indigenous peoples, differ greatly from region to region. There is no standardized literary dialect, and Russian remains the language of administration, education, and publishing. Most Siberians speak standard Russian along with at least one of the regional dialects and often the language of the regional indigenous group.

The majority of the Siberians are Orthodox, although most major religions are represented in the region. The religious beliefs of the Siberians have been heavily influenced by the animist and shamanistic beliefs of the indigenous peoples. Many traditions brought by the colonists from pre-revolutionary Russia have long since disappeared in European Russia.

NATIONAL HISTORY: Originally inhabited by nomadic Turkic and Mongol tribes, the vast area remained divided until most of the southern territories were united under the rule of the Mongol Golden Horde in the thirteenth century. At the disintegration of the Mongol's vast empire most of the region was included in a Tatar successor state, the Khanate of Sibir. The name comes from a Mongol word meaning "sleeping land."

The first Europeans to penetrate the region were Slavic traders from the mercantile republic of Novgorod in the thirteenth century. The traders, seeking furs, made contact with many of the tribal peoples of western Siberia. Cossacks in the service of the Russian tsar crossed the Urals in 1518 to conquer Sibir—the name of the conquered state applied to the entire area east of European Russia. A series of Cossack forts gradually expanded Russian territory in the face of resistance by the native peoples. The first settlers, mostly Cossacks and peasant serfs seeking land and independence in Siberia's vast spaces, expanded along the rivers, the only means of transport and communication.

Organized as a Russian province in 1710, Siberia became a place of exile, a dumping ground for deportees, political prisoners, recalcitrant serfs turned over for deportation by landlords, convicted prostitutes, and Jews who failed to pay their taxes. The deportation of Polish insurgents, revolutionaries, and captured members of antitsarist groups began in 1825. The attitudes and ideas of the political exiles, often well educated and antigovernment, spread through Siberian society, becoming part of the political culture. By 1890 there were an estimated 100,000 Polish rebels, 40,000 Russian criminals, 50,000 political prisoners, and over 5,000 wives who had voluntarily joined their prisoner-husbands in Siberian exile, often taking their children with them.

There was no organized colonization until the mid-nineteenth century, and the region grew slowly due to the resistance of the indigenous peoples east of the Ural Mountains. The abolition of serfdom in 1861 freed thousands of land-hungry peasants. Offered free land in underpopulated Siberia, thousands crossed the Urals to settle the valleys of the Ob and Yenisei Rivers. The completion of the Trans-Siberian Railroad in 1891–92 facilitated settlement, and over three million Slavs had migrated to Siberia from Europe by 1914. Most colonists settled along the main transportation lines, contributing to the growth of industry in the new Siberian cities. The new arrivals, generally adopting the speech and antigovernment attitudes of the earlier immigrants, joined a society in many ways more similar to the frontier regions of Canada and the United States than European Russia.

The Siberians, through long contact with exiled revolutionaries and political prisoners, were among the first to espouse revolutionary ideals as Russia slowly collapsed during World War I. The overthrow of the monarchy in February 1917 met with jubilation. Exiles and revolutionaries, suddenly freed, eagerly joined the revolution.

A Siberian national movement had existed since the late nineteenth century but had enjoyed little popular support until the revolution. In August 1917 the nationalists formed a Siberian parliament. Promised autonomy, the nationalists supported Russia's new democratic government until its overthrow by the Bolsheviks in October 1917. On 7 December 1917, one day after the Tomsk *soviet*, or council, declared Siberia under Bolshevik rule, a hastily convened All-Siberian Provisional Council declared Siberia autonomous. A Siberian Duma, or congress, met to confirm the region's autonomy in January 1918. The Duma authorized the formation of a national army from the thousands of Siberian soldiers deserting the front. On 26 July 1918, troops of the Tomsk *soviet* forcibly closed the Duma and arrested many of its members.

Many of the parliamentarians fled east to Omsk, where the anti-

Bolshevik White government of Adm. Aleksandr Kolchak quickly suppressed the national movement. The Whites opposed any movement that proposed the secession of any part of Holy Russia.

Siberia's independence was made briefly possible instead by the Czech Legion, Czech and Slovak prisoners of war trying to return to Europe via the Trans-Siberian Railway to Vladivostok and then by ship to France. The Czech Legion overthrew the *soviet* of Western Siberia and captured Omsk on 7 June 1918. The Siberian government, ignoring Kolchak's threats, officially severed all ties to Bolshevik Russia and on 4 July 1918 declared the vast region an independent republic.

An All-Russian Provisional Government, formed by tsarist officers and supported by the White forces of Admiral Kolchak, set up a rival government on 4 November 1918. On 18 November 1918 Kolchak's troops overthrew the separatist Siberian government and took control of the administration. Recognized as the legitimate government by the Western allies, Admiral Kolchak led the White forces in Siberia as civil war spread across the region. Kolchak, allied to the Czech Legion, fought the advancing Bolsheviks, but when a great anti-Bolshevik offensive was defeated in November 1919 the White forces collapsed. Members of the Social Revolutionary Party, emboldened by Bolshevik successes against Kolchak, declared the formation of a provisional government of Siberia. Within a day the revolt had been brutally suppressed and hundreds of Siberian nationalists were executed. By 1920 most White resistance had collapsed, and by 1922 Siberia was Soviet. Admiral Kolchak was captured and shot, as were most leaders of the Siberian national movement.

The Soviet government up to World War II treated Siberia as a colony to be exploited. During the war, the Soviet government transferred many industries and large numbers of workers eastward, away from areas threatened by the German advance. The rapid industrialization was accompanied by the need for workers in the less accessible districts. Siberia became the site of the infamous Gulag, the string of labor camps to which millions were deported during Stalin's long rule, from the late 1920s to 1953. The deportees were used as slave labor for mines and the construction of dams, railroads, and cities. Siberia's vast resources propelled the Soviet Union to superpower status, but the living and working conditions of ordinary Siberians barely attained the levels of developing Africa. An estimated 20 million people perished in the Gulag.

The population grew rapidly from the 1950s, but without losing its unique Siberian cultural characteristics. Up to 1958, the numerous labor camps contained large numbers of Siberians, peasants who had resisted collectivization, Jews, ethnic minorities from the border regions, members of religious groups, state officials fallen from favor, and anyone who crossed local officials. The prisoners, increasingly released under the post-Stalin premiers, mostly stayed in the region as settlers. Other colonists, moving east from overcrowded European Russia, became the most fervent supporters of the Siberian way of life.

The Soviet liberalization of the late 1980s loosed a torrent of Siberian grievances. Mikhail Gorbachev, in a tour of central Siberia over two days in September 1988, was constantly assailed over poor housing, scarce food, and inadequate medical care. Gorbachev acknowledged that the Siberians had cause for complaint and promised government attention to their problems. The Siberian nationalist movement, dormant for decades, reemerged at the same time, with demands that Siberia become the sixteenth republic of the Soviet Union. The split between the Siberian region and the Far East, lying on the Pacific Ocean, became a political division; the two regions increasingly went their own ways.

The Soviet Union collapsed and the communist government gave way to the new Russian Federation in August 1991. The revived Siberian national movement, now with a strong environmentalist strain, no longer suppressed, won widespread support. The activists pressed for the closure of the industries, mines, and other Soviet-era installations that had heavily polluted many areas of the formerly pristine region. Radioactive and industrial wastes, carelessly dumped for over 40 years, had damaged the fragile ecosystem and destroyed most of the region's rivers and other natural resources. Siberian industrial emissions had contributed heavily to the threat of global warming. Siberian nationalist pointed to the fact that the effects of even a small temperature rise globally would be exaggerated in the north, by melting the upper parts of the region's permafrost and thereby turning huge areas of Siberia into mush. The thousands of Soviet-era buildings constructed on stilts would sink.

Many activists fear that Russia's new capitalism, with its unchecked race for profits, will finish the destruction begun under Stalin's rule. The Russian government and the new capitalist class want to realize income from Siberia's vast resources as fast as possible, with little in the way of environmental safeguards. Even the more moderate nationalists support autonomy as a means of buying time for Siberia. The wholesale sell-off of Siberian resources to foreign firms has aroused great bitterness. Ordinary Siberians are frustrated by corrupt officials and courts, confiscatory taxes, and the Russian government's focus on Europe. To many of the region's inhabitants, democracy poses a serious threat to their homeland.

In the aftermath of the Soviet disintegration, in 1991, Siberian political demands changed to republic status within the new Russian Federation, while more militant groups debated the issue of Siberian independence. Russian government plans to continue closing unprofitable or unproductive mines and industries stirred the debate over Siberian autonomy. In February 1993, responding to Siberian charges that the region was still treated as a colony, the government officially ended the practice of exiling convicted criminals there.

In January 1994, the governments of several provinces withdrew from the Siberian Agreement, originally set up as an economic organization by the Siberian regional governments in 1992. The governors of the regions accused the organization of becoming overly politicized. During the Russian political crisis of late 1993, the leaders of the organization threatened to declare a Siberian republic and to blockade the Trans-Siberian Railway.

Growing demands for full disclosure of the Stalinist crimes in Siberia led to the uncovering of mass graves in several areas in the 1990s. The move to rewrite the fictitious Soviet history of Siberia became a focus of nationalist feelings. In 1999 an estimated 40% of the Siberian population was descended from the exiles shipped to Siberia from European Russia.

The economic hardships of the Russian change to a market economy have caused a massive exodus of Russian bureaucrats, miners, and other workers back to European Russia, an exodus estimated at over four million people between 1991 and 2001. The Siberian nationalists, gaining strength with each perceived desertion, declare that when all the Russians have gone home, the Siberians—the descendents of Cossacks, exiles, and freed serfs—will regain control of their vast and potentially wealthy homeland.

SELECTED BIBLIOGRAPHY:

Brower, Daniel R., and Edward J. Lazzerini, eds. *Russia's Orient: Imperial Borderlands and Peoples, 1700–1917.* 1997

Forsyth, J. *A History of the Peoples of Siberia: Russia's North Asian Colony 1581–1990.* 1992.

Motyl, Alexander J. *Siberia: Worlds Apart.* 1998.

Thubron, Colin. *In Siberia.* 2000.

Sicilians

Sicilianos

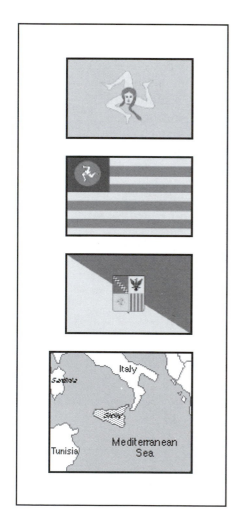

POPULATION: Approximately (2002e) 7,550,000 Sicilians in Italy, concentrated in Sicily, but with sizable populations in other parts of the country. Other large Sicilian communities live in Germany, Switzerland, and France. Outside Europe there are Sicilian communities in South America, especially Argentina and Brazil, the United States, Canada, and Australia.

THE SICILIAN HOMELAND: The Sicily homeland is an island off the southern Italian Peninsula, separated from the mainland by the narrow Strait of Messina. The island, the largest and most densely populated in the Mediterranean Sea, is roughly triangular in shape. There is an imbalance in the population distribution, with the population concentrated in the coastal zones while the interior is almost uninhabited. Lying 90 miles north of the African coast, Sicily is mostly a broad, hilly plateau rising in the northwest to volcanic Mount Etna, the island's highest point. Sicily has long been know for its fertility, its pleasant climate, and its scenic beauty. Sicily and the smaller nearby islands—the Egadi Islands, the Lipari Islands, the Pelagie Islands, Pantelleria, and Ustica—form a semi-autonomous region of the Italian republic. Region of Sicily (Sicilia): 9,925 sq. mi.—25,706 sq. km, (2002e) 5,217,000— Sicilians 94%, other Italians, Albanians, and others 6%. The Sicilian capital and major cultural center is Palermo, (2002e) 684,000, metropolitan area 948,000, the largest city on the island. The other important cultural center is Catania, (2002e), 337,000, metropolitan area 829,000.

FLAG: The Sicilian national flag, the unofficial national flag, is a yellow field bearing the national symbol, the Trinacria, three legs and the Medusa head. The flag of the national movement is the flag of the World War II independence movement; it has nine horizontal stripes of yellow and red bearing a blue canton on the upper hoist charged with the Trinacria on a red circle. The official flag of the region of Sicily is a diagonal bicolor of red over yellow bearing the coat of arms centered.

PEOPLE AND CULTURE: The Sicilians are a diverse nation, having had contact with a great variety of ethnic groups and physical types. Sicily has been inhabited for over 10,000 years. The Sicilians are of mixed ancestry, being the descendents of the island's original Celtic and Latin inhabitants, with admixtures of the island's many conquerors—Phoenicians, Carthaginians, Greeks, Romans, Vandals, Ostrogoths, Byzantines, Normans,* French, Catalans,* Spaniards, Savoyards,* Austrians, Neapolitans*, and Piedmontese.* Sicily's position in the mid-Mediterranean aided the evolution of the distinct Sicilian culture and the originality of its customs, art, and traditions. Sicilian culture retains many characteristics of more rural regions, also the result of its isolation and distance from mainland culture. The Sicilian culture, developed during two thousand years of foreign rule, incorporates many customs and traditions not found on the mainland and has spawned the Mafia, Sicily's infamous export to the world. In certain parts of the island the Mafia is virtually a second government, a standard of conduct, and a system of enforcement. The quality of life in Sicily is conditioned by a generally poorly developed economy, characterized by high unemployment and frequently leading to emigration, exploitation, or crime.

LANGUAGE AND RELIGION: The Sicilian dialect is a Romance language using borrowings from French, Greek, Spanish, and Arabic; it is as distinct from standard Italian as is Romanian. The language is spoken in seven major dialects—Western Sicilian or Trapani, Messinese or Messina, Catania-Siracusa, South-east Sicilian, Nissa-Enna, Agrigento, and Palermo. Sicilian remains the dialect of daily life for most of the islanders, although the majority are bilingual in standard Italian. There is still a significant linguistic minority in the Piana degli Albanesi, near Palermo, where Albanian is spoken.

The Sicilians are devoutly Roman Catholic and among the most conservative of the Italian peoples. Historically the Roman Catholic Church has had enormous influence in the region, particularly in times of weak governments or foreign rulers. The church provided a refuge and a center of Sicilian culture. Although religious observance has fallen since the 1950s, the church remains important as a center of rural life and of urban education and social systems.

NATIONAL HISTORY: Originally inhabited by Sicani, Elymi, and Siculi tribes, probably of Celtic origin, the island was early divided into numerous small territories. Phoenicians established trading centers as early as the eighth century B.C. Between the eighth and sixth centuries B.C.,

Greeks founded colonies that grew into great and powerful cities in the east of the island. Syracuse, the island's leading Greek city and a center of Greek culture and Mediterranean trade, in the fifth century B.C. gained hegemony over the other Greek cities. The mountainous center of the island remained under the authority of the Siculi and Sicani, who increasingly adopted Hellenistic culture.

The Syracusans successfully resisted a Carthaginian invasion at Himera in 480 B.C., but by the fourth century B.C. the western part of the island was under Carthaginian control. Carthaginian control of western Sicily involved the island in the conflicts between Rome and Carthage known as the Punic Wars. In 246 B.C. Roman legions invaded the island and took control of Carthaginian Sicily, and by 210 all of Sicily had come under Roman rule.

Rome's first overseas possession, Sicily was divided into large estates, a debilitating economic legacy that persists to the present. The chief events of Roman history in Sicily were two serious insurrections of slaves, in 135–132 B.C. and 102–99 B.C. The collapse of Roman power left the island without defenses, and Germanic tribes from northern Europe overran the island. The Vandals, led by Gaiseric, took control of the island in A.D. 440. In 493 the Vandals ceded the island to the invading Ostrogoths. Byzantines forces of the Eastern Roman Empire led by general Belisarius took control of the island in 535 and imposed Greek Byzantine culture.

Muslim Arabs, called Saracens, conquered the island from nearby North Africa in 827–31. The Saracens created a remarkable civilization on the island, incorporating the earlier Roman and Byzantine traditions into a enlightened, advanced culture. Sicily's Muslim rulers practiced a tolerance of religious and ethnic minorities unknown in the rest of Europe. The enlightened Muslim government fostered education, agriculture, art, and the sciences; it administered a civilized state far ahead of the European culture of the time. The island flourished as a center of trade between Europe and North Africa.

The Norman conquest of Sicily mirrored the 1066 Norman conquest of England. A large force led by Roger de Hauteville left Normandy for Sicily in 1061; they achieved victory 30 years later. Under the Hauteville dynasty the Normans adopted much of the more advanced Saracen culture, particularly the tolerance that allowed a mixed population of Normans, Muslims, Latins, Greeks, and Jews to live in peace and prosper. The most enlightened state in Europe from 1072 to 1266, Sicily enjoyed a "Golden Age" that was a forerunner of the later European Renaissance of the fourteenth to sixteenth centuries. The brilliant Hauteville court did much to introduce Arabic learning to Western Europe.

Norman rule in Sicily was replaced in 1194 by that of the Hohenstaufen dynasty of Germany. The Hohenstaufen Holy Roman Emperor Frederick II shifted the center of the empire to Sicily and southern Italy. The cultural brilliance of his court at Palermo was renowned throughout Western Europe.

The pope bestowed the kingdom on Charles of Anjou, as king of Naples and Sicily, in 1266. Harsh and intolerant French rule ended the brilliant Sicilian civilization of the Saracens and Normans. A 1282 Sicilian rebellion culminated in the massacre of all the French on the island, the "Sicilian Vespers." Freed of French rule, the Sicilians chose the Catalan king, Peter III of Aragon, as their new ruler in 1295. Ruled as a separate kingdom until 1409, Sicily then became part of Aragon. The merger of Aragon and Castile in 1469 in the united Spanish kingdom brought an end to all Sicilian autonomy.

With the accession of the house of Habsburg to the Spanish throne in the early sixteenth century the government was further centralized, and Spanish governors were sent to Sicily to enforce imperial rule. Corruption increased, and the island came under the influence of a handful of powerful nobles and churchmen. Sicily declined during the long period of Spanish rule.

Sicily remained Spanish until 1713, after which it was held briefly by Savoy and Austria before coming under the Bourbon monarchs of the Kingdom of the Two Sicilies. Although the feudal privileges that had held the Sicilians in virtual serfdom were renounced in 1812, the island remained under the domination of Naples, the kingdom's capital. The Sicilians unsuccessfully rebelled against the Neapolitans in 1820. The Sicilians again rebelled in 1848, the main cause being the corruption and brutality of government under the rule of the Bourbon King Ferdinand. Several thousand Sicilians faced the Neapolitan garrison in January 1848. In little over a month, the rebels overran every royalist stronghold except Messina. In May 1848 the Neapolitans returned, and the Sicilian rebel movement crumbled.

In 1860 Giuseppe Garibaldi, during yet another Sicilian revolt, landed with a thousand volunteers, who quickly overthrew Bourbon rule on the island. Garibaldi relinquished his Sicilian conquests to a newly united Italian kingdom, under the Piedmontese house of Savoy, in 1861. Sicily was neglected by the central government even after unification, and the island's basic economic and social problems remained. Dominated by the Piedmontese, the national government possessed little understanding of the southern regions of Italy. Sicily's traditional landholding system, control by a few large aristocratic estates, remained unchanged, and the Sicilians remained poor and backward. Burdensome taxes and military conscription intensified Sicilian resentment and led to an abortive rebellion in Palermo in 1866.

The Mafia emerged to serve a vital purpose, to offer Sicilian peasants a means of justice outside the always unequal Italian law. Carried to the Americas by Sicilian emigrants, the Mafia remained a strong force among immigrant communities in the Western Hemisphere. Challenged by leagues of rebellious workers and peasants, in 1894 the Italian government proclaimed martial law in Sicily. Mutual suspicion characterized north-south relations in Italy until 1915, when the Italians entered World War I.

In 1922, promised glory and reforms, the Sicilians supported Mussolini's Fascist takeover of Italy. However, Sicilian support of the Fascists waned following government efforts to curtail the Mafia in 1927–28. Fervently anti-Fascist by the time Italy joined World War II, the island's nascent nationalist movement provided fertile ground for British, and later American, agents. Encouraged by the Allies, the nationalists carried out a guerrilla war against the Italian Fascists and their Nazi allies.

When Allied troops invaded Sicily in 1943, they were welcomed as liberators. Supported by the Allies, the nationalist leader Turiddu Giuliano declared Sicily independent on 10 July 1943 and began to organize the first independent Sicilian state in history. The Allies, however, in an attempt to persuade the Italian government to withdraw from the war, abruptly ended their support of Sicilian separatism. In late 1943 Italy changed sides in the war and Italian troops invaded the island, finally defeating the nationalists in a vicious eight-week war. With widespread popular support, the rebels continued to fight a guerrilla war in the west of the island. In 1945 the Sicilian nationalists pled their case before the newly formed United Nations, but the Sicilian rebellion collapsed following the mysterious death of Giuliano in 1950.

Decades of neglect forced thousands of Sicilians to emigrate in the 1950s and 1960s to the booming northern Italian regions or to the Americas. The forced emigration provoked strong resentment and a resurgence of nationalist sentiment in the 1970s. The polarization of Italy, marked by a rise of anti-southern sentiment in the rich northern regions, gave the nationalist movement new impetus in the 1980s.

Sicilians claimed that collusion between the Italian government and the Mafia had maintained an iron grip on the island since the separatist war in the 1940s and had left Sicily a neglected dependency, with incomes little more than half the Italian average. The unholy alliance kept social protest to an absolute minimum until cooperation collapsed in the late 1980s. The reemergence of the nationalists showed in the voter support for nationalist issues in the March 1994 local elections. The industrialization of the island had not absorbed the surplus labor force, and many Sicilians emigrated to northern Italy, Germany, Switzerland, North and South America, and Australia.

Sicily's economy remained relatively underdeveloped, and emigration continuing into the 1990s to escape high unemployment and poverty. Some heavy industry, based on the oil–refining and chemical industries expanded rapidly after the 1970s, but at a tremendous cost to the natural environment. Pollution in many areas virtually stripped the land of vegetation, leaving behind a scarred landscape, dead rivers, and a growing environmentalist wing of the Sicilian national movement. The most dangerous trend lay in indiscriminate speculative housing construction, with no respect for natural surroundings, cultural heritage, or the dangers of volcanoes and other natural hazards.

In local elections in 1996, small numbers of candidates campaigned on a platform to split Sicily from Italy and to turn the island into the "Hong Kong of the Mediterranean." The openly separatist organizations gained one seat in the regional parliament, the first time since the early 1950s that an openly separatist group had gained widespread support on the island.

Sicily has experienced a resurgence of the Mafia, which remains a serious problem to the development and modernization of Sicilian society. In March 2000 bulldozers began demolishing illegal buildings, including a church, a luxury restaurant, and a number of homes built in the Valley of the Temples, near Agrigento. Building in the region had been outlawed over thirty years before. Government officials from Palermo and Rome attended the demolition to stress their commitment to protect the Sicilians' precious historical legacy increasingly threatened by illegal construction, often linked to the Mafia.

The Sicilians increasingly look to the European Union for a brighter future. After thousands of years of conquerors, hundreds of years of neglect, and decades of underdevelopment, they view united Europe as a chance to regain control of their island.

SELECTED BIBLIOGRAPHY:

Facaros, Dana, ed. *Sicily*. 1998.
Finkelstein, Monte S. *Separatism, the Allies and the Mafia: The Struggle for Sicilian Independence 1943–1948*. 1998.
Robb, Peter. *Midnight in Sicily*. 1999.
Seindal, Rene. *Mafia: Money and Politics in Sicily 1950–1997*. 1998.

Sikhs

Punjabis; Punjabi Sikhs

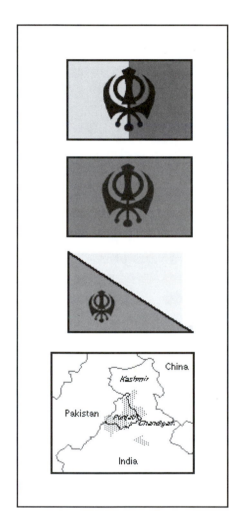

POPULATION: Approximately (2002e) 20,200,000 Sikhs in India, concentrated in the northwestern state of Punjab and the adjacent union territory of Chandigarh. There are sizable Sikh communities in the neighboring states of Haryana, Kashmir and Jammu, and Rajastan. Outside India there are large Sikh communities in the United Kingdom, Germany, Canada, the United States, Australia, and New Zealand.

THE SIKH HOMELAND: The Sikh homeland, called Khalistan ("Land of the Pure"), lies in northeastern India, consisting of a flat, fertile plain traversed by several important rivers. The word "Punjab" is a compound of two Persian words signifying "the land of five waters," for the five major rivers of the region—although since the partition of India in 1947 only two of the rivers lie within the state. Sikhs form the majority both in Punjab and the neighboring territory of Chandigarh, which forms a capital territory shared with the state of Haryana. *State of Punjab*: 19,448 sq. mi.—50,370 sq. km, (2002e) 24,689,000—Sikhs 63%, Punjabi Hindus 34%, Punjabi Muslims 2%, other Indians 1%. *Union Territory of Chandigarh*: 44 sq. mi.—114 sq. km, (2002e) 926,000—Sikhs 55%, Hindus 43%, other Indians 2%. The Sikh capital and major cultural center is Amritsar, (2002e) 961,000, metropolitan area 1,117,000. The other important cultural centers are Chandigarh, (2002e), 821,000, metropolitan area 1,214,000, the official capital of Punjab, and Ludhiana (2002e) 1,526,000.

FLAG: The Sikh national flag, the flag of the national movement, is a vertical bicolor of yellow and pale blue bearing two crossed black swords centered and backed by a black spear, its point enclosed in a black circle.

The traditional Sikh flag is an orange triangle bearing the black swords and spear.

PEOPLE AND CULTURE: The Sikhs, a religious and military sect founded in the fifteenth century, are among the newest of India's national groups. Ethnically the Sikhs are the descendents of the pre-Aryan Dravidian peoples and the Aryan tribes that entered India from the northwest during the second millennium B.C. Successive waves of invaders, including Greeks, Persians, Kusans, and Huns, added to the diversity of the earlier social or caste groups. Sikh folklore, ballads of love and war, fairs and festivals, and the Punjabi-language Sikh literature are characteristic of Sikh cultural life. About 30% of the Sikhs of Punjab are urbanized, living in the region's large cities and agricultural towns; about 70% are still dependent on agriculture. The Sikhs are one of the most visually distinctive groups in India, as orthodox males wear beards and turbans, and usually the ceremonial sword, the *kirpan*. In November 1999 several Sikh leaders attempted to introduce a new calendar to replace the lunar calendar, which is also used by the Hindus. The decision caused a serious crisis among the Sikh leadership in March 2000.

LANGUAGE AND RELIGION: The Sikh language, a dialect of Eastern Punjabi called Gurumkhi, closely resembles western Hindi in vocabulary but uses the Gurumkhi script, which was devised by the Sikh guru Angad in the sixteenth century and is the alphabet of the Sikhs' sacred texts. Punjabi (or Panjabi) is the official language of the state of Punjab, which is the heartland of the Sikhs; it is spoken in six subdialects in the Sikh regions. The language is one of 14 recognized by the Indian constitution.

The Sikh religion, called Sikhism, is an integral part of Sikh culture. The Sikh religious and military sect, created by Guru (teacher) Nanak, is based on a monotheistic creed, the fundamental identity of all religions, and the knowing of God through religious exercises and meditation. Sikh religious beliefs, which prohibit tobacco and alcohol, command Sikh adherence to the "Five Ks"—*kesha*, long, uncut hair wrapped in a turban; the *kangla*, a wooden or ivory comb; the *kacha*, military knee britches; the *kara*, a steel bracelet; and the *kirpan*, the Sikh sword. There is a potential division within the Sikh community between those who have undergone the baptism ceremony and those who practice the original system but do not adopt the distinctive lifestyle. There is no official priesthood within Sikhism or any widely accepted mechanism for policy making.

NATIONAL HISTORY: The Sikh nation emerged in the fifteenth century as the result of an attempt by a religious teacher, Guru Nanak. to reconcile hostile Hindus and Muslims. The Sikhs, opposed to idolatry, religious ritual, the maintenance of a priesthood, and the caste system, rapidly gained adherents. The egalitarian creed appealed to prosperous landowners and peasants alike. All took the name "Singh," meaning "Lion,"on becoming members of the new faith. In 1574 the faithful built a new capital city, Amritsar, around the spiritual center of their new religion, the Golden Temple. Sikhism was established and directed by a succession of 10 gurus, who codified the precepts of the religion between 1467 and 1708. The execution of Guru Arjun in 1606 by the Mughal emperor began the sect's change from a pacifist group to a militant one. By the late seventeenth century the Sikhs had consolidated as a people and had begun to develop as a military power.

Goviad Singh, in the 1690s, created a powerful military unit, the Khalsa, meaning "the Pure," based on the Five Ks. The militarization of the Sikhs, hastened by a Muslim invasion in 1710, evolved as an anti-Muslim movement. The Sikh movement was an open challenge to the rule of the Muslim Mughals. Imperial forces invaded the region and captured some important Sikh strongholds but could not crush the movement. The Mughal troops, however, swept the Sikhs from the plains back into the Himalayas. In 1715 the Sikh leader, Banda Bahadur, together with hundreds of his followers, was captured by the Mughal governor of Punjab. They were all executed, and the threat of the emergence of an autonomous non-Mughal state in the Punjab in the early eighteenth century disappeared. The Sikh warriors returned to their homeland and submitted to Mughal rule.

A prolonged struggle between the Sikhs, the Mughal rulers of India, and the powerful Afghans to the north continued the militarization of the Sikhs. By 1764–65 the Sikhs had established control in the Punjab and extended their authority to the adjacent provinces of Multan, Kashmir, and Peshawar. The Muslims declared holy war against the Sikhs in 1826 but were resoundingly defeated in 1831. The Sikh victory over the Muslims brought Sikh warriors to the borders of British territory. Tension on the border provoked the first Anglo-Sikh War in 1845. A second Anglo–Sikh conflict in 1848–49 resulted in the British annexation of the Sikh heartland in the Punjab.

Impressed by the Sikhs' military prowess, the British recruited Sikh soldiers for the colonial army. By the late nineteenth century the Sikh units formed the backbone of Britain's colonial forces in India. When the Indian Mutiny broke out in 1857, the Sikhs remained loyal to the British and took a prominent role in suppressing the uprising. For this loyalty and aid they were rewarded by grants of land. The proportion of Sikhs in the British army was increased. During World War I, Sikhs formed more than a fifth of the British Indian army.

Sikh revivalist movements in the late nineteenth century centered on the activities of the Assembly of Lions, the Singh Sabha, which moved a majority of the Sikh population toward their own ritual systems and away from Hindu customs. The revival culminated in the Akali mass movement in the 1920s to take control of the Sikh temples, the *gurdwaras*, from

Hindu managers and place them under the control of an organization representing the Sikhs.

Serious violence between Sikhs and Muslims, the majority in western Punjab, broke out with the beginning of World War I in 1914. Anti-Muslim sentiment pushed the Sikhs to embrace the growing Indian national movement, particularly the Sikh soldiers returning from military duty in Asia and Europe. In 1919 British general E.H. Dyer ordered soldiers to fire on a huge crowd of Sikh demonstrators in Amritsar. The massacre left 379 dead and over 1,200 wounded. The massacre, called the Jallianwala Bagh massacre, hardened Sikh opposition to continued British rule.

Sikh leaders after World War II began negotiations on the creation of a Sikh homeland separate from both India and Pakistan, to be called Sikhistan or Khalistan. The British authorities initially agreed to separate Sikh independence, but pressured by Indian leaders Jawaharlal Nehru and Mohandas K. Gandhi, reneged on the agreement and terminated the negotiations. Unable to move ahead with their plans for independence, the Sikhs, promised religious and cultural autonomy, attached themselves to India. Over vehement Sikh protests the British authorities partitioned their homeland in the Punjab between India and Pakistan, setting off massacres that left thousands dead. Approximately 2.5 million Sikhs fled to India from Pakistani West Punjab, often in protected caravans miles long.

The feeling that they had been duped by Indian leaders when the promised autonomy and concessions were denied spread through the Sikh community soon after Indian independence in 1947, provoking a peaceful campaign for a separate Sikh state within India. In 1956 the government agreed to the creation of a linguistic state, but with a Punjabi-speaking Hindu majority. Following serious Sikh agitation, the largely Hindu districts of the state were separated to form the new state of Haryana in 1966, leaving a truncated Punjab with a slight Sikh majority.

Lack of land and overpopulation led to widespread emigration in the 1960s, mostly to the United Kingdom, Canada, and after immigrations restrictions were relaxed in 1965, to the United States. The Sikh diaspora numbered over a million by 1974.

The union territory of Chandigarh, constituted on 1 November 1966, was made the joint capital of the two states of Punjab and Haryana. The Indian government proposed to add Chandigarh to Punjab as the new state capital, but the move was opposed by the Hindu population of Haryana, and the political situation remained as it was. The Sikhs, although participating in the state government of Punjab in Chandigarh, increasingly looked to their holy city, Amritsar, as their capital.

The energetic Sikhs, many of whom had begun as refugees in 1947, achieved India's highest standard of living by the 1970s in the wake of the Green Revolution of the late 1960s. Material prosperity gave the Sikhs new confidence. In 1973 the Akali Dal political party released the Anand-pur Sahib Resolution, which called for greater autonomy for an enlarged Punjab. In 1980 a sustained campaign was launched in support of Sikh self-rule. In 1982 violence broke out between Sikhs and Hindus.

Increasing mistrust of the Sikhs by the Indian government was reciprocated, as the Sikhs withdrew into nationalism. In the mid-1980s an increasingly vocal minority began a campaign to win support for secession and the creation of an independent Sikh state to be called Khalistan. The nationalist territorial claims included Punjab State, Chandigarh, and the Sikh-populated regions of Haryana and Rajastan States.

Nationalist organizations proliferated as the national movement splintered between groups advocating violence and nonviolent factions. Extremists like Jarnail Singh Bhindranwale won the support of many younger, devout Sikhs. Amid growing separatist violence the Indian authorities imposed direct rule from New Delhi in October 1983. Five months later the nationalists took control of the Sikh's holiest shrine, the Golden Temple, and its precincts in Amritsar. The government of Indira Gandhi, unable to stop the growing terrorist attacks in Punjab, Haryana, and Delhi, gave permission to launch Operation Bluestar: Indian police and troops attacked the Sikh separatists sheltering in the Golden Temple, leaving over 500 dead, including Jarnail Singh Bhindranwale. The Sikh's dream of Khalistan had its first martyrs.

The Sikh revenge—the murder of Prime Minister Gandhi by her Sikh bodyguards on 31 October 1984—set off violent anti-Sikh rioting. Hindu mobs roamed the Sikh neighborhoods of Delhi, burning cars, homes, and businesses. They perpetrated a massacre of Sikhs that left over 3,000 dead and thousands more wounded and homeless. The Hindu-Sikh rioting was the worst religious violence since the 1947 partition of the subcontinent. Amid the continuing turmoil, a group of nationalists, led by Jagjit Singh Chohan, declared the independence of Khalistan on 30 April 1986. The secession, crushed by security forces, set off a renewed and even more violent campaign to win independence. Despite numerous attempts at a negotiated settlement, a climate of violence and chaos continued in Punjab.

In 1985 the moderate nationalists of the Akali Dal Party won the Punjab State elections, and presidential rule from New Delhi was lifted. Because of the inability of the Akali Dal government to deal with Hindu-Sikh violence, presidential rule was restored in Punjab and thereafter extended by six-month increments until scheduled elections in June 1991. The elections were postponed due to violence in the state and in September 1991 were indefinitely postponed. Elections were finally held in February 1992, ending more than five years of direct rule from New Delhi. Only 28% of the eligible voters participated, due to a boycott called by both militant and moderate Sikh groups.

The terrorist campaign by radical Sikh nationalists, and the often brutal official reprisals, had taken over 20,000 lives by 1992. In March 1993, Sikh militants set off 13 car bombs across Bombay, killing over 200 people, in one of the worst atrocities of the Sikh separatist campaign. An investigation blamed a Muslim crime family for the bombs, but many moderate Sikhs denounced the separatist violence and affirmed their support of greater self-government through peaceful means. The crisis in the Punjab, India's breadbasket, was one of the most serious nationalist threats to the fabric of multinational India.

In 1994, six factions of Akali Dal met at the Golden Temple and demanded that the Sikhs be granted a separate region in a new Indian confederation. The violence of the 1980s and early 1990s declined, although 1995 was declared by militant leaders to be the year for the revival of the Khalistan Movement.

Members of Akali Dal staged a sit-in at the Lok Sabha, the lower house of India's parliament, to protest government inaction on claims that over 3,000 of those that had officially disappeared during the Punjab insurgency of the 1980s and early 1990s had actually been killed and cremated by the Indian security forces. In January 1997, India's National Human Rights Commission began to investigate the alleged murders and cremations.

Over 69% of the people in Punjab state turned out to vote in state elections in 1997, the first elections not boycotted by Sikh nationalists since 1980. The vote gave Akali Dal a majority in the local government. The peaceful election was seen as a triumph for moderate Sikhs who opposed the violence of the Sikh uprising.

In July 1997 there were reports that five Sikh militant groups were attempting to resuscitate the insurgency that had been largely contained in 1993. A number of militants were arrested, and explosives and weapons were found. Growing links between militant Sikhs and Kashmiris* were formalized in a new organization called Kashmir-Khalistan International. On the fiftieth anniversary of India and Pakistan's independence, on 15 August 1997, Sikhs in many parts of the world demonstrated in favor of an independent Khalistan.

The Indian government in 1998 accused Pakistan of supporting the resurgent Sikh national movement with arms and training following the arrest of two militants who had allegedly been trained in Pakistan to attack well-guarded government officials. There were also allegations of a campaign to recruit young Sikhs with no previous criminal records. Recruiting reportedly continued when nearly a million Sikhs gathered in Punjab to celebrate the 300th anniversary of the founding of the Khalsa on 8 April 1999.

Isolated acts of violence and arrests of reported Sikh militants indicate that a small militant minority continue to use violence to press for Sikh autonomy or independence, but the majority of the Sikh population has rejected a return to violent conflict.

In June 2001, Jagjit Singh Chohan, the self-styled president of Khalistan returned to India after 21 years of exile in Britain. He announced that he would continue his "peaceful advocacy" of an independent Khalistan. At the height of the separatist campaign in the 1980s, Chohan declared Punjab a separate Sikh nation, opened some foreign embassies, and issued passports and a new currency. His return caused consternation among government officials who fear a return of Sikh militancy.

SELECTED BIBLIOGRAPHY:

Gupta, Dipankar. *The Context of Ethnicity: Sikh Identity in a Comparative Perspective.* 1996.

Mahmood, Cynthia Keppley. *Fighting for Faith and Nation: Dialogues with Sikh Militants.* 1997.

Singh, Patwant. *The Sikhs.* 2000.

Tatla, Darshan Singh. *The Sikh Diaspora: The Search for Statehood.* 1999.

Sikkimese

Sikamis; Danjongka; Bhotias-Lepchas; Bhutia-Rong; Nunpas

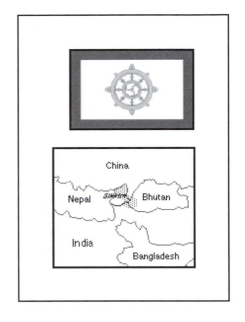

POPULATION: Approximately (2002e) 192,000 Sikkimese in South Asia, concentrated in the northern Indian state of Sikkim, with large Sikkimese communities in adjacent areas of Nepal, India, and Bhutan.

THE SIKKIMESE HOMELAND: The Sikkimese homeland occupies the high valleys of the southern slopes of the Himalayas of northeastern India. Mount Kanchenjunja, the third-highest peak in the world, lies on Sikkim's western border. Most of the region is mountainous, and rivers flow through deep valleys, intersecting the state and hindering transport and travel. The Sikkimese are concentrated in the high valleys of the Himalayas in the northern and eastern parts of the state. Sikkim was annexed to India as a state in 1975. *State of Sikkim (Denjong—the Valley of Rice)*: 2,744 sq. mi.—7,107 sq. km, (2002e) 553,000—Sikkimese 30%, Gorkhas* 62%, other Indians 8%. The Sikkimese capital and major cultural center is Gangtok, (2002e) 33,000. The other major cultural center is Rongphu (Rongpo), (2002e) 13,000, the center of the Lepcha population.

FLAG: The Sikkimese national flag, the flag of the former kingdom, is a white field, bordered in red, bearing a centered gold and red Buddhist wheel, the *Chakra*.

PEOPLE AND CULTURE: The Sikkimese include three closely related groups—the Lepchas, Bhotias, and Limbus. The earliest inhabitants of the region—the Naong, Chang, Mon and other tribes—apparently assimilated into the larger Lepcha group. The Lepchas, also called Rong, are thought to have been the earliest inhabitants of the region, but they have adopted many elements of Bhotia culture, and the two peoples are now closely related in both culture and language. The Bhotias are mainly pastoralists in the high mountains, while the Lepchas usually live in the more remote mountain valleys. While some intermarriage has occurred between the two groups, they tend to retain their ancient identities. The Sikkimese culture, although showing strong Tibetan influences, retains a character derived from the fusion of the Bhotias, Lepchas, and Limbus and their pre-Buddhist cultures. Buddhist lamasaries and monasteries are repositories of Sikkimese culture, with renowned artistic treasures, religious paintings, and bronze images. It is common for a woman to have more than one husband, usually brothers.

LANGUAGE AND RELIGION: The language of the Bhotias, called Sikkimese or Denjonke, is the most widespread of the three Tibeto-Burman languages spoken by the Sikkimese peoples. It belongs to the southern Tibetan group of Tibeto-Burman languages. The Lepcha language, spoken in three major dialects, belongs to the Kuki-Chin group of the Tibeto-Burman languages and is written in its own script. The Limbu language is closely related to Bhotia and is spoken in southeastern Sikkim and adjacent areas of West Bengal. The language of the Bhotias, formerly the official language of the kingdom, is widely spoken as an intergroup language across northern and eastern Sikkim.

The Bhotias are Tantrayana Buddhists, belonging to the sect of Lamaism practiced by the neighboring Tibetans.* The belief system teaches that right thinking, ritual sacrifices, and self–denial enable the soul eventually to reach nirvana, a state of eternal bliss. The Sikkimese have retained many beliefs that are thought to predate their Buddhist religion, including belief in spirits, both good and evil. The Tibetan dalai lama is recognized as the religious head by the Sikkimese Buddhists. A small number, about 1% of the population, has converted to Christianity, the result of Christian missionary activity in the region. The Lamaist religion is the major element in the fusion of the three Sikkimese into a viable national group. The Namgyal Institute of Tibetology has one of the largest collections of Tibetan books in the world. Shamanism is still prevalent in the more remote areas, particularly among the Lepchas.

NATIONAL HISTORY: Sikkim has been inhabited for thousands of years, although little is known of the history of the Sikkimese prior to the seventeenth century. An early center of trade between China, India, and Tibet, the region maintained ties to regions far beyond the Himalayas. The state's name is derived from the Limbu words *su him*, meaning "new home." The Lepchas formed a state, the Rong kingdom, ruled by the Namgyal dynasty of Tibetan origin, in the fourteenth century. Tibetan migrants, the Bhotias, settled in the kingdom between the fourteenth and sixteenth centuries. The Bhotias paid tribute to the Lepcha rulers of the region.

The Bhutia's religion, Mahayana Buddhism, known as Tibetan Lamaism, became the state religion in 1630 with the conversion of the Bhotia leader, Pentsho Namgyal. The adoption of Lamaism strengthened religious and cultural ties to Tibet. In 1642 Pentsho Namgyal established the kingdom of Sikkim. The king, called the *chogyal*, extended his rule over a large area of the Himalayan highlands, although Sikkim remained a virtual dependency of Tibet until the nineteenth century.

The Sikkimese fought a series of territorial wars with both the Bhutanese and Nepal beginning in the mid-eighteenth century. The warlike Gorkhas* invaded the kingdom several times in the late eighteenth and early nineteenth centuries. In 1814–15 the Gorkhas were driven back with the assistance of British forces. The Gorkhas who remained in the kingdom, mainly in western Sikkim and the Tarai, were later called the Gorkhalis. During this period the largest immigration of Nepali Gorkhas began. The British restored the Gorkha-controlled regions to Sikkim in 1816 in return for Sikkimese support during the Anglo-Nepalese War of 1814–16. By 1817 Sikkim had become a de facto protectorate of the British Empire.

The Sikkimese king accepted British military protection against the continuing Gorkha threat, but in 1835 the British authorities forced the cession of the southern part of the kingdom, including Darjeeling, to direct British rule. Frontier incidents between the Sikkimese and the British led to the British annexation of additional territory from the kingdom in 1846 and 1849. To counter Tibetan claims to the newly ceded districts the British encouraged immigration from Nepal; the immigrants also moved into southern Sikkim. In 1861 Sikkim's status as a British-protected state was formalized by a treaty with the Bhotia-dominated royal government.

The treaty left the issue of sovereignty undefined. The British were given rights to free trade and to construct a road through Sikkim to Tibet. In 1890 an agreement between the British and the Tibetans defined the border between Sikkim and Tibet. The Tibetans, having claimed Sikkim as a tributary state for hundreds of years, acknowledged the special relationship of British India with the Sikkimese kingdom. A British political officer was appointed to assist the king, in the administration of the kingdom's domestic and foreign affairs. The British political officer, in effect, became the ruler of the Sikkimese state.

Nepalese Gorkhalis continued to move to British Bengal and Sikkim after 1900. The Nepalese influx caused much ethnic tension between the indigenous peoples and the newcomers. The Gorkhalis, culturally and religiously distinct from the Buddhist, Tibetan-oriented Sikkimese, moved into most of the southern districts in such numbers that the Sikkimese were soon a minority in the state.

Sikkim's separate treaty relations allowed the kingdom to survive the consolidation of the Indian states in 1947. On 15 August 1947, the day the British withdrew from India, the king declared Sikkim an independent state. Political and social unrest, a result of Gorkha demands for rights equal to those of the ruling Sikkimese, persuaded the king to sign a treaty of protection with India on 15 December 1950. The agreement gave the Indian government the right to control defense, foreign affairs, and communications. Gorkha demands for increased rights within the kingdom led to renewed unrest in the late 1950s and early 1960s. In 1961 the Gorkhas were granted full political and cultural rights, including the vote.

Sikkim remained the main trade route between India and Tibet until the border was closed in 1962. The same year, Chinese troops from Tibet invaded the northern parts of India, threatening the tiny Himalayan state. Indian troops were rushed to the border, but fighting was mostly confined to other regions of the Indian-Chinese border.

In 1963 the Namgyal heir married an American heiress, Hope Cooke, the "Grace Kelly of the East." On 2 December 1963 the heir, Gyalsay Palden Thonduys Namgyal, succeeded to the throne, and his American wife became the queen, the *gyalmo*. The gyalmo promoted Sikkimese culture, arts, and crafts. The queen's foreign background became a political issue as political parties formed in the 1960s.

The National Party, which enjoyed royal patronage, represented the Sikkimese peoples, the Bhotias, Lepchas, and Limbus. The Gorkhalis formed the National Congress Party, while the State Congress Party was supported by India. Both of the Congress parties called for popular rule, the main obstacle being the monarchy and safeguards for the minority Sikkimese population.

In 1965 China renewed Tibet's old claim to Sikkim, and two years later fighting broke out on the Tibetan border. Indian troops aided the Sikkimese to defend the state, and an Indian-constructed road ended Sikkim's long isolation. The Indians withdrew when the Chinese threat ended.

In the early 1970s wealthy landlords sought to reduce the chogyal's power amid a deepening political crisis aggravated by Indian-sponsored Gorkha rioting. In early 1973 the royal family was forced to flee, although the king returned later in the year. Unable to quell renewed Gorkha rioting, the king requested assistance from the Indian government. On 4 July 1974 the king signed the state's first constitution, in which he gave up his absolute rule and created a constituent assembly. Safeguards for the Sikkimese minority and popular government were introduced. Renewed Gorkha rioting and increasing tension brought a renewed Indian military intervention. The Indians, despite international condemnation, stayed in the tiny state to overthrow the royal government and place the king under house arrest. The Indians revoked the titles of the royal family and the Sikkimese nobility as they extended their control of the small state.

The Indian parliament in April 1975 voted to annex Sikkim to the Indian union. A referendum of dubious legality, but with widespread Gorkha support, confirmed on 15 April 1975 the abolition of the monarchy and Sikkim's union with India. On 16 May India annexed Sikkim, ignoring the protests of the king and the opposition of the neighboring states and international governments. Sikkim became the 22d state of the Indian Union on 15 May 1975.

To undermine the continuing Sikkimese opposition the Indian government sponsored the migration of Indians from the lowlands to the newly annexed region, but the movement served only to unite the three Sikkimese peoples. In 1981–83 serious disturbances shook the state as nationalists demanded the expulsion of the newcomers and the restoration of Sikkimese independence under United Nations auspices. In 1982 the exiled chogyal died in the United States. The Indian government countered growing Sikkimese opposition by dissolving the state government and imposing direct rule from New Delhi in 1984. A year later the government restored the state government following renewed disturbances and protests. Indian immigrants since 1985 have added to the growing Hindu population in the state, but the growing rift between the Gorkhas and the newcomers has also added to the ethnic tension of the late 1980s and 1990s.

In 1990 Sikkimese nationalist leaders declared the annexation of Sikkim to be illegal and reiterated their demands for the restoration of the kingdom. The Indian government acknowledged the illegality of the annexation and issued an official apology but refused to discuss the kingdom's restoration. However, as a conciliatory gesture, the government opened the state to visitors, the first since 1978.

In November 1994 state elections the Sikkimese nationalists won a substantial portion of the vote. The nationalist resurgence has become an embarrassment for the Indian government, which had claimed that Sikkimese nationalism had faded away under the benefits of Indian rule.

The Gorkhas, once the vanguard of Indian intervention in Sikkim, increasingly want to join their southern districts to the Gorkha region of neighboring West Bengal state to form a new Gorkha state within India. The increasing split between the Sikkimese-populated northern districts in the Himalayas and the Gorkha lowlands in the south fueled a revival of Sikkimese nationalism in the 1990s. The majority of the Sikkimese support the creation of a new Sikkimese state with redrawn borders and substantial autonomy within the Indian federation, but a vocal minority seek to restore Sikkimese sovereignty in a truncated Sikkimese state in the high Himalayas.

A Gorkha strike in southern Sikkim and the Darjeeling region of West Bengal isolated the Sikkimese for several days in February 2001. The strike closed the NH-31 A, the only highway connection between Sikkim and central India. The lack of mail, newspapers, and other goods from the south was applauded by Sikkimese activists, who reminded the Sikkimese that they were too dependent on India and must regain control of communications and government functions affecting Sikkim.

SELECTED BIBLIOGRAPHY:

Bajpai, G.S. *China's Shadow over Sikkim: The Politics of Intimidation*. 1999.
Rao, P.R. *Sikkim: The Story of Its Integration with India*. 1978.
Rustomji, Nari. *Sikkim: A Himalayan Tragedy*. 1987.
Singh, K.S. *Sikkim*. 1993.

Sindhis

Sindis; Sindudeshis

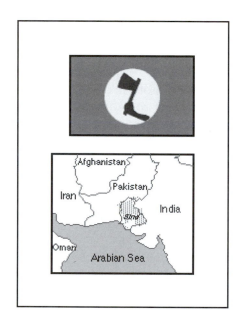

POPULATION: Approximately (2002e) 16,800,000 Sindhis in Pakistan, concentrated in the southern province of Sind. Outside the region there are Sindhi communities in other parts of Pakistan, in the United Kingdom, Canada, and the United States.

THE SINDHI HOMELAND: The Sindhi homeland, called Sind or Sindh, occupies a region of flat plains in the lower Indus River basin and its outlet to the Indian Ocean. The province is roughly divided into three parts—the Kirthar Range in the west, the Indus River basin in the center, and the desert belt in the east. Locally the Indus River is called the Sindhus River. Except for the irrigated Indus Valley, the province is arid and has scant vegetation. Immigration has resulted in an ethnically mixed population. Sind forms a province of the Islamic Republic of Pakistan. Province of Sind (Sindhu Desh): 54,407 sq. mi.—140,914 sq. km, (2002e) 32,929,000—Sindhis 46%, Mohajirs* 32%, Pushtuns* 8%, Baluch* 7%, Punjabis 5%, other Pakistanis 2%. The Sindhi cultural center is Hyderabad, (2002e) 1,273,000, metropolitan area 1,359,000, which also has a large Mohajir population. The other important cultural centers are Larkana, (2002e) 399,000, and Sukkur, (2002e) 366,000. Karachi, (2002e) 10,261,000, the official capital of Sind, is increasingly identified as a Mohajir city.

FLAG: The Sindhi national flag, the flag of the national movement, is a red field bearing a centered white disc charged with a black forearm and hand holding a black hatchet.

PEOPLE AND CULTURE: The Sindhi are a mostly rural people of mixed Aryan, Arabic, and Baluch background. The urbanization of the Sindhi began only in the 1970s, so that the Sindhi culture remains a rural culture, traditional and conservative. The Sindhis comprise a number of regional and cultural divisions, including the Mehs, Muhannas, Sammas, Lakhas, Lohanas, Nigamaras, Kahahs, Channas, Sahtas, Bhattis, Thakurs,

Jats, Lorras, Jokhia, and Burfats. There are about 3.5 million Hindu Sindhis, most being refugees from Muslim Pakistan now living in adjacent areas of India. Most Sindhi women wear the *burkha* in public, a loose-fitting black dress that covers the body from head to toe. Sindhi culture is slowly dying due to urbanization and modernization and the predominance of Mohajir culture and the Urdu language, particularly in southern Sind.

LANGUAGE AND RELIGION: The Sindhi language is a northwestern Indo-Aryan language spoken in six major dialects, including Dukslinu, or Hindu Sindhi. Both the Arabic and Gurumukhi or Persian script are used. The Pakistani national language, Urdu, the language brought to Pakistan by the Mohajirs, and Sindhi are both taught in provincial schools. During the British era, Sindhi was the language of administration and law at all levels. The Sindhi literary language is based on the Vicholi or Central Sindhi dialect spoken around Hyderabad. Due to the various influences and cultures, Sindhi developed in unique ways. Although it is most often written in the Arabic script, it draws equally from roots in Sanskrit and Arabic-Persian. The Sindhi language is India is giving way to the regional languages, particularly Hindi.

The Sindhis of Pakistan are overwhelmingly Muslim, both the Sunni and Shi'a branches. The mostly rural Sindhis have retained a very conservative, even antiquated belief system that often combines pre-Islamic with Islamic customs and traditions. There are smaller groups of Ahmadis,* Sikhs,* and Christians, the latter the result of missionary activity under British rule.

NATIONAL HISTORY: Ancient Sind was the center of the ancient Indus Valley civilization, as represented by the remains of large, sophisticated cities over 4,000 years old. Little is known of the region until it was conquered by the Persians of Darius I in 510 B.C. The culture and language of the Persian conquerors became predominant. Sind fell to Greeks of Alexander the Great in 326 B.C.; it later formed part of the Buddhist Mauryan Empire following the Greek withdrawal. Over the next centuries Sind retained considerable autonomy under the nominal rule of various states and empire. The region fragmented into a number of small states in the fifth century A.D.

Due to the proximity of the sea, the Sindhis evolved as a seafaring people, plying the ancient trade routes in Asia and North Africa. Contact with many peoples living around the Indian Ocean added to the cosmopolitan character of the Sindhi coastal cities. Over the centuries the Sindhis absorbed many smaller groups and also cultural traits from other peoples.

Invading Arabs overran their region in 711–712; it was the first area of the subcontinent to be brought under Islamic rule. The Arabs' new religion, Islam, spread from its foothold in the port cities to the inland districts over the next decade. Ruled as part of the Muslim empire, the Caliphate, the Arab governors of As-Sindh established their own dynastic rule in the tenth century. Sind later came under the control of Turkic peoples and in the fourteenth century became part of India's Mughal Empire. The Sindhis asserted their independence under their own amirs in the eighteenth century. The Sindhi homeland was united except for Khairpur, which formed a separate state in the northwest.

A British military campaign defeated the Sindhis in 1842–43. The British authorities added the conquered Sind states to the British province of Bombay. In 1861, with the exception of Khairpur, the Sindhi territories were consolidated in a single district, which was annexed to the Bombay Presidency. Religious tension between Muslims and Hindus stimulated the growth of both Sindhi nationalism and Muslim separatism in the late nineteenth century. Under British rule Sind was a neglected hinterland of Bombay. The Sindhi national movement mobilized in the 1930s in an effort to separate Sind from Bombay province.

Sindhi society was dominated in the early twentieth century by a small number of major landowners, the *waderas*. Most people were tenant farmers, contract workers equivalent to serfs. Unlike in other parts of British India, a Sindhi middle class barely existed. The Sindhis suffered unremitting poverty, and the feudal landlords ruled with little concern for outside authority. A series of irrigation projects in the 1930s served only to increase the wealth of large landowners when the arid lands were made more productive.

Communal tension escalated after World War I, raising Sindhi demands for separation from Hindu-dominated Bombay Province. Sporadic rioting and violence continued even after Sind became a separate province in 1937. Reformist legislation that was intended to improve the lot of the Sindhi poor had little success. The endemic rioting and disturbances reached serious proportions during and after World War II, as the British government prepared for the partition of British India into the two states of India and Pakistan.

Sind, as a Muslim majority region, joined the new Pakistani state in 1947. Sind's eastern border became the scene of massacres and other outbreaks of violence as Hindus fled to India and Muslims to Pakistan. The two main obstacles to peace in Sind were the oppressive feudal system and the sudden departure of the Sindhi Hindus, who had formed the bulk of the middle class. The flight of the Hindu merchants and professionals left the province without an indigenous educated class. The vacuum was filled by the Urdu-speaking Muslims crossing into Pakistan from northern India, the Mohajirs. The result was a radical alteration of the ethnic makeup of Sind. In 1947, 95% of the population was Sindhi, but by 1951 over 50% of the urban population in Sindh was made up of people whose mother tongue was Urdu. The proportion of Mohajirs reached 80% in Karachi and 66% in Hyderabad.

The arriving Mohajirs, having lost properties in India, took over the properties of the Hindus who had fled to India, further alienating the Sindhis. The initially accommodating Sindhis saw their province and resources literally taken over by the newcomers and found themselves in a constant confrontation with the Pakistani government, dominated by the Mohajirs and the Punjabis. Multiethnic Karachi, dominated by the better educated Mohajirs, was separated from Sind to form a Pakistani federal capital district. The city, with a population of 308,000 in 1939, had grown to a metropolis of over 1.2 million by 1951. The Mohajirs' language, Urdu, the predominant language of the newly designated capital, was adopted as Pakistan's official language even though its use was mostly restricted to the influential refugee population and put the Sindhis and other non-Urdu speakers at a disadvantage in terms of education, jobs, and culture. The Pakistani government abolished the ancient provinces in 1955.

Under the political and economic domination of the more sophisticated, urbanized Mohajirs, Sindhi resistance evolved into cultural and linguistic nationalism in the 1960s. In 1967 the predominantly Sindhi Pakistan People's Party formed under the leadership of Zulfikar Ali Bhutto and in 1970 won control of the Pakistani government. Bhutto's home province, Sind, was reconstituted with its capital at Karachi. The Sindhi provincial government passed a law making Sindhi the only official language of the province in 1972, which exacerbated the growing rift between the Sindhis and the Mohajirs and set off serious Mohajir rioting.

The Bhutto government, vehemently opposed by Pakistan's majority Punjabis, in alliance with the Mohajirs, was overthrown by the army. In 1979 Zulfikar Bhutto was hanged by the military government. Bhutto's wife and his daughter, Benazir, took over the Pakistan People's Party as the party of Sindhi nationalism. Bhutto became a Sindhi martyr as Sindhi nationalism flared across the province. Rising Sindhi nationalism was particularly focused on control of Karachi, with its multiethnic population.

Mohajir demands for a greater say in running Sind province in the early 1980s aggravated the already poor relations between the Sindhis and the Mohajirs. A growing Sindhi alienation provoked widespread nationalist and ethnic violence in 1983–85, leaving over 6,000 dead in Sindhi and Mohajir rioting. In December 1986, the worst ethnic violence since 1947 swept the province, quieting only with the virtual military occupation of the Pakistani army. Sindhi opposition had tended to take nonviolent forms, in contrast to that of the other national groups in Pakistan, but that trend began to erode as regional tension continued to compound in the early 1980s.

Benazir Bhutto won the Pakistani elections in 1988 to become the first female prime minister of a Muslim country. Bhutto's election victory temporarily ended nationalist demands for separation from Pakistan. Disappointed by Bhutto's refusal to grant Sindhi autonomy and her political alliance with the Mohajirs, however, the Sindhis renewed their support for nationalist groups. The nationalist resurgence sparked renewed rioting in 1989–90.

Sind province in early 1990 was poised on the brink of massive civil strife; both urban and rural areas experienced high levels of ethnic tension and sporadic communal confrontations. Violent antigovernment demonstrations in Karachi, organized by the Mohajirs in February 1990, led to serious fighting between the Mohajirs and Sindhi nationalists of the Jiya Sindh movement. The arrest of Qadir Magsi, the Sindhi nationalist leader, in May 1990, following machine-gun battles in Karachi and Hyderabad, further inflamed Sindhi sentiments. The army was deployed throughout the province. Bhutto's government was ousted in August 1990, pushing many moderate Sindhi political groups to form closer ties to the increasingly vocal nationalists. The Pakistani government accused the Indian government of supporting Sindhi separatism to offset alleged Pakistani aid to the nationalists Kashmiris* and Sikhs.

In 1991, the Sindhis, already fearful of becoming a minority in their homeland due to continuing immigration of Pushtuns and Baluchis from other parts of Pakistan, were faced with yet another immigrant group. The Pakistani government began to repatriate Biharis, the "stranded Pakistanis," from Bangladesh. The 250,000 Biharis, left behind when Bangladesh seceded from Pakistan in 1971, were intended to be resettled mostly in Sind province. The Sindhi nationalists protested by calling a general strike, but violence quickly broke out with bomb attacks on strikers in Hyderabad. In 1993 the first 300 Biharis were repatriated, in a move seen by the Sindhis as part of a long-running conspiracy by the Punjabi–dominated Pakistani government to eleminate the Sindhi majority in the province.

Benazir Bhutto, with Sindhi support, again became prime minister of Pakistan in 1993. Her election increased the polarization between the Sindhis and Mohajirs. The Bhutto government determined to decimate the Mohajir national leadership as a political entity in Sind. Bhutto's electoral defeat in 1998, followed shortly after by yet another military coup, again left the Sindhis as outsiders in Pakistan.

Sind, the most lawless and alienated of the turbulent Pakistani provinces, has become the most serious threat to Pakistan's fragile unity. The province, like Pakistan itself, has become virtually ungovernable and is split between hostile national groups. The Sindhis have grown increasingly resentful of their subordinate status within Punjabi-controlled Pakistan and by the uncontrolled influx of immigrants into Sind. In 1995 the Mohajir leaders claimed that their national group had surpassed 50% of the population of Sind, and they demanded social, economic, and political power commensurate with their numbers. The claim was quickly refuted by the Sindhis, but because the government had been unwilling to carry out a census in the region since 1981, the claims and counter-claims continued.

Each of the groups in Sindh claims that its numbers are rising and therefore demand a greater role in governing Karachi and all of Sindh. The Mohajir leader, Altaf Hussain, in 1996, suggested the creation of a separate Mohajir province in southern Sind.

The chairman of Jiya Sindh, Dr. Qadir Magsi, accused the Pakistani government of siphoning off Sindhi wealth from oil, gas, coal, and the port fees to finance the armed forces. He also alleged that the Sindhis were excluded from all major national institutions and threatened that the Sindhis would demand secession if their national and political rights were not recognized.

Violence flared between Sindhis and Mohajirs in the east of the province in 1997, partly over preliminary census results. In March 1998, the Pakistani government completed its first census in 17 years. The Sindhis resisted the results, fearing it would lead to a decrease of their political power in favor of the Mohajirs, whose numbers continued to grow due to immigration and natural population growth.

In October 1998 the Sindhis joined with the Pushtuns, Baluchis, and other non-Punjabi national groups in a new organization, the Pakistan Oppressed Nations Movement, to warn that Pakistan might collapse if they were not given equal rights. The central government reacted by suspending the Sindhi provincial government and placing Sind under direct federal rule, supposedly to curb lawlessness and fight terrorism in the province.

The Pakistani military overthrew a corrupt civilian government in October 1999 and declared a state of emergency. The military, traditionally centralist, announced in April 2000 plans for the devolution of central government power to local levels. The devolution plan would include direct elections at village and district levels. The Sindhi leadership replied that the plan sounded similar to those put into effect under previous military governments, plans that had only increased centralization and Punjabi domination.

Karachi symbolizes Sindhi frustrations with the rest of Pakistan. The city is an explosive mixture of poverty, rampant population growth, crime, and ethnic antagonism. Sindh, according to the nationalists, is the victim of Pakistan's failure to forge a sense of unifying nationhood. The Sindhis are now believed to form a minority in their homeland, which fuels resentment and separatism.

The Sindhi national movement continues to suffer from factionalization. The more moderate groups, probably supported by the Sindhi majority, prefer wider autonomy within a democratic, federal Pakistan. The militants demand secession from chaotic Pakistan and the creation of a separate Sind republic, but the national movement is divided in often antagonistic factions; Sindhi unity remains elusive. The policies of successive Pakistani governments have conspired to produce the present conflict in which the Mohajirs are fighting to maintain their privileged position and the Sindhis, experiencing the phenomenon of an emerging middle class, are laying a vociferous claim to what they consider to be their due.

SELECTED BIBLIOGRAPHY:

Abbott, J. *Sind: A Re-Interpretation of the Unhappy Valley.* 1992.
Burton, Richard F. *Sind Revisited.* 1997.
Khuhro, M.J. *Sind through the Centuries.* 1982.
MacLean, Derryl N. *Religion and Society in Arab Sind.* 1997.

Sioux

Lakotas; Dakotas; Nakotas; Dahoctah

POPULATION: Approximately (2002e) 215,000 in the United States and Canada, with over 100,000 concentrated in South Dakota, and smaller communities in North Dakota, Montana, Nebraska, and Minnesota. About 10,000 live in the Canadian provinces of Manitoba and Saskatchewan. Population figures vary greatly due to the official policy of counting only registered members of the official tribal groups, yet many Sioux live off the reservations and participate only sporadically in community life.

THE SIOUX HOMELAND: The Sioux homeland occupies part of the Great Plains in the north–central United States. The region, mostly flat prairie, includes the Badlands, mostly barren desert; it rises to the forested Black Hills in southwestern South Dakota. The traditional Sioux lands are now mostly lost; the remaining lands are in small reservations in South Dakota, North Dakota, Montana, Nebraska, and Minnesota. Overlapping Sioux land claims, based on the various nineteenth-century treaties, include about 77,210 sq. mi.—200,000 sq. km in the present-day state of South Dakota and neighboring states. The unofficial Sioux capital is Wounded Knee, (2002e) 2,000. The major cultural center is Rapid City, in South Dakota, (2002e) 58,000, urban area 89,000.

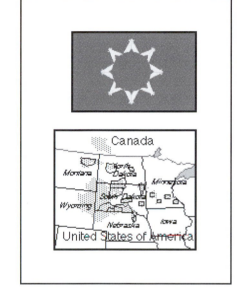

FLAG: The flag of the Oglala Sioux, popularly considered the national flag of the Sioux nation, is a red field bearing a centered circle of eight stylized teepees.

PEOPLE AND CULTURE: The Sioux, popularly called the Great Sioux Nation, are a native American people, the descendents of the tribes that once controlled most of the Great Plains of the north–central United States and Canada. The nation comprises seven tribes, called the Seven Council Fires. The Lakota Sioux, the Teton or Western Sioux tribes, include the Sicangu (Brulé), Hunkpapa, Miniconjou, Ogalala, Oohenupa (Two Kettles), Itazipacola (Sans Arc), and Sihasapa (Blackfoot). The Santee or Eastern Sioux, the Dakota, include the Teton, Wahpekute, Mde-wakanton, Wahpeton, Sisseston, Yankton, and Yanktonai. The Assiniboine and Stoney peoples of Canada, the Yankton or Central Sioux, call themselves and their language Nakota. Collectively the Sioux prefer to be called Dakota (Santee), Lakota (Teton), or Nakota (Yankton), depending on their dialect group. A rich oral history relates the values, culture, and spirituality of the Sioux nation. The Sioux share many cultural characteristics with the other Plains societies.

LANGUAGE AND RELIGION: The Sioux speak dialects of the Dakota branch of the Hokan-Siouan language group. The use of the Sioux dialects is widespread in some communities, although English is the first language for the majority. The language is spoken in three major dialects, Dakota, Nakota, and Lakota. The Santee Sioux speak Dakota and the Yankton Sioux originally used Nakota, but many adopted the Dakota dialect in the mid-1800s. The Teton Sioux speak the Lakota dialect. The three dialect groups are closely related, with 90 to 95% intelligibility among the dialects.

Traditionally the Sioux's belief system revered a Great Spirit, whose breath, the stars, formed a canopy over the nation. The sun and the earth figured prominently in this tradition. The Sioux religion allowed them to live in harmony with their surroundings and the universe. Warfare and supernatural visions were closely connected; totems and magic signs were used to protect the bearers from their enemies. Their religious system recognized four powers presiding over the universe, each in turn divided into hierarchies of four. The buffalo had a prominent place in religious beliefs. In the nineteenth century many Sioux adopted Christianity. The present religious beliefs often mix Christian and traditional beliefs. Many of the Christians belong to the Native American Church.

NATIONAL HISTORY: Several theories concerning the origin of the Sioux trace their birth to the Black Hills of South Dakota, which are sacred to them. Others claim they migrated to the area from the woodlands of present Minnesota. The seven original bands of the Sioux nation were joined in an alliance called the Oceti Sakowin, the Seven Council Fires. The name Sioux, short for *nadouessioux*, meaning "little snakes," came from the Ojibwe,* the Sioux's ancient enemy.

French Jesuit missionaries first encountered the people they called the Sioux near Sault Sainte Marie in the early seventeenth century. The tribes, living in small agricultural villages, probably numbered some 50,000 when the first Europeans visited their lands. The tribes were divided into a northern group occupying the valleys of the Missouri River and its tributaries, and a southern group living in the upper Mississippi Valley. In the late seventeenth century the Sioux migrated to the southwest to escape hostile neighbors, particularly the Ojibwe equipped with firearms by the

Europeans. The tribes finally settled in the Mille Lac region of present Minnesota.

The horse, introduced into the southwest by the Spanish, appeared on the Great Plains at the beginning of the eighteenth century and revolutionized the life of the plains peoples. By the mid-eighteenth century the Lakota had abandoned agriculture and had moved out onto the flat, northern plains, where they evolved a mobile culture based on the hunting of buffalo. The Sioux tribes, in the early nineteenth century, dominated a vast area of the Great Plains, with their spiritual center in the Black Hills, which they occupied around 1775.

At the beginning of the nineteenth century, the Sioux tribes dominated a vast region of prairies, mountains, and river valleys embracing most of present-day South Dakota, and parts of North Dakota, Montana, Wyoming, Nebraska, Iowa, Wisconsin, and Minnesota. The U.S. government purchased the northern plains as part of the vast territory sold by France in 1803, the Louisiana Purchase. American officials signed treaties with the Sioux in 1815, 1825, and 1851, but each time the government ignored the terms of the treaty. The 1851 First Treaty of Laramie formally recognized the Sioux as entitled to a huge tract of land in the West and recognized the Sioux nation as an independent political community, a sovereign nation.

Distrust of American intentions and the steady advance of the American frontier pushed the Sioux tribes westward. The wanton destruction of the buffalo herds on which the Sioux depended finally provoked violence in 1856. The Sioux tribes until 1861 attempted to remain at peace, roaming the plains in winter and returning to the sacred Black Hills each spring to conduct religious ceremonies and to summer in the cooler highlands. The Sioux, under increasing pressure from land-hungry American settlers, rose in 1862 and killed over 800 settlers and soldiers in Minnesota.

Government plans to build the Powder River Road across important hunting grounds in the Bighorn Mountains to Bozeman, Montana, brought the western tribes into the war. Red Cloud, an Oglala chief, led thousands of warriors in a campaign to halt the road's construction. The U.S. government eventually acknowledged a military stalemate in the second Treaty of Fort Laramie in 1868. The government agreed to abandon the road and guaranteed the Sioux exclusive possession of a large territory west of the Missouri River. Trapped by the devastation of the once great buffalo herds, and under increasing military pressure, the Sioux agreed to turn over huge tracts of land to the government. They agreed to move before 1876 to territory that would be reserved in perpetuity for the Lakota Nation.

An expedition into Sioux territory led by Gen. George Custer in 1874 discovered gold in the sacred Black Hills. The resulting gold rush provoked war. General Custer and 200 soldiers died on the Little Big Horn

River in June 1876. The Battle of the Little Big Horn was the last major Lakota victory in the long war to preserve their lands and way of life. Soon after the battle the hard-pressed Sioux tribes surrendered. In direct violation of the 1868 treaty the victors seized the Black Hills in 1877 and drove the Sioux bands into the barren Badlands to small reservations in the most arid parts of their former lands. Chiefs Sitting Bull, Crazy Horse, and Gall refused to take their bands into the reservations. Crazy Horse was killed following his surrender in 1877. Sitting Bull escaped to Canada but returned to the United States in 1881.

The Ghost Dance religion, which spread through the tribes in the late nineteenth century, preached the coming of a savior, a return to the old nomadic way of life, and reunion with the dead. The Sioux, who had suffered harsh privations while confined to their reservations, saw the new religion as their only hope. The U.S. authorities, believing that the movement was disturbing the uneasy peace with the Sioux, ordered the arrest of the leaders. Sitting Bull was killed in 1890 by Indian police taking him into custody. A band of starving Sioux warriors fled the reservations and took refuge in the Badlands, followed by their families. They were captured and brought in December 1890 to Wounded Knee, where a scuffle broke out and an army officer was wounded. Without warning soldiers opened fire, and within minutes nearly 200 men, women, and children had died. The massacre at Wounded Knee ended the last major conflict of the so-called Sioux Wars.

Under the original treaties and agreements signed with the federal government in the late 1800s, reservation lands were owned communally. A well-meaning U.S. senator, Henry Dawes of Massachusetts, saw the reservation system as racial segregation that reduced the Sioux and other reservation groups to paupers. His answer was to dissolve the reservations and distribute the land to individuals. Private ownership would ensure the Sioux protection from encroachment by homesteaders and miners, who continually tried to move in on reservation lands. The 1887 General Allotment Act, known as the Dawes Act, authorized the government to survey reserved lands and to assign farm plots to individuals.

Instead of bringing the Sioux a measure of security, the law separated them from their lands. When the reservations were divided, government agents of the Bureau of Indian Affairs (BIA) gave some Sioux land that could never be irrigated, much less farmed. Family members where often allotted lands at opposite ends of the reservations. Once each Sioux was given an allotment, the Interior Department bought up "surplus" reservation land—often the most desirable tracts on the reservation—and opened it to non-Sioux homesteaders or the railroads. The practice prompted "land runs," in which white settlers lined up at reservation boundaries to wait for a gunshot signifying the opening of new territory. Within four years of the passing of the Dawes Act, the BIA was leasing allotted lands to non-Sioux. Other Sioux were cheated out of their land, creating islands of "fee" land within the reservations.

Plagued by disease, alcohol, and unemployment, the small reserves became notorious for abject poverty and desolation. In 1920 when new laws allowed the tribes to sue for their rights, a small band of educated Sioux filed the first in a long series of court cases seeking to win the return of stolen lands through the justice system. In 1924 the government granted the Indian tribes U.S. citizenship, rights few Sioux were equipped to use. The allotment system was finally ended in 1934, but much damage had already been done. When Congress passed the Dawes Act in 1887, there had been 138 million acres of Indian reserved land in the United States. By 1934, that number had fallen by 65%, to just 48 million acres.

Younger Sioux began to leave the reservations in the 1960s, a time of political turmoil, sit–ins, demonstrations, and fiery speeches. Most Sioux left their reserved lands seeking greater educational and employment opportunities. A growing number of the educated Sioux turned to activism and launched a campaign to open investigations into conditions on reservations and treatment of the reservation Sioux. Militancy centered on the 1868 treaty, with demands that the government honor its terms, beginning with the return of the sacred Black Hills. In the Lakota language the Black Hills are called *wamaka ognaka onakizin*, the Sanctuary of Everything That Is.

Hundreds of activists occupied the town of Wounded Knee in 1973 and held out for 70 days. Leaders of the Oglala Sioux, as the crisis deepened, declared the sovereignty of the region and prepared to send a delegation to the United Nations, but they were blocked by federal authorities. The siege ended with over 300 arrests, but also with promises to initiate talks on Sioux grievances.

In 1980 the U.S. Court of Claims ruled that the federal government had violated the 1868 Second Treaty of Fort Laramie and that the Sioux should be awarded $106 million for lands illegally taken, but that the Black Hills would not be returned to Sioux control. The Sioux nation refused the offer, not only because of the Black Hills but because the money was only a fraction of the real worth of the stolen lands. In 1987 a bill introduced in the Senate would have reaffirmed the Sioux's 1868 boundaries, but did not cover all of the lands agreed to in the 1868 Fort Laramie Treaty and was rejected by the tribal councils.

The Sioux reservations, virtually undeveloped enclaves, where up to three–quarters of the inhabitants are unemployed and income levels are not better than in the poor states in Africa and Asia, continue to fuel the Sioux national movement. Lawyers, not warriors, became the heroes of the movement, fighting in the courts for the sovereign rights the Sioux had never surrendered.

Leaders of the Sioux and the neighboring Northern Cheyenne, the signatories of the 1851 and 1868 treaties of Fort Laramie, in 1991 charged the U.S. government with infringement of the tribal territorial sovereignty. On 14 July 1991, they reaffirmed their sovereignty and established the Confederacy of the Black Hills. The declaration attempted to terminate the colonial occupation of the territory defined as "permanent Indian territory," in the two treaties. They specifically rejected U.S. sovereignty, based as it is on discovery and conquest.

Many Sioux returned in the 1980s and 1990s to their culture, having drifted away in search of jobs, security, or simply to leave behind the dismal life of the reservations. In 1990, the U.S. census counted 103,000 registered Sioux in the United States. Activists claim that the number represented only half the Sioux population, as many of those living away from the reservations were not registered as tribal members.

In 1998 a controversy over a "ghost shirt," taken from a Sioux brave during the Battle of Wounded Knee a century before, animated Sioux nationalism. The shirt, in a museum in Glasgow, Scotland, was seen by a visiting Sioux tourist in 1990 and reported to his tribe. The tribal leaders demanded the return of the shirt, thought to have arrived in Glasgow with Buffalo Bill's Western Show in the early 1890s. The shirt was finally returned following mobilization of Scots* opinion in favor of the Sioux demand.

The Sioux embarked on a new revolution in the 1990s. When this revolution ends some time in the twenty-first century, Sioux lands will no longer be controlled by the Bureau of Indian Affairs (BIA) or by the non-Sioux ranchers, farmers, loggers, and miners who lease land on the reservations. The aim of the Sioux nationalism is an economically sovereign, independent, and self-sufficient community, a part of the American mosaic and part of the global economy. The Sioux revolution, rather than violent headlines, armed takeovers, or battle cries, is to be a matter of soil surveys, changes in the laws governing land inheritance, the control of capital and negotiations over leases. The new revolution is both political and economic; its ultimate aim is to free the Sioux of paternalistic control. Most reservations remain economic colonies, where the BIA manages the land and non-Sioux reap the profits.

The Sioux reservations, the scene of uncontrolled exploitation, are heavily polluted. Forty years of uranium mining in the Black Hills have left rivers poisoned. Radioactive sands from the tailings have been scattered over the Sioux lands, and the people are suffering devastating health defects. The U.S. government is pressuring the tribal councils to accept nuclear waste on their lands in exchange for financial compensation. The Sioux may be coerced into accepting the dumps, much as the largest gold mine in the country, in the Black Hills, is being mined against the wishes of the indigenous people.

Government funds set aside to compensate the Sioux for the loss of the

Black Hills, $100 million in 1980, had grown, with interest to $570 million in 2001. They refuse to touch the money, claiming that to do so would be selling their heritage. Many government officials view the Sioux attitude as foolish pride, but Sioux leaders reply that pride is all they have left. To some, it's just land, something to be bought and sold. But to the Sioux, it's Paha Sapa, the Black Hills. It is sacred ground, and not for sale—even for a half billion dollars.

SELECTED BIBLIOGRAPHY:

Caes, Charles J. *Sign of the Sioux*. 2000.
Hedren, Paul L. *Fort Laramie and the Great Sioux War*. 1998.
Lazarus, Edward. *Black Hills, White Justice: The Sioux Nation versus the United States, 1775 to the Present*. 1999.
Lund, Bill. *The Sioux Indians*. 1998.

Sorbs

Srbi; Sorbischs; Sorabes; Sorben; Sorbians; Lusatians; Wends; Wenden

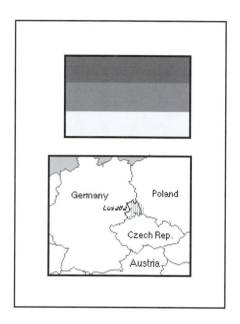

POPULATION: Approximately (2002e) 643,000 Sorbs in central Europe, most in the eastern German states of Brandenburg and Saxony, and with some 40,000 in adjacent areas of Poland. Outside the region there are Sorbian communities in Berlin, other parts of Germany, in Australia, and in Texas in the United States.

THE SORBIAN HOMELAND: The Sorbian homeland lies in east-central Germany and southwestern Poland, a region of rolling hills and forests, particularly the large Spree Forest around Cottbus. The region extends north from the Lusatian Mountains lies mostly between the Elbe and Oder Rivers and is traversed by the basin of the Spree River. The hilly and fertile southern section is known as Upper Lusatia, the sandy and forested northern part is Lower Lusatia. Lusatia, the Sorb homeland, has no official status; the historical region forms the districts of Bautzen, Görlitz, Kamenz, Niesky, and Zittau of the German state of Saxony, and Callau, Cottbus, Forst, Guben, Hoyerswerda, and Weisswasser districts of Brandenburg state, along with the Zgorzelec district, the western part of the Polish province of Zielona Góra. The historical district, called Luzicka Serbja by the Sorbs, is called Lausitz in German and Luzyce in Polish. *Region of Lusatia/Luzyce (Luzicka Serbja/Luzia)*: 4,933 sq. mi.—12,776 sq. km, (2002e) 1,116,000—Germans 54%, Sorbs 43%, Poles 2%, others 1%. The Sorbian capital and major culture center is Bautzen, called Budysin in the Sorbian language, (2002e) 41,000. Other important Sorbian culture centers are Cottbus, called Khociebuz in Sorbian, (2002e) 108,000, and Görlitz, called Zhorjelc, including the Polish half of the city, called Zgorzelec, with a combined population (2002e) 112,000.

FLAG: The Sorb national flag, the flag of the national movement and the unofficial flag of the Lausitz region, is a horizontal tricolor of blue, red, and white.

PEOPLE AND CULTURE: The Sorbs, calling themselves Srbi, are a West Slav nation, also called Lusatians or Wends. The smallest of the West Slav nations, they are related to the neighboring Poles and Czechs but have retained their distinct culture and language. In the Middle Ages the term "Wends" was applied by the Germans to all the Slavs inhabiting the area between the Oder, Elbe, and Saale Rivers. Culturally, the majority of the Sorbs have assimilated into German culture while retaining their own traditions and customs. Part of the Sorbian population, in the Spree Forest, has preserved their traditional dress. The Sorbs have retained their traditional ties to the neighboring Poles and Czechs, and since 1989 there has been a general revival of the Sorbian culture and language. The German-speaking Sorbs, speaking a German dialect with marked Slavic admixtures, retain many Slavic characteristics and are increasingly aware of their unique culture and heritage.

LANGUAGE AND RELIGION: The Sorbian language, Serbscina, of the West Slavic language group, is spoken in two major dialects—Upper Sorbian, which resembles Czech and is spoken around Bautzen; and Lower Sorbian, spoken around Cottbus, in its spoken form closer to Polish. A third dialect, called Eastern Sorbian, considered a subdialect of Upper Sorbian, is spoken in Polish Lusatia. In Germany a majority of the Sorbs now speak German, with only some 200,000 able to understand Sorbian and only 60,000 using the language as the language of daily life. Among the latter, speakers of the Upper Sorbian dialect predominate. Since German unification, Sorbian has been accepted as a minority language and is authorized in local government and education.

The majority of the Sorbs are Lutheran, making them the only Slav nation with a Protestant majority. The Roman Catholic minority is concentrated in the border districts on both sides of the Polish border. There are a large number claiming no religion, the result of decades of persecution of religion and official atheism.

NATIONAL HISTORY: Two small Slavic tribes, the Milceni and Luzici, subgroups of the larger Sorb tribe, settled the region east of the River Elbe in the seventh and eighth centuries. The tribes controlled most of present Saxony and founded towns that later developed into the great Saxon cities, Dresden, Leipzig, and Chemnitz. They continued to migrate west until their expansion was checked by Charlemagne's Franks in the ninth century at the Saale River.

Called Wends, they soon came into conflict with the Germanic peoples moving into their territory in the tenth century. The Germans conquered the region in A.D. 928, but German control of the area east of the Elbe collapsed during a Sorb rebellion in 983. The Germans regained the region, only to lose it to the Poles in 1002. Lusatia was incorporated into Poland in 1018 but returned to German rule in 1033, absorbed by the states of Meissen and Brandenburg. Slavic Lusatia was centered on the

Neisse and upper Spree Rivers, between the present-day cities of Cottbus on the north to Dresden in the south.

During their periodic rebellions against both German and Sorb landlords, the Sorb peasantry would also repudiate Christianity. Saxons* and Brandenburgers launched a crusade to Christianize the Sorbs in 1147, a crusade authorized by the Roman Catholic church. The Sorbs had already begun to adopt Christianity, so the crusade served the ends of German expansion rather than the propagation of the faith. The Germans inflicted great loss of life, and the onslaught drove many of the Slavs east across the Oder and Neisse rivers. The survivors offered little opposition to German colonization of the Elbe-Oder region. German nobles and merchants seized the conquered lands and reduced the Sorbs to serfdom. The Germans relegated urban Slavs to restricted sections or to districts outside the city walls of their conquered towns and cities. The Sorbs were subjected to a ruthless Germanization, and severe economic restrictions were applied.

Seven Sorb cities in the southeast, free cities of the Holy Roman Empire, formed in 1346 a defensive alliance, the Lusatian League. The cities preserved considerable independence from the surrounding German states and maintained the Sorb language and culture. The Czechs of Bohemia took control of Lusatia in 1368, temporarily easing the pressure to assimilate into German culture. Divided into two margravates, Upper and Lower Lusatia, in the fifteenth century, the Sorb lands were partitioned and often changed hands. The Saxon annexation of the margravates reunited the area under Saxon rule in 1635, after the Peace of Prague. The majority of the Sorbs gradually absorbed German culture and language, retaining their own ancient customs and dialects as family or village traditions.

Most of the Sorbs accepted the Lutheran Reformation in 1530, their conversion to Protestantism stimulating a cultural and national revival. A written form of the Sorbian language was devised in order to publish the New Testament in 1548; a Lutheran catechism followed in 1574. In the Spree Forest and the highlands, the Sorbian language remained the first language of the Slav population; the isolated regions became bastions of the beleaguered language and culture. In the Germanized lowlands and in the towns and cities, German slowly gained prominence as the language of daily life.

The Saxon kingdom, allied to Napoleonic France, lost its northern districts, including Lower Lusatia, to victorious Prussia in 1815. The Prussians instituted an intense Germanization policy in the region, forcing the Sorbs of Lower Lusatia to adopt German names and to relinquish their language and Slavic traditions. The western section of Lower Lusatia was completely Germanized, and the number of Sorbian speakers was greatly reduced. The eastern districts experienced a similar assimilation after 1871.

The Sorbs of Upper Lusatia, remaining under more lenient Saxon rule, published the first grammar in the Upper Sorbian dialect in 1830, and the first dictionary in 1840. Reunited in the German Empire in 1871, the Sorbs experienced a national revival, with the first grammar in Lower Sorbian published in 1891. Resistance to forced assimilation sparked the growth of Sorb nationalism in the late nineteenth century. To escape harsh Prussian rule, many Sorbs emigrated, mainly to Texas and Australia.

The Slavic nationalism that swept Poland and the Czech lands in the mid-nineteenth century acquired many parallels in Lusatia. The first openly nationalist organization, Macica Serbska, formed in the late nineteenth century. The German parliament declared in 1908 that German must be the spoken language of the empire and placed official restraints on the Sorb cultural and national revival. An organization known as Domowina (Nation), formed in 1912, pressed for Sorb secession from the German Empire.

The Sorbs, conscripted to fight fellow Slavs when war broke out in Europe in 1914, became openly anti-German by late 1918. In November 1918, as defeated Germany collapsed in revolution, Sorbian leaders declared the autonomy of Lusatia and dispatched a delegation to Berlin to negotiate the peaceful secession of Lusatia from Germany. Rebuffed by the German government, the Sorbs declared Lusatia independent of Germany on 1 January 1919. A Sorbian delegation traveled to the Paris Peace Conference in 1919 to seek recognition under U.S. president Woodrow Wilson's call for the self-determination of Europe's minority peoples. Their appeals ignored, the Sorbs were forced to surrender to invading German troops.

In the postwar German reorganization the states of Saxony and Prussia again divided the Sorbian homeland. By 1920, due to intense pressure to assimilate, only 170,000 used Sorbian as their first language; over 600,000 were able to speak both Sorb and German. The number of Sorbian speakers fell rapidly under the policies of the postwar German government. In 1929 the Sorbs won the right to use their language in education and religion, but the concessions fell far short of the cultural autonomy demanded by Domowina and other national organizations.

National Socialists, called Nazis, in control of Germany from 1933, persecuted the Sorbs as "subhuman Slavs" and banned the use of their language. All remnants of the Sorbian culture were suppressed. In 1938 Domowina was banned and its leaders condemned to Nazi concentration camps. Finally liberated by the German defeat in 1945, the Sorbs attempted to win Allied support for independence. In an exchange of territories the Americans withdrew from the region and allowed the Soviets to occupy Saxony and Lusatia. Western and central Lusatia was incorporated into East Germany in 1949, while the portion of Lusatia east of the Neisse River was ceded to Poland.

The East German government, encouraged by the Soviet Union, for a time in the late 1940s contemplated setting up an autonomous Sorb state. The plans gained little support from the East German communist authorities and stimulated the growth of Sorb regionalism. The Soviet authorities, although supporting cultural autonomy and the façade of self-determination on the Soviet model, remained unsympathetic to national movements in Eastern Europe. They quickly suppressed the Sorbian movement and imprisoned the nationalist leaders, although communist nationalities policy guaranteed the right to use their language and to maintain their distinctive culture. In the early 1950s the inhabitants of three Sorb villages in the new Polish province of Zielona Góra were deported to German territory.

In 1952, over Sorbian protests, their homeland remained divided among two of the new districts that were created out of East Germany's historical regions. The government encouraged Sorbian education and made Sorbian an official language in Lusatia. Ethnic awareness revived in the 1960s and 1970s as the Sorbs created cultural centers, newspapers, radio stations, theaters, schools, folk ensembles, and publishing houses.

Sorb nationalism reemerged as communism in East Germany collapsed in 1989. The nationalists dared to show their forbidden flag at a national rally in Bautzen for the first time since 1945. Sorbian nationalists leaders, citing the medieval Lusatian League as justification for their claims to sovereignty, put forward plans for an autonomous Sorbian homeland.

Nationalist demands for a separate Sorb state within united Germany were ignored in the rush to German reunification in October 1990. Mass unemployment and economic hardships followed unification, giving rise to a wave of German intolerance of "foreigners," including the Sorbs, who did not fit the vision of a pure "Fatherland" propagated by the more radical German nativist organizations. A new wave of vandalism in the region by right-wing radicals in the late 1990s were directed mainly at the Sorb language, including commercial, street, and directional signs.

In 1997 the German government pledged to protect and foster the languages and cultures of the national and ethnic minorities that had traditionally lived in Germany, the largest of which is the Sorb national group. In July 1997, the Saxon state government passed a law to protect the Sorb minority. The new Saxon law granted the Sorbs broad cultural and linguistic rights. The law, together with a recently negotiated agreement between Saxony and Brandenburg states, ensured a steady flow of state financing for educational and cultural activities. The state government was reacting to a federal government announcement that it would cut grants to the Sorbs from $9.5 million to five million by 2007.

The prospect of Polish and Czech membership in the European Union has raised hopes that a larger Slavic presence in the integrated European federation will aid the Sorbs' efforts to retain their language and culture and to reverse the decades of assimilation into German culture. The Sorbs have resisted assimilation for over a thousand and now focus on formalizing their position as the first Slav nation in the European Union.

SELECTED BIBLIOGRAPHY:

Baker, Peter. *Slavs in Germany: The Sorbian Minority and the German State Since 1945.* 2000.

Michalk, Siegfried. *German and Sorbian in Lusatia.* 1990.

Neilsen, George R. *In Search of a Home: Nineteenth-Century Wendish Immigration.* 1989.

Stone, Gerald. *The Smallest Slavonic Nation: The Sorbs of Lusatia.* 1972.

South Sulawesis
Buginese-Makassarese; Bugis-Macassarese; Bugi-Taena

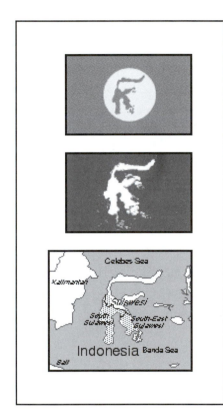

POPULATION: Approximately (2002e) 9,755,000 South Sulawesis in Indonesia, concentrated in the South and South-East Sulawesi provinces of the island of Sulawesi. There are South Sulawesi enclaves in other provinces of Sulawesi, and there are sizable South Sulawesi communities in the other islands of the archipelago, particularly Maluku, Sumatra, Java, and Kalimantan.

THE SOUTH SULAWESI HOMELAND: The South Sulawesi homeland lies in Southeast Asia, forming the southern two-thirds of the island of Celebes, Sulawesi in the Malay languages. The island consists of a central mountainous region and several long peninsulas enclosing large gulfs. The forested region is dotted with shallow lakes. Many of the South Sulawesis live in the large port cities, but the majority are located in small villages scattered along the coastline, rivers, and major highways. Although nationalists claim the entire island, the homeland embraces the provinces of South and South-East Sulawesi. *South Sulawesi*: 38,461 sq. mi.—99,613 sq. km, (2002e) 10,437,000—South Sulawesi (Buginese and Makassarese) 78%, Mandarese 11%, Coastal Malays and Javanese 10%, other Indonesians 1%. The South Sulawesi capital and major cultural center is Makassar, until 1999 called Ujung Pandang, (2002e) 1,177,000, metropolitan area 1,305,000. Other important cultural centers are Palu, (2002e) 179,000, and Kendari, (2002e) 162,000.

FLAG: The South Sulawesi national flag, the flag of the national movement, is an orange field bearing a white disk charged with a map of the island centered. The flag of the South Sulawesi Coalition is a green field bearing a map of the island in white.

PEOPLE AND CULTURE: The South Sulawesis are ethnic Malays, comprising the numerous Buginese and Makassarese and the smaller Mandarese groups of the large island of Celebes (Sulawesi). They are the culturally dominant group and are spread across the southern two-thirds of the island. A proud people, they view themselves as superior to the other peoples of the island. South Sulawesi culture, early influenced by the Indian civilizations, is unique and retains many traditions unknown in other parts of the archipelago. Although the traditional village economy is based on rice cultivation, the South Sulawesis are famed as a maritime people and control much of the interisland trade in the region. The Buginese, numbering about 5.8 million, originated in Makassar, in the southwest of the island, where they were well known for their valor and nautical skill. The closely related Makassarese, numbering about 2.6 million, who remained in the southwest, are considered the heart of the South Sulawesi nation. The smaller Mandarese, numbering about a million, live around the Gulf of Mandar north of Makassar.

LANGUAGE AND RELIGION: The South Sulawesis speak the Buginese and Makassarese languages of the South Sulawesi group of the Austronesian language family. Both of the closely related languages are spoken in numerous regional dialects. The Bone, or Boni, dialect is the central literary dialect of the Buginese. The Gowa, or Goa, dialect is the major dialect spoken by the Makassarese. An early Indian form of writing was adopted, forming the basis of a long literary tradition. The Bugis-Makassar syllabary is still in use; over many centuries thousands of manuscripts were written in it on banana leaves. The manuscripts, called *lontara*, reveal the history of the region and are a source of local pride.

The South Sulawesis are staunch Sunni Muslims, often more militant than other Muslim peoples of the Malay Archipelago. They celebrate Islamic feasts and fasts in ways that are heavily influenced by spiritualism, belief in unseen gods, and ancestor worship. One group of Buginese retains the pre-Islamic religion called Tuanni, involving the worship of several gods. They believe that certain illnesses and misfortunes are inflicted on people by the spirits of fire, air, earth, and water. Local gods are believed to dwell on mountain peaks as well as in soil, plants, and animals. The souls of the ancestors are also believed to exert direct influence on the everyday life of their descendents.

NATIONAL HISTORY: The island was originally populated by peoples moving south from the southern Philippines and by waves of migration from Polynesia. The original Melanesian inhabitants were pushed into the inaccessible mountains, an area that was already inhabited by tribal peoples who practiced head-hunting. The coastal inhabitants were among the early Malay converts to Buddhism. They adopted many Indian customs, including a hierarchical society under a raja.

The South Sulawesis began as river pirates and merchants, but as they expanded their piracy onto the open waters and began to use chain mail, they gained a reputation for being invincible on land or at sea. The South Sulawesis also engaged in interisland trade and shipped as seamen. Originally one people, the Buginese, left the homeland in the southwest to migrate north and east, settling and dominating most of the island. Known for their skills as sailors, they traded and raided across a large portion of the Malay Archipelago. They levied nominal customs duties in Makassar and other port cities, bringing prosperity and a trading culture that stretched from the Malay Peninsula to the Philippines.

The South Sulawesi homeland was split in the thirteenth century between two powerful states, the Buginese state of Boni and the Makassarese state of Gowa, leading to later divisions in the South Sulawesi peoples. In the sixteenth century Islam arrived, becoming the major religion in the southern portion of the island. The Muslims in the souther part of Sulawesi united under the Muslim sultan of Makassar. Many confederations existed within the small kingdom, establishing the basis of today's discussions of federalism and increased local autonomy.

The Dutch established a trading post at Makassar in 1609, gradually extending their influence across the southern Buginese and Makassarese states. Shifting their alliances between Boni and Gowa, the Dutch were able to weaken both. A series of wars between the South Sulawesis and the Dutch led to the conquest of the sultanate of Makassar during the Makassar War of 1666–69, but the Dutch were unable to conquer the Buginese, although they overcame several of the smaller Buginese states.

In the 1700s the growing sea power of the Buginese allowed them to control a considerable empire including parts of the Malay Peninsula, Borneo (Kalimantan), and Sumatra. The Dutch considered the Buginese the most serious threat to their colonial interest in the East Indies. South Sulawesis began to emigrate from their island homeland to places in the Malay Archipelago not yet reached by Westerners. Buginese emigrants established settlements on the mainland Malay Peninsula and by 1710 had established a state in Selangor. From their base in Selangor they extended their rule to Riau and other areas of northern Sumatra in 1722. Throughout the eighteenth century, sporadic conflicts erupted between the Buginese and the expanding Dutch empire.

The expansion of the Buginese jeopardized the Dutch trading empire, especially the important tin trade. In the 1770s, the Buginese and Makassarese, assisted by the Melayus* of Riau, attacked the Dutch in Malacca, the major Dutch port on the Malay Peninsula. The Buginese leader Raja Haji led a fleet to the Malay Peninsula and was killed fighting Dutch forces in 1784. Later conflict between the Buginese and the Melayus weakened both and resulted in the end of Buginese supremacy in the region after 1800. In the early 1800s the Buginese state of Boni fought a series of wars with the neighboring Makassarese Gowa, further weakening the two related nations. Between 1837 and 1860 the South Sulawesis fought against encroachments by Dutch, Spanish, and British colonial forces.

Dutch rule was gradually established in both the north and south of the island of Celebes. Dutch missionaries established churches and mission stations, mostly among the northern ethnic groups in the latter half of the 1800s. Dutch influence was strong in the north but remained weak in the South Sulawesi territories in the south.

Some of the South Sulawesi states maintained a precarious independence well into the twentieth century. The Dutch subdued the last sovereign states, Boni and Gowa, in 1905–1906 and 1911, respectively. The colonial government divided the island into two regions, the State of Celebes in the south, and the Residency of Manado in the north. During the 1920s and 1930s the Buginese rebelled several times, constantly threatening Dutch control of the island.

Japanese troops overran the Dutch defenses in 1942 and took control of the island. The occupation authorities, to gain local support, sponsored nationalist groups and promised eventual independence. Some of the island's many ethnic groups collaborated, but the South Sulawesis, viewing Japan as just another conqueror, terrorized Japanese troops moving into the interior of the island.

In September 1945, the Japanese surrendered to the advancing Allies. The Muslim peoples of the south supported a nationalist movement that attempted to create an independent South Sulawesi state, but it was not recognized by the returning Dutch administration or by Indonesian nationalists on Java. Between 1945 and 1949 there were sporadic battles between the South Sulawesi nationalists and the Dutch and Indonesian nationalist forces for control of the island.

The island of Celebes was included as an autonomous state in the new federated United States of Indonesia in 1949. When the Javanese-dominated central government refused to grant the promised autonomy and erected a unitary Republic of Indonesia, rebellion broke out in the Christian north of the island, soon spreading to the south, where the South Sulawesis rejected Javanese domination. On 2 March 1957, a military coup overthrew the Indonesian government. Taking advantage of the chaos, the Celebes army commander and a 51-member council, mostly South Sulawesis, formally withdrew the island from the Indonesian republic and declared it a sovereign state. The nationalists cited Javanese insensitivity and economic grievances—the central government took 80% of the revenues from the island for development projects on Java. The rebels demanded self-government and that 70% of the revenues collected in the Celebes be spent there.

In early 1958 negotiations between the South Sulawesi rebels and the government broke down. On 16 February 1958 the nationalist leaders, reportedly supported by the U.S. Central Intelligence Agency, declared the independence of the island as the Celebes Republic. All ties to the Indonesian government were severed. Indonesian troops were airlifted to the island, where heavy fighting finally ended the secession in May 1958. Nationalist insurgents, called Permesta, continued a guerrilla war until 1961.

Alarmed by the growing communist strength on Java, the South Sulawesis again rebelled in 1965. The rebellion spread across the south of the island, but factional fighting between rival groups weakened the movement. Indonesian troops quickly crushed the rebellion. The central government changed the name of the island to Sulawesi and divided the island into four separate provinces. Many towns and cities were also renamed, including the South Sulawesi capital, Makassar, which became Ujung Pandang.

Oil was discovered in the region in the 1970s and became an important part of the island's economy. The government's policy of transmigration, moving excess population from the central islands of Java and Bali to the southwestern peninsula of Sulawesi, began in the 1960s and continued until the 1980s. The tension and economic impetus created by the settlement of tens of thousands of culturally and linguistically distinct Javanese raised South Sulawesi demands for an end to the transmigration program and for a more equal distribution of revenues by the Jakarta government.

Opposition to Javanese domination continued to fuel nationalist sentiment in the south of the island. In early November 1987 thousands of Buginese and Makassarese students took part in protests against government economic policies and against the lack of cultural and political autonomy. The protests turned to riots in Ujung Pandang. Fearing that the rioting would spread, the authorities ordered soldiers to open fire on the crowds, killing and injuring many of the protesters.

Prodemocracy demonstrations and nationalist unrest were again met with armed troops in 1996. Rioting again broke out in Ujung Pandang in September 1997, leaving whole neighborhoods in ruins and many dead and injured. The rioting, the worst in the city's history, resulted from a clash between South Sulawesis and Chinese merchants.

A relaxation of military control of the region in August 1999 allowed autonomists and separatists to step up their activities. Nationalists demanded a referendum on the unification of the island of Sulawesi, greater political autonomy, and an apology for the massacres that accompanied the reconquest of the breakaway state in the late 1950s.

Religious violence that shook the Molucca Islands to the east beginning in 1998 spread to Sulawesi in May 2000. Although Christians and Muslims had lived in peace for decades, sporadic fighting now erupted between rival gangs in Poso, in the southeast. The fighting spread until over 4,000 homes had been destroyed and over 200 people had been killed. In one village near Poso, 40 Muslims were rounded up in the local mosque, where they were massacred with machetes. Political leaders on both sides exploited communal tension to win ethnic support, dividing the island along religious lines.

The Indonesian government passed local autonomy laws in 1999, ending decades of highly centralized government. The promised autonomy is still distant, but the violence engendered by the growing Indonesian instability is spreading. There have been frequent clashes between Christians and Muslims, and between ethnic Chinese traders and local groups. The term "autonomy" means different things to different people. To the growing South Sulawesi regionalist movement, it means a chance to redress decades of centralizing government and achieve greater control over local affairs and resources. To the small, but also growing, national movement, it is a first step to full sovereignty.

In April 2000, street rallies were held in Makassar protesting the dismissal of the minister of industry and trade, Yusuf Kalla, the only South Sulawesi in the Indonesian government. The rallies soon turned into pro-independence demonstrations. Student leaders demanded transparent government and an explanation for Kalla's dismissal. Viewing the ousting of Kalla as a rejection of South Sulawesis from the national government, several leaders threatened to support independence for Sulawesi.

The increasing influence of radical, political Islam in the region was examined following the terrorist attacks in the United States in September 2001. Local leaders rejected terrorist tactics and violence, but a growing number of militants have embraced the radical doctrines.

SELECTED BIBLIOGRAPHY:

Amal, Ichlasul. *Regional and Central Governments in Indonesian Politics: West Sumatra and South Sulawesi, 1949–1979*. 1984.
Anweiler, Charles. *South Sulawesi: Towards a Regional Ethnic Identity*. 1994.
Freiberg, Timothy, ed. *South Sulawesi Sociolinguistic Surveys*. 1987.
Harvey, Barbara. *Permesta: Half a Rebellion*. 1977.

South Vietnamese

Kinh; Gin; Jing; Ching; Annamese

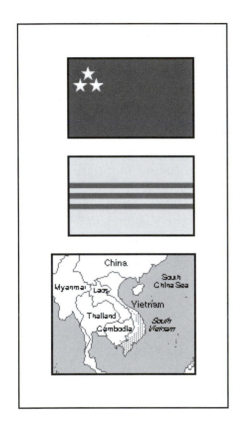

POPULATION: Approximately (2002e) 30,100,000 South Vietnamese in Vietnam. Outside the country there are South Vietnamese communities numbering about two million in neighboring countries of Southeast Asia, in Europe, Australia, and in the United States, where over a million live.

THE SOUTH VIETNAMESE HOMELAND: The South Vietnamese homeland lies in central and southern Vietnam, a region of mountainous interior plateaus, the Central Highlands, and fertile lowlands on the coastal plains on the South China Sea and the Gulf of Thailand, and in the delta of the Mekong River, a flat, often marshy region. South Vietnam has had no official status since the defeat of the South Vietnamese in 1975. The territory of the former republic forms the central and southern provinces of the Socialist Republic of Vietnam. *South Vietnam (Viet Nam Cong Hoa)*: 67,108 sq. mi.—173,810 sq. km, (2002e) 35,146,000—South Vietnamese 78%, Chinese 10%, Montagnards* 3%, Khmer Krom,* Chams,* and other Vietnamese 9%. The South Vietnamese capital and major cultural center is Ho Chi Minh City, called Saigon by the South Vietnamese, (2002e) 3,377,000, metropolitan area 5,595,000. Other important cultural centers are Danang, (2002e) 444,000, metropolitan area 792,000, and Hue, (2002e) 267,000, in central Vietnam.

FLAG: The South Vietnamese nationalist flag, the flag of the anticommunist national movement, is a blue field bearing three white, five-pointed stars on the upper hoist. The South Vietnamese national flag, the flag of the former republic, is a yellow field charged with three narrow, horizontal red stripes centered.

PEOPLE AND CULTURE: The South Vietnamese are part of the Vietnamese nation, separated from the North Vietnamese by a distinct history from World War II to 1975. Despite over 25 years of communist rule, the southerners remain a people apart. Discrimination continues against anyone whose family was associated with the former Saigon regime or the Americans, as do the cultural and historical differences between the two peoples. Culturally the South Vietnamese mostly ignore communist ideology and maintain the culture that flourished under American influence and the French colonialists before them. The legacy of South Vietnam endures in a mood of hard-driving materialism fueled by funds sent by the South Vietnamese diaspora of more than two million worldwide. Remittances from overseas were estimated at over three billion dollars in 1999.

LANGUAGE AND RELIGION: The South Vietnamese speak the Central (Hue) and Southern dialects of Vietnamese, a language of the Annamese-Muong language group. There are only minor dialectical differences between the South and the North Vietnamese, despite the tremendous cultural and historical differences. The language is written in the Latin alphabet. English and French are widely spoken, particularly in Ho Chi Minh City and other urban areas.

The majority of the South Vietnamese are Buddhists, with large Roman Catholic and indigenous religious minorities. Three popular sects are based in the South. The Cao Dai sect mixes Buddhist, Islamic, and Christian teachings and counts among its saints not only Buddha and Jesus but Victor Hugo and Joan of Arc. The Hoa Hao and Bin Xuyen sects are based on Buddhist traditions. All three are centers of resistance to communist rule. The communist leadership regards the three million Roman Catholics with particular suspicion, associating them with the former French colonial rulers and also because of the close relations that Catholics had with the former South Vietnam regimes. The small Protestant minority is also viewed with suspicion.

NATIONAL HISTORY: The Viet peoples originated in the valley of the Red River in the north. The Red River region was conquered by the Chinese in 214 B.C. A separate Viet state, Annam, emerged in A.D. 923 and finally threw off Chinese domination in 1428. Expanding south, the Viet state, called Dai Viet, defeated the Chams in 1471, extending their authority to the area of present Danang.

The kingdom was divided in 1558, with the north, later called Tonkin, ruled from Hanoi and Annam in the south centered on Hue. The Annamese conquered the remainder of the Cham lands and in the eighteenth century conquered the Mekong River delta from the Khmers, taking control of the major city of Saigon in 1776. The Annamese dynasty was overthrown in 1778, and southern Vietnam split into several small states. In 1802 a Hue general reunited the states in a reconstituted Annamese empire under the Nguyen dynasty.

French Catholic missionaries converted many to Catholicism in the early nineteenth century. In 1858 persecution of Catholics and mistreatment of French nationals provided a pretext for French intervention. A French military force occupied Saigon in 1859 and annexed the provinces of Cochin China between 1862 and 1867. Cochin China became a French colony in 1884, while the northern Viet states, Annam and Tonkin, became French protectorates.

A Vietnamese nationalist movement, based in northern Tonkin, became active in the early twentieth century. By 1930 the national movement, called the Vietminh, was dominated by the communists and led by Ho Chi Minh. Forming a guerrilla army during the Second World War, the communists established a regime at Hanoi following the Japanese defeat. On 9 March 1945 Vietnam was declared independent by Emperor Bao Dai of the Nguyen dynasty.

Ho Chi Minh laid claim to all of Vietnam, but the French refusal to give up the southern region, Cochin China, provoked war in December 1946. Between 1946 and 1948 the communists in the north eliminated thousands of political and religious nationalists. Over 800,000 Roman Catholics fled to the South to escape communist rule.

The French authorities supported a rival Vietnamese government in Saigon in early 1950, and in February 1950 requested U.S. military aid. By the time the French suffered their decisive defeat at Dien Bien Phu in May 1954, the United States was paying 80% of the French war costs. As a temporary expedient Vietnam was partitioned, the South under Emperor Bao Dai, supported by the French and Americans, and the North under Ho Chi Minh's communists. Elections and reunification were scheduled for July 1956.

In an attempt to create a stable government, the South Vietnamese accepted Ngo Dinh Diem as prime minister. Diem quickly overthrew the monarchy and, fearing a communist victory in the Vietnamese elections, declared the Republic of Vietnam independent on 26 October 1955. The new government won recognition by most of the world's noncommunist states. In 1956 war broke out between the two Vietnams, and a procommunist guerrilla group, the Viet Cong, began to operate in the South.

In 1963, in protest against the anti-Buddhist policy of the Roman Catholic–dominated Diem government, several Buddhist monks poured gasoline over themselves and set themselves on fire. Diem also suppressed the nationalist Cao Dai sect. The rising Buddhist rebellion in the south marked the beginning of the end for Diem, who was executed during a military coup in November 1963.

The Viet Cong infiltrated villages and towns across South Vietnam, making it difficult to identify antigovernment elements. U.S. troops, introduced in 1955, were to number over half a million by 1969. As preparations were being made for the New Year celebrations in January 1968, more than 85,000 Viet Cong and North Vietnamese regulars simultaneously attacked all major cities and important military installations in the South, in what became known as the Tet Offensive. Most of the attacks were repulsed by the South Vietnamese and their American allies, but the communist troops held out for more than three weeks within the thick walls of Hue's old citadel. About 70% of the city was destroyed or badly damaged, and more than 7,000 lives were lost in the battle to retake Hue. Many of the casualties were South Vietnamese civilians who worked for the government and had been murdered or buried alive by the communists, along with all foreigners living in the city. The Hue massacre hardened South Vietnamese attitudes to the communist North.

South Vietnam, in spite of despotic rule and the ongoing war, developed a dynamic capitalist economic aided by increasing American economic and military aid. However, in the United States the mounting American casualties provoked massive antiwar demonstrations and pressure to disengage. A 1973 truce, the Paris Peace Accords, formally ended American participation in the war. The U.S. troops were withdrawn, having suffered 57,000 casualties.

In early 1975 the North Vietnamese launched an offensive at Banmethuot. The South Vietnamese government ordered the defenders to withdraw. The withdrawal became a headlong retreat, the fleeing soldiers accompanied by hundreds of thousands of panicked South Vietnamese civilians. In violation of the 1973 accords, the North Vietnamese rolled south, spreading chaos through the republic. On 21 April 1975, South Vietnamese president Nguyen Van Thieu resigned and fled to Taiwan. The last American helicopters, rushed by South Vietnamese frantic to escape the communists, left the surrounded city of Saigon, ending a shameful page in the history of the Vietnam War.

The North Vietnamese, rather than acting like the liberators they claimed to be, became arrogant conquerors. Tens of thousands of Southern officials, clergy, conscript soldiers, members of anticommunist groups, and intellectuals who failed to escape were ultimately imprisoned in reeducation camps. Over the next decade over a million South Vietnamese fled, mostly in small boats. Exile nationalists organized to aid the refugees and to work for the restoration of the republic. In 1979 the communist government agreed to an "orderly departure" program, which allowed some 100,000 to leave legally, in exchange for foreign currency.

The majority religion of the South, Buddhism, was suppressed in the late 1970s. In 1981 the Buddhist Church of Vietnam (UBCV) was officially dissolved, though it continues to exist underground. The Buddhist hierarchy has been one of the country's most important centers of unarmed resistance, first against the Roman Catholic–dominated Saigon regime and then, after the North Vietnamese victory in 1975, against the communist rulers in Hanoi. Following the fall of South Vietnam, resistance also formed around the socioreligious sects, the Cao Dai and Hoa Hao. Until accommodation with the government was reached in the mid-1980s, there was considerable armed resistance in areas inhabited by members of the two sects. Renewed confrontations and demonstrations broke out among the sect members in 1996.

South Vietnamese nationalism, suppressed since 1975, reemerged in the late 1980s, strengthened by a wave of nostalgia for the former republic. Southern grievances added to the unrest, particularly the communist regime's greater concern for preserving "revolutionary" memorials than for saving the rich cultural heritage of the South. Nationalists launched guerrilla military operations in the South in 1986, 1993, and 1996, but to little effect.

The introduction of *doi moi*, economic reforms, in 1986 exacerbated the tension between the richer, more dynamic South and the poorer, economically backward North. Nonetheless, the government, wishing to improve international relations, released between 1990 and 1995 its 100,000 or more political prisoners, mostly former military officers and members of the South Vietnamese government.

In May 1992 the Vietnamese government adopted a new, highly centralized constitution to combat "archaic autonomy demands" and "localism." The authorities in March 1993 announced the arrest of a large number of South Vietnamese charged with attempting to destabilize and split Vietnam. In spite of continuing tension, in 1993 more Vietnamese returned than left the country, for the first time since 1975.

The government crackdown on the South of the early 1990s, particularly on the Buddhist and Catholic clergy, provoked the largest antigovernment demonstrations in Saigon since the 1975 invasion. In Ho Chi Minh City the police foiled a 1993 plot, or plots, to set off bombs in the city. Four Vietnamese who had returned from the diaspora were given long jail sentences, while six others and 10 local residents received shorter sentences. In November 1993 a number of Buddhist monks were sentenced to prison following serious disturbances in Hue.

The government euphemisms "opponent forces" and "enemies within" are increasingly applied to the restive southerners. As economics replaced ideology as the prime nationalist issue in the 1990s, discontent and resentment fed a nationalist resurgence. Although South Vietnam is still 30 years ahead of the North in development, it has fallen far behind its former competitors—Thailand, Malaysia, and the Philippines—though no fault of the entrepreneurial South Vietnamese.

In late 1995 the United Nations voted to close the remaining refugee camps in Southeast Asia and repatriate the 40,000 peoples still living in the camps. The United States in April 1996 decided to accept everyone who could prove association with the former South Vietnamese government or the U.S. forces during the Vietnam War.

Ten years after economic reforms were introduced, in 1996 the communist government faced difficult choices. The economy was expanding, especially in the still freewheeling South, far from the political preoccupations of the northern capital. But the inequalities between the North and South were widening. In the South the U.S. dollar was the currency of choice. Although the northern provinces were progressing, the economy of the southern provinces, with their free market tradition, were growing even faster. South Vietnam remained what it always had been—wealthier, gaudier, and more independent minded.

Communist Party cadres seem unable to regain control of the South other than through placement of North Vietnamese at every layer of the bureaucracy. Corruption is rife. Prostitution, drugs, and gambling have reappeared, and some intellectuals in Saigon are looking back wistfully at the "Golden Era" of South Vietnam, from 1955 to 1975, and farther afield to the pluralist political systems of the industrialized democracies. In 1998 the Communist Party leader, Do Muoi, claimed that Ho Chi Minh City was a hotbed for hostile forces. Entrepreneurs cannot be comrades.

A widespread cultural purge was launched by the government in 1996. Police raided karaoke bars in Ho Chi Minh City to ensure that no banned pre-1975 music was being played, particularly the romantic "yellow music" popular in South Vietnam during the war and among the Vietnamese diaspora. Signs with foreign brand names were covered up with tape, black paint, and newspaper in an effort to enforce a Vietnamese-only decree. Video shops were also raided as police looked for "foreign pollution" from the West.

The important Vietnamese diaspora still recognizes the South Vietnamese flag and anthem and vehemently oppose the communist regime. Overseas Vietnamese maintain links to underground groups operating in the South and funnel funds and arms to anticommunist and nationalist organizations. On 13 September 1998, ceremonies honoring the 50th anniversary of the flag of the Republic of Vietnam drew crowds in France, the United States, and Australia.

In 1997–98 the party responded to the increasing southern challenge by waging a mass campaign against social evils, nostalgia for the pre-1975 South Vietnam, "backsliders," those nostalgic for the prosperity and freedom of the former South Vietnam republic, and unwelcome Western influences. In a surprise move, the Vietnamese government released more than 7,000 prisoners between September and November 1999. Most were convicted common criminals, but some were prominent religious and political dissidents.

The Vietnamese government announced in early 2000, as part of the 25th anniversary of Vietnamese unification, that the Ho Chi Minh Trail of the Vietnam War era was to be turned into a national highway, paralleling the famous Vietnam War route that wound through Vietnam and Laos. The highway is being constructed in eastern Vietnam in an effort to unite the two parts of the country, which are now linked only by the narrow Route 1, which suffers frequent damage from storms, floods, and landslides.

Increasingly the South Vietnamese are asking how the Communist Party can justify its monopoly on political power while following policies it once denounced as "capitalist." To many South Vietnamese, particularly the more nationalistic diaspora, however, the party is now less interested in justifying its control than in prolonging it. The government fears that every time the economy is liberalized, it will be South Vietnamese businessmen and investors who take most advantage, while the poorer north falls further behind both politically and economically. The communist leadership seems prepared to accept lower economic growth if it helps keep the South under control.

The lessons of the Soviet Union, Yugoslavia, and Czechoslovakia have not been ignored by the party in Hanoi or by the would-be democratic entrepreneurs of Saigon. Vietnam, unified for nearly three decades, remains one country, but with two distinct halves. Unemployment, social unrest, and the prospect that the country could snap in two are the three greatest worries for the communist government in Hanoi. Foreign reporters visiting the country in 2000–02 noticed that the South Vietnamese dared to talk about themselves as southerners rather than as Vietnamese.

SELECTED BIBLIOGRAPHY:

Dacy, Douglas. *Foreign Aid, War and Economic Development, South Vietnam 1955–1975.* 1986.
Givhan, John B. *Rice and Cotton: South Vietnam and South Alabama.* 2000.
Jamieson, Neil L. *Understanding Vietnam.* 1993.
Taylor, Philip. *Fragments of the Present: Searching for Modernity in Vietnam's South.* 2000.

Southern Azeris

Southern Azerbaijanis; Azerbaydzhanis; Azeri Turks; Iranian Azeris; Azaris; Turki

POPULATION: Approximately (2002e) 18,500,000 Southern Azeris in Iran, concentrated in the northwestern provinces of East and West Azerbaijan. It is difficult to determine the exact number of Southern Azeris in Iran, as official statistics are not published detailing Iran's ethnic structure. Estimates of the Southern Azeri population range from as low as 12 million up to 40% of the population of Iran—that is, nearly 27 million. Outside the South Azerbaijan region there are large Southern Azeri communities in Tehran and the other cities between Tehran and the Southern Azeri homeland, particularly Hamadan, Karai, and Qazvin; in Iraq, with a Southern Azeri population of between 500,000 and 1.5 million; 50,000 in Syria; and about 700,000 in Turkey.

THE SOUTHERN AZERI HOMELAND: The Southern Azeri homeland extends south from the Aras (Araks) River, which forms the international border between Azerbaijan and Iran. Most of the region is mountainous, but it also includes the lowlands around Lake Urmia and some of Iran's most fertile lands. The Azeri

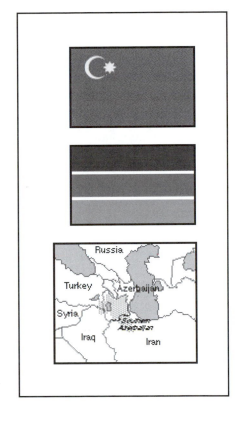

homeland in northwestern Iran is made up of three provinces, West and East Azerbaijan and Ardabil, although the Azeris also inhabit adjacent areas in Zenjan and Hamadan provinces, and the Astara, Gazvin, and other areas of northwestern Iran. *Region of Azerbaijan (Azerbaychan)*: 42,277 sq. mi.— 104,497 sq. km., (2002e) 7,322,000- Azeris 72%, Kurds* 20%, Persians (Iranians) 6%, other Iranians 2%. The Azeri capital and major cultural center is Tabriz, (2002e) 1,210,000. Other important cultural centers are Orumiyeh, called Uromeiyeh by the Southern Azeris, (2002e) 481,000, and Ardabil, called Ardebil locally, (2002e) 349,000, metropolitan area 466,000.

FLAG: The Azeri national flag, the flag of the National Liberation Movement of Southern Azerbaijan (NLMSA), is a red field bearing a small white crescent moon and an eight-pointed star on the upper hoist. The flag of the United Azerbaijan Organization, which seeks unification with the Republic of Azerbaijan is a horizontal tricolor of blue, red, and green with the stripes separated by narrow white stripes.

PEOPLE AND CULTURE: The Azeris are a Turkic people, the descendents of early Caucasian peoples with later Persian and Turkic admixtures. The clan-type family structure remains common among the Azeris of Iran. The clan, the *hoj*, is usually named after a common ancestor. Clan members shared pastureland and were bound to provide mutual aid to each other. They frequently acted as a unified entity in business dealings. It was also common for up to 40 members of an extended family to live together in large dwellings, called *gazma*. Landless peasants, the *tavyrga*, made up the lowest social class. The Azeri population of the former Soviet Union and Iran, although separated by political borders for nearly two centuries, retain strong cultural and linguistic ties. The Southern Azeri culture is a mixture of Turkic and Persian (Iranian) elements, with borrowings from Caucasian peoples and the neighboring Kurds. The Turco-Iranian Islamic heritage remains predominant, as Persianization has never been actively promoted to any extent. The sense of identity remains very strong, although specific forms of cultural expression are prohibited by the Islamic government.

LANGUAGE AND RELIGION: The Southern Azeris speak a Turkic language belonging to the Southwestern or Orguz branch of the Turkic language family. The Southern Azeri language differs considerably from the Northern Azeri language spoken in the Republic of Azerbaijan, both in sound and in basic structures. The Southern Azeri language is spoken in 12 regional dialects. The language has a literary tradition, based on the Tabriz dialect, that dates back to the fourteenth century. Arabic or Persian script is used by the Azeri literary language in Iran. Azeri serves as the somewhat hybrid lingua franca of northwestern Iran. The Azeri language under the Islamic regime was removed from official use in all areas, including schools, courts, government offices, and the army, though the 15th article of the Iranian constitution guarantees the use of local languages for literature lessons in elementary education. The Azeri Turkish language is the most important factor that differentiates the Southern Azeris from the rest of the Iranian population.

The majority of the Iranian Azeris belong to the Jafari sect of the Shi'a branch of Islam, the predominant sect in Iran. A minority, mostly along the border with Azerbaijan and around Lake Urmia, adhere to the Sunni rite. Islam plays a significant role in peoples lives, particularly since the 1979 Islamic revolution, but religion is not a key identifying factor in the relationship with the rest of Iran. The Shi'a and Sunni differences are sensitized and demarcated, and intercommunal violence is just below the surface. A small number of Southern Azeris are Bahais.*

NATIONAL HISTORY: The Azeri homeland is thought to have been settled by the ancient Medes in the eighth century B.C. The region formed part of successive Persian empires and is traditionally the birthplace of Zoroaster, the founder of Persia's pre-Islamic religion. A Persian governor, Atropates, appointed by Alexander the Great, established an independent Mede kingdom in the region in 328 B.C. Known as Atropatene or Media Atropatene, the region, lying on the major invasion route between Asia and Europe, was often conquered by migrating armies.

Claimed by the Parthians and later by Persia, continuous Persian control was not firmly established until the third century B.C., when Azerbaijan became a province or satrapy of the Persian Empire. Except for a brief period of Byzantine control in the early seventh century, the area remained Persian until the Arab conquest of the region.

The Muslim invaders of the seventh century forcibly converted the inhabitants to Islam. The area was ruled by the Muslim empire, the Caliphate, until the eleventh century, when it was conquered and settled by migrating Seljuk Turks. The conquerors adopted the Islamic region, but the Turkish language and the culture of the conquerors replaced the earlier Persian influences in the region. In 1136 the Seljuk Turks created the Atabek state of Azerbaijan under Shams ad-din Ildeniz. The boundaries of the state eventually extended from Tbilisi in Georgia to encircle the southern half of the Caspian Sea and extended into present-day Iraq. The state collapsed with the Mongol conquest of the region in 1225.

For centuries the Azeri homeland formed a frontier district at the confluence of the competing Turkish and Persian empires. The Safavid dynasty, established in 1499, from its beginnings in Southern Azerbaijan restored internal order in the Persian empire from its capital at Tabriz. By 1551 all of Azerbaijan was under Safavid rule. The Shi'a sect was established as the state religion in Safavid Persia.

Wars between Safavid Persia and the Turkish Ottoman Empire marked the next several centuries in the region. Between 1578 and 1603 the Azeri homeland again fell to Turkish rule; however, in the seventeenth century Azerbaijan was once again under firm Persian control. As Safavid power waned, Russia and the Ottoman Empire vied for power in the region. In 1720 a Sunni religious leader led a rebellion in the north and asked for help from the Ottoman Turks. The Russian government uses this upheaval to occupy the coastal regions of Azerbaijan. Between 1750 and 1813 both Northern and Southern Azerbaijan were divided and ruled by local khans.

The Russian Empire annexed the northern Azeri territories piecemeal from a weakened Persia between 1805 and 1813. The territories taken by the Russians were formally ceded by Persia in the treaties of Gulistan in 1813, which divided Azerbaijan into Russian and Persian spheres at the Araz (Araks) River. Southern Azerbaijan remained under Persian rule, as a separate satrapy with its capital at Tabriz. Russian attempts at further expansion to the south were mostly unsuccessful. The two parts of the Azeri homeland developed in separate ways at a time when national self-consciousness was not strong enough to resist the imposed cultural and political influences. The division played an essential role in creating the modern distinctions between South and North Azerbaijan.

The Azeri population in Persia, affected by the nationalism spreading across the border from Russian Azerbaijan, although less developed than their northern kin, also began to espouse nationalism as a reaction against the corrupt and feudal rule of the Persian state. The Russian government often cooperated with the Persian authorities to combat the growing nationalism in the region. Southern Azeri nationalists claimed a territory of 65,600 square miles (170,000 sq. km) of northwestern Iran as national territory.

The Azeri national movement led to the formation of specifically Azeri political parties. The most important, Hemmat (Endeavor), the Muslim Marxist party, formed in Russian Azerbaijan in 1904 and quickly spread to Iranian Azerbaijan. Party members participated in the 1906 revolution in Persian Azerbaijan, with national-territorial demands put forward during serious disturbances in 1908–1909. The second revolution in Persia in 1909 gave the Russian government the opportunity to occupy Persian Azerbaijan, but the troops were later withdrawn under the terms of economic and political agreements with the Persian government.

During the repression that followed, the nationalist political party, Mussavat (Equality), and other political parties were forced underground while the rioters were put down by Cossack troops in the service of the Persian government. Mussavat was founded in 1911 with supporters in both Russian and Persian Azerbaijan, although historical factors combined to ensure different responses in the two regions. Nationalist sentiment, based on the idea of a united Azeri homeland and promoted by the newly formed political parties, spread rapidly on both sides of the international border. Russian and Persian government policies restricted contacts between the two halves of the Azeri nation, but clandestine contacts continued, particularly between Mussavat activists in Russia and nationalists in Persian Azerbaijan.

Religious unity in terms of their Shi'a Islam and cultural closeness to the Persians in language and religion moderated the impact of nationalism in South Azerbaijan until after World War I, as did the threat of Russian aggression. Many Southern Azeris held important posts in the Persian government, which tempered the social and economic demands of the small nationalist organizations.

Nationalist leader Sheykh Khiyabani led a serious revolt in 1920. He created a separatist government called Azadistan, or "Land of the Free," but his movement collapsed following his arrest and execution. He is now a hero of the Southern Azeri national movement.

The Northern Azeris, effectively independent with the collapse of tsarist Russia in 1917, declared Russian Azerbaijan independent on 28 May 1918. The pull of Azeri nationalism fueled the growth of separatist sentiment in Tabriz, but Persian troops effectively blockaded the new border and cut communications between the two Azeri peoples during the Russian Civil War. The victorious Bolsheviks declared former Russian Azerbaijan a Soviet republic on 1 May 1920, and all remaining contacts between the Northern and Southern Azeris ended, although clandestine contacts continued.

Azeri nationalism, during the purges and oppression in the Soviet Union in the 1920s and 1930s, shifted to Iranian Azerbaijan, where many Mussavat leaders had taken refuge. Supported by nationalists in Tabriz, the exiled Azeri leadership continued to work for a free, united Azeri nation, although local grievances and interests often overrode the idea of Azeri unity. In 1938 Iranian Azerbaijan was reorganized into two separate provinces in an attempt to dilute growing Southern Azeri nationalist sentiment.

During World War II the Soviet Union and the United Kingdom requested transit rights, which were refused by the Iranian government. On 25 August 1941 the two allies sent troops to occupy Iran, the Soviets in the northern provinces, and the British in the south. A tripartite agreement signed on 29 January 1941 stipulated that the occupying troops would leave within six months of the end of the war.

Southern Azeri communists of the Tudeh Party, in alliance with the nationalist groups, formed the Democratic Party of Azerbaijan. With Soviet support, the Southern Azeris declared the independence of Iranian Azerbaijan as the Azerbaijan Democratic Republic on 20 July 1945. The Soviet government, despite earlier promises, at first refused to withdraw its troops. The Southern Azeri republic collapsed in 1946, following Stalin's withdrawal of the Soviet troops as part of a new oil deal with the Iranian government.

The prohibition on contacts between Soviet Azeris and Iranian Azeris became increasingly hard to enforce as the use of radios became widespread in the 1950s, allowing the Azeris in the Soviet Union to lend covert aid to their kin suffering under the oppressive rule of the imperial Iranian government. The Azeris represented the middle class in the stratified society, dominating the bazaars and providing two-thirds of the army officers and many of Iran's intellectuals, writers, and teachers. Despite the repression of the shah's government the Southern Azeris prospered economically.

The prelude to revolution in Iran spurred a renewed interest in the Southern Azeris' ties to their northern kin and in their unique culture and language. With the fall of the shah of Iran's government in 1979 Azeri nationalism reemerged in opposition to the excesses of the revolutionary clique. Southern Azeri opposition to the Islamic Revolution fueled nationalist rioting in Tabriz and other large cities. The Azeri spiritual leader Ayatollah Shariamadari was placed under house arrest in Tabriz after his followers clashed with Revolutionary Guards during nationalist rioting in the city. In 1983 the Democratic Party of Azerbaijan and the leftist Tudeh Party were officially dissolved by Iran's Islamic government. In a massive crackdown hundreds of party members and suspected Southern Azeri nationalists, including many women, were imprisoned. Of the many Azeri language publications that emerged after 1979, by 1984 only one remained.

The relaxation of Soviet rule in the late 1980s began a series of events that fueled the rapid growth of Southern Azeri nationalism. Azeri demonstrators on the Iranian border tore down the border posts and the frontier fence that divided the two halves of the Azeri homeland, while Northern Azeri leaders called for independence for a "Greater Azerbaijan."

The Iranian Islamic government, no longer trying to export its Islamic revolution to the Northern Azeris, and increasingly aware of the effect of the independence movement in Soviet Azerbaijan on its own Azeri population, cracked down on antigovernment activities in Tabriz. Envoys to Moscow demanded a curb on the Azeri drive to independence in Baku. Pressured by the Iranian government, which had contended with rising Southern Azeri nationalism in Iran since the 1979 revolution that installed an Islamic state, the Soviet authorities finally sent troops to Baku, raising tension across the region.

In August 1991 the Soviet Union collapsed, and Northern Azerbaijan became independent as the Azerbaijan Republic. The event led to a rise of Southern Azeri nationalism and diffusion of national identity into the higher social strata. The national movement in the region continued to win support, but three major groups emerged. The first consisted of religious leaders, industrialists, and bureaucrats closely tied to the Iranian state; this group supported the unification of Northern Azerbaijan with Iran. The second group, led by intellectuals, supported the democratization of Iran and national-territorial autonomy for the Southern Azeris. The third group was represented by a growing number of political organizations and nationalist groups that supported the independence of South Azerbaijan.

The Iranian government sought to prevent the formation of a truly independent and prosperous Azerbaijan Republic and to minimize its influence in Southern Azerbaijan in order to ensure the territorial integrity and internal stability of the Islamic state. They also wanted to prevent the integration of the Turkic-speaking nations and to prevent the increase of U.S. and Turkish influence in Azerbaijan and Central Asia. To this end, the Iranian government supported the Christian Armenians against their fellow Muslim Azeris in the Caucasian conflict in Nagorno-Karabakh. Repressive measures toward all signs of Southern Azeri activism increased in the mid-1990s. Four Southern Azeri political parties and groups merged under the Front for the Independence of South Azerbaijan in 1996.

Increasing discontent with the Islamic government led to widespread disturbances in 1999. Student demonstrations swept the major South Azeri cities, the first large indication of the popular rejection of the policies of the conservative religious leaders who control Iran. Clashes between demonstrators and the security forces in Tabriz resulted in a number of deaths in January 2000. Many Southern Azeri leaders fled to Baku in June and July 2000 to escape an Iranian round-up of nationalist leaders in Tabriz. The detention of Mahmud Ali Chehragani, a leading advocate of Southern Azeri rights, became the focus of newspapers in the Azerbaijan Republic and international human rights organizations.

Small demonstrations, the first serious show of defiance by nonpolitical Southern Azeris, were held in Tabriz and other cities in late 2001. The fall of the Islamic government of Afghanistan in December led to calls for the democratization of Iran and autonomy for the Southern Azeris.

SELECTED BIBLIOGRAPHY:

Atatbaki, Touraj. *Azerbaijan: Ethnicity and Autonomy in Twentieth Century Iran.* 1993.
———. *Azerbaijan: Ethnicity and the Struggle for Power in Iran.* 2000.
Nissman, David B. *The Soviet Union and Iranian Azerbaijan.* 1987.
Swietochowski, Tadeusz. *Russia and a Divided Azerbaijan.* 1993.

Southern Cameroonians

Anglophones; Ambazonians

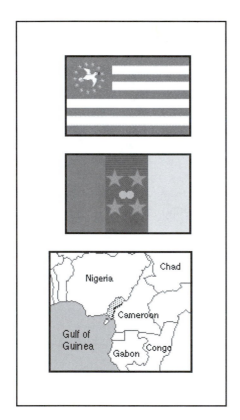

POPULATION: Approximately (2002e) 2,761,000 Southern Cameroonians in Cameroon, concentrated in the two western provinces of Northwest and Southwest. Outside the region there are Southern Cameroonian communities in other parts of Cameroon, in neighboring Nigeria, and in the United Kingdom and the United States.

THE SOUTHERN CAMEROONIAN HOMELAND: The Southern Cameroonian homeland lies in the western highlands of Cameroon, stretching from the Adamawa Plateau to the coast at Mount Cameroon, just east of the international border with Nigeria. The densely populated region is separated from francophone Cameroon by the Mungo River; it is the center of Cameroon's oil and agricultural wealth. The region, popularly called Western Cameroon, comprises the provinces of Northwest and Southwest. *Region of Western Cameroon (Federal Republic of Southern Cameroons)*: 16,324 sq. mi.—42,281 sq. km, (2002e) 3,131,000—Southern Cameroonians 71%, other Cameroonians 29%. The Southern Cameroonian capital and major cultural center is Buea, (2002e) 84,000. The other important cultural centers are Bamenda, (2002e) 149,000, and Kumba, (2002e) 101,000.

FLAG: The Southern Cameroonian national flag, the flag of the national movement, has nine pale blue and white stripes with a pale blue canton on the upper hoist charged with a white dove carrying an olive branch within a circle of 13 gold stars. The flag of the Southern Cameroonian National Council (SCNS) is a vertical tricolor or green, red, and yellow, bearing two yellow, overlapping yellow circles surrounded by four gold stars on the red stripe.

PEOPLE AND CULTURE: The Southern Cameroonians are a group of at least 50 Bantu peoples united by their history and the English language. The major groups include the Kakas, Tikar, Ambas, Berbers, Bamilekes,* Bayangs, Mambilas, Bamouns, Ibos,* and Ibibios.* They include many peoples of the savanna region and are divided into many small kingdoms ruled by kings called *fons*. They form part of the regional-cultural group known as the highlanders, or grasslanders. The historical divisions into numerous small kingdoms has led to a proliferation of nationalist and local interest groups and has hindered the movement for sovereignty. The Southern Cameroonian culture combines indigenous foundations and the influence of the British colonial structure. Many of the indigenous traditions evolved as religious or ceremonial rituals in the small kingdoms. The region is an amalgam of various cultures, variously Bantu, German, British, and French. The British influence and language have come to define the political body, education, and the state structure. The British influence is still paramount in education, writing, language, politics, administration, and the performing arts, effectively separating the Southern Cameroonians from the French-speaking Cameroonians.

LANGUAGE AND RELIGION: The Southern Cameroonians speak dozens of Bantu languages, but they use an English pidgin and standard English as a lingua franca. The introduction of French into regional schools in 1972 continues to be a very sensitive issue. Linguistic discrimination in favor of French continues to be a serious problem, undermining the educational system established under British rule. The majority of the inhabitants of the region speak over two dozen languages belonging to the Grasslands group of Southern Bantu languages. English is widely used as an intergroup language.

Officially the majority of the Southern Cameroonians are Christians, both Protestant and Roman Catholic. Smaller groups adhere to traditional beliefs, particularly in the less accessible areas of the highlands, and there is a small Muslim population in the north. Many of the religious traditions combine customs and rituals from all three traditions.

NATIONAL HISTORY: Thought to have originated farther to the north, the Bantu tribes moved into the highlands to escape Muslim invaders in the eleventh century. Over several centuries numerous small chiefdoms emerged, often warring among themselves. Some 90 of the small tribal states united in the fifteenth and sixteenth centuries to form a powerful confederation in the southern highlands. The confederation began to decline in the eighteenth century, its disintegration hastened by the secession of the Bamoun states.

The early European presence was confined to the coastal ports and the acquisition of slaves. British explorers, pushing inland from the slave ports, made contact with most of the kingdoms by the early nineteenth century. Despite its considerable influence among the highland tribes in the region, the government of the United Kingdom made no colonial claims. Malaria prevented significant European settlement or conquest until the late eighteenth century.

During the late eighteenth and early nineteenth centuries, Fulani Muslims from the north raided the region, seeking slaves and loot. Many of the Bantus fled south and west to the less accessible areas of the highlands. The slave trade, both among the coastal Europeans and the northern Muslims, was largely suppressed by the mid-nineteenth century.

Christian missions established a presence in the late nineteenth century. The mostly English-speaking missionaries converted many of the inhabitants to Christianity but also, more importantly, established mission schools and introduced modern education. Christian missionaries continue to play a role in the region.

In 1884 several chiefs signed a protectorate agreement with German explorer Gustov Nachtigal, laying the foundation for Germany's annexation of what it called the Kamerun colony. German rule, specifically its forced labor and curtailment of the powers of the traditional chiefs, incited sporadic rebellions up to World War I. Taken by British troops from Nigeria when war broke out in 1914, German Kamerun was partitioned between Britain and France in 1916. In 1922 the allied powers established mandate governments under the auspices of the new League of Nations. The boundary between the two mandates, drawn without consideration for the region's traditional frontiers, gave the French control of three-fourths of the former German colony. The British mandate covered two regions—Northern Cameroons, mostly Muslim, and Southern Cameroons, more advanced and with a Christian elite. The two Cameroon mandates developed completely independent of each other. The two territories, under different administrative systems and using different languages, had little in common except the divided Bamileke-Tikar-Bamenda ethnic community and a shared past as a German colony.

After World War II, the Cameroon mandates were renewed under the auspices of the new United Nations as trust territories in 1946. The Southern Cameroonians again protested the colonial division, which cut through several tribal groups. The British and French authorities met in Kumba in May 1949 and again in December 1951 to work out a program that would satisfy Southern Cameroonian demands, but the sides failed to reach an agreement.

Following a 1953 constitutional crisis, the southern and western regions of the British Cameroons were divided; the Northern Cameroons was incorporated as a region of Nigeria, while the Southern Cameroons was included in Nigeria's Eastern Region. In 1954 the representatives of the Southern Cameroons demanded a separate government. The region was then constituted as a federal territory, with its own legislature, in 1954.

Planned independence for the French Cameroons, announced in 1958, stimulated a discussion on the future of the British Cameroons. The prime minister of the Southern Cameroons, John Ngu Fonchu, went to the UN in 1959 expressly to ask for time to prepare the territory for complete independence before exploring the question of unification with either Cameroon or Nigeria. The UN refused the option of independence, believing that the territory would be a financial and economic liability. The refusal was in violation of the UN Charter, which guaranteed automatic full independence for all trust territories.

An antigovernment rebellion against the domination of the Muslim north, which was favored by the French authorities, erupted among the Bamilekes*, who straddled the border between the two Cameroons. The smaller Bamileke population in the British mandate supported the rebellion, but the violence was restricted to the French zone. The Bamilekes and other groups, divided by the mandate boundaries, pressed for unification of the Cameroon mandates.

On 11 February 1961 the inhabitants of the British Cameroons voted on the future of the territory, although the only options on offer were union with Nigeria or with Cameroon. In Northern Cameroons the mostly Muslim population voted in favor of joining neighboring Nigeria, while the Southern Cameroonians voted, mostly on ethnic grounds, to join the newly independent Republic of Cameroon, the former French mandate. In 1962 the southern part of the British trust territory joined Cameroon within a new Federal Republic of Cameroon. On 1 October 1961 the former British Southern Cameroons became the federated state of West Cameroon, and the French-speaking Republic of Cameroon became the state of East Cameroon. Each state had its own prime minister and legislature, sharing only a joint presidency. In 1966 all political parties were outlawed, except that of the francophone government, the Union National Camerounaise.

Ahmadou Ahidjo, a French-educated Muslim Fulani, was chosen president of the federation with the votes of the French-speaking majority. The federation functioned fairly well until February 1972, when Ahidjo, following a referendum favored by the francophone majority, unilaterally discarded the federal constitution and abolished all federal legislative, judicial, and administrative institutions. A new constitution removed all Southern Cameroonian autonomy and established a unitary state in Cameroon. Regional leaders protested the change but had no legal means of fighting the virtual annexation in May 1972 by the larger French-speaking East Cameroon. West Cameroon was divided into two new provinces, Northwest and Southwest. Government policies pressed assimilation and the political subjugation of the anglophone region.

President Ahidjo resigned as president in 1982 and was succeeded by Paul Biya, from the southern Bulu-Beti ethnic group of French Cameroon. Opposition in the western provinces to the increasingly autocratic Biya government formed around the English-speaking elite in the early 1980s, particularly following the official change of name to La République du Cameroun, in 1984. Most of the groups advocated a return to the former federal system that allowed the anglophone provinces considerable cultural, political, and economic autonomy. More militant groups supported a demand for complete separation and the independence of the former Southern Cameroons voiced by the leadership of the Ambazonia group in 1985. The confiscation of land and its auction to companies associated with the Biya government aggravated the situation in the late 1980s.

Cameroon's turn toward democracy, demanded by international aid donors following the end of the Cold War, rekindled old tribal and regional tension. Violence flared between the francophone supporters of the government and the increasingly marginalized anglophones. The introduction of multiparty politics led to an escalation of Southern Cameroonian opposition. In 1989, a newly formed group, the Cameroon Anglophone Movement, collected thousands of signatures from the region's elite to legitimize a push for anglophone rights. The rights issue became even more important following the discovery of oil on the Bakassi Peninsula on the Nigerian border.

Supposedly free elections, held in October 1992, polarized Cameroon and fueled the nascent Southern Cameroonian national movement, allied to the largely antigovernment Bamilekes of the western provinces of francophone Cameroon. The government responded by placing the western provinces under emergency military rule, but it failed to stem the growth of the Southern Cameroonian national movement based on the distinct culture and the English language of the region. President Biya won flawed multiparty elections in 1992 and 1997.

In early 1993 rumors that the English-speaking Southern Cameroons were preparing to secede circulated amid a wave of strikes and disruptions that accompanied demands for the return of a federal system and guarantees of language and minority rights. The national movement greatly affected Cameroon's richest area in the English-speaking western provinces. After 1992 the continuing confrontation pitted French-speaking gendarmes against the English-speaking Southern Cameroonians, adding language to the volatile mix of ethnic tension and economic problems.

Regional leaders, at meetings in Buea in April 1993 and Bamenda in May 1994, intensified their demand for a return to federation. The Bamenda declaration stated that should the Cameroon government either persist in its refusal to engage in meaningful constitutional talks or fail to engage in such talks within a reasonable time, the anglophone leadership would proclaim the revival of the independence and sovereignty of the Southern Cameroons. The nationalists, including nonelected and retired politicians, clergy, *fons*, and chiefs, formed the Southern Cameroons Advisory Council, which plays an advisory role to the growing national movement.

An informal referendum was held in the two western provinces from 1 to 30 September 1995. Ignored by the central government, dominated by the more numerous French-speaking Cameroonians, nationalists took their case to the UN in 1995. They presented a petition against the virtual annexation of their homeland by the francophone majority and asked the world body to correct the error of the 1961 union and to honor Article 76 of the UN Charter and grant the Southern Cameroons independence as a former trust territory. The petition continues to languish, awaiting a hearing by the UN Security Council.

A new constitution, adopted by the Cameroonian government in 1996, further eroded anglophone influence in the state. Nationalists organized an informal referendum on independence; over 85% of the adult respondents supported independence through a negotiated constitutional separation from Cameroon.

Militants attacked government facilities in Northwest Province during rioting in March 1997. Over 300 were arrested; most were later released, but of the 75 that remained in custody, six subsequently died of abuse or lack of medical care. There are reports of a number of dead and wounded in violent confrontations. In 1999 the Cameroonian government set up a military tribunal to try 87 nationalists arrested between 1995 and 1997. The majority of the nationalists were sentenced to lengthy prison terms after a blatantly unfair trial conducted entirely in French.

On 30 December 1999, Justice Alobwede Frederick Ebong formally proclaimed the restoration of Southern Cameroons sovereignty and independence. He and other nationalists leaders were arrested and later condemned to death for treason. The independence declaration was condemned by many Southern Cameroonian groups as premature and illegal; the arrests and condemnations led to widespread protests and increasing nationalist activities.

Following large pro-independence demonstrations in Buea and Limbe in January 2001 hundreds of Southern Cameroonians were arrested. The two western provinces remain under the virtual occupation of the state security forces. The highly mobilized and active Southern Cameroonian national movement is dedicated to regaining autonomy or failing that, separation from Cameroon, but they stress that they will pursue a peaceful, legal campaign.

SELECTED BIBLIOGRAPHY:

Asuagbor, Greg. *Democratization and Modernization in a Multilingual Cameroon.* 1998.

Krieger, Milton H. *African State and Society in the 1990s: Cameroon's Political Cross-roads.* 1998.

Mukong, Albert, ed. *The Case for Southern Cameroons.* 1990.

Nkwi, P., and B.F. Nyamnjoh, eds. *Regional Balance and National Integration in Cameroon.* 1997.

Southern Mongols

Inner Mongolians; Mongols of the Forty-Nine Banners

POPULATION: Approximately (2002e) 6,110,000 Southern Mongols in China, concentrated in the Inner Mongolia Autonomous Region, with smaller communities scattered across northern China, particularly in Xijiang Uyghur Autonomous Region and the provinces of Qinghai and Gansu.

THE SOUTHERN MONGOL HOME-LAND: The Southern Mongol Homeland, popularly called Southern Mongolia, occupies a vast inland plateau of rolling grasslands in north-central China between the border with the Republic of Mongolia and the Great Wall, a massive structure originally built to protect central China from nomadic Mongols and other peoples to the north. Most of the region is agricultural, with few industrial centers. The region forms the Inner Mongolia Autonomous Region of the People's Republic of China. *Nei Monggol Zizhiqu/ Inner Mongolia Autonomous Region (Southern Mongolia)*: 454,633 sq. mi.—1,177,499 sq. km, (2002e) 24,776,000—Han Chinese 74%, Southern Mongols 20%, Hui*

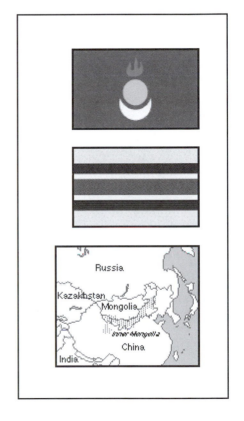

4%, other Chinese 2%. The Southern Mongol capital and major cultural center is Hohhot, called Khokekhota by the Southern Mongols and Kukuhoto by the Northern Mongols, (2002e) 724,000, metropolitan area 1,038,000. Other important cultural centers are Baotao, called Bozhen by the Mongols, (2002e) 697,000, metropolitan area 1,246,000, and Chifeng, called Ulanhad, 255,000, metropolitan area 470,000.

FLAG: The South Mongolian national flag, the flag of the Inner Mongolian People's Party, is a blue field bearing the *soyonbo*, an ideogram of mystical symbols—a red flame, a yellow sun, and a white crescent moon. The traditional Southern Mongol flag, the flag of the former Southern

Mongol federation, is a yellow field bearing a centered horizontal red stripe bordered by narrow white stripes inside wider pale blue stripes.

PEOPLE AND CULTURE: The Southern Mongols are the descendents of the historical Forty-Nine Banners of Inner Mongolia, mostly belonging to the Chahar, Bairin, Khorchin, Kharachin, and Ordos (Tumet) tribes. The tribes are organized in six leagues—Huna in the north, Khingan in the center, Qirin in the southwest, Jooda in the south, and Chahar and Silingol in the southeast. The name Inner Mongolians is often applied to all the Mongols in China, including the historically distinct Eastern Mongols* of the northeastern districts of Inner Mongolia. Assimilation, official policy since 1947, has progressed rapidly in some regions, although a re-culturation, begun in the 1980s has begun to reverse the growing threat to the survival of the Southern Mongol culture.

LANGUAGE AND RELIGION: The Southern Mongols speak a variant of Khalkha Mongolian called Peripheral, or Inner, Mongolian. The language, also called Southern-Eastern Mongolian, shows a clear Chinese influence. The language is spoken in four major dialects—South Mongolian, Ordos, Chahar, and Harachin—and a number of subdialects. The Chinese majority has mostly settled in the area in the twentieth century, particularly after World War II. The Mongol language was banned for use in education in 1957 but was reinstated for primary education in 1973. Southern Mongolians who are unable to speak Mandarin Chinese are now considered illiterate. The Southern Mongolian language is written in the standard Inner Mongolian script.

The Southern Mongols adhere to Mahayana Buddhism, also called Tibetan Lamaism. As in Tibet the dalai lama is revered as the spiritual leader. Traditional Mongol beliefs were shamanistic, involving an unseen world of gods, demons, and spirits. Shamans were depended on to cure the sick, communicate with the spirits, and control daily events. In the late 1500s Tibetan Buddhism was introduced, and most Southern Mongols embraced the new faith, although they retained many of their shamanistic traditions. About half the Southern Mongols, after decades of Marxist teachings, are either atheists or nonreligious. Many younger Southern Mongols are returning to the animist beliefs of their forefathers.

NATIONAL HISTORY: Historically the region marked the boundary between the settled agriculturists and the nomadic steppe tribes. Originally occupied by the Chahar and Tumet tribes, the immense plains south of the Gobi Desert were often overrun by other nomadic Mongol tribes. Tribal wars and raids on the settled peoples to the south brought the tribes into conflict with the ancient Chinese Empire. To contain the fierce Mongol peoples, several states of the North China Plain combined their efforts in 658 B.C. to construct an enormous defensive wall, the Great Wall, which extended some 1,500 miles along the northern border of the empire. The massive construction was finally completed in 204 B.C.

Genghis Khan, the ruler of a small tribe called the Mongols, extended his rule over neighboring tribes and in 1206 A.D. established the first unified Mongol state. The establishment of the Mongol Empire brought prestige and expanded trade to the southern Mongols tribes. A Mongol army, built into an efficient fighting force around a core of highly mobile cavalry, eventually conquered most of the known world, from the east coast of China to the Danube River.

The Mongol Empire disintegrated into several successor states in the late thirteenth century. A Mongol dynasty, the Yuan, ruled all of China from 1271 until the Mongols were finally expelled in 1377–78. Hostility to the Mongols helped to unite China under successive Chinese dynasties. When the disintegration reached the Mongol heartland, the Southern Mongols united in a loose confederation of leagues (principalities), the Forty-Nine Banners of Inner Mongolia.

The Manchus, a Tungus people from the northeast, conquered the Southern Mongol confederation in 1635. The Manchus then moved south to conquer China in 1644. The conquered Southern Mongol lands were added to Manchu China, effectively separating Inner and Outer Mongolia. To counter continuing Mongol resistance to Manchu rule, the emperor issued a decree that promised the Mongols of the Forty-Nine Banners renewed independence, under their own laws, should there be a change of dynasty in China. The Manchus organized Inner Mongolia into "banners" and leagues, and promoted trade through itinerant merchants.

Han Chinese immigration to the provinces of Outer China, the provinces populated by non–Chinese minorities, remained restricted until 1878. In that year, to relieve severe land pressure the Manchu government opened the borderlands to Chinese settlement. Sporadic violence and resistance accompanied the colonization of Inner Mongolia in the 1880s and 1890s.

In 1904 the Mongol demonstrations turned to rioting, which spread across the region, with attacks on immigration offices and Chinese settlements. Both the Russians and Japanese enlisted Mongol mercenaries as auxiliaries during the Russo-Japanese War of 1904–1905. Serious antigovernment disturbances continued up to the revolution that overthrew the Manchu dynasty in 1911. Northern, or Outer, Mongolia, under Russian influence, was declared independent of China in 1912.

In 1915 the Russian and Chinese governments, opposed to Mongol sovereignty, forced several Mongol leaders to sign the "Kiakhta Agreement," which effectively divided historical Mongolia between the two states. The Mongols of the Forty-Nine Banners, invoking the seventeenth-century Manchu decree, informed the new Chinese republican government of their intention to secede. The government refused to recognize the decree and dispatched troops to suppress the national movement. In 1916, 24 of the Southern Mongol princes presented a memorandum to the government stating that unless the Manchu dynasty was restored, they would secede, under the Manchu decree. Savage Chinese reprisals depopulated entire principalities.

The Japanese, in control of neighboring Manchuria from 1931, encouraged resurgent Mongol nationalism in the 1930s. To counter Japanese influence, the Chinese government granted autonomy to Inner Mongolia in 1932. The Japanese took control of Eastern Mongolia, historically part of Manchuria, in 1933. Taking advantage of chaotic conditions in China, the Southern Mongols declared the historical principalities of the Forty-Nine Banners autonomous on 23 April 1934. On 8 December 1937, in advance of the Japanese invasion of China, the Southern Mongolian Prince Teh Wang proclaimed independence and signed a cooperation agreement with neighboring Manchukuo, the Japanese-dominated state of the Manchus.*

In January 1938 the Japanese took control of the region and imposed a Japanese-dominated government on the region. The Mongols of Xinjiang joined a regional revolt in 1944. The puppet Mongol state collapsed with the Japanese defeat in 1945. A Mongol army of 80,000 moved south from the communist Mongolian People's Republic to occupy the region. Welcomed as liberators from both the Japanese and the Chinese, the Mongols drove out the last of the Japanese forces and held off both sides in the widening Chinese civil war. The Southern Mongols erected a provisional government and organized a referendum on unification with Mongolia. The Chinese communists, embroiled in the civil war, appealed to their ally, the Soviet Union. Joseph Stalin asserted his influence with the Mongolian government, effectively blocking Southern Mongol unification with Mongolia and forcing the withdrawal of the Mongol army from Inner Mongolia.

The Chinese communists moved into the region in 1947, quickly suppressing the Southern Mongol nationalist movement and killing or displacing tens of thousands. As part of the communist nationalities policy, a theoretically autonomous Inner Mongolian region was created for the Southern Mongol people, and in 1949 the government granted the region the hypothetical right to secede from China.

Despite official policies of cultural autonomy, the communist government pressed assimilation and the sinicization of the Southern Mongols. Many national customs were prohibited, and the Mongol dialects were discouraged. Government-sponsored immigration soon made the Mongols a minority in their traditional homeland. In 1947 only 14% of the population of Inner Mongolia was Han Chinese. By 1951 the Southern Mongols in Inner Mongolia were outnumbered two to one; in 1957 they numbered only one in every eight; and in 1980 they constituted just one out of every 17 people.

The pluralist language policies of the late 1940s were felt by the Chinese government to have contributed to the segregation of the nationalities in China. In 1957 the Communist Party banned the use of the Southern Mongol language and writing system. Primary education using the Mongol language was ended, and all schools were ordered to teach only in Mandarin Chinese.

The ecological consequences of the massive population transfer devastated local life. Many Southern Mongols were forced to give up their nomadic way of life and adopt the farming existence of the Chinese settlers. Lush pasturelands were overfarmed to the point of turning into desert. Nuclear testing further poisoned the environment.

Southern Mongol nationalism reemerged during the destruction and violence of the Cultural Revolution in 1966–67, but strict censorship kept details from reaching the West. Buddhist monasteries were vandalized, and most of the Buddhist priests disappeared during the Cultural Revolution. Any display of Mongol culture was used as evidence of Southern Mongol separatism. For over a decade the region remained under tight government control, with all signs of dissent quickly eradicated. Wearing traditional Mongol robes rather than the conformist "Mao suits" was dangerous, and public meetings in the Mongol language were forbidden. On the pretext that the Southern Mongols were preparing to fight for independence, hundreds of thousands of Red Guards were sent to the area. According to Communist Party documents revealed in 1981, between 20,000 and 50,000 Mongols were killed, 120,000 were tortured and maimed, and 790,000 were arrested.

The situation improved only in the early 1970s, when the Southern Mongols were officially recognized as one of China's ethnic minorities. Demonstrations against the communist government began again with a student protest in 1981 in Hohhot against those responsible for the deaths and destruction of the 1960s and 1970s.

The turbulence of the collapse of communism in neighboring independent Mongolia in 1990–91 and the crushing of the democracy movement in China gave the resurgent nationalists new impetus. In March 1992 details leaked out to the West of growing unrest and nationalist demands for the government to honor the promise made in 1949 to allow the Southern Mongols to secede from China if they wished. In April 1994, over 4,000 national leaders signed a letter to Beijing protesting against the policies of the Communist Party and the Chinese People's Liberation Army.

The increasing pollution of the Southern Mongol homeland includes the dumping of nuclear waste from all over China and from Germany and other European countries. The disposal of the wastes has become a lucrative sideline for the army, which controls the disposal sites, as well as many other industries in the region. In 1987, government troops oversaw the arrival of 4,000 metric tons of nuclear waste from West Germany. Over strong local protests, this first large foreign consignment was buried in the Gobi Desert.

The Chinese authorities began a crackdown on antigovernment activity in the region in 1991. Cultural groups, environmentalists, and antinuclear organizations were grouped with the nationalists and targeted for repression. Since 1995, the nationalists have absorbed many of the groups, including strong environmental and antinuclear wings. The Inner Mongolian People's Party was formed as an umbrella group in 1997.

The Southern Mongol nationalist movement remains small in number, poorly equipped, loosely united, and geographically dispersed. Militants based in Europe and the United States remain its most active sector. Support within Inner Mongolia is ambivalent at best, given the economic situation and memories of the Cultural Revolution and the mass starvation of World War II. The nationalists increasingly encompass environmentalists, anti–nuclear testing groups, religious organizations, and opponents of the recently imposed limits on the number of children. Moderate nationalists work for more autonomy, as promised in the Chinese constitution. Severe floods struck the region in August 1998, renewing grievances that the region remains neglected and underdeveloped.

In the 1990s, the Southern Mongols formed a close political alliance with the Tibetans* and Uighurs.* Representatives of the three nations participated in a peace march in the northwestern United States in March 1998. The marchers, beginning in Portland, Oregon, on 10 March, walked north across the state of Washington, stopping often to address curious crowds and fellow walkers or to accept invitations from colleges and universities to talk about the situation of non–Han Chinese in China. On 20 April 1998 Americans, Canadians, Tibetans, Southern Mongols, and Uighurs participated in a ceremony at the "peace arch" on the international border between the United States and Canada.

Demonstrators marching in Hohhot and other cities in September 2001 were reportedly arrested by security forces. The demonstrators demanded language and cultural rights, and economic development to match that of the pampered provinces of China's east coast.

SELECTED BIBLIOGRAPHY:

Amitai-Preiss, Reuven, and David O. Morgan. *The Mongol Empire and Its Legacy.* 1998.
Kessler, Adam T. *Empires beyond the Great Wall: The Heritage of Genghis Khan.* 1997.
Rahul, Ram. *Mongolia, between China and the U.S.S.R.* 1989.
Sneath, David. *Changing Inner Mongolia: Pastoral Mongolian Society and the Chinese State.* 2000.

Southern Sudanese

Anyidis; Imatongese

POPULATION: Approximately (2002e) 7,500,000 Southern Sudanese in Sudan, including over a million refugees in Northern Sudan, with hundreds of thousands of refugees also in the adjacent states of Ethiopia, Kenya, Uganda, and the Democratic Republic of the Congo. Outside the region many Southern Sudanese refugees have been admitted for resettlement in the United States, Canada, several European countries, and Australia and New Zealand.

THE SOUTHERN SUDANESE HOME-LAND: The Southern Sudanese homeland occupies a vast region in the southern part of Africa's largest state, the Republic of the Sudan, south of the 13th parallel. The region, traversed by the White Nile and its tributaries, is characterized by the Great Sudd Swamp and extensive rain forests. During the rainy season much of the region becomes swampland, with channels of deep water running through it. Southern Sudan has no official status; it embraces the Al-Istiwa'iyah (Equatoria), A'Ali An'Nil (Upper Nile), and Bahr al-Ghazal (Bahr-el-Ghazel) provinces of Sudan. *Southern Sudan (Imatong)*: 250,215 sq. mi.—648,053 sq. km, (2002e) 6,775,000—Southern Sudanese 88%, Northern Sudanese 11%, other Sudanese 1%. The Southern Sudanese capital and major cultural center is Juba, (2002e) 147,000. Other important cultural centers are Wau (Waw) (2002e) 106,000, and Malakal, (2002e) 93,000.

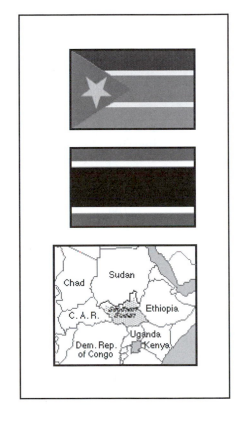

FLAG: The Southern Sudanese national flag, the flag of the national movement, is a horizontal tricolor of black, red, and green, the stripes divided by narrow white stripes, bearing a pale blue triangle at the hoist charged with a large five-pointed gold star. The flag of the proposed Southern Sudanese republic is a black field bearing narrow red and white stripes on the bottom and top.

PEOPLE AND CULTURE: The name Southern Sudanese is an inclusive name given to the varied peoples who live in the three southern provinces of Sudan. The Southern Sudanese peoples, although they are marked by physical and many common cultural features, encompass a large number of black African tribes closely related to the peoples of the neighboring countries, but not to the Arabs and Arabized peoples of northern Sudan. The major Southern Sudanese tribes include the more numerous Nilotic peoples who make up about three-fifths of the Southern Sudanese population in the northern districts—the Dinkas, Nuers, Shilluks, and Anauks. The Dinkas are the largest group, making up about 40% of the regional population. The Nilo-Hamitic tribes live in the south, the Bari,* Murles, Didingas, Boyas, Toposas, Lotukos, Mundaris, and Kabwes. Sudanic tribes are concentrated in the southwest—the Azandes, Kreisch, Bongos, Moros, and Madis. Most of the Southern Sudanese are river people, inhabiting the fertile lowlands along the White Nile and its tributaries. The tribal groups are divided into clans, which often cut across tribal lines. Intermarriage between tribal groups is common. Ties to ethnic communities are deeply rooted and are not forgotten, even by those who flee to northern urban centers. A distinct Southern Sudanese national identity has developed only since the 1950s.

LANGUAGE AND RELIGION: The majority of the Southern Sudanese people speak English as a lingua franca, as 32 major languages are spoken in the region. Most of the languages belong to the Eastern Sudanic branch of the Nilo-Saharan language group; Niger-Congo languages, such as Zande, are spoken in southern Equatoria. The largest of the regional languages, Dinka, serves as an intertribal language over much of the northern districts of Southern Sudan. The largest of the other regional languages are Moru, Avokaya, Baka, Didinga, Kakwa (Bari), Lango, Lopit, Toposa, Zande, spoken in Equatoria; Nuer, Shilluk, Murle, Anauk, and Atuot, and spoken in Upper Nile; and Luwo (Luo), the major language in Bahr al-Ghazal.

Most of the tribes retain traditional beliefs, with a large and influential Christian minority. The Christians, converted by European and American missionaries, benefited from missionary education and now form the political and cultural elite in the region. Animist beliefs revolve around an all-powerful spirit, with various tribal names, who is regarded as the creator of all things. Sorcery and divination remain powerful elements of the region's pre-Christian beliefs.

NATIONAL HISTORY: The region has been inhabited since ancient times. Egyptian slavers raided the tribes of the region, which they called the "Land of the Slaves," as early as 2800 B.C. The present tribal population is believed to have begun settling in the region before the tenth century A.D. They remained divided into tribal groups, engaging in intertribal warfare and cattle raids. Protected by formidable natural barriers and having little contact with the outside world, the tribes retained a nomadic existence adapted to the annual migrations of their cattle herds, the local measure of wealth.

Islam was introduced to the tribes of Northern Sudan in the seventh century, gradually becoming the dominant religion of the region. The koranic ban on enslaving Muslims led to raids on the pagan black tribes to the south. Many of the tribes fled farther south to the relative safety of the swampy lowlands along the lower Nile.

Muslims from the north, searching for slaves and ivory, began to penetrate the swampy Sudd in the 1840s. Slave raids depopulated many regions, as whole villages were captured and sent north into slavery. The Arabs slavers were followed by European explorers who claimed the region on behalf of colonial empires. In 1874 the United Kingdom decreed an end to slavery and launched military campaigns against the Arab gangs that had already devastated many tribes.

During the European scramble for African colonies, the British, French, and Belgians became interested in present-day southern Sudan. In 1892, the French occupied Bahr al-Ghazal and the western Upper Nile up to the town of Fashoda, now called Kodok. By 1896 they had established a firm base. The French intended to annex the region to French Sudan in central-west Africa. Conflicting European territorial claims brought Britain and France close to war in 1897. Two years later Britain's territorial claim was confirmed by international agreement.

Favoring indirect rule, through the traditional tribal leaders, the British separated the region from the Arab-dominated northern districts of Sudan. Although the Sudan officially remained a unified territory under its own colonial administration, the southern districts were governed as effectively separate territories. The separation of northern and southern Sudan was the result of acute and irreconcilable geographical, political, and cultural differences. In 1928 the last of the southern tribes to resist British control submitted.

Separate ordinances of government in the South laid the foundation for complete separate educational, socioeconomic, and political development as well as a strict control on the issue of passports and permits for traveling between northern and southern Sudan. Educational opportunities offered the Southern Sudanese were never in Arabic-speaking Khartoum but in English-language institutions in Britain's eastern and southern African colonies. The colonial language policy approved English as the official language of the South and adopted tribal languages such as Dinka, Nuer, Bari, Latuka, Shilluk, and Zande as regional languages. Administratively the region was closer to the neighboring British territories of Kenya and Uganda than to the Muslim North.

At the end of World War II, the British administration convened the Sudan Administrative Policy conference in Khartoum in 1946. The conference created an advisory council for northern Sudan, but the same resolution recommended that the South remain under colonial rule for another 10 to 15 years should the North opt for independence. The resolution was rejected by the northern Sudanese. The Southern Sudanese were not represented at the conference.

Tribal leaders united in 1950 to form the Southern Liberation Party, which advocated federal status within Sudan and an equal share of the development programs. Southern resistance to Arab domination became a major impediment to Sudanese independence in the early 1950s. The British authorities continued to favor a plan to give the Southern Sudanese an opportunity to decide their own future. Under intense pressure from the oil-rich Arab states, the British government finally agreed to the integration of the southern provinces in a unified, independent Sudanese state, in spite of the impassioned opposition of the region's tribal leaders.

On 15 August 1955, amid rising tension, the Southern Corps, the local militia formed under British rule, mutinied, killing its Arab officers and several hundred Arab civilians. The mutiny set off anti-Arab violence across the southern region of the Sudan. In spite of the growing crisis, Sudan became independent in 1956; the British transported 8,000 Muslim troops to the south in Royal Air Force planes. The troops of the Southern Corps, although assured of safe conducts by the British, were rounded up and tried in Muslim courts. Many were executed by firing squads, and thousands more imprisoned.

The Arabized northern Sudanese–dominated new Sudanese government, viewed by many in the South as the new colonial power—refused all concessions to Southern Sudanese self-rule. The rebellion spread across the south as the region's many tribes united against domination by the Muslim, Arabized northern Sudanese. The conflict was the result of the arbitrary colonial boundaries that brought together two fundamentally different ethnic and religious groupings. The war also stemmed from the chronic underdevelopment of the South and the government exploitation of its natural wealth, which includes oil.

The rebel forces split in the early 1960s along tribal lines, and the national movement splintered into a number of rival groups. The largest organization, the Sudan People's Liberation Movement (SPLM), led by John Garang and supported by the majority Dinka and Nuer tribes, attempted to create an independent state in 1969. Sudan's Arabic rulers finally agreed to Southern Sudanese autonomy and a regional parliament in 1972, ending over a decade of civil war.

Relations between the Southern Sudanese and the government deteriorated rapidly following the division of the region into three separate provinces in 1981, a clear violation of the autonomy agreement. In late 1983 the government abrogated the 1972 autonomy agreement and officially extended strict Muslim shari'a law to the South, ending the last vestiges of Western law and justice. Rebellion again erupted in the region, which, with only 17 miles of paved roads, quickly declined into a premodern condition.

The rebels, in control of all but the main towns by 1987, were unable to provide for the civilian population. In the first five years of the renewed rebellion over two million fled the fighting, leaving behind over 250,000 dead of starvation and disease. Southern leaders accused the Sudanese government of blocking international aid in order to terrorize and starve the southern region into submission. A government scorched-earth policy displaced hundreds of thousands of civilians, aggravating the food crisis.

The lack of tribal unity, a major obstacle to final victory, led to serious splits in the rebel ranks in late 1991, mostly between factions favoring autonomy and their opponents advocating an independent Southern Sudan. The tribal splits involved not only such tribes as the Toposa, armed by the Khartoum government, but the two largest ethnic groups, the Dinka and the Nuer. Several rival nationalist groups emerged from the movement's factional rift, and heavy fighting often broke out between rival groups.

The Southern Sudanese rebellion, which had continued for all but 10 of the years since Sudanese independence in 1956, was originally launched to win equality and autonomy for the southern tribes, but by the early 1990s the conflict had became a war of survival for the beleaguered Southern Sudanese. In March 1992 a government offensive, the largest in decades, pushed south on four fronts, aided by the split in the rebel leadership.

In September 1993 the neighboring states of Ethiopia, Eritrea, and Uganda acted as mediators in talks between the government and the southern leaders. The negotiations collapsed almost as soon as they opened, over continuing Southern Sudanese demands for their own government. In February 1994 the government launched an offensive across the southern provinces. The advance, adding to the chaos already created by the southern factional fighting, created another 150,000 refugees, bringing the estimated number of refugees to 4.5 million. The conflict, complicated by the tribal factionalism in the South, continued to widen the gap between the two halves of Sudan.

The success of the government offensives and the continuing factional fighting among the Southern Sudanese forces nearly led to the collapse of the rebellion in 1995. Some factions went over to the government, further complicating the political situation in the region. The rebel leadership, faced with defeat, reorganized and sought alliances among their former enemies fighting the Islamic government.

Seven northern opposition groups forged an alliance with the Southern Sudanese and the Nuba* to form the National Democratic Alliance in late 1995. None of the dissident organizations or rebel national groups were strong enough to overthrow the National Islamic Forces alone; the alliance was a precarious grouping of widely differing aims and ideologies, including northern political parties that had participated in former Sudanese governments and had fought the Southern Sudanese rebels.

In April 1997 five rebel factions opposed to the SPLM signed an agreement in Khartoum to end the civil war. The agreement provided for a four-year transition government in Juba, followed by a referendum on the future of the South. The government agreed that Southern Sudanese would no longer be subject to shari'a Muslim law and would exercise legislative rights based on their traditional tribal laws. The agreement also provided for an amnesty and the repatriation of thousands of refugees. The agreement was rejected by John Garang of the SPLM. The Sudanese government demanded in February 1998 that fighters of the five groups that signed the peace accord lay down their arms. Despite the signing of the accord, the Sudanese parliament in March 1998 approved a draft constitution, its first since 1984, asserting that Sudan was a unitary state in which Islam was the state religion. Most of the groups rejected further contact with the Sudanese government.

The stalemated war, by the late 1990s, was an ongoing crisis of cease-fires, peace negotiations, shifting alliances, and massive suffering. Two successive poor harvests and the continuing displacement of hundreds of thousands of refugees produced yet another food crisis in early 1998. Malnutrition in some areas reached 30–40% of the population. The war brought not only famine and disease but the resurrection of slavery, as Baggaras, Muslim, Arabicized nomads from northern Sudan, armed by the Islamic fundamentalist government, rampaged through the devastated region enslaved thousands of Dinkas and stealing food aid. The numerous cease-fires have not covered activities by the government-armed militias, to which the Sudanese government deny any link. By 1999, the number of deaths as a result of the war was estimated at over two million.

In March 1999, Omar el Bashir, president of Sudan, faced with rebel advances in several areas, regional isolation, and a declining economy, reversed decades of its policies toward the South by accepting the idea of separation of Southern Sudan. A government spokesman announced that a referendum on self-determination would be held in Southern Sudan before the end of an interim period agreed to by all parties. The leaders of the rebel groups dismissed the statement as yet another maneuver in one of the world's longest-running wars. Many Southern Sudanese felt that after decades of fighting, massacres, famine, and suffering, it had become impossible for the Southern and northern Sudanese to coexist in a unitary Sudanese state.

When oil began to flow from fields in the northern districts of Southern Sudan in 1999 the Sudanese government, which had exploited divisions between the largest of the Southern Sudanese tribes, the Nuers and Dinkas, began a new policy of expelling or exterminating the non-Arabic populations in and around the oil-producing centers. Offensives by the Sudanese army and the paramilitary militias renewed fighting in many areas in 2001. Southern Sudanese rebels attacked the oil-producing areas, claiming the government uses oil revenues to buy weapons.

The referendum on independence, agreed to by the Sudanese government in 1994, remains just a promise. In 2001–2 the rebels hold 80% of the southern provinces, but the government is slowly persuading neighboring states to end support of the rebel groups. The so-called holy war, decreed by the Sudanese government, has fizzled due to unwilling conscripts and a military structure overburdened with officers whose only credentials are Islamic piety.

SELECTED BIBLIOGRAPHY:

Daly, M.W., and Ahmad Alawad Sikainga, eds. *Civil War in Sudan*. 1993.
Lesch, Ann Mosely, ed. *The Sudan: Contested National Identities*. 1999.
O'Ballance, Edgar. *Sudan: Civil War and Terrorism, 1956–1999*. 2001.
Petterson, Donald. *Inside Sudan: Political Islam, Conflict, and Catastrophe*. 1999.

Southerners
Dixielanders; Rebels; Confederates

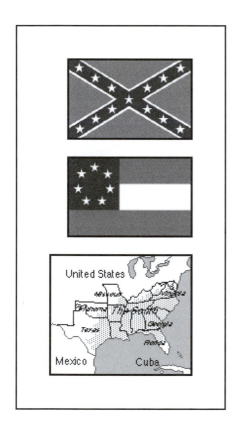

POPULATION: Approximately (2002e) 46,000,000 Southerners, based on the number of people who consider themselves by heritage and culture to be Southerners. Southerners are concentrated in the southeastern United States, in the region known as the Deep South, with smaller communities in the neighboring states of Texas and the Middle or Upper South.

THE SOUTHERN HOMELAND: The Southern homeland, popularly called Dixie or the South, lies in the southeastern United States, a region of indefinite boundaries usually considered to be bounded on the north by the Mason-Dixon Line. The region, the most populous region of the country, stretches from the temperate zone in the Mid-Atlantic states of Virginia and North Carolina and includes a wide variety of climatic and topograpical zones, including the fertile cotton and crop lands, the tropical areas in Florida and along the coast of the Gulf of Mexico, and the vast cattle lands of western Texas. The South, defined by the states that seceded in 1861, includes Alabama, Arkansas, Florida, Georgia, Louisiana, Mississippi, North Carolina, South Carolina, Tennessee, Virginia, and Texas. A wider definition of the South also includes the states of Maryland, the District of Columbia, Kentucky, West Virginia, Delaware, Oklahoma, and Missouri. *The South (Dixie/Confederate States of America 1861):* 752,178 sq. mi.—1,948,132 sq. km, (2002e) 71,188,000—Southerners 60%, black Americans 16%, other Americans 24%. The major Southern cultural centers are Dallas and Houston in Texas, Miami, Jacksonville, and Tampa-St. Petersburg in Florida, Atlanta in Georgia, Norfolk and Richmond in Virginia, New Orleans in Louisiana, Charlotte in North Carolina, Nashville and Memphis in Tennessee, Birmingham and Montgomery in Alabama, Jackson in Mississippi, Little Rock in Arkansas, and Charleston in South Carolina.

FLAG: The Southern national flag, the former battle flag of the Confederacy, is a red field bearing a blue saltaire outlined in white bearing 13 white stars. The other popular Southern flag, which is often used by those opposed to the negative image of the battle flag, is the so-called Stars and Bars, which has three vertical stripes of red, white, red, bearing a square blue canton charged with 7 white stars.

PEOPLE AND CULTURE: Southerners are considered one of the major branches of the American nation, being the descendants of the original European settlers of the southern colonies established by settlers from the British Isles in the seventeenth and eighteenth centuries. By far the largest of the three original Anglo-American cultural areas, the South has always been the most idiosyncratic with respect to national norms. Although there are great regional differences between the inhabitants of the vast area, the cultural heritage of the Deep South remains the focus of modern Southern culture. Southern culture is still observable in almost every realm of activity, including the rural economy, regional dialects, diet, folklore, politics, architecture, recreation, and social customs. Only in the twentieth century has material culture and economic activities begun to converge with the rest of the country. The Texas subregion is so large, distinctive, self-assertive, and vigorous that the Texans* have acquired so strong and divergent an identity that Texas is now considered a separate region. The name Dixie stems from the bank notes issued in New Orleans in 1860 and used largely by the French-speaking residents that were imprinted with dix, French for 10, leading to the adoption of the name Dixies, or Dixie Land, which was applied to the Louisianans and eventually to the whole South.

LANGUAGE AND RELIGION: The Southerners speak standard American English, but have retained a number of regional dialects grouped together as Southern. The dialects vary greatly from the soft cadences of Virginia to the twang of the Appalachian accents to the distinct regional speech of Louisiana. The dialects, greatly influenced by the speech of the former black slaves, resulted from the interaction of the English-speaking colonists and the need to adapt their speech to that of their workers.

Southern religion, mostly based on Protestant sects, but with sizable Roman Catholic and Jewish minorities, remains one of the pillars of Southern society. The so-called Bible Belt, the fundamentalist Christian heartland of the middle South, has influenced attitudes to religion and its core influence across the region.

NATIONAL HISTORY: The vast and fertile region was occupied by a number of materially advanced tribal peoples when the first European settlement was established at Jamestown in Virginia in 1607. The first settlers were almost purely of British stock, not outwardly different from those who settled in New England or the Middle Atlantic, but in terms of motives and social values and more conservative in retaining the rural values and the family and social structures of premodern Europe.

The South's climate, coupled with abundant rainfall, offered seventeenth- and eighteenth-century European settlers an opportunity to raise lucrative crops for export if an adequate permanent labor could be found. The source of this labor was found, slaves made available for purchase through the international slave trade. From this unique situation arose the plantation system which above all distinguished the South from the other regions of the United States. By 1790, black slaves and freemen constituted about a third of the total Southern population and almost the entire workforce. The adaptation to a starkly unfamiliar physical habitat, accentuated the South's deviation from other culture areas.

Historically Southerners such as George Washington and Thomas Jefferson dominated politics in the early years of the United States, which was established following the Declaration of Independence in 1776 and Southerners predominated among the signers of the Declaration. Southern intellectuals and political leaders claimed that the Constitution of 1787 established a compact of sovereign states rather than a unitary nation-state, a controversary that led to a widening rift between North and South in the nineteenth century.

The North's early nineteenth century development was characterized by free labor, commercial vigor, and agricultural diversity while the South remained tied to the slave economy and cotton. By the 1850s the question of the extension of slavery into the western territories was the central issue uniting the North and bringing it into conflict with the South. On the eve of the Civil War there were 19 free and 15 slave states, the boundary generally following the Mason and Dixon Line, the Ohio River, and except for Missouri, lay below latitude 36°30'. Only about a sixth of white Southerners were slaveowners.

Economically the cotton-producing South looked to the British textile industry for its market and opposed the growing politico-economic power of the industrializing North. The Southern social identity remained based on a rural slave-owing gentry, presenting a sharp contrast with that of the North, for it stressed a genteel, aristocratic lifestyle rather than one based on the perceived accumulation of money.

In the period between the American Revolution and about 1830, the North passed from mild opposition to strong condemnation of slavery and the Southern plantation system. In response, white Southerners rose to defent their "peculiar institution," supporting it on the ground of biblical teachings, economic necessity, the supposed racial superiority of whites, and the necessity of a well-ordered and secure society.

Southern separatism in defense of states' rights and slavery culminated the secession of 1860–61. Following the election of Abraham Lincoln in 1860 the gulf between the North and South widened. Secession swept the region, first with several states of the Deep South seceding, but by October 1861 the new Confederacy consisted of 11 states and recognized delegations from Missouri and Kentucky. The Civil War, fought from 1861 to 1865, was fought by Southerners defending slavery as well as states' rights. During the Civil War, called by Southerners the War between the States, officially neutral Maryland and Kentucky contributed over 200,000 troops to the Southern cause although many state officials were imprisoned and held without trial. The Confederacy was aided by the Five Civilized Tribes that had been driven from their homes to Indian Territory in Oklahoma, the Cherokees,* Choctaws, Seminoles, Chickasaws, and Creeks.

The Civil War was the first to target civilian populations in an attempt to destroy the ability of the South to resist. The devastation of whole regions to deny support to the Southern army wrought immense damage to croplands, lost livestock, and burned towns and cities. It took four years of grim, unrelenting warfare and enormous numbers of casualties and devastation before the Southerners could be defeated in April 1865. The war ended with near half a million dead and a legacy of bitterness and defeat in the South that lasted for a century.

Economic and cultural recovery was very slow, hampered by military occupation and imposed state governments. The birth of the Klu Klux Klan, which was organized in an effort to reassert Southern control of the region, dates from the 1880s and included many Confederate war veterans. Eventually the Klan, like many other organizations, became identified with racism and violence. The Southerners' continued insistence on the inferiority and subordination of blacks through a system of legalized racial barriers known as Jim Crow laws resulted, particularly when the Reconstruction ended with the withdrawl of Union troops in 1877, in the replacement of slavery with black sharecropping, the political system of one-party politics, and the social and racial segregation supported by law and custom. Southern blacks were gradually disenfranchised and forcibly segregated within the larger Southern society.

The South voted as a block from the 1850s to 1970, when Southerners began to see that the Democratic Party was becoming dominated by Northern liberals. Many Southerners turned to the Republican Party as the only alternative, but by the early 1990s many were also disillusioned with Republican policies. Small nationalist and pro-heritage groups began to win support with their policies of nonracial nationalism and pride in the Southern cultural and historical heritage. As early as 1948, the governor of South Carolina, Strom Thurmond, ran for the presidency of the United States on the State Rights Party (Dixiecrat) ticket.

Until the early 1930s the South remained an impoverished and undiversified region. Chronic overproduction of cotton, with attendant low prices, forced many farmers, both black and white, into sharecropping between 1880 and 1930. The Great Depression of the 1930s led to a total bankruptcy of the cotton industry, which was not relieved until federal New Deal legislation intervened to provide payments for reducing cotton acreage and for unemployed cotton workers. Migration to the cities, a trend that accelerated during World War II, greatly changed the traditional rural character of the South. After World War II the South began to experience a sustained surge in growth and industrialization.

Efforts to end the traditional racial segregation of the South was prompted by the 1954 U.S. Supreme Court decision that public school segregation was unconstitutional. The civil rights movement in the 1960s polarized the South as blacks registered to vote and liberals from the North, many university students, came to the region to aid in the voter registration and to march in civil rights demonstrations. The movement proved a catalyst with the racism of the Old South giving way to a more moderate majority and to desegregation of the region's schools and other institutions. The adoption of the Civil Rights Act of 1964 and the Voting Rights Act of 1965 institutionalized the advances in black rights and profoundly altered the biracial system that had been in place throughout the century since the end of the Civil War.

Population growth remained slightly above the national average after 1940 but was almost twice the national average after 1970. In contrast to earlier decades when out-migration was the answer to underdevelopment, by the 1960s the South was experiencing a net in migration. Consistant with population growth, urbanization, and industrialization, per capita incomes increased rapidly for both whites and blacks. Politically the traditional Democratic control of the South disappeared, with Republicans coming to power in many Southern states.

In the late 1990s, several states reopened civil rights murder cases thirty years later. Most of the momentum to reopen the cases comes from a defiant group of young Southern lawyers and prosecutors, determined to discover the truth before time puts the suspects beyond reach or completely erodes the evidence. Many of the new Southern generation grew up when the passions of the civil rights movement were still fresh in people's minds. The cases are also easier to investigate now. In the 1960s, the Klan and similar organizations were still very powerful and violent and many witnesses feared death or retaliation.

In the 1990s, several nationalist organizations, including the Southern Party, garnered considerable attention throughout the region. Looking to the example of the Parti Québecois in Canada and the Scottish National Party in the United Kingdom, the Southern Party (SP) and other political groupings advocated home rule for the South with eventual independence through a democratic referendum. Several of the Southern political organizations, including the Southern Political Alliance (ASP), a loosely organized confederation of Southern political parties, have branches in all of the Southern states and also among Southern communities in the North and in the western United States.

The question of displaying the Southern flag, the former battle flag of the Confederacy, generated considerable controversy in 1999–2002. Several of the states of the Deep South either displayed the flag along with their state flags or the symbol had been incorporated into the state symbols after the Civil War. Many black organizations, led by the National Association for the Advancement of Colored People (NAACP), demanded that the Confederate symbols be eleminated as they represented racial discord and the legacy of slavery. Marchs, counter-marches, and heated arguments surrounded the discussion on the state symbols of South Carolina, Georgia, and Mississippi and the flying of the Confederate flag throughout the region. A massive NAACP boycott of South Carolina tourism ended when the South Carolina government agreed to take down the Confederate battle flag that flew alongside the state flag above the dome of the state house in Columbia on 1 July 2000. Many black Southerners claim that displaying the Confederate flag is a symbol of racism and slavery while nationalists denounced the NAACP campaign against the flag as "cultural genocide." Nationalists lament the use of the flag by racists and radicals, which makes it a symbol of hate to many across the South.

In 2000, nationalists urged Southerners to write Southerner in the ethnic classification of the national census and to extend the practice to any government, school, or corporate form that asks for ethnic or national identity. Nationalists want Southerners to be accepted as a national minority. Southern nationalists want to overcome the negative image of Southern nationalism projected by such white supremacist groups as the Klu Klux Klan or the Aryan National Front and to appeal to the sentiments of black Southerners. Nationalists claim that their heritage is being given away in the name of political correctness.

A small number of nationalists sighed a Declaration of Southern Cultural Independence in March 2001, describing it as the first step in what they hope will be the second secession of the South. More moderate nationalist groups advocate home rule for Dixie with less interference from the federal government.

In April 2001, voters in a referendum in the state of Mississippi decided to retain their state flag, which includes the Confederate battle cross, unlike similar votes in South Carolina, Florida, and Georgia. Mississippi, America's poorest state, is now the only Southern state to retain the old battle cross as part of its state flag. The old Confederate battle flag has taken on a post–civil rights symbolism revered by conservative Southerners as the symbol of their history and culture, while black Southerners detest the flag as an antiquated symbol of slavery. In most cases throughout the South, pressure from white businessmen has been as great as that from black politicians. The conflict over the flag is often seen as a rearguard action in the long battle between mostly rural white traditionalists and the urbanized proponents of the New South.

Literally and symbolically, Southerners have been defined as being in opposition to America. From the historical realities of slavery and the Civil War, Reconstruction, and the Jim Crow laws to the myths and symbols of the current debates over the meaning of the Confederate battle flag. Southerners find themselves, or place themselves, at odds with the understood meaning of America itself. Southerners remain keenly sensative to the attitudes and relations with other Americans, who adopted aspects of Southern culture that appealed, like Coca-Cola, but rejected many aspects of Southern culture that define the distinctive and important region. As William Faulkner observed, the past is never ending down there.

SELECTED BIBLIOGRAPHY:

Goldfield, D.R. *The South for New Southerners*. 1991.
Grammer, John M. *Pastoral and Politics in the Old South*. 1999.
Kirby, Jack Temple. *The Counterculture South*. 1996.
Wilson, C.R. and Willian Ferris, eds. *The Encyclopedia of Southern Culture*. 1989.

Suvadivians

Huvadu

POPULATION: Approximately (2002e) 63,000 Suvadivians in the Maldive Islands, concentrated in the three southernmost atolls of the archipelago. There are Suvadivian communities in the northern Maldives, particularly around the capital, Male, and in southern India and Sri Lanka.

THE SUVADIVIAN HOMELAND: The Suvadivian homeland lies in the southern Maldive Islands, a chain of about 1,300 small coral islands in the Indian Ocean. Suvadiva comprises the most southerly atolls of Attu (Addu), Suvadiva, Fua Mulak, and Haddummati, renamed following the Suvadivian rebellion in the late 1950s. The Maldive Islands are one of the smallest and poorest states in the world. The atolls lie about 275 miles (443 km) south of Male and some 400 miles (644 km) southwest

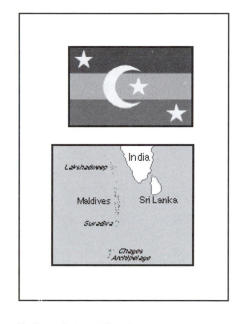

of Sri Lanka. The atolls are made up of many small, low-lying islands in three clearly defined groups. None of the islands is more than six feet (1.8 meters) above sea level. Barrier reefs protect the islands from the destructive effects of the yearly monsoons. "Atoll" is a local word adopted by Europeans to describe a cluster of small islands around a central lagoon. Suvadiva has no official status; the region comprises Gaaf Alif (Suvadiva North Huvadu) and Gaaf Dhaal (Suvadiva South Huvadu), Siin (Attu/ Addu), Gnaviyani (Fua Mulaku), and Laam (Haddummati). *Suvadiva*: 30 sq. mi.—78 sq. km, (2002e) 66,000—Suvadivians 96%, other Maldivians 4%. The Suvadivian capital and cultural center is Thinadhoo, called Suvadiva locally, (2002e) 6,000. Other important cultural centers are Hithadhoo, (2002e) 11,000, and Fuvahmulah, (2002e) 8,000.

FLAG: The Suvadivian national flag, the flag of the national movement, is a horizontal tricolor of blue, red, and green bearing a large white crescent moon and a five-pointed star centered and small white five-pointed stars on the upper hoist and lower fly.

PEOPLE AND CULTURE: The Suvadivians are the descendents of early

Sinhalese migrants from Sri Lanka. The Suvadivians, unlike other Maldivians, have retained much of their ethnic heritage as they rarely intermingle with other groups. While the northern Maldivians are of mixed Indian, Sinhalese, and Arabic descent, the Suvadivians remain primarily of Sinhalese descent. The majority of the population lives by fishing, as fish abound in the reefs, lagoons, and waters around the islands. Sea turtles are also caught for food and for their oil, a traditional medicine. Only about 20 of the Maldivian Islands have more than 1,000 inhabitants, making the southern atolls the most densely populated in the country. The population is spread across a large area of the Indian Ocean.

LANGUAGE AND RELIGION: The Suvadivians speak a dialect of Dhivehi, a Sinhalese language akin to the Elu, or Old Sinhalese, that is spoken throughout the Maldive Islands. Dialect differences between the Suvadivian dialect as spoken in the four southern atolls are pronounced, as the dialect retains more of the original Sinhalese brought by early settlers than the dialects spoken in the northern Maldives. English is also spoken in the islands, and it is taught in primary schools.

The Suvadivians are Sunni Muslims, living in one of the most restrictive Muslim states in the world. Many Suvadivians, particularly on the more remote islands, retain their animistic practices, trusting charms, mantras, and *fandita*, or spirit men, to protect themselves from evil spirits. The spirit men protect their occupations by using Islamic terms and chanting Arabic-sounding incantations. The Maldives have one of the highest percentages of divorce in the United Nations; some 85% of all marriages end in divorce. Many people have up to 10 spouses, and marriage vows are casual.

NATIONAL HISTORY: The atolls were settled by migrants of unknown origin in ancient times. The island group was probably known to the ancient seafaring peoples of South Asia, but the first mention of them appears in chronicles of traders from the Indian mainland and Ceylon, later called Sri Lanka, in the second century A.D. The atolls, sparsely inhabited and of little interest to outsiders, remained isolated from the major trade routes farther north.

The Buddhist islanders were converted to Islam by Arab traders who brought the new religion to the northern Maldives in 1153. Many of the Arabs remained in the northern atolls, where they mixed with the local population. Islam gradually spread to the Suvadivian atolls, displacing the Buddhism originally brought from Sri Lanka. The Didi clan, of Arab descent, eventually ruled the entire Maldive chain.

European navigators visited the region in the fifteenth century. The islands held out little interest for the explorers, who were looking for spices and trade. The most lasting effect of the European visits were diseases brought by the sailors. The local populations, with no immunity to the alien diseases, were often devastated.

In the sixteenth and seventeenth centuries the atolls suffered raids by pirates from the Malabar Coast of southeastern India. The sultan of the Maldives in the late 1600s sought the protection of Dutch forces in Ceylon. The Dutch sent ships to protect the islands but also placed them under Sinhalese authority. Sinhalese islanders from Ceylon settled in colonies throughout the archipelago. In the north they mixed with the Maldivians, but in the southern atolls, which had few indigenous inhabitants, they formed the majority and eventually absorbed the original population. Isolated and self-sufficient, the Suvadivans of the southern atolls thereafter remained of nearly pure Sinhalese descent, rarely mixing with outsiders or with the Maldivians of the north. Their culture and dialect remained intact.

The Maldive group came under British control during the Napoleonic Wars, when the Netherlands was absorbed by the French and the British assumed the task of keeping the French from taking over the Dutch colonial possessions. In 1796, British forces occupied Dutch Ceylon, which had controlled the Maldive Islands. The British presence was very slight, and in the southern islands life continued in its traditional way. In 1815, when Europe was reorganized at the end of the Napoleonic Wars, the British retained control of Ceylon and the Maldives. In 1887 the British formally proclaimed a protectorate over the sultanate of the Maldives.

At the outbreak of World War II, the British built a naval and air base on Gan Island in the southernmost atoll of Attu. The base brought employment and relative prosperity to the inhabitants of the atoll, and its influence spread throughout the southern islands. The based was closed at the end of the war in 1945.

The British authorities proposed to reactivate the base on Gan in 1956. The Maldivian protectorate government resisted the move, claiming that it violated Maldivian neutrality. Nonetheless the British reopened the base, supported by the Suvadivians, who benefited from the British presence in their islands. A Maldivian government representative sent to order the Suvadivians to stop working for the British was attacked. The inhabitants of the southern atolls rebelled and threw off Maldivian control. The rebel leader, Abdallah Afif, declared the southern Maldives independent as the United Suvadivian Republic on 18 January 1958.

The Suvadivians requested British recognition of their new state and sought military aid. The British government refused to recognize the secessionist government, but as relations with the Maldivian government were strained, it sent material aid to the islands, which roused strong feelings in the northern Maldives. Negotiations between the British and Maldivian governments continued through 1959 and 1960, finally coming to an agreement that gave Gan Island to the British in exchange for the British withdrawal of assistance to the rebel republic and military help in suppressing the Suvadivian rebellion.

In March 1960, Maldivian government troops invaded the atolls of Suvadiva and Haddummati but did not interfere with the British occupation of Attu. The Suvadivan government collapsed with the end of British assistance in 1962. Abdullah Afif fled to the then British colony of Seychelles, where he was granted political asylum. The islands were placed under the rule of a committee under the sovereign control of the Maldivian sultan. The last rebels surrendered on the more remote islands in 1963.

The Maldive Islands gained full independence on 26 July 1965, setting off a period of unrest in the Suvadivan atolls. The Maldives became a republic in 1968, following the military overthrow of the sultan. In 1976 the British gave up the base on Gan and their radio installations in the other islands; the Suvadivans thereby lost 800 jobs and their major source of outside revenue. In 1977 the Soviet Union tried to negotiate the use of the Gan base (which was near the U.S. base on Diego Garcia in the Chagos Archipelago), but the Maldivian government declined.

In the 1980s the Suvadivans proposed to reactivate the former Royal Air Force base on Gan as an airport, in order to attract tourists, but the proposal was put aside following an attempted coup in the Maldivian capital, Male, in 1988. The Maldivian government requested Indian military aid to repel the rebels, whose origins were unknown. The threat to the Maldivian power center and the lack of direction from the national government revived demands in the southern atolls for greater control of their homeland and its resources, including the former British base.

Power in the Maldives remains in the hands of a small, wealthy elite based in Male, in the north, a fact that is much resented among the Suvadivians of the south. The Maldive Islands are fairly prosperous, with one of the highest per capita incomes in South Asia, but because of a rapidly growing population, particularly in the southern atolls, with a large fraction under 20 years of age, frustration is growing with the conservative, elitist government in Male.

Increasingly the Suvadivians are going their own way rather than waiting for decisions to be made hundreds of miles to the north. The need for rapid economic development to keep up with population growth, according to local leaders, requires greater local control over resources and decision making. Another local concern is a projected long-term rise in the sea level, which would prove disastrous to the low-lying coral islands.

SELECTED BIBLIOGRAPHY:

Gayoom, Maumoon Abdul. *The Maldives: A Nation in Peril.* 1998.
Kelly, Robert C. *Country Review: Maldives 1998/1999.* 2000.
Maloney, Clarence. *People of the Maldive Islands.* 1980.
Ngcheong-Lum, Roseline. *Maldives.* 2000.

Swabians

Schwäbisch; Suabians; Suevians

POPULATION: Approximately (2002e) 8,851,000 Swabians in Germany, mostly in southwestern states of Baden-Württemberg and Bavaria, where about 1.7 million Swabians reside. Sizable Swabian communities live in Berlin and other areas of the German Federal Republic. Outside Europe there are large Swabian populations in the United States, Canada, and South America.

THE SWABIAN HOMELAND: The Swabian homeland, Schwaben in German, lies in southwestern Europe, a fertile region drained by the Rhine (which forms the international border between Germany and France), the upper Danube, and the Neckar Rivers. The southern districts are mostly rolling hills and include the Black Forest, the Lake of Constance (the Swabian Sea), and the Swabian Jura Mountains. Much of the region is forested, although the river valleys, particularly along the Rhine, are among the most fertile regions in Europe. The territory known as Swabia is divided; most of it is included in the German state of Baden-

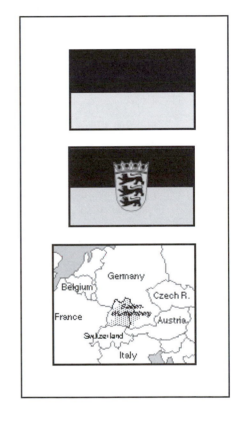

Württemberg, and the smaller eastern region is part of the state of Bavaria.

State of Baden-Württemberg (Land Baden-Württemberg): 13,803 sq. mi.—35,750 sq. km, (2002e) 10,584,000—Swabians 88%, Bavarians* 8%, French 2%, other Germans, Turks, Spaniards, Italians, Portuguese 2%. The Swabian capital and major cultural center is Stuttgart, (2002e) 578,000 (metropolitan area 2,336,000). Other important Swabian cultural centers are the Badenese capital of Karlsruhe, (2002e) 279,000 (metropolitan area 584,000), and Augsburg, (2002e) 254,000 (metropolitan area 419,000), the leading city of Bavarian Swabia.

FLAG: The Swabian national flag is a horizontal bicolor of black over yellow. The official flag of Baden-Württemberg is the same black over yellow bicolor with the addition of the coat of arms, a yellow crowned shield bearing three black lions.

PEOPLE AND CULTURE: The Swabians are a southern German people related to the Bavarians, the Alsatians,* and the Swiss-Germans. The Swabian nation includes four historically distinct divisions—the Swabians in the center, the Badenese in the west, the Franconians in the north, and the Eastern Swabians in Bavaria. The Swabian groups, although historically divided, are united by culture and language. The Swabians tend to be more blond and Nordic than other southern Germans, although culturally they have much in common with the neighboring Germanic peoples. The Swabian culture has many borrowings from the French due to close geographical proximity. In the 1980s and 1990s younger Swabians took a new interest in their culture and dialects, which were quickly declining.

LANGUAGE AND RELIGION: The Swabian language is a group of related High German dialects spoken in southwestern Germany. The language is more distinct than Bavarian from standard German and is only about 40% intelligible to speakers of standard German. Swabian is spoken in two major dialects, Black Forest and Alpine, while a closely related dialect, Alemannic or Alemannisch, is spoken by the Badenese in the west. The western dialects of Swabian blend into Alemannic, most of the dialects being mutually intelligible. Swabian and Alemannic differ from other German dialects in not having undergone the second *lautverschiebung*, or vowel change. The Swabians can be readily distinguished by their characteristic pronunciation of both the Swabian dialects and standard German. A Swabian dictionary was compiled in the early 1990s, followed by Swabian-German, Swabian-English, and Swabian-French dictionaries. Standard German has replaced the dialect as the first language in the urban areas, although the dialects remain the language of daily life in the home and in rural areas.

Religiously the Swabians are divided; Protestants are concentrated in the northern districts, Roman Catholics in the southern districts and Bavaria. Secular life has led to a sharp decline in religious participation in the region, although in the Alps and the Black Forest traditional religious beliefs still form an important part of daily life.

NATIONAL HISTORY: The Celtic-populated region was colonized as part of the Roman Empire when the tribes of the Black Forest were finally subdued in A.D. 83. The decline of Roman power allowed the Germanic Alemanni tribe to occupy the region in the first and second centuries A.D while still under Roman rule.The Suevi (or Suebi) later migrated to the area. The mingling of the peoples evolved a unique Germanic-Celtic-Roman culture, which flourished under nominal Roman rule in the third and fourth centuries.

One group of Suevi, allied to the Vandals and the Alans, continued south to conquer the Iberian Peninsula in 407. Absorbing the Hispano-Romans, they apportioned the territory among the various chiefs. By 411 the Suevi were established in northern Portugal and Galicia, and by 452 in Castile. They ruled the region until 469, when they were defeated by the Visigoths. Eventually they merged with the other peoples of the area and lost their distinct identity.

The Roman province remained stable until the fourth century, when pressure from Goths and Burgundians* forced the Suevi to expand westward. In 476, shortly after the fall of Roman power, the Alemanni tribes set up an independent state embracing present Alsace, most of Switzerland, and southwestern Germany. Farther east, the Suevi were conquered by the Franks under Clovis in 496; they formally remained part of the Merovingian and the later Carolingian Frankish empires until the ninth century. The Alemanni had come under Frankish rule in the sixth century, but Merovingian rule was not powerful, and Swabia was virtually independent by 689. It was brought under control in the 730s and 740s by Charles Martel, the founder of the Carolingian dynasty, who deposed the hereditary dukes of Swabia and subdivided the area into a number of counties.

Charlemagne's death in 843 was followed by the division of the empire between his three sons. By the Treaty of Verdun, the Carolingian lands were formally distributed; Swabia became part of the kingdom of Louis the German. The southern districts were included in the duchy of Swabia, and the north was added to the Franconian duchy. The entire Swabian region, known as Alamannia or Alemannia, became one of the five stem duchies of medieval Germany. The name, Aleman or Alemanni, is still used by the French and Spanish to mean "German." In 1079 the duchy, with its capital at Augsburg, was bestowed on the house of Hohenstaufen, which established the imperial dynasty in 1138. On the extinction of the dynasty in 1268, Swabia broke up into a number of small secular and ecclesiastic holdings and lost its political identity.

The most powerful of the Swabian regional states were Baden in the west and Württemberg in the east, while the Habsburgs gained control of Breisgau and other districts in the south in the fourteenth century. Most of the Swabian towns had obtained the status of free imperial cities, virtually independent city-states, by 1300. Their wealth, built on commerce and industry, made them the most powerful elements in the region. They consolidated their power in a series of leagues, starting in 1331. The Swabian League of 1376–89 successfully opposed the German emperor but was eventually defeated by the count of Württemberg. The most important Swabian League was that of 1488–1534, which was formed for the purpose of maintaining internal stability in the Swabian homeland. When the Holy Roman Empire was organized in "circles" in the sixteenth century, the Swabian Circle was created, with its capital at Augsburg.

The commercial revolution in Europe in the fifteenth and sixteenth centuries decreased the power of the imperial cities; international trade became more important than local agriculture or crafts. The activities of the Fugger and Welser banking families, based in Augsburg, made Swabia a center of trade between northern and southern Europe.

Most of the petty Swabian states, including the Habsburg fiefs, accepted the Protestant Reformation in the sixteenth century, but the countryside remained divided between Catholics and Protestants, as it has to the present. The area suffered a sharp loss of population during the religious wars that swept Europe, sending thousands of Swabians to settle Hapsburg lands newly reconquered from the Turks in southeastern Europe.

The French Revolution of 1789 forced the Swabian states to choose sides as Europe descended into war. Baden and Württemberg initially joined the allies fighting Napoleon and French expansion but were later forced by French forces to switch sides at the Peace of Lunéville in 1801. Napoleon in 1806 raised the duke of Baden to the status of grand duke, and the duke of Württemberg to the status of king. Most of the small Swabian ecclesiastic and feudal holdings were annexed, and the free imperial cities and small principalities constituting eastern Swabia were ceded to Bavaria. Baden and Württemberg again switched sides before Napoleon's final defeat and participated in the Congress of Vienna as victorious states. Massive Swabian migration to Eastern Europe in the 1820s and 1830s, particularly to Galicia and Bukovina, reinforced earlier German migrations to the Hapsburg provinces in eastern Europe.

Western, particularly French, influence in Swabia, always strong, resulted in the adoption of liberal constitutions in Baden and Württemberg. The social and cultural life of the Swabian states reflected their ties to the West, while conservative Prussia held sway in most of the German states. Anti-Prussian sentiment, which remains today, resulted from heavy-handed Prussian pressure to join the Zollverein, the German Customs Union, in 1835, and from the suppression of popular revolutions during the upheavals of 1848–49. Between 1849 and 1851 tens of thousands of Swabians emigrated to escape grinding poverty or domination by the hated Prussians. In 1866 Baden and Württemberg sided with the Austrians in the Austro-Prussian War and shared Austria's defeat. The south German states were forced to pay large indemnities and to sign military alliances with Prussia.

Prussian political influence increased, and in 1870 the Swabian states joined the North German Confederation, and a year later the Prussian-dominated German Empire. The Swabians fought as Prussian allies in the Franco-Prussian War of 1870–71, although many felt that they had more in common with the neighboring French than with the Protestant Prussians of eastern Germany. Prussia, with 65% of the German Empire's area and 62% of its population, was able to exert enormous pressure on the smaller German states. In 1890 the German Empire became more militaristic under the rule of Emperor William II, who was very unsympathetic to the Catholic-dominated southern German states.

The troops of Baden and Württemberg joined those of the other German states when war broke out in Europe in 1914. The Swabians, whose territory lay on the border with France, felt they would lose no matter who won the war, but with initial German victories war fever blunted Swabian misgivings. Following a French air raid on the Badenese capital, Karlsruhe, in 1916, however, the Badenese government attempted to secede from the empire and to negotiate a separate peace with the allies; they were prevented by Prussian troops. As defeat for the Central Powers loomed in October 1918, strikes and anti-Prussian rioting erupted across the region.

Strong movements for secession from Germany gained support, but in November the German government surrendered, throwing the nation into chaos. Revolution swept the region, and the rulers of Baden and Württemberg were deposed. Provisional republican governments were formed in Baden and Württemberg, which incorporated the formerly independent duchies of Hechingen and Hohenzollern-Sigmaringen. Political moves during 1918–19 toward a merger of the two states of Baden and Württemberg were unsuccessful, but they strengthened Swabian identity.

An attempted communist coup in Berlin had local repercussions as separatism again gained support. The French, who saw the breakup of the German Empire as a solution to their security problem, supported separatism in Baden and Württemberg, but in 1919 the two states, with governments dominated by moderate political parties, joined the new Weimar Republic. The new federation, like the former empire, was dominated by Prussia, and tension between the Prussians and the southern Germans, particularly the Swabians and Bavarians, was felt in all areas of political life. In 1921 membership in monarchist organizations was made a criminal offense.

The Swabians continued to oppose Prussian domination throughout the turbulent 1920s and 1930s. Anti-Prussian sentiment remained a strong ingredient in the Swabian nationalist movement, which continued until the early 1930s. The rise of the Nazis in Germany was also resisted. The Swabians, with their long tradition of stable democracy, included one of only five districts in Germany to elect stable, democratic parties to state governments in the postwar period. In 1933, when Adolf Hitler came to power, he sent in SS and SA troops to quell the remaining Swabian opposition, on the pretext that the Baden and Württemberg state governments were unable to maintain order. Many of the Swabian opposition leaders were sent to concentration camps, while others fled across the frontier into France. In the late 1930s, the Swabian majority, along with the other German peoples, supported Hitler's nationalist, anticommunist crusade. Air raids and heavy fighting in the northern districts devastated Swabia, especially the cities of Mannheim, Karlsruhe, and Heidelberg. In early 1945 Baden and Württemberg were occupied by French and American troops.

Following the German surrender, the states of Württemberg and Baden were placed under American and French occupation. On 6 December 1951 a referendum was held in four voting districts—North Baden, South Baden, North Württemberg, and South Württemberg-Hohenzollern. The Swabians voted 69.7% in favor of the creation of a new "South-West State." The largest vote against was in South Baden, where 62.2% voted in favor of the reestablishment of the two states of Baden and Württemberg. In 1952 the states were united to form the new state of Baden-Württemberg. Stuttgart, the Swabian capital since 1482, was chosen as the capital of the new, united Swabian state.

Swabia formed an important element in the postwar German economic recovery. The culture of the region in the postwar years became less Swabian and took on more of the pan-German culture. Standard German became the language of the cities. The industrialized cities of the region were rebuilt and were among the most prosperous in Germany in the 1960s and 1970s.

In the late 1970s, the Swabians began to take a new interest in their unique culture and dialects. Centuries of close contact with the French and other nations on their borders made the Swabians among the most enthusiastic about closer European integration in the 1970s and 1980s. The Swabian cultural revival and the growth of regionalist sentiment were reinforced by the rivalry between the northern and southern German states in the late 1980s. The Swabians, unlike the northern Germans, with their aging heavy industries and high unemployment, consistently had the lowest unemployment in Germany, and very high economic growth; only the Bavarians surpassed them.

The Swabians continue to press for more autonomy and a greater say in the European Union. Nationalists and regionalists cite the medieval Swabian Leagues as the model for a sovereign Swabia within united Europe. Swabians generally opposed moving the federal capital from Bonn to Berlin, fearing a return of Germany's former centralized government.

The German federation allows for considerable local autonomy, which has curtailed the growth of radical nationalism in areas with strong national identities. The Swabians, who built Baden-Württemberg into a powerhouse with their ingenuity and diligence, retain a sense of historical national identity and a powerful sense of local pride. Swabian politicians believe that the trend in Europe is shifting governmental power to regional and local levels as national borders are erased while the economy of Europe becomes united.

SELECTED BIBLIOGRAPHY:

Craig, Gordon A. *The Germans*. 1991.
Elias, Norbert, ed. *The Germans*. 1996.
Gress, D.R. *A History of West Germany, 1945–1988*. 1989.
Shlaes, Amity. *Germany: The Empire Within*. 1991.

Szeklers

Székelys; Székelyek; Szekely; Szekelars; Seklers; Secui

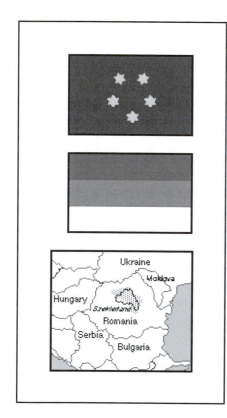

POPULATION: Approximately (2002e) 1,125,000 Szeklers in Romania, concentrated in the eastern Transylvanian counties of Covasna, Hargita, and Mures. Outside the region there are Szekler communities in neighboring Transylvanian counties and in Hungary.

THE SZEKLER HOMELAND: The Szekler homeland lies in eastern Transylvania, forming part of the Transylvanian Basin, where it rises to the Transylvanian Alps and the Eastern Carpathian Mountains. Szeklerland occupies the upper valleys of the Mures and Olt Rivers. Since the 1910 census, the number of Hungarian-speakers has decreased in all Transylvanian counties save those of the Szekler heartland. The Szekler homeland, called Székelyföld, forms the Romanian counties of Covasna (Kovászna), which is 75% Szekler; Hargita (Harghita), which is 85% Szekler; and Maros (Mures), 41% Szelker. *Szeklerland/Székely Region (Székelyföld)*: 6,542 sq. mi.—16,943 sq. km, (2002e) 1,163,000—Szeklers 61%, Romanians 33%, Germans 3%, Roms* 3%. The Szekler capital and major cultural center is Tîrgu Mures, called Marosvásárhely by the Szeklers, (2002e) 163,000. Other important cultural centers are Miercurea-Ciuc, called Csíkszereda (Szeklerburg), (2002e), 46,000, Odorheiu, called Székelyudvérhely, (2002e), 38,000, and Sfîntu Gheorghe, locally called Sepsiszentgyörgy, (2002e) 66,000.

FLAG: The Szekler national flag is a blue field bearing five six-pointed yellow stars centered. The traditional flag of the nation, is a horizontal tricolor of red, green, and white.

PEOPLE AND CULTURE: The origins of the Szeklers is a controversial question. According to their own tradition, they are the descendents of Attila's Huns. Historically the Szeklers were one of the three privileged nations of Transylvania. The Szeklers, who call themselves Székely, came into Transylvania either with or before the Magyars, the Hungarians. Their traditional organization and hierarchy was of the Turkic type, and the Szeklers were probably of Turkic origin, possibly related to the Avars.* The Szeklers remain a separate nation and are recognized by the Romanian government as a distinct national group. Historically the Szeklers were considered noble, thus owing military service to their rulers but not required to pay taxes. Their former military organization is still evident in the vestiges of the clan system that made up the Szekler nation. Originally there were seven territorial clans, each called a *szék*. The fiercely independent Hungarian-speaking Szeklers have retained their language, customs, and institutions from the late Middle Ages to the present. The Hungarian-speaking Csángós east of the Carpathian Mountains are closely related to the Szeklers, having been separated by Szekler migrations in the Middle Ages and in the eighteenth century.

LANGUAGE AND RELIGION: The language of the Szeklers is a dialect of Hungarian, which they adopted by the eleventh century. Their dialect, called Szekel, is the easternmost of the Hungarian dialects and contains many borrowings from Romanian, German, and Turkish. Many scholars consider the dialect so distinct from standard Hungarian that it could represent a separate branch of the Magyar language. It is not intelligible to speakers of standard Hungarian, which is also spoken by the Szeklers.

The Szeklers are mostly Protestant, having adopted the Reformation from neighboring German groups. As they have historically done, the Szeklers represent a bulwark of Protestantism in Eastern Europe. Szekler churches have traditionally formed the center of Szekler life, both secular and religious, and the core of a culture surrounded by an ethnically and dialectically different majority.

NATIONAL HISTORY: Historically the Transylvanian basin formed part of the Roman province of Dacia, where Latin culture and speech were predominant. From the third century A.D. the region was overrun by tribes moving into the weakened Roman Empire. Barbarian invasions destroyed Roman culture, but not the Roman's language, which became the basis of the later Romanian language. Magyar tribes, the ancestors of the Hungarians, are thought to have entered the region in the fifth century.

In the ninth century, the Szeklers, Turkic-speaking tribes, were known to have settled the valleys of eastern and southeastern Transylvania. It is not known whether they came into Transylvania with or before the Magyars. Szekler tradition tells that their ancestors fled east to settle in Transylvania following the Frankish defeat of the Avars in 797. Christianity was introduced to the Szekler tribes in the late ninth and the early tenth centuries. The first fortified parishes were established in the most important Szekler villages, which became important crossroads and the centers of religious life.

Transylvania, with its mixed population, was brought under the control of the Hungarian crown in 1003. By the eleventh century the Szeklers had adopted the Magyars' Hungarian speech. Wars with Bulgars and Petchengs forced the majority of the Magyar tribes to move farther west into present Hungary, leaving the Szeklers in the Transylvanian Basin to hold the eastern districts of the Hungarian kingdom. Autonomous Szekler settlements were established along the eastern frontier in the Mures and Olt Valleys in the thirteenth century. The Szekler clan organizations, covering seven districts, were under the leadership of a bailiff, the *ispán*, of all Szeklers. The bailiff represented the local power of the Hungarian kings. The general conclave of the Szeklers is first mentioned in royal documents in 1344.

The Hungarian administration of Transylvania was headed by a royal governor, a *voivode*. Society was divided into three privileged nations—the Szeklers, the Magyars, and the Saxons—and the nonprivileged class of serfs, mostly Romanian Vlachs. Following a Vlach peasant revolt in 1437, the three privileged nations renewed their historical alliance, and suppression of the Vlach peasants increased. The majority of the Szeklers formed part of the landed gentry, owning large estates worked by Vlach serfs, although a minority were urban dwellers.

The Szeklers, with their own military and civil organization, enjoyed broad autonomy under the Hungarian crown and were, without exception, regarded as of noble birth and exempt from taxation. In the sixteenth century, the majority of the Szeklers accepted the Protestant Reformation, most adopting Calvinism, while others became Unitarians or remained Roman Catholic.

The Turks defeated the Hungarians in 1526, and Transylvania was separated as an autonomous principality under Turkish protection. The Báthory family, which came to power in Transylvania in 1571 with Szekler support, ruled the region as princes under Ottoman, and briefly under Austrian Habsburg, suzerainty until 1602. In 1604 Stephen Bocskay led a rebellion against Austrian rule, and in 1606 he was recognized by the Austrian emperor as prince of Transylvania. Under Bocskay's successors Transylvania experienced a golden age as the bulwark of Protestantism in Eastern Europe and as the only European country where Roman Catholics, Calvinists, Lutherans, and Unitarians lived in relative peace and mutual tolerance. Only the Orthodox Vlach Romanians were denied equal rights.

The Turkish defeat near Vienna in 1683 increased Austrian influence in the region, and in 1699 the Ottoman Empire ceded Transylvania to the Austrians. A widespread Szekler revolt fought the creation of an Austrian civil government in the region. In 1711 the Szeklers were defeated, and Austrian control was firmly established in eastern Transylvania. The Austrians maintained the status of the three privileged nations, but during the eighteenth century their privileges declined. Austrian attempts to press the Szeklers into service as border militia met with widespread resistance. In

1763 a large number of Szeklers who sought to escape recruitment were massacred at Mádéfalva (Siculeni).

The revolutionary upheavals of 1848 were greeted in Transylvania by a proclamation of union with Hungary. The proclamation, supported by the Magyars and Szeklers, was opposed by the Saxons, the Vlach Romanians, and the Austrians. The Szeklers and Magyars promised the Romanians abolition of serfdom in exchange for their support, but the Romanians rejected the offer, and a revolt spread among the Romanian peasants. In the fighting that followed the Szeklers, led by Aron Gábor, were defeated in 1849 near Tîrgu Mures and lost their remaining autonomy and privileges. Austrian military rule, from 1849 to 1860, was disastrous for the Szeklers but greatly benefited the Romanian peasants, who were given lands confiscated from the defeated Szeklers.

Transylvania became an integral part of the Hungarian kingdom in 1867. The Romanian population, forming about half the Transylvanian population, having enjoyed brief equality under Austrian rule, were again reduced to the domination of the Hungarian-speaking military and land-owning classes. The growth of a particular Szekler national consciousness began following the imposition of Hungarian rule and evolved in the late nineteenth century. In 1879 the Székely National Museum was founded at Sfîntul Gheorghe, and a Szekler-supported Cultural Society of Transylvania was established in 1885.

In 1918, following the defeat of Austria-Hungary, the Szeklers, Magyars, and Saxons of Transylvania attempted to erect an independent republic to perpetuate their favored positions. The minority-dominated Diet of Transylvania declared the independence of the province on 28 October 1918, but the allies early in the war had supported Romanian claims. The Transylvanian Romanians on 1 December 1918 declared the union of Transylvania and Romania; Romanian troops invaded the region and suppressed the Szekler independence movement. By the terms of the Treaty of Trianon, Hungary formally ceded the entire region, including the seven Szekler districts, to Romania. Thousands of Magyars left Transylvania to settle in Hungary, but the Szeklers, seeing themselves as a separate nation, not as Hungarians, remained in their eastern Transylvania homeland.

The large Szekler estates were broken up, and holdings were limited to 300 acres, while those in the "old kingdom" of Romania were allowed up to 1,250 acres. In 1921 the Szeklers complained of Romanian suppression of thousand-year-old Transylvanian institutions by Orthodox officials sent from the East. In 1929 the government placed restrictions on language and religious rights in an attempt to assimilate the non-Romanian populations.

When World War II broke out both Hungary and Romania were allied to the Axis powers. In 1940, over strong Romanian protests, the Vienna Award gave Hungary about two-thirds of Transylvania, including the

Székelyföld, which again formed Hungary's eastern frontier. In 1944 war broke out between Hungary and Romania, facilitating Soviet occupation of both countries.

A communist government installed in Bucharest at the end of the war moved to integrate the non-Romanian minorities; however, a small autonomous region was created in 1952. The autonomous province, called the Magyar Autonomous Region, was superseded in 1960 by the Mures Magyar Autonomous Region, further divided in 1968 into two nonautonomous districts, Mures and Hargita. During the 1956 Hungarian Revolution there was rioting in Szeklerland in support of the revolutionaries. The demonstrations led to executions and imprisonment for the leaders, who were accused of separatist plotting.

In 1971 the Romanian government prohibited the use of the ancient place names and allowed only the Romanian names to be used. Decrees passed in 1974 undermined the foundations of Transylvania's Szekler and Magyar past. Hungarian-language schools and publications were forcibly closed.

During the 1980s, under Romania's communist dictator, Nikolai Ceausescu, new restrictions were placed on the non-Romanian minorities, and the government pressed assimilation. In October 1985 the government further curtailed Szekler cultural activities. The sorry state of the Romanian economy aggravated tension, as the Szeklers tended to be more prosperous than the majority Romanians.

In the late 1980s the Szeklers looked to liberalizing Hungary, as Romania remained under the Stalinist Ceausescu regime. Decades of oppression and communist mismanagement had impoverished the potentially prosperous area, but Transylvania remained the most advanced of the Romanian regions. In December 1989, government attempts to silence a Magyar Protestant minister in the city of Timisoara, in the southwestern region of Banat, sparked a revolution that spread rapidly across Transylvania and the rest of Romania. Fighting and violence accompanied the overthrow of the Ceausescu dictatorship, although the Szekler region remained relatively calm.

The end of the communist suppression opened the old disputes in eastern Transylvania and renewed Szekler demands for language, cultural, and religious rights. Romania's new president, Ion Iliescu, demonized the Hungarian-speaking minorities as a fifth column of the Hungarian government. The creation of ultranationalists Romanian groups, particularly Vatra, antiminority and anti-Semitic, contributed to the growing unrest. In March 1990 radical Romanian nationalists, formerly supported by the communist government, attacked Szeklers demonstrating for autonomy in the city of Tîrgu-Mures. The attacks were the most serious ethnic violence in the region since World War II. In 1992 the ultranationalists took 11%

in national presidential elections, winning most of their votes from Romanians in Transylvania.

The Szeklers, threatened by rabid Romanian nationalism and unable to count on the Hungarians of western Transylvania or the Hungarian government, increasingly developed their own national identity. Demands for a special status, with Szekler language and cultural guarantees, were sent to the Romanian government in 1995. Unlike the Hungarians and Germans of Transylvania, the Szeklers had no other homeland. Following local elections in 1998, the national movement split into two groups, the militants calling for autonomy and the creation of a Szekler homeland, and moderates favoring cooperation with other groups in Transylvania to achieve collective self-determination. The split led to the loss of the mayoralty in Tîrgu Mures to the rival Romanian candidate in 1999. A March 2000 poll showed that 85% of the Szeklers supported some form of autonomy but feared a repeat of the ethnic violence of 1990.

In late 1999, Romanian president Emil Constantinescu signed the Law on Restitution of Illegally Confiscated Agricultural and Forest Lands. The law was particularly significant for the Székely region, where 851 sq. mi. (2,205 sq. km) stood to be returned to the Szeklers of Covasna and Harghita Counties. New laws on language use, cultural rights, and self-government, pressed on Romania by the European Union (EU), also stood to benefit the Szekler nation.

The Hungarian government in mid-2000 reiterated its stance that the Transylvanian peoples historically connected to Hungary were not welcome to settle in Hungary. A new law, to be passed before Hungary joins the EU, would further restrict the rights of Hungarian-speaking minorities from neighboring countries to work or live in Hungary. However, in April 2001 the Hungarian government announced plans to extend protection to ethnic Magyars (including the Hungarian-speaking Szeklers) outside the borders of Hungary, making them elegible for education and health benefits, emploment rights, and other opportunities. In 2002 the Hungarian government plans to issue cards that would confer such rights, but not the right to vote, to non-Hungarian Magyars.

The Szeklers, among the most pro-European of the peoples of Eastern Europe, see integration in the continental federation as the salvation of their isolated homeland. The election of a new government in Romania in the autumn of 2000 was seen by the Szeklers as another inept group of ex-communists, but by late 2001 the economy had begun to recover and Romania's chances of joining the European Union improved considerably.

SELECTED BIBLIOGRAPHY:

Biro, Sandor. *The Nationalities Problem in Transylvania 1867–1940.* 1992.
Carta, Gabor, ed. *History of Transylvania.* 1994.
Gerard, Emily. *The Land beyond the Forest: Facts, Figures and Fancies from Transylvania.* 2001.
Laszlo, Peter, ed. *Historians and the History of Transylvania.* 1993.

Tabagonians

Tobagans; Tobagoans; Tobagonians

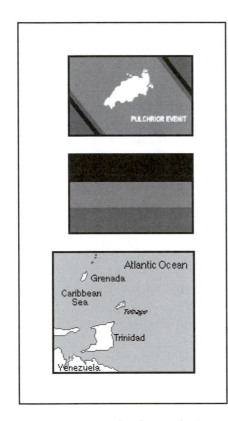

POPULATION: Approximately (2002e) 58,000 Tabagonians in the West Indies, concentrated in Tobago, a constituent part of the Republic of Trinidad and Tobago. Outside Tobago there are Tabagonian communities in Trinidad, the United Kingdom, the United States, and Canada.

THE TABAGONIAN HOMELAND: The Tabagonian homeland lies in the southeastern Caribbean, forming an extension of the chain of mountain-top islands that extends north from the South American mainland. The island has a volcanic ridge in the center, which gently slopes to the coastline. The dominant feature of the island is the mountains, particularly Main Ridge, an extension of Trinidad's North Range. *Island of Tobago (Republic of Tobago)*: 116 sq. mi.—300 sq. km, (2002e) 54,000—Tabagonians 88%, other West Indians 12%. The Tabagonian capital and major cultural center is Scarborough, (2002e) 2,000, urban area 9,000.

FLAG: The flag of the nationalist movement is a green field bearing red and black triangles on the lower hoist and upper fly, and with a centered yellow outline of the island and the Latin motto *Pulchrior Evenit*, meaning "She becomes more beautiful." The unofficial national flag is a horizontal tricolor of black, green, and red.

PEOPLE AND CULTURE: The Tabagonians are a West Indian nation, more closely related to the peoples of the islands to the north than to the Trinidadians of the larger island of the joint state. Primarily the descendents of the African slaves brought to the island by sugar planters in the eighteenth and early nineteenth centuries, the Tabagonians have developed a distinct island culture, part of the West Indian Creole culture, but with many unique traditions, foods, and customs. There are small numbers of East Indians, Europeans, Chinese, and people of mixed ancestry.

LANGUAGE AND RELIGION: The Tabagonians speak standard English, but the language of daily life is the Tabagonian dialect of Lesser Antillean Creole, the patois spoken in the Caribbean islands from the Virgin Islands south to Tobago, including St. Vincent, Antigua, Grenada, and other English-speaking islands. The Tabagonian dialect is classified as a Southern dialect of the Eastern group of the English-based Atlantic Creole group of dialects. Using many local words and forms, the dialect is intelligible only with difficulty to speakers of Trinidadian Creole.

The majority of the Tabagonians are Christians, mostly Roman Catholic or Anglican. Rastafarianism, popular on Trinidad, has some adherents on the island, but many continue to practice a particular island blend of Christianity and traditional beliefs brought to the island from Africa.

NATIONAL HISTORY: The island was inhabited by indigenous groups moving north through the Caribbean from the South American mainland. The original inhabitants, the Arawaks, were later conquered and absorbed by the more warlike Caribs. By the thirteenth century, the Arawaks had virtually disappeared on Tobago, while the Caribs regularly raided the remaining Arawak population on Trinidad.

Tobago was sighted and named by Christopher Columbus in 1498. He claimed the island for Spain, but it remained virtually untouched by the Spanish colonial authorities. The first settlers, a group of English colonists, were driven from the island by the fierce Caribs in 1616. In 1632 the Dutch took control of the island, but from 1654 to 1683 it was a colony of the duchy of Courland, in what is now northern Lithuania. Throughout the seventeenth and eighteenth centuries the island changed hands several times, variously controlled by the English, French, and Dutch. By the early eighteenth century the indigenous peoples of the island had disappeared, killed, sold into slavery, or been absorbed by the large slave population.

The British attempted to settle Tobago in 1721, but the French captured the island and transformed it into a plantation colony dominated by a small Dutch and French planter minority. African slaves were brought in from the other French Caribbean islands and later directly from Africa. The island was ceded to the British in 1763, but in 1768 France gained control of it again; British authority was not finally established until 1797. In 1814 the island was confirmed as a British colony by the Treaty of Paris, which ended the Napoleonic Wars.

The citizens of the island, mostly Dutch, recognized British rule, but in fact the island remained virtually self-governing. The island's development as a sugar colony began under British rule and continued to expand until the 1820s, when its importance began to wane. The emancipation of slaves throughout the British West Indies in 1834–38 resulted in the collapse of the sugar economy, leading to the flight of most of the European population. The slave population remained on the island, surviving mostly as subsistence farmers.

Unlike neighboring Trinidad, Tobago was granted its own bicameral legislature, which remained the instrument of self-government until 1874. Tobago remained a separate colony until 1888. It was united with Trinidad in 1888–89, although the Tabagonians retained their own legislature and tax system, and became part of the joint colony of Trinidad and Tobago in 1899 as a separate administrative district.

In 1925 constitutional reform added new elected members to the Trinidad and Tobago Legislative Council, allowing some degree of self-government. Continued agitation on both islands, particularly a damaging series of strikes and riots in 1937, led to a grant of universal suffrage in 1945. For about 10 years after the grant of universal suffrage, politics in the colony, particularly in Tobago, was characterized by individualism and confusion.

After World War II, when decolonization reached the Caribbean, Tabagonians began to press for separate status from Trinidad but were opposed by the Trinidadians and the British authorities. The Trinidad-based People's National Movement (PNM) won local elections in 1956 and formed the first party-based cabinet government in the islands. The joint colony attained independence in 1962 under a PNM government. Tobago's first parliamentarian, Alphonse Philbert Theophilus "Fargo" James, became the spokesmen for Tabagonian interests. He remains a national hero and the inspiration for the modern separatist movement.

The PNM won six consecutive elections and held power in the state from 1956 to 1986. Domination by the Trinidadians and the PNM produced continuity and stability but was accompanied by growing economic problems and social unrest. Anti-Trinidadian sentiment exploded in Tobago in the early 1970s with widespread disturbances.

The oil boom in 1973–81 brought sudden prosperity to most sectors, including more remote Tobago, and helped to reconcile Tabagonians to continued unification with Trinidad. The island entered a period of rapid development, fueled by tourism and oil revenues. The construction of an international airport at Crown Point, on the western tip of the island, opened formerly isolated Tobago to greater contacts with the world.

The collapse of oil prices, along with the PNM's failure to curb widespread corruption, led to a revival of separatist sentiment among the Tabagonians. In 1977 a group of nationalists of the Fargo House Movement raised the separatist flag on the island. Legislation passed in 1980 gave the Tabagonians considerable autonomy and established a separate Tobago House of Assembly of 15 members. In 1987, in response to continued separatist agitation, Tobago was granted full internal autonomy.

The growth of East Indian political power in the late 1990s further threatened the ties that bind the two islands. Trinidad, with its half-black and half–East Indian population, tends to neglect the needs of the smaller, less populated Tobago while the two major ethnic groups fight for supremacy. With few citizens of East Indian heritage, the Tabagonians, mostly descended from the island's African slaves, have increasingly little in common with the inhabitants of the larger island except the desire to share in Trinidad's oil wealth.

The National Alliance for Reconstruction (NAR), which began as a genuinely multiracial party in both islands in the early 1990s, lost support on Trinidad but not in Tobago. In the 1995 elections, the NAR held on to the two parliamentary seats in Tobago but won few votes in Trinidad, becoming the major political part of Tobago interests. Anti-Trinidadian sentiment led to the two NAR parliamentarians forming a political alliance with Trinidad's East Indians in opposition to the Trinidadian black-dominated PNM.

A new museum opened in Scarborough in mid-1999 that traced the history of the Tabagonian people from Africa, through slavery, to the present. The museum, part of the reculturation of the Tabagonians, represented one of the first national treasures of the small island nation.

Government corruption and political uncertainty in mid-2001 further alienated the smaller island from the larger and more powerful Trinidad. Tabagonian leaders demanded greater autonomous powers to counter growing separatist support on the island.

SELECTED BIBLIOGRAPHY:

Kelly, Robert C. *Country Review: Trinidad and Tobago 1999/2000.* 1999.
Ledgister, F.S.J. *Class Alliances and the Liberal Authoritarian State: The Roots of Post-Colonial Democracy in Jamaica, Trinidad and Tobago, and Surinam.* 1998.
Mahabir, Cynthia. *Crime and Nation-Building in the Caribbean: The Legacy of Legal Barriers.* 1985.
Malaki, Akhil. *Development Patterns in the Commonwealth Caribbean: Jamaica and Trinidad and Tobago.* 1996.

Tahitians

Polynesians; Society Islanders; Maohi

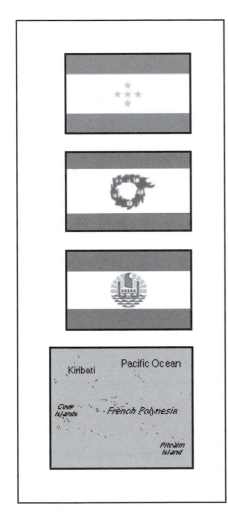

POPULATION: Approximately (2002e) 191,000 Tahitians in French Polynesia in the South Pacific. There are Tahitian communities living in the other French Pacific possessions, and in metropolitan France.

THE TAHITIAN HOMELAND: The Tahitian homeland, officially called French Polynesia, comprises an archipelago of 130 islands lying in the southwestern Pacific Ocean some 2,000 miles south of Hawaii. The Society Islands are the most westerly of the group and the most important in terms of land area and population. Most of the islands are of volcanic origin, with highly eroded volcanic cones and deep, radiating valleys. The most populated of the islands are Tahiti and Moorea, situated in the eastern Windward group, the Iles du Vent. Tahiti since 1946 has formed a territory of the French republic. *Territory of French Polynesia/ Territoire de la Polynésie Francaise (Porinetia Farani/Tahiti)*: 1,522 sq. mi.—3,943 sq. km, (2002e) 245,000—Tahitians 77%, Chinese (called Demin) 12%, French 10% (local French 6%, metropolitan French 4%), other Pacific Islanders 1%. The Tahitian capital and major cultural center is Papeete, (2002e) 30,000, urban area, 115,000.

FLAG: The flag of the Independent Front for the Liberation of Polynesia (Tavini Huiraatira) has three horizontal stripes of blue, white, blue with a centered cross of five gold stars. The flag of the Hau Tahiti group has horizontal stripes of red, white, red, the white twice the width and bearing a green wreath centered. The official flag of French Polynesia is the same red, white, red flag with a centered pirogue, a Tahitian war canoe, with five rowers.

PEOPLE AND CULTURE: The Tahitians are a Polynesian people, descendents of early migrants from Southeast Asia, speaking a Polynesian language of the Malayo-Polynesian language group. On the major islands the Tahitians have some European and Chinese admixture, but on the outer islands the Tahitians have retained the traditional culture. Tourism and urbanization have had adverse influences on the Tahitian culture, although official support and protection since the 1980s has helped to reverse rapid assimilation into French culture.

LANGUAGE AND RELIGION: The Tahitian language is the most important of the several Polynesian languages spoken in the islands. The languages belong to the Polynesian branch of the Malayo-Polynesian (Austronesian) group of languages. The other languages are Austral, also called Tubuai-Rurutu, also of the Tahitic branch of the Polynesian languages, spoken in the Austral Islands by about 10,000 people; North and South Marquesan, of the Marquesic branch, spoken by about 12,000 peoples; and Tuamotuan or Pa'umotu of the Tahitic branch, on Tuamotu, spoken by about 10,000 people. The peoples of the outer islands are slowly switching to Tahitian. Both French and Tahitian are official languages in French Polynesia.

Most Tahitians are Christians, the result of nineteenth-century missionary activity. The largest group, about half of the population, belongs to various Protestant sects. About a third are Roman Catholic. Since the 1970s there has been a movement to resurrect parts of the traditional belief system of the islands.

NATIONAL HISTORY: Archaeological evidence points to the settlement of the northern Marquesas as early as 200 B.C. from western Polynesia. In subsequent migrations, the Polynesians from the Marquesas migrated to Hawaii (Hawai'i) about A.D. 300 and reached the Society Islands by the ninth century. Tahitian tradition asserts that migrants from Samoa settled the islands in the fourteenth century A.D. Over the next century the settlers spread through the far-flung archipelago.

Large chiefdoms were established on Tahiti, Bora-Bora, and Raiatea. Ruled by chiefs or kings, the widely separated islands often engaged in interisland warfare, the inhabitants of each island constituting a separate nation. The Polynesians constructed their villages along the water; the interiors of the islands remained nearly uninhabited and were often considered sacred. Teriaroa, north of Tahiti, was set aside as a royal retreat, and Taputapuatea, on the island of Raiatea, was the archipelago's most sacred shrine.

European contact with the islands was gradual. Portuguese navigator Ferdinand Magellan sighted Pukapuka in the Tuamotus in 1521. The Marquesas were sighted and charted by Spanish explorer Alvaro de Mendaña in 1595. No other Europeans visited the islands until the Dutch explorer Jacob Roggeveen encountered Makatea, Bora-Bora, and Mapuiti in 1722. The expedition of Samuel Wallis sighted the central islands of Tahiti and

Moorea in 1747. Capt. James Cook arrived in 1769, accompanied by a party of scientists from London's Royal Society; in their honor he named the archipelago the Society Islands. Again visited by Cook in 1773 and 1777, the idyllic islands figured in the drama of the HMS *Bounty*, which visited Tahiti in 1788. The inadvertent introduction of European diseases devastated the island populations, drastically reducing the population in the nineteenth century.

British and French missionaries became active in the islands in the early nineteenth century, their activities intensifying the European rivalry for influence. The missionaries introduced European morality, but also Western-style education and medicine. Missionary-educated children, often the sons of chiefs, often rose to important positions in the royal government of Tahiti.

The history of the Society Islands is virtually that of Tahiti, the largest and most populous island of the group. In 1841 Queen Pomare IV of Tahiti sought French assistance against British encroachment and two years later agreed to a French protectorate. In 1846, however, the queen appealed unsuccessfully to the British to block the formal French annexation of Tahiti. Queen Pomare died in 1877. Her son and heir, Pomare V, was forced to abdicate in 1880, and his abdication was followed by French annexation. As late as 1888, the inhabitants of Rimatara and Rurutu sought British protection but were refused. In 1903 the various island groups were consolidated to form the colony of French Polynesia.

The islands were governed by a naval government as the Colony of Oceania until 1885. A French government decree provided for a French civil government and a general council, representing all the islands, which had some control over fiscal policies. The powers of the council were curtailed in 1899, and in 1903 it was replaced by an advisory council. French economic development, accompanied by imported Chinese labor, generally ignored the native Tahitians.

At the outbreak of war in Europe in 1939, many French troops were withdrawn from the islands. To ensure the loyalty of the islanders, the French government promised French citizenship at the end of the conflict. In 1940, after the fall of France, the island's voters chose to side with the Free French of Charles de Gaulle, and many Tahitians fought with the Allied armies.

The French government in fact granted citizenship in 1946 and made the islands an overseas territory of the French republic. The authorities in the 1950s extended parts of the French welfare system to the islands, bringing relative prosperity at a time when the Tahitians were gradually changing from traditional ways of life to the more urbanized life of the French community.

The colonial government extended the powers of the local territorial assembly in 1957. The next year Pouvanaa a Oopa, the vice president of the government council, announced a plan to secede from France and form a sovereign Tahitian republic. He was arrested, and the movement collapsed. Local powers were again curtailed. His plan, supported by leftist French politicians, marked the beginning of the modern Tahitian national movement; however, the proposal shocked the conservative Tahitians, who marched in what was probably the world's first procolonial demonstration. In November 1958 the islanders voted to make their islands a French overseas territory administered by a governor and a territorial assembly.

The extension of French monetary subsidies and the advent of tourism dramatically raised living standards and ended the islands' long isolation during the 1960s. By the early 1970s the modernization of the islands had turned Tahiti into the most urbanized island in the South Pacific south of Hawaii. New government statutes granted more local autonomy in 1977, but the pro-independence and pro-autonomy political groups continued to call for popular election of the president and for greater autonomy or outright independence.

Between 1962 and 1966 over 15,000 French soldiers, bureaucrats, and technicians arrived in the islands to prepare for French nuclear tests on Mururua Atoll, 500 miles southeast of the main island, Tahiti. The European influx and the beginning of nuclear tests in 1963 spurred the growth of Tahitian nationalism. Over the next decade nationalist's demands for autonomy or independence gained widespread support in the islands.

Reports that the nuclear tests threatened the islands' health and environment mobilized the population in the 1970s and 1980s. In response to worldwide pressure the tests were moved underground on Fangataufa in 1975. Several nationalist groups formed, and in 1976 they demanded autonomy for the islands. A year later the more militant groups called for immediate independence, an end to nuclear testing in their homeland, and the repatriation of all mainland French. In 1980 elections nearly all the island political parties, including those representing the Europeans, supported greater autonomy or independence.

The French authorities, not willing to lose the nuclear test site or the lucrative tourist trade, rejected the autonomy demands. In 1982 a majority in the territorial assembly announced support for independence, and nationalist groups threatened a violent separatist campaign like that in New Caledonia. Fearing that the growing nationalist sentiment could erupt in violence, the French government hastily granted autonomy in September 1984.

In the mid-1980s, political parties, environmental and human rights groups united to protest the continuing nuclear testing. In 1985, media attention focused on the South Pacific when the French secret service blew up a ship, owned by the Greenpeace environmental group, that was preparing to leave the harbor in Auckland, New Zealand, to protest near Mururoa atoll. An environmental activist was killed in the blast.

The Tahitian economy benefited as a supply base for the nuclear test site, with many Tahitians working as laborers and cooks. Income for the tests were valued, as unemployment was high, but growing worries over the health and environmental hazards diminished Tahitian support by the early 1980s. The French managed to contain dissent, mainly by the use of money, but opposition continued to grow.

Nationalism in the late 1980s was tempered by the increase in the generous government subsidies, by which the islands enjoyed the highest standard of living between Hawaii and New Zealand. The growth of militant separatist groups in the late 1980s pushed the islands toward independence. In June 1989 the nationalists called a boycott of local election, a boycott that 90% of the voters honored. In June 1991 the imposition of new taxes set off rioting, the riots quickly turning into a mass pro-independence movement that eventually forced the resignation of the local French administration.

In 1992, President François Mitterand of France announced a moratorium on nuclear tests in the islands, but they were resumed in 1995 under Jacques Chirac. In 1996, the French government signed the Treaty of Rarotonga, which created a nuclear-free zone in the South Pacific and supported the prohibition of nuclear testing in Polynesia. The decision to stop the tests was a major victory for the Tahitians, as well as for environmental groups worldwide. The French authorities finally acknowledged that there had been leaks of toxic waste. The claim that the wastes did not pose a health and environmental hazard was disputed by local groups.

In May 1996, the French authorities approved a new statute of internal autonomy that gave French Polynesia additional control over immigration, marine resources, and relations with other Pacific states. The desire for self-rule, seen as the only means to preserve Tahiti's ancient culture, has fueled the dramatic rise of Tahitian nationalism. However, though there is widespread support for independence, the French monetary subsidies, valued at $2.2 billion in 2002, may prove too difficult for Tahiti's prosperous and sophisticated population to give up.

SELECTED BIBLIOGRAPHY:

Aldrich, Robert. *France and the South Pacific since 1940*. 1994.
Firth, Stewart. *Nuclear Playground*. 1987.
Levy, Robert I. *Tahitians: Mind and Experience in the Society Islands*. 1975.
Stone, William Standish. *Idylls of the South Seas*. 1995.

Tai

Thai; Tribal Thai; Tay; Phuy Thay; Phu Tay

POPULATION: Approximately (2002e) 1,570,000 Tai in Southeast Asia, concentrated in the northwestern provinces of Vietnam (with 1,380,000), northern Laos (140,000), southern China (70,000), and northeastern Thailand, with a population of about 35,000. Outside the region there are Tai communities in other parts of Southeast Asia, in France, Australia, and the United States.

THE TAI HOMELAND: The Tai homeland lies in Southeast Asia, occupying the upland valleys of the northern reaches of the Annamese Cordillera around the headwaters of the Red (Song Hong) and Black (Song Da) Rivers. The Tai heartland in Vietnam comprises areas in the highland provinces of Lai Chau, Son La, Hoa Binh, Lao Cai, and Nghe An. The region is densely forested, with level land accounting

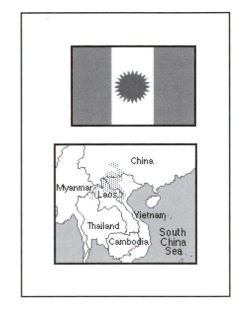

for no more than 20% of the area. The forested Tai highlands rise steeply from the Red River delta, which forms the major part of northern Vietnam. The Tai homeland has no official status in Vietnam or Laos. In China the Tai, called Dai, have some cultural autonomy in the so-called Autonomous Dai County in Yunnan. The Tai capital and major cultural center is Hoa Binh, (2002e) 94,000. Other important cultural centers are Son La, called Thai Tong by the Tai, (2002e) 19,000, and Lao Cai, (2002e) 36,000 The other important Tai cultural center is Phongsali, (2002e) 18,000, the center of the Lao Tai. The Tai center in China is Hekou in Yunnan, (2002e) 42,000.

FLAG: The Tai national flag, the traditional flag of the Black Tai, has three vertical stripes of blue, white, and blue, bearing a centered red sun with 24 rays.

PEOPLE AND CULTURE: The Tai nation is a Thai people living in northern Vietnam, Laos, Thailand, and southern China. The Black and White Tai were named for the color of their women's blouses. Related to the Thais and Laotians, they form a distinct people with a common historical origin and shared cultural characteristics. The Tai include the Tai Dam (Black Tai) and Tai Khao (White Tai), and the subgroups, the Tai Deng (Red Tai), Tai Muoi, Tai Thanh (Man Thanh), Tai Muong (Hang Tong), and the Phu Thay in Laos. There is considerable controversy over the classification of the Red Tai—whether they forms a group equal to the Black and White Tai, or a subgroup of one or the other. The classification of the different groups is clear in some areas of northwestern Vietnam, but in other areas the division between Black and White is not clearly defined, and many groups use local names. The practice of calling group by their location is widespread. Each of the tribal groups has its own cultural traits, including food, clothing, and architecture, although they share the basic culture and language. A common marriage tradition has the man live with the wife's family until the couple's first child is born, when they move to the house of the husband's family. Funeral rites are also important, with elaborate rites to see off the dead to the other world. Socially the Tai are patriarchal; the eldest male is the head of the local tribal group. Historically the Tai have been known for their independence and self-reliance. The White Tai have been more influenced by Vietnamese culture that the Black Tai, but both continue to consider themselves part of the officially recognized Tai nationality in Vietnam and Laos.

LANGUAGE AND RELIGION: The Tai language belongs to the Tay-Thai (Thai-Kadai) language group. Until the twentieth century the Tai dialects were not literary languages, but they have a valuable legacy of myths, legends, ancient tales, versed stories, and folksongs. The Tai dialects are tonal, with dialectal differences often in the number of tones used and in pronunciation. The various dialects are mutually intelligible, although the major differences between the Black and White Tai is that of language. Each group has a distinct writing system. Contact with the many different languages of Southeast Asia has led to the adoption of many words from different sources.

One of the few Thai groups not strongly influenced by Buddhism, the Tai retain their traditional beliefs, except for small Buddhist and Christian minorities each making up about 5% of the population. Ancestor worship is an important part of the belief system, as are the spirits of heaven, earth, and other natural phenomenon. Traditional ceremonies are held to pray for good crops, healthy children, and peace. The Tai often seek help through supernatural spirits and objects. They believe in a multiple-personality soul and have rites for recalling the soul and strengthening individual personalities within. They also belief in spirit guides and locality spirits, which are identified with different levels of society. These spirits must be appeased to avoid curses and receive blessings. A growing number of Tai consider themselves nonreligious, mostly due to the official atheism of the Vietnamese and Laotian governments. Despite official disapproval of superstitious practices, however, most Tai continue to be influenced by such practices as astrology, geomancy (divination), and sorcery.

NATIONAL HISTORY: The Tai began migrating south from central and southern China due to relentless Chinese military pressure. The migrating groups conquered and absorbed many peoples, taking on many of their cultural traits. The Tai were often at war with neighboring peoples or among themselves before settling the mountains and high valleys of Southeast Asia. Some 2,500 years ago the Tai peoples split, the Northern Tai* remaining in present southern China while other Tai groups migrated south, where they settled several widely scattered areas. Over many centuries invasions by Chinese and other peoples pushed the Tai peoples into the less accessible mountain regions.

The Tai developed their own indigenous culture through contacts with other Tai and non-Tai groups and later influences from China and India. The trade route from Guangxi in China south to present Thailand helped to spread Tai culture through much of Southeast Asia. This trade route marked the first known migration of Tai-speaking peoples as merchants and settlers moved into northern Vietnam. Around 900 A.D., a second migration moved west and south from the Tai homeland in present Vietnam to people central and southern Thailand and Laos.

The spread of Buddhism in Southeast Asia failed to reach the mountainous Tai homeland in the isolated upper basins of the Black and Red Rivers. While the majority of the Thai peoples adopted Buddhism, the Tai retained their traditional beliefs, which are believed to have remained consistent with the beliefs of the wider pre-Buddhist Thai population. The introduction of Buddhist culture to the lowland Thai peoples of Thailand and Laos began the long cultural separation of the Black and White Tai peoples, who remained tribal in structure and traditionally Thai in culture. The highlands between Laos and Vietnam, although settled on both sides by the Tai people, were divided by the rulers of the two states in the mid-seventeenth century.

French colonial forces took control of Indochina in the mid-nineteenth century. Before the arrival of the French, the highland Tai lived in isolation from the lowland Vietnamese population. The consolidation of French rule, in the 1860s, increased contacts between the Tai and Vietnamese. The colonial authorities were interested in the Tai highlands for plantation agriculture, allowing the Tai linguistic and cultural autonomy. The Tai districts were administered separately from the rest of French Vietnam and Laos. Conferring special status on the Tai homeland gave the French a free hand in cultivating the largely unexploited highlands, where their administrators and Christian missionaries also set up schools, hospitals, and leprosariums.

Conflicts soon arose between the Tai and the French colonists, who were seen as exploitative interlopers. The colonial authorities eventually overcame the unrest and distrust and developed some of the highland regions, where they established large rubber, tea, and coffee plantations using local labor. The boundary with China to the north was delineated under the French-Chinese treaties of 1887 and 1895.

During World War II, the government of Thailand, allied to the Japanese, attempted to recruit among the Tai of the region, then under the control of the French Vichy government, but with little success. Communist propaganda also failed to win many converts in the region, as the ideology was closely tied to particular Vietnamese nationalism. Famine struck the region in 1944–45, causing many deaths and a strong antigovernment sentiment that persists to the present.

After the end of the war the French colonial administration returned but faced a widespread nationalist uprising in northern Vietnam. Following the French defeat at the town of Dien Bien Phu just west of the Tai territories in 1954, Vietnam was divided into North and South Vietnam at the 17th parallel, the North under a communist regime, the South under a right-wing regime supported by France and the United States. North and South Vietnam dealt with their respective minorities quite differently. The North Vietnamese, recognizing the traditional separatist attitudes of the tribal minorities, initiated a policy of accommodation by setting up two autonomous zones in return for acceptance of Vietnamese communist political control.

The communist Chinese government in the early 1950s formally claimed the northwestern provinces of Vietnam as historical Chinese territory, partly based on the ethnic affinities of the Tai and Northern Tai (Zhuang) peoples living on both sides of the border. Agreements were reached in 1957–58 between the two governments to respect the colonial boundaries, but border incidents continued, and Chinese support of dissidents continues to fuel unrest in the Tai highlands.

The Tai of China during the Chinese Cultural Revolution of 1965–76 were often uprooted and sent to the countryside to settle the borderlands. The increased contacts between the Tai in China and their kin in Vietnam and Laos began a modest cultural revival in all three areas, which was supported by the Thai government beginning in the late 1970s.

During the long nationalist war against the French, then the Americans, the communist North Vietnamese mostly ignored the Tai regions except those near the border with China. Despite South Vietnamese and American clandestine efforts to provoke resistance to the Hanoi regime, little opposition formed among the Tai during the Vietnam War. They saw the conflict as a war between the Vietnamese and preferred to leave the painful issue to the lowlanders.

Only after the defeat of the South Vietnamese* in 1975 was an effort made to integrate the Tai into Vietnamese national life. Minority cadres were sent into the region to lay the groundwork for socioeconomic development, but resistance to government practices continued to cause unrest. In February 1979, Chinese forces invaded northern Vietnam, but an expected Tai uprising failed to materialize. The boundary between Vietnam and Laos, never until then precisely delimited, was finally defined by a treaty signed in 1977 and ratified in 1986.

The Tai had virtually no real representation in government in any of the countries in which they live, although they are nominally represented by government functionaries. The living conditions of the Tai continue to lag behind those of the lowland peoples of Vietnam and Laos. In more remote areas, "backward customs and practices" remain unchanged despite official government disapproval. In the 1980s and 1990s official Vietnam government claims that closer unity and greater harmony were being achieved were belied by the government's frequent attacks on "narrow nationalism" among the highland Tai. Although the number of Tai officials expanded, by 1989 only a small portion of the functionaries serving in the Tai provinces were ethnic Tai.

Under the Vietnamese and Laotian government programs of population distribution, lowlanders continue to emigrate to the Tai highlands. Tai leaders, in 1996–97, responding to greater openness in Vietnamese society, denounced the continuing ingrained Vietnamese biases against the non-Vietnamese minorities and the official policies that encouraged the lowland peasants to move into the ethnic Tai regions. Unrest in 1997 in the northern province of Thai Binh was officially blamed on minority opposition to economic reform, which the minorities blame for their growing poverty.

The Tai region is closed to journalists and most outsiders, so information is difficult to obtain or validate. Reports of unrest in the region, particularly in 1999, included stories of a growing movement for cultural and political self-government based on the traditional communist nationalities policy espoused by the Vietnamese and Laotian governments but never applied to the Tai nation.

In April 2001 the Communist Party of Vietnam named a new leader, Nong Duc Manh, who is from the northern hills and is partly of Tai ancestry. His nomination, seen as a move toward greater liberalization, was welcomed by the Tai leaders who continue to chafe under restrictive government regulations. Manh is member of the Tai ethnic minority but thought to be Ho Chi Minh's illegitimate son. Tai leaders appealed to Manh to rein in the brutal communist police and Vietnamese army that continue to murder ethnic minorities over land disputes and preceived antigovernment statements.

SELECTED BIBLIOGRAPHY:

Asian Minorities Outreach. *The Peoples of Vietnam.* 1998.
Harrell, Steven, ed. *Cultural Encounters on China's Ethnic Frontiers.* 1996.
Nguyen, Dac Tri. *Ethnic Minorities in Vietnam.* 1972.
Van, Dang Nghiem. *Ethnological and Religious Problems in Vietnam.* 1998.

Taiwanese
Formosans; Hoklo

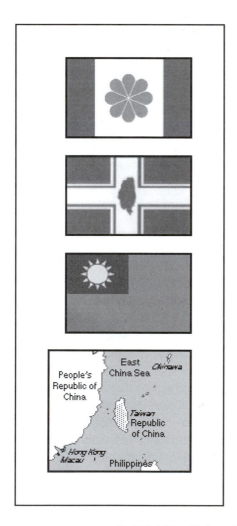

POPULATION: Approximately (2002e) 17,090,000 Taiwanese in the Republic of China, which includes Taiwan and some smaller islands in the Taiwan Strait, which separates the island of Taiwan from the Chinese mainland. Outside the region there are sizable Taiwanese communities in Singapore, the Philippines, and other parts of Asia, and in Europe, the United States, Canada, and Australia.

THE TAIWANESE HOMELAND: The Taiwanese homeland lies in the South China Sea, a large mountainous island north of the Philippines and south of Japan. Taiwan lies 90 miles east of the Chinese mainland across the Taiwan Strait and includes a handful of tiny islands in the Strain of Taiwan and just off the coast of mainland China. Officially Taiwan forms a province of the Republic of China, since 1949 the only Chinese province controlled by the republic's government. The government of the rival People's Republic of China considers Taiwan a province in rebellion against the rightful government of united China. *Republic of China/Chung–hua Min-kuo/ Taiwan*: 13,895 sq. mi.—35,997 sq. km, (2002e) 20,346,000—Taiwanese 84%, Mainland Chinese (called Mainlanders) 14%, Kaoshans 2%. The Taiwanese capital and major cultural center is Taipei, (2002e) 2,653,000, metropolitan area 7,438,000. Other important cultural centers are Kaohsiung, (2002e) 1,334,000, metropolitan area 2,469,000, Taichung, (2002e) 894,000, metropolitan area 2,061,000, and Tainan, (2002e) 694,000, metropolitan area 770,000.

FLAG: The Taiwanese national flag, the flag of the nationalist movement, is a white field bearing two broad green vertical stripes on the hoist and the fly and bearing a centered eight–petaled red flower. The official flag of the Republic of China is a red field bearing a blue canton on the upper hoist charged with a white twelve-rayed sun. The flag of the largest Taiwanese national party, the Democratic Progressive Party, is a green field divided by a centered white cross bearing a green map of the island at the center of the cross.

PEOPLE AND CULTURE: The Taiwanese are a Chinese people, descendents of early Fujianese and Hakka migrants from the mainland provinces. The island's language and culture have absorbed many non-Chinese influences from the indigenous Malay minority, the Kaoshan, the Europeans and Americans, and from the Okinawans* and Japanese who controlled the island for various periods of its history. Taiwanese culture, which has diverged considerably from that of mainland China, has evolved as the national culture of the island. About 360,000 people belong to several aboriginal tribal groups of Malay descent, mostly in the more rugged eastern part of the island.

LANGUAGE AND RELIGION: The Taiwanese speak a Min dialect closely related to the language spoken in mainland Fujian, there called Hokkien or Fukien. Mandarin Chinese, the language of the mainland Chinese who dominated the island since 1949, is the official language of the Republic of China. Mandarin is mainly spoken in Taipei and the five largest provincial cities where the mainland Chinese settled in 1948–49. The language of the Taiwanese majority, called Taiwanese or Min Nan, is the Taiwanese dialect of the dominant language spoken in Fujian province opposite the island. Taiwanese is considered the true national language. There are two subdialects, Sanso and Chaenzo, which are mutually intelligible only with some difficulty. A minority of the Taiwanese, about 11% of the population, speak the Hakka dialect of Chinese.

The majority of the Taiwanese, about 93%, adhere to traditional religions, a mixture of Buddhism, Confucianism, and Taoism. There is a small but influential Christian minority, numbering about 4.5% of the population. Other religions include the animist beliefs of the Kaoshans, and a small Muslim minority.

NATIONAL HISTORY: The large island of Taiwan was sparsely populated by Malayo-Polynesian aborigines related to the inhabitants of the Philippines to the south until the seventh century A.D. In the next centuries small groups of Chinese settlers from the mainland opposite crossed the narrow strait. The growing Chinese population gradually forced the Malay Kaoshan tribes into the eastern mountains.

In the seventeenth century thousands of refugees fleeing mainland upheavals settled on the island, making the Chinese population the dominant group. Isolated from the mainland, the islanders developed a distinct culture and island dialects quite distinct from the nearby Chinese provinces across the Strait of Taiwan. The few contacts with China were mainly through refugees fleeing upheavals on the mainland.

Portuguese sailors sighted the island in 1590, calling it Ilha Formosa, the Beautiful Island. In 1624 the Dutch East India Company established forts in the south and in 1641 gained control of the entire island. Meanwhile, the Manchus* invaded China in 1644, overthrowing the Ming dynasty in the north and moving south against the various warlords who controlled the region. An estimated 100,000 Chinese from the coastal provinces fled across the narrow waterway to the relative safety of Taiwan.

A Ming loyalist, Cheng Ch'eng-kung, called Koxinga, a Chinese general fleeing the Manchu conquest of China, with the help of angry islanders, expelled the Dutch in 1662 and established an independent kingdom. Koxinga was determined to use Taiwan as a base for an invasion to retake the mainland from the Manchus. He died before the invasion could be organized. Twenty years later Manchu forces from the mainland defeated Koxinga's grandson and conquered the island in 1683. The Manchus made Taiwan part of China for the first time in its history.

The Taiwanese, having developed independently of the mainland, resented Chinese domination and attempted to throw off Manchu rule in 1721. Brutally crushed by imperial troops, the uprising and its aftermath sparked a tradition of antigovernment and antimainland tendencies. Frequent unrest and rebellions kept the island on the margins of Chinese interest.

Japan, expanding rapidly during the late nineteenth century, became interested in the island's potential, one of the reasons for war with China in 1895. Resisting the cession of the island to the victorious Japanese, the Taiwanese declared the island independent on 23 May 1895 and appealed for international support to save their island from a colonial occupation. The Japanese quickly suppressed the republic and all Taiwanese opposition.

Exploited for the Japanese home market, the undeveloped island was organized with new transportation systems, industries, and cities. Without attempting mass Japanese settlement, the colonial administration pressed assimilation and the use of the Japanese language in daily life. The improvements to Taiwan's agriculture and infrastructure made it the most advanced Chinese-populated region in Asia other than Singapore. The Japanese authorities planned to use Taiwan as a military base and as the breadbasket of the growing Japanese empire.

The Kuomingtang (KMT), the Nationalist Party, in control of mainland China following the overthrow of the Manchu dynasty in 1911, was increasingly caught up in a spreading civil war with the Chinese communists and ignored the situation on Taiwan. Neither the KMT nor the communists of Mao Tse-tung cared to challenge Japanese control of the island while fighting a vicious civil war for control of the mainland.

Taken from the defeated Japanese by American troops in 1945, Taiwan was turned over to the wartime allies, the KMT. The Nationalists established the island as a safe base in the civil war, which resumed on the mainland following the Japanese defeat. A Taiwanese provincial government, installed by the KMT government of the Republic of China, proved as corrupt and incompetent on Taiwan as the KMT had been on the mainland. The provincial authorities used harsh measures to put down Taiwanese nationalist sentiment and a popular pro-independence movement.

In 1947, careful to profess continued support of Chiang Kai-shek's Nationalist Chinese government, the unhappy Taiwanese rebelled against the provincial government in Taipei. In spite of the rebels' appeals for the removal of the corrupt and brutal provincial authorities, the Nationalist government withdrew 10,000 troops from the fight against the communists and sent them to pacify the island. In February 1947, savage reprisals against rebels and suspected sympathizers left 28,000 dead, generating Taiwanese bitterness and resentment that continues to the present. The massacre virtually eliminated a generation of Taiwanese professionals and intellectuals. The day, remembered as "2–28," still serves as a rallying cry of the anti-KMT Taiwanese.

The communist victories in 1948 and 1949 sent a flood of refugees to the island from all over China. In December 1949, Chiang Kai-Shek's Nationalist government fled to the island. By 1950 over two million Nationalist supporters had arrived on Taiwan. Even though the Nationalist government controlled just one province, Taiwan, it maintained that it represented the only legitimate government of all China. Both the KMT and the mainland communists agreed that Taiwan was part of China. Taiwan was to be just a temporary staging area before the army returned to the civil war on the mainland, but only the timely outbreak of the Korean War, which brought American forces to protect its strategic interests in the region, prevented Mao Tse-tung from invading Taiwan.

The Nationalist government imposed martial law on the island, banned all political parties except the KMT, outlawed the Taiwanese language in favor of Mandarin, and persecuted Taiwanese nationalists as traitors. The mainland Chinese minority dominated the political, cultural, and economic life of the island. Constant tension across the Strait of Taiwan provided an excuse for dictatorial rule.

Taiwan was governed under martial law while the KMT concentrated mostly on Taiwan's economic development. The KMT government received much material and financial aid from the United States, which saw Taiwan as both an anticommunist bastion in a tense area and a possible forward military base should the need arise.

The Nationalist government's increasing isolation in the 1970s, as many countries switched diplomatic recognition to the mainland's communist government, provoked a resurgence of Taiwanese nationalism. America's toleration of the authoritarian and corrupt KMT was also wearing thin. The death of Nationalist leader Chiang Kai-shek in 1975 began a decrease in rhetoric about unification with the mainland. In 1979 the United States broke relations with the KMT government of the Republic of China and established relations with the People's Republic of China on the mainland, although economic and military agreements continued to provide some degree of security amid the growing diplomatic isolation.

Meanwhile, the Taiwanese national identity and the pro-independence opposition were getting stronger. The Taiwanese nationalists demanded that Taiwan, effectively independent since 1949, take its place among the countries of the world, but opposition to Taiwanese nationalism was the only point on which the Nationalists of the KMT and mainland communists continued to agree.

Prodded by the Americans, Chiang Ching-kuo, Chiang Kai-shek's son and heir, ended martial law, legalized opposition parties, eased press restrictions, and lifted the ban on the Taiwanese language in 1987. The political reforms set the stage for democratic parliamentary elections in 1992. Taiwanese political parties, legalized after four decades of suppression, rapidly gained support with calls for democracy, independence for the wealthy, industrialized state, and an end of domination by the Mainlanders.

The island had incomes nearly equal to the mainland's in 1950, but by the late 1990s Taiwanese incomes were ten times higher. Taiwanese nationalists claim that the Taiwanese, not the Mainlanders who came in 1949, are responsible for Taiwan's economic miracle. Assured, rich, and, unlike the Mainlanders, with no spiritual ties to the mainland, the Taiwanese see little need to maintain the KMT fiction that it is the only legitimate Chinese government. The often-repeated threat of a communist invasion should Taiwan declare independence remains the major impediment to the Taiwanese desire to take their place among the nations of the world.

The Kuomingtang, which ruled the island from 1949, was notorious for nepotism, corruption, and unfair elections, but by the mid-1990s the democracy process embraced by the Taiwanese had established the first Chinese multiparty democracy. Debate on Taiwanese independence became acceptable within the mainstream of domestic politics. The political liberalization and the increased representation of opposition parties opened public debate on the island's national identity.

In the spring of 1994, the democratic pro-independence opposition initiated a campaign to lead Taiwan to full independence. A popular campaign, the "New Name, New Flag, New Anthem" campaign won widespread support with its call for Taiwan to declare independence openly and to end the de facto independence that had prevailed for nearly 50 years.

The pro-independence groups, including the Democratic Progressive Party (DPP), opposed the ruling party's traditional stand that the island will eventually reunify with mainland China. The independence movement's program includes a sovereign Taiwanese state, membership in the United Nations (UN), and normal state relations with mainland China. During the 1990s, the KMT lost its grip on local government to legalized opposition parties, but at a national level it remained dominant, having controlled the island without serious challenge since 1949.

The president of the Republic of China, Lee Teng-hui, the first native Taiwanese leader of the KMT, outraged mainland Chinese leaders in 1999 with his insistence on Taiwan's equal status with the mainland. By demanding that the government of the People's Republic deal with Taiwan as an equal, he proposed Chinese recognition of the island's de facto independence.

In March 2000, the Taiwanese voted for the president of the Republic of China for only the second time. The presidential campaign drew threats from the government of the People's Republic of China, including a threat of war if the Taiwanese continued to delay talks on reunification. The candidate of the openly pro-independence DPP, Chen Shui–bian, a native Taiwanese, was elected by pro-independence and anti-KMT groups, as tension between the island and mainland increased dramatically. Chen Shui-bian concluded that a declaration was unnecessary because Taiwan was effectively sovereign. He repeated his campaign pledge not to declare independence unless the confrontation with China turned violent.

Most Taiwanese are content with their de facto independence as the Republic of China. Although they would like to participate in the UN and other world bodies, they want neither to risk conflict with the mainland nor surrender to a unification with the mainland, with which they disagree. The question of whether Taiwan and the Taiwanese should be part of China remains an open and increasingly politicized debate.

A public opinion poll in June 2000 found that over 45% of the population considered themselves Taiwanese, a distinct national identity, against just 14% who consider themselves Chinese. The change dramatically demonstrates the changes that have occurred since the 1980s, when all Taiwanese considered themselves Chinese. The remainder felt that they have "dual identities."

The first three ships to sail from Taiwanese territory to the Chinese mainland since 1949 arrived in the ports opposite Taiwan in early January 2001. The transportation links ended yet another of the long-sustained prohibitions that have divided the two Chinese states. Nationalists claim that it is part of the normalization of relations between Taiwan and China, but the Beijing government rejects this interpretation.

Parliamentary elections in December 2001, for the first time gave the DPP more seats than the KMT. The electoral result was a shattering defeat for the KMT, once the most powerful political party in East Asia. The DPP victory was an endorsement of policies that increasingly accept the premise that the Taiwanese are not interested in maintaining the fiction that their island represents just a province, effectively rejecting claims by the Republic of China and the KMT and the People's Republic of China on the mainland.

SELECTED BIBLIOGRAPHY:

Hsiau, A-Chin. *Contemporary Taiwanese Cultural Nationalism*. 2000.
Long, Simon. *Taiwan: China's Last Frontier*. 1990.
Shambaugh, David, and Frank Dikotter, eds. *Contemporary Taiwan*. 1998.
Watchman, Alan M. *Taiwan: National Identity and Democratization*. 1994.

Talysh

Talushon; Talish; Tolish; Talush; Talyshi; Talesh; Talishi

POPULATION: Approximately (2002e) 340,000 Talysh in Azerbaijan and Iran, with about 140,000 concentrated in the Lenkoran, Astara, Lerik, and Massallin regions of southern Azerbaijan, and an estimated 200,000 in the Ardabil, Gilan, and Zenjan provinces of Iran. Talysh nationalists claim that the Talysh account for 11% of Azerbaijan's population, or about 850,000, and have a national population in Azerbaijan and Iran of over two million.

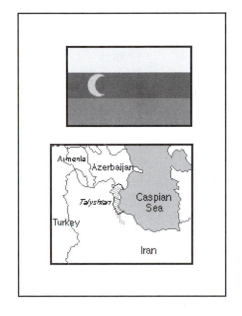

THE TALYSH HOMELAND: The Talysh homeland, called Talyshtan, occupies a varied landscape southwest of the Caspian Sea in Azerbaijan and Iran. A land of sharp contrasts, the Talysh homeland occupies the high, forested Talysh Mountains, sloping down to the subtropical coastal plain on the Caspian Sea south of the Viliazh-Chai River and north to the dry Mugani Steppe. Talyshtan has no official status in Azerbaijan or Iran, and until 1991 there was little cross-border communication. The region comprises the four districts of Lenkoran, Astarin, Lerik, and Massallin in Azerbaijan, and the Astara district of Gilan Province in Iran. *Talyshstan*: 5,498 sq. mi.—14,239 sq. km, (2002e) 546,000—Talysh 64%, Azeris 21%, Gilakis* 13%, others 2%. The Talysh capital and major cultural center is Lankaran, called Lenkoran by the Talysh, (2002e) 51,000. The other important cultural centers in Iran are Astara, (2002e) 31,000, urban area 53,000, which straddles the Azeri-Iranian border, and Hashtpar, (2002e) 34,000.

FLAG: The Talysh national flag, the flag of the national movement, is a horizontal tricolor of white, red, and green bearing a gold crescent moon on the red stripe near the hoist.

PEOPLE AND CULTURE: The Talysh, calling themselves Talushon, are an Iranian people of mixed Iranian and Caucasian ancestry known throughout Azerbaijan for their intellectual abilities and literacy. They tend to be more highly educated and more literate than the surrounding peoples. The Talysh culture, similar to that of the Azeris, combines elements of Caucasian, Turkish, and Iranian origin but has retained customs and traditions not found among other groups in the region. Traditionally a rural people whose economy and culture revolved around cattle raising, the Talysh since the late 1970s have been urbanizing at a rapid rate. In 1979, only about 1% of the Talysh lived in towns, but by 1994 an estimated 22% did. Talysh women in Iran continue to wear veils and robes that completely cover their bodies, but in more secular Azerbaijan they have mostly abandoned traditional dress for Western-style clothing. Traditionally the Talysh marry young; the bride's family is required to pay *kebin*, the bride price, which consists of money and such items as carpets and utensils. Talysh nationalists claim that the related Takestanis of Iran, who number about 250,000, are part of the Talysh nation.

LANGUAGE AND RELIGION: The language of the Talysh, Talyshi, is a northwestern Iranian language with a strong admixture of Caucasian and Azeri borrowings. The language spoken in Azerbaijan, Northern Talyshi, is spoken in four major dialects that roughly correspond to the four regions with Talysh majorities—Astarin, Lenkoran, Lerik, and Massallin. Under Soviet policies, the Talysh literary language disappeared; Azeri is now used as the literary language. The majority are bilingual, speaking both Talysh and Azeri, and some are even trilingual, also speaking Russian or Iranian. The language is closely related to that of the Gilakis in Iran, and it is spoken in two major dialects that gradually merge into Northern Talyshi around Astara. Central Talyshi is centered on the Asalem-Hashtpar area along the Caspian littoral, and Southern Talyshi is spoken around Shandermen, Masal, Masule, and in the surrounding mountains in central Gilan.

The Talysh, like the majority of the Azeris and Iranians, are mostly Shi'a Muslims, with a Sunni Muslim minority. Some elements of their pre-Islamic religion remain, such as reverence for trees and groves. Some of their most sacred sites are trees. The Talysh also believe in the presence of both good and evil spirits. The most dangerous spirit is Alazan, the Red Woman, who is believed to attack women during childbirth, as well as newborn babies. The Sunni minority in Iran has suffered discrimination and abuse under the Islamic government since the early 1980s.

NATIONAL HISTORY: The Talysh are believed to be an ancient indigenous people of the region, with roots in the Talish Mountains thousands of years ago. Nomadic Caucasian tribes as early as 1500 B.C. migrated south to settle the fertile plains and marshlands along the Caspian Sea. Traditionally the Talysh economy revolved around cattle raising in the highlands. The culture evolved around the seasonal activities associated with their herds.

In their early history, both Persian and Caucasian peoples settled in the mountains, and the Talysh evolved from the mixture of the two peoples.

By the sixth century B.C. most of the Talysh lands were included in a satrapy (province) of the ancient Persian Empire. Conquered by the Macedonians of Alexander the Great in 334–331 B.C., the region later formed part of the Greek province of Media Atrophene. In the second century B.C. the Persians reconquered the Caspian region.

Invading Arabs conquered and overran the southern Caspian region in A.D. 641, bringing with them their new religion, Islam. From the coastal settlements, Islam was carried into the Talish Mountains, and the Talysh tribes, over many decades, were finally converted. From the tenth century, Talyshstan formed part of the newly established linguistic and culture frontier between the Turkic peoples, who had conquered the territory to the north between the eleventh and thirteenth centuries, and the Iranian peoples. Devastated by the Mongols in the thirteenth century and by the forces of Tamerlane a century later, Talyshstan had declined to a poor, backward region when the Persians regained control of the Caspian provinces in 1592.

Explorers and Cossacks spearheaded the Russian expansion into the Turkish and Persian lands in the sixteenth century. English traders moving south from Russia opened the area to trade with the West. Cossacks overran the Talysh lowlands in 1636 and caused considerable damage before withdrawing. In 1722 the Russians took Talyshstan from Persia and held the region for 10 years, finally returning the region to Persia in exchange for territorial concessions in the Caucasus. The Talysh tribal groups began to unite into a larger defensive unit, although politically they remained under local tribal chiefs and sheiks.

Sheik Seid Abbas established a united Talysh khanate in the mid-eighteenth century. His son Muhammad inherited the throne in 1747 and expanded Talysh control to the lowlands. At his death in 1786 Russia and Persia were competing for influence in the region. The Talysh resented Persian encroachments and nearly constant military pressure, and the khanate developed a pro-Russian policy.

The Talysh khan, Mir-Mustafa, appealed to the Russians for protection against the Persians in 1795, and in 1802 the Russian government proclaimed a protectorate over Talyshstan. The Persians contested Russian influence in the region until the Treaty of Turkmanchai, which recognized Russian authority in 1813. The heartland of the Talysh khanate officially became Russian territory, and the political sovereignty of the Talysh was dissolved. Under British pressure, the Persian government delineated the northern border in the late nineteenth century in a way that effectively divided the Talysh nation between the Russian and Persian Empires.

In Persian Talyshstan, opposition to the excesses and neglect of the Persian monarchy erupted in open rebellion in 1905. A British-Russian agreement signed in 1907 divided the weak Persian state into spheres of influence. In 1909 Russian troops crushed the rebellions in northwestern

Persia, which re-formed as an anti-Russian movement in 1912. In 1917, with their country collapsing in revolution, the Russian troops withdrew from Gilan and Talyshtan.

In 1920 the Soviets, victorious in the Russian Civil War, established control over the northern Talysh region. In May 1920, Soviet forces invaded Iran in support of Talysh and Gilaki rebels fighting the Persian government. The rebels, aided by Soviet troops, declared the region independent of Persia as the Persian Soviet Socialist Republic, and a new government began to redistribute lands traditionally held by absentee Persian landlords, religious bodies, the Persian state, and the Persian crown. The Talysh enthusiastically supported the Soviets, in the hope that their divided nation would be reunited, but in 1921, in exchange for generous oil concessions from the Persian government, the Soviet forces withdrew and the rebel republic collapsed. The border was reestablished, and Talyshstan remained divided.

During the Soviet period the subtropical Talysh lowlands were set aside for large-scale projects such as tea and citrus cultivation. The Talysh lands were nationalized, and the people were forced to join *kolkhozes*, communal farms. Many found work in the oil industry in Baku or in the fishing fleets on the Caspian Sea.

Soviet policy encouraged the assimilation of the Talysh into the more numerous Azeri community, with whom they shared many cultural traits and their Shi'a Muslim religion. According to the Soviet census of 1926, there were 77,039 Talysh in Soviet Azerbaijan, but subsequent censuses counted them as ethnic Azeris. To further assimilation, the Soviet authorities abolished the Talysh Latin alphabet and replaced it with Russian Cyrillic in 1939, forcing those Talysh who were literate to turn to Azeri publications. Azeri, along with Russian, was the official language of the region; education, local administration, and entertainment were all in Azeri. By 1959, relative few people in the region identified themselves as Talysh. Soviet ethnographers assumed that the Talysh, as planned, were disappearing as a separate nation and were being absorbed by the more numerous Azeris. For several decades the Talysh in the Soviet Union virtually disappeared as a people.

The Iranian government also pressed assimilation, declaring that there where no minorities in Iran, though more than 40 different national groups inhabited the country. Because the Talysh and other non-Iranian groups supposedly formed tribal groups of Iranians, they were not counted separately in national censuses. Following the Islamic revolution in 1979, all Muslims in Iran were considered Iranians.

The Soviet authorities, convinced that the Talysh had disappeared, did not try to count them in the censuses of 1970 or 1979; however, in the early 1980s, agitation and demands for limited cultural freedom forced the authorities to reconsider. Previously considered a branch of the Azeris, the Talysh began to demand separation and recognition as a distinct nationality.

In the late 1980s, during the liberalization of Soviet society under Mikhail Gorbachev, it became increasingly clear that a core of Talysh clung to their mother tongue and culture, and refused to assimilate into either Azeri or the Russian-dominated Soviet culture. The reforms in Soviet society allowed the Talysh to organize and recover their national identity. The revival of the Talysh nationality loosed a torrent of economic, political, and cultural grievances. The Soviet authorities, forced to count the Talysh as a separate ethnic group in the 1989 census, were surprised to find that 21,914 people in the region stubbornly registered themselves as Talysh in spite of official pressure to register as ethnic Azeris.

Since the independence of Azerbaijan in 1991, many younger Talysh have rejected the assimilation projected by the Azeri government. New interest in their language and culture has spurred the formation of an autonomy movement, with a small, but growing, separatist movement in the Talysh homeland. Government figures estimate the Talysh population of Azerbaijan at less than 2% of the population, but nationalists claim a much higher number, estimating that 11% of the total population of Azerbaijan is ethnic Talysh. The different figures would seem to be based on language rather than ethnic origins. The Talysh are being drawn back into the revived Talysh culture and language.

Cross-border contacts between the Talysh in Azerbaijan and in Iran has stimulated the rebirth of the Talysh nation. A new appreciation of their music, ancient literature, and folk culture has been reflected in cultural events in Talysh towns on both sides of the border.

On 12 August 1993, Talysh rebels, led by Alikram Gumatov, Rahim Gaziev, and Avaz Ramazanov, proclaimed the independence of a Talysh republic called the Talysh-Murgan Republic, in coordination with an antigovernment coup in northern Azerbaijan. Iranian troops were rushed to the border, and the Azeri military moved in to suppress the rebellion, forcing the leaders to flee to Russia. Gaziev, former defense minister of Azerbaijan, was extradited by the Russian authorities. Many Talysh were arrested and sentenced to prison. The leaders were sentenced to death for high treason in 1996. Gumatov reportedly died in prison in 1997, setting off demonstrations across the region, but he was later confirmed alive in solitary confinement in an Azeri prison.

The Azeri government ratified contracts on the exploration and development of the Talysh–Deniz and Lenkoran-Deniz offshore oil fields, offshore near the Talysh homeland. The development of the fields in 1998–99 brought much-needed employment to the region, but also gave the growing national movement an economic base.

In October 2001, for the first time, the Talysh defied the Islamic authorities of Iran and staged a peaceful march to the Iran-Azerbaijan border in support of their right, as the major national group on both sides of the border, to cross without excessive formalities. Leaders of the Talysh in Azerbaijan supported the demands.

SELECTED BIBLIOGRAPHY:

Kashani-Sabet, Firoozeh. *Frontier Fictions: Shaping the Iranian Nation, 1804–1946.* 2000.

Olson, James S., ed. *An Ethnological Dictionary of the Russian and Soviet Empires.* 1994.

Sicker, Martin. *The Bear and the Lion.* 1988.

Swietochowski, Thadeusz. *Russia and Azerbaijan.* 1995.

Tamils

Thamils; Tamuls; Tamili; Tamals; Damulians; Dravidians

POPULATION: Approximately (2002e) 70,855,000 Tamils in South Asia, 67 million concentrated in Tamil Nadu State and the neighboring states of India, and 3.5 million in the Northern and Eastern Provinces of Sri Lanka. Outside the region there are large Tamil communities in Canada, the United States, the United Kingdom, Germany, South Africa, Malaysia, Singapore, Fiji, Mauritius, Réunion, and various Caribbean states.

THE TAMIL HOMELAND: The Tamil homeland lies in South Asia, occupying the southeastern coastal zone at the tip of India east of the Eastern Ghats and the coastal regions of the north and east of the island of Sri Lanka, just southeast of the Indian mainland. Indian Tamilland forms the state of Tamil Nadu and the union territory of Pondicherry; Sri Lankan Tamilland comprises the Northern and Eastern provinces of Sri Lanka, which are included in the North-East Autonomous Zone. *State of Tamil Nadu*: 50,180 sq. mi.—129,966 sq. km, (2002e) 62,735,000—Tamils 83%, Andhrans* 8%, Kannarese 3%, Malayalis* 2%, other Indians 4%. *Union Territory of Pondicherry:* 183 sq. mi.—474 sq. km. (2002e) 991,000 – Tamils 93%. *North-East Autonomous Zone of Sri Lanka (Tamil Eelam)*: 7,296 sq. mi.—18,826 sq. km, (2002e) 2,645,000—Tamils 77%, Moors (Muslims) 12%, Sinhalese 10%, other Sri Lankans 1%. The Tamil capital and major cultural center is Madras, called Chennai by the Tamils, (2002e) 4,539,000, metropolitan area 7,113,000. The capital and major cultural center of the Sri Lankan Tamils is Yapanaya, called Jaffna in the Tamil language, (2002e) 162,000. Other important cultural centers in Sri Lanka, Tirikunamalaya, called Trin Komali locally, (2002e) 83,000, and Madak-

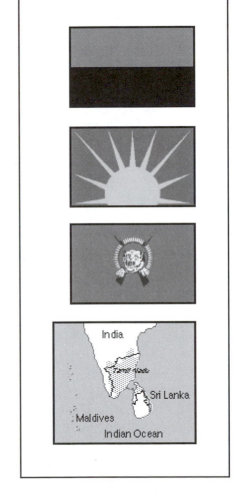

alpuwa, called Batticaloa, (2002e) 64,000. Other important cultural centers in India are Coimbatore, known as Koyampattur to the Tamils, (2002e) 1,245,000, metropolitan area 1,614,000, Madura, called Madurai by the Tamils, 1,262,000, metropolitan area 1,408,000, and Pondicherry, Puttucheri in Tamil, (2002e) 313,000, metropolitan area 570,000.

FLAG: The unofficial flag of the Indian Tamils, the flag of the Free Tamil Movement, Tamil Nad, is a horizontal bicolor of red over black. The national flag of the Sri Lankan Tamils is a red field bearing a yellow half at the bottom and 11 yellow rays radiating to the hoist, top, and fly. The flag of the largest of the Sri Lankan nationalist groups, the Liberation Tigers of Tamil Eelam (LTTE), is a red field charged with a yellow roaring tiger's head in a circle of short yellow rays.

PEOPLE AND CULTURE: The Tamils are a Dravidian people, generally smaller and darker than the Aryan peoples of northern India and southern Sri Lanka. The Tamil population of South Asia is divided between the states of India and Sri Lanka. They represent one of the indigenous peoples of the subcontinent and claim to be the original pre-Aryan settlers of Sri Lanka—where they are now divided into two distinct groups, the descendents of the early settlers, and the Indian Tamils, brought to the island in the nineteenth century. The two groups of Tamils in Sri Lanka had little social contact with each other until the mid-twentieth century. The caste system is still strong, even though discrimination has been banned by the Indian and Sri Lankan constitutions. The Tamil diaspora, living in areas in many parts of the world, is united by the shared Hindu religion, Dravidian Tamil language, and over 3,000 years of history.

LANGUAGE AND RELIGION: The Tamil language is a Dravidian language, belonging to the Tamil-Malayalam branch of the Southern Dravidian language group. The language is written in its own script. Tamil is the oldest cultivated Dravidian language, with a rich literature that extends back to the early Christian era. There exist a number of local dialects, the major dialect regions being the northern and eastern areas combined, the western area, the southern area (split into at least four major dialects of Madurai, Tirunelveli, Nanjiland, and Ramnad), and Sri Lanka (Ceylon). Correlated with the social position of the speaker are a number of speech forms; a major division occurs between the Brahmin and the non-Brahmin varieties. In addition, there is a sharp dichotomy between the formal language and informal speech. The language issue is at the center of the Tamil movement, which calls for the de-Sanskritization and de-Brahminization of Tamil culture, language, and literature. Tamil has official status in India, Sri Lanka, and Singapore. Many of Sri Lanka's Muslim population, popularly called Moors, speak Tamil as their first language.

The great majority of the Tamils are Hindus, although their form of

Hinduism, called Traditional Hinduism, is less rigid and more relaxed than that of northern India, where Brahminism prevails. About 3% of Tamil Nadu's population adheres to Brahminism, which is seen by most Tamils as elitist and anti-Dravidian. Tamil schools of personal religious devotion, called *bhakti*, go back at least to the sixth century A.D. In recent decades atheism has spread, probably as a protest against Brahmin ritualism. There are also Jains (mostly in northern Tamil Nadu), Christians, and Muslims (particularly in eastern Sri Lanka).

NATIONAL HISTORY: The Dravidian peoples, once dominant in almost all of present-day India, were driven south from the Indo-Gangetic Plain by invasions of Aryan tribes from the Iranian Plateau between 2000 and 1700 B.C. The Aryan northerners adopted the Hindu beliefs of the Dravidians but developed a form of the religion that enshrined a rigid caste system, relegating the Dravidians and other indigenous peoples to the lower rungs of society. The Aryans also developed an elaborate priestly ritual, called Brahminism, which was rejected by the Dravidian peoples moving south to escape Aryan rule. In the south the Dravidians gradually divided into a number of distinct groups, the most important the Tamils, Kannarese, Malayalis, and Andhrans.

Buddhist Aryans from northern India conquered the island of Sri Lanka in the fifth century B.C. The island was the center of an advanced Buddhist culture when it fell to Tamil invaders from the Indian mainland in 235 B.C. The Hindu Tamils ruled the island as an aristocratic elite until the resurgent Buddhists overthrew Tamil rule in 101 B.C.

The Tamils halted the Aryan advance from northern India while expanding their rule in the Dravidian south. Under the powerful Chola dynasty, the Tamils crossed the narrow strait to reconquer Sri Lanka in A.D. 1017. The Tamils spread across the north of the island and down the eastern coast, bringing them into the Tamil kingdom. In the twelfth century most of the remaining Sinhalese fled the regions under the control of the Tamil kingdom, moving into the south and west as the Tamils expanded into the central districts of the island. Centuries of sporadic war continued to divide the island.

For over three centuries the Chola kings supported a flourishing social and economic life and a great flowering of Hindu Tamil culture in southern India and northern Sri Lanka. The use of Roman gold and lamps and the consumption of European wine testify to the extensive foreign trade carried on by the Tamil kingdom. A declining power in the thirteenth century, the Tamil kingdom fell to invading Muslims in 1279. A century later the resurgent Tamils drove the Muslims from their homeland on the Indian mainland.

The Portuguese established the first European base on the coast of mainland Tamilland. Taking advantage of the nearby Sri Lanka's ethnic and religious conflicts, they took control of several coastal areas in the north of the island. In 1639 the English opened a post at Madras, followed by the French, who established a base at Pondicherry in 1673. The Portuguese gradually extended their authority over Sri Lanka until the Dutch ousted them from the entire island in 1658. The French and British established footholds on the island in the late eighteenth century; the island came under British colonial rule in 1796. The British added the Tamil north of Sri Lanka to the Madras government on the mainland, which governed it until 1833.

Madras became the center of British power in South Asia. The city developed rapidly as one of the three cornerstones of British India. The stability and peace of British rule generated an important Tamil cultural revival in the late nineteenth century, notable for a literature that drew on ancient Tamil traditions.

The British authorities in Ceylon, as Sri Lanka was called during the colonial period, gave the Tamil and Sinhalese areas separate colonial administrations. Plantation agriculture, introduced in 1815, required additional labor; thousands of Tamils were brought to Ceylon from the Indian mainland between 1830 and 1850. To differentiate the mainland and Sri Lankan Tamils, the newcomers were called "Indian Tamils." Christian missionaries, restricted to the Tamil-populated Jaffna Peninsula, gave the Tamils a head start in education, heightening ethnic tension, as the Tamils advanced more rapidly than the Sinhalese.

The Tamil cultural revival of the late nineteenth century fueled a parallel national movement in southern India in the early 1900s. The first distinctly Tamil interest group, the Self Respect Movement (Suya Mariyathai Iyakam), formed in 1921, and the first openly secessionist program was espoused by a Tamil political party in 1925. Tamil nationalism merged into the Indian nationalist movement that spread across the subcontinent in the 1930s.

Imposition of Hindi, India's Aryan national language, in Tamil Nadu started in 1937, when the government of Madras Presidency made Hindi a compulsory subject in schools. Anti-Hindi protests spread across the region in 1938. Several protesters were killed, becoming martyrs to the anti-Hindi movement.

Ethnic strife continued to divide British Ceylon. The resentment of the majority Sinhalese manifested itself in bloody pogroms and the seizure of Tamil lands in the early decades of the twentieth century. The attacks on the Tamils continued up to World War II. Only the British presence prevented even more violent ethnic confrontations. The dour and hardworking Tamils prospered under British rule; ethnic Tamils held most of the clerical and administrative jobs in the British colonial government of Ceylon.

The British province of Madras, made a separate autonomous province of British India in 1937, gave the Tamils a territorial base. Led by the

Justice Party, the Tamils demanded the separation of their homeland from British India under a separate government like that of Burma. The British began to dismantle their empire after World War II, granting independence to India in 1947 and to Ceylon in 1948. The Tamils, minorities in both India and Ceylon, turned to regionalism and nationalism in the late 1940s.

The Sinhalese-dominated government of Ceylon immediately after independence disenfranchised the Indian Tamils—that is, the nineteenth-century migrants from the mainland—which greatly curtailed Tamil voting power and political strength. Official discrimination and a law establishing Sinhala as the only official language provoked serious clashes and rioting in 1956, 1958, and 1961. Determined to protect Tamil interests, Tamil national leaders, backed by a nonviolent campaign for linguistic and cultural rights, petitioned the government for limited autonomy.

The Indian government, dominated by the Aryan northern states, ignored growing demands for Tamil autonomy in the late 1940s, leading to a widening of the demands to cover the Dravidian southern states of India. Tamil nationalists promoted a united Dravidian state in the south, but the neighboring Dravidian peoples, remembering past Tamil domination, rejected the proposal. Particularist Tamil nationalism gained support following the separation of the non-Tamil districts of Madras into distinct linguistic states between 1953 and 1956.

The Dravida Munnetra Kazagham (DMK) was formed in India by a coalition of nationalist and cultural groups in the late 1950s. Initially anti-Aryan and anti-Brahmin, the DMK led a secessionist campaign in the early 1960s in opposition to the imposition of Hindi. In 1965, following a series of violent pro-independence demonstrations, the Indian prime minister, Jawaharlal Nehru, made advocating secession a criminal offense. The DMK, in order to continue operating legally, changed its focus to Tamil autonomy and won control of the state legislature in 1967. The state legislature voted to change the state's name from Madras to Tamil Nadu, the Tamil Nation, in 1968. The Tamil nationalist movement of the mid-1960s was the first serious threat to Indian unity.

A new Sri Lankan constitution approved in 1972 changed the island's name back to Sri Lanka and institutionalized Buddhism as the state religion, completely ignoring Tamil rights. Moderate Tamil nationalists led a nonviolent resistance, which government ministers dismissed as a mere nuisance. Militant nationalists, seeing no prospect for progress by nonviolent means, demanded independence for the north and east of the island in 1975. Anti-Tamil rioting swept the island; Sinhalese mobs attacked Tamil areas, murdering, raping, and looting Tamil businesses and homes. In retaliation the militant Tamil nationalists, led by the Liberation Tigers of Tamil Eelam (LTTE), launched a terrorist campaign against Sinhalese domination.

The Indian government dissolved the Tamil Nadu state government in 1976, accusing its authorities of corruption and support of Tamil separatism. The suspension of the Tamil government initiated a long period of tension between the Tamils and the Indian government. The Indian government's covert support of Tamil separatism in Sri Lanka while refusing to discuss greater Tamil autonomy in India escalated Tamil distrust of the Indian government in the early 1980s.

Anti-Tamil rioting resumed in Sri Lanka in 1981–83, the worst ethnic violence in over 30 years of confrontations. Too late to stop the violence overtaking the island, the Sri Lankan government in 1984 offered the Tamils limited concessions and power sharing. The Tamil leaders rejected the limited offer and repeated their demands for autonomy and an end to Sinhalese settlement in Tamil districts. Attempts to reach a negotiated settlement collapsed in 1985.

Tension between the Tamils and the northern-dominated Indian government increased in the 1980s, partly over the question of Tamil rights in both India and Sri Lanka. The Indian government detained over 10,000 Tamils following serious antigovernment rioting in 1984. Another 19,000 were arrested when disturbances and rioting resumed in 1986.

Heavy fighting between separatists, armed by Tamil sympathizers in India, and the Sri Lankan military swept the northern districts of the island in 1986. To avert civil war in Sri Lanka, the Indian government brokered a compromise that provided for the disarming of the Tamil rebels under an Indian military force that would temporarily occupy the Tamil region. The pact, accepted by most Tamil groups, was rejected by the LTTE. Reaction to the Indian intervention in Sri Lanka raised nationalist sentiment in Tamil Nadu to levels not seen since the secessionist crisis of 1965–66.

The Indian troops, at first viewed as the saviors of the Tamils of Sri Lanka, by late 1987 were seen as oppressors. Skirmishes between LTTE guerrillas and the Indian troops turned into running battles. Badly mauled by the separatist forces and no longer welcomed by the Sri Lanka government, the Indian troops withdrew in 1989–90. The LTTE took control of much of the region as the Indians left, battling rival Tamil groups and government troops. Violence erupted between Tamils and the Muslim Moors unwilling to accept their rule in the Eastern Province, which, unlike the Tamil-majority Northern Province (96% Tamil), is 42% Tamil, 33% Moor, and 25% Sinhalese. By June 1990 over 30,000 had died.

In January 1991, the Indian government again imposed direct rule on Tamil Nadu and Pondicherry, the former French enclave on the Tamil coast. The imposition was accompanied by the arrest of between 15,000 and 20,000 Tamils, officially to avert widespread violence by separatists and supporters of the Sri Lankan Tamils' fight for independence. The

LTTE extended the Sri Lankan war to the Indian mainland, on 21 May 1991 assassinating Rajiv Gandhi, the prime minister of India during the Indian occupation of northern Sri Lanka in the 1980s. Gandhi's assassination was reportedly carried out with the active support of dissident Tamils in Tamil Nadu.

The Indian and Sri Lankan governments, beginning in 1992, increased military and political cooperation to oppose the growing Tamil nationalist movement in both countries. In April 1993 an LTTE suicide assassin blew up Sri Lanka's president, Ranasinghe Premadasa. The Sri Lankan military took control of Jaffna in December 1995, driving the Tamils from their last major city on the island. The Tamil campaign for independence became one of the world's most violent and long-lasting separatist wars, and seemingly one of the most intractable.

The Tamil movement in India, which has remained mostly nonviolent, in the late 1990s focused on economic and political issues. Domination by the northern Aryans of the central Indian states continued to fuel demands for greater cultural autonomy and wider powers of self-government for Tamil Nadu.

A measure of autonomy for the north and east of Sri Lanka was accepted in 1998 by many of the war-weary Tamil minority, but the LTTE rejected local self-government and insisted upon an independent homeland for Tamils on the island. The LTTE retook Jaffna from government troops in early 2000, facilitating Tamil acceptance of government offers to attend peace talks. Assassinations of moderate Tamil politicians and Sri Lankan government officials continue to divert attention from efforts to reach an agreement to end the long-running war, which had cost over 60,000 lives by late 2001.

Nationalist sentiment, particularly strong in Sri Lanka, around Madras on the Indian mainland, and among the Tamil diaspora, often focuses on the unity of all Tamil territories in South Asia in a Greater Eelam. The majority of the population of Tamil Nadu support demands for greater autonomy within India, while supporting the Eelam Tamils of Sri Lanka, but only a minority seek complete separation from India.

The United States, Canada, and the United Kingdom, all with sizable Tamil communities who have supported the Tamil separatists in Sri Lanka, branded the LTTE a terrorist organization. The decline of support pushed the Tamils to negotiate with a new government that won elections in December 2001.

SELECTED BIBLIOGRAPHY:

Fuglerud, Ivind. *Life on the Outside: The Tamil Diaspora and Long-Distance Nationalism.* 1999.

Krishna, Sankaran. *Postcolonial Insecurities: India, Sri Lanka, and the Question of Nationhood*. 1999.

Ramaswamy, Sumathi. *Passions of the Tongue: Language Devotion in Tamil India*. 1998.

Wilson, A. Jeyaratnam. *Sri Lankan Tamil Nationalism*. 1999.

Tannese

Tannans; Tafeans; Tanese; Tanians

POPULATION: Approximately (2002e) 30,000 Tannese in Vanuatu in the South Pacific, concentrated in the Tafea district, the five southern islands of the archipelago, particularly Tanna, with about 24,000, and Erromango, with 2,000. Outside the home islands, there are Tannese communities in Port Vila, on Efate, the capital of the country, and in other northern islands. There area also Tannese communities in Fiji and Australia.

THE TANNESE HOMELAND: The Tannese homeland lies in the South Pacific, comprising the five islands of the southern group of the Vanuatu Archipelago: Tanna, Anatom, Futuna, Erromango, and Aniwa. The islands, volcanic in origin, lie about 60 miles south of the central island of Vanuatu, Efate. Mount Yasur on Tanna is one of the highest active volcanoes in the world, giving the island some of the most fertile land in the South Pacific. The five islands form the Tafea district of the Republic of Vanuatu. *Tafea District (Tanna)*: 875 sq. mi.—2,266 sq. km, (2002e) 29,000—Tannese 84%, other Vanuatuans 16%. The Tannese capital and major cultural center is Isangel, (2002e) 2,000.

FLAG: The Tannese national flag is a pale blue field bearing a centered green five-pointed star against a narrow yellow circle centered. The flag of the John Frum Movement has five green and red horizontal stripes with the Tannese flag as a canton on the upper hoist. The flag of the Tafea Movement, the official flag of the Tannese state proclaimed in 1980, has five red and green stripes with a brown canton on

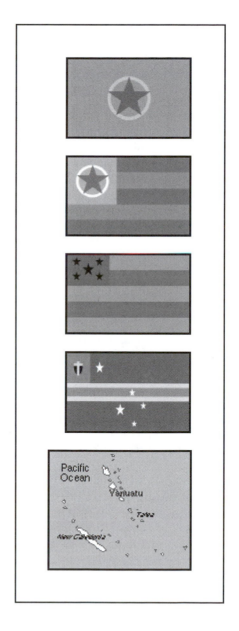

the upper hoist bearing five black stars. The official flag of Tafea Province is a blue field bearing yellow, red, and yellow horizontal stripes centered behind five white stars and a small green canton on the upper hoist bearing a black shield with a yellow cross.

PEOPLE AND CULTURE: The Tannese are a Melanesian people, the inhabitants of the five southern islands of the Vanuatu Archipelago. Taking their name from the largest and most important of the islands, Tanna, the Tannese retain their traditional culture, which remains strong in the islands. The "cargo cults" that began in the late 1930s have had a profound religious and political influence on the islanders. Long isolated from the administrative centers of the archipelago, the Tannese retain many customs and traditions that have disappeared elsewhere.

LANGUAGE AND RELIGION: The Tannese speak several South Vanuatu dialects of the Oceanic subgroup of the Austronesian languages. The mutually intelligible dialects—Kwamera, Lenakel, North Tanna, Southwest Tanna, Whitesands (Napuanmen), Aneityum, and Sie (Eromanga)—differ considerably from the dialects of central and northern Vanuatu. The dialects are further divided into a number of subdialects. The South Vanuatu dialects are thought to have been influenced by later Pacific migrations. The dialect spoken on Aneityum is particularly difficult for other Vanuatuans to understand. Education is principally conducted in English and French; Bislama, the national language of Vanuatu, is used as a second language, but many in the southern islands do not understand it.

The majority of the Tannese are Christians, mostly Protestant, but with an important and influential Roman Catholic minority. The conversion of the islanders by nineteenth-century missionaries became part of the British-French rivalry in the islands, with the British supporting Protestantism and the French the Roman Catholics. The rivalries still remain, although the John Frum movement has since the 1930s taken on much of the belief system of the islanders.

NATIONAL HISTORY: The original settlers of the islands are thought to have formed part of a migration from Southeast Asia or Taiwan in Neolithic times. Moving south through the Philippines and Indonesia, they eventually fanned out across the Pacific from the region of New Guinea, crossing the sea in highly seaworthy outrigger canoes. Archeological evidence indicates that the northern islands of Vanuatu were settled by about 1300 B.C. from Melanesian islands to the west. After that there were successive waves of migration to the islands. The earliest date for settlement on the southern islands is 420 B.C.

Around A.D. 1200, a highly stratified society developed in central Vanuatu with the arrival, according to tradition from the south, of the great chief Roymata. His death was marked by elaborate rituals, including the burying alive of one woman and one man from each of the clans in the central and southern Vanuatu islands.

European contact began with the Portuguese navigator Pedro Fernández de Quirós in 1606, although contact with the islanders was minimal. The next to visit the islands were the French explorer Louis-Antoine de Bougainville in 1768 and Capt. James Cook in 1774. Cook was the first European to visit Tanna and the smaller southern islands, having been drawn by the glow of Tanna's active volcano. He mapped the entire archipelago and named it the New Hebrides, after the Scottish islands. He requested permission to climb Tanna's volcano, but because of a traditional taboo he was refused. His ship anchored in a small bay, which he named Port Resolution, later renamed Isangel.

European traders and missionaries settled in the islands in the 1840s, but their impact on the Tannese was minimal. Significant cultural influences began only after the 1860s, when British and French planters settled in the islands and thousands of Tannese who had been indentured workers or had been captured by "blackbirders" began to return to the islands from the plantations of Fiji, New Caledonia, and northern Australia. Many established new forms of political influence with the aid of Protestant missionaries. Supported by the missionaries, who supplied education and advice, Tannese leaders began to compete against European traders and planters encroaching on the islands.

To protect the interests of the mainly British missionaries and the primarily French planters in the archipelago, in 1887 the British and French governments established rudimentary political control through a joint commission. This was succeeded in 1906 by a formal Anglo-French condominium. British and French commissioners retained responsibility over their respective nationals and jointly ruled the indigenous groups. This odd arrangement had only a slight impact on Tanna and the southern islands, whose main European contacts continued to be either with European missionaries or planters.

Cargo cults began in the South Pacific during the late 1930s but remained small and isolated until World War II. Tanna became a major Allied base in the war against Japan in 1942. Free-spending black American troops inspired the Tannese cargo cult. The Americans built a huge base, which, when the war ended, they left to the Tannese. According to tradition, one of the villagers asked an American who he was. The American answered, "John, from America," which the Tannese heard as "John Frum." An early emblem of the cargo cult was a red cross, as many goods arriving in the islands were Red Cross relief materials.

To the islanders it seemed that the visitors possessed unimaginable riches without doing anything that in the least resembled work. This perception led to the conclusion that the strangers, instead of fishing or farming, lived by talking or by manipulating bits of paper. In the Melanesian moral system, riches were exclusively the result of labor. Many felt that the whites must have fooled the gods with magic into misdirecting all the wealth the islanders saw from people who had done work—real work, such as farming—and who as a result received nothing. The Tannese had to call the gods' attention to the situation, and they hit on white rituals as the key.

They devised a set of ceremonies, dressing in approximations of military uniforms and conducting drills. They set up a miniature air base with a control tower and radio antenna—a vine strung between two poles. The chiefs would utter magic phrases asking for the riches to come based on what they had overheard from the American and European soldiers.

John Frum was believed to have returned in spirit when development brought to the Tannese many of the riches they had sought during the years after the end of World War II. In the early 1950s, the cargo cult became the John Frum Movement and developed into an important anticolonial movement in the southern islands of the New Hebrides. The movement emerged over such concerns as land ownership; over a third of the best island lands were owned by foreigners.

The Forcona Movement, also called the Four Corners Movement, developed as a political and religious movement opposed to the anglophone political parties and the influence of the Presbyterian Church. The movement, supported by the French planters, became openly secessionist, demanding separate status for the five southern islands. The French-British condominium authorities reacted to the growing power of the John Frum and Forcona Movements by prohibiting the wearing of uniforms and the raising of flags. Both the John Frum Movement and the Forcona Movement, however, were supported by the French, who hoped to retain a foothold in the islands as decolonization neared. Cult leaders were allowed to form private militias, to which the French authorities donated funds and vehicles.

Tanna was thrown into turmoil in 1973 as independence fever swept the New Hebrides. A French government delegate asked for the mediation services of the colonist Antoine Fournalli, who gained the confidence of the five chiefs of the southern islands. Fournalli proclaimed himself king of Tanna, and on 24 March 1974 proclaimed the Nation of Tanna independent, with the support of the major chiefs. The new Tannese government demanded that all British and French leave the islands within eight days. French troops took control of Isangel, the Tannese capital, setting off a widespread revolt against the Europeans. On 29 June 1974 a joint French-British forced landed on Tanna from the central island of the New Hebrides, Efate, and secured the islands. Fornelli was captured and deported to New Caledonia. The Tannese leaders of the Forcona Movement were sentenced to prison terms, adding to the anti-Efate feeling in the islands.

The Tanna revolt fueled the growth of nationalism in the islands, both an anti-European and anti-Efate mass movement. The flag of the revolt was adopted as the Tannese national flag, which flew over the island alongside that of the John Frum Movement, the largest political organization in the southern islands.

The decolonization of the South Pacific islands fueled the secessionist movement in the southern islands, which was supported by the French planters, who feared that a program of land reform would deprive them of their large plantations. A third political movement, the Kapiel Alliance, supported by the animist Tannese of the interior, became openly separatist as independence neared in the late 1970s.

Independence for the New Hebrides was agreed upon at a Paris conference in 1977 between the British, French, and representatives of the New Hebrides political elite from the central island of Efate. Elections were held, and in 1979 a constitution was drawn up for all the islands. On 1 January 1980, a second Tannese attempt to secede was made, with a unilateral declaration of independence. The new state was named Tafea, from the first letter of the names of each of the five southern islands. French officials who had encouraged the revolt disappeared shortly before the independence proclamation. British forces invaded the islands in May 1980, ending the secession on the 26th. The secessionist flag and the leaders of the revolt were seized.

On 30 July 1980, the New Hebrides became independent under the name Republic of Vanuatu, which translates as "our land forever." The integrity of the new country remained under threat for some time, although the Tannese participated in the national government. Members of the John Frum Movement were elected to parliament in the 1980s and 1990s. The Tannese continue to hold John Frum ceremonies on a weekly basis, often as a tourist attraction, but also as a sort of town meeting or local government. Conflicts are resolved, grievances voiced, and wishes declared. All tourists on the island are welcome to join in.

SELECTED BIBLIOGRAPHY:

Bonnemaison, Joël. *The Tree and the Canoe: History and Ethnography of Tanna*. 1994.
Ferea, W. *Cargo Cults and Development in Melanesia*. 1984.
Lindstrom, Lamont. *Working Encounters: Oral Histories of World War II Labor Corps from Tanna, Vanuatu*. 1989.
Quirk, Tom, Tim Duncan, and Richard de Lautour. *The Clever Country as a Cargo Cult: National Needs and Higher*. 1990.

Tatars

Volga Tatars; Kazan Tatars; Tatarians; Tartars

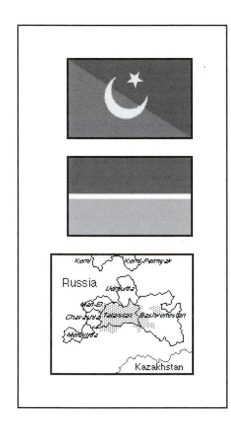

POPULATION: Approximately (2002e) 7,121,000 Tatars in Russia and the other states of the former Soviet Union, 6,620,000 in Russia, and with smaller numbers in Belarus and Ukraine. Outside Europe, sizable Tatar communities live in Siberia, the Central Asian states, particularly Kazakhstan, and the Russian Far East.

THE TATAR HOMELAND: The Tatar homeland lies in eastern European Russia, occupying the steppe lands, the low, rolling hills of the Volga and Kama River valleys. In the east the region rises to wooded uplands, with extensive plains in the river valleys and the Chuvash Plateau to the west. Rich in natural resources, Tatarstan is a leading producer of oil and natural gas and is the starting point for the "Friendship" pipeline to Eastern Europe. Tatarstan, the core of the Tatar homeland, is a member state of the Russian Federation. *Tatarstan Republic (Tatarstan Respublikasi)*: 26,256 sq. mi.—68,002 sq. km, (2002e) 3,746,000— Tatars 51%, Russians 40%, Udmurts* 4%, Chavash* 3%, Maris* 2%. The Tatar capital and major cultural center is Kazan, (2002e) 1,106,000, metropolitan area 1,245,000. The other important cultural center is Naberezhnye Chelny, called Challi by the Tatars, (2002e) 514,000.

FLAG: The flag of the Tatar national movement is a diagonal bicolor of green over red, divided lower hoist to upper fly, bearing a centered white crescent moon, horns pointing down, and a five-pointed white star. The Tatar national flag, the official flag of the republic, is a horizontal bicolor of red over green, the colors separated by a narrow white stripe.

PEOPLE AND CULTURE: The Tatars are a Turkic nation of mixed ancestry, the largest of the non-Russian peoples of the Russian Federation. They are descended from the Volga Bulgars, Turkicized eastern Finns, and the Turkic tribes of the Golden Horde. Extensive mixing with the other peoples of the Volga River basin over the centuries has changed the physical aspect of the Tatars, who are now mostly European in culture and appearance, with a range from blond hair and blue eyes to almost Mongol physical features, resembling Central Asians. The Tatars are divided into several subgroups. The Mishars are Turkicized eastern Finns, descendents of Meschera and Mordvins,* who speak a western dialect of Tatar. The Teptiars, Tatars who migrated east after the Russian conquest of Kazan and settled among the Bashkorts, speak a dialect that mixes Tatar and Bashkort. The Kryashans or Kreshans are Tatars that converted to Christianity. Although they remain Tatar in culture and language, they have been the most susceptible to assimilation into Russian culture. The Tatars have a long urban tradition; about 71% of the Tatars lived in urban areas in 2001.

LANGUAGE AND RELIGION: The language of the Tatars is a Uralian language of the northwestern Kipchak Turkic language group of the Altaic languages. Spoken in three major dialects—Middle Tatar or Kazan, Western Tatar or Mishar, and Eastern Tatar or Siberian Tatar—the language is further divided into a number of subdialects and several mixed dialects, including Astrakhan, Kasim, Tepter, and Uralic. The literary language is based on the Kazan dialect. Assimilation or Russification, government policy during the Soviet era, had a particular impact on language. Between 1959 and 1989 more than 8% of the Tatar population adopted Russian as their preferred language; however, since 1991 that trend has reversed.

The Tatars are the most northerly of the Muslim peoples; the majority of the Tatars are Sunni Muslims of the Hanafite rite. Many still observe pre-Islamic rites such as *sabantuy*, the ancient spring agricultural festival, which has its origins in shamanism. Some pre-Islamic beliefs, such as the "evil eye," still exist. There is an important Orthodox Christian minority, called the Kreshen, who number about 320,000 and have helped to maintain historical Tatar ties to the neighboring Christian Finnic and Slav peoples. They were converted to Christianity during two campaigns of forced conversion in the seventeenth and eighteenth centuries.

NATIONAL HISTORY: The name "Tata," later "Tatar," was first used among nomadic tribes living in northeastern Mongolia and the area around Lake Baikal in the fifth century A.D. Migrating west, the Tata mixed with the Kipchak and other Turkic peoples, and they first appeared in the lower Volga River basin in the eighth century. From the ninth to the twelfth centuries the Tatars formed a national state with its capital at Bolgary Velikiye. The Tatar state traded with China and Central Asia, and it developed a high level of culture. Mixing with the Finnic, Slavic, and Bulgar peoples of the Volga region, the Tatars became more European in physical aspect with each generation.

Traditionally, an embassy from the Muslim caliphate in Baghdad came to the region in the year A.D. 922. A congress of the tribes met and adopted the new religion, Islam, as the state religion, also replacing their ancient Turkic script with the Arabic of the Muslim emissaries. The adoption of Islam and contact with the Muslim peoples to the south stimulated art and learning.

The Tatars were conquered and absorbed into the Mongol Golden Horde in 1236. Many Tatars fought in the Mongol armies that invaded Europe in the thirteenth century. The Mongol and Turkic peoples of the Golden Horde merged and became known in Europe as simply as "Tatars"; the invasion led by Batu Khan into Central Europe in 1241 is known as "the Tatar invasion."

After Genghis Khan's enormous Mongol Empire disintegrated, the Tatars established several successor states, including the khanates of Astrakhan and Kazan. Kazan, founded as the capital of the Volga Tatars in 1401 in the Volga-Kama region, became the capital of the new Khanate of Kazan in 1445. In 1502 the Tatars defeated the remnant of the Golden Horde and expanded west to the Ural Mountains. The powerful khanate extracted tribute from the Slav states west of the Urals, including the Muscovite state, as the price of continued independence. Rich on tribute and trade, the khanate fostered a great flowering of Tatar culture, arts, and literature.

In 1486 the Tatar khanate and the growing duchy of Moscow signed a treaty of eternal peace. The Tatar's former vassals, the Russians, led by Ivan IV, called the Terrible, the grand duke of Moscow, ignored the treaty and invaded and conquered the Tatar Kazan state in 1552–53. The Tatar capital, Kazan, finally fell following a two-month siege. As part of the official policy of suppressing Islam, Tsar Feodor ordered the destruction of all mosques in the Tatar homeland. The Tatar Khanate of Astrakhan was conquered in 1556. Even though Ivan IV had ruthlessly suppressed the Tatars' Islamic religion, the family of the last khan and the Tatar aristocracy were absorbed into the tsarist aristocracy, greatly facilitating the annexation of the vast region.

The most advanced of the Turkic peoples, the Tatars became the middlemen between the imperial government and newly conquered Turkic peoples over the next three centuries. They earned a favored position within the expanding Russian Empire as commercial and political agents, teachers in Muslim regions, and administrators of the newly won Muslim territories in Central Asia.

Tatar resistance to Russification and forced conversion to Orthodox Christianity generated sporadic revolts and violence in the seventeenth and eighteenth centuries. The Tatar revolts prompted a new imperial policy, the colonization of the vast Volga Basin by more reliable Christian Slavs. In 1708 Kazan Province was established and became the center of the Slavic colonization of the Volga Basin. Persecution of the Muslims reached its peak in 1742, when new and more repressive laws were adopted.

Thousands of Slav colonists settled in the area over the next century. The resilient Tatars, despite steady pressure to assimilate, tenaciously clung to their language and their highly stratified culture. Their Islamic religion, banned for two centuries, was again allowed during the reign of Catherine the Great. The law on building mosques was rescinded in 1766.

A large middle class evolved by the 1880s, the first to emerge in a Muslim society in Russia. A progressive religious outlook, emphasis on modern education, an increase in publication, and general political activity stimulated the rapid growth of national consciousness. The high literacy rate and well-developed national culture stimulated a national revival in the late nineteenth century. The first openly nationalist group formed in 1906, advocating independence, socialism, and the expulsion of the Slavs.

Officially exempted from military conscription until 1916, the Muslim Tatars felt few of the effects of World War I until revolution swept the empire in February 1917. As civil government collapsed Tatar nationalists and Slav Mensheviks (a moderate Russian political wing opposed to the Bolsheviks) took control of the Volga region. Vehemently against the atheism of the Bolsheviks in power following the October 1917 coup, and threatened by advancing Bolshevik forces, regional leaders formed the state of Idel–Ural, encompassing present-day Tatarstan, Bashkortostan, and Orenburg Provinces. The Tatar leaders declared the sovereignty of Idel-Ural on 24 January 1918. In April 1918, the Bolsheviks overran the territory and suppressed the Tatar national movement. Many Tatar leaders were arrested and subsequently disappeared.

Militarily allied to the anti-Bolshevik Czech Legion, made up of freed prisoners of war, the nationalists returned to rout the Bolsheviks in the region. With the other non-Russian peoples of the Volga the Tatars formed the Idel-Ural Federation, which was declared independent on 30 September 1918. The expanding Russian Civil War brought violence and destruction to the Tatar homeland as the Whites and Reds fought for control. In 1920 the victorious Soviets took control of the Tatar lands, which were absorbed into the new Russian Federation, the largest component of the Soviet Union, as an autonomous republic.

Although the Tatars were one of the largest nations of the new Soviet Union, they were not granted union republican status but were given only autonomous status within the autonomous Soviet Russian Federation on 27 May 1920. The boundaries of the new autonomous republic were drawn to include only about a third of the total Tatar population and to ensure an ethnic Russian majority.

The Tatars, feared and hated since the Mongol-Tatar conquest of Russia, were not trusted by the new Soviet regime; the Soviet leader, Joseph Stalin, later reportedly said that the Tatars had as much chance of achieving union republic status as of seeing their ears. Mass purges eliminated all members of the Tatar government and a greater part of the intelligentsia during the 1920s and 1930s. Intermittent purges continued until the death of Stalin in 1953. The systematic Russification of the Tatar population continued until the 1970s.

The discovery of extensive petroleum reserves in Tatarstan during World War II hastened industrialization but drew a large influx of Slav workers. By 1975, the Tatar population of the republic had fallen to just 37% of the total. Minority status quickened a national revival that converged with the liberalization of Soviet life in the late 1980s. In 1989 the Tatars celebrated the 1,100th anniversary of the adoption of Islam in the Volga region.

The reforms introduced by Mikhail Gorbachev in the late 1980s raised expectations among the Tatars that old grievances would finally be addressed. Demands for full republican status within the Soviet Union led to a declaration of sovereignty by the Tatar republican government in August 1990.

The complete collapse of the Soviet Union in August 1991 set in motion a strong Tatar nationalist movement and sparked huge pro-independence rallies in Kazan. A number of nationalist groups formed, the more moderate advocating greater self-government within a new democratic Russia, while militants demanded a declaration of independence before undertaking negotiations with the new Russian state. in a referendum on sovereignty in March 1992, 61% favored independence. As a result of the referendum, later in March the president of Tatarstan, Mintimer Shaimiev, refused to sign a new Russian federation treaty, and in November 1992 the Tatar parliament approved an amendment declaring Tatarstan a sovereign state freely associated with the Russian Federation.

In December 1992, nationalists in Tatarstan, Chuvashia, and Mari-El lobbied for the formation of a confederation of the peoples of the Volga and Ural regions. It was planned to be initially a social and cultural union, the union later evolving into a political union. The plan for an Idel-Ural state was opposed by the Russian central government and was never implemented.

Tatar national leaders, in spite of growing pressure from the Russian government, stubbornly insisted that Tatarstan's relations with Russia and other states must be governed by treaty. In July 1993 the Tatars negotiated 12 bilateral treaties with Russia. In February 1994 the Tatar leaders of the republic approved a treaty to normalize relations with the Russian Federation and finally signed the 1992 federation treaty. The treaty, revised through two years of often acrimonious negotiations, covered a number of the points that the Tatars insisted on, including the recognition of Tatarstan as a sovereign state freely associated with the federation and the right to legal secession.

Russian leaders, including President Boris Yeltsin, denounced Tatar separatism and warned that the loss of Tatarstan would be a strategic and economic disaster for the Russian Federation. Tension between the republic's Tatars and Russians worsened with the influx of Tatars from other parts of the former Soviet Union, particularly refugees fleeing violent disorders in the Central Asian republics.

The Tatars outside Tatarstan, including related nations like the Bashkorts, established closer economic and cultural ties after the demise of the Soviet Union. In August 1997 the second World Congress of Tatars was held in Kazan, with representatives of the many Turkic nations in Russia and the former Soviet Union, and delegates from the large Tatar diaspora.

In the late 1990s Tatar demanded that their language be given official status in the neighboring Republic of Bashkortostan, where activists claimed the Tatars were more numerous than the titular group, the Bashkorts. The controversy was based on the fact that some Tatars had begun to assimilate into Bashkort culture in the republic. Bashkort leaders argued that to declare Tatar an official language in their homeland would make their people subject to "Tatarization" in their own republic. The debate became one of the focal points of Tatar nationalist activity.

The Tatarstan government signed a friendship and cooperation treaty with the Chechens* in May 1997, but the subsequent war in Chechnya was a sobering example to the militants demanding full independence. As a result of the war on the Muslim Chechens an increase in religious awareness was observed in all social and age groups among the Tatars. However, the re-Islamization of the Tatars was more a manifestation of national consciousness than the militarization of their Islamic religion. In 1998–99, the Tatar government pursued an Islamic-based foreign policy of its own, separate from that of the Russian Federation. President Shaimiev offered to loan funds to Iraq, visited Muslim states like Egypt and Malaysia, and hosted Islamic leaders and conference in the Tatar capital.

In July 2000, the Russian parliament passed new laws to abolish all provisions on sovereignty in the constitutions of six Russian republics, particularly Tatarstan. Constitutional provisions considered to contravene the federal constitution were ordered revoked. The Tatar government attempted to have the decisions revised, militants were outraged, and nationalist feelings reached the levels of 1991–92.

The terrorist attacks on the United States in September 2001 emphasized the growing influence of political Islam. The Russian government accused militant Tatars of having ties to terrorists in early October 2001. A *madrassa* (religious school) known for zealotry in Tatarstan, where many young Muslims trained, was closed, and Wahhabism, the radical Islamic movement exported by Saudia Arabia, was banned in Tatarstan.

On 14 October 2001 over 2,000 people gathered in Kazan to mourn those who defended the city against Ivan the Terrible in 1552. Some burned the Russian state symbols and historical maps. Leaders of moderate nationalist groups criticized mistaken policies toward ethnic groups within

Russia and growing federal pressure on Tatar legislators. Demonstrators called on the Tatarstan government to adopt an act on full independence for Tatarstan and the creation of an Idel-Ural confederation in the Volga region, reject Russian passports and the creation of their own, and law enforcement and military bodies under local Tatar authority, effectively ending the Russian colonial occupation of their homeland.

SELECTED BIBLIOGRAPHY:

Alexseev, Mikhail A. *Center-Periphery Conflict in Post-Soviet Russia: A Federation Imperiled.* 1999.

Frank, Allen J. *Islamic Historiography and "Bulghar" Identity among the Tatars and Bashkirs of Russia.* 1998.

Kondrashov, Sergei. *Nationalism and the Drive for Sovereignty in Tatarstan, 1988–1992: Origins and Development.* 1999.

Rorlich, Azade-Ayse. *The Volga Tatars: A Profile in National Resilience.* 1986.

Tavoyans

Tavai; Tavoyan-Merguese; Dawei-Myeik

POPULATION: Approximately (2002e) 1,205,000 Tavoyans in Myanmar, concentrated in the southern division of Tenasserim. Outside the region there are Tavoyan communities in other parts of Myanmar, in India, and in Thailand.

THE TAVOYAN HOMELAND: The Tavoyan homeland, called Tenasserim or Tanintharyi, extends in a narrow coastal strip over 600 miles (970 km) along the Gulf of Martaban of the Andaman Sea south to the Isthmus of Kra. Separated from Thailand by the Bilauktaung Mountains, the Tenasserim Division stretches along the Andaman Sea, and includes the Mergui Archipelago, some 900 islands, including the large islands of Mali, Kadan, Letsok-aw, Lanbi, and Zadetkyi. The majority of the Tavoyans live in the coastal regions of the Tanintharyi Division, which remains the least populated area in the country. Tenasserim, officially called Tanintharyi, forms a division of the Union of Myanmar. *Tenasserim Division (Taninthayi)*: 16,735 sq. mi.— 43,344 sq. km, (2002e) 1,335,000—Tavoyans 61%, Karens* 28%, Mons* 6%, Shans* and Burmans 5%. The Tavoyan capital and major cultural center is Dawei (Tavoy), called Tavai by the Tavoyans, (2002e) 115,000. The other important cultural center is Mergui, called Myeik locally, (2002e) 147,000.

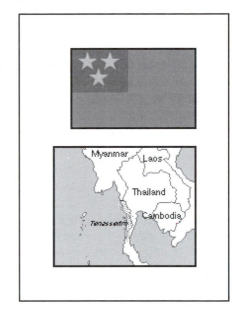

FLAG: The Tavoyan national flag, the flag of the Myeik-Dawei United Front (MDUF), is a pale blue field bearing a red canton on the upper hoist charged with three gold, five-pointed stars.

PEOPLE AND CULTURE: The Tavoyans are a people of mixed Burman, Karen, Thai, and Malay background. Although related to the Burman majority of the Irrawaddy Delta, the Tavoyans consider themselves a separate nation, but it is not recognized by the military government of Myanmar. Officially the Tavoyans are considered a branch of the dominant Burman nation. The Tavoyans include the Tavoyans in the north, the

Merguese in the south, and the Malay Salons, also called Sea Gypsies, living in the offshore islands. The Tayoyans' long seafaring tradition and intermarriage with neighboring peoples led to cultural differences with the central Burmans, who are essentially valley dwellers. The Tavoyan culture shows a complex mixture of Burman, Thai, and Malay influences.

LANGUAGE AND RELIGION: The Tavoyans and Merguese speak distinct southern dialects of the Burman language; the Tavoyan dialect, called Tavoya or Tavoyan, is often considered a separate language. The dialects belong to the southern branch of the Burmish group of the Tibeto-Burman languages. Extensive borrowings from neighboring languages, particularly Karen and Thai, make the Tavoyan-Merguese dialects difficult for speakers of standard Burman to understand. Nationalists claim that the dialects, particularly the central Tavoya dialect, form a national language historically separate from Irrawaddy Burman.

The majority of the Tavoyans are Buddhists, belonging to the Therawada branch of the religion. Cultural influences have shaped the religious beliefs of the Tavoyans, particularly the beliefs in spirits that guide and protect fishermen. Thai cultural influence has historically been very important. There is a Muslim minority, mostly in the islands and along the southern coast.

NATIONAL HISTORY: The coastal zones were inhabited by migrants, probably from the Tibetan Plateau, in the third century A.D. The immigrants absorbed the region's earlier inhabitants and developed as a seafaring people, divided into a number of small kingdoms. In the eleventh century the kingdoms were attached to the Burman state under the kings of Pagan. The coastal groups were again independent following the overthrow of Pagan by invading Mongols in the thirteenth century.

For centuries the Tavoyans lived in autonomous communities only nominally under the authority of Thai or Burman kings. Whichever of the two kingdoms was paramount extended its authority to the isolated region. The coastal and island peoples developed a culture based on independence, fishing, and seafaring, bringing them into contact with other maritime peoples around the Andaman Sea.

The Burmans of the Irrawaddy Valley, with Portuguese assistance, conquered the region and incorporated the Tavoyans into their resurgent state in the mid-sixteenth century. The Burman authorities allowed Dutch, Portuguese, and British ships to trade in the Tavoyan ports, bringing European influences and rivalries. The Burman kingdom fell into decay, and petty states replaced the central authority in the late 1600s. Thai influence then became strong in the Tavoyan region, after centuries of Burman-Thai conflict for control of the rich coastal areas. Mergui was made the capital of the Thai province in the early eighteenth century.

The Tenasserim coast was again brought under Burman rule in 1763 after Burman forces drove the Thais from the area in a series of wars that ended with complete Burman control in 1767. Burman attempts to assimilate the Tavoyans, Merguese, and other peoples of the region were often brutal but ultimately failed to eliminate the Thai and other influences incorporated into the local culture.

Conflicts between the Burman state and the expanding British Empire led to the First Anglo–Burmese War in 1824–26. The victorious British took control of the outer provinces of Tenasserim and Arakan. Under British rule, the region, always far from the centers of Burman power, was further separated from the Burman society of the Irrawaddy Delta. In December 1826 the Burmans attempted to regain control of Tenasserim but were driven back by the British. Tenasserim was made a separate province of British India until the formation of Lower Burma in 1862.

Christian missionaries became active in the region, particularly in the coastal port cities, bringing Western-style education and medicine to the region. Although they won few converts among the Buddhist and Muslim population, their influence was substantial among the small, politically active elite. The introduction of Western-style education has left a more lasting legacy than the attempts to win converts to Christianity.

In the late nineteenth century the region was relatively prosperous, with pearl fishing in the islands, trade in the port towns, and rubber production in the hinterlands. The Tavoyans generally supported British rule, while rejecting influences from the Burman heartland.

Tenasserim remained part of British India until 1923, when the province, along with the other parts of historical Burma, were separated under a new Burmese government within British India. Although somewhat neglected in the first decades of the twentieth century, the Tavoyans continued to prefer British to Burman rule. In 1937 the government of Burma was separated from India, and Tenasserim was included in spite of pleas and demands for separate status.

During World War II, the Burmans initially supported the invading Japanese, who promised Burman independence, but the Tavoyans remained loyal, often fighting the Japanese in guerrilla groups or acting as guides for allied troops later in the war. With Japanese defeat in 1945, the Burmans began to demand independence from Britain, fueling a Tavoyan movement for recognition and protection of their distinct culture. The newly formed Burmese government refused to recognize the Tavoyans as a distinct national group, claiming they formed a branch of the Burman peoples.

Burma was granted independence in 1948, with guarantees for regional and ethnic autonomy for the various groups included in the new state. Tenasserim was generally ignored by the central government, which was soon faced with widespread rebellions by various ethnic groups, including the neighboring Karens and Mons. The Karen rebellion had particular influence on Tavoyan attitudes toward the increasingly autocratic central government in the late 1940s and early 1950s.

The Tavoy homeland in coastal Tenasserim remained relatively calm during the turbulent 1960s and early 1970s. The widespread poverty and oppression of the Burmese state was offset by the increasing self-reliance of the Tavoyans. Relying on their traditional pursuits, particularly fishing, they distanced themselves from both the Burmese government and dozens of groups fighting for greater self-government around the periphery of the country. The creation of ethnic states for the largest non-Burman ethnic groups in the late 1970s outraged the Tavoyans, whose demand for their own state was rejected on the grounds that they were ethnic Burmans speaking somewhat divergent Burman dialects.

The government's refusal to grant the Tavoyans even limited local autonomy fueled a regionalist movement, which spawned a nationalist wing by the early 1980s. The movement, reportedly armed and trained by the Burmese Communist Party, launched an armed insurgency in 1979. The Tavoyans' seafaring and smuggling traditions made it difficult for government troops to control the region. By 1983, Tavoyan rebels held the zone between the Thai border and the government-held towns of Tenasserim and Lenya.

The military government suppressed a widespread prodemocracy movement in Burma in 1988. The suppression that followed ended Tavoyan hopes that Burma could be converted into a democratic federation of states. The junta renamed the country "Myanmar" in 1989, the ancient Burman name, but the State Law and Order Council (SLORC), the ruling military junta, suppressed any sign of antigovernment sentiment.

The government policy of forced labor is a serious concern to the Tavoyans. During the monsoon season of 1993–1994, somewhere between 120,000 and 150,000 people were conscripted to participate in railway construction. Hundreds died from accidents, diseases, or fatigue. Reportedly, soldiers working for the SLORC estimated that about 30,000 people would die before the 100-mile railway between Ye and Tavoy is completed.

The Unocal Oil Company of the United States, in partnership with Total Oil of France, signed a contract with the Burmese military government in February 1995 to extract and transport natural gas using a pipeline from the Yadana Field, 43 miles off the Tenasserim coast. The gas pipeline, running 218 miles (350 km) underwater and 41 miles (66 km) across southern Tenasserim to Thailand, was constructed by forcibly displacing the population in its right of way. Those that resisted were killed or arrested.

The most notorious forced labor project, however, is the Total and Unocal-sponsored gas pipeline. The pipeline stretches from the wells at the Gulf of Martaban all the way through the Division to Thailand. In addition to the ecological damage effected by the massive project, numerous villages along the route were uprooted, and the homeless villagers were simply put to work on the pipeline.

The Unocal/Total venture provides the brutal, bankrupt military government of Myanmar with much-needed revenue but is also linked with forced relocations, forced labor, and hundreds of deaths at the hands of government troops. Unocal and Total have repeatedly denied any responsibility for the massive human rights abuses that accompanied the construction of the gas pipeline. The construction of the Ye-Tavoy railway brought even more suffering. It is widely believed that the railway will be used to bring equipment and more troops to the area when it is finished in 2002. Unocal and Total claim they will not use the railway, but they have contracted with the troops it brings to provide security against Tavoyan and Karen rebels along the pipeline. The pipeline project has become the most important economically to the Myanmar government, particularly as many governments, including the United States, have attempted to ban new investment in the country so long as the savage military regime remains in power.

Tenasserim, separated from central Burma by the Mon and Karen states, where active insurgencies continue, had become a center of a new Tavoyan insurgency in the mid-1990s. The largest of several Tavoyan organizations, the MDUF, allied to other insurgent minorities, fought pitched battled with government troops in several areas in the late 1990s. Thousands of Tavoyans sought refuge across the border in Thai territory to escape forced labor and other government brutalities.

The SLORC, renamed the State Peace and Development Council (SPDC) in 1997, is the most widely criticized and brutal regime in Asia in the early years of the twenty-first century. The importance of the growing oil and natural gas production in Tenasserim is demonstrated by the fact that by 1998 the Tavoyan homeland was the most militarized region in the country. The gas pipeline began to operate in late 1998.

In January 1998 renewed fighting broke out after peace talks failed. A major government offensive against the Karens in the highlands displaced thousands of Tavoyans living between the coast and the Karen-held regions. The Tavoyans were subject to summary executions, arbitrary arrests, forced labor, rape, and other forms of oppression. In some areas the military demanded that one person from each household, bringing their own food and blanket, work on military-owned rubber, oil palm, and cashew plantations. Those unable to go had to hire someone as a substitute, a policy that favored the more prosperous elements of the region.

Tavoyan nationalists, charging the large oil companies with propping up the repellent Myanmar military dictatorship, engaged in a campaign of sabotage in 1999–2001, using hit-and-run raids on the pipeline in the rugged interior. The MDUF, in an alliance with 26 other national organizations and antigovernment groups, continues to fight the military government, which locally means the gas pipeline that crosses their national territory and the government troops that protect it. The majority of the Tavoyans live in rural areas, the so-called Black Areas, considered free-fire zones by the Myanmar military.

In addition to the railway and pipeline projects, the SPDC conscripted forced laborers in 2001 to partake in the beautification of tourist attractions and infrastructure. In the cities forced laborers toiled to build airports, buildings, roads, harbors, and even parks and golf courses.

SELECTED BIBLIOGRAPHY:

Fisher, Frederick. *Myanmar*. 2000.

Mirante, Edith T. *Burmese Looking Glass: A Human Rights Adventure*. 1994.

Sinha, Rameshwar P., and Surya Dandekar. *South-East Asia: People's Struggle and Political Identity*. 1998.

Smith, Martin. *Ethnic Groups in Burma: Development, Democracy and Human Rights*. 1994.

Telenganas

Telenganans; Telinganas; Telanganas; Telangis; Tolangans

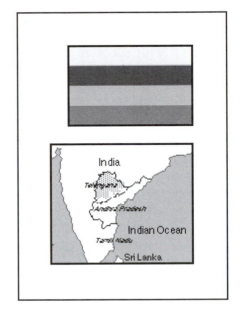

POPULATION: Approximately (2002e) 31,400,000 Telenganas in India, concentrated in the Telengana region of the state of Andhra Pradesh.

THE TELENGANA HOMELAND: The Telengana homeland lies in the highland Deccan Plateau of central India. The region, mostly low mountains in the Eastern Ghats, interspersed with fertile plains, includes the basin of the Krishna River. Telengana forms the nine interior districts of the state of Andhra Pradesh in south-central Asia. *Region of Telengana*: 44,999 sq. mi.—116,548 sq. km, (2002e) 37,498,000—Telenganas 77%, Andhrans* 16%, Hyderabadis (Urdu-speaking Muslims) 5%, others 2%. The Telengana capital and major cultural center is Hyderabad, called Haidarabad locally, (2002e) 3,710,000, metropolitan area 6,671,000. Other important cultural centers are Warangal, (2002e) 653,000, and Nizamabad, (2002e) 348,000.

FLAG: The Telenganan national flag, the flag of the national movement, has four horizontal stripes of white, blue, orange, and green.

PEOPLE AND CULTURE: The Telenganas are a subgroup of the Telugu nation of south-central India. The distinct Telengana identity grew out of a sense of regional identity rather than out of a sense of ethnic identity, language, religion, or caste. The regional identity encompasses the Telugu-speaking Telenganas, the Muslim Urdu-speaking population around Hyderabad, and several smaller non-Telugu groups. Telengana identity developed over several centuries of separation from the coastal Andhrans, who were under British rule, while the Telengana region remained under the feudal control of the princely state of Hyderabad. Culturally the Telenganas differ considerably from the Andhrans, having absorbed many Muslim influences and traditions. The cultural evolution of the Telengana under different historical circumstances resulted in the occurrence of recognizable variations in dialect, in the caste structure, and in habits.

LANGUAGE AND RELIGION: The Telenganas speak the northwestern dialects of Telugu, a Dravidian language belonging to the great Dravidian group spoken across southern and central India. Linguistic affinity did not form a firm basis for unity between the two disparate regions of Telengana and Andhra, from which the state of Andhra Pradesh was formed, because the two Telugu-speaking peoples were separated by hundreds of years of cultural and economic differences. Next to Hindi, Telugu is the largest linguistic unit in India, but the sharp dialectal differences between Telengana Telugu and Andhra Telugu make each dialect difficult for speakers of the other to understand. Telengana Telugu has absorbed many Urdu words and forms, with Urdu influence more marked in the dialect spoken around Hyderabad, but less so in the northern districts. The Urdu language spoken around Hyderabad is different from the Urdu of Pakistan, being a mixture of Urdu, Telugu, and Hindi.

Telengana religion revolves around the traditional Hinduism of the region, which has long been influenced by early Buddhism and the later Muslim domination of the region. Ceremonies that mix both Hindu and Muslim traditions are common in the Hyderabad region; Hindus take part in Muslim celebrations, and Muslims participate in Hindu rites.

NATIONAL HISTORY: Telengana was the location of several ancient Hindu kingdoms, including the ancient Andhra state, which flourished from 250 B.C. to A.D. 250. The Andhrans spread from the coastal region to conquer most of the Deccan Plateau of the Telengana by the third century B.C.

The Kakatiya dynasty of Warangal, in the twelfth and thirteenth centuries, extended Andhran power across the region both militarily and culturally. The Telugu language became paramount throughout much of the Deccan Plateau. At the same time the Muslims established themselves in the north, invading and conquering Warangal in 1323, beginning the separation of the Andhrans into two distinct divisions.

The Muslims erected the Bahmani Sultanate, which eventually split into the five kingdoms of the Deccan, one of which, Golconda, was centered on the city of Golconda, just five miles from present Hyderabad. The Deccan states fell to the Moguls under Aurangzeb in 1687–88 and were incorporated into the Muslim Delhi Sultanate.

The Telenganas, under Muslim rule, slowly absorbed much of the dominant culture, which also influenced their language and traditional way of life. Coffee replaced tea as their favored drink, holy days were based on the Muslim calendar, and Muslim restrictions on women were adopted.

In 1713, a Mogul general, Asaf Jah, had himself named viceroy of the Mogul possessions in the Deccan. In 1722, when the Mogul Empire collapsed, Asaf Jah took control of the region and in 1724 declared the independence of Hyderabad with himself as *nizam-al-mulk*, or prince. The state, often called the Nizam's Domains, included a large Telengana population, which was dominated by the Urdu-speaking elite of the state.

The Telengana region remained feudal and underdeveloped in comparison with the British-ruled Telugu-speaking Andhrans of the northern districts of the Madras Presidency. The first attempt to mobilize the Telenganas on the basis of their Telugu language was the establishment of the Hyderabad State Congress in 1938. By 1941 the Telengana movement had come under the leadership of leftist nationalists seeking to overthrow the Hyderabad government and to establish a Soviet-style government.

After World War II, the British government prepared India for independence, accepting the need to partition the region into two states, predominantly Hindu and secular India, and Muslim Pakistan. The princely state of Hyderabad, dominated by the Urdu-speaking Muslim population concentrated in the city of Hyderabad, remained under the rule of the *nizam*. Beginning in July 1946, communist-led guerrilla bands began overthrowing local feudal systems and organizing land reform of the Telugu-speaking regions of Hyderabad, collectively known as Telangana.

When India became independent in 1947, the seventh *nizam*, Mir Osman Ali Khan, vacillated, seeking separate independence or affiliation with Muslim Pakistan. The Telengana uprising, supported by the Communist Party, in the districts of Nalgonda, Khammam, and Warangal was met by the Razakars, the Muslim militia of the pro-*nizam* Muslimeem Party, leaving over 4,000 Telenganas dead. The Telengana insurgency was used as an excuse for Indian army intervention in September 1948. In November 1949 the Hyderabad state had been overthrown and forced to accede to the Indian Union. By October 1951, the violence of the Telengana movement had been suppressed, but demands for separation from Hyderabad continued to fuel the nationalist movement.

The Telengana revolt of 1946–51 and the electoral victories of the nationalists in 1952 led to the division of Hyderabad State along linguistic lines in 1956. The commission in charge of Hyderabad considered establishing a separate Telengana state, but the decision was eventually made to merge Telengana with the Andhra state, established in 1953 from the Telugu-speaking regions of the former British Madras Presidency, to form the new state of Andhra Pradesh. Even moderate Telenganas resented the name of the new state, which reflected only the identity of the dominant Andhrans.

An agreement covering the first five years of union gave the Telenganas certain advantages in revenues and development, education, and local government. A Regional Council for Telengana was to be responsible for economic development. The informal system of political and economic sharing quickly collapsed over complaints about how the agreements and guarantees were to be implemented. The selection of Hyderabad as the state capital led to a massive immigration of Andhran civil servants. Andhran landlords brought up large tracts of land, which was less expensive than in the Andhra districts. The Telenganas felt discriminated against in education, employment, and government.

Telengana discontent intensified in 1969, when the unification guarantees were scheduled to lapse. Student agitation for the continuation of the agreement spread across Telengana, though most Telenganas felt that the agreement had been violated by the leaders of the Andhra region. Government employees and opposition groups threatened to support the students. New agreements on revenue sharing and local government employment failed to appease the separatists, and violent mob attacks on railroads, highways, and government facilities spread across the Telengana, threatening civil war in the state. Police fired on demonstrators, killing 23 people, according to official figures.

The nationalists, led by M. Chenna Reddy, founded the Telengana People's Association, which fielded candidates in local elections on a separatist platform. A high court ruling in 1972 upholding pro-Telengana employment policies in state government set off months of violence as agitation in the Andhra region became violently anti-Telengana. Chenna later switched to the Congress Party and was elected chief minister of Andhra Pradesh. He announced that Telengana separation was no longer an issue and that Andhra Pradesh was an integrated state. Nationalist groups denounced him as a traitor, but the violence of 1969 and 1972 did not reoccur.

Differences between the two regions were serious and complicated. Telengana had a less developed economy than Andhra, but with a larger revenue base, mostly because alcoholic beverages were taxed rather than prohibited. The Telenganas feared that their meager resources would be used for development in Andhra and rejected planned dams on the Krishna and Godavari Rivers, which would not benefit their homeland. The better educated Andhrans had an advantage in government and education in the united Telugu state.

The Telengana movement demanded redress for economic disadvantages, the writing of a separate Telengana history, and establishment of a sense of cultural distinctness. The nationalist Telenganas were often branded Naxalites, as the communist insurgents in the area were known. Government statements equating Telengana separatism with communist agitation and violence complicated the issue in the 1970s.

Naxalites, Marxist guerrilla bands, used violence to press their demands for land redistribution and peasant rights in the 1970s and 1980s. Assassinations of government officials, attacks on army barracks and police commissaries, and terrorist acts kept the region in turmoil. The Naxalite campaign overshadowed Telengana nationalism throughout the 1980s and early 1990s.

In 1999, the Indian government decided to delay decisions on the creation of new states, mostly due to the opposition of the Telugu Desam Party, the major political party of the Andhrans and a major component in the Indian coalition government. The Andhrans feared that the creation of new states would reactivate the demands for a separate Telengana state.

In October 2000, Telengana leaders visited New Delhi to secure endorsement for a separate Telengana state. Government leaders objected to clauses in the petition that referred to exploitation by the Andhran rulers of the state and to their making Telengana a virtual colony for promoting the interests of the ruling class from the coastal Andhra region.

The question of Telengana separation is one of the most serious problems facing southern India, with the potential for violence growing with each year that the issue is ignored or postponed. Telengana continues to be known as the land of poverty, injustice, and extremist violence, and it remains last by all development parameters in Andhra Pradesh. The Telenganas have been demanding separation from Andhra since 1948, but the movement has taken on new life in the late 1990s over economic and cultural grievances. The local Congress Party leaders, partly because their party is out of power both locally and nationally, have espoused the Telengana Movement. The Telengana region is considered a traditional stronghold of Congress while the Andhrans support the nationalist Telugu Desam Party. In early 2000, 41 Congress Party representatives submitted a memorandum to Mrs. Sonia Gandhi demanding the creation of a separate Telengana state.

The Telengana region is potentially rich, with many natural resources. Seventy percent of the catchment area of Krishna and Godavari Rivers is in Telengana; however, less than 12% of the available water is allocated to Telengana needs. Over 70% of the state's power is generated in the region, but the Telenganas pay higher prices than the coastal Andhrans. Telengana education, literacy, and employment opportunities continue to fall farther behind the more developed Andhra region.

Growing nationalist violence in the region is blamed on an unresponsive government, severe poverty, and a lack of opportunities. Many younger Telenganas, driven into desperation and extremism, have embraced Telengana nationalism as a means to demonstrate their grievances. A long series of broken promises, unimplemented development schemes, and continued cultural and political domination by the Andhrans fuels the demands for separation and creation of a self-governing Telengana homeland.

The creation of new states within India in late 2000 reactivated the Telengana Movement. Demonstrators clashed with police and with Andhran nationalists in several areas. The demonstrators demanded that the

Telenganas had the same right to separate sovereignty as the peoples of the new states created in northern India. Several Telengana leaders stated that the Telenganas would have suffered less had the state of Hyderabad maintained its independence.

SELECTED BIBLIOGRAPHY:

Bernstorff, Dagmar, and Hugh Gray. *The Kingmakers: Politicians and Politics in Andhra Pradesh.* 1998.

Lalini, V. *Rural Leadership in India.* 1991.

Palanithurai, G., and R. Thandavan. *Ethnic Movement in India: Theory and Practice.* 1992.

Sangathana, Stree S. *We Were Making History: Women in the Telangana People's Struggle.* 1989.

Terek Cossacks

Terskie Kazaki; Ter Cossacks; Kazaki Ter; Kazaky Ter; Kazaki Terek; Kazaky Terek

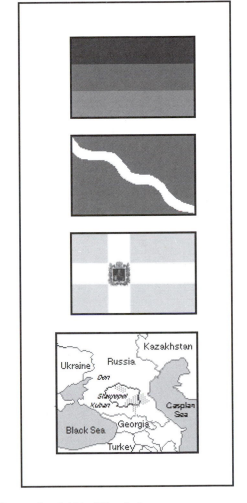

POPULATION: Approximately (2002e) 848,000 Terek Cossacks in Europe, mostly in the Stavropol Krai and the Dagestan, North Ossetian, and Chechen republics of southern European Russia. Outside the region there are Terek Cossack communities in other parts of Russia, particularly Moscow and central Russia, and in Central Asia and Siberia.

THE TEREK COSSACK HOMELAND: The Terek Cossack homeland lies in the North Caucasus, occupying the Stavropol Plateau and the Terek River basin, mostly north of the Terek River in southern European Russia. The northern foothills of the main Caucasian range lie in the southern part of the region, while the northern lands, including the Stavropol Plateau, are mostly dry steppe. Terek has no official status; the region, one of the three Cossack provinces of the North Caucasus, forms Stavropol Krai (Stavropol Territory) of the Russian Federation. The historical Terek Cossack territory is presently divided between Stavropol Territory and the republics of Dagestan, Kabardino-Balkaria, Chechenia, and North Ossetia. Terek Cossack nationalists also claim the Naursky and Shelkovsky Districts of the Chechen Republic and the Kizylar District of Dagestan. *Stavropol Krai (Stavropol Territory/Terek)*: 25,676 sq. mi.—66,501 sq. km, (2002e) 2,701,000—Russians 51%, Terek Cossacks 24%, Ukrainians 18%, Chechens* 3%, Karachais,* Nogais,* and Turkmens 4%. The Terek Cossack capital and major cultural center is Stavropol, (2002e) 346,000, founded as a Cossack fort in 1777. The other major cultural centers are Vladikavkaz, (2002e) 313,000, the historical capital of the Terek host *(voisk)*, and Pyatigorsk, (2002e) 133,000.

FLAG: The Terek national flag, the flag of the former republic, is a horizontal tricolor of black, green, and red. The flag of the Terek Cossack national movement is a blue field crossed by a wavy, diagonal white stripe, representing the Terek River, upper hoist to lower fly. The flag of Stavropol Territory, based on the historical flag of the Terek Cossacks, is a yellow field bearing a white cross with the territorial coat of arms centered.

PEOPLE AND CULTURE: The Terek Cossacks, the third largest of the Cossack peoples of Russia, are concentrated in the east and southeast of the Stavropol Territory. They evolved from Don Cossacks* moving south in the eighteenth century, with admixtures of Khazars, Circassians, other Slavs, and Turkic groups. A major subgroup, the Greben Cossacks, also called the Skoi, still inhabit the northern districts close to the territory of the Don Cossacks. The Terek Cossack culture is laced with North Caucasian elements, which reflect long association with the Ossetians, Cherkess,* and Nogais. In the north, among the Greben Cossacks, cultural borrowings from the Chechens are more important. Not recognized by the Russian government as a separate cultural and national group, the Terek Cossacks claim national status on the basis of their history, dialect, and geographic location. The Terek Cossacks have incorporated more influences from different ethnic groups than have the other Cossack hosts.

LANGUAGE AND RELIGION: The language of the Terek Cossacks is a Cossack language that incorporates Russian, Ukrainian, Caucasian, and Turkic elements. The language, not inherently intelligible to speakers of Russian, is spoken in two major dialects—Terek in the south and east, and Greben in the northern districts. The Terek dialect incorporates borrowings from various Caucasian and Turkic languages, and it retains many antiquated Russian forms, making it one of the most divergent of the Cossack dialects. Standard Russian is used as the group language, but the Cossack dialect remains the language of the home.

NATIONAL HISTORY: The Russian Empire began to expand into the North Caucasus, the Muslim lands between the Black and Caspian Seas, in the sixteenth century. The Slavs captured the region traversed by the lower Volga River in 1554–56 and pushed into the North Caucasus region in 1557. Although the region was claimed by Russia in 1598 and scattered Cossack settlements were established, the Ottoman Turkish resistance to the Russians delayed colonization for over two centuries. The Cossacks built a fort at Terka on the Terek River, where various groups from the upper Volga came to settle. In addition to the Greben and Volga Cossacks, groups of Don Cossacks joined the growing community in the Terek River basin.

The region became subject to the Russian Empire in 1721. In 1777 the Cossacks, called "Terek" after the river, established a fort at present Stavropol, which became the center of the Slavic colonization of the North Caucasus. In 1784 the key fortress of Vladikavkaz was founded by the

Terek Cossacks in the lower Caucasus Mountains. Cossack territory north of the Terek was organized as the Terek Cossack homeland, part of the Caucasus Line, the line separating the Slav settlement and Caucasian territories, in 1836.

The Cossack groups spearheading the Russian expansion governed themselves, under elected leaders called *atamans*, in return for military service and oaths of personal loyalty to the Russian tsar. In 1861 the Terek Cossack lands were combined with the newly conquered highlands of the Caucasus Mountains to form Terek Province. The lands of the Muslim Chechens and Ingush* north of the river were confiscated, and the Muslims were driven from their lands into the less productive mountains.

The Terek Cossacks formed the first line of defense between the Slav lands to the north and the subject Caucasian territories to the south. Although their traditional rights were curtailed in the eighteenth and nineteenth centuries, their military skills allowed the Cossacks to continue as a group distinct from the general public. The Terek Cossacks' pride in being completely free was replaced by pride in soldierly service. Total loyalty to the tsar, but not the Russian state, became a tradition among the Terek Cossacks.

Holding their lands in common, the Terek Cossacks became large-scale landlords in the late nineteenth century. The abolition of serfdom in Russia sent a wave of landless peasants to the region, most settling on the Cossacks' communal lands as tenant farmers. The better educated and more prosperous Cossacks dominated a large area of the North Caucasus up to World War I.

The Orthodox Christian Terek Cossacks were charged with keeping the Muslims tribes in Terek Province under close military control. In the latter part of the nineteenth and the early part of the twentieth centuries, the tsarist government used Cossack troops to perpetrate pogroms against the Jews. Cossack troops were used on a large scale in the suppression of the Russian Revolution of 1905, and during the strikes and demonstrations that erupted during World War I.

Elite Cossack military units were sent to the front when war began in 1914. The Cossack units were decimated as Russia slipped into chaos and supplies failed to reach the troops. In February 1917 the discontented Terek Cossacks, freed from their oath to the tsar by revolution, began to desert and return to their homeland. Like the other Cossack hosts, the Terek Cossacks restored their ancient traditional forms of elected *atamans* and self-government. In March 1917 the Terek Cossacks elected a new leader and formed a military government to fill the void as the tsarist civil government collapsed. The new Terek Cossack government, virtually independent, was formed on military lines.

The Muslim peoples and the Terek Cossacks put aside decades of tension when a new force threatened them both. The Bolshevik coup in October 1917 forced the peoples of the region to participate in a cooperative government. On 20 October 1917 the Terek-Dagestan government declared its sovereignty, as a temporary expedient until a legitimate Russian government could be reestablished. The cooperative state, called Terek-Dagestan, collapsed in December 1917 as fighting broke out between the Terek Cossacks and the Chechens and Ingush. The Muslim tribes attempted to recover lands in the Terek lowlands lost to the Cossacks in the eighteenth and nineteenth centuries.

Two Bolshevik statutes officially reduced the Cossacks to the status of other Russian peoples. The statutes, greatly resented among the Terek Cossacks, fueled support for the nascent national movement. The Terek Cossack military government on 4 March 1918 declared the Terek Cossack territory independent of Bolshevik Russia. The Terek leaders tried to ensure the security of their new republic by proposing a union of the states seceding from Russia, or failing that, a federation with the other Cossack peoples of the North Caucasus—the Don Cossacks to the north and the Kuban Cossacks* to the west.

In November 1918 invading Bolsheviks overran most of the Terek Cossack republic and surrounded the Terek Cossack forces. The Bolsheviks began a reign of terror against the anti-Bolshevik groups. The Soviet authorities confiscated Cossack properties and lands, redistributing them to the pro-Bolshevik Russians and their Chechen and Ingush allies. The Soviets allowed the looting of Cossack towns and *stanitsas* (villages), while thousands of Terek Cossacks faced eviction and persecution. In January 1919 Kuban Cossacks finally broke through the Bolshevik lines to rescue the embattled Terek Cossack forces, but the tide of the Russian Civil War was turning against the anti-Bolshevik forces, known as the Whites. By 1920 the victorious Red Army had regained control of most of the Terek region.

The Terek Cossack territory was divided among several governments in the region. Part of the traditional Terek lands was added to northern Dagestan in 1922, but in 1938 all the land north of the Terek River was added to Astrakhan Province. Lands formerly belonging to the Greben or North Terek Cossacks were added to Dagestan in 1923, then to Chechnya in 1957. Vladikavkaz, one of the major centers of the Terek Cossacks, was included in several North Caucasus territories before becoming the capital of the autonomous Republic of North Ossetia in 1944.

The new Soviet authorities ended all the Cossacks' traditional privileges and dismantled the Terek Cossack military structure. Terek Cossack leaders who failed to escape were deported or executed, and thousands of Cossacks died in purges between 1920 and 1938. Despite resistance, in the early 1930s the Cossacks were engaged in collective farming, Cossack cavalry units were forbidden, and many Terek Cossacks had been resettled in Kazakhstan and in a number of areas in Siberia. The Soviets banned the use of the Cossack language and reclassified the Cossacks as ethnic Russians, carefully suppressing their separate history and culture. Not until 1936 were the Cossacks again allowed military training and to serve in the Red Army.

Thousands of fervently anti-Soviet Terek Cossacks joined Nazi Germany's anticommunist crusade during World War II, often facing Cossack units serving in the Red Army. The German advance in the Caucasus reached the Terek homeland in 1942. Many Terek Cossacks welcomed the invaders as liberators from hated Soviet rule. In 1944–46 the Soviet authorities meted out punishment for the Terek Cossack collaboration with deportations and mass executions. The severe oppression continued until Joseph Stalin's death in 1953.

A general Cossack cultural and national revival, begun among exile groups in Europe and the United States after World War II, started to penetrate slowly the closed Soviet territories in the 1960s and 1970s. The exile publication of the first Cossack dictionary, along with works on Cossack culture and history, stimulated a renewed interest in the suppressed Terek Cossack nation. A parallel movement among the Muslim Caucasian peoples led to increasing tension in the 1980s; Terek Cossack cemeteries were vandalized in many areas, and isolated homesteads were burned.

The Cossack revival accelerated in the late 1980s with the introduction of reforms to the Soviet system by Mikhail Gorbachev in 1987. Terek Cossacks began to rebuilt their communities, re-creating the Terek Cossack host and reviving their traditions and culture. The revived Terek Cossack national identity stimulated the traditional hostility between the Terek Cossacks and the Chechen Muslims of Chechnya to the south. In April 1990 serious ethnic clashes erupted as the conflict, frozen but not resolved by communist rule, again became a factor in the politics of the region.

During the last years of the USSR, Terek Cossack organizations experienced a sudden revival in the region. In 1990, Cossack associations were formed in traditional areas of the Terek lowlands. The largest, the Low–Terek Cossack Association, led by Alexandr Elson, which called for the reunification of all Terek Cossacks and the recovery of traditional Terek Cossack territories.

At first the goals of the majority of the Terek Cossack associations were cultural and historical in nature—to preserve Cossack traditions and promote the historical accuracy of Cossack lifestyles. The Terek Cossacks later began to demand local self-administration and the return of traditional lands. The Terek Cossack Host, based in Vladikavkaz, was formed as a centralized government and umbrella group for Terek Cossack associations.

The collapse of the Soviet Union in August 1991 split the growing national movement. One faction, centered on Stavropol, demanded official recognition as a separate people and on 17 November 1991 proposed the creation of a separate Terek Cossack republic within the reconstituted Russian Federation. The other faction, based in Vladikavkaz, unofficially resumed the ancient Cossack tradition of defending Russia's southern frontier with the Muslim lands. Terek Cossacks fought for the Russian-dominated Dniestrian Republic against the Moldovans and joined Russia's traditional allies the Serbians in the wars that raged through the Balkans. The Terek Cossacks living away from the Caucasian frontier were markedly less militant than the groups living in the Caucasian foothills, and relations were often strained between the moderates and the more radical Vladikavkaz-based mother organization.

In mid-1992, a decree signed by Russian president Boris Yeltsin rehabilitated the Cossacks. The decree granted them the status of a distinct ethnic group and gave them the right to receive land free of charge. The decree also called for the use of Cossack forces to protect Russia's borders, although some Terek Cossacks have refused military duty outside their traditional homeland.

In July 1993 the Stavropol regional parliament began a debate on whether to declare the territory a republic and to restore the name Terek, banned by the Soviets in 1920, but as the differences between the republics, regions, and territories making up the Russian Federation began to blur, sentiment for republic status waned. In the late 1990s the Terek Cossacks pressed for the replacement of local governments, in areas with Terek Cossack majorities, with the traditional *ataman* boards of government.

In 1997, the Russian government passed a law allowing for the official registration of the Cossack Hosts. On 12 February 1997, the Terek host won the official right to bear arms and to maintain order in the territories in which its members resided. The Terek Cossacks in the later 1990s became more politically assertive. Renewed violence in 1996–97 marked a dramatic increase in the ethnic tension in the region. Attacks on Terek Cossacks in northern Chechnya left 26 dead, dramatically raising tension in the Terek Cossack regions. By June 1999, over 5,000 Terek Cossacks had been mobilized to guard Terek Cossack settlements in the North Caucasus. Many local and regional governments have simply incorporated these new forces into their local constabularies.

The *ataman* of the Terek Cossack host, Aleksandr Voloshin, called in 1999 for the Naursky and Shelkovsky Districts of Chechnya to be transferred to Russia proper and added to a proposed Terek Cossack Republic. Voloshin rejected the territorial changes by force advocated by militant nationalists, but did not rule out actions by individual Terek Cossack bands.

Voloshin, in October 2001, claimed that the growing ethnic violence in the Caucasus is caused by Islamic radicalism, particularly in neighboring

Chechnya. He echoed the Russian government's claim that Islamic groups had infiltrated the region and were engaged in terrorism.

SELECTED BIBLIOGRAPHY:

Barrett, Thomas M. *At the Edge of the Empire: The Terek Cossacks and the North Caucasus Frontier, 1700–1860*. 1999.
Feodoroff, Nicholas V. *History of the Cossacks*. 1999.
Groushko, Mike. *Cossack: Warrior Riders of the Steppes*. 1993.
Sgorlon, Carlo. *Army of the Lost Rivers*. 1998.

Texans

Texicans

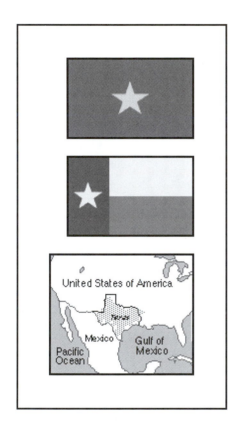

POPULATION: Approximately (2002e) 15,500,000 Texans in the United States, concentrated in the southwestern state of Texas. Outside the state there are sizable Texan communities in neighboring states and in other parts of the United States.

THE TEXAN HOMELAND: The Texan homeland lies in the south-central United States along the Gulf of Mexico. On the international border between the United States and Mexico, Texas is the second largest of the states of the Union, stretching north from the humid, subtropical Gulf Coast to the high plains and the western desert, which is subject to droughts and frequent sandstorms. Far from merely wide, arid plains filled with cattle and cowboys, the vast territory of Texas comprises a number of distinct landscapes and regions. Texas is a state within the United States. *State of Texas*: 26,807 sq. mi.—691,030 sq. km, (2002e) 21,674,000—Texans (Anglo-Texans 54%, Hispanics 24%, blacks 12%) 90%, other Americans 10%. The Texan capital and major cultural center is Austin, (2002e) 684,000, metropolitan area 1,197,000. Other important cultural centers are Houston, (2002e) 1,996,000, metropolitan area 4,603,000, Dallas, (2002e) 1,231,000, Fort Worth, (2002e) 553,000, Dallas-Fort Worth metropolitan area 5,033,000, and San Antonio, (2002e) 1,182,000, metropolitan area 1,607,000.

FLAG: The flag of the nationalist movement is a blue field bearing a centered gold five-pointed gold star. The national flag, the official flag of the state, is a horizontal bicolor of white over red with a broad blue stripe at the hoist bearing a centered white five-pointed star.

PEOPLE AND CULTURE: The Texans are of mixed background, about 54% of European descent, 12% black, and 24% Hispanic. Many Texans also have some Indian ancestry. The Germans are the most numerous of the European element, while the Hispanic population is of mixed Tejano, native Texan, and immigrant populations from Mexico and other parts of Latin America who have adopted the Texan way of life. The Texans, although of diverse ancestry, share a unique folk culture that mixes elements of America's southern and western cultures with native Indian and Tejano, Mexican, and black influences. The Texan culture, popularly called "Tex–Mex," includes a distinctive popular culture—with its own festivals and traditions, including a particular cuisine, music, and dialect—that is the basis of the American culture of the state. The Texans pride themselves on being self-sufficient and independent. Texans claim that Texas is a way of life and a way of thinking.

LANGUAGE AND RELIGION: The Texan dialect is a southwestern dialect of American English. The dialect combines elements of the dialects spoken by Southerners* along with many borrowings from Spanish, the second language of the state. Rice University and other institutions of higher learning offer courses in the Texan dialect.

NATIONAL HISTORY: The region was sparsely inhabited by several distinct indigenous peoples when the first Europeans visited the region in the early 1500s. The name "Texas" is derived from *tejas* or *teyas*, a Spanish corruption of the Caddo words, one of the indigenous people's word for "friends" or "allies." It gradually came to denote the vast region north of the Rio Grande and east of New Mexico.

In 1519 the region was included in the Spanish colony of New Spain, later known as Mexico. The Spanish explorers Cabeza de Vaca and Francisco Coronado visited the interior in 1541. The first European settlement was made at Ysleta, near present El Paso, in 1682, although effective settlement only began in 1715. The French established a colony at Matagorda Bay in 1685, which made the Spanish take settlement in Texas seriously.

In the early eighteenth century, Spanish Roman Catholic missionaries established a string of missions, notably Mission San Antonio, popularly called the Alamo, in 1718. Four hundred thirty-three Spanish families were granted land in what was then known as Tejas by the Spanish crown. The great *ranchos* established by the landowning families covered most of Tejas and parts of the present-day states of Oklahoma, New Mexico, Kansas, Colorado, and Utah. In 1820 Moses Austin of Virginia secured Spanish permission to began a colony in the sparsely populated region.

Mexico broke away from the Spanish Empire in 1821, claiming Tejas, or Texas, as part of its national territory. Other than the wealthy owners of the Spanish land grants and their imported workers, few settlers moved into the region from Mexico. Sparse settlement prompted the Mexican government to employ American entrepreneurs to encourage American immigrants to settle in Texas, hoping the Americans would check the hostility of the indigenous peoples in the huge territory. Although Roman

Catholicism was the official religion in Mexico, the Mexican government allowed the Americans their own religions and some political autonomy, although settlers had to swear allegiance to Mexico. Each settler family was granted 4,428 acres of rich farmland for just a few pennies an acre. The settlers were exempted from paying customs duties on imports for seven years, and some taxes were waived for 10 years.

American settlers outnumbered the Tejanos by 1820. Many Americans from the South moved to Texas, bringing their black slaves to establish cotton plantations in the fertile southeast. The Mexican government outlawed slavery in 1829, incurring the enmity of the southern settlers. By 1835 over 30,000 Americans had settled in the province, outnumbering the Mexican population by 10 to one.

Mutual hostility escalated in Texas as the Americans became contemptuous of the Mexicans, who seemed unable to form an effective government, and the Mexicans grew fearful of American expansionism. The Mexican government abolished the region's federal status and dissolved the provincial government. Texas was joined to the province of Coahuila to the south, giving the expanded province a definite Mexican majority. The authorities imposed strict restrictions on the American population.

Texicans, as they called themselves, both Anglo-Americans and Mexicans, became disgruntled with Mexican rule, particularly after Gen. Antonio López de Santa Ana established dictatorial rule in 1833 and abolished Mexico's decentralized federal system. The Texicans rebelled against the Santa Ana government, prompting Santa Ana himself to march on Texas to crush the rebels. The Texican rebels swept through the scant Mexican garrisons south of the Rio Grande. American volunteers poured across the border, among them such legendary figures as Davy Crockett and Jim Bowie. A Tennesseean, Sam Houston, took control of the Army of Texas to face the large army led by Santa Ana moving into the territory from the south.

Despite orders to blow up the old mission at San Antonio, 185 Texicans and Americans fortified the mission and held off 4,000 Mexican troops for 11 days, giving Houston time to organize in eastern Texas. To the last man, the defenders of the Alamo died fighting. During the siege of the Alamo, independence from Mexico was declared on 2 March 1836 at the Texas capital at Washington-on-the-Brazos. After burning the bodies of the Alamo's defenders, Santa Ana pushed on until he confronted Houston's army of 738 Texicans beside San Jacinto Creek. Under the battle cry "Remember the Alamo," the Texicans annihilated Santa Ana's army, suffering only two Texican dead and 23 wounded. Santa Ana, captured by the Texican rebels, offered to recognize Texan independence in exchange for his release. In 1842 a second Mexican invasion threatened, forcing the Texans to prepare for war and to move their capital from Austin, in the invasion's path, to Houston in the southeast.

The new Republic of Texas exchanged ambassadors with the United States, Mexico, and many European states, but in the face of threats by Mexican claims, sentiment for incorporation in the United States grew rapidly. After a 10-year struggle to maintain a viable independent state, in 1845 the majority of the population voted for annexation. Texas entered the United States as a slave state on 19 February 1846, with Austin as its capital. The American annexation of the Texas republic was one of the causes of the Mexican-American War of 1846–48. More than 12 million acres in Texas were taken from the Mexicans in a land rush that more than doubled the population by 1850.

The state ceded vast areas in present-day New Mexico, Colorado, Oklahoma, and Kansas to the U.S. government. Sam Houston, who had led Texas to independence, became governor in 1859 but was deposed when he opposed Texan secession over the issues of state's rights and slavery. On 1 February 1861 Texans declared the secession and independence of the Republic of Texas, which formed a military alliance with the other seceding states in the American South. Thousands of Texans participated in the American Civil War from 1861 to 1865. In 1865 slavery was officially ended, and Texas was placed under military occupation. The bitter Reconstruction period, dominated by northerners, is still an open issue in the state. On 30 March 1870 Texas was readmitted to the Union.

In the late nineteenth century, thousands of European immigrants arrived in Texas. The new immigrants adopted the unique Texan way of life, often becoming the most Texan and patriotic sector of the growing population. The immigrants spread out across the huge state, most settling in small rural communities. The Texans developed one of the strongest regional cultures in the United States, with its own cuisine, dialect, and traditions. The Texans' quasi-nationalistic identity was related at least in part to their history and proximity to Mexico.

Oil was first discovered in 1901, becoming an important resource in the course of World War I. Oil transformed the state's economy. The Germans, attempting to entice Mexico into the conflict, promised to return Texas and its oil to Mexican control but failed to convince the Mexican government. Before and after the war immigration to the state continued, both from other American states and from Europe, Mexico, and other areas of the world.

The desegregation era after World War II again raised the question of states' rights, which had long been an issue for the independent-minded Texans. During the 1950s and 1960s, both blacks and Hispanics began to throw off the domination of the past and demand their rights as Texans.

Descendents of the original Spanish and Mexican landowners banded together, trying to get compensation for lands appropriated by American settlers after the Texas war of independence. In 1976 the over 2,000 descendents of the 433 original families formed the Association de Reclamantes. A class-action suit was filed against the Mexican government, which had originally given the lands away without compensation. The claims should ultimately total about a billion dollars, with as many as 25,000 Texans eligible for compensation.

Texas was 60% rural in 1930, but by 1950 it was 60% urban. The urbanization of the Texans accelerated in the 1960s and 1970s. By 1980 four out of every five Texans lived in urban areas, which had not kept up with the state's phenomenal growth. The urban areas absorbed the continuing immigration, which was needed for the growing economy but was often resented by the Texans as diluting their culture and Americanizing their traditional way of life.

One option for Texas, short of independence, incorporated in the 1845 annexation agreement, gives Texas the right to divide into as many as five states, which would give Texans four more governors and eight more senators.

The oil industry, which shaped the Texas economy and way of life for the first decades of the twentieth century, began to wane in the early 1980s. By 1984 Texas only had 7.5 billion barrels of oil that could be profitably extracted. The Panhandle area of north Texas was especially hard hit by the oil recession of 1985–86.

In the mid-1980s various groups formed in the state to halt the "Californization" of Texas. The groups generally opposed the heavy immigration to the state and interference of the federal government in the affairs of Texas. A survey carried out by Texas A & M University in 1986 showed that nearly 20% of Texans felt that their state would have been better off never having joined the Union. In the late 1980s Texans regained their confidence after three years of economic recession.

The Prince of Wales made an official visit to Texas in February 1986 to participate in the celebration of the anniversary of the declaration of Texas independence. The prince presented a painting of the former embassy of Texas in London. The celebration was the scene of demonstrations by the small number of separatists who called for a return to the status of an independent republic.

Texan nationalists, a small minority among the Texan population, believe that the Lone Star State was illegally absorbed into the Union in 1845 and therefore remains a sovereign nation. Separatists decry the tremendous increase in the power of the central government since the mid-twentieth century. Claiming that Texas became a great state because individuals were allowed to develop without undue interference from government, nationalists want Texas to secede and resume its former independence.

A nationalist group, the Republic of Texas, took its argument that Texas remains a sovereign republic and that the annexation to the United States was illegal to the Supreme Court of Texas, which dismissed the case for lack of jurisdiction. The group has also petitioned the International Court of Justice at The Hague, but the judges refused to hear the application. The U.S. State Department also refused to give the separatists a hearing.

The group argues that since Texas was an independent country in 1845, and states make agreements by treaty, the United States could annex Texas only by treaty. The idea of annexing Texas by a joint resolution of Congress was denounced at the time but passed by a majority in each house, allowing Congress to admit Texas as a state. The group's claim that the joint resolution was unconstitutional echoed objections from many in the legislature at the time. The majority of the Senate Committee on Foreign Relations voted against the Texas resolution on that ground in 1845. Texas's annexation marked the first time in history that a sovereign state voluntarily relinquished its freedom to become part of another state. With a minimum of publicity, the group declared the independence of the Republic of Texas on 27 December 1995. The attorney general of Texas threatened court action if the group persisted in representing the Republic of Texas as an official government.

In the 1990s, Hispanics and blacks used the power of the ballot to elect city officials, influence state decisions, and move into the Texan power structure. The increasing influence of the non-Anglo Texans moderated the old conservative attitudes that had marked Texan traditions since the days of the republic.

Texans remain a distinct American people, proud of their past and sure of their place in the world in the future. Their distinct history and diversity, they say, is what makes Texans unique. The separatist demand that Texans be allowed to vote on the independence issue is rejected by the vast majority, who point to the fact that Texas enjoys considerable autonomy under the American system. Others reject the referendum demand on the grounds that their ancestors already voted on the issue in 1845 and opted overwhelmingly for statehood within the Union.

The question of what makes Texas different from other American states has many answers, but one of the most important is that the Texans, not the U.S. government, own the land they call their homeland. It is extraordinary that Texas contains virtually no public land, while other western states are a checkerboard of federal land. The land issue was settled when independent Texas joined the Union in 1845, at which time they retained title to their lands. Although urbanization, immigration, the 1980s recession, and the North American Free Trade Association (NAFTA) have loosened Texans' ties to the land, some 55% is still owned by large *ranchos*.

Texas remains a nation-state in all but name. The Texans remain Texans when they leave the state, even to live in other states or abroad. The Texas economy, with about 40% of its trade with neighboring Mexico, is unlike that of the other American states and has many of the characteristics of a national economy. Texans enthusiastically embraced NAFTA, which further opened its borders to trade with Mexico. The NAFTA secretariat is located in Dallas, and the North American Development Bank is based in San Antonio.

With the departure of George Bush for Washington in 2001, the opposition in Texas has begun to pass legislation that reverses many of Bush's least-liked stances. Many, including the increasingly vocal regional and pro-Texas groups, call the reversal an open rebellion against Bush's policies that left Texas in a mess.

SELECTED BIBLIOGRAPHY:

Davidson, Donald. *Regionalism and Nationalism in the United States.* 1990.
Kraemer, David F. *Texas Politics.* 1998.
Nachman, Mark E. *A Nation within a Nation: The Rise of Texas Nationalism.* 1988.
Richardson, Rupert N. *Texas, the Lone Star State.* 1996.

Tibetans

Tibate; Tebilians; Bhotias; Wei; Weizang; Dbus; Phoke; Zang

POPULATION: Approximately (2002e) 6,550,000 Tibetans in China, concentrated in the Tibetan Autonomous Region, formerly Outer Tibet, in the southwest and the province of Quinghai and the western districts of Sichuan, Yunnan, and Gansu, which together formed Inner Tibet. Outside the region there are Tibetan communities in India, where about 150,000 Tibetans live, including the Tibetan government-in-exile, as well as in Europe, the United States and Canada, and in Nepal, Bhutan, and other adjacent areas in the Himalayas.

THE TIBETAN HOMELAND: The Tibetan homeland, often referred to as the "roof of the world," occupies the vast Tibetan Plateau in the Himalayas of southwestern China. Nestled among some of the earth's highest mountain range, most of the plateau lies above 14,000 feet (4,267 meters) above sea level, making Tibet the highest inhabited area in the world. The relatively level northern part of the plateau, the Northern Plain, is bordered on the north by the Kunlun Mountains. The Tibetan homeland is split between several Chinese provinces and the autonomous region of Tibet, formerly Outer Tibet.

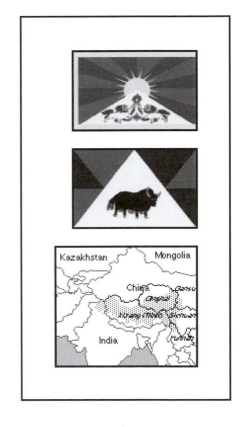

Tibetan Autonomous Region/Xizang Zizhiqu (Bod/Bod Rang-skyong-Ijongs): 471,660 sq. mi.—1,221,599 sq. km, (2002e) 2,805,000—Tibetans 71%, Han Chinese 28%, other Chinese 1%. The Tibetan capital and major cultural center is Lhasa, called Lha-sa by the Tibetans and Lasa by the Chinese, (2002e) 113,000, metropolitan area 377,000. Other important cultural centers are Xigaze, called Shigatse, (2002e) 34,000, and Qamdo, called Chamdo locally, (2002e) in western Tibet. The most important Tibetan center in Qinghai is Qumalai, (2002e) 11,000. The major cultural center outside China is Dharamsala, in northwestern India, the unofficial capital of the Tibetan government-in-exile.

FLAG: The Tibetan national flag has a central yellow sun with twelve red and blue stripes or rays at the top, hoist, and fly; a white triangle at the bottom, its point touching the center of the sun, is charged with two white dragons holding the national symbols; the flag is bordered on all but the fly by narrow yellow stripes. The flag of the National Democratic Party of Tibet (NDPT) has a blue and red design with a large white triangle, point to the top, bearing the image of a yak.

PEOPLE AND CULTURE: According to legend the Tibetan people originated from the union of a monkey and a female demon. The Tibetans are a Mongoloid people with two distinct strains, the brachycephalic (or round-headed) and the dolichocephalic (or long-headed) people. The former, predominant in the cultivated river valleys, are more closely related to the early Chinese and Burmans. The latter, found mainly among the nomads of the northern districts and in the noble families of central Tibet, more closely resemble the Turkic peoples. The Tibetans are divided into three major divisions—the Tibetans of Outer Tibet, the Amdo Tibetans in the north, and the Kham Tibetans in the east—further divided into 15 subgroups. The Tibetan religion is closely tied to the Tibetan culture and way of life. Prior to the imposition of communist rule, Tibetan life revolved around the religious calendar. Most Tibetans are seminomadic, constantly moving their herds of yaks, cattle, goats, and sheep to new pastures. Polyandry, which permits a woman to have several husbands, remains socially accepted and very common, except among the Amdo, who are usually monogamous. The ability to withstand the severe weather conditions of the Tibetan Plateau has made the Tibetans one of the most rugged peoples in the world. By the early 1980s the Han Chinese migrants outnumbered the Tibetans of the Tibetan Plateau in all areas except central or Outer Tibet, the area that constitutes the Tibetan Autonomous Region.

LANGUAGE AND RELIGION: The Tibetan language, called Tibetic or Bodic, belongs to the Tibeto-Burman group of the Sino-Tibetan language group. The language is spoken in four major dialects, Central, Southern, Northern, and Western. Each of the dialects represents a group of related dialects divided by region and history. The dialect of Lhasa, part of the Central group, forms the basis of the literary language, which is written in a very conservative script of Indian origin from the ninth century. A 1995 survey revealed that 40% of Tibetans in China are illiterate or semiliterate and that more than 70% of the population has no formal schooling.

An isolated mountain people, the Tibetans are the heirs of an ancient civilization but are more defined by their religion, a variant of Mahayana Buddhism known as Tibetan Buddhism or Lamaism. The religion is an historical blend of several Asian religions with a strong occult aspect and many pre-Buddhist animist practices. The Tibetans believe in numerous gods and spirits, and they constantly strive to appease them with chants, rituals, and sacrifices. The continuing cycle of death and reincarnation is central to the belief system. There is a small Muslim minority in the south-western districts.

NATIONAL HISTORY: The Chinese T'ang chronicles of the tenth century place the Tibetans' origin among the nomadic, pastoral Ch'iang tribes recorded about 200 B.C. as inhabiting the great steppe northwest of China. The region, where various ethnic elements met and mingled for centuries, was dominated by the early tribes that absorbed other groups by conquest or alliance.

Nomadic tribes, possibly originating in Ladakh to the southwest of the massive plateau, created a sophisticated theocratic kingdom following the introduction of Buddhism around A.D. 630. The Buddhist religion merged with the pre-Buddhist Bon religion to produce a unique system of beliefs and rituals. The kingdom expanded in the eighth century into the Mongol lands to the north and the lowlands south of the Himalayas. The Tibetan kingdom first established relations with China during the T'ang dynasty (618–906), beginning centuries of resistance to Chinese incursions and conquest. At the height of its power, in the eighth century, the Tibetans controlled the Silk Route and exacted tribute from the T'angs.

The kingdom disintegrated in the tenth century, and invading Mongols conquered much of Inner Tibet in the thirteenth century, eventually extending their influence to mountainous Outer Tibet. In 1270 the Mongol emperor of China, Kublai Khan, was converted to Lamaism by the abbot of the Sakya Lamasery. The abbot later returned to Outer Tibet to become Tibet's first priest-king. During China's Ming dynasty (1368–1644), Tibet was ruled as an independent kingdom under its own Pagmodru, Rinpung, and Tsangpa dynasties.

Tibet's religious leaders in the sixteenth century accepted the reform sect of Mahayana Buddhism, Gelugpa (the Victorious Order of the Yellow Hat), under the spiritual leadership of the dalai lama. The reform movement emphasized a more secluded, meditative life as a way to enlightenment. The founder of the new sect, Tsong-kha-pa, died in 1419, but his branch of Lamaism continue to spread.

China came under the rule of the Manchus* in the latter half of the seventeenth century. To avoid maintaining a military force, the fifth dalai lama negotiated a protective alliance with the Manchu emperor in the 1650s. The Manchus, having incorporated Inner Tibet into their growing empire, established nominal rule over Outer Tibet in 1720, although the Tibetan secular and religious hierarchy remained in control.

Over the next century the British gained control of the vassal kingdoms south of the Himalayas. The Tibetans repeatedly rejected British overtures in the mid-nineteenth century. The British first saw Tibet as a trade link to China but later viewed the region as a route for Russian advances that might endanger India. When the Tibetans rebuffed a demand for trade concessions, the British dispatched an expedition to occupy the country in 1903–1904. The British occupation force coerced the dalai lama to sign a treaty that opened several Tibetan cities to outsiders in 1904. Two years later the British signed a treaty with China, without Tibetan participation, that recognized Chinese suzerainty over Tibet.

The Manchus, to reinforce their claim, sent a Chinese force to Tibet in 1910, driving the dalai lama and many followers into exile in British India. The Chinese Revolution, which overthrew the Manchu dynasty in 1911, seriously weakened Chinese control of Outer Tibet, and Tibetan soldiers ultimately succeeded in driving the Chinese from the kingdom. The thirteenth dalai lama returned from exile in India to declare Tibet independent of republican China on 18 February 1912. The Tibetans, in control of Outer Tibet, laid claim to the historical territory of Inner Tibet, still under Chinese rule. In 1918 the Tibetans fought off a second Chinese invasion.

Tibet was organized as a Buddhist theocracy ruled by the dalai lama; only 3% of the Tibetan population controlled all the land—noble families, feudal lords, and some 6,000 lamaseries. Of the Tibetan majority 5% were slaves, 20% Buddhist monks, and the remainder serfs attached to the feudal estates and lamaseries. The dalai lama, the god-king, was both the religious and secular head of the Tibetan state.

Tension between the Tibetans and the Chinese government continued, primarily over the Chinese treatment of the Tibetan majority in Inner Tibet. A brief border war in 1931–33 ended with the loss of additional Tibetan territory north of the Yangtse River in present Qinghai. The Tibetan ruling class declined offers of outside help, fearing that new influences would undermine their position. Opening to the outside world could have posed a credible deterrence to Chinese claims, allowing Outer Tibet, like Outer Mongolia, to maintain a precarious independence to the present.

China's growing civil war and the later war with Japan eased pressure on the kingdom in the 1930s and early 1940s. The Chinese Civil War, suspended during the last years of World War II, resumed in 1945. Four years later the Chinese communists emerged victorious and set about consolidating their authority. On 30 October 1950 the Chinese invaded eastern Tibet, overwhelming the poorly equipped Tibetan troops. An appeal by the dalai lama to the United Nations was denied, as were pleas to the British and Indians. In 1951 the Chinese forced the dalai lama to sign a new treaty and to accept garrisons on the southern borders.

The supreme communist leader, Mao Tse-tung, announced his intention to change the Tibetan-majority population of Inner Tibet to a Chinese majority of five to one. To that end he launched massive immigration to the region in 1954. In 1956 the Tibetans in the colonization region revolted, determined to reunite their region with Outer Tibet under the rule of the dalai lama. Refugees from the fighting in the east carried guerrilla warfare to central Tibet, leading to a popular uprising against the Chinese in Lhasa in March 1959. The Chinese army invaded, driving Tenzin Gyatso, the fourteenth dalai lama, and 87,000 refugees into exile in India. The tension raised by the invasion intensified Chinese disagreements with India, which had given asylum to the refugee Tibetan government, and in 1962 Chinese forces invaded northern India, setting off fighting in several areas along the India-Tibet border.

Determined to crush the Tibetan culture, the communist government ordered the destruction of 6,125 ancient lamaseries, murdered over 100,000 Tibetans in mass executions, and began to settle millions of ethnic Chinese in the traditionally Tibetan lands. During the upheavals of the Cultural Revolution, from 1966 to 1976, most of the remaining shrines and lamaseries were reduced to rubble by zealous Red Guards. The priceless collections of ancient manuscripts stored in the lamaseries were publicly burned. Of the 6,254 lamaseries in existence in 1959, only 13 survived the onslaught. Between 1963 and 1971 no foreigners were allowed to enter Tibet.

Persecution of the Tibetan population in China abated in the late 1970s with the end of the Cultural Revolution, but repression resumed when the Tibetans renewed their claims to autonomy or independence. The Chinese government invested in the economic development of Tibet and in the early 1980s attempted to open a dialogue with the dalai lama, who continued to lead a nonviolent campaign to save the Tibetan nation from genocide. With outside help and contributions, the reconstruction of some of the destroyed lamasaries was undertaken in the 1980s.

Intrigue and acrimony followed the death in 1989 of the second-ranking religious leader, the panchen lama. The Chinese authorities and the exiled dalai lama ran separate searches to find his reincarnation. In 1995 the Chinese placed the boy chosen by the dalai lama under house arrest and installed their own candidate. The panchen and karmapa lamas, the second- and third-ranking lamas of the Tibetan religion, under the control of the Chinese government, were groomed as "patriotic" lamas, who could be relied upon to do the Communist Party's bidding when the time comes to choose a new dalai lama.

Pro-independence demonstrations in Lhasa in 1988 spread across the region to districts in Inner Tibet in 1989. The authorities imposed martial law and countered the nationalist upsurge with thousands of arrests and increased suppression. In 1989, over fiery Chinese protests, the dalai lama was awarded the Nobel Peace Prize, an acknowledgment of his and his nation's peaceful campaign to regain their lost freedom.

The dalai lama renounced his previous insistence on complete separation of Tibet from China in December 1990, proposing instead that Tibet and China should form a loose confederation. In September 1994 the dalai lama again warned China that the Tibetans could turn to armed rebellion if the government oppression continued. In March 1995 he put forward a plan for a referendum of all Tibetans, both those living under Chinese rule and those living in exile, to determine their wishes for the future of their threatened nation. The Chinese government condemned the plan and the Tibetans' efforts to involve the UN and other international bodies as just another ploy to win independence for Tibet. The incorporation of Hong Kong into China in 1997 under a formula called "one country, two systems" offered a new policy that could allow the Tibetans considerable autonomy in their homeland.

The National Democratic Party of Tibet was formed as the first democratic political party in the history of Tibet. Founded in September 1994 as an initiative of the Tibetan Youth Congress, the party's objective was to safeguard and strengthen the democratic process inaugurated by the dalai lama in the 1960s and to ensure that the Tibetans' commitment to democracy remained firm and resolute, with clear and unequivocal direction in the struggle for the restoration of Tibetan independence.

In 1998, a leading lama, Argya Rinpoche, based at the Kumbum monastery in Qinghai, escaped to exile in India. One of the most important Tibetan religious leaders, Ugyen Trinley Dorje, the third-ranking lama in Tibetan Buddhism and the head of the Karmapa order, also escaped from Tibet in late December 1999 to India. The flight of the seventeenth karmapa lama, who is venerated by all major branches of Tibetan Buddhism, was another embarrassment to the Chinese government, which had attempted to control the young leader. The escape of the Chinese recognized lamas underlined the worsening treatment of Tibetan Buddhists in China.

Official denunciations of the dalai lama, who promotes dialogue, nonviolence, and accommodation, increased in 2000. His program of negotiations and autonomy was dismissed and distorted with accusations of covert support of violence to secure Tibetan independence. During celebrations in Dharmsala in early December 2000, the dalai lama proposed a new effort to resolve the Tibetan problem by sending a delegation to Beijing to open long-delayed talks on Tibetan autonomy. An estimated one million Tibetans have been killed since the Chinese occupation in 1959, but the Tibetans continue to defy the communist authorities.

The Chinese government announced plans in June 2001 for a new railway to link Golmud in Qinghai and Lhasa in Tibet, making it possible to travel by train from Beijing to Lhasa, was applauded by many, but not the Tibetans, who see the rail link as making colonization even easier for the Chinese government. The railway was the focus of Chinese celebrations in Lhasa in July to celebrate the 50th anniversary of the "peaceful liberation" of Tibet. Posters went up in the city in Tibetan saying there is nothing to celebrate, as for the last 50 years the Tibetans had known only "blood and tears."

SELECTED BIBLIOGRAPHY:

Kerr, Blake. *Sky Burial: An Eyewitness Account of China's Brutal Crackdown in Tibet.* 1993.

Lehman, Steve, ed. *The Tibetans: A Struggle to Survive.* 1998.

Paff, Joseph. *Tibetans.* 2000.

Shakya, Tsering. *The Dragon in the Land of Snows: A History of Modern Tibet since 1947.* 1999.

Tigreans

Tigrayans; Tigrai; Tegray; Tegaru

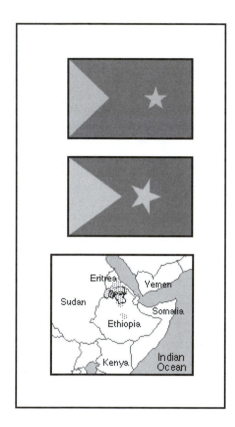

POPULATION: Approximately (2002e) 7,300,000 Tigreans in the Horn of Africa, concentrated in the Tigray state of Ethiopia, with a Tigrean population of 5.5 million, and the central districts of neighboring Eritrea, with 1.8 million. Outside the region there are sizable Tigrean communities in other parts of Ethiopia, particularly in the capital, Addis Ababa.

THE TIGREAN HOMELAND: The Tigrean homeland is located in northern Ethiopia. Centuries of erosion, deforestation, and overgrazing have left the region with dry and treeless hills and plains in the central highland, with more fertile land in the lowlands to the west, and escarpments in the east. The fertile irrigated land and the lowlands along the rivers produce abundant food, but the region remains subject to seasonal droughts. The historical province of Tigray, comprising administrative zones and a special zone, forms the Tigray state of the Federal Democratic Republic of Ethiopian. *State of Tigray (Tigre)*: 39,372 sq. mi.—101,973 sq. km, (2002e) 3,957,000—Tigreans 94%, Amharas* 3%, Erob, Kumama, and other Ethiopians 3%. The Tigrean capital and major cultural center is Mekele, (2002e) 122,000. The important cultural center is Aksum, (2002e) 33,000.

FLAG: The Tigrean national flag, the flag of the Tigray People's Liberation Front, is a red field bearing a yellow triangle at the hoist and a yellow five-pointed star near the point of the triangle. The official flag of Tigray state has the same basic design and colors, with a slightly larger star turned on its side.

PEOPLE AND CULTURE: The Tigreans are a Semitic people, descendents of ancient migrants from the Arabian Peninsula who mixed with the indigenous Cushitic peoples of northeastern Africa. Considered the closest to the original settlers, the tall, handsome Tigreans have intermarried less than the other Semitic peoples of the region. The Tigrean culture, in both Ethiopia and Eritrea, retains many traditions and customs that have disappeared from the culture of the Amharas, the other large Semitic nation in northeastern Africa. The Tigreans of Eritrea are often called Tigrinya, the original name of the early Tigrean peoples. The Tigreans believe that they have a historical kinship with other Tigreans regardless of their place of residence. Coffee is a ceremonial drink; the "coffee ceremony" is a part of any important negotiations or ceremonies.

LANGUAGE AND RELIGION: The Tigrean national language, called Tigrinya, is a Semitic language belonging to the Ethiopian group of Semitic languages in northwestern Africa. Tigrinya, spoken in both Ethiopia and Eritrea, is the Semitic language most closely related to Old Ethiopian, Ge'ez, the language spoken in the fourteenth century and retained as the language of the Ethiopian Orthodox religion. The language is written in the Fidel script, which developed from the ancient Phoenician-Sabean script.

The majority of the Tigreans are Coptic Christians, estimated at about 90% of the total; a minority, the Jabarti, between 8 and 10%, are Sunni Islam and form a trading class that has maintained the Tigreans' close contacts with neighboring Muslim peoples. Smaller groups have adopted evangelical Christian beliefs introduced by European and American missionaries. The Coptic Orthodox Church is an integral part of the Tigrean culture, and the major events of the year revolve around the church calendar. It is estimated that there is a Coptic priest for every 92 Tigrean Christians.

NATIONAL HISTORY: The Tigreans claim descent from the Sabeans of ancient Sheba, the legendary monarchy on the Arabian Peninsula. Tigrean tradition has a Sabean migration, led by Menelik, the son of Israel's King Solomon and the queen of Sheba, crossing the Red Sea to settle the Tigrean highland around the year 1000 B.C. Menelik is credited with bringing the Ark of the Covenant from the Temple in Jerusalem to Aksum, the capital of the Semitic kingdom, known as the Aksumite Empire, that the Sabeans created. Authentic records from the first century A.D. confirm that the early Ethiopian state centered on Aksum. The empire controlled present northern Ethiopia, Tigray and Amhara, and parts of Sudan.

Frumentius of Tyre, called Abba Salama by the Aksumites, converted the Aksumite king to Christianity in A.D. 330. The new religion rapidly spread among the sophisticated population of the empire. The Semitic Christian inhabitants of the empire, spreading across the Ethiopian highlands, gradually separated and evolved as two separate nations—the Tigreans in the north, and the Amhara in the west and south. Together the two nations expanded the empire to include many tribal peoples in the lowlands to the south and east.

The introduction of Islam in the seventh century confined the Christian peoples to the highlands, a Christian island surrounded by hostile Muslim states. In the eighth century Muslims overran Tigre, and the center of Christian power shifted south to the Amhara lands. The Christian reconquest, led by the Amharas, of Tigre relegated the resurrected kingdom to a secondary position in the Amhara-dominated empire.

Nevertheless, the Tigreans, by controlling the Red Sea ports, became prosperous from the caravan routes that reached the seat of the Ethiopian empire to the south. After losing the coastal region to the Ottoman Empire in the sixteenth century, the Tigreans lost status and influence and came under the direct political domination of the Amhara, generally under the rule of the princes of Gonder or Shoa. The Tigrean homeland was under constant threat in the nineteenth century from Egyptian, Sudanese, British, and Italian armies intent on penetrating the Ethiopian interior in the highlands.

The Tigreans increasingly shifted their culture and loyalty away from the Amharas during the intense civil strife in the empire in the seventeenth and eighteenth centuries. In the early nineteenth century Tigre broke away under its *ras* (prince), Mikhail Suhul. Tigre was reconquered by Theodore, an Amhara chief, who was crowned as the Ethiopian emperor in 1855. In 1868 the succession passed to the prince of Tigre, only to be usurped, with Italian assistance, by the Amhara leader, later known as Menelik II. Increasing tension between the two peoples culminated in a widespread Tigrean uprising in the 1880s. The imperial army defeated the Tigrean rebels with great brutality. The Tigrean prince and many leaders were exiled, and reprisals decimated the Tigrean nobility.

Threatened by Italian expansion from their colony in Eritrea, the Tigreans joined the Amharas to defeat an Italian invasion in 1895–96, the first major defeat of a European force in northeastern Africa. The campaign against the Italians began the Tigrean opposition movement in Ethiopia. Emperor Menelik deployed an army of 80,000 into Tigray to oppose the Italians, but without adequate provisions, forcing the soldiers to live off the land. According to Tigrean nationalists, the number of Tigreans killed defending their homes far outnumbered the number of Italians killed in battle.

Determined to erase the shame of their 1895 defeat, a mechanized Italian army returned to defeat the feudal Ethiopian forces in Tigray in 1935. Once again the inhabitants suffered. Under Italian rule from 1935 to 1941 the region was governed by officials appointed from the Italian administration in Addis Ababa.

British forces from Kenya liberated Ethiopia early in World War II. Ethiopia's emperor, Haile Selassie, returned in 1941 amid rising Tigrean demands for special status and the right of their *ras* to return to Tigre. Their appeals ignored, the Tigreans rebelled in 1943, the Weyane Rebellion, intent on separating from Ethiopia under their prince. In early September the rebels drove the government troops from Mekele and on 11 September 1943 declared Tigre independent. Fearing the destabilization of the entire Horn of Africa, the British occupation forces in neighboring Eritrea aided the imperial forces in reconquering the breakaway state. Continued Tigrean resentment and resistance evolved into the modern liberation movement.

In the early 1970s the government moved against the nationalists, forcing the movement underground. A popular revolution, initially supported by the Tigreans, overthrew the feudal Ethiopian monarchy in 1974. The revolutionary government was soon dominated by a Marxist clique, the Derg, made up of mostly Amhara army officers. Mengistu Haile Mariam was made chairman of the Derg, which assumed the functions of government.

In October 1974, the Derg ordered Ras Mengesha Seyoum, the governor of Tigray and member of the Tigrean royal family, to relinquish his office and surrender to the authorities. He fled to the bush and organized Tigrean resistance to the new Marxist regime. The anti-Christian stance and the widespread nationalizations of the Mengistu government helped rekindled the Tigrean rebellion. In 1975 the Tigray People's Liberation Front (TPLF) was formed as a coalition of nationalist, Marxist, and democratic groups to lead the Tigrean insurrection. The TPLF eliminated most Tigrean opposition and adopted Marxist rhetoric. Initially the TPLF leadership advocated the creation of an independent Tigrean-Eritrean federation. By 1978 the Tigreans had driven the Ethiopian forces from 90% of Tigre. The TPLF held its first congress in the spring of 1979, reaffirming its goal of complete independence for "Greater Tigre," including the territory separated after the 1943 Weyane Rebellion.

Drought and famine, exacerbated by government refusal to allow relief supplies to enter rebel areas, took thousands of lives in 1984–85. The Marxist Ethiopian regime barred food aid from the region, using hunger as a weapon against the Tigrean rebels. Tigreans accused the government of bombing crops and animals in an effort to keep the famine from ending. In spite of ideological differences and splits between the pro-autonomy and pro-independence factions, the Tigreans continued to advance against the Soviet-supported Ethiopian forces.

The TPLF, led by Meles Zenawi, became the key political force in the antigovernment coalition, the Ethiopian Peoples' Revolutionary Democratic Front, which was formed in 1989 and included Eritreans, Oromos,* Amharas, Western Somalis,* and other ethnic groups.

Abandoned by their Soviet allies during the turmoil in the Soviet Union in 1989, the Ethiopian military began to crumble. The forces of the insurgent alliance, led by the Tigreans, moved on the Ethiopian capital, Addis Ababa, in 1990. Mengistu suddenly resigned and fled to exile in

Zimbabwe. In late May 1991 the rebels occupied the city and overthrew the hated communist government.

In 1992–93 the coalition government of Ethiopia began to split along ethnic lines as the other groups rebelled against Tigrean hegemony. The independence in 1993 of Eritrea, in which half the total population is Tigrean, reduced Tigrean influence, although the TPLF remained the most powerful partner in the Ethiopian government. The Oromos and others withdrew from the government as ethnic violence and tension returned to the multiethnic state. In the Tigrean heartland nationalists began a campaign to win support for the independence of Tigre in a federation of independent states.

The Tigrean national movement, split between the faction that supported a federal system in Ethiopia and a growing faction seeking to follow Eritrea to independence, remained the most important component in Ethiopia's postcommunist government. In December 1994 the Tigrean-dominated Ethiopian government approved a new constitution that allowed any of the new federation's ethnic regions to secede peacefully if a referendum proved that independence was the wish of the region's majority. The pro–independence faction of the Tigrean national movement publicly welcomed the new law, but militant Tigrean leaders admitted that with broad Tigrean autonomy within the newly created federal Ethiopian state support for separatism had waned since 1991.

Many of Ethiopia's diverse peoples view the Ethiopian government as Tigrean dominated, stripping other regions of resources for the benefit of the Tigrean homeland in the north. This attitude contributed to the dramatic growth of antigovernment sentiment and organization in the 1990s. Tigrean regional forces operated in collaboration with Eritrean forces to invade the neighboring Afar region in December 1995. The combined forces, mostly ethnic Tigreans, pushed Afar rebels toward the desert area and away from the border regions. Cooperation between the Tigrean-dominated Ethiopian and Eritrean governments began to deteriorate in 1997, with minor border incidents and cross-border accusations.

In September 1997 a new Islamic rebel group, the Oromo-Somali-Afar Liberation Alliance, accused the Tigreans and Amharas of imposing their Judeo-Christian hegemony on Ethiopia. The growing Islamic movement, particularly strong in the east and south of the country, expanded as an anti-Christian, anti-Tigrean mass movement. The call for the establishment of an Islamic state in Ethiopia, supported by several radical Arab governments, was one of the reasons that the Ethiopian government embarked on a nationalistic border war with neighboring Eritrea in 1998.

Tigrean nationalism, put aside during the early 1990s, began to reappear in the late 1990s. Tigrean nationalists in the Ethiopian government expanded the borders of the Tigrean state, first at the expense of neighboring Ethiopian provinces, then of neighboring Eritrea. Although the Tigreans claim close kinship with the Tigrean population of Eritrea, tension rapidly grew in the region. The border dispute with Eritrea, growing from a minor dispute over some arid territory, by 1999 had displaced over 125,000 Tigreans. The Ethiopian government mobilized the former guerrillas of the TPLF to reinforce the border forces. The war ended in 2000 with Ethiopian forces occupying a swath of Eritrean territory, including several important Tigrean towns.

The increasingly autocratic Ethiopian government, although still dominated by ethnic Tigreans, has alienated a growing number of Tigreans, particularly members of the former landowning and aristocratic classes. Opposition leaders in Tigray state have been arrested or harassed. Several fled to exile in Djibouti or Eritrea in 1999–2001 after denouncing the lack of real federalism in Ethiopia.

Increasing tensions in Tigray was opposed by the virtual occupation of Mekele and southern Tigray by military police, mostly drawn from the south of Ethiopia. The police, known as Wopo, have little in common, linguistically or culturally, with the Tigreans, leading to a growing number of incidents.

SELECTED BIBLIOGRAPHY:

Abbay, Alemseged. *Identity Jilted or Reimagining Identity: The Divergent Paths of the Eritrean and Tigrayan Nationalists Struggles*. 1998.

Lata, Leenco. *The Ethiopian State at the Crossroads: Decolonization and Democratization or Disintegration*. 2000.

Zartman, William, ed. *Collapsed States: Disintegration and Restoration of Legitimate Authority*. 1995.

Zegeye, Abebe, and Siegried Pausewang, eds. *Ethiopia in Change: Peasantry, Nationalism, and Democracy*. 1994.

Tiv

Munshi; Mitshi; Munchi

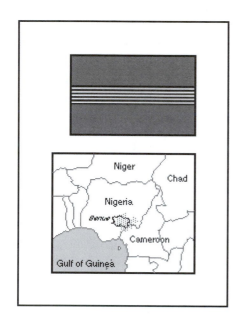

POPULATION: Approximately (2002e) 5,200,000 Tiv in Nigeria, concentrated in the eastern state of Benue and adjacent areas of Nassarawa, Taraba, and Cross River States. Outside the region there are Tiv communities in northern Nigeria, in Lagos, and in the southeast. Sizable Tiv communities also live in neighboring Cameroon, Europe (mostly in the United Kingdom), and the United States.

THE TIV HOMELAND: The Tiv homeland, Tivland, lies in the Middle Belt region of east-central Nigeria in the basin of the Benue River and the foothills of the Bauchi Plateau to the north. The lush river valley is heavily wooded, with much fertile land under cultivation. The region is situated between the southern Christian states and the northern Muslim states of Nigeria. Tivland has no official status but forms the federal state of Benue in Nigeria. *State of Benue (Tivland)*: 17,437 sq. mi.—45,161 sq. km, (2002e) 5,039,000—Tiv 73%, Idomas 18%, Jukum 7%, other Nigerians 2%. The Tiv capital and major cultural center is Makurdi, (2002e) 253,000. The other important cultural center is Gboko, (2002e) 170,000. The center of the Tivs of Taraba State is Wukari, (2002e) 81,000.

FLAG: The Tiv national flag, the flag of the national movement, is a green field bearing twelve narrow black and white horizontal stripes across the center.

PEOPLE AND CULTURE: The Tiv are a Bantu people living in the area thought to be the center of the early Bantu migrations to the south and southeast. They form the largest of the Plateau peoples, the fourth-largest ethnic cluster in Nigeria, with a population of eight million. All the Tiv are thought to be related through a common ancestor who lived 17 to 25 generations ago. For centuries Tiv culture stressed equality, but the introduction of cash crops has created classes, something unknown in the past. The Tiv, mostly farmers, are somewhat less developed than the other major national groups in Nigeria. Strongly linked patrilineages bind large portions of the ethnic group into named nonlocal segments based on real and putative concepts of descent. Local organization, land tenure, inheritance, religious beliefs, law, and allegiances are all related to this sense of lineage relationship. "Munshi," the name give the Tiv by the Muslims to the north, is considered pejorative.

LANGUAGE AND RELIGION: The Tiv language is a non-Bantu language of the Tivoid (Tiv-Batu) group of Benue-Congo languages of the Niger-Congo group. The language is used in initial primary education in the region. Many Tiv speak English as a second language, the result of continuing missionary activity. The Tiv language includes Tiv proper and the related dialects of the Tivoid group, Abong, Batu, Bitar, Evand, and Iceve-Maci.

The majority of the Tiv are Christians, with evangelical groups gaining converts in recent decades. Pre-Christian traditions remain very strong, including belief in spirits, charms, and sorcery. Prayer to spirits and the ghosts of departed lineage leaders forms an important part of local ceremonies. Witchcraft, called *tsav*, is not necessarily evil; it can be used for the good of the community.

NATIONAL HISTORY: Tiv legend states that they are the descendents of Adam, who had two sons—the first, Tiv, the ancestor of the Tiv nation; and another who became the ancestor of all others. Their homeland to the east of the Benue Valley is thought to have been the center of the great Bantu migrations. Linguistic evidence suggests that the Bantu speakers originated in the region before moving south and southeast to populate much of Africa.

The fragmented tribes of the region were ruled by "drum chiefs" who controlled small clan and tribal areas. Historically the Tiv developed as enemies of the Ibos* to the southwest, the dominant tribe between the Tiv and sea. The early Tiv tribes established wide trading and cultural contacts with neighboring peoples. In the sixteenth century, the western Tiv were included in the great medieval empire of the neighboring Jukum, the Kwararafa kingdom, which encompassed most of the present Plateau peoples.

In the eighteenth century a large Tiv migration moved from Cameroon to the Benue Valley, then under Jukum control. The Tiv settled as mainly rural farmers and did not interfere with Jukum administration. The *aku uka*, the Jukum king, was the only paramount ruler in the area and was respected by the Tiv immigrants.

Hausa* slavers from the north raided Tivland for slaves for centuries. In the 1700s the Hausas shipped thousands of Tiv slaves north along the Trans-Saharan trade routes to servitude in Muslim North Africa. The Muslim Hausas, forbidden to enslave fellow Muslims, preyed on the pagan tribes, sowing terror among the Tiv peoples.

In the early nineteenth century, nomadic Fulani Muslims conquered the Hausa states to the north, forming a great Muslim empire in present northern Nigeria. Under Muslim pressure the Jukum state collapsed, and the Tiv again became self-governing in small tribal groups. Muslim Hausas and Fulani settled in the Benue region, soon dominating commerce and trade.

In the mid-1800s European missionaries penetrated the region but were allowed to work only in the non-Muslim regions of northern Nigeria. They began the conversion of the pagan tribal peoples. Missionary schools introduced the Tiv to Western education and established contacts with the outside world. The idea of nation and state, new to the Tiv, began a modest cultural movement in the late nineteenth century.

The Tiv remained highly fragmented politically, making domination by the Muslim Hausas and Fulani easy to maintain. One of the last of the major Nigerian areas to be brought under British rule, British conquest of northern Nigeria was aided by a widespread revolt of the Tiv and Jukum against Muslim rule in the 1890s. The British conquest of the Muslims to the north allowed the colonial administration to assert its power in Tivland. Living in autonomous village units, the Tiv resented British attempts to place them under the rule of a centralized political unit under a British-authorized chief. In the early 1920s the British authorities placed about half the Tiv villages under the rule of a Jukum chief, which was a total failure. The Tiv rioted, and the colonial authorities were forced to rescind Tiv inclusion in non-Tiv chieftaincies. British control of Tivland was not definitely established until the mid-1920s. Continued Tiv expansion in population created a densely populated farming region.

The authorities gave up trying to impose chiefs on the independent-minded Tiv and instead erected a three-tiered system of councils established at kindred, clan, and tribal levels. In 1927 the traditional practice of bride price was abolished, causing considerable agitation, as did the British practice of conscripting labor for the mines and industries outside under-developed Tivland. In the 1920s and 1930s, amid growing unrest and discontent, witch-hunting outbursts swept the region. Forced labor continued until the early 1940s, contributing to considerable anti-British feeling among the Tiv.

The rapidly expanding Tiv were the largest ethnic group in the Middle Belt by the 1940s, over three times more numerous than their Jukum rivals. Tiv migrants began to move from their overcrowded homeland into the Wukari Division to the east, which the Jukum considered their homeland. The British, worried about the Tiv expansion, organized the Jukum and smaller groups in the Wukari Federation Council, which excluded the Tiv, who were considered immigrants.

The Tiv chiefs in the 1940s, seeing the advantages accruing to the Muslim emirates to the north, pressed the British authorities to set up a local

Tiv government similar to them. British rejection of the plan, and an attempt to impose a Muslim chief led to rioting and rebellion in the region. Tiv warrior groups attacked government installations and fought pitched battled with neighboring peoples, particularly the Jukum. In 1947 the British established the office and title of Tor Tiv, with rights and duties similar to the northern Muslim emirs.

Along with the other non-Muslim national groups included in the Muslim-dominated region of Northern Nigeria, the Tiv formed the Northern Non-Muslim League in 1945 to fight for the rights of the tribes living in the region. In 1950 the organization changed its name to the Middle Zone League (MZL). The MZL led a campaign for separation from Northern Nigeria and the formation of a fourth region in Nigeria. The league was divided among several ethnic groups, leading to the formation of several factions. In the late 1950s, under the leadership of a Tiv, J.S. Tarka, the league became the Middle Belt Movement, with support almost exclusively among the Tiv. Led by missionary-educated Tiv, the organization demanded the creation of a Middle Belt region and separation from the Muslim north.

Excluded from the government of Nigeria's Northern Region, as independence neared for Nigeria, the Tiv joined the colonial army in large numbers. Tension surrounding the preparations for independence touched off Tiv rioting against inclusion in the Northern Region at independence. Over 2,000 people died in the ethnic violence that swept Tivland in the early 1960s. Tiv attacks on Muslim Hausas and Fulani in their homeland added to the growing violence.

In the pre-independence elections, the United Middle Belt Congress (UMBC), formed in 1955, won a decisive victory in Tivland, with 85% of the Tiv vote. Feeling left out of the Northern Region government at independence, the Tiv rioted again in August 1960. UMBC supporters rampaged, attacking police stations, court officials, Northern Region government officials, and tax collectors. Spurred by the growing competition between the Muslim economic elite and the emerging Tiv merchants and traders, the bloody riots turned into anti-Muslim crusades of over 50,000 people. Over 30,000 buildings were burned at the height of the riots.

Tivland fell into anarchy; the law and government were unable to function. Factions within the Tiv national movement pressed for a unilateral declaration of independence. The violence in Tivland became one of the most serious threats to the integrity of the new Nigerian state. The Nigerian government sent in the army to quell the rioting; over 5,000 Tiv were arrested. The new Nigerian government feared that the unrest would spread through the Plateau peoples, posing a serious threat to the unity of the state.

The Tiv refused alliances with the Northern or Southern regional groups as tension grew in the early 1960s. Most Tiv supported the Tiv Progressive Union, the major organization in the UMBC. Three years of tension again erupted in violence in 1964. Fighting between the Tiv and the Hausa-Fulani groups in the region quickly spread through the Benue Valley. Hundreds died before the military brought the revolt under control. Tiv separatism posed a major threat to the Hausa-Fulani domination of the Northern Region.

In 1966 the Northern Region moved toward secession from Nigeria. Muslim troops in the north attacked immigrant Christian groups, especially Ibos from southeastern Nigeria. Many Tiv helped to hide their former enemies from Muslim mobs, saving many Ibo lives. The north, if it seceded from Nigeria, would include Tivland, which would make the Tiv a small non-Muslim minority in a Muslim state. To counter Muslim influence, some Tiv groups allied with the southern political parties, while other remained linked to the northern groups.

The crisis in the north waned as the Ibos in the southeast pressed for secession in 1966–67. The Tiv, with many serving in the Nigerian military, supported the federal cause when the Ibos seceded as the Republic of Biafra. The federal government, in an effort to dampen secessionist sentiment in other regions, created new ethnic states. Tivland became part of the new North-Eastern state, but sentiment for an exclusively Tiv state continued.

During the early months of the Nigerian civil war, Tivland, lying just north of secessionist Biafra, formed the front line. Following Biafran defeat in 1970, demands for a separate state were renewed. Benue State was carved out with a Tiv majority, which satisfied the more moderate nationalists. After 1976, federalism and local autonomy blunted militant Tiv nationalism.

Nigeria continued to be governed by Muslim-dominated military or corrupt civilian governments in the 1970s. The Tiv, one of the most ethnocentric nations in Nigeria, developed a nationalist sentiment in opposition to Muslim domination and military dictatorships. Periodic violence between the Tiv and neighboring peoples continued to disrupt the region.

Hausa cultural and political influence in the 1990s led to some assimilation to the Hausa language, dress, and residential arrangements. Hausaization was particularly strong in the northern Tiv districts. In reaction, Tiv militants mobilized to support a cultural revival and a reculturation of the Tiv nation. Marginalized politically and economically, the Tiv attempted to survive by assimilation or by embracing militant nationalism.

Trouble resurfaced with local elections in 1987 when the Tiv gained powerful positions at local and state levels in Taraba against strong Jukum opposition. Jukum mobs attacked the Tiv in the region in 1990–92, driving many back to their homeland in Benue. The number of deaths or injured is unknown, but there were massive burning of houses, businesses, and schools, accompanied by looting. Among the dead were children and pregnant women.

A growing dispute between the Tiv and the neighboring Jukum, particularly in the Wukari region of Taraba state, fueled a revival of nationalist sentiment in the late 1990s. The conflict had numerous causes, including land disputes, traditional rule, political authority, and fears of domination and marginalization. The conflict, which began in the 1940s, erupted again in 1997.

New elections in 1996 and 1997 were peaceful in Wukari, primarily because the Tiv were not represented. Jukum refusal to allow Tiv representatives on local councils in Taraba State mobilized the entire Tiv nation. The federal government, preoccupied with disputes in other parts of the country, mostly ignored the growing conflict. Tiv militants claimed that the region forms part of their traditional homeland and wanted the Wukari District transferred from Taraba to Benue. The continued high population growth of the Tiv continued to create a need for more and more farmland.

Negotiations began in 1997, but the Jukum accused the Nigerian government of allowing high-ranking Tiv military officers to manipulate government decisions in their favor. Many of the Tiv displaced from the lands on which they had lived for decades or even centuries joined unofficial militias. The 80,000 refugees in the Tiv homeland became a fertile breeding ground for radical Tiv nationalism.

Pressure for land is growing in the crowded region, reinforcing ethnic identities and violence. With ethnic conflicts between the Tivs and neighboring Jukum and Hausas growing more serious, the Tivs formed militias to protect Tiv villages in disputed districts.

The conflict, one of the most violent since the Nigerian civil war of 1967–70, has been mostly ignored by the federal government. In early 1999 the Jukum had still not yet reopened Tiv schools and health facilities. The century-long tension between the Tiv and Jukum could be the spark for a new threat to Nigeria's integrity. Centrifugal forces being generated by the quest for control of oil resources in the south, and the introduction of Islamic Shari'a law in the north are pushing the Tiv into nationalism.

Renewed fighting in the region in 2001 left hundreds dead and as many as 50,000 homeless in fighting between Tivs and Hausa groups. Fighting started when young men from the Tiv ethnic group attacked a village in Nassarawa state north of Benue after the killing of a traditional Tiv leader. The problems are made more serious by the Tiv migration to the north into areas traditionally inhabited by peoples forming part of the Hausa groups. At least 35,000 Tiv people are reported to have fled the state, and some are now living in squalid refugee camps in Benue.

In late October 2002, in response to the death of 19 soldiers by a local Tiv militia in early Oct, the Nigerian army moved into Benue and Taraba states. Army units attacked 4 villages in Benue, reported killing over 200 Tivs in indiscriminate massacres. Demonstrations broke out in Makurdi, quickly turning anti-government and openly nationalist.

SELECTED BIBLIOGRAPHY:

Anifowose, Rem. *Violence and Politics in Nigeria: The Tiv and Yoruba Experience.* 1982.
Badru, Pade. *Imperialism and Ethnic Politics in Nigeria, 1960–96.* 1998.
Bohannan, Paul. *The Tiv: An African People from 1949 to 1953.* 2000.
Makar, Tesemchi. *The History of Political Change among the Tiv in the 19th and 20th Centuries.* 1978.

Toros

Batoros; Batooros; Tooros

POPULATION: Approximately (2002e) 945,000 Toros in Uganda, concentrated in the western regions of Kabarole and Kasese Districts. Outside the region there are sizable Toro populations in the Ugandan capital, Kampala, and other areas of southern Uganda.

THE TORO HOMELAND: The Toro homeland occupies a region of rolling grasslands west of the Ruwenzori Mountains in southeastern Uganda, forming part of the great savanna that runs from Sudan to Rwanda. Toro lies in the Lake Region of East Africa, occupying the high plateau between Lake Albert, Lake George, and Lake Edward. Toro forms the Kabarole, Kasese, and Bundibugyó Districts of the Republic of Uganda. In 1993 the Kingdom of Toro was partially restored. *Kingdom of Toro*: 5,233 sq. mi.—13,556 sq. km,

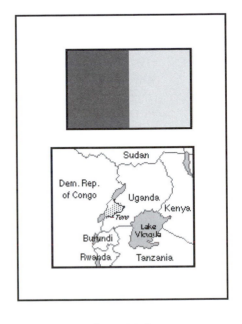

(2002e) 1,647,000—Toros 56%, Ruwenzoris* (Konjos 27%, Ambas 13%), Kigas 2%, other Ugandans 2%. The Toro capital and major cultural center is Fort Portal, called Kabarole by the Toros, (2002e) 44,000. The other important center is Kasese, (2002e) 24,000.

FLAG: The Toro national flag is a vertical bicolor of blue and yellow. The flag of the kingdom (not shown) is the same bicolor bearing a centered brown drum backed by crossed white spears and flanked by erect lions, the drum surmounted by a red ceremonial mask.

PEOPLE AND CULTURE: The Toros are a Bantu people of the Western Lacustrine group, which inhabits the region around Africa's great lakes. The Toros comprise two distinct groups—the tall, lighter-skinned Hima, descendents of pastoralists who migrated into the region from the northeast; and the shorter Iru, the Dark People, descendents of the original Bantu population. The complex Toro culture is the product of acculturation between the two groups. During the Amin and Obote dictatorships of the 1960s and 1970s, the traditional differences between the Toro Hima and Toro Iru began to break down as they united around a shared culture and language and against a common enemy. The Toro clan system, formerly exclusively Hima or Iru, now crosses ethnic lines. Descent is patrilineal, and named lineages within a clan are not hierarchically organized.

LANGUAGE AND RELIGION: The Toro language, Lutoro, is a Bantu language of the Western Lacustrine group of the Nyoro-Ganda languages of the Benue-Congo language family. The language is basically Bantu but has many roots that show Nilotic influences. Many words have clear linkages to the Nilotic languages spoken north and east of the Nile River. The language became a written language under the influence of the early Christian missionaries. Like many African languages, Lutoro has not kept pace with the introduction of world culture or technology, which has fueled a movement since 1995 to revive the language. Education for children over 10 years of age is in English, which is spoken as a second language throughout the kingdom. Toro reverence for their king is displayed by the fact that there exists a completely different vocabulary for use when addressing the king.

The majority are Christian, about 85%, with a minority adhering to traditional beliefs based on ancestor worship and veneration of the Toro king. Many Toros see Christian and traditional rituals as equally valuable sources of spiritual power. They observe the rituals of their Christian religion scrupulously, along with their equally careful practice of the ancient rituals and ceremonies. Many use traditional charms to protect their homes, children, and crops from curses. Appeals are often made to ancestors through the services of a diviner or sorcerer.

NATIONAL HISTORY: There are conflicting legends about the origins of the Toros. One legend asserts that the Toros are the indigenous people of Toro and that they originated from the Batembuzi and Bagabu, who are believed to have been the first inhabitants and rulers of the earth. Other traditions are related to the Bito dynasty, which originated to the north. Most Toro believe that the legendary Batembuzi kings created the earliest centralized political organization in the area and that they were succeeded by the Cwezi and then by the Bito, Nilotic people who came from the north.

Bantu agriculturists settled the lowlands, probably before A.D. 1100, settling in autonomous villages united only by culture and tradition. Around 1500 tall Hamitic herdsmen, possibly from present Ethiopia, conquered the region around the highland lakes. The invaders created a large, centralized kingdom dominated by a Hamitic aristocracy. The warlike nomads relegated the more advanced Bantu to a lower class of serfs, craftsmen, farmers, and herdsmen forbidden to own cattle, the measure of Hamitic wealth.

The lakes region formed part of the extensive Kitara kingdom, centered east of Lake Albert. The land was owned the Hamitic aristocracy and was worked by Bantu serfs and herdsmen. The Hamitic elite slowly absorbed the Bantu language and many of the cultural traits of the conquered peoples, gradually becoming a people of mixed race and culture.

Nilotic invaders from the north conquered the Kitara kingdom in the sixteenth century. The Nilotes divided the region into a string of small independent kingdoms. The area west of the Blue and Ruwenzori Mountains formed Bunyoro, the kingdom of the Nyoros.* About 1830 a Nyoro prince, Kaboyo, broke away from the kingdom and with his followers created a separate kingdom in the southern districts between Lake Albert and Lake Edward. Toro formed one of the cluster of independent kingdoms, which included Bunyoro, Buganda, Ankole, Karagwe, Rwanda, and Burundi.

Toro society became stratified into the Hima and Iru, the cattle-owning aristocracy and the Bantu workers. The relationship between the two groups was more one of caste than class distinctions. Socially and economically, there was a symbiotic relationship, with the Iru trading beer and other agricultural products for meat, milk, and hides. Cattle remained the symbol of wealth and power in the kingdom.

The prince, the first *omukama* (king) of Toro, Kaboyo Kasusunkwanzi, controlled the lowlands but only nominally ruled the mountainous west. The inhabitants of the region in the Ruwenzori Mountains, the Konjo and Amba, considered primitive by the cultured lowlanders, acknowledged the authority of Toro's government, while maintaining only minimum contact.

The hereditary Toro kings of the Bito dynasty, which also ruled neighboring Bunyoro, were considered to have magical powers and formed the focus of the Toro religious beliefs. The king was assisted by a hierarchy of chiefs and a standing army. In time of war all able-bodied men in the kingdom would be called upon to serve defense of the homeland. The advanced Toros, despite the sophistication of their kingdom, maintained many unique traditions, such as fattening aristocratic maidens on milk until they weighed about 300 pounds (136 kg)—the more weight the greater the beauty. Iron weapons and a monopoly on salt allowed the Toros to prosper from the trade that passed through the lake district.

European explorers who visited the kingdom in the 1850s were amazed to find a sophisticated culture and state system. Over the next decades the kingdom established trade relations with the British. The kingdom signed a diplomatic treaty with the British authorities in 1890. Five years later, reacting to interest by other European powers, the British declared Toro a protected state. The king finally signed the protectorate agreement in 1900 and with British assistance consolidated his authority; in 1906 he brought the mountain tribes under direct Toro rule. The Rukurato, the Toro parliament, became a partly elected legislature under British influence, allowing the Konjos and Ambas some say in the government of the kingdom.

Christian missionaries entered the kingdom in the early twentieth century, establishing both Protestant and Roman Catholic missions and schools. The majority of the kingdom's inhabitants converted to Christianity. The growing Christian presence began to undermine the king's power, traditionally based on the magic and rituals of the old religion.

Throughout the colonial period, the Toros remained less developed than the neighboring nations, partly due to British neglect but also to the Toros' unwillingness to enter voluntarily into protectorate status. Gandas* from the neighboring kingdom of Buganda became the agents of British imperialism; many Gandas moved into Toro as government functionaries, traders, and colonial soldiers. Local Toro national resistance to British colonialism began as an anti-Ganda movement.

Long isolated from the central authority of the kingdom, the Konjos rebelled in 1919. The Konjo rebels repulsed the king's troops but met defeat when British forces were dispatched. Though serfdom and slavery gradually disappeared, the dominant Toros continued to discriminate against the Ruwenzori peoples in education, administration, and the economy. The discrimination, only partly ethnic and cultural, was accentuated by the inaccessibility of the Ruwenzoris' mountain homelands.

The colonial authorities gradually reduced the power and independence of the kingdom, although in 1949 legislation was passed recognizing the king's right to regulate local government within the protectorate of Uganda. Encouraged by the British, who believed that Ugandan independence was still decades away, the kingdom became the focus of Toro nationalism and identity. In 1953 the Toro royal government demanded federal status and the extension of the Lutoro language to all the kingdom's schools, even in the non-Toro Ruwenzori district.

The issue of Toro nationalism intensified as independence for Uganda neared in the late 1950s. Toro nationalism grew in an effort to keep the revenues from the Kilembe Copper Mine for themselves, and over what they perceived as lesser treatment for their *omukama*. Activists demanded that the *omukama* of Toro be granted the same privileges as the kabaka, the king, of Buganda, Uganda's largest and most powerful kingdom.

The rapid growth of Toro nationalism paralleled the growing nationalism of the Konjo and Amba, in a reaction to increasing assimilation. The two mountain peoples demanded separation from Toro and the creation of a separate Ruwenzori district within Uganda. The threat to the kingdom's territorial integrity raised Toro demands for recognition as an independent state before future relations with Uganda were regulated. On the eve of Ugandan independence the kingdom adopted a new constitution that ignored the Ruwenzori people's demands for official recognition of the kingdom's three peoples.

In 1962 the Toro accepted semifederal status within the newly independent Ugandan state. Toro nationalists, somewhat mollified by official recognition of the kingdom, blocked Konjo and Amba efforts to separate in a distinct district. In early 1963 the mountain tribes rebelled, and on 13 February 1963 they declared independence as the Republic of Ruwenzuru, basing their claims to the entire Toro kingdom on historical possession and assertions that the Toro had migrated to the region from Bunyoro and should return to their original homeland.

Uganda's independence government, dominated by northerner Milton Obote, had little sympathy for the traditional Bantu monarchies in the southern districts. In 1967 the Obote government abolished the kingdoms as centers of local nationalism and separatism, and in 1970 the Ruwenzori rebels were finally defeated.

The Ugandan government, overthrown in a coup led by Idi Amin in 1971, gained infamy as Africa's most brutal. Initial Toro support of Idi Amin in the belief that he would restore the kingdom quickly disappeared. Princess Elizabeth of Toro formed part of Amin's administration, but she was later framed and dismissed. Persecution of the Christians fueled a revival of Toro separatism as the Amin excesses accelerated. A strong secessionist movement in Toro ended in 1972 with the murder or disappearance of the majority of Toro's leadership.

In 1980 Obote again took control of Uganda but met with stiff resistance in the southern Bantu regions. A Bantu supported resistance movement, led by Yoweri Museveni, rallied the peoples of the former southern kingdoms. Obote's efforts to destroy the rebels led to a greater loss of life, about 300,000 people, than even the murderous Amin had caused. Museveni finally took control of devastated Uganda in 1986, forming the country's first government controlled by the southern Bantus. The relative freedom, after two decades of terror and destruction, rekindled Toro nationalism. The land issue, involving claims to territories taken from Toro during the colonial period and turned over to rival tribes, became the focus of the growing national movement.

In July 1993, with Museveni government approval, the Toro kingdom was partially restored, and Patrick Olimi Kaboyo in 1995 was crowned as the twelfth king of Toro in Fort Portal. The monarchy became a cultural expression, without its former political and administrative powers. The Konjo and Amba of Bundibugyó District initially refused to relinquish the former royal lands they had occupied, but in March 1994 senior members of the Ruwenzori movement acknowledged the new king, officially ending the conflict that had begun three decades before. The Ruwenzori rebellion resumed in the late 1990s.

The Ugandan government's emphasis on cash crop production in the 1980s and 1990s aided economic recovery. Devastated during the 1960s and 1970s by civil wars and brutal dictatorships, the Toros had slipped back to a premodern existence. The economic resurgence paralleled the cultural and political revival of the kingdom.

Rebel groups in the Ruwenzori Mountains mounted raids on Toro towns in the western districts in early 2000, disrupting the tourism and farming industries. The rebels, mostly based among the Ruwenzoris, sought to separate the mountainous west from the Toro. Reaction to the threat to split their ancient kingdom raised nationalist tension in the kingdom to levels not seen since the early 1960s.

Toro nationalism, led by the Protestant minority, at the turn of the twenty-first century was less separatist than federalist. Many saw the king and the traditional legislature as the logical extensions of Ugandan federalism. A completely restored Toro within a Ugandan federation would safeguard the Toro culture and traditions, while federalism and regional autonomy would support the moderate nationalist demands against the more radical aims of the small militant minority. Many Toros support nationalism on the belief that had the kingdom seceded in 1962 as a member state of the British Commonwealth, they would have escaped the devastation, ruin, and massacres of the Amin and Obote years.

Increasing violence between the Toros and migrants from other areas of western Uganda, particularly the Kigas, became a serious problem in 1997–98, and by early 2002 had destabilized many of the rural areas. Many people fled to the relative safety of the towns and cities.

SELECTED BIBLIOGRAPHY:

Ingham, Kenneth. *The Kingdom of Toro in Uganda.* 1965.
Jamison, Marton, ed. *Idi Amin and Uganda.* 1992.
Ofcansky, Thomas P. *Uganda: Tarnished Pearl of Africa.* 1996.
Twesigye, Emmanuel K. *African Monarchies and Kingdoms of Uganda.* 1995.

Tripuris

Tippera; Tipperah; Tiperas; Tipuras; Usipi; Boroks

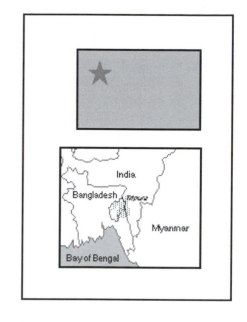

POPULATION: Approximately (2002e) 1,520,000 Tripuris in South Asia, concentrated in Tripura state in northeastern India, with sizable communities in neighboring Indian states and adjacent areas of Bangladesh, with a Tripuri population of about 100,000.

THE TRIPURI HOMELAND: The Tripuri homeland lies in northeastern India, comprising a finger of land surrounded on the north, west, and south by Bangladeshi territory. The Tripuris are predominantly rural; most of the towns and cities have Bengali majorities. Most of the Tripuris live in the foothills surrounding the western plains, and the Gumti, Dharmanagar, and Khowari Valleys. Tripura forms a state of the Indian union, the smallest of the seven northeastern states. *State of Tripura (Twipra):* 4,035 sq. mi.—10,451 sq. km, (2002e) 3,234,000—Bengalis 65%, Tripuris 29%, Meitheis* 4%, other Indians 4%. The Tripuri capital and major cultural center is Agartala, (2002e) 263,000, metropolitan area 355,000.

FLAG: The Tripuri national flag, the flag of the national movement, is a pale blue field bearing a single green five-pointed star on the upper hoist.

PEOPLE AND CULTURE: The Tripuris comprise 19 groups of Mongoloid ancestry that represent the indigenous people of the region, including the Tipra (Tippera), Reang (Riang), Debbarma, Chakma, Halam (Malsum), Usai, Jamatia, Kaipeng, Noatia, Koloi, Wrangkhal, Mog (Mogh), Garo, Lushai, Darlongs, and Bangcher. The Tripuris, ethnically related to the Bodos,* have a rich historical, social, and cultural heritage that is totally distinct from that of the lowland Bengalis. The Tripuris marry only within their own tribe, and polygamy is permitted, although it is increasingly rare. Traditionally slash-and-burn agriculturists, most Tripuris are now settled farmers. The Tripuris, constituting 85% of the total population in 1949, have been reduced to a minority in their homeland, numbering just 29% of the total in 2000. Only about 5% of the population of the urban areas is Tripuri. Bengali immigration to Tripura is seen by the indigenous Tripuris as a form of genocide. Discrimination by the Bengali majority is widespread; the Tripuris are viewed as poor, careless, and lazy.

LANGUAGE AND RELIGION: The Tripuri language, Kok Borok or Kakbarak, belongs to the Baric or Bodo languages of the Tibeto-Burman language group. It forms a lingua franca of the 12 largest groups of the indigenous Tripuris and the other Tibeto-Burman dialects spoken by tribal peoples in the state. The five major dialects are Jamatia, Noatia, Riang (Tipra), Halam, and Debbarma. Debbarma is spoken by the former royal family and is the basis of the Tripuri literary language. Bengali and Tripuri are the official languages of the state, and Tripuri is used in primary schools in the state. The language is spoken in three major dialects, Debbarma, Riang, and Halam. Many Tripuris also speak English, the result of missionary activity.

The majority of the Tripuri are Hindu, with sizable Christian and Buddhist groups. Religious practices often mixed with pre-Hindu traditions and customs. The small Christian minority, about 1% of the Tripuri population, is made up of tribal converts. Traditional beliefs include worship of the gods of fire, water, and the forest. The Tripuris believe that they must appease these spirits in order to have bountiful harvests. They believe that they are surrounded by spirits that affect their daily welfare and health, and that after death each person goes to an underworld and begins reliving his or her previous life.

NATIONAL HISTORY: Migrants from the upper reaches of the Yangtsekiang and Hwangho Rivers in western China migrated south along the rivers, traditionally settling the high Tripura valleys around A.D. 65. The common reference to the Mongoloid peoples as Kiratas and Cinas in early Indian texts indicates that they settled the region before the Christian era. They gradually expanded their settlement and ruled over the whole of Tripura. Successive waves of migration established a number of distinct tribal groups.

The early history of the Tripuris is chronicled in the *Rajamala*, an account of the largely legendary early maharajas of Tripura. The ruling class adopted the Hindu religion brought to the region by Aryan invaders from the west. In the late seventh century the Tripuris established a state structure in Tripura, one of the subcontinent's earliest Hindu states. The Tripuri evolved a sophisticated, settled society in the isolated high valleys. The maharaja of Tripura-Missip maintained personal relations with the chiefs of the various tribes. According to the *Rajamala* and later chronicles, a total of 184 kings ruled the state up to 1949.

The Bengali population of the surrounding lowlands converted to Islam in the tenth century, separating and isolating the Hindu kingdom. The Mankiya dynasty, founded in 1280, strengthened the state's defenses against Bengali incursions from the lowlands. The written history of Tripura begins with Dharma Manikya, the maharaja from 1431 to 1462. During his reign and that of his successor, Dhanya Manikya, who ruled from 1463 to 1515, Tripuris suzerainty was extended over much of Bengal, Assam, and Myanmar in a series of remarkable military conquests. The Bengalis finally overran the Tripuri state in 1625, incorporating Tripura as a dependency of the Muslim Mughal empire. The Tripuris expelled the Bengalis and maintained a precarious independence into the eighteenth century.

British officials, from their expanding base in Bengal, visited Tripura in 1725, calling the highland region Hill-Tippera. Soldiers of the Muslim Mogul Empire conquered Tripura in 1733 but allowed the kingdom to retain nominal independence as a tributary state. In 1765 the Moguls detached part of the kingdom, called the district of Tippera, as a separate Mogul ruled region. The Mogul action turned the Tripuri against their Muslim overlords. The power of the Moguls effectively ended in 1803, and the British rapidly took control of former Mogul territories. In 1808 the Tripuris established direct treaty relations with the British Empire. The Tripuri maharaja formally ceded the district of Tippera to the British, to become a separate district of British Bengal. From 1808 each successive Tripuri ruler had to receive investiture from the British colonial government.

The kingdom preserved its traditional feudal system as a separate British protectorate and ally. In 1905 Tripura was attached to the new province of Eastern Bengal and Assam. During World War I the maharaja furnished troops to aid his British ally. During World War II Tripuri enthusiasm for Britain noticeably waned until a Japanese thrust into Indian territory nearly reached Tripura. Spurning Japanese overtures and promises of independence, the Tripuris rallied to the Allied cause.

The British authorities, soon after the end of World War II, began preparations to grant independence to British India. The Tripuris expressed their desire for separate status, but the state was believed too small to maintain itself. The British recommended that Tripura become part of Assam, a proposal that was vehemently rejected on historical, linguistic, and ethnic grounds. The king, Bir Bikram, died on 17 May 1947, leaving a power vacuum and a 15-year-old successor at a time when the British were preparing to leave India and a large-scale influx of Bengalis arrived in the state, fleeing communal rioting in neighboring Muslim areas.

The Tripuris resisted growing pressure and officially remained under nominal British rule when India and Pakistan were declared independent on 15 August 1947. The Indian government reported that the Bengali refugees were planning to depose the king and merge Tripura with Pakistan. The British withdrawal and increasing threats from neighboring Muslim East Pakistan aggravated the crisis. The young king and his mother, the regent, fled to New Delhi, seeking Indian aid against the Muslim conspirators. As a condition for giving help, the regent was made to sign the Tripura Merger Agreement on 9 September 1949. The agreement provided official protection for the cultural and political autonomy of the Tripuri nation but led to the annexation of Tripura to India on 15 October 1949. The annexation ended 1,300 years of Tripuri independence. The nationalists denounced the accession and Indian rule as illegal.

Thousands of Hindu Bengali refugees from Muslim East Pakistan settled in Tripura rather than in areas vacated by Muslims leaving for Pakistan. The refugees, called "settler refugees" by the Tripuris, began an immigration flow that eventually swamped the Tripuris. Appeals to the Indian government to block further immigration were ignored. Muslim Bengalis, searching for arable land, began to enter the fertile valleys of Tripura illegally in 1951. The Tripuris were dispossessed of their lands and resources, trade, and access to local government services. Many were driven farther into the less productive hill areas.

Administered directly from New Delhi as a separate territory, the Tripuris continued to reject proposals for union with neighboring Assam. On 1 September 1956 the Indian government granted the region a degree of autonomy as a union territory. Included in the Northeastern Areas Reorganization Act of 1971, Tripura became a full state of the Indian union, under a government dominated by the growing Bengali majority.

The Indian government's inability or unwillingness to stem the illegal immigration in the 1960s and 1970s spurred Tripuri nationalism. Members of Tripuri tribes formed the first avowedly separatist organization in 1978, the Tripura National Volunteers (TNV). Gaining support in the state, and with ties to other nationalist organizations in India's turbulent northeastern region, the Tripuri nationalists called for an end to India's illegal control of Tripura and for the expulsion of all Bengali migrants.

The more sophisticated Bengalis by the early 1970s controlled the economy and had gained control of the most fertile agricultural land. With the economy in their hands and the Indian government favoring them, the Bengalis captured political power in Tripura.

Confronted with the growing threat to their existence and the loss of their means of survival, the land, the Tripuris, led by the TNV, launched an armed struggle in the early 1980s. The resulting ethnic and religious conflict spread across the state, leaving over 800 dead in violent clashes. The continuing clashes and the growing Tripuri separatist campaign in the 1980s focused on the migrant Bengali population. Over 200,000 Bengalis fled the violence to the protection of camps set up by the Indian government.

The Indian government finally agreed to take drastic measures to end illegal immigration. A memorandum on settlement was signed between the Indian and Tripuran governments and the TNV in August 1988. A 30-

member Tripura Tribal Areas Autonomous District Council was formed in the Tripuri majority districts. Several factions split from the TNV over opposition to the agreement, and subsequent government inaction led to a resurgence of violence in 1989. To the present, not all the terms of the agreement have been implemented, partly due to disagreements and fighting between the various Tripuri nationalist factions.

A Tripuri nationalist boycott of state elections in June 1991 allowed India's predominant Congress Party to take control of the state. In late 1991 party cadres attacked Tripuri nationalists and burned the headquarters of legal opposition parties, while the Congress Party–controlled police turned a blind eye. The growing violence provoked the Tripuri leaders to demand the creation of a separate tribal state within Tripura. The increasing polarization of the state's population hampered the nationalists and autonomists in their efforts win greater independence. In April 1993 the Bengali-supported Left Front took power after winning state elections.

The Tripuris, outvoted in local elections, are increasingly marginalized culturally and economically in their homeland. Several of the many nationalist organizations that formed in the 1970s and 1980s have adopted a platform of separatism, feeling that there is no other option left but to fight for the restoration of the sovereignty and independence of Tripura. The only political party led by Tripuris, the Tripura Upajati Juba Samiti, has been co-opted by India's Congress Party.

Nationalists leaders in the mid-1990s set three preconditions for the Indian government in response to its proposal to a proposal for a peaceful resolution. The conditions included declaring foreigners all migrants to the state after 15 October 1949 who were not listed in the 1951 voter list; holding peace negotiations in a third country under UN mediation; and considering the sovereignty of Tripura to be not negotiable under any circumstances. The Indian government rejected the Tripuri conditions, and the vicious ethnic fighting continued. The Indian government deployed thousands of troops in the region in May 1997. By 1998 over 30,000 Tripuris had been forced from their homes by armed factions of the Bengali community, often supported by Indian military units.

Tripura is governed under the counterinsurgency Armed Forces Special Powers Act (AFSPA), which allows the police and military broad powers. It has also been declared a "disturbed area," on the recommendation of the Bengali-dominated state government. These declarations empower any noncommissioned officer to apply maximum force without any limitation on mere suspicion—amounting to wide powers to shoot to kill with virtual impunity. More than 135 students, youth, and peasants have been killed under the AFSPA since it was imposed on 15 February 1997. Innocent Tripuri civilians are imprisoned without trial, and reportedly many women have been raped with impunity. The Left Front government exempted the Bengali-populated areas from the AFSPA.

Food distribution, disrupted by the growing tribal insurgency, led to famine and many deaths in the tribal areas in the early 1990s. The situation was aggravated by the arrival of some 55,000 refugee Jummas,* mostly Tripuri and Chakma, fleeing military offensives in the Chittagong Hill Tracts of Bangladesh.

In 1993 many of the Tripuri factions joined a new umbrella group, the Tripura People's Democratic Front (TPDF), which also included members from the other indigenous groups. The TPDF included both cultural and political organizations, as well as a military wing that has attacked police and military units in the state. The factionalism of the national movement severely hampered efforts to present a united front in the ongoing conflict with the Bengali majority. In 1997 several important organizations joined the new group in an effort to consolidate Tripuri unity, but factional fighting resumed.

The National Liberation Front of Tripura and several other organizations were banned in April 1997 for secessionist and terrorist activities. In March 1999, the Bangladeshi army attacked nationalist camps in the Tripuri territory in the Chittagong Hill Tracts and arrested a number of Tripuri activists. Kidnapping and murder, mostly politically motivated, were widespread. From 1997 to 2000 over 1,200 people were released after ransoms were paid, although many remain in the custody of armed insurgent groups. Thousands of soldiers belonging to various state and national security forces have been deployed in the state to combat the rising nationalist rebellion.

Tripuri nationalists of the insurgent group turned political party, the TNV, wrested control of the autonomous district council from the ruling Left Front in April 2000, an unusual victory for the seriously divided and factionalized national movement. Independent guerrilla activities have weakened the Tripuris' collective action, and the varied demands make it difficult for local and central governments to negotiate greater autonomy and limits on Bengali immigration. The creation of various armed Bengali groups to defend against or avenge Tripuri insurgent attacks has greatly increased violence.

In March 2001 the Tripura Chief Minister, Manik Sarkar, requested the Union government to initiate a ceasefire in Tripura. A similar call was made, in July, by a delegation representing some insurgent groups. A delegation from the Indian government visited Tripura in September, 2001 to study the situation and take necessary steps to contain insurgency. Many Tripuri insurgents surrendered their arms and returned to their villages following the arrival in the state of additional security troops in early 2001.

The level of violence in Tripura has also been heightened by the emergence of militant Bengali organizations such as the United Bengali Liberation Front (UBLF) and Amra Bangali (We Are Bengalis) since 1999.

Violence between Tripuris and Bengalis has resulted in hundreds of dead and injured.

SELECTED BIBLIOGRAPHY:

Bhattacharjee, S.R. *Tribal Insurgency in Tripura: A Study in Exploration of Causes.* 1990.
Bhattacharyya, Suchintya. *Genesis of Tribal Extremism in Tripura.* 1991.
Gan-Chaudhuri, Jagadis. *A Political History of Tripura.* 1986.
Singh, K.S. *People of India: Tripura.* 1996.

Tuaregs
Touregs; Twaregs; Tourage; Imacaghen; Imajighen

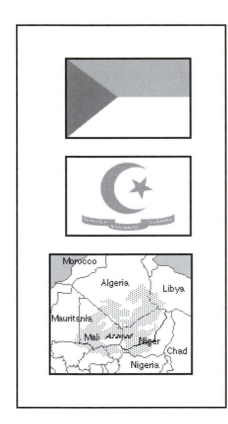

POPULATION: Approximately (2002e) 3,100,000 Tuaregs in north-central Africa, concentrated in the Sahara and Sahel regions with about 1,460,000 in Niger, 1,025,000 in Mali, and 500,000 in Algeria, Bukina Faso, Libya, Mauritania, and Nigeria. Outside the region there are large Tuareg populations living in the urban areas south of the Sahara in Niger and Mali.

THE TUAREG HOMELAND: The Tuareg homeland, called Tamazgha, lies in the central Sahara and on the edges of the Sahel in the south. The process of colonization divided the Tuareg homeland, which now forms parts of Algeria, Niger, Mali, Burkina Faso, and Libya. The region includes the Aïr and Ahaggar Mountains and the fertile Sahelian Plains along the Niger River and in the Tilemai Valley. The Tuareg heartland in northern Niger and Mali, the Nigerian department of Agadez and northern districts of Tahoua and the Malian regions of Gao, Tombouctou, and Kidal, forms the region called Azawad, where the Tuaregs want to establish an autonomous state. *Region of Azawad*: 485,668 sq. mi.—1,257,874 sq. km, (2002e) 1,621,000—Tuaregs 80%, Songhai 14%, Djerma 4%, other Nigerians, other Malians 2%. The Tuaregs' major cultural centers are Tombouctou, called Timbuktu by the Tuaregs, (2002e) 58,000, and Gao, (2002e) 106,000 in Mali, Tahoua, (2002e) 88,000, Agadez, called Agades, (2002e) 111,000, and Arlit (2002e) 76,000 in Niger, and Tamanghasat, called Tamoust by the Tuaregs, (2002e) 61,000, and Ayn Salah, (2002e) 32,000 in Algeria.

FLAG: The Azawad flag, the flag of the Tuareg nationalist movement, is a blue over white bicolor with a red triangle at the hoist. The flag of MOREHOB, the Revolutionary Movement of the Blue Men, is a white field bearing a blue crescent moon and a five-pointed star over a banner bearing the name of the organization.

PEOPLE AND CULTURE: The name Tuareg, singular Targi, is used to identify numerous diverse groups of nomadic or formerly nomadic people who share a common language and history. The Tuaregs are a Berber people, descendents of the Zenaga Berbers, a Caucasian people with later black African and Arabic admixtures. Tuareg society is divided into three distinct classes—the nobles, the *Heratin*; agriculturists and artisans; and the descendents of former slaves, the *bellah*. Unlike most Muslim communities the Tuareg are a matriarchal people, the unveiled women enjoying freedom and respect. Unlike most Islamic societies, marriage is monogynous. The Tuareg men wear the veils, and their traditional clothing, including veils and turbans, is dyed indigo. The blue dye used in the veils and clothing of the Tuareg nobles frequently transfers to the skin, giving the Tuaregs the name the "blue men of the Sahara." The seven major Tuareg tribes are the Kel Ahaggar and Kel Ajjer of southern Algeria, the Kel Adrar of northern Mali, the Kel Aïr of northern Niger, the Kel Geres of the plains, the Allemmeden Kel Dennek in the east, and the Aullemmeden Kel Atatam in the west. The tribes are further divided into regional tribes and clans with traditional territories that often cross international borders. The constant struggle to exist in one of the earth's harshest environments has bred a passionate devotion to the desert and a strong sense of national identity.

LANGUAGE AND RELIGION: The Tuareg language—called Tamahaq, Tamajaq, Tamachaq, Tamajeq, Tamahaq, or Tamajeg, depending on the region—is a Berber language. The language is spoken in numerous regional dialects. In spite of their dispersal over a very large geographical area, all of the Tuareg tribes speak closely related dialects of Tamachek, a Berber language with its own script called Tifinagh or Shifinagh, the only Berber language to have retained its own alphabet. Traditionally, only Tuareg women were able to read and write, and the tradition of the Tuaregs was essentially oral. The language was prohibited for public use in many areas until the early 1990s.

The Tuaregs adhere to the Maliki sect of Sunni Islam, which incorporates many nonorthodox, magical elements. The sect is based on the teachings of the great prophet, El Maghili, who lived among the Tuaregs in the early sixteenth century. Music is often used to cast out evil spirits, and amulets for protection from lonely spirits haunting the desert. The relative recent Islamization of the Tuaregs did not affect certain customs and traditions that are much older. The belief in various spirits, called *djinns*, is widespread. Divination is accomplished using the sacred writings of Islam, the Koran.

NATIONAL HISTORY: Tuareg legends place their origins on a large island in the Atlantic Ocean. According to the legends, when their island home disappeared, the only survivors were traders stranded in the port cities of North Africa, the survivors becoming the ancestors of the Tuareg nation. The Zenaga Berbers, a settled farming people in North Africa, were pushed or fled into the southern desert during the Arab invasion of North Africa in the seventh and eighth centuries. Retaining their Berber language and culture, the refugees adapted to a nomadic existence in the vast reaches of the arid Sahara. Tuareg means "the forsaken of God," a name given them by the Arabs. The Tuaregs referred to themselves simply as "the free men." By the end of the fourteenth century, the Tuaregs had established themselves as far south as the present northern border of Nigeria.

The tribal groups formed large confederations that controlled regional trade and united in defending traditional territories. Often warring among themselves, the Tuaregs lived by raiding sedentary settlements, trading along the trans-Saharan routes, and extracting protective fees from caravans and travelers. The Tuaregs migrated south during the eleventh century and occupied the fertile valleys on the desert's southern edge, where they erected several Tuareg states. Converted to Islam, the states amassed great wealth as the southern terminals of the caravan routes that crossed the Sahara and linked the Muslim Tuaregs to Muslim North Africa. The cities of Agades, Gao, and Timbuktu, the Tuaregs' spiritual capital, became noted centers of Muslim culture and learning, instrumental in the spread of Islam through much of Central Africa.

The Tuareg confederations gradually fell to the expanding medieval empires of Songhai, Ghana, and Mali. These empires were in turn destroyed by invading Moroccans in 1591. Several small Tuareg states, notably Agades and Gao, established following the Moroccan withdrawal, recovered control of the trans-Saharan trade routes and the markets for salt, gold, ivory, and slaves. The Tuaregs controlled the trans-Saharan caravan routes between the trading centers on the southern edge of the Sahara Desert and the Arabic territories north of the desert. Many Tuareg tribes prospered on trade and by raiding caravans that refused to pay protection.

In the late eighteenth century six Tuareg confederations—Ahaggar, Ajjer, Tadamakat, Aïr, Ouadalan, and Adagh—dominated a large empire in the grasslands of the southern Sahara. Mounted Tuareg warriors habitually raiding the settled black African tribes for slaves to ship north along the caravan routes to North Africa. Pushed southward by more powerful peoples, several of the confederations allied with various states of the Hausas* against the Fulani empire of Sokoto in the late eighteenth century. The Tuareg raids and slavery set pattern for relations with the black African tribes south of the desert that persist to the present.

Lying far from Africa's coasts, the Tuareg homeland escaped European attention until the late nineteenth century. In 1890 the French proclaimed a protectorate in Aïr and the southern Tuareg regions, but French troops attempting to enter Tuareg territory in 1898 met fierce resistance. Their lands eventually divided among several French colonies, the Tuaregs were finally subdued by a French military expedition in 1906. The confederations were stripped of their political power by the colonial administration.

The Tuaregs, with German backing and encouragement, launched a rebellion in 1916 and remained a threat to the European colonies until defeated by a combined French and British force. The Tuareg noble class was nearly decimated in the fighting against mechanized European columns before fighting ended in early 1919. The Tuareg rebellion soon resumed in response to French conscription, taxes, and forced labor. Unable to suppress the Tuareg tribes militarily, the French authorities formed an alliance with Tuareg leaders in 1923. In return for Tuareg aid in policing the black African tribes as part of France's colonial army, the Tuaregs enjoyed extensive autonomy in their own territories, administratively separated from those of the black African tribes to the south. In 1954 the French authorities recruited Tuaregs to fight in the growing Algerian war of independence.

The southern black tribes, quicker to accept French culture and education, began to dominate the colonial administration and to lead the drive for independence from France. Fearing domination by their former slaves, the Tuareg demanded the creation of an autonomous state in the northern districts of French West Africa and southern Algeria in 1959. Ignored by the French authorities, the Tuareg territories remained part of the colonial territories that became the independent states of Niger, Mali, Algeria, and Upper Volta (Burkina Faso) in the early 1960s.

The postcolonial states, ruled by one-party governments, mostly excluded Tuareg participation, which aggravated ethnic tension. Forced to live in countries where they were not accepted, the Tuareg became marginalized culturally, socially, and politically. Open rebellion erupted in 1963 and was not completely crushed until the governments of Mali, Niger, and Algeria joined forces two years later. Government attempts to force the nomadic Tuareg to settle provoked renewed resistance in many areas in the 1960s and 1970s.

Severe drought and famine devastated the Tuareg lands in the 1970s. Particularly severe in 1973–74, 1977–78, and 1985, the droughts and the ensuing famines killed up to 100,000 Tuaregs and decimated their herds of cattle, goats, sheep, and camels. Their herds gone, many of the starving nomads moved into refugee camps or the squalid slums of the larger cities. During the drought of 1984, many Tuaregs lost most of their camels; many were forced to settle, mostly in shantytowns around the larger cities or in small villages that soon swelled into towns.

Resentment of the governments, which did little to aid the stricken Tuaregs, stimulated the beginning of the modern Tuareg national movement. Libyan radio broadcasts in the early 1980s incited Tuaregs in Mali and

Niger to revolt. Younger Tuareg men were offered incentives to join the Libyan army of Muammar Qadafi, who claimed the Tuaregs as ethnic kin. Many Tuareg armed refugees began to return to Niger and Mali in 1990. A nationalist group, the Revolutionary Movement of the Blue Men, known by its initials, MOREHOB, gained supporters in all Tuareg areas.

In May 1990, a Tuareg band from Libya attacked a police post at Tchintabaradene in northern Niger, killing several policemen and stealing their weapons. The Nigerian government sent young, inexperienced soldiers drawn from the southern black tribes. When the soldiers were unable to find the suspects, they went on a rampage, killing hundreds of unarmed Tuareg civilians. The Tuaregs of Niger rebelled, and the unrest soon spread to the Tuareg districts of northern Mali. Paramilitary groups organized and armed by the Niger and Mali governments attacked across the region. The brutal repression cost hundreds of Tuareg lives and forced many more to seek refuge in Mauritania and Algeria. The paramilitaries moved through the Tuareg regions looting, raping, and summarily executing local leaders. Many of the refugees died of starvation, cold, and epidemics. The suppression of the Tuaregs was mostly ignored by the international community. Tuareg sources claim that thousands of their people died in the attacks and massacres.

Several agreements and cease-fires were negotiated and signed during the 1990s. Although the agreements mostly failed, most of the Tuareg nationalist groups joined the peace process in 1995. Some of the 150,000 refugees began returning from Algeria, Burkina Faso, and Mauritania under UN supervision. Some groups returned to armed rebellion in Niger in 1997. According to Nigerian government sources, the last group of armed Tuareg rebels surrendered in June 1998. In March 1999, representatives of 14 Tuareg groups signed a declaration that denounced the government for delaying the implementation of the peace accords, particularly the release of Tuaregs detained on rebellion charges.

The Tuareg rebellion, despite numerous cease-fires and attempts at negotiations, continues as a major threat to the integrity of the postcolonial states, while a negotiated settlement receded farther with each violent confrontation. The Tuaregs are an underprivileged minority in several of the world's poorest countries, though they are the region's former masters. In 1999–2001 the region was generally calm, but the Tuareg grievances remained unresolved and Tuareg nationalism was still a powerful force.

The terms of the 1995 agreement have yet to be fully implemented. The Tuaregs face enormous difficulties whether they try to maintain their nomadic life or become more integrated into the black-dominated cultures of Mali and Niger. Tuareg leaders, claiming that only they can inhabit the semi-arid lands of the Sahara without destroying them, continue to demand a sovereign Tuareg state, to be called Azawad.

In Niger many of the former rebel leaders have been given government positions, but thousands of former rebel fighters remain in camps or have returned to the rebellion. Of the 6,000 former rebels, 2,000 have been integrated into the military, the police, customs, and other branches of government. Another 4,000 former rebels and their families have yet to be integrated into Nigerian society. In theory, under the terms of a second term signed in 1998, the former rebels are no longer armed, but sporadic skirmishes continue in northern Niger, and in Mali. Most Tuaregs have resigned themselves to a settled way of life, but they retain their spirit of independence.

The President of Niger, Tanja Mamadou, has lit a 'flame of peace' to incinerate more than a thousand weapons at a ceremony in Agadez in September 2000. The bonfire—greeted by applause and ululations from a crowd of several thousand—was aimed at highlighting the end of Tuareg wars in northern Niger, following the peace accords of 1995 and 1998. The Tuareg leader, Mohamed Anako, used the occasion to announce the dissolution of several rebel movements and militias.

The Tuareg rebellion, although considered ended or at least dormant, has left a legacy of lawlessness in the northern parts of Niger and Mali. In October 2001 attacks on tourist groups by freedom fighters turned bandits highlighted the growing problem. Many Tuareg fighters, unlike their leaders, have not accepted the peace accords.

SELECTED BIBLIOGRAPHY:

Bernus, Edmond. *Tuaregs*. 1991.
Bourgeot, Andre. *Tuareg Societies: Nomadism, Identity, Resistance*. 1995.
Dayak, Mano. *Tuareg: The Tragedy*. 1992.
Nicolaisen, Johannes, ed. *The Pastoral Tuareg: Ecology, Culture, and Society*. 1998.

Turkomans

Turkmens; Torkomanis; Trukhmeny; Turkmanis; Turkomanis; Iraqi Turks; Trukhmenis

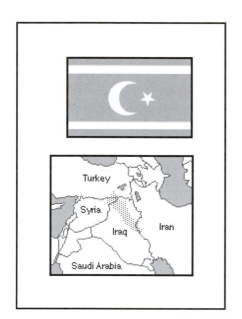

POPULATION: Approximately (2002e) 2,840,000 Turkomans in the Middle East, concentrated in northern Iraq, with smaller populations in adjacent areas of Iran, Syria, and Turkey. Outside the region there are large Turkoman communities in Baghdad (with about 300,000), Damascus, and other large cities outside the homeland. There is a small community in northern Jordan, and there are groups in Europe, the United States, Canada, and Australia. Turkoman nationalists claim a national population of over four million, with 3.5 million in Iraq.

THE TURKOMAN HOMELAND: The Turkoman homeland occupies a long swath of territory from south-central Turkey across Syria and northern Iran to the Iran-Iraq border. The Turkoman population live in a series of cities, towns, and villages across a wide strip of Iraq territory from Baghdad and the Iranian border to the Turkish-Syrian borders. The Turkoman heartland in northern Iraq comprises the provinces of Mosul, Irbil (Arbil), Al-Tamim, Salahaddin, and Diyala. According to Turkoman sources, Mosul is 40% Turkoman, Irbil (Arbil) is 35% Turkoman, Al-Tamim is 65% Turkoman, Salahaddin is 60% Turkoman, and Diyala is 33% Turkoman. The Turkoman capital and major cultural center is Kirkuk, called Kerkuk by the Turkomans, (2002e) 702,000. The other important Turkoman cultural centers is Irbil, called Arbil by the Turkomans, (2002e), 1,068,000.

FLAG: The Turkoman national flag, the flag of the nationalist movement, is a pale blue flag bearing a centered white crescent moon and a five-pointed star with narrow white horizontal stripes at the top and bottom.

PEOPLE AND CULTURE: The Turkomans are considered the third national group in Iraq, with smaller numbers in Syria, with about 100,000, in Iran, and Turkey. The Turkomans, often called simply Turks, are more closely related to the Southern Azeris* than to the Turks of Turkey. Traditional Turkoman society was characterized by a distinct economic division between herders and farmers. The division was present in almost every tribe, settlement, and family. The division still exists; the rural Turkomans are divided into two groups. Clashes between the two groups often came to violence, especially as sedentary farmers began keeping herds and required more pasture lands. The remnants of clan and tribal federations are still evident in the strong sense of family loyalty. Tribal identity is reinforced by a tradition of marrying within the tribal group.

LANGUAGE AND RELIGION: The Turkomans speak dialects of South Azerbaijani, which is popularly called Turkoman in Iraq and Syria. The Kirkuk dialect is the basis of the standard and literary language in Iraq, but the dialects spoken in Syria and Turkey differ considerably and are considered closer to Osmanli Turkish than to South Azerbaijani. Turkoman in Iraq is written in Arabic script, but there is little literature. The language is not a written language in Syria. Many read Arabic or Kurdish, but most are illiterate in their own language, which they speak at home or within the group. In Iraq the language is banned from public use, education, or communications, while in the northern protected zone, Kurdish is the official language.

The majority of the Turkomans are Sunni Muslims, with a small Shi'a minority. Around 30,000 Turkomans, called Kale Gavuru, have adopted Christianity. In Iran the Turkomans have suffered discrimination due to their status as Sunni Muslims in the predominantly Shi'a Muslim Iran. Like many Turkic nomads or former nomads, the Turkomans have not been as deeply influenced by Islam as are the sedentary Turks. In spite of the outward conformity to Islam, mysticism and other pre-Islamic religious traditions are still prevalent.

NATIONAL HISTORY: Early in the seventh century nomadic Turkic-speaking tribes from Central Asia and Azerbaijan began to settle the foothills of the mountainous north of Mesopotamia. The settlement of the Turkomans continued in the ninth century, at the time when most of the Middle East was ruled by the Muslim Caliphate. The migration of the Turkic tribes continued steadily for several hundred years and increased dramatically at the height of the Turkic Seljuk empire in the Middle Ages. The Seljuk Turks were the first to use the name "Turkoman" for the various Turkic-speaking tribes in Mesopotamia.

Turkoman soldiers and officers were recruited to serve in the army and as palace guards of the Abbasid caliphs in the eighth century. The recruitment of these Turkic tribes increased sharply during the reign of Al Mu'Tasim, whose mother was Turkoman, in the early ninth century. The Turkomans in the government gained political power with the assassination of Al-Mutawakkil in 861 and the installation of Al-Muntasirin as caliph. The Abassid caliphate was ruled by Turkomans from then on; successive caliphs were installed and removed as mere figureheads until the thirteenth-century Mongol invasion.

The majority of the Mongol forces that invaded Mesopotamia in 1258 were ethnic Turkic peoples from Central Asia. These forces devastated large parts of the region before settling and eventually being assimilated by the local Turkoman population. The importance of the region declined following the destruction of irrigation systems, trade centers, and local administrations. Turkoman tribes lived by raiding Persian caravans and eventually became involved in slave trading. Slave raids became so frequent in the fifteenth and sixteenth centuries that many settled communities built walls and other fortifications.

Early in the sixteenth century, the Azeris invaded Mesopotamia under Shah Ismail. Although Azeri control was short-lived, this period brought the settlement of Turkic peoples around Baghdad, Najaf, and Karbala. The various Turkic tribes that settled in Mesopotamia over many hundreds of years came to be collectively called Turkoman. Although scattered over a large area they shared language, culture, and religion. Mutual social, religious, economic, and political factors considerably influenced the relations and distribution of the Turkoman population. For centuries, the Turkoman territories were considered a buffer zone separating the Arabs from the Kurds.*

The Mesopotamia region became part of the Turkish Ottoman Empire in the sixteenth and seventeenth centuries. Turkish administration divided the region into various provinces under local governors, who enjoyed broad powers. The corrupt local authorities, rather than distinguish between local Arabs, Kurds, or Turkomans, treated all Muslims as one group, with only the Assyrians* and other ethnoreligious groups subject to restrictions and special taxes. Many Turkic tribal groups were settled in the region by the Ottomans to repel tribal raids along important trade routes and around military garrisons. Many Turkomans were settled at the entrances of the valleys that gave access to the Kurdish areas. This historical role in the region led to strained relations with the Kurds.

The Ottoman Empire joined the Central Powers during World War I and shared their defeat in 1918. British and French forces occupied Mesopotamia, dividing the region into mandates under the new League of Nations in 1920. Most of the Turkoman territories were included in the new Iraq mandate, although the Mosul region was contested by Turkey. The French controlled the western districts in Syria, and some northern Turkomans were included in the new nationalist Republic of Turkey to the north.

Under the terms of the 1925 Iraqi constitution, the non-Arabic minorities had the right to use their own language in schools and government offices, and to have their own national press. In 1932 the mandate was ended, and Iraq became a kingdom. The government of the new Iraqi kingdom recognized the religious, linguistic, and cultural rights of the non-Arab national groups, and it made Turkoman an official language in the

Kirkuk region. The declaration was the first to officially recognize the Turkomans as a separate nation in Iraq. The Turkomans of Syria and Turkey were excluded from local government and faced discrimination in health, education, and representation. The Turkish government in 1958 outlawed the Turkoman language, insisting on the use of the Turkish language instead.

After World War II, successive Iraqi regimes restricted minority rights. In 1972 the government, under Arab radicals, prohibited study in the Turkoman language and banned Turkoman media. A new constitution adopted in 1973 made no reference to the Turkomans. Saddam Hussein became president of Iraq in 1979 at the head of a radical regime that began a 10-year war with neighboring Iran. The regime banned all public use of the Turkoman language and pressed Arabization in the early 1980s.

Shortly after the Iranian revolution in 1979, the Iranian Turkomans rebelled against the new Islamic government. They demanded autonomy, official recognition of their language, and representation in local revolutionary councils dominated by Shi'a Muslims. The rebellion was shortly crushed, and their demands were ignored. Many of the Turkomans in west-central Iran fled across the border into Iraq. Afterward, the Iranian Turkomans suffered from the excesses of the Revolutionary Guards. In 1983, violence broke out when the Revolutionary Guard tried to prevent Turkoman women from working on farms and going about unveiled. Continuing persecution caused many Turkomans to flee to Iraq or Turkey in the 1980s.

The Hussein government in Iraq adopted a policy of assimilation of minorities in 1980. Government relocation programs moved thousands of Arab families to the Turkoman and Kurdish areas of northern Iraq in the 1980s in an effort to Arabicize the region. Hundreds of Turkoman villages and towns were destroyed to make way for Arab migrants, who were promised free land and financial incentives. Turkoman names of many settlements were changed to Arabic names. In September 1989, a resolution was passed barring Turkomans from acquiring real estate in Kirkuk. A new Iraqi constitution in 1990 recognized only Arabs and Kurds as peoples.

The Iraqi government of Saddam Hussein invaded and annexed the neighboring state of Kuwait in August 1990. An international coalition led by the United States finally drove the Iraqi forces from Kuwait in early 1991, setting off revolts among the Shi'a population of southern Iraq and among the Kurds, Assyrians, and Turkomans of northern Iraq. To protect the region, the coalition forces set up an autonomous Kurdish state in northern Iraq, effectively dividing Iraq in two parts. The Turkoman population, divided between the autonomous Kurdish region and central Iraq, generally supported any force that would protect them from the excesses of the Hussein regime.

In 1992 Turkomans from all areas attended an opposition congress held in Kurdish-controlled northern Iraq. The desire for autonomy and the right to speak their language were the major themes of the conference. The new Republic of Turkmenistan, which became an independent state in Central Asia in 1991, was seen as a rallying point for the Turkomans of the Middle East.

The official policy of Arabization meant the forced relocation of ethnic Turkomans in 1994–96, particularly in the large city of Kirkuk. Often a Turkoman was arrested, not to be released until the his family had sold its properties to Arab buyers and accepted relocation to southern Iraq or to the Kurdish autonomous region in the north. The policy formed part of a terrorist campaign carried out against the non-Arab populations under the control of the Iraqi government.

The Turkomans, traditionally nonpolitical, began to mobilize against the repression. In April 1995 they formed the Turkoman Front as their official representative in the autonomous zone in northern Iraq. The front subsequently split into factions, some allied to the various Kurdish factions, others seeking a national state separate from the Kurds and Assyrians in northern Iraq. Turkoman disunity made resistance to oppression very difficult to maintain.

Fighting between the two main Kurdish factions led to a serious split in the autonomous region in northern Iraq in 1996. Iraqi military forces, in alliance with one of the Kurdish Democratic Party, invaded the autonomous region in August 1996. Many opposition Kurds, Assyrians, and Turkomans in Kirkuk and Arbil were arrested during the operation, particularly the Turkoman leaders in Kirkuk and Arbil. Members of Turkoman nationalist organizations were also rounded up, with many imprisoned in camps in southern Iraq. Over 250 Turkomans were executed, disappeared, or arrested during the operation.

As part of the continuing policy of Arabization, the Iraqi authorities forced thousands of Turkomans from their homes in Kirkuk in September 1996. Ethnic Arabs were moved to the region, which has a substantial Turkoman population, in an effort to change the demography of the Kirkuk and Irbil regions. Many Turkomans, forced from their homes, fled across the border into Iran, where they were allowed to remain in refugee camps. Turkoman resistance led to fighting in the region in October, leading to another flow of refugees into the Islamic Republic of Iran.

A number of Turkoman members of the Turkoman Front were publicly executed by the Hussein regime in Baghdad in 1996–97. Those executed, mostly Turkomans from the Kirkuk region, had been charged with secession and threatening the integrity of the Iraqi state. Several were executed for participating in a coup attempt against Saddam Hussein in 1996.

In October 1997, Turkomans from across Iraq participated in the first Turkoman Congress, organized by the umbrella group, the Turkoman Front; it adopted a Turkoman constitution. Turkoman associations from

Europe, the United States, Canada, and Australia/New Zealand also participated. The congress also adopted Istanbul Turkish as the official written language in place of the present Arabic, and it adopted the Latin alphabet. Addressing the historical question of who is and is not Turkoman, the congress decided that belonging to the Turkoman nation is unconditional and that anyone who considers him or herself Turkoman and is loyal to the concept of the Turkoman national idea is a Turkoman. The Turkomans agreed to seek a civilized, democratic, and peaceful path toward the realization of their national goals. They reserved the right to defend themselves against those who threatened their national existence. The agreed goal of the Turkoman nation is the achievement of inalienable rights within the boundaries of Iraq through the adoption of a multiparty, parliamentarian system that respects basic human and national rights.

The delegates at the congress also refused to recognize the decisions of the Iraqi regime that are against the principles of the Turkoman people's rights. They demanded the right to return to the lands from which they were forcibly displaced or compensation for the properties and agricultural lands that were seized by the governmental organization. Compensation for the victims of forced relocation for political reasons was also agreed upon. A second national congress, in February 1999, adopted a more nationalistic doctrine.

Turkomans in all regions have been marginalized and mostly excluded from government positions. Their distinct identity is not recognized in Iraq, and they have suffered discrimination in Turkey, Syria, and Iran. They do not figure in national censuses, and linguistic rights are denied, even in areas where they form a majority. The Iraqi government let it be known that any Turkoman registering as ethnic Turkoman in the October 1997 census would be deprived of all rights and deported. Thousands of Turkomans registered as ethnic Arabs to ensure the security of their lives and possessions.

The Council of the Turkmen Front, which meets twice a year, met in February 1999 to work out a strategy concerning the Washington Agreement, brokered between the two major Kurdish factions in northern Iraq. The Turkomans were excluded from the agreement, but any political change is of vital interest to the Turkoman nation, which remains divided between the Kurdish autonomous area in the north and the Iraqi government of Saddam Hussein in central Iraq. At the meeting and subsequent conferences, Turkoman leaders stressed the ethnic diversity of Iraq, demanding that agreements and governments recognize the demographic structure of the region in a balanced way. The Turkomans are especially anxious that the United States, with considerable influence with various Kurdish factions, recognize their existence as a distinct national group. The Turkomans oppose the policies of Turkey in the region, particularly the extended alliance between Turkey, the United States, and the Kurdish Democratic Party, which severely restricts Turkoman rights.

A Turkoman congress in 2001 put forward a plan for a federation of autonomous states to replace the hated Ba'ath Party regime in Baghdad. The plan envisioned autonomous states or regions for the Sunni Arabs, the Shi'a Arabs, the Turkomans, the Kurds, and the Assyrians.

SELECTED BIBLIOGRAPHY:

Demirci, Fazil. *The Iraqi Turks Yesterday and Today.* 1992.
Krueger, J. *The Turkic Peoples.* 1997.
Stuart, Murray, ed. *Not on Any Map.* 1997.
Warner, Geoffrey. *Iraq and Syria 1941.* 1979.

Tuvans

Tyva; Tuvinians; Tuwa; Tuba; Uriankhai; Uryankhays; Tannu; Soyoty; Soyony

POPULATION: Approximately (2002e) 280,000 Tuvans in Central Asia, concentrated in the Republic of Tuva in the Russian Federation, with 245,000, with another 35,000 in adjacent areas of Mongolia, and a few hundred in China.

THE TUVAN HOMELAND: The Tuvan homeland, sometimes called the "Land of the Eagle," occupies the valley of the lower Yenisei River in southern Siberia, between the Sayan Mountains on the north and the Tannu–Ula Mountains on the Mongolian border. Much of the Tuvan homeland is desert, but there are extensive grazing lands and some agriculture on the great plains between the Tarbagata River and the Khinghan Mountains. There is considerable mineral wealth, but it has not been developed. A monument near Kyzyl, the capital of the republic, marks the geographic center of the Asian continent. Most of the traditional Tuvan lands are included in Tuva Ulus, a constituent republic of the Russian Federation. *Tuva Ulus (Republic of Tuva/Tyva Respublika):* 65,380 sq. mi.—170,544 sq. km, (2002e) 309,000—Tuvans 67%, Russians 28%, Mongols 3%, others 2%. The Tuvan capital and major cultural center is Kyzyl, (2002e) 103,000.

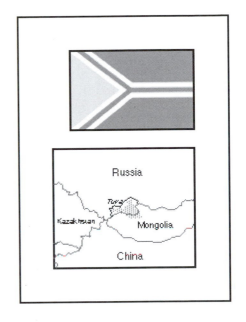

FLAG: The Tuvan national flag, the official flag of Tuva Ulus, is a pale blue field bearing a yellow triangle at the hoist outlined by narrow white stripes that extend in parallel stripes to the fly.

PEOPLE AND CULTURE: The Tuvans are a people of mixed background, physically resembling the Mongols but culturally and linguistically more closely related to the Turkic peoples. Historically they are a mixture of Turkic, Mongol, Samoyedic, and Kettic groups. The Turkic and Mongol strains predominate in western Tuva, the Samoyeds in western and eastern Tuva, and the Kets in eastern Tuva. Historically the Tuvan nation has been divided into two subgroups—the Eastern Tuvans and the Western Tuvans—which are further divided into tribal groups. In spite of the damage that over four decades of Soviet rule inflicted on the Tuvan nation, education and professional training made great strides. The majority are literate and the number of trained doctors, engineers, and other professionals is much higher than in neighboring Mongolia. The majority of the Tuvans are herdsmen and hunters, but some, in recent years, have taken up cereal farming. Since 1991 ethnic Tuvans returning to the region from China have introduced vegetable farming. Traditionally the Tuvans on the steppe lands lived in large felt tents called *gers* or *yurts*, while those in the mountains lived in round tents made from bark. The modern Tuvans are more likely to live in urban settlements in permanent brick houses or highrise residential blocks. The Tuvan culture is noted for its rich oral epic poetry and its music. The Tuvans are famous for their singing; some are able to sing with two voices simultaneously, one voice usually a lower drone and the second a high-pitched flutelike sound. This singing is called *khoomei*, or throat singing. This two-note singing is unique to Tuva, part of Mongolia, and to some Tibetan monks.

LANGUAGE AND RELIGION: The Tuvan language, called Tuvin, is a Northern Turkic language of the Altaic language group. The language, closely related to Uighur spoken in Chinese Xinjiang, has literary status in the Tuvan Republic, but the Tuvan minority in neighboring Mongolia use Khalkh Mongol as their literary language. Five distinct dialects of Tuvin are spoken in Russia, with sharp dialectical differences—Central, Western, Northeastern or Todzhin, Southeastern, and Tuba-Kizhi. Kokchulutan and Khöwsögöl are the major dialects spoken in Mongolia and China. In spite of the inroads made by the Russian language, Tuvin remains the mother tongue of 99% of the Tuvan population in Russia. Until the imposition of Soviet rule in 1944, very few Tuvans were able to read or write. The dialect spoken around Kyzyl forms the basis of the literary language, which is written in the Cyrillic alphabet. There are sharp dialectal differences due to the rugged nature of the landscape, which once restricted travel. Russian is spoken by many as a second language.

The Tuvan religion is Lama Buddhism, and the dalai lama of Tibet is revered as the spiritual leader of the Tuvan nation. An estimated 2% of the Tuvans have converted to Orthodox Christianity, and evangelical Christian organizations have become active since 1991. An estimated third of the Tuvan adult population consider themselves nonreligious, as a result of decades of official atheism. The Tuvans were traditionally shamanists, believing in an unseen world of gods, demons, and ancestral spirits. Even today Buddhist beliefs are mixed with earlier shamanistic traditions and beliefs; the majority believe that all natural elements contain spirits that must be appeased with offerings. The people remain dependent on shamans, medicine men, to cure the sick by magic and communicate with the spirits. The soul is believed to remain in the body for seven days, then depart for the "kingdom of the dead," reaching its ultimate destination on the 49th day. The traditional religion, like the Tuvan culture, is experiencing a revival since the collapse of the Soviet Union in 1991.

NATIONAL HISTORY: Traditional history has the Tuvans under the rule of a Turkish khanate in the sixth century. Chinese and Uighurs* then held the region for a century each, until the Yenisei Kyrgyz took control of the Tuvan homeland in the ninth century. The Tuvans were first mentioned in the chronicles of travelers of the tenth century A.D. as a herder people living in clan groups ruled by hereditary or elected chiefs. They inhabited the grasslands of the mountainous area north of the Silk Road, the ancient trade route between China and the Mediterranean.

The Mongols conquered the region in the thirteenth century, and the Tuvan tribes lived under nominal Mongol authority for three centuries. The Mongol Golden Horde ruled the region from 1207 to 1368, after which Tuva was dominated by Eastern Mongols* until the sixteenth centuries. The Altyn khans held the region until around 1650, when the Dzungarians took military control of the region.

The Tuvan tribes, often warring among themselves, emerged as an identifiable cultural groups in the early eighteenth century. In the 1700s Tibetan Buddhism, or Lamaism, reached the Tuvans through contact with the Mongols. The new religion was adopted as the national religion, but the earlier shamanistic traditions were also retained, producing a unique blend of beliefs. In 1757–58 the Manchus* of China took control of the Tuvan territories. Under Manchu rule the Tuvan homeland was incorporated into Manchu Mongolia as the Uriankhai, or Urjanchai, region.

Russian explorers came into contact with the Tuvans around 1860, when the Treaty of Peking between China and Russia opened the region for trade. Russians began to move into the territory as Manchu power waned in the 1870s. Over the next two decades several thousand Russians settled in the fertile river valleys. The Slavic settlers, drawn to the region known as the Asian Switzerland, gradually took authority. Tuvan nationalists, with Russian support, organized a national government during the 1911 Chinese Revolution, which overthrew the Manchus. On 18 December 1911 the Tuvans declared their independence from China.

The Tuvans, bowing to the demands of the republic's influential Russian population, accepted Russian protection against renewed Chinese and Mongol claims when war broke out in Europe in 1914. The Russians proclaimed the region a protectorate and assumed responsibility its defense and foreign affairs. A 1915 agreement between the Russians, Chinese, and Tuvans left Tuva autonomous but under Chinese influence. The majority of the Tuvans lived in rural areas or small villages, often working for members of the aristocracy in a feudal system of local loyalties.

The Russian Revolution of 1917, which led to a breakdown of civil government in the region, allowed the Tuvans to again assert the independence of their homeland. In early 1918 local Bolsheviks, supported by their Russian counterparts, rebelled against the Tuvans' traditional ruling class. The revolution, which further weakened the Tuvan government, left the region nearly defenseless when the Russian Civil War spilled into the region. Alternately occupied by Red and White armies, the Tuvan homeland was the scene of severe fighting from 1918 until the Bolshevik victory in 1920. During the civil war the Chinese attempted to reassert their authority in the region, but with the White defeat and the Bolshevik occupation of Mongolia, the Tuvan homeland came under firm Red control.

The Bolshevik authorities overthrew the feudal Tuvan lords, and on 14 August 1921 Tuvan and Russian socialists declared the state an independent people's republic called the Tuvinian People's Republic, popularly called Tannu Tuva, for its towering Tannu Mountains. The Tuvans organized their state along traditional lines, but with a functioning parliament called the Great Huruldan, which elected a second branch of the legislature, the Little Huruldan. The establishment of Tuvan autonomy helped the Tuvans to resist Mongol attempts to gain control of the region.

Tuvan independence was finally confirmed by treaties with neighboring states in 1924–26, but in 1931 the Soviet government forced the Tuvans to disenfranchise the traditional ruling class and to reorganize as a communist state, the world's third. To reinforce the break with the past, the Soviet authorities destroyed nearly all of the region's 49 Buddhist monasteries, killing, imprisoning, or exiling the monks and traditional healers. Tannu Tuva remained an independent communist state until Soviet troops occupied the capital city in October 1944 during World War II, leading to the Soviet annexation of the country in 1945, supposedly at the request of the region's population.

In spite of the Stalin-era repression, the Tuvans continued to send petitions and to pressure local government officials until the Soviet government finally granted their homeland the status of an autonomous republic in 1961. The new status guaranteed at least some cultural autonomy, although the Tuvans were forbidden contact with neighboring peoples. The majority of the Tuvan population continued to pursue their traditional way of life and mostly left the painful issue of politics to the Russian minority.

The Tuvans began to urbanize in the 1970s, leading to increasing industrialization, strengthened by the discovery of huge asbestos deposits. A rapid industrialization program, launched by the Soviet authorities, caused major ecological and health programs for the Tuvans.

In the late 1970s and early 1980s, the anti-Buddhist policies of the Soviet authorities were relaxed as Moscow attempted to exploit the Buddhist religion as part of its international "peace" campaigns. In 1980, as part of this program, the president of communist Mongolia was allowed to pay an official visit to the region. In 1985 another high-ranking Mongolian delegation visited the autonomous republic.

The liberalization of Soviet life, which began in 1987 under Mikhail

Gorbachev, allowed the Tuvans to reestablish long-forbidden ties to the neighboring peoples, particularly the Mongols. Closed to foreigners for over two decades, the Tuvan homeland was finally opened to travel in 1988.

Tuvan nationalist groups support widening international contacts of the Tuvan republican government. Tuvans recall that their homeland was annexed by their huge neighbor twice in just 30 years, in 1914 and 1944, without protest from the outside world.

Freed of Soviet constraints, Tuvan nationalism reemerged, with calls for increased Tuvan language education, help in rebuilding destroyed Buddhist monasteries, and for closer ties to the related peoples of southern Siberia and Mongolia. More militant groups called for secession and the resumption of Tuvan independence.

In June 1990, large demonstrations rocked the Tuvan capital; demonstrators demanded the dismissal of the local government and denounced as illegal the annexation of their state in 1944. In July and August 1990 demonstrators regularly clashed with Soviet police dispatched to regain control. The clashes left hundreds dead or injured. Over 3,000 ethnic Slavs fled the escalating violence.

The disintegration of the Soviet Union in 1991 raised nationalist demands for autonomy and self-determination. More radical groups called for the resurrection of the former independent republic; however, in September 1991 nationalist leaders acknowledged that after nearly half a century of Soviet rule they suffered from a lack of trained administrators and that immediate independence would be impossible.

The name of the republic was changed from Tuva Autonomous Soviet Socialist Republic to the Republic of Tuva. In July 1992 the Free Tuva Party, the largest of several nationalist groups, agreed to suspend its campaign for a referendum on independence in exchange for a pledge that a self-determination clause would be included in the new Russian constitution. In August 1992, the group again called for a referendum on secession.

In late 1991 a Buddhist community was officially registered in the Tuvan Republic, and efforts were begun to rebuild the Tuvan capital's great monastery. Sacred Tuvan religious scrolls, spirited away and hidden in 1921, were returned to the reopened Tuvan Buddhist center in Kyzyl in late 1992. The return of the scrolls, symbols of Tuvan religious devotion and sovereignty, was seen as yet another step to the restoration of the Tuvan nation.

An acrimonious border dispute with neighboring Mongolia, including cross-border theft of livestock, led to stricter security measures in territories adjacent to the Mongolian border. The Free Tuva group demanded the creation of a national guard free of Russian control.

In May 1993, Tuva's parliament amended the republic's constitution to include a provision for secession from Russia. In 1995, under federal political and economic pressure, the constitution was again amended to remove clauses that clashed with the constitution of the Russian Federation.

In April 1997, Sherig-ool Oorzhak, a pro-Russian candidate, was reelected as president of the republic. A reduction of pro-secessionist sentiment reflected the improvement of the local economy and the increasing autonomy allowed within the Russian Federation. Attempts to curtail local autonomy in 1999–2000 again raised nationalist sentiment. Growing differences between President Sherig-ool and the parliament resulted in the postponement of local elections in 1998 and 2000.

The major factor in the region is Tuva's economic dependency on the Russian state. This both contributes to and undercuts nationalist agitation. Although nationalist sentiment is widespread, the economic constraints continue to mitigate demands for full independence. Anti-Russian attitudes, at least in part, are manifestations of economic problems. If economic conditions continue to improve, Tuvan nationalism could again become a major factor in the republic.

SELECTED BIBLIOGRAPHY:

Krueger, J. *The Turkic Peoples.* 1997.

Leighton, Ralph. *Tuva or Bust!* 1991.

Thomas, Nicholas, and Caroline Humphrey, eds. *Shamanism, History, and the State.* 1994.

Vainshtein, Sevyan. *Nomads of South Siberia: The Pastoral Economy of Tuva.* 1980.

Twa

Twas; Batwa; BaTwa; BaTwas; Buti; Mbutis

POPULATION: Approximately (2002e) 85,000 Twa in east-central Africa, concentrated in the republics of Rwanda, with 20,000, and Burundi, with 40,000, with smaller numbers in adjacent areas of Uganda, where 15,000 live, and the Kivu region of Congo, with a Twa population of about 10,000.

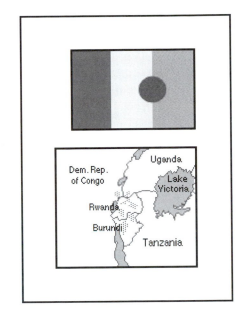

THE TWA HOMELAND: The Twa homeland lies in the Great Lakes region of east-central Africa, although most of the region is now inhabited by other national groups. The Twa live in the rain forests of the high mountains and plains, and they function in economic symbiosis with the pastoral Tutsis and the agricultural Hutu. The Twa homeland has no official status in any of the countries in which the Twa live. The Twa capital and major cultural centers are Bunyambili in Rwanda and Matana in Burundi.

FLAG: The Twa national flag, the flag of the national movement in Rwanda, is a vertical tricolor of blue, white, and pale green, bearing a red circle on the division between the white and green stripes.

PEOPLE AND CULTURE: The Twa are a Negroid pygmy people belonging to the Southern group of Africa's pygmy peoples. The Southern group, also known as the Lake Kivu potters, live in scattered groups in the Great Lakes region. Their chief physical traits of the Twa are short stature, averaging less than five feet (1.5 meters), short legs, and long arms. Generally their skin is yellowish to reddish brown. Throughout central Africa there are an estimated 170,000 pygmy peoples, scattered from Cameroon to Uganda. The Twa see themselves as a colonized nation, first by agriculturists, then by pastoralists, and finally by the Europeans. Each colonizer put growing pressure on the original forest of the area, turning their homeland into farmland, pasture, commercial plantations, and protected areas for conservation or military exercises. The Twa were incorporated into the dominant societies at the very lowest level. This low status, their small numbers, and the dispersal of their communities contributed to their extreme political weakness and the serious difficulties they have encountered in asserting their rights or resisting exploitation and violence. Neighboring peoples will not eat or drink with them, allow them into their houses, or accept them as marital or sexual partners. They are not allowed to take water from community wells, and their communities are segregated from others, forcing them to live on the outskirts of population centers, on marginal land unwanted by others. These practices are less rigid in urban areas, but many underlying biases against the Twa remain. A gentle, peaceful people, the Twa have the ability to camouflage themselves in the forest; they were overlooked for centuries.

LANGUAGE AND RELIGION: The Twa, due to their subjugation by stronger peoples and their long association with the Bantu Hutus, adopted the language of the larger ethnic groups. The Twa speak the national languages of Rwanda and Burundi; in Rwanda they speak the Rutwa dialect of Kinyarwanda, and the Twa of Burundi speak the Rutwa dialect of Kirundi. The languages belong to the Niger-Congo subgroup of the Bantu languages. The small Buti of Uganda have retained their original language, which is reportedly very difficult to learn. Promotion of Twa education among the young, both boys and girls, is now considered of primary importance for the survival of the Twa.

Most Twa are nominally Christian, mostly Roman Catholic. Traditionally the Twa believe that a god named Tore created the world and remains as the supreme being. Tore is identified with the forest, since for them everything is dependent on it. They call on Tore for assistance only during times of crisis. He is usually summoned by a trumpet blast, which is supposedly an imitation of his voice. Some groups believe that after creating the first humans, Tore was no longer interested in the world and withdrew to the sky. Belief in forest spirits also remains strong.

NATIONAL HISTORY: The pygmies are considered the original inhabitants of central Africa, perhaps having originated in the Great Lakes region of east-central Africa. The Ituri forest in Kivu has reportedly been occupied by pygmies for over 4,000 years. Historically, the geographic environment of the Great Lakes region erected an effective barrier to all but the most determined invaders.

Bantu Hutu agriculturists moved into the region between 1000 and 1200 A.D. Later migrations of the tall Tutsi pastoralists from the north established a stratified society with a Tutsi aristocracy, a Hutu serf and artisan class, and the Twa increasingly marginalized and driven from the best and most fertile lands. The three groups lived in relative harmony until the Tutsi began to consolidate and expand their power in the core areas. Social distinctions became the reality, relegating the indigenous Twa to the lowest levels of society.

The Tutsi monarchies, established in the seventeenth century, remained in place when German colonial rule was extended to the region in the early late nineteenth and early twentieth centuries. In 1923 the territories of Ruanda-Urundi became a Belgian mandate under the new League of Nations. Neither the Germans nor the Belgians paid much attention to the forest dwellers, particularly the Twa, who inhabited areas not economically interesting to the colonial powers. Their major contribution to the colonial state was as a tourist curiosity for wealthy Western travelers.

Independence for Rwanda and Burundi, as well as the end of the Tutsi monarchies in the 1960s, began a long series of ethnic confrontations between the Tutsi minority and the larger Hutu majority. Both groups often targeted the small Twa groups that inhabited the marginal areas favored by rebel or military groups. Massacres in the late 1960s carried out by the Hutus in both countries against the former Tutsi rulers also decimated the Twa.

In the 1950s and 1960s, deforestation and discrimination forced many Twa to abandon the traditional hunter-gatherer existence and to adopt the way of life of neighboring peoples. By the early 1970s the last forest-dwelling groups were forced out of the forest and denied further access to it. As late as 1980, most Twa had lived undisturbed by alien cultures. Their nomadic way of life had formed an integral part of the rain forest ecosystem.

Renewed ethnic strife in the Rwanda and Burundi led to peace agreements in the early 1990s, but when the presidents of the two countries were killed in a plane crash on their way to a regional meeting in April 1994, widespread violence broke out. Many Twa fled to the sanctuary of their traditional forest homes as the ethnic conflicts spread. In Rwanda, the Hutu-dominated government participated in a massacre of the Tutsi population, forcing hundreds of thousands of refugees, including many Twa, to flee. An estimated 500,000 people were killed in the violence, since labeled genocide, including about half of Rwanda's 40,000 Twa.

The Twa, forced from their traditional forest homes, had to adjust quickly to totally new living conditions in countries in the grip of ethnic fighting. Forced to live in close contact with other peoples led to a dramatic increase in diseases, including leprosy. Exploitation by Bantu farmers, including distributing alcohol or material goods, then demanding labor in exchange, was common. Impressed into virtual slavery, the Twa men were unable to provide for their families. As a result hunger became endemic.

The Twa, led by Charles Uwiragiye, organized to defend themselves and their interests. The Association for the Promotion of the Batwa (APB) sought to give the Twa a voice in the devastated region. APB aims were to defend the rights and interests of Batwa of Rwanda: to act as intermediary for the Batwa community in its contacts with national and local authorities, to promote the socio-economic and political development of the

Twa, with the emphasis on primary health care, education and employment and the promotion of the Twa culture.

Demands for an autonomous region were rejected by the new governments, but international attention aided the Twa and their efforts to protect themselves and their way of life. The Twa had few resources to fall back on during the Rwandan crisis of October 1993–June 1995. Their lack of mobilization allowed both sides in the conflict to label them as both victims and perpetrators. Mobilization since 1995 has aided the survivors to tell their side of the story. Charles Uwiragiye traveled to Europe in 1994–96 in an effort to enlist support for his beleaguered small nation.

The democratization of Rwanda and Burundi in the late 1990s pointed out the special vulnerability of the minority Twa in the region. The governments instituted policies to protect the surviving Twa as an especially vulnerable group. Support of greater education, projects that allow Twa families to become self-sufficient, and employment for Twa in government departments at various levels are the major focus of the programs. Equality with other citizens, particularly in Rwanda, remains the most important nationalist demand. Government educational and health programs do not normally include the Twa.

Fighting in eastern Congo in 1996–97 threatened the Twa living in the areas and the many people still in refugee camps set up during the upheaval in Rwanda. Representatives of the Rwandan Twa sent a group to the region to aid those caught up in the fighting, helping many refugees and Congolese Twa to cross the border to the relative security of Rwandan territory.

The situation for the Twa in central Africa remains critical and very sensitive. The Twa face serious problems in reestablishing their communities following the disruptions, massacres, and political uncertainty of the 1990s in Rwanda, Burundi, and Congo. The Twa need urgent, active, and effective international assistance to survive in the twenty-first century. Their disadvantaged position in the past and their continued vulnerability demands special care by governments and aid organizations to ensure equal treatment in terms of repatriation and rehabilitation. The Twa themselves are suffering from losses and divisions caused by war, making it difficult for the Twa to undertake meaningful activity on their own behalf.

The insecurity of Twa subsistence strategies have contributed to their increasing poverty and marginalization from the rest of society. In all areas they face discrimination in employment, education, and access to local administration. Other national groups hold extremely negative stereotypes of the Twa, despising them as uncivilized or subhuman, without intelligence or moral values. In recent years the Twa have been stereotyped as poachers, notably of the region's dwindling number of gorillas.

Throughout their homeland, the Twa have been dispossessed of almost all of their traditional lands and have only a tenuous claim to the remainder. Deprived not only of their traditional way of life but of fertile farm-lands, they have been forced to become tenants or client farmers. Pottery, a low-status craft traditionally reserved for them, has become their major occupation and primary economic activity, except in Rwanda, where an estimated 70% are reduced to begging.

In the late 1990s Western human rights and aid agencies campaigned for a Twa biosphere reserve, possibly in the Ngungwe forest in eastern Rwanda and western Tanzania. Although they have gained some support, including from the major Twa nationalist groups, time is crucial, as tree cutting and destruction of the habitat continues. An autonomous homeland may be the last, perhaps only, hope for the survival of the Twa nation.

European and Asian logging concerns are currently endangering the basis of the Twa existence. Bantu slash-and-burn peasants are advancing into the remaining rain forests on newly built logging roads. Increasingly numbers of Twa are being forced into permanent villages, where they are threatened by disease, hunger, and exploitation by the advancing farmers. In the first years of the twenty-first century, the Twa are among the poorest people in the world, without rights or wealth, perhaps the world's most neglected national group.

During July 2000, a conference was held in Kigali, Rwanda, highlighting the plight of the indigenous forest peoples, or pygmies of central Africa. According to Kalimba Zephyrin, director of the community of Indigenous People of Rwanda, the situation of the Twa has hardly improved since the 1994 genocide. Most Twa are marginalized and landless, suffering from poverty and high mortality rates. They are not integrated into society and government administration and are still the victims of inter-state and inter-ethnic conflicts in which they are not active participants. Despite this, great efforts are being made by the Twa themselves to improve their situation and become self-supporting.

SELECTED BIBLIOGRAPHY:

Dostert, Pierre Etienne. *Africa 1997*. 1997.
Duffy, Kevin. *Children of the Forest: Africa's Mbuti Pygmies*. 1996.
Haskins, J. *From Afar to Zulu*. 1995.
Jones, Schuyler. *Pygmies of Central Africa*. 1989.

Tyroleans

Tiroleans; Tirolese; Tyrolese; Tirolos

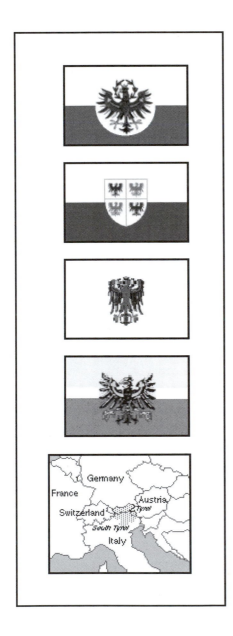

POPULATION: Approximately (2002e) 1,496,000 Tyroleans in south-central Europe, concentrated in the Tyrol state of Austria and the Alto-Adige region of Italy. Outside the region there are Tyrolean communities in other parts of Austria, in Germany, and in the United States and Canada.

THE TYROLEAN HOMELAND: The Tyrolean homeland occupies a mountainous region of high alpine valleys between the Bavarian Alps in the north and Ötzaler Alps in the south. Tyrol is famed for its idyllic beauty but has only limited natural resources, so tourism is the major industry. Tyrol, divided in 1919 between Austria and Italy, forms the Austrian state (bundesland) of Tyrol, consisting of North Tyrol (Nordtirol) and East Tyrol (Osttirol), and the Italian region of Trentino–Alto Adige (Trent-Tiroler Etschland), which is divided into two provinces, Bolzano (Bozen) and Trento (Trient). Historical Region of Tyrol (Tirol/Tirolo): 10,139 sq. mi.—26,259 sq. km, (2002e) 1,635,000—Tyroleans 91% (Tyroleans 37%, Trentines 29%, South Tyroleans 25%), other Austrians and other Italians 9%. The Tyrolean capital and major cultural center is Innsbruck, (2002e) 113,000. Other important Tyrolean cultural centers are Bolzano, called Bozen in German, (2002e) 95,000, the capital of South Tyrol in Italy; Trento, called Trient in German and Trent in English, (2002e) 106,000, the capital of the Trentine Tyroleans; and Merano, locally called Meran, (2002e) 35,000, the region's historical capital.

FLAG: The Tyrolean national flag is a horizontal bicolor of white over red charged with a centered white disc bearing the national symbol, the red Tyrolean eagle. The unofficial flag of the autonomous region of Trentino–Alto Adige is a horizontal bicolor of white over blue bearing a centered shield of four quarters, two bearing the red Tyrolean eagle and two bearing the black eagle of Trent. The Tyrolean eagle centered on a white field is the flag of the South Tyrol. The flag of the Trentines is a horizontal bicolor of white over red bearing the black eagle of Trent centered.

PEOPLE AND CULTURE: The Tyroleans are an alpine people comprising the Tyroleans, including the South Tyroleans, in the north, and the Trentines (Trentinos, Trentini), in the center and south. The two Tyrolean peoples share a collective history that spans over a thousand years of coexistence in their mountain homeland. The Tyroleans also share their Roman Catholic religion and a common alpine culture that supersedes the linguistic diversity of the region. Activities relating to music, literature, and the performing arts involve all the national groups, including the small community of Ladins,* who form the third of the traditional Tyrolean peoples. Multilingual festivals and cultural events are subsidized by the provincial governments.

LANGUAGE AND RELIGION: The language of the Tyroleans and South Tyroleans is an alpine dialect of High German. The Trentines speak an alpine dialect of Italian. The majority of the Tyroleans and South Tyroleans are fluent in both standard German and the Tyrolean dialect, which is closely related to the language spoken by the Bavarians* to the north. The Trentines are mostly Italian-speaking, using both standard Italian and a distinct Gallo-Italic dialect that remains the language of daily life in Trento province. Many of the Tyrolean peoples speak both German and Italian. Bilingualism is supported by the regional government in Italy and is a condition for competition for jobs in the public service.

The Tyroleans are overwhelmingly Roman Catholic, which is a major component in the regional alpine culture. Historically ruled by ecclesiastical authorities, the region remained a Catholic stronghold during most of its history. The church has lost influence in the twentieth century, but the majority of the population still considers themselves Roman Catholic.

NATIONAL HISTORY: The mountainous region north of Roman Italy was the home to a number of Celtic tribes that prevented communications between Italy and the Roman possessions in Gaul and Germania. Between 25 and 15 B.C. Emperor Augustus directed several military campaigns that ultimately defeated the Celtic tribes. Some of the tribes were decimated, while others were sold as slaves and deported to far-flung corners of the empire. The surviving tribes readily adopted the Romans' Latin speech and culture and became influential citizens of the vast empire.

The Roman frontiers completely broke down during the fourth century, and the Germanic tribes moved south. Bavarians took control of most of the region in 680. Avars* moving into the region from the east contended with the Bavarians for control of the Danube River valley. The Avars left only superficial traces in the country, but the Bavarian clans who settled in the Tyrol developed a distinctive alpine culture and eventually split from the Bavarians as a separate people in the highlands. St. Vigilius, the first bishop of Trent, converted the Trentino and South Tyrol to Christianity in the late fourth and early fifth centuries.

In the eighth century, the Franks absorbed the region into their expanding empire. "Tirol" originated as a family name, derived from the castle of Tirol near Merano. The southern Tyrolean districts were given to the powerful bishops of Trent and Brixen by Conrad II in 1027. In the north the counts of Tyrol and Montfort gained control of the Tyrolean districts.

In 1342 the Tyrolean peoples adopted a constitution, the first of its kind in Europe. The Hapsburgs gained control of the northern part of Tyrol in 1363, gradually extending their influence throughout the region. The Tyrolean province was held by a junior branch of the Hapsburgs but was united with the main Austrian possessions in 1655.

Over the next centuries, the Tyroleans and Trentines developed a common alpine culture unique to the region. The common culture and religion transcended the linguistic issue, while the majority of the population used the Tyrolean German dialect for communication between the region's isolated alpine groups.

The secularized bishoprics of Trent and Brixen were awarded to Austria in 1802, during the Napoleonic Wars. Three years later, defeated Austria was forced to cede all of Tyrol to Napoleon's ally, Bavaria. Andreas Hofer, now a Tyrolean national hero, united the diverse Tyrolean peoples to drive the Bavarians and French from the region. He defeated the Bavarians so decisively at the second Battle of Berg Isel in August 1809 that they were forced to evacuate the province. Hofer was finally captured and executed in 1809, but his followers held out in mountain strongholds until Tyrol returned to Hapsburg control in 1815. The rebellion against the Bavarian occupation strengthened the historical and cultural ties among the Tyrolean peoples. The poem "Sandwirth Hofer," by Julius Mosen, is still the Tyrolean anthem.

The Tyroleans formed a distinct national group in the multi-ethnic Hapsburg empire, with ties of loyalty to the Hapsburg monarchs, but not to the Austrians—seen by the Tyroleans as a distinct, lowland nation. In the latter part of the nineteenth century, as revolutionary ideas fed nationalist movements across Europe, the Tyroleans developed a distinct nationalism, seeking greater cultural and political freedom within the empire.

Italian irredentism, the movement to incorporate Italian-speaking parts of the Austro–Hungarian Empire into newly united Italy, gained some support in Trentino after 1878, but the majority of the Italian-speaking

Trentines, separated from Italian influence since the fourteenth century, remained markedly unaffected by calls to Italian unity. Progressive and prosperous, in the 1880s and 1890s the Tyrol was one of the few regions of the vast Hapsburg empire where ethnic strife remained virtually unknown. The Italian government, promised the Italian-speaking areas of Austro-Hungary, joined the allies in 1915. Italy's entry into World War I turned Tyrol's pristine alpine valleys into battlefields and opened a serious rift between the German-speaking Tyroleans and Italian-speaking Trentines.

A Tyrolean national movement, opposed to the war and rejecting Italian territorial claims, gained support among the Tyroleans in the north. In October 1918, as defeat for the Austro-Hungarian Empire loomed, the Tyroleans took control of the regional civil administration. Local leaders, hoping to save their nation from division, organized a referendum in the Tyrolean Diet, which voted overwhelmingly for secession and independence. Tyrolean nationalist leaders, citing point number ten of President Woodrow Wilson's Fourteen Points, independence for the non-Austrian peoples of the empire, rejected both Austrian and Italian claims to the Tyrol. On 24 April 1919, when it had become clear that the Italian government was determined to annex the southern districts, including the German-speaking South Tyrol, the nationalists declared the Tyrol independent. The Tyrolean nationalists began to erect a confederation of Swiss-style autonomous cantons, with German, Italian, and Ladin as official languages, but again the allies intervened to prevent secession. At the Paris Peace Conference the allies assigned northern Tyrol to the new Austrian republic. The mainly Italian-speaking Trentino and the South Tyrol, with its 250,000 German-speaking Tyroleans, came under the authority of the Italian kingdom.

Italy's Fascist government, installed in 1922, and the leftist Austrian government pressed assimilation in their respective Tyrolean territories. In the south, despite promises of autonomy for the South Tyroleans, the Fascist authorities closed all Tyrolean schools, newspapers, and publications and in 1926 ordered the South Tyroleans to change all place and family names to Italian. The Fascist government sponsored immigration from the backward, culturally and dialectically distinct southern Italian regions. This immigration raised tension, not only with the German-speaking Tyroleans in South Tyrol but also between the immigrants and the culturally distinct Trentines. By 1939 95% of public offices in Italian Tyrol were held by Italians from outside the region.

The nationalist tension in Italian Tyrol reverberated in Austrian Tyrol. A militia sent from "Red Vienna" to suppress the Tyrolean national movement brought the region close to civil war in the early 1930s. The German annexation of Austria in 1938, welcomed in the anti-Austrian but pro–German Tyrol, proved a disaster. The German annexation of South Tyrol, following Italy's World War II surrender in 1943, briefly reunited the region; over 60,000 Tyroleans had moved to the north Tyrol before Germany's defeat in 1945.

At the end of the war, the South Tyroleans and the Austrian government presented a plan for the reunification of South Tyrol with Austria, but in the autumn of 1945 the Allies rejected the proposal. Over 150,000 South Tyroleans signed a demand for a plebiscite, and on 5 May 1946 hundreds of thousands marched through Innsbruck demanding Tyrolean unification. On 5 September 1946, the Paris Agreement provided for autonomy for the German-speaking South Tyroleans. Trentine politicians and interest groups tried to have the autonomy statute extended to the historically and culturally distinct Trent province. In 1948 the new Italian constitution provided for a united autonomous region combining Bolzano (South Tyrol) and Trento provinces in the region of Trentino–Alto Adige, giving the region considerable autonomy.

A democratic postwar Austrian government continued to champion the cause of the South Tyroleans. Agreements between Austria and Italy provided for limited autonomy in 1964, the accord designed to head off a growing campaign of violence and sabotage by South Tyrolean nationalists in Italy. The Südtiroler Volkspartei (SVP) became the major political party in German-speaking South Tyrol. The party, seeing that revision of borders and unification of the Tyrol were currently impossible, worked for increased autonomy for the South Tyrolean minority in Italy.

In the 1960s the concept of a collective historical past emphasizing the shared alpine culture gained support among both German and Italian-speaking Tyroleans. As tension increased between the Tyrolean peoples and the influx of newcomers from southern Italy, new demands were put forward for increased autonomy for the entire Trentino–Alto Adige region. Only after the escalation of terrorist acts by radical South Tyrolean groups in the late 1960s did the Italian government acknowledge the ethnic problem in the region. In 1972 the Italian government instituted a new autonomy statute for the region. In Austrian Tyrol the idea was paralleled by the growth of a strong regional movement. On the Italian-Austrian border, nationalists erected signs showing the artificially and unjustly fragmented Tyrol, with "Never forget Tyrol" printed on large signs. Radical Tyrolean nationalists put forward a plan for an autonomous federation of Tyrol, South Tyrol, Trentino, and Vorarlberg.

The increasing Italianization of the Trentino-Alto-Adige was demonstrated by the language issue. In 1987 only 67% of the population of the province of Bolzano spoke German as their first language, down from over 90% in 1919. The language issue fueled the growth of more radical groups in the 1980s, particularly Ein Tirol (One Tyrol). A series of bombings kept the separatist issue in the news in the late 1980s and early 1990s.

The integration of Europe and the reunification of Germany stimulated a resurgence of Tyrolean nationalism in the 1990s. The possibility of re-unification within a federal Europe stimulated nationalist sentiment across the region. Resentment of the mass migration from southern Italy, beginning in the 1950s, reversed decades of assimilation and reinforced the Trentine participation in the common alpine nationalism.

On 15 September 1991 nationalists from all the Tyrolean areas demonstrated on the frontier at the Brenner Pass, demanding a referendum on reunification of Tyrol within a united Europe. Faced with rising nationalism, the Italian government agreed to greater autonomy in 1992. In 1995, Austrian intelligence agents discovered that armed groups and members of rifle clubs calling for Tyrolean cultural and political unity had attended paramilitary training camps in the region. The Italian government in 1996 rejected a proposal for a joint bureau to represent the Tyrolean peoples in the European Union.

The Tyroleans are unusually pro-European, hoping that a united Europe will hasten the reunification of their homeland. When Austria became a member state of the European Union (EU) on 1 January 1995, the two halves of the Tyrolean nation were in theory, but not in reality, reunited. The politics of South Tyrol, long dominated by the SVP, began to change in the 1990s with the creation of opposition nationalist groups. In elections for the local assembly in 1998, the SVP received 56.6% of the vote, but other, often more radical, groups won wider support than any time since the 1960s.

Hundreds of protesters blocked roads near the Brenner Pass in June 2000 to protest increased traffic on the highway that traverses their delicate alpine environment. The protesters, from both sides of the frontier, demand greater control of the traffic, which has doubled since 1990, seriously threatening the region's fragile ecosystem. The protests demonstrated the growing environmental faction of the Tyrolean movement for greater local control.

Dislike has grown among the Tyroleans in Austria for the system known as *proporz*, under which Austria's two major political parties, the Socialists and the People's Party, have shared power and patronage between them since the Second World War. Most positions in public service and state industries, including schools and hospitals, are allocated by *proporz*. Even janitors and committees that select juries are part of the system. Protests include voting for the far-right Freedom Party and continuing demands for more local control, self-government, and closer ties to South Tyrol in a proposed European region.

SELECTED BIBLIOGRAPHY:

Alcock, Anthony Evelyn. *The History of the South Tyrol Question*. 1989.
Hofmann, Paul. *South Tyrol and the Dolomites*. 1995.
Proctor, Alan. *The Tyrol*. 1986.
Toscano, Mario. *Alto Adige, South Tyrol: Italy's Frontier with the German World*. 1994.

Udmurts

Udmorts; Ud-Murts; Vudmurts; Odmorts; Votiaks; Votyaks; Ary; Arianes; Otiakis

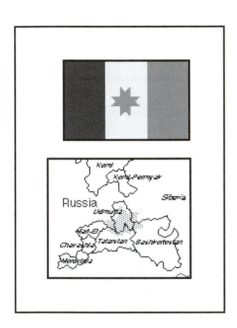

POPULATION: Approximately (2002e) 1,020,000 Udmurts in Russia, concentrated in the Udmurt Republic, a member state of the Russian Federation, but with sizable communities in neighboring republics of Bashkortostan, Tatarstan, and Mari El, and the Russian regions of Kirov, Perm', and Sverdlovsk. There are scattered communities in Siberia and the Far East. The only large community outside Russia is the 16,000 Udmurts living in Kazakhstan in Central Asia. Nationalists claim a national population of up to 1.5 million.

THE UDMURT HOMELAND: The Udmurt homeland lies in eastern European Russia, mostly a highland region between the Vyatka and Kama Rivers and the forested foothills of the Ural Mountains. The region, lying 620 miles (1,000 km) northeast of Moscow, is largely low and hilly, with wide river valleys. Railroads are the main form of transportation, with important trunk lines crossing Udmurtia, which forms part of the Ural industrial region. Although soil fertility is low, cereal crops are cultivated. The Udmurt Republic, raised to the status of an autonomous republic within Soviet Russia in 1934, since 1992 has been a member state of the Russian Federation. *Udmurt Republic (Udmurt Eljkun)*: 16,255 sq. mi.—42,101 sq. km, (2002e) 1,620,000—Russians 46%, Udmurts 43%, Tatars* 8%, Maris* 1%, Bashkorts* 1%, others 1%. The Udmurt capital and major cultural center is Izhevsk, called Izhkar in the Udmurt language, (2002e) 654,000. The other important Udmurt cultural centers are Glazov, called Glaskar in Udmurt, (2002e) 106,000, the historical capital of the Udmurt nation, and Votinsk, called Votka in Udmurt, (2002e) 101,000. Elabuga, called Alabugo in Udmurt, in Tatarstan, is also an important cultural center, (2002e) 67,000.

FLAG: The Udmurt national flag, the official flag of the republic, is a vertical tricolor of black, white, and red bearing a red eight-pointed star, representing the sun, centered on the white.

PEOPLE AND CULTURE: The Udmurts are a Finnic people, one of the nations that make up the eastern branch of the Finno-Ugric peoples concentrated in the Volga River basin of eastern European Russia. They are known as the "people of the woods," and the forests have had a great impact on their mentality, industry, and way of life. The Udmurt nation, one of the oldest eastern Finnish nations, is made up of three major divisions—the Udmurts, divided into northern and southern groups, in the south; and the Besmerians or Besermyans, of Tatar or Chavash* origin but assimilated into the Udmurt culture and language. Known for their folk crafts, embroidery, weaving, and wood carving, the Udmurts have retained their traditional culture in spite of centuries of assimilation pressures. The Udmurt weaving and embroidery, in the three basic colors of red, black, and white, remains an important part of the folk culture. Along with the Irish, the Udmurts have the highest proportion of red-haired people in Europe. Known for their hospitality and obstinacy, they are considered the most hardworking of the Finnic peoples of the Urals. The Udmurts consider the former Russian name for their nation, Votyak, as disparaging and offensive. In recent years the numbers of Udmurts has increased due to the former practice of registering as ethnic Russians for social, political, and employment advantages.

LANGUAGE AND RELIGION: The language of the Udmurts, Udmurt Kyl, is a Permian language of the Finno-Permian branch of the Finno-Ugric languages. The language, related to the language of the Komis,* is considered one of the oldest of the Finno-Ugric language group. It is spoken in two major dialects—North Udmurt or Vesermyan (Besermyan), spoken by the Besmerians; and South Udmurt, also known as Southwestern Udmurt, spoken by the Udmurts. The two Udmurt dialects are distinct but are mutually intelligible. The literary language is based on a transitional dialect between the North and South dialects. The Cyrillic alphabet used by the language was developed in the eighteenth century, and the first Udmurt grammar was published in 1775. There are only very minor dialectal differences among the scattered Udmurt population. The so-called city Udmurts have adopted Russian as their first language, with about 70%, mostly in smaller towns and rural areas, continuing to consider Udmurt their first language.

The Udmurts are mostly Russian Orthodox, but a minority has retained traditional beliefs, which include ancestor worship. Officially only about 55% claim membership in the official Russian Orthodox Church, while many others belong to the Old Believers or other sects. Evangelical groups have been active in the region in the 1990s, and many Udmurts have adopted their more liberal and exciting Christianity. Many retain their traditional beliefs, and holy groves and other shrines from the Udmurts' pre-Christian religion are maintained as centers of veneration. A minority, mostly in Bashkortostan, adopted Islam from the Muslim Bashkorts.

NATIONAL HISTORY: The ancestors of the Udmurts lived in the region between the Kama and Vyatka Rivers in Neolithic times. They emerged as an identifiable ethnic group in the sixth century A.D. in the present-day Kirov region and Tatarstan. Divided into tribes, the Udmurts appeared as an identifiable ethnic group in the sixth century A.D. The tribes survived by slash-and-burn agriculture, hunting, fishing, and trade with neighboring peoples. Until the conquest of their homeland by the Chavash in the eighth century, the Udmurts controlled a large territory north of the Volga River. Influenced by the Bulgar Chavash, the Udmurt tribes settled in agricultural villages in the fertile river valleys. The Udmurts remained under nominal Chavash rule until the thirteenth century.

Slavic traders and explorers from the Novgorod republic visited the northern Udmurt districts in the early twelfth century, and in 1174 Novgorodian colonists founded fortified settlements north of the Vyatka River. The Udmurts fiercely resisted the Slav colonization but gradually lost ground to the Slavs and abandoned their traditional lands in the north. Originally called Arans by the Russians, they were later referred to as Perm, a term also applied to a number of different Finnic peoples, and still later Votyaks.

The Golden Horde of the Mongols, advancing from the southeast, conquered and devastated the Udmurt lands in 1236–37, forcing many Udmurts to take refuge in the unconquered Slavic region to the north. With the breakup of the Golden Horde, in the fourteenth century, the southern Udmurts came under the rule of the successor state of the Tatars and were included in the Khanate of Kazan. The Udmurts in the north came under the control of the Slavic Vyatka Republic. By the late fourteenth century most of the Udmurts had accepted the Christian religion, brought to the region by Orthodox monks, although they retained their traditional beliefs or adopted Islam from their Muslim neighbors.

The northern Udmurts came under the rule of the Russians of the Duchy of Muscovy (Moscow) in 1489 following the conquest of the Vyatka Republic. The conquest of Kazan by the Muscovites in 1552 reunited the Udmurt peoples under Russian rule, although Kama Udmurt rebels continued to fight the Russians until 1558. Then began a period of the forced conversion to Orthodox Christianity. They were sometimes offered tax incentives or exemption from serving in the imperial army, but more often soldiers would arrive in Udmurt villages and force all the inhabitants to stand in the snow while an Orthodox priest read the liturgy and the *zakon bozhii*, God's Law, to them; they were then considered Orthodox Christians and were given Christian—that is, Russian—family names. The majority of the Udmurts only superficially accepted Christianity, and those living near Tatars and Bashkorts also adopted elements of Islam.

The Udmurts moved farther to the east and north, leaving the banks of the largest rivers, where the invaders were well established. The best and most fertile lands were confiscated and controlled by absentee Russian landlords, and poverty became widespread. The local Udmurt population, including the large Orthodox community, suffered a harsh Russian colonial rule. By the seventeenth century most Udmurts were tied to the large Russian estates in the region as serfs, unpaid agricultural workers. Kept in ignorance and poverty, the Udmurts' only escape was the lower ranks of the Orthodox priesthood. The small Udmurt population in the Kama River area produced the first educated minority, made up mostly of clergy, the spark that began an Udmurt cultural revival in the late nineteenth century.

The second half of the nineteenth century was marked by the rapid development of industry and culture in the region. Regional enterprises began to draw in large numbers of Udmurts, creating an urbanized class of workers. In 1899 the main railway line of the Perm-Cotlas route crossed Udmurtia, aiding its industrial development.

The vast majority of the Udmurt population lived in rural isolation until World War I. In 1910 the first literary works appeared in the Udmurt language; the development of a separate literary language accelerated the cultural and national revival. Thousands of illiterate Udmurt soldiers, sent to the front in 1914, began to desert and return home following the overthrow of the tsar in February 1917. The returning Udmurt soldiers formed a self-defense force as civil government collapsed.

The growth of national consciousness accelerated after the revolution. In the summer of 1917 the Udmurts convened a national congress, which voted for autonomy in a federal, democratic Russia, as promised by government agents. The Bolshevik coup in October ended the debate and thrust the non-Russian peoples of the Volga Basin into closer cooperation. The Udmurts began to erect a state as part of a federation of non-Russian states in the region.

Invading Bolshevik forces of the new Red Army occupied Udmurtia in March 1918. The Bolshevik authorities quickly suppressed the Udmurt national movement and transferred the capital of the region from the Udmurt city of Glazov to the mostly Russian industrial city of Izhevsk. To win Udmurt support, the Soviets distributed the lands of the great Russian estates to the former Udmurt tenant farmers. On 5 January 1921, following the Soviet victory in the Russian Civil War, the regional authorities, as part of the Bolsheviks' nationalities policy, established an autonomous Udmurt province.

The provincial Soviet government moved in 1921–22 to confiscate the agricultural lands distributed to the Udmurt farmers in 1918, which provoked a widespread revolt. Between 1920 and 1922 thousands of Udmurts perished in the fighting or from famine and disease. Thousands fled to escape the famine that decimated the population as a result of the civil war and revolt. In the 1930s the remaining Udmurt lands were confiscated and collectivized, and their dispossessed owners forced to settle on government communes. By 1937 tens of thousands had been deported, and Udmurt intellectuals had been nearly annihilated.

Despite the harshness of Soviet political rule, the Udmurts advanced in education and culture, particularly after gaining republic status in 1934. In 1922 only 22% of the region's population was literate, and only 10% of that small number were ethnic Udmurts. By the time World War II began in June 1941, Udmurt literacy had become widespread, and a number of writers and intellectuals were promoting the Udmurt culture, although they were forced to write and publish in the Russian language.

As part of the Ural industrial zone, during World War II Udmurtia received large industries and populations displaced by the war farther west. The Slavic influx reduced the Udmurts to a minority in their homeland, their minority status stimulating the first stirrings of modern Udmurt nationalism in the late 1940s and early 1950s. Until Stalin's death in 1953 the Udmurts, like the other non-Slav peoples of the region, were under intense pressure to assimilate into the wider Soviet culture, and all signs of dissent or Udmurt nationalism were harshly suppressed.

The Udmurts began to urbanize in the 1970s; the populations of many regional towns and cities doubled between 1969 and 1979. Urbanization produced a modern generation of Udmurts, educated in Russian and hardly aware of their unique history. Udmurt assimilation, well advanced by 1980, began to reverse in the late 1980s as young Udmurts took a new interest in their culture and language.

The Soviet liberalization initiated by Mikhail Gorbachev in the late 1980s accelerated the reculturation of the Udmurts. As strict Soviet controls disappeared, cultural and nationalist groups formed, demanding official status for their language, the opening of a specifically Udmurt university, and a change from the Russian Cyrillic alphabet to the Latin alphabet used in the West.

The government of the autonomous Udmurt republic, pressed by the growing Udmurt national movement, declared Udmurtia a sovereign state in October 1990. The Udmurt parliament then declared that federal laws were valid in the republic only when confirmed by the parliament. Following the disintegration of the Soviet Union in August 1991, militants advocated independence within a Volga federation, but the majority of the Udmurts feared the uncertainties of independence, while asserting their rights within the Russian Federation. The moderate nationalist groups believed that real autonomy would ensure that the Udmurts had not replaced Soviet domination for an equally oppressive Russian domination.

In the years since the emergence of the Russian Federation from the collapsing Soviet Union, the number of ethnic Udmurts has risen dramatically. To escape persecution or to gain economic advantages during the Soviet era, many Udmurts had registered as ethnic Russians, but since 1991 many have again assumed their traditional designation as ethnic Udmurts. The government of their homeland, the largest part of which forms an autonomous republic within the Russian Federation, has fostered the use of the Udmurt language and sponsors cultural activities, including traditional religious rituals. Political organizations, such as the Udmurt National Center, an umbrella coalition of nationalist, ecologists, and cultural groups, work for greater autonomy for the Udmurts.

The decline and low status of the Udmurt language became the focus of the growing nationalist movement dedicated to the revival of the Udmurt culture. In 1996 the republican legislature passed a national education bill that guaranteed the people the right to receive all forms of education and to be educated in their own language. Until then Udmurt was taught mainly in rural primary schools, and only as a preparation for entry in the Russian-language educational system.

The Udmurts have maintained a surprisingly cohesive sense of identity to the present. In spite of centuries of assimilationist pressure, the Udmurts in the 1990s demonstrated a strong sense of national identity. In the late 1990s, more than 80% of the Udmurts considered Udmurt as their first language, and an estimated third of the total Udmurt population, mostly living in rural areas, did not understand Russian. They also retained many elements of their traditional animistic religion. Closer ties to the other non-Russian nations of the Volga-Ural region are strengthening demands for greater local control of resources, education, and cultural activities.

SELECTED BIBLIOGRAPHY:

Colton, Timothy, and Robert Levgold, eds. *After the Soviet Union.* 1992.

Kirkow, Peter. *Russia's Provinces: Authoritarian Transformation versus Local Autonomy.* 1998.

Milner-Gulland, R.R., ed. *Cultural Atlas of Russia and the Former Soviet Union.* 1998.

Warhola, James W. *Politicized Ethnicity in the Russian Federation: Dilemmas of State Formation.* 1996.

Uighurs

Uygurs; Uyghurs; Uyghers; Uigurs; Uighuirs; Wei Wuer; East Turkestanis; Kashgar Turki

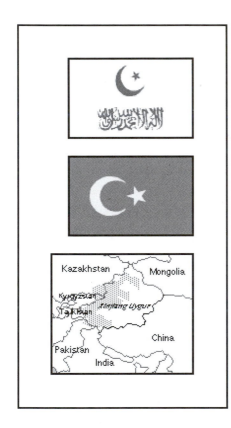

POPULATION: Approximately (2002e) 10,538,000 Uighurs in Central Asia, concentrated in the Xinjiang Uyghur Autonomous Region of northwestern China, with about 500,000 in the neighboring Central Asian states. Outside the region there are sizable Uighur communities in Europe, Turkey, Australia, Canada, the United States, Pakistan, and Russia. Population estimates are difficult, as no reliable census figures are available. The government acknowledged 8.5 million in 1996, but nationalists claim a population of 15 to 22 million.

THE UIGHUR HOMELAND: The Uighur homeland, known to nationalists as East Turkestan, comprises five distinct geographic regions—the Dzungarian Basin, the Tien Shan Mountains, the Tarim Basin, the Ili Basin, and the Kunlun Mountains. The huge region includes vast stretches of arid dunes and forbidding mountains that contain oil reserves estimated at up to 40 billion tons, accounting for nearly two-fifths of China's total. The region is dotted with the notorious *laogai*, slave labor camps. Most of the population is rural, concentrated in numerous oases that lie between the deserts and mountains. *Xinjiang Uyghur Autonomous Region (East Turkestan/Shärqiy Türkistan/Uighuristan)*: 635,829 sq. mi.—1,646,797 sq. km, (2002e) 21,624,000—Uighurs 46%, Han Chinese 42%, Kazakhs 7%, Hui* 4%, Kyrzyz 1%, Manchus,* Southern Mongols.* The Uighur capital and major cultural center is Wulumuqi (Urumchi), called Ürümçi by the Uighurs, (2002e) 1,118,000, metropolitan area 1,512,000. Other important cultural centers are Yining (Kuldja), called Kuldca by the Uighurs, (2002e) 220,000; Kashi (Kashgar), locally called Qäsqär, (2002e) 193,000; Shihezi, called Sihänzä, (2002e) 190,000, and Shache (Yarkand), locally called Yäkän, (2002e) 82,000.

FLAG: The flag of the nationalist movement is a white field bearing a small blue crescent moon and a five-pointed star centered above the Sha-hada, in blue Arabic script, reading "There is no God but God, Mohammed is the Prophet of God." The Uighur national flag, the flag of the East Turkestan movement, is a blue field charged with a large white crescent moon and a five-pointed star near the hoist.

PEOPLE AND CULTURE: The Uighurs, called Wai Wuer by the Chinese, are the descendents of the Dzungars (Left Hand), the left wing of the hordes of the medieval Mongol Empire. They are ethnically, culturally, and linguistically related to the Turkic peoples of Central Asia. The descendents of the traders of the Silk Road, the Uighurs still dominate the bazaars of Xinkiang, although the majority are farmers, living in rural areas. The Uighur are the most numerous of the 40 different national groups that inhabit the region. In the 1980s the very high Muslim birthrate and an exodus back to the Chinese heartland again made the Uighur the largest national group and reestablished a Muslim majority. Despite government programs to redress the situation, about 90% of all Uighurs live below China's established poverty line. Nationalists claim that at least one million Uighurs have died as a result of government policies and repression between 1949 and 1999, and another half-million have been driven into exile.

LANGUAGE AND RELIGION: The Uighur language, Vigus or New Uighur, is a language of the Uighur-Chagatai branch of the Turkic languages. It is spoken in several regional dialects and numerous subdialects; the literary language is based on the Taranchi dialect. The Arabic script, adopted in the eleventh century, remains the basis of the Uighur literary language, although officially the script has been replaced by the Latin alphabet, adapted to suit Chinese phonology in the 1960s and 1970s. The Arabic script was reintroduced in 1987. The Uighur language became a focus of Chinese assimilation efforts following unrest in the late 1990s. Under the pretext that "language must serve the unification of the motherland," a fierce campaign is under way to Sinicize the Uighur literary language. Until the communist takeover of Xinjiang in 1949, the literary language contained almost no Chinese words. Steps have been taken to introduce Chinese words and expressions. Around 70% of schools in the region teach in Chinese, and about 60% of the Uighurs are illiterate in their own language.

The Uighurs are a Sunni Muslim people, as are the related Kazakh, Kyrzyz, Tajik, and Uzbek minorities of Xinjiang. Prior to adopting Islam in the tenth and eleventh centuries, the Uighurs practiced Buddhism or shamanism. Suppressed during the antireligious Cultural Revolution in the 1960s and 1970s, Islam has revived and is again a vigorous part of the Uighur culture. Like most Central Asians, the Uighurs practice a form of folk Islam, a blend of Muslim beliefs and animistic rituals. Men traditionally wear an embroidered cap called a *doppa*, while the women of the more conservative families cover their faces with veils.

NATIONAL HISTORY: Possibly the human race's earliest home aside from Mesopotamia, the vast Central Asian plateau has been contested by the Turkic and Chinese peoples for thousands of years. The ancient Turkic cities, important stops on the Silk Road, the caravan routes that linked China and the Mediterranean, knew many conquerors. The Uighurs are mentioned in the chronicles of the Chinese Han dynasty, which that ruled from 206 B.C. to A.D. 220. Ancient Greek, Iranian, and Chinese sources included references to Uighur tribes living west of the Yellow River.

The Uighurs established their first national state in 744 under Kutluk Bilge Kul. His son, Moyunchur, subdued neighboring Turkic peoples, consolidated the kingdom, and extended his rule to Lake Baikal in the north and India in the south. A large Chinese invasion was defeated in 751 by a combined force of Uighurs, Arabs, and Tibetans.* The Uighur kingdom reached its apex in the late eighth century, but their power and prestige began to decline under a series of wars and weak leaders. In 795 a new dynasty was established that promoted religion and culture but became embroiled in wars with the Kyrgyz to the north. In 840 the Kyrgyz overran the Uighur state and took control of the capital.

Militarily absorbed by the Mongols of Genghis Khan, the Uighurs formed the left wing of the Mongol-Turkic hordes that eventually conquered most of the known world. Islam, traditionally introduced by Arab invaders in 934, spread rapidly along the Silk Road and was embraced by the Uighur tribes. Numerous small states founded in the fourteenth century gained fame as centers of Muslim learning and tolerance. The Uighur cities, centers of world trade, boasted large populations of disparate ethnic and religious groups, extensive libraries, elaborate mosques, and opulent palaces and public buildings.

China's Manchu rulers dispatched a huge army, which overran the region in a swift campaign in 1756–59, effectively ending the celebrated ethnic and religious tolerance of the region. Interethnic conflicts and sporadic rebellions constantly threatened Chinese rule. Great Britain held all of India with just 30,000 troops, while Manchu China in 1825 required a garrison of over 100,000 to control the region's rebellious Muslim tribes. Between 1759 and 1862 the Uighurs rebelled 42 times.

A widespread Muslim rebellion in 1863–66, encouraged by Russian and British agents, loosened China's hold. Russian troops occupied Kuldja and the Ili Valley in 1871, and the British supported Uighur efforts to create a separate state centered on Kashgar. The Kashgar kingdom was recognized by the Ottoman Empire, tsarist Russia, and the United Kingdom. The Chinese reconquest in 1876–78, marked by savage reprisals, drove thousands of refugees to seek shelter in neighboring Russian territory.

Sinkiang, later called Xinkiang, meaning "new dominion" or "new territories," was annexed to the Manchu Chinese empire on 18 November 1884. The region was divided into four administrative regions, while the Uighurs, who were considered "rebellious," were subjected to a policy aimed at destroying their pride and self-respect. The various national groups living in the region were divided and discord encouraged. All cities, towns, and counties were given Chinese names. Uighurs were forced to marry Han Chinese, wear Chinese dress, and show exaggerated respect for Chinese officials. Local government officials were given the right to punish at their discretion, including executions. Any complaints against Chinese officials brought brutal reprisals against those who made the complaints, their families, and often their towns or villages. The feudal Chinese administration executed thousands of Uighurs, up to a million according to Uighur nationalists. Another 500,000 fearing Chinese suppression, escaped to neighboring countries, including Russia and Afghanistan, and 200,000 were forced from the southern districts to the Ili Valley as forced labor, to provide food for the Manchu Chinese forces stationed in the area.

The Muslims again rebelled as news reached the region of the overthrow of the Manchu dynasty in 1911, beginning several decades of instability and turbulence in Chinese Turkestan. The first Chinese republican leader, Dr. Sun Yat Sen, acknowledged the Turkish peoples' rights, but after his death in 1924, power passed to Chiang Kai-shek, who was far less tolerant of the minority nations. Thousands died opposing the assimilation policies of the Chinese Kuomintang government. In 1931 the Uighurs rebelled and drove all Chinese officials from the territory. Aided and encouraged by the Soviet Union, on 23 January 1934 the rebels declared Xinjiang independent of China as the Islamic Republic of East Turkestan. Undermined by Soviet duplicity, the new state fell to returning Chinese troops.

A renewed Muslim revolt in 1936–37 culminated in the virtual collapse of Chinese control of Xinjiang in the early years of World War II. In June 1943 the Kazakhs rebelled in the north, soon joined by the Uighurs and other Muslim peoples. In 1944 the Mongols joined the revolt. The rebels took the last Chinese garrison, Kuldja, in January 1945 and on 13 January 1945 declared the independence of the Republic of East Turkestan, under a government led by Ali Khan Türe.

The Soviet government, fearing the affects of the revolt on Soviet Turkestan, pressured the rebel government to negotiate with the Nationalist Chinese government of Chiang Kai-shek. After eight months of talks the rebels agreed to accept political autonomy and to disarm. The Nationalist authorities, as soon as the rebels had laid down their arms, began a brutal retribution. The Nationalist betrayal eventually cost Chiang Kai-shek a major defeat in the civil war with the communists: the entire region went over to the Red Chinese without a fight in late 1949. After the nearly bloodless communist victory in Xinjiang, 100,000 soldiers were put to work clearing land for farming, creating a vast agricultural colony and a strong frontier defense garrison.

Communist rule, consolidated in 1949, proved as harsh as that of the Nationalists. Mao Tse-tung completely ignored his own promises of autonomy. To dilute the region's Muslim majority, the government sponsored mass colonization beginning in 1954. From only 3% in 1950, the proportion of Han Chinese grew to nearly 50% in 1975. In 1955, the region was organized as a nominally autonomous region of the Chinese People's Republic. Targeting the region for forced assimilation during the Chinese Cultural Revolution in 1966–76, Chinese cadres destroyed thousands of mosques and shrines, and paraded learned religious and cultural leaders through the streets with pigs' heads, anathema to Muslims, dangling around their necks. Public prayer was banned, Koranic schools closed, and Han settlers raised pigs in Muslim neighborhoods.

Isolated from the outside world, Xinjiang became the government's dumping ground. Numerous labor camps were established to hold thousands of "criminals," mostly political prisoners, not only from the province but also from eastern China. The goods produced by unpaid prison labor were often exported for profit. The use of the region as a dumping ground also extended to the environment. China's nuclear test facility was located in the region and numerous tests have been carried out. The authorities have steadily dumped toxic wastes across the region in ways that poisoned both the land and the water. Many Uighurs suffer from the health effects of the nuclear testing and the careless disposal of toxic wastes.

The excesses of the Cultural Revolution gave way to a more relaxed communist administration, and in 1981 the region's four major non-Chinese languages regained official status. A limited number of mosques reopened, and some religious schools reopened, but the momentous changes already under way across the Soviet border had begun to spread to the region.

Supported by the newly independent states of western Turkestan on their western border, the Uighur national movement became a potent force. Nationalism grew rapidly in the 1980s and culminated in an abortive insurrection in April 1990. The Uighurs, joined by Kirgzyzs and Kazakhs, again rose up against Chinese rule. In April in the remote town of Akto, more than 1000 residents, furious at not being allowed to build a mosque, took to the streets. More than 60 people were killed in clashes with Chinese troops. In July 1990 the authorities in Xinjiang announced the arrest of 7,900 people in a crackdown on "criminal activities of ethnic splittists and other criminal offenders."

In early March 1993 Uighur nationalists took their message and their plea for independence to the United Nations, but they received little open support. Separatist violence in 1996–97 led to a crackdown, but it was moderated by China's reluctance to alienate Islamic governments in the Middle East. Riots and demonstrations in various cities were met by force, leaving a number of Uighurs dead. Nationalists claimed that hundreds died in the uprising of 1996–97, although news from the region is censored and difficult to obtain. Much of the violence goes largely unreported; journalists and diplomats are prevented or discouraged from visiting the region. The demonstrations in Xinjiang sparked parallel demonstrations in support of Uighur rights in Washington, Istanbul, London, and in various Muslim countries.

The Chinese response to Uighur unrest was typically ruthless. Military experts estimate that the Chinese government stationed a million troops in the region. Nationalists claim that over 1,000 people were executed between 1997 and 2000, and that over 10,000 activists or sympathizers were arrested.

Despite its size, three times that of France, Xinjiang has just six official entry points by land and only one by air. Chinese government control even extends to time. The cities of Xinjiang, thousands of miles east of Beijing, must maintain the same time zone as the capital, with the absurd result that the region is dark almost until noon during the winter.

The Uighurs have resisted assimilation for decades, relying on their cultural, linguistic, and geographic differences to combat Chinese influences. They claim they have nothing in common with the Han Chinese or their culture to the east but remain a Central Asian nation—historically, religiously, linguistically, and culturally related to the Turkestani peoples to the west. In the late 1990s, the politically and economically struggling Central Asian states responded to Chinese offers of increased trade and investment by curbing Uighur agitation in their territories.

The Uighur national movement remains factionalized and divided, particularly since the death in 1995 of Yusuf Alptekin, a former official of their short-lived republic in the 1940s. However, a conference in 1999 of the Uighur National Congress, involving most of the major national groups, began the process of forming a viable, united national organization.

The economic situation worsened as China's eastern provinces progressed, leaving the far northwest to stagnate. The Uighurs receive little benefit from their oil wealth; Uighur separatists claim that almost all of the industrial and technical positions are reserved to entice Han Chinese to migrate to Xinjiang, while large numbers of Uighurs remain unemployed, adding to the rising incidence of crime and drug trafficking. Rail and oil pipeline links to Central Asia and its growing production of oil and natural gas were extended to the border near Kashgar in 1999, making Xinjiang important as a link to the natural resources of the former Soviet republics of Central Asia. The improvement of rail and road links is seen by the Uighurs as a government preparation for yet another influx of Han Chinese.

The Uighurs are fervently Muslim but see their cause as anticolonial, not Islamic. The Chinese government, attempting to discredit the national movement, accused it of having links to Islamic extremist groups in Pakistan and Afghanistan in November 2001, following the terrorist attacks in the United States. What little foreign support it receives comes mostly from the Uighur exile communities in Turkey and other European countries and in North America. Most world governments ignore the plight of the Uighurs, preferring not to jeopardize trade links with the Chinese government.

Official suppression of dissident Uighurs increased in late 2001, portrayed as part of the world's fight against Islamic extremists. Although most Western nations have carefully differentiated between terrorist and nationalist groups, the Chinese government brands all nationalists in Xinjiang as terrorists.

SELECTED BIBLIOGRAPHY:

Benson, Linda. *The Ili Rebellion: The Moslem Challenge to Chinese Authority in Xinjiang 1944–1949*. 1990.

Cheng, Jack. *Sinkiang Story*. 1977.

Forbes, Andrew. *Warlords and Muslims in Chinese Central Asia*. 1986.

Rudelson, Justin Jon. *Oasis Identities: Uighur Nationalism along China's Silk Road*. 1998.

Ural Cossacks

Ural'skie Kazaki; Transcaspian Cossacks

POPULATION: Approximately (2002e) 140,000 Ural Cossacks in the former Soviet Union, concentrated in the Ural River valley of western Kazakhstan. There are Ural Cossack communities in adjacent areas of the Russian Federation. Outside the region there are Ural Cossack communities in Germany, Canada, the United States, and Australia.

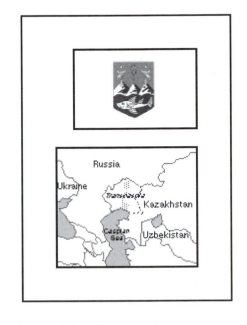

THE URAL COSSACK HOMELAND: The Ural Cossack homeland occupies a vast plain, part of the Caspian Depression, in western Kazakhstan. Much of the region is sparsely populated salt steppe or desert, with the majority of the population concentrated in the fertile lowlands along the river and around the northern shore of the Caspian Sea, where there are extensive marshes. The Ural Cossack homeland, locally called Caspia or Transcaspia, has no official status, forming the Kazakh provinces of Batis Kazakhstan and Atirau. *Batis Kazakhstan-Atirau (Transcaspia)*: 165,945 sq. mi.—429,796 sq. km, (2002e) 977,000—Russians 36%, Kazakhs 22%, Ural Cossacks 12%, others 30%. Ural Cossack capital and major cultural center is Oral, called Uralsk in Russian, (2002e) 188,000. The other important cultural center is Atyaü, called Guryev by the Russian-speaking population, (2002e) 137,000.

FLAG: The Ural Cossack national flag, the flag of the national movement, is a white field bearing the Ural Cossack coat of arms comprising a blue sea, three hills, and the various traditional symbols of the group.

PEOPLE AND CULTURE: The Ural Cossacks are a distinct Slavic people, one of the 11 historical Cossack hosts of Russia. Although their homeland is now in the Republic of Kazakhstan, they form a subgroup of the Russians. Their ancestry includes Slavs, Kazakhs, Turkmens, Germans, Ukrainians, and other Turkic peoples, with the Slavic strain predominant. National identity is based on the their geographic location, dialect, and distinct history. The Ural Cossack culture stresses independence and self-reliance. Their motto, "Always on horseback, ready to fight" remains to the present, although the majority are now settled farmers or industrial workers in the region's towns and cities. The military traditions of the past, revived in the 1990s, have again become an integral part of the culture. The name "Cossack" derives from the Turkic word *"kazak,"* which means "free man" or "adventurer."

LANGUAGE AND RELIGION: The Ural Cossacks speak a dialect of the Cossack language that incorporates extensive borrowings from Kazakh and Tatar. The dialect, which developed in the isolation of the early settlements, emerged as a distinct dialect in the early eighteenth century. The majority of the Ural Cossacks speak standard Russian, but few have bothered to learn Kazakh, the official language of the country that now includes their homeland.

The religious beliefs of the Ural Cossacks belong to the Orthodox tradition in Russia, although a substantial minority are Old Believers, a schematic sect that broke with the Russian church in the seventeenth century. Many fled persecutions in European Russia to settle in the region, where their conservative beliefs spread among the Cossack settlements.

NATIONAL HISTORY: The vast steppe region was nominally controlled by small Kazakh tribes, who lived a nomadic way of life. The first Slavic settlers were deserters from the Don Cossacks to the west. They were later joined by refugees fleeing reprisals for peasant uprisings, bandit groups, and escaping serfs. They organized small bands in the region, which was virtually beyond government control.

The extension of Russian administration to the region gave the communities greater coherence and unity. Regulations were adopted allowing the groups, called the Ural Cossacks, to maintain their traditional independence in exchange for personal loyalty to the tsar and military service. In 1591 Tsar Fyodor created a regiment of Ural Cossacks.

The Cossacks settled on the right bank of the Ural River to protect the colonists from attacks by Kazakh tribes. In the early seventeenth century, they established a fortified line, the Lower Yaik Line, from Mukhranov, near Orenburg over 450 miles (724 km) to Chunev, where the Ural empties into the Caspian Sea. The infertility of much of the territory made it unsuitable for farming; fishing and cattle herding became the major economic occupations. The Ural Cossacks made their capital at Yaik, founded in 1613 and renamed Uralsk in 1775.

All Ural Cossack males were required to serve in the armed units from their eighteenth to their twentieth birthdays, and outside the territory from the age of 20 to 25, as often as needed. Most Ural Cossacks served a total of 12 years, three of them outside their homeland. The *ataman* of the Ural Cossacks served as the elected leader during peace but had despotic powers during time of war.

The revolt of Stenka Raza in 1667 against the tyranny of the tsar brought the Cossacks of the region into full rebellion. When the revolt collapsed, they were punished with sanctions, deportations, and a loss of part of their historical independence. The Ural Cossack Army, called the Yaitsk Army until 1775, participated in the widespread uprising in 1707 led by the Don Cossacks.* Emelian Pugachev capitalized on the grievances of the Ural Cossacks to lead them in revolt in 1773. The movement spread up and down the Ural River and westward to the Volga Basin. When the rebellion was crushed, the Ural Cossacks lost their remaining independence. Control was transferred from their elected *ataman* to an appointed leader. From 1782 the Ural Cossack Army was managed by the government of Astrakhan or the governor-general of Orenburg. In 1803 provisional regulations about military service were introduced, provoking considerable unrest.

The military units formed part of the Cossack units raised to fight Napoleon's invasion of Russia in 1812. Many of the Ural Cossacks, skilled in tracking and living off the land, terrorized the retreating French troops.

In the mid-nineteenth century the Ural Cossacks participated in the Russian conquest of the Central Asian territories just to the east. New provisional regulations governing the administration of the Ural Cossack homeland were introduced in 1868. Matters pertaining to the civil administration were to remain with the Ural Cossack Army but were subordinated to common local bodies. Military matters were left to the governor-general of the newly formed Ural Province, who was also appointed as the *ataman* of the Ural Cossacks. In 1874 several thousand Ural Cossacks and their families were exiled to Central Asia in the region of the Aral Sea for disobedience toward the new regulations.

During World War I, the Ural Cossack Army supplied nine cavalry regiments, one battery, one Life Guard squadron, nine special and reserve squadrons, and two steppe teams, totaling over 10,000 men. The Ural Cossack Army remained part of the imperial army from the early seventeenth century to 1917, not only as a fighting unit but also providing the tsar's own squadron of Life Guards.

The revolution that ended the monarchy, and therefore the oath of personal loyalty to the tsar, freed the Ural Cossacks from any obligation to the new Russian state. As chaos spread following the Bolshevik coup in October 1917, they joined the anti-Bolshevik Whites, and the Ural region became an anti-Bolshevik stronghold. An estimated third of all male Ural Cossacks died in the bloody Russian Civil War.

In 1920, after the White defeat, the Ural Cossack community was officially disbanded by the new Soviet government. Cossack traditions, associated with the precommunist Russia, were forbidden. Thousands escaped and fled west, most settling in Germany. There they maintained their military discipline as the Ural Cossack Choir, under the direction of Andrei Soloeich. Their early military training, vocal talent, and discipline laid the foundation of success but also maintained their small nation in exile.

In 1936 the Soviet dictator, Joseph Stalin, realizing that Germany was becoming a serious threat, decided to rehabilitate the Cossack hosts as military units. The Ural Cossacks were again allowed to train, carry arms, and eventually to fight in the Red Army when Germany invaded in 1941. Many Cossacks, especially those living in exile, joined the Nazi campaign against the hated Soviet Union. Some 28,000 Cossacks and their families were in northern Italy when the war ended. They crossed the Alps into Austria and were confined to camps by the British authorities. Eventually they were forcibly repatriated to the Soviet Union, most to perish by execution or in the Gulag in Siberia.

The Ural Cossacks never forgot their history or their heritage. When the Soviet Union began to relax its stringent hold on society in the late 1980s, the Ural Cossacks began to organize and mobilize their demoralized nation in an effort to restore their pre-Soviet status. When the Soviet Union collapsed in 1991, the Ural Cossacks found themselves living in a foreign country, the new republic of Kazakhstan.

In 1991 the Ural Cossacks were legally registered as a cultural society, but the registration was withdrawn when the group organized itself as a Cossack host, claiming the right to carry arms. Demands for cultural and political autonomy followed, particularly calls for annexation to the Russian Federation. The inclusion of the Ural Cossacks in the Union of Cossacks of the Volga and Ural in 1993 was opposed by the Kazakhstan government. Relations between the leadership of the host and the government continued to deteriorate over demands for the Cossacks' traditional self-government.

On a visit to Moscow in 1995, Kazakh foreign minister Kasymzhomart Kokayev was confronted with demands by Russia's foreign minister for consultations on the situation of Cossacks in Kazakhstan. The issue of the large Russian-speaking population in northern Kazakhstan occupied much of the meeting, but the increasingly problematic Ural Cossacks also received attention as part of the contentious Caspian Sea issue of oil, pipelines, and territorial claims. The Ural Cossack leaders had demanded autonomy or annexation to Russia and insisted on their traditional right to carry weapons. The Kazakh authorities arrested two leaders, including Ural Cossack *ataman* Nikolai Gunkin, whose followers threatened to kidnap Kazakh emissaries to Russia in reprisal. The Ural Cossacks warned that they would cut roads and impose an economic blockade of Kazakhstan if Gunkin was put on trial for irredentist activities. Gunkin was later given a three-month sentence in a corrective labor institution, which was dropped on appeal. Gunkin then attempted to run in legislative elections, in an apparent effort to gain immunity from prosecution.

In May 1999, reacting to the confiscation by Kazakh authorities of traditional Cossack costumes, the Cossacks threatened to emigrate, leaving the Ural region depopulated, a serious economic threat. Some concessions by the Kazakh government ended the crisis, but demands for greater self-government, and cultural, linguistic, and educational rights continued to color relations between the Ural Cossacks and the government.

Ural Cossacks seek an autonomous homeland in the region, but most have refused to become embroiled in the contentious issue of oil drilling in the Caspian lowlands, which both Russia and Kazakhstan claim. The Cossacks claim that theirs is a separate issue. They have denounced discrimination against their Cossack-Russian language, the closing of Russian language schools, attacks on Orthodox churches, the dismissal of Slavs from high-level posts in the civil service, and the arrest of Ural Cossack leaders for nationalist activities.

Despite Kazakh government efforts to maintain their authority in the Ural region, the rise of the Ural Cossack militias has seriously threatened government control. The revival of their military tradition has added yet another layer to the already tense ethnic, religious, and political relations between the Slavs and the Kazakhs. The poor state of the economy and the growing importance of the region's petroleum reserves have added economic issues to the nationalist revival. Their geographic location, at the edge of Russian territory, has allowed ultranationalist forces in Russia to use the Ural Cossacks as a cause and an example of the persecution of Slavs in the "near abroad."

The majority of the Ural Cossacks in the region would be content with some measure of self-government, religious and cultural freedom, and education in their own language. Government attempts to introduce Kazakh into the school system and the local administrations have been met with serious resistance. The Ural Cossacks see themselves as a distinct Slavic national group—not exactly Russian, but not Kazakh either. The growth of national identity, which began with the collapse of the Soviet Union in 1991 and continued with the Ural Cossacks' situation as a minority in a new country, is now one of the most serious ethnic problems facing the Kazakhstan government.

SELECTED BIBLIOGRAPHY:

Chinn, Jeff, and Robert Kaiser. *Russians as the New Minority: Ethnicity and Nationalism in the Soviet Successor States.* 1996.
Groushko, Mike. *Cossack: Warrior Riders of the Steppes.* 1993.
Nikitin, N.I. *The Origin of the Cossacks of Siberia.* 1999.
Ure, John. *The Cossacks.* 1999.

Uralians

Uralnaks; Ural Russians; Uralsk Russians

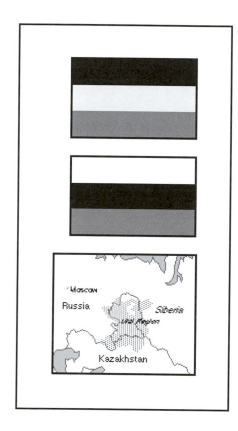

POPULATION: Approximately (2002e) 12,050,000 Uralians in the Russian Federation, concentrated in the Ural *oblasts* of Perm, Sverdlovsk, Chelyabinsk, and Kurgan. Outside the region there are Uralian communities in the neighboring provinces and republics, in Moscow, and in various parts of Siberia and Central Asia.

THE URALIAN HOMELAND: The Uralian homeland lies in central Russia on both sides of the southern Ural Mountains, which divide Europe from Asia. The Ural Region stretches from the Arctic Ocean to the Kazakhstan border, occupies the steppe lands and foothills of the Urals in eastern European Russia and the vast Ural Steppe in western Siberia. The Ural area, densely forested and rich in minerals, is one of the major industrial regions of the Russian Federation. The region comprises the provinces *(oblasts)* of Perm, Sverdlovsk, Chelyabinsk, and Kurgan. *Ural Region*: 198,571 sq. mi.—514,296 sq. km, (2002e) 12,076,000—Uralians 92%, Bashkorts* 4%, Permyaks* 1%, other Russians 3%. The Uralian capital and major cultural center is Yakterinburg (2002e) 1,263,000, metropolitan area 1,390,000. Other important cultural centers are Chelyabinsk, (2002e) 1,082,000, metropolitan area 1,216,000, and Perm, (2002e) 1,006,000.

FLAG: The Uralian national flag, the flag of the regional movement, is a horizontal tricolor of black, yellow, and green. The flag of the republic declared in 1918, a horizontal tricolor of white, black, and green, is the flag used those advocating a separate Ural Republic.

PEOPLE AND CULTURE: The Ural Russians, calling themselves Uralnaks, are the descendents of early Cossack settlers, freed serfs, and later Slav settlers who were transferred wholesale to the region before and during World War II. Historically and physically removed from the European Russian heartland, the Uralians see themselves as Russian but separate, belonging neither to the European Russians to the west nor the Siberians* to the east. The descendents of pioneers and later groups unwanted in European Russia, the Uralians have developed many unique traditions and customs, often borrowing from the Bashkorts and other non-Russian peoples. The Uralians are highly urbanized; the majority live in the region's large industrial cities. Economic grievances and a shared sense of neglect and distance from the centers of power in the old Soviet Union led to the development of a distinctly Uralian identity.

LANGUAGE AND RELIGION: The Uralians speak several Russian dialects with marked Ukrainian, Cossack, and Turkic borrowings. In the south, the major influence has been from the neighboring Bashkorts; in the north, the dialects have been influenced by words and phrases taken from the Komis* and Permyaks. In the isolated highlands, forms and expressions that have disappeared elsewhere in Russia remain in use.

The majority of the Ural peoples are Russian Orthodox, with an influential Roman Catholic minority—mostly suspect religious groups, deported from Russia's western provinces during and after World War II. The region's early isolation served as a refuge for various dissident religious groups, such as the Old Believers, a schismatic sect of the Orthodox church.

NATIONAL HISTORY: The original inhabitants of the region, Finnic Permian peoples in the north and Turkic tribes in south, came under loose Mongol rule in the thirteenth century. The Tatars,* absorbed into the Mongol hordes, gained control of the Volga River basin and much of the southern Ural Mountains at the breakup of the Mongol Empire in the fourteenth century. The powerful Tatar khanates of Kazan and Sibir extracted tribute from the Slavic peoples west of the Ural Mountains, often holding sway as far west as Moscow.

The Ural Mountains were known to the medieval Slavs as the Stone Belt. Slav explorers and fur traders from the Novgorod republic began to penetrate the region in the twelfth century, setting up trading relations with the indigenous peoples. The expanding Russian state, the Moscovite duchy, extended its authority west of the mountains in the fifteenth century, and in 1552 the Russians defeated the Tatars and absorbed the Khanate of Kazan. The conquest of Kazan and the subsequent conquest of Sibir in 1581 opened the way for European colonization. Slavic colonists settled the western slopes of the Urals, founding the town of Perm, named for the Permian peoples, in 1568. The region's mineral wealth led to the establishment of the first ironworks in the 1630s.

The Slavic colonists, spreading across the more fertile areas from their center at Perm, absorbed or displaced the earlier populations of Bashkorts, Udmurts,* Komis, Permyaks, and other Finnic and Turkic peoples. Cossacks moved out to found a string of forts on the eastern slopes and on the Ural Steppe beyond. The Cossacks established Yekaterinburg in 1721 and Chelyabinsk in 1736. Civilian colonists accompanied or followed the Cossacks as they pushed into the frontier districts. When a substantial Slav population had settled in the region, they began to demand annexation to the Russian empire, which would bring additional troops to protect them against attacks by hostile tribes. The Yekaterinburg region was annexed by Russia between 1726 and 1762, and the southern districts after 1731. The history of the region is remarkably similar to the expanding of the frontier in eastern North America.

The territory, rugged and mountainous, and far from the centers of Russian life in European Russia, grew slowly in the eighteenth and early nineteenth centuries. The freeing of the serfs in the Russian Empire in 1861 brought an influx of land-hungry colonists. The freed serfs were allowed to take possession for free of parcels land formerly held by the region's Turkic and Finnic peoples. The colonists received little practical government help and suffered incredible hardships. Isolated and neglected, they developed a strong antigovernment, anti-European attitude that exists to the present. The construction of the Trans-Siberian Railroad to Kurgan in the 1890s opened the way to the mass colonization of the Ural Steppe and of the high plateau of the middle Urals. The population nearly doubled between 1890 and 1910.

Thousands of military conscripts from the region were sent to the front when war began in 1914. Disheartened and disillusioned, they mostly deserted and returned home following the Russian Revolution in February 1917. The returnees enthusiastically joined the revolution that was spreading from European Russia. After the Bolshevik coup overthrew the Provisional Government of Russia in October 1917, the region was roamed by armed bands—pro-Bolshevik, anti-Bolshevik, and a small separatist group made up of deserters and Cossacks trying to protect their homeland from the spreading civil war.

Bolshevik forces, including local groups, took control of most of the region in March 1918, but their hold extended to only a few of the major towns and along the railway. The Czech Legion, Czech and Slovak prisoners of war trying to return to Europe via the Trans-Siberian Railroad through Siberia, became stranded in the region as the fighting spread. An organized military group, the Legion established its headquarters at Chelyabinsk, which became a haven for the various anti-Bolshevik factions. The Czech Legion fought the Bolsheviks for control of the vital railroad and the major centers of population in the southern Ural Mountains.

Nationalists in Ekaterinburg proclaimed the Provisional Regional Government of Ural, known by its Russian initials, VOPU, in early 1918. The VOPU government was opposed by the anti-Bolshevik White forces. When Admiral Aleksandr Kolchak, the self-designated Supreme Ruler of

Russia, took control of Ekaterinburg he ordered the execution leaders of the Uralian national movement. The last Romanov tsar, Nicholas II, was overthrown during the early months of the revolution. He and his family were arrested by the new Provisional Government and transported as prisoners to the east, away from areas held by their supporters, the remnants of the imperial army. As chaos spread, the Romanovs fell into the hands of the members of the newly formed Ural *soviet*, or Bolshevik council. Held prisoner in Yekaterinburg, the former imperial family became the object of an anti-Bolshevik White offensive. On 16 July 1918, as the rescuers neared, the Soviet authorities, possibly on Lenin's orders, executed the entire family.

By 1920, the Whites had been defeated and the Urals region had come under firm Soviet rule. Soviet economic experimentation and the crushing of anti-Soviet groups in European Russia sent a steady stream of deportees to the Urals in the 1920s and 1930s. Slave labor camps, begun under the authority of Joseph Stalin, the Soviet dictator after 1924, expanded rapidly. The prisoners, working in abysmal conditions, were forced to construct road, dams, and tunnels. After 1929, when collectivization of all land was begun, many of the remaining free tracts were forcibly colonized by *kulaks*, formerly free farmers, persecuted and deported from the European provinces.

The outbreak of war in 1941, when Stalin's ally Adolf Hitler suddenly ordered his forces to invade the Soviet Union, drastically changed the Urals. During the war much of the Soviet Union's heavy industry, as well as the workers and their families, threatened by the Nazi advance, were transferred to the Urals region. The rapid increase of population required an administrative reorganization. In 1943 Chelyabinsk and Sverdlovsk were organized as separate administrative provinces.

In the 1950s and 1960s, the region, with its inadequate housing, aging industries, and lack of amenities, became a center of unrest. Industrial workers formed the core of groups demanding improved housing and working conditions. By 1965, the region had been labeled a problem region by the ministers in Moscow. Conditions continued to deteriorate in the 1970s and early 1980s, with growing shortages of basic goods and food.

The liberalization of Soviet life in the late 1980s finally allowed decades' worth of grievances to be voiced openly. Grievances ranged from neglect and disdain by the centers of power in European Russia to massive pollution, which was doing great harm to the health of the inhabitants. Demands for an end to the economic control by ministries in Moscow led to demands for political as well as economic autonomy. Protests against receiving fewer privileges in taxation than the Russian heartland and too little local control of resources sparked a movement for local autonomy. The movement, which began as an economic revolt, opened the way for a torrent of additional, local grievances, from poor living standards to a lack of school books, to demands for the protection of local dialects and cultural traditions.

In June 1993 the Sverdlovsk Oblast unilaterally declared itself a member republic of the Russian Federation, with the greater independence associated with that status; by October the other Ural provinces had voted to do so as well. To pressure Moscow to accept their bids, the provinces began to withhold taxes and block government directives. In December 1993 Russia's president, Boris Yeltsin, dismissed the provincial leader of Sverdlovsk, Eduard Rossel. Ministers in Moscow labeled the region a separatist center that threatened Russia's territorial integrity.

In May 2000, the Russian government, in an effort to curb the powers of the powerful rulers of the various region, divided the country into a number of planning regions. The new Ural Region, stretching from the Kazakhstan border north to the Arctic Sea, was placed under the control of the former interior minister, Pyotr Latyshev. His authoritarian manner led to confrontations with local leaders, particularly the powerful governor of Sverdlovsk. In late October 2000, the government used a court ruling to remove Alexander Rutskoi, an ex–fighter pilot, regionalist leader, and governor of the Kurgan Oblast.

In late 2000, the federal government took control of most local agencies that had been run by the provincial governments. Appointments of local government loyalists or transferees from Moscow or other areas of European Russia were keenly resented. The government crackdown on local autonomy proved to be unimpressive as production remained static, economic grievances continued, and popular unrest spread.

In the decade since the collapse of the Soviet Union, thousands of European Russians have left the region to return to the Russian heartland. Many, drawn by the higher wages paid during the Soviet region, had little in common with the Uralians and were often resented for their privileges. Their departure reinforced the felling in the Urals of the differences between the Uralians and other Russians. Although economically the region is still trying to recover and to update aging industries, the Uralians have received little from the federal government, reinforcing the sentiment of "them" and "us."

SELECTED BIBLIOGRAPHY:

Alexseev, Mikhail A., ed. *Center-Periphery Conflict in Post-Soviet Russia: A Federation Imperiled.* 1999.

Harris, James R. *The Great Urals: Regionalism and the Evolution of the Soviet System.* 1999.

Kirkov, Peter. *Russia's Provinces: Authoritarian Transformation versus Local Autonomy?* 1998.

Stavrakis, Peter J., ed. *Beyond the Monolith: The Emergence of Regionalism in Post-Soviet Russia.* 1997.

Uttarakhandis

Uttarkashis; Garhwalis-Kumaonis; Uttaranchalis

POPULATION: Approximately (2002e) 7,370,000 Uttarakhandis in northern India, concentrated in the Himalayan state of Uttaranchal in northern India. Outside the region there are Uttarakhandi communities in neighboring areas of Nepal and Tibet, and in the United Kingdom, Canada, and the United States.

THE UTTARAKHANDI HOMELAND: The Uttarakhandi homeland occupies a rugged area in the Himalayas in northern India. Much of the region is uninhabitable; most inhabitants are in the densely populated river valleys. Forests cover about two-thirds of the region and contain many species not found anywhere else. The five headstreams of the Ganges all rise in Uttarakhand, although an acute shortage of water exists there. The region forms the state of Uttaranchal in India. *State of Uttaranchal (Uttarakhand)*: 19,740 sq. mi.—51,125 sq. km, (2002e) 8,615,000—Uttarakhandis 85%, Bhotias 12%, other Indians 3%. The Uttarakhandi capital and major cultural center is Dehra Dun, locally called Dehradun, (2002e) 348,000, metropolitan area 471,000. The other important cultural centers are Hardwan, locally called Haridwar, (2002e) 191,000, and Haldwani (2002e) 139,000.

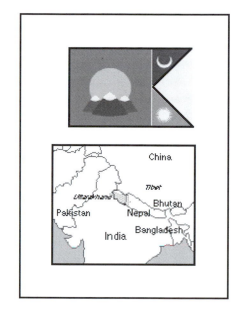

FLAG: The swallowtail Uttarakhandi national flag, the flag of the national movement, is a green square bearing a yellow sun behind three brown snow-capped mountains, with two black and blue triangles bearing a white crescent moon and a multirayed white moon.

PEOPLE AND CULTURE: The Uttarakhandis are a Pahari people, known to upper-class Indians as their loyal Pahari servants, whose honesty, gentleness, and hard work are renowned. Pahari means "hill person," a name applied to all the highlanders in northern India. The name is often used pejoratively; the hill tribes are relegated to the lowest rungs of the Hindu hierarchy and are treated as *harijans*, untouchables. The Uttarakhandis, mostly descended from the early Tibetans,* are divided into two major groups, the Garhwalis and Kumaonis, and several castes, mostly based on former tribal divisions, including the Bothias, closely related to the Tibetans, in the north. The Uttarakhandis are noted for having given disproportionately large numbers of their sons to the defense of the Indian state—because many of their young have been unemployed and turn to the military as a means of survival. The majority live a traditional agrarian-pastoral way of life; unlike in the plains, there is no indigenous trader class. Women have high status and form the core of the nationalist and environmental groups.

LANGUAGE AND RELIGION: The Uttarakhandis speak several related Central Pahari languages. The two major languages are Garhwali and Kumauni, which belong to the Northern group of the Indo-Aryan group of Indo-European languages. Both languages are spoken in a number of geographical dialects, including groups in Tibet and Nepal. Janusari, Tharu, and Tehri are smaller related Indo-Aryan languages spoken in the region. The Central Pahari languages are so diverse that one valley may not be able to communicate with a neighboring valley. The Bhotias in the northern districts speak a language related to Tibetan. Crumbling buildings, absentee teachers, and steeply falling enrollment have increased illiteracy in the last decades. Hindi is fast supplanting the indigenous languages of Uttarakhand, particularly in the urban areas. English is the language of the educated elite and is taught in some schools; the Pahari languages of Garhwali and Kumaoni are rarely taught.

Most of the Uttarakhandis are Hindu or Buddhist, but all retain many traditional shamanistic traditions and beliefs. The people of the valleys are mostly Hindus, with smaller numbers of Buddhists and Christians. There are small Muslim groups, particularly the Gujjar herders in the southeast. The Hindus and Buddhists both adhere to a Hindu-Buddhist tradition that mixes elements from both religions, and both rely on *lamas* to conduct ceremonies and rituals. Village or local deities remain important in local religious traditions.

NATIONAL HISTORY: The region, known since ancient times as Uttarakhand, the "northern tract" or "higher tract," was populated by Munda Dravidian tribes when the Aryan peoples entered northern India from Iran over 2,000 years ago. Called "the land of perpetual snow," Uttarakhand was identified by the early Hindus as the abode of the gods, a holy place. The Aryans pushed the indigenous peoples into the less accessible hill country to the north, where they mixed with the Tibetans. Divided into a number of small states in the twelfth century, often warring among themselves, the hill tribes remained divided and easy prey to invaders.

The Panwar dynasty united the small kingdoms of Garhwal in A.D. 1517, at the same time that the Chand dynasty from Rajastan united neighboring Kumaon, leading to three centuries of prosperity and stability. Silkworms brought to Kumaon from Nepal and Tibet began a tradition of silk production that continued for over 200 years. The local dynasties became increasingly despotic, and open revolts broke out in the mid-sixteenth century, but when the Mughal emperors swept the plains of Hindu resistance to Muslim rule, unity became a matter of survival. The kingdoms retained their independence and a diplomatic presence at the Mughal court as tributary states.

In 1610, English traveler William Finch visited Garhwal, describing a wealthy and advanced Himalayan kingdom often at war with the neighboring state of Kumaon. In 1624 the two states were united after Garhwal defeated Kumaon. A series of strong kings in the late seventeenth and early eighteenth centuries fought wars with neighboring Tibet and the Nepali tribes and eventually established a lasting peace between the Garhwalis and Kumaonis. The region slid into anarchy in the early 1790s; internecine strife and court intrigues ripped apart the political, administrative, and military foundations of the kingdom.

In 1790, fierce Gorkhas* invaded from Nepal, overrunning Garhwal in 1795 and Kumaon in 1803. For twelve years the Gorkhas pillaged the region, even logging the best trees of the lower foothills, beginning a serious pattern of deforestation. The Uttarakhandis mostly abandoned their terraced fields and silk works to escape the ravages of the Gorkhas, many taking refuge in the higher altitudes.

The British feared that the Gorkhas would join with the Sikhs* to the west to resist British influence. When the local Uttarakhandi king requested British aid, the colonial government sent troops, which defeated the Gorkhas. In the process of pacifying the region after the Anglo-Gurkha War of 1816, the British annexed Kumaon and half of Garhwal. A small princely state, centered on Tehri, was established for the descendents of the Garhwal kings.

Organized commercial logging to feed Britain's industrial revolution severely impacted many areas. Large tracts of virgin forest were cleared and then given to immigrants from the overcrowded lowlands. The economic devastation of the hill communities and the erosion of the ancient cultural and societal ties to the forests resulted in self-destructive protests against colonial rule, felling of trees, and setting forest fires. Many young Uttarakhandis, unable to make a living, joined the colonial military forces, laying the foundations for a famous regiment known as the Gahrwal and Kumaon Rifles.

The Home Rule League, organized in the hills, brought the independence movement to Kumaon and later to Garhwal. The growth of Indian nationalism in the 1920s and 1930s stimulated a parallel situation in the neglected hill tracts. The first demand for Uttarakhand statehood was put forward, on linguistic, racial, and cultural grounds, at a session of the Congress Party in 1928.

Sikhs from western Punjab settled in the lowlands during and after the division of British India into India and Pakistan in 1947. The influx of lowlanders continued in the 1950s and 1960s, leading to the loss of ancestral lands. Many unsophisticated Uttarakhandis were forced to work as laborers for the new masters, who gained control of their lands through unlawful means.

Uttarakhand became part of the new Indian state of Uttar Pradesh in 1949. Communist members of the Indian legislature advocated in 1952 setting up a separate state in the hill areas of Uttar Pradesh. Many Uttarakhandis supported leftist political groups, the only national political organizations interested in the statehood movement.

The ancient trade routes with Tibet were closed in 1950 when the Chinese invaded and occupied the Tibetan heartland. The closing of the routes led to social and economic dislocation. The traditional north-south trade was redirected to the plains, impacting on the cultural and economic life of the Uttarakhandis. The brief border war between China and India in 1962 led to the rapid development of roads to the border area, further opening up the forest lands to exploitation. Water shortages became acute as the broad-leaf trees that had once protected streams disappeared from the landscape.

Deforestation and the introduction of a money-based economy into the hills dramatically dislocated many Uttarakhandi communities. The Garhwal Rifles and other Indian army regiments continued to receive many young recruits from the region. Although the region had been accustomed to the emigration of working-age men, the new economic realities propelled a vastly larger number south to the plains in search of work. Entire villages were abandoned as poverty and the monetary demands of the new economy squeezed more and more Uttarakhandi families off their ancestral lands. Thousands of women were left to sustain their families on remittances and backbreaking work on small plots of land.

At the beginning of the 1970s the combined hardship and adversity of hill life had prepared the Uttarakhandis to respond radically to the powers destroying their lands and livelihoods. Alcoholism and growing social problems impacted the region negatively. Effectively mobilized by the anti-alcohol groups, the first nationalist organizations appeared as village-based cooperatives. The movement became a distinctly nonviolent, grassroots movement, with a more radical wing that attracted many young activists. Early successes centered on saving the forests. The scope of the movement widened as more issues came to the fore. In 1979 the Uttarakhand Revolutionary Front was formed to fight for separation from Uttar Pradesh.

Beginning in the 1980s, the Uttarakhandis began to agitate for self-government and autonomy. Long disenchanted with the centralization of state power in Delhi and in the Uttar Pradesh capital, Lucknow, they based their demand for statehood on the neglect and underdevelopment of their homeland. Having so little to lose, the Uttarakhandis continued to defy state and federal authorities and to fight for their rights. Feelings between the hill and plains peoples of Uttar Pradesh led to demonstrations and violent clashes.

In August and September 1994, thousands participated in mass demonstrations demanding separation from Uttar Pradesh. The demonstrations were met with repeated acts of violence; police fired on the crowds, killing 25 and injuring many more. The police then went on a rampage, raping and looting. Internal divisions, politicking, and severe economic repercussions of the widespread strikes and sabotage deflected and deflated the Uttarakhandi movement for a time. Two years later, in 1996, when the Indian prime minister announced the formation of a 26th state, the movement revived, but it stalled in the legislature in 1998.

The opponents of the Uttarakhand movement, supported by the timber, resin, and liquor interests, have attempted to divide the region along tribal and political lines. The worsening law and order crisis in Uttar Pradesh, one of the largest and most populous of the Indian states, reverberated in the hill zones with increased violence and crime.

The numerous social movements of the Uttarakhand region are based on participatory democracy, in sharp contrast to the violent and divisive party politics of the plains. Following the violence of the 1990s, a small militant wing put forward a plan for an independent Uttarakhandi state, a neutral sanctuary in a turbulent region. Revenues collected in the region in 1992–93 compared favorably with neighboring Nepal and showed that Uttarakhand could survive as a financially viable state.

Many of the thousands of Uttarakhandi men who migrated to the plains over the last decades ended up as menial workers in wealthy households. Others enlisted with the military, the easiest escape for male youths from the Himalayas. Uttarakhandi women have to survive on remittances from husbands or sons in the plains. Few Uttarakhandis have climbed out of poverty without also leaving their own culture to assimilate into middle-class Indian culture.

The Uttarakhandis often point to parallels between their small nation and the neighboring Tibetans. The Tibetans also struggle over control of natural resources, and as in Tibet the indigenous Uttarakhandi minority is losing out to the majority. The best agricultural lands of the foothills have been seized by corrupt state officials and immigrants from the plains. As in all of Uttar Pradesh, the state of the roads is deplorable, transportation is very difficult, and many areas are virtually cut off from the modern world.

A Uttar Pradesh Reorganization Bill was introduced to the Indian parliament in 1998 but stalled following opposition from state officials and others who feared that should the Uttarakhandi succeed, many other groups in India would put forward demands for separate states. A move to separate the southeastern Udham Singh Nagar and Hardwar districts on the grounds that the majority were Punjabi-speaking began the mobilization of the Uttarakhandis in the late 1990s.

An integral part of the growing national identity is the fight to save the ancient monuments of the region. A Himalayan heritage center set up in 1997 aims to sustain the traditional culture of the Uttarakhand region. The refusal of the Uttar Pradesh government to acknowledge responsibility for the violence in 1994 led to monthly protest rallies in remembrance of the movement's martyrs.

A severe earthquake in March 1999, which killed over 2,000 people, exposed the ineptitude of the Uttar Pradesh state services. Government relief material disappeared, often to later appear for sale in markets. Financial aid promised by the state government never appeared. The state's dismal response to the crisis reactivated the Uttarakhandi agitation for a separate state to be carved out of the hill districts.

More than 30 organizations joined in 1999 to relaunch the Uttarakhand Movement, vowing not to give up until the separate state was created. The Uttar Pradesh Reorganization Bill, introduced in August 2000, finally allowed the Uttarakhandis to create a separate state within the Indian Union, but many obstacles remained, and Uttarakhandi patience was wearing thin. Several militant leaders called for the secession of Uttarakhand in early 2001 if no progress was made. Citing the success of Bhutan and Nepal in maintaining their independence, the leaders demanded a referendum not only on separation from Uttar Pradesh but from the Indian union.

In mid-2000, the Indian government finally approved the separation of the Uttarakhandi region from the state of Uttar Pradesh. The state, named Uttarachal, was split from Uttar Pradesh on 8 November 2000 and admitted to the Indian Union as the twenty-sixth state. The majority of the Uttarakhandis welcomed statehood, which gives them more control over their natural resources and protection for their threatened culture and language. A militant minority, in early 2001, stated that statehood was not the answer to the many problems faced by the Uttarakhandis as sovereignty was still compromised.

SELECTED BIBLIOGRAPHY:

Farooqui, Amar. *Colonial Forest Policy in Uttarakhand, 1980–1998.* 1998.
Negi, S.S. *Uttarakhand: Land and People.* 1995.
Singh, Gopal. *South Asia: Democracy, Discontent and Societal Conflicts.* 1998.
Trivedi, V.R. *Autonomy of Uttarakhand.* 1995.

Vemeranans

North Vanuatuans; Santos

POPULATION: Approximately (2002e) 65,000 Vemeranans in Vanuatu, concentrated in the northern islands of Espiritu Santo, Malo, Aoba, Maewo, and the Torres and Banks groups.

THE VEMERANAN HOMELAND: The Vemeranan homeland lies in the South Pacific, forming the three northern districts of the Republic of Vanuatu—Sanma, Penema, and Torba. The islands are of volcanic origin and generally mountainous, with active volcanoes and rugged interiors, and low coral plains devoted to plantation agriculture. The islands are heavily wooded, with broad, fertile, well-watered valleys. *Region of Vemerana*: 2,443 sq. mi.—6,328 sq. km, (2002e) 72,000—Vemeranans 89%, French 1%, Vietnamese 1%, Chinese and other Vanuatuans 9%. The Vemeranan capital and major cultural center is Luganville, locally called Santo or Santo Town, (2002e) 9,000.

FLAG: The Vemeranan national flag, the flag of the republic in 1980, is a pale blue field bearing a centered green five-pointed star. The flag of the Na-Griamel Party is a blue field bearing clasped hands centered with the party's name at the top and a white five-pointed star on the bottom. The official flag of the region is a blue field bearing six five-pointed white stars on the center and the fly and white meshed gears on the hoist.

PEOPLE AND CULTURE: The Vemeranans are Melanesians, part of the large Melanesian population of the western South Pacific. Of mixed Australoid and Polynesian ancestry, the Vemeranans are divided into tribal groups based on island affiliation. Most of the Vemeranans live in rural communities, although an important urban center is growing up around the regional capital, Luganville, which is also called Santo locally. About 45% of the population of the islands is under 20 years of age, increasingly alienated from the traditional farming and fishing of their parents. The Vemeranans do not leave their country in large numbers, unlike some other Pacific Islanders, although in the past a number went to French New Caledonia to work in the nickel industry.

LANGUAGE AND RELIGION: The language of the islands comprises a group of dialects of Bislama, the English-based national language of Vanuatu. The language is spoken in a number of regional varieties, with more French influence in the dialects spoken in the northern Vemerana islands. Melanesian languages and dialects remain the languages of daily life, but most are not mutually intelligible. Education is primarily conducted in English and French. About 40,000 of the Vemeranans are bilingual in their local dialects and French, with about 5,000 speaking only their Melanesian language and others speaking Melanesian dialects, Bislama, English, and French; many speak three languages or more. The Melanesian dialects are spoken languages with oral traditions; Bislama is the literary language.

The majority of the Vemeranans are Christians, converted by French missionaries in the nineteenth century. Roman Catholicism is the predominant denomination; there are also Presbyterians, Anglicans, and, increasingly, evangelical sects. A significant number, while professing Christianity, maintain their allegiance to traditional rituals and activities, including grade-taking, the division of young men into fraternal groups, and the killing of pigs.

NATIONAL HISTORY: The islands were settled by Australoid peoples related to the Aborigines* of Australia. Later Polynesians spreading through the islands in large family canoes settled some of the islands. The fusion of the two groups produced the present Melanesian population as early as 1000 B.C. The inhabitants of the northern islands of Vanuatu are descended from the first inhabitants of the region. The islands to the south were settled hundreds of years later.

Melanesians were divided into tribal and clan groups, often warring and raiding among themselves or against tribes on other islands. Isolated for many centuries, the tribes developed several distinct although related cultures. Local dialects also developed on each of the islands, often splitting along tribal or regional lines.

The first European known to have visited islands was Portuguese explorer Pedro Fernandes de Queiros in 1606. He named the largest of the archipelago Australia del Espiritu Santo. The islands were virtually forgotten by the Europeans until the arrival of French explorer Louis de Bougainville in 1768. He was followed in 1774 by the British explorer James Cook, who called the islands the New Hebrides after his Scottish homeland. Conflicting claims to the archipelago by France and Great Britain led to a clumsy compromise, by which both powers exerting influence in the islands.

French and British missionaries, planters, and traders came to the islands in the 1800s; the French predominated on Espiritu Santo and the northern islands. French missionary stations and schools were the first contact with Europeans for many of the islanders. Western education and Christian concepts greatly changed the rhythms of daily life.

The extension of plantation agriculture in Australia and other areas of the South Pacific led to raids by European "blackbirders," slavers who sold captured islanders to European planters in Fiji and other areas. French plantations using Melanesian labor were established in the northern islands, particularly fertile Espiritu Santo. Later, when the Melanesians proved unsuited to plantation labor, indentured workers were imported from Asia.

The British and French governments divided responsibilities in the islands but were unable to agree on judicial matters; as a result, French subjects were under French law, and the British in the islands were subject to British law. The non-European islanders were thus faced with a bewildering dual set of laws, two judicial systems, two police establishments, and two colonial administrations. On 20 October 1906, after years of controversy, the islands were established as a condominium with joint Franco-British control. The two colonial powers established parallel French and British administrations.

Planter society brought much prosperity to the islands, many educated Melanesians adopted European lifestyles. The islands, particularly Espiritu Santo and the northern islands under French domination, prospered until the market for plantation agricultural products began to dwindle in the early 1920s.

The islanders remained loyal to the colonial powers during World War II, particularly after the Vichy French were expelled by British, American, and Free French troops in 1941. Allied bases were established in the islands, which had not been reached by the Japanese. In 1942 the United States constructed on Espiritu Santo a huge air and naval base that was used as a staging area for the invasions of the Japanese-held islands to the north. The bases, garrisoned by Americans and Europeans, brought back some of the earlier prosperity and raised expectations. Cargo cults proliferated, with promises of Western-style prosperity to be brought by the planes that supplied the bases.

In 1957 an appointed advisory council, including British and French commissioners, virtually controlled the government of the New Hebrides. The decolonization movement sweeping Africa, Asia, and the Pacific was echoed in the islands, particularly in the northern island of Espiritu Santo, whose inhabitants resented the New Hebrides government on Efate, in the central islands.

Jimmy (Moli) Stevens, a mixed-race rice planter and hereditary chief, founded the pro-French political party, Na-Griamel, seeking autonomy for the northern islands under French tutelage. The autonomy movement, unofficially supported by the French authorities, won widespread support as an anti-Efate mass movement. On 27 December 1975 the separatist leaders proclaimed the independence of the Na-Griamel Federation. The breakaway state was ended by colonial troops, and the region was reintegrated into the New Hebrides in 1977.

The advisory council continued to control the New Hebrides government until 1975, when a representative assembly, some of whose members were elected, was created. Serious disagreements among the various political parties delayed implementation of the assembly until 1978. As the New Hebrides moved toward independence, the Na-Griamel became openly separatist, demanding separation of the northern islands under French protection. The separatists were openly supported by French planters who feared that the new government of the archipelago would nationalize French-owned plantations.

In September 1979 a new constitution guaranteed French language rights, established a Council of Chiefs to preserve Melanesian customs and culture, and erected regional assemblies in Espiritu Santo and other outlying areas. In November 1979, Na-Griamel lost its majority in the Espiritu Santo Regional Assembly. Riots broke out as the separatists claimed they had lost because of voter fraud.

Na-Griamel leader Jimmy Stevens and several hundred followers, calling themselves Vemeranans, after the historic name for the northern islands, and armed with bows and arrows, attacked government offices in Luganville, supported by French planters armed with shotguns. The rebels took the British district commissioner hostage, and on 25 May 1980 the Vemeranan leaders declared the independence of the Republic of Vemerana. The Vemeranan revolt was reportedly financed by the United States–based Phoenix Corporation, which wished to set up a tax-free haven, with few government controls and open capitalism.

On 28 July 1980 the New Hebrides was granted independence as the Republic of Vanuatu. The new prime minister appealed to the United Nations for help in maintaining Vanuatu's territorial integrity. Other Pacific states, fearing secessionist groups in their own countries, sent troops to aid the new Vanuatu government. Nearby Papua–New Guinea sent 150 troops, the British sent Royal Marines, and the French provided a contingent of police. In July 1980 the British and French forces were withdrawn amid increasing violence and several clashes with the Vemeranan rebels. The Vemeranans formed a loose alliance with the Tannese,* who had rebelled in the southern group of the Vanuatu islands.

Jimmy Stevens and other Vemeranans were captured by Papuan troops in late July 1980, and the rebellion was effectively ended. Over 700 rebels fled to French New Caledonia, and some 1,000 people were eventually arrested. Stevens was tried and sentenced to 14 years in prison. Other Vemeranan leaders were imprisoned or deported. Stevens claimed that the French had reneged on agreements to support the new state. Most of the captured rebels were tried, but in the mid-1980s several were still held in prison without trial.

The Na-Griamel movement was converted into a regional political party, the Na-Griamel Party, which represented the interests of the francophone, largely Roman Catholic, northern islands. The party fielded candidates in regional and national elections from 1983, winning considerable support with demands for regional autonomy and greater control of cultural and economic aspects.

The Vanuatu government, increasingly leftist and dominated by an anglophone, Protestant minority, formed close political ties with Libya and the Soviet Union in the mid-1980s, alarming the conservative Vemeranans of Espiritu Santo and the smaller northern islands. The Na-Griamel Party, in the 1980s and the 1990s, continued to represent the Vemeranan secessionist sentiment against the increasingly left-leaning government of Vanuatu.

In late 1988 the rift between the francophone and anglophone supporters of the separate political parties again came to a head as the francophone leaders demanded more representation. In the late 1980s, to preempt renewed support for separatism in the northern islands, the Vanuatu authorities created a federal system of government, creating regional assemblies and local administrations. The Vemeranan demands for greater autonomy were repeated in the mid-1990s, revealed the remaining underlying ethnic and regional divisions that continued to threaten the unity of Vanuatu.

Dozens of people were arrested and often ill treated by police and military officers during mass arrests under a four-week state of emergency in 1998. The government suspended most constitutional human rights guarantees in January following widespread rioting and looting, mostly on Efate, but soon extending to Espiritu Santo. Protests were prompted by a report on official corruption in the federal and regional governments.

Nationalists in the northern islands point to the hypocrisy of the Vanuatu government, which vocally supports self-determination for the Melanesian populations of New Caledonia and Irian Jaya in Indonesia but continues to deny the same to the Vemeranans of the northern part of the archipelago.

SELECTED BIBLIOGRAPHY:

Doorn, Robert J. *A Blueprint for a New Nation: The Structure of the Na-Griamel Federation.* 1982.

Lindstrom, Lamont. *Knowledge and Power in a South Pacific Society.* 1991.

Miles, William F.S. *Bridging Mental Boundaries in a Postcolonial Microcosm: Identity and Development in Vanuatu*. 1998

Premdas, Ralph R. *Politics and Government in Vanuatu: From Colonial Unity to Post-Colonial Disunity*. 1988.

.

Venetians

Venezianos; Venetos

POPULATION: Approximately (2002e) 3,670,000 Venetians in Europe, mostly in the northeastern Veneto region of Italy. Other Venetian communities live in other parts of Italy, particularly Rome, and an estimated 100,000 inhabit the western districts of the republics of Croatia and Slovenia. Outside Europe there are important Venetian communities in the United States, Brazil, Germany, Switzerland, Australia, and Argentina.

THE VENETIAN HOMELAND: The Venetian homeland is made up of two distinct topographical areas: the mountain ranges of the Carnic and Dolomite Alps in the north, and the Venetian Plain in the south. The lowland region, the Venetian Plain, lies on the Gulf of Venice, an arm of the Adriatic Sea, and includes the valleys of the lower Adige, Po, and Piave Rivers. The region, coextensive with the ancient region of Venetia, comprises the provinces of Venezia, Padova, Rovigo, Verona, Vicenza, Treviso, and Belluno. Veneto now forms a semi-autonomous region of the Italian Republic. *Region of Veneto (Venezia)*: 7,095 sq. mi.—18,376 sq. km, (2002e) 4,528,000—Venetians 78%, Lombards* 3%, Ladins,* Tyroleans,* Friulis,* and other Italians 19%. The capital and major cultural center of the Venetians is Venice, Venezia to the Italians, (2002e) 274,000, built partly on 118 islands in the Lagoon of Venice. Other important Venetian cultural centers are Verona, (2002e) 255,000, and Padua (Padova), (2002e) 211,000.

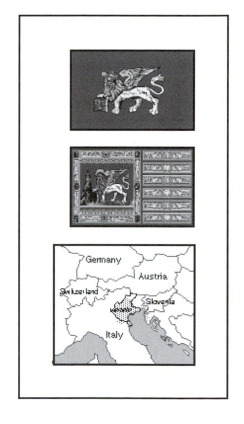

FLAG: The flag of the national movement is a red field bearing the lion of Venice centered. The Venetian national flag, the official flag of the region of Veneto, is a yellow field charged with a red square on the hoist bearing the lion of Venice in yellow and outlined in a yellow and red design, the same design reflected in six horizontal stripes on the fly.

PEOPLE AND CULTURE: The Venetians are a northern Italian people, the descendents of the medieval Venetians, who created a vast Mediterranean empire. The Venetian culture, which incorporates both Mediterranean and Alpine influences, has borrowed many traits and customs from the peoples that were once ruled by the Venetian Empire. The Greeks of the former Byzantine Empire had great influence on the culture, particularly Venetian architecture. More oriented to Vienna and the north than to Rome and the south, the Venetians have maintained their distinct identity, which has strengthened in recent years as part of the nationalist reculturation of northern Italy.

LANGUAGE AND RELIGION: The language of the Venetians is a distinctive dialect that has incorporated many influences from the neighboring Slavic, Rhaetian, and Germanic peoples. The present Venetian language is not the language of the "Serene Republic," as the Venetian city-state was once known, but a variety of dialects that vary from region to region, although they all derive from a common Venetian matrix. The dialect is very different from standard Italian; the Venetians are mostly bilingual, speaking their own Venetian language as well as standard Italian. Venetian is spoken by 60% of the inhabitants of the region and is used as the first language by 35% of the population. About a quarter of the population, particularly in rural areas, have a poor grasp of standard Italian. The language is spoken in three major dialects—Istrian, Trentine, and Venetian. There is a continuing debate over the language; many outside the region claim it as a dialect of Italian, while many Venetians argue that it is a separate Romance language. As Venetian is not taught in area schools, only a small minority can write properly in the language, which was the official language of the Serene Republic for centuries.

The Venetians are overwhelmingly Roman Catholic, although religious practice has slipped greatly since World War II. Traditionally the calendar revolved around church holidays and celebrations, but secular life has taken a toll on church influence. In recent years evangelical sects have gained some influence in the region. There is a Protestant minority, mostly in the foothills of the Alps in the northern districts.

NATIONAL HISTORY: The Veneti, an Illyrian people, are thought to have settled the Venetian Plain by 1000 B.C. In the north, the high mountain valleys were home to various Celtic tribes. In the second century B.C. the region came under Roman rule, and Venetia and Istria were joined by Emperor Augustus to form a separate province, with its capital at Aquileia. The city of Aquileia, and the second city of the Roman province, Padua, dominated the region and evolved as centers of Roman culture. Padua eventually became an important city of Italy, second only to Rome in wealth and culture.

Military and political power began to collapse in the northern Roman provinces in third century. Eventually the remaining Roman defenses were overrun. Barbarian tribes invaded the region in the fifth century A.D. In 452 the Huns, led by Attila, moved across the Venetian Plain, destroying everything in their path. Germanic Lombards later invaded the region from the west. The inhabitants of the once-flourishing city of Aquileia, to escape the destruction, fled to the defensible islands of the Venice Lagoon. The Byzantine Empire, the eastern part of the Roman Empire, gained control of the region in the sixth century. Although Byzantine political power was nominal, cultural influences remain to the present.

The inhabitants of the small island communities of the Venetian Lagoon united in 697 to elect the first *doge* (duke) to rule over the new island state. Well situated to control the flourishing maritime trade, the island communities grew and prospered. In the ninth century the central islands joined to form the city of Venice. It was not until the tenth century that important towns, and later free communes, developed in the region. Cities such as Verona and Padua grew powerful under the rule of noble families, but the republic of Venice gradually became dominant. By the late eighth century Venice gained power and eventually broke free of Byzantine rule.

The Venetians began to expand their authority over nearby mainland territories, winning control of the plains east of the Adige River and expanding to conquer the islands and coastal regions of Dalmatia, across the narrow Adriatic. Venetian control of both sides of the Adriatic Sea, allowed the republic to control trade between Europe and the East.

The lion on the Venetian flag is the symbol of the evangelist St. Mark, the patron of Venice. Mark was buried in Alexandria in Egypt, which later came under Muslim rule. His remains were stolen, hidden under a load of pork, and taken by ship to Venice in 828. His remains were later placed in the ornate basilica that bears his name.

The fourth Christian crusade against Muslim control of the Holy Land, led by the Venetian *doge* Enrico Danolo in 1204, turned instead on the Christian capital of the Byzantine Empire, Constantinople. The treasures looted from Christendom's largest and wealthiest city financed Venice's rise to power. The Venetians emerged as the rulers of a colonial empire made up of several Mediterranean islands, including Crete and parts of the Greek mainland.

All Venetian citizens shared in the bounty of the golden age of the republic, but the patrician merchants increasingly obtained political power and eventually formed a ruling oligarchy. In reaction to an unsuccessful conspiracy in 1310, a Council of Ten was instituted to punish crimes against the state. The Ten, supported by a formidable secret police, acquired increasing power; the *doge* eventually became a figurehead.

Venetia, the mainland territory under the control of the Republic of Venice, in the fourteenth and fifteenth centuries extended from Lake Garda to Dalmatia. Venetian colonies were founded around the northern

Adriatic under the rule of the Council of Ten. By the early fifteenth century, the Adriatic was often called "the Venetian lake."

In 1380–81 Venice, then known as the "queen of the seas," defeated the rival Republic of Genoa to become the premier Mediterranean maritime power. In the fifteenth century, at the height of its power, Venice extended its rule to the former free cities of the eastern Po Valley to become an extensive Italian state, one of the wealthiest and most powerful in Europe. Its ambassadors, the creators of the modern diplomatic service, represented Venetian interests in every court in the known world. The Most Serene Republic of Venice was the most powerful state of the Western world in the fifteenth and sixteenth centuries.

The emergence of the Ottoman Empire of the Turks challenged Venetian dominance of the Mediterranean; the decline of Venice is usually dated from the fall of Byzantine Constantinople to the Turks in 1453. Sporadic wars between the fifteenth and eighteenth centuries gradually shrank the republic's overseas empire, as colony after colony fell to Turkish rule. Even though the republic declined in power between the fourteenth and sixteenth centuries, in those years its cities experienced a great flowering of culture and arts—the Renaissance. The naval battle of Lepanto in 1571 gave the Venetians renewed standing in Europe by ending the predominance of Turkish seapower, but the respite was not to last.

The decline of Venetian power was accompanied by a increasing intolerance, particularly of Jews, and led to the growing power of the Inquisition between 1550 and 1670. The empire continued to decay, losing Cyprus to the Turks in 1571, Crete in 1669, and the Peloponnesus in 1715. The territorial losses ended Venetian dominance of trade in the eastern Mediterranean.

The Venetian state in the eighteenth century was aristocratic and politically stagnant. The republic, in spite of frantic efforts to maintain its neutrality, fell without a shot to Napoleon's forces in 1797. Napoleon traded most of the Venetian territories to Austria in exchange for lands in the Low Countries. Briefly joined to Napoleon's Kingdom of Italy from 1805 to 1814, Venice returned to Austrian rule following Napoleon's final defeat.

In 1848, during the Risorgimento, the unification of Italy, the Venetians, led by Daniele Manin, rebelled against Austrian rule and heroically resisted a siege until 1849. The rebels proclaimed Venetian independence as the Republic of St. Mark. Opposed to Venetian moves to unite with the Kingdom of Sardinia, Manin resigned, but he returned in 1849 to lead Venetian opposition to the reimposition of Austrian rule.

The Kingdom of Italy, united in 1860–61 under the Sardinian king, sided with Prussia in the Austro-Prussian War of 1866. As a reward Prussia backed the Italian annexation of the Venetian territories from Austria. The annexed territories were called Tre Venezie, the Three Venices—Venezia

Euganea, the area around Venice; Venezia Giulia in the northeast; and South Tyrol, called Venezia Tridentina even though it had never been under Venetian rule.

The new Italian kingdom adopted a Tuscan dialect spoken around Florence as its national language. The dialect, very unlike the Venetian dialect, was generally rejected in Veneto. Linguistic nationalism increased as Veneto industrialized in the late nineteenth century, bringing the first immigrants from southern Italy, part of the same migration that sent millions of southern Italians to the Americas. The first recorded incidence of violence between the migrants and anti-immigrant Venetians took place in Verona in 1889.

The poor state of the economy of united Italy forced many Venetians to emigrate. Nationalists now claim that up to three million left the region between 1870 and 1910. The emigrants spread to other parts of Europe, and many sailed to new lives in the Americas, but without losing touch with the homeland.

Italy remained virtually a collection of regions until the early twentieth century. The Italian Fascist government launched a campaign to eradicate Italy's many regional languages in 1922; the campaign was largely unsuccessful in Veneto. The beginning of radio broadcasts in the 1930s helped to spread standard Italian to the region, but the predominance of the Venetian language continued through World War II.

After World War II 60% of the Venetian population still used the Venetian dialect in daily life. The percentage began to decline only with the arrival of mass media in the 1950s and 1960s. The postwar economic boom in northern Italy further eroded the use of the Venetian dialect. Standard Italian became the lingua franca used by Venetian supervisors and the thousands of southern Italians moving north to work in the booming industries in the postwar period.

Resentment of the dialectically and culturally different southern Italians became an issue in the 1960s. Serious anti-immigrant sentiment and violence began to grow in the 1970s, along with increasing frustration with the notoriously inefficient and overstaffed government in Rome. Moves toward European integration raised fears that Veneto and the other industrialized northern regions would be unable to compete in Europe under the burden of Rome's bloated bureaucracy and the channeling of northern taxes as massive development aid to the corrupt and backward southern regions. In the late 1980s, nationalists formed the Liga Veneta, the Venetian League, which formed part of the autonomist Northern League, which in turn grouped several autonomist organizations from regions across northern Italy.

Venetian nationalism, as exemplified by the dramatic spread of national sentiment in the late 1980s and early 1990s, was still mainly autonomist, the majority of the nationalists favoring political and economic autonomy within a federal Italy. In late 1994 nationalists in the city of Venice accused members of the Italian government of having more interest in looting the public purse than in the neglected heritage of Venice and other decaying historic cities in the region.

In September 1996 Umberto Bossi, leader of the coalition Northern League, declared the "federal republic of Padania" independent from the rest of Italy. The so-called republic stretched from the Po River to Italy's northern border and included the cities of Turin, Milan, Bologna, and Venice. The declaration was not to take effect for up to 12 months, in order to enable a Northern League provisional government, formed earlier in the year, to negotiate a treaty of separation with the Italian government. While the Northern League and the regional autonomist organizations were founded on a federalist platform, Bossi had redefined the coalition's goals and had begun calling for the region's secession. Although opinion polls showed little support for secession in Veneto, analysts said that the movement tapped into a growing discontent among northerners. In response to such concerns, the Italian parliament had been working to pass constitutional reforms aimed at giving local leaders a stronger voice in national government and at changing the country's tax structure.

In early December 2000, a group of separatists, using a homemade tank, occupied St. Mark's Square, the historic center of Venice. Taking control of the bell tower, they raised the flag of independent Venice. The nationalists were arrested and tried but were later released. Many considered the occupation a publicity stunt, but others supported the idea of an independent Venetian republic within the European Union.

Poor roads, a lack of infrastructure, and government bureaucrats are all targets of Venetian grievances. The massive corruption and crime scandals that have reached the highest circles of the Italian government and the economic elite have spurred the growth of Venetian nationalism and increasing calls for a separate Venetian state, tied to a federal Italy or an independent Padania, within a united, federal Europe. The Venetians, with their long and separate history, often see the Italian government as a "foreign" presence in their homeland.

SELECTED BIBLIOGRAPHY:

Carello, Adrian N. *The Northern Question: Italy's Participation in the European Economic Community and the Mezzogiorno's Underdevelopment.* 1989.

Levy, Carl, ed. *Italian Regionalism: History, Identity and Politics.* 1996.

Norwich, John Julius, and Peter Dimock, eds. *A History of Venice.* 1989.

Thubron, Colin. *The Venetians.* 1988.

Veps

Vepse; Vepslaines; Bepslaanes; Lyyudiniks; Lüdilaines; Kayvans; Tyagalazhet; Vepsians

POPULATION: Approximately (2002e) 40,000 Veps in Europe, about half living in Finland and half in northwestern Russia, where they are concentrated in the Republic of Karelia and the regions of Vologda and St. Petersburg. Outside Europe there is a Vep community in Kemerovo Oblast in Russian Siberia. Vep activists claim a national population in excess of 70,000 in Russia.

THE VEP HOMELAND: The Vep homeland, popularly called Vepsia, lies in northwestern European Russia between three lakes— Ladoga, Onega, and Beloye Ozero—and around the Oyat, Kapscha, Pascha, and Ivoda Rivers, east of Lake Ladoga. The homeland of the Veps has no official status in Russia; since the foundation of the independent Russian Federation in 1991 the Veps have worked to

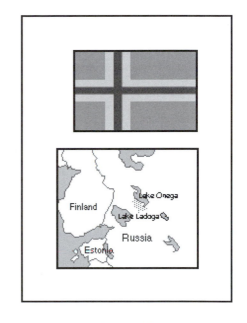

unify the three Vep territories into a single autonomous unit. The northern Veps, called the Äänis, live in the Republic of Karelia around the town of Äänisjärv, on the southwestern shore of Lake Onega, south of the Karelian capital, Petrozavodsk. The central Veps, the most numerous group, live in the St. Petersburg region, on the Oyat River and its tributaries. The southern group lives on the border between St. Petersburg and Vologda Oblasts, on the Lid River. Some Veps live in St. Petersburg and other nearby towns. The Vep capital and major cultural center is Sheltozero, called Shoutar'v by the Veps, (2002e) 4,000.

FLAG: The Vep national flag, the flag of the regional movement, is a pale green field bearing a light blue Scandinavian cross outlined in yellow.

PEOPLE AND CULTURE: The Veps are a Finnic people of the White Sea–Baltic group, culturally and linguistically related to the neighboring Karels.* The Veps are divided into three major groups, the Northern Veps (Ylä-Vepsä), the Central Veps (Vepsä), and the Southern Veps (Ala-Vepsä). Called Chud until the Russian Revolution, "Vep" was retained only by the Southern Veps, but the name has been revived as part of the Vep national movement. Vep nationalists claim a much larger population, as many registered in successive Soviet censuses as ethnic Russians for political or economic reasons. There is a growing sense of Vep identity and a desire to revive their unique culture and language. The Vep population in Finland, mostly refugees who fled the Vep homeland during the Winter War and World War II, have provided financial and educational aid to the Vep national revival. The Russian name for the Veps, Chukhar or Chukhna, is often used prejoratively.

LANGUAGE AND RELIGION: The language of the Veps, called Vepsian, is a Balto-Finnic language of the Finno-Ugric language group. The language, closely related to Karelian and Finnish, is written in the Latin alphabet. Veps is spoken in three major dialects—Southern Veps, Central Veps, and Prionezh or Northern Veps. The dialects correspond to the three major divisions of the Vep nation. The language is now taught in some primary schools but is not compulsory. Most Veps are bilingual in Russian and often speak Karelian or Finnish as well. The Vep language is now recognized as one of the official languages of the Republic of Karelia, a member state of the Russian Federation. A written Veps language was created in the 1930s but was soon discontinued. A new literary language based on the Latin alphabet has been promoted since the late 1980s.

The majority of the Veps adhere to the Russian Orthodox Church, with many retaining pre-Christian customs and traditions. The indigenous religious beliefs, over several centuries, became part of the Vep Orthodox observances. Traditional shrines, in particular sacred groves, remain an important part of Vep beliefs and are places of pilgrimage.

NATIONAL HISTORY: Finnic tribes, from the Volga River basin, migrated to the west and settled the territories around the Baltic Sea and lakes Ladoga and Onega, probably by the eighth century. Early chronicles mention the Veps in the region, and by the ninth century, as mentioned in Slavic chronicles, the Veps were known as a separate people that populated the region between the large lakes. They lived in clan groupings, with few ties beyond the clan level. In the tenth century, they were mentioned as a people called the "Visu" in the journals of Arab travelers.

Many of the Vep clans came under the political control of the Slavic Republic of Novgorod, as a merchant state that controlled much of northern Russia in the fourteenth and fifteenth centuries. The Vep homeland was invaded by Germans and Swedes expanding their territories to the east, but the majority of the clans remained under Novgorodian rule until 1478, when Great Novgorod fell to the expanding Russian state called Muscovy (Moscow). In 1485 the Vep territories were annexed to the growing Russian empire of the Grand Principality of Moscow.

The northward expansion of Russian settlement reduced the Veps to a minority in their traditional homeland. Russian colonists formed a wedge in the Süväri Basin, which divided the Northern and Central Veps. The intrusion of Russian colonists on the tributaries of the Süväri and Jüvenjoe Rivers also divided the Northern Veps from the related Ingrians* and Karels. Forcible conversion to the Orthodox religion, schooling only in the Russian language, and the close proximity of Russian settlements began the long process of the assimilation of the Veps into Russian culture.

The small Finnic nations of the region were often in the middle of the quarrels between the expanding Swedish and Russian states. The western Vep clans formed part of the medieval Karel state, which came under Swedish rule in 1617. At the end of the Northern War between Sweden and Russia in 1721, all the Vep territories came under the rule of the Russians. Under tsarist rule, the region became backward and poverty stricken; it was known chiefly as a place of exile for political prisoners and criminals.

In the mid-nineteenth century, under the influence of the Westernized Finns, the Veps, then numbering over 70,000, experienced a cultural revival and took renewed interest in their language, literature, and culture. The Finns of neighboring Finland, incorporated into the Russian Empire in 1809, became the champions of the smaller Finnic nations of northwestern Russia.

An official government policy of Russification was introduced in 1899, and the Veps came under intense pressure to assimilate. Their language was prohibited in publications and in education, but materials smuggled into the region from Finland kept the Veps in touch with the nationalist movement that was growing there. In the past, the Veps, and also the other Finnic peoples of the region, suffered discrimination and were suspect as not loyal to the tsarist, thereafter Soviet, state. Ethnologists working in the region in the late nineteenth century were of the opinion that the small nation would shortly be extinct.

The first Russian revolution, in 1905, stimulated the first stirrings of Vep nationalism. Vep activists took to the streets to call attention to a long list of grievances. Among the concessions granted by the Russian government were an end to the policy of Russification of the Finnic minorities and more linguistic and cultural freedom. The opening of Vep schools and appearance of Finnish publications began to reverse decades of forced assimilation.

The beginning of World War I in 1914 accelerated the growth of nationalism in nearby Finland, with a parallel increase in activity in the Vep territory. The overthrow of the tsarist government in 1917 threw the region into chaos; escaped prisoners and political exiles were suddenly freed from the many prison camps. As the tsarist administration collapsed, the Veps, following the lead of the Finns, created a nationalist administration to administer the official national population of over 35,000. However, the Vep government, opposed by many of the local Russians, remained for the most part a government in name only.

The arrival of British interventionist troops in March 1918 gave the Veps a degree of protection. The British and allied troops, landed at Murmansk and Archangel in support of an anti-Bolshevik government, took control of much of the territory, driving local Bolsheviks underground. During the Russian Civil War, the Finns invaded the region and were welcomed by the Veps as liberators from hated Russian rule. The Western interventionist forces were withdrawn in 1919 as the Red and White Russian forces fought for control.

The Red Army defeated the remaining White forces in the region in early 1920, and the last of the foreign troops were withdrawn. The imposition of Soviet rule, particularly the Soviet nationality policy, was quite promising for the Veps and even seemed to aid the national awakening that began in the nineteenth century. The Soviet authorities created 24 administrative units in the Vep homeland, some of which were grouped into two national districts, Vidla in the Leningrad region and Shoutjärve in the Karelian Autonomous Republic.

The reversal of the earlier nationalities policy and the collectivization of Vep agriculture in the late 1920s caused severe disruptions. In 1928, to escape the forced collectivization, some Southern Veps emigrated as homesteaders to the new lands in Siberia, particularly the Kemerovo Oblast. In spite of the hardships of collectivization, Vep culture advanced under Soviet rule. Schools in the Vep language were opened, and a written language, in the Latin alphabet, was created on the basis of the Central Vep dialect.

A department of minorities established in the Leningrad District Council engaged in compiling the Vep written language. A system of spelling was worked out similar to the Latin alphabet system created for the Karels of Tver. The first book published in the Latin alphabet, in 1932, was a primer; altogether more than 30 books were printed in the Vep language. By 1934 all the Vep schools had been supplied with textbooks in their native language. Finnish academics visiting the Vep region in 1934 reported a national population of over 50,000, with large families and the widespread use of the Vep language in domestic life. The period of Soviet support, however, was short-lived.

The Stalinist policy of forced assimilation and oppression of minorities, begun in 1937, hit the Veps particularly hard. All national cultural activities were stopped, and the assimilation of the Veps by "accelerated methods" was ordered. Vep schools were closed, textbooks were burned, teachers were imprisoned, and many intellectuals disappeared or were executed. In 1939, before a third autonomous district, Shimjärve, planned for the Leningrad region could be formed, the national districts already in existence were liquidated and their leaders eliminated. The Vep autonomous districts were parceled out between the Karelian Autonomous Soviet Socialist Republic and the Leningrad and Vologda Oblasts. The Veps of Shimjärve abandoned their homes and settled in the villages and towns of the Northern Veps.

War between Finland and the Soviet Union broke out in 1939. The Winter War divided the Veps, then estimated to number over 60,000, between those wishing to aid the related Finns and those so terrified of the Soviet administration that they wished to ignore politics. During World War II, called the War of Continuation by the Finnic peoples, Finnish troops occupied part of the Vep region. The occupation authorities established a Finnish educational system, and many Vep volunteers joined the Finnish military, where they formed the Kindred Battalion. In 1944 the Finns were defeated and were driven back into Finland by the Red Army. Thousands of Finnic refugees fled their homelands as the Russians advanced, including an estimated half of the total Vep population. Those that stayed or were unable to escape faced severe punishment for collaborating with the Finns.

After the war, younger Veps began a mass migration to the towns, thereby moving into Russian linguistic and cultural environments. Soviet census figures were always suspect; the data from the 1959, 1970, and 1979 censuses were not objective but reflected the arbitrary power of local officials in recording nationalities. In identification documents and housing registers of the village Soviets, Veps often misrepresented their nationality out of fear or false shame. By the late 1970s the population claiming Vep nationality was mostly over the age of 40, reflecting the assimilation of the younger Veps into the urban Russian population. The feeling of national identity was very low, and the prospect for the future was bleak.

The social and political reforms introduced into Soviet society by Mikhail Gorbachev in the late 1980s began the reculturation of the Veps. Under Gorbachev's regime, Soviet officials acknowledged the Stalinist terror that had decimated the Veps in the late 1930s. A national district was reestablished for the Northern Veps, but aspirations for a united administrative unit for all Vep regions were met with powerful Russian resistance. A Veps Cultural Society was formed in 1989, the first openly Vep association since 1937.

The Vep language was adopted by as an official language by the government of the Republic of Karelia following its declaration of sovereignty in 1990. Following the collapse of the Soviet Union and the creation of the new Russian Federation in 1991, various Vep nationalist associations were formed to promote the revival of the Vep culture and language. Very few Veps actually knew how many Veps lived in the region or exactly where they lived. In 1998, Vep activists in Finland estimated the national population, both declared and registered as other nationalities, at over 70,000 in Russia. Activists claimed that assimilation was the result of the lack of a common Veps administrative territory, and they demanded a separate Veps homeland, an autonomous region that would allow the Veps the same rights as other national groups in the Russian Federation.

After more than 50 years of Russification and social oppression, the Veps are rebuilding their ethnic identity and cultural institutions. A Veps national village community was established at Sheltozero in January 1994, comprising 14 villages and hamlets. The community has become the focus of the Veps revival in Russia. Finnish financial and material aid, including books, educational materials, and cultural support has helped Vep activists to continue the reculturation of the small Vep nation.

SELECTED BIBLIOGRAPHY:

Allison, Roy. *Finland's Relation with the Soviet Union 1944–84.* 1985.

Maude, George. *The Finnish Dilemma: Neutrality in the Shadow of Power.* 1976.

Paasi, Anssi. *Territories, Boundaries and Consciousness: The Changing Geographies of the Finnish-Russian Boundary.* 1997.

Smith, Graham, ed. *Nation-Building in the Post-Soviet Borderlands: The Politics of National Identities.* 1998.

Vojvodines

Voyvodines; Voivodines; Voyvodinans; Voyvodina Serbs

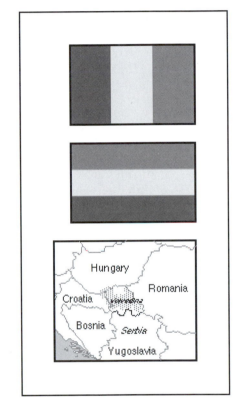

POPULATION: Approximately (2002e) 1,645,000 Vojvodines in Yugoslavia, concentrated in Vojvodina in the northern part of the Republic of Serbia. Outside the region there are Vojvodine communities in Belgrade, the Serbian capital, and in the neighboring states of Croatia, Romania, and Hungary. There are small Vojvodine groups in western Europe and North America. Vojvodine activists often count the non-Serb groups of the province as part of the Vojvodine nationality, including the 300,000 Hungarians and smaller numbers of Slovaks, Croatians, Montenegrins,* and other less numerous groups.

THE VOJVODINE HOMELAND: The Vojvodine homeland occupied the southern part of the Pannonian Plain in northern Serbia in Yugoslavia. The plain has only two mountains, Fruska gora and Vrsaki breg, and is mostly flat with many lakes and rivers, the most important the Danube. Wine has been produced in the region for over 2,500 years. The province is the most hetrogeneous area in Serbia with members of 26 national groups living there. Vojvodina forms a province of the Republic of Serbia, a constituent state of the Yugoslav Federation. *Province of Vojvodina (Pokrajina Vojvodina):* 8,304 sq. mi.—21,506 sq. km, (2002e) 1,928,000—Vojvodines 52%, Hungarians 12%, Serbians 8%, Slovaks 3%, Croats 3%, Montenegrins 2%, Romanians 2%, other Yugoslavs 18%. The Vojvodine capital and major cultural center is Novi Sad, (2002e) 176,000, metropolitan area 260,000.

FLAG: The Vojvodine national flag, the flag of the national movement, is a vertical tricolor of blue, yellow, and green. The same colors, but in a horizontal tricolor, is the flag used by the League of Social Democrats of Vojvodina, the Vojvodina Coalition, and several other autonomist and separatist political organizations.

PEOPLE AND CULTURE: The homeland of the Vojvodines is geographically situated at the junction of the Orthodox eastern Europe and the western Latin and Roman Catholic Europe. The influences from both have produced a culture that blends many traditions in a unique middle-European nation. The Vojodines view themselves as a central European nation unlike the Serbs, seen as a Turkish-influenced Balkan people. The cultural traditions and heritage were enriched by the historical interaction of the various national groups. The Vojvodines adopted elements of other cultures into their own, particularly in arts, music, and the religious traditions of both Orthodox and Catholic groups. The Hungarian population dropped from nearly 340,000 in 1991 to just under 300,000 in 2001, mostly due to emigration to Hungary or Western Europe.

LANGUAGE AND RELIGION: The Vojvodines speak Serbian, the official language of Serbia and the Yugoslav Federation. The language, spoken in the Vojvodina dialect, has incorporated influences from many neighboring languges, particularly Hungarian, German, and Slovak. The language is a western dialect of the South Slavic language known as Serbo-Croatian. Like the Serbian spoken in central Serbia, the dialect is written in the Cyrillic alphabet, but in recent years has been adapted to the Latin alphabet, which is used by the Hungarians and some of the other smaller national groups. The literary language is based on standard Serbian, the Stokavian dialect spoken around Belgrade.

The Vojvodines are mostly members of the Serbian Orthodox Church, although their practices and traditions have incorporated many aspects of the Roman Catholicism of the neighboring peoples of Vojvodina. The Hungarians are mostly Roman Catholic, about 80%, with the remainder adhering to Calvinist Protestant groups.

NATIONAL HISTORY: Plentiful fertile land, available water, and a mild climate drew migrants to the region since the paleolitic period. Some stayed in the plain for short periods of time, but evidence of the first permanent settlements of farmers and cattle herders date to 6000 to 3500 B.C. Celtic warrior tribes, migrating from western Europe, settled the plain around 400 B.C. The Scordisc, a branch of the Boie tribe, settled the region between the Danube and Sava Rivers.

Latin culture, introduced following the Roman conquest in the second half of the first century B.C. introduced better tools and arms and induced the inhabitants to move out from their fortified villages. Commerce flourished as the major trade routes increasingly crossed the Vojvodina Plain. The Romans built cities and roads, developed literacy, and maintained a strong civil and military authority. The city of Sirmium, now called Sremska Mitrovica, emerged as a major Roman cultural center at the end of the third century A.D. The city was the birthplace of many Roman emperors; Aurelian, Probus, Decius, Trainus, Maximinus, and Gracium.

During the great migrations, in the fifth and sixth centuries, the ancestors of the Serbs settled the Balkan Peninsula and spread north to the Pannonian Plain. The Magyars, later called Hungarians, invaded and conquered the plain in the ninth century. The newcomers settled among the Slav and Romanian populations. The region became part of the medieval Hungarian kingdom. Christianity was introduced in the early eleventh century.

To the south the Serbs established the state of Raska, which reached its height of power and culture between the twelfth and fourteenth centuries. The Serbian Orthodox Church was recognized as an independent entity in 1219. Orthodoxy became the major religion among the northern Serb clans of the Pannonian Plain.

Ruled by Hungarian or Croatian governors called bans, the territory was popularly called the Banat. In 1233, King Andrew II of Hungary established the Banat of Severin, a frontier province whose defense was entrusted to the crusading Knights Hospitalers.

Turkish expansion in the Balkans in the thirteenth century, culminating in the defeat of the Christian kingdoms at Kosovo in 1389. A Hungarian victory over the Turks at Belgrade in 1456 divided the Serbs between Turkish and Hungarian rule. The Turks occupied central Serbia in 1459. Many Serbs moved north to the Banat. The Serbs in the Hungarian kingdom, although they retained their Orthodox religion, mostly adopted the culture of the Westernized Hungarians. In 1526, the Turks defeated the Hungarians, setting the stage for the Turkish domination of the Banat region in 1552.

The Hungarians recognized the Hapsburg claim to the Hungarian throne in 1687. The victory of the Austrians and Hungarians against the Turks culminated in the Peace of Kalowitz in 1699, which ceded Vojvodina and other territories to the Hapsburgs of Austria. By the Treaty of Passarovita in 1718, the Banat was made an Austrian military frontier province known as the Banat of Temesvar.

The Austrian emperor made the Serbs the guardians of the southern frontier against the Turks, and in return the Serbs were granted privileges that included the right to elect their own leader, the *vojvod*. Empress Maria Theresa of Austria placed the Banat under civilian rule in 1751 and sponsored the settlement of thousands of German-speaking colonists. In 1799, the Banat passed to Hungarian rule, but had developed considerable autonomy before being brought under Hungarian rule in 1814. In 1849, portions of Backa and Banat were combined and given the name Vojvodina as part of the crownland of Croatia-Slavonia.

Extensive land reclamation and railway construction brought many Hungarian colonists, entrepreneurs, and officials. Stimulated by improved communications, large Hungarian estates underwent rapid commercialization. Agricultural wage labor replaced the traditonal Vojvodine peasantry, so that socially and economically the region acquired much of its modern character. During the last quarter of the nineteenth century, Vojvodina became known as the "breadbasket of the empire."

In Vojvodina, as in Croatia and Bosnia, the better political position of the Serbian-speaking population led to increasing clashes. The call to Serb nationalism eminating from Belgrade found fertile ground. Serbian expansion at the expense of Ottoman Turkey fueled the growth of Serb nationalism in the southern Austro-Hungarian Empire, particularly following the liberation of Old Serbia and Kosovo from Turkish rule in 1912. Disturbances and anti-Hungarian agitation became more frequent as tensions increased in Europe. In June 1914, the Austro-Hungarian heir, Archduke Ferdinand was assinated by a Serb nationalist in Bosnia. The empire declared war on the Kingdom of Serbia, quickly drawing in most of the European states and eventually much of the world.

The London Declaration of 1915 recognized that the Serbian majority territories of the Austro-Hungarian Empire, such as Vojvodina, Lika, and Bosnia, should become part of the Serbian kingdom at the end of the war. In 1918 a Serb-dominated congress declared the union of Vojvodina with the new Kingdom of the Serbs, Croats, and Slovenes although the allies during World War I had promised through a secret agreement to give the Banat to Romania. The Banat was partitioned, the western part joined to the new South Slav kingdom, the eastern districts were incorporated into Romania.

Differences between the Vojvodina Serbs and the Serbs of central Serbia surfaced soon after the incorporation of Vojvodina in 1918. The Serbs of the region, increasingly calling themselves Vojvodines to differentiate themselves from the Serbs of the Old Kingdom, chafed under the excessively bureaucratic and corrupt government of Belgrade. Their traditional ties to the West, to Hungary and Austria, made them suspect and the new border controls ended long-standing trade and cultural exchanges. The kingdom, renamed the Kingdom of Yugoslavia in 1929, was dominated by the Serbs of Belgrade and the south, the supporters of the Serbian monarchy. During the inter-war period, the Serb-dominated Yugoslav government sponsored the settlement of Serbs from other regions in Vojvodina while pressuring ethnic Hungarians to emigrate.

The fascist armies of Germany, Italy, Hungary, and Bulgaria invaded Yugoslavia in April 1941. The Hungarians took control of Vojvodina. Suppression of Serb institutions and efforts to assimilate the Vojvodines led to widespread support for the Serb communist partisans active in central Serbia to the south. Violence and atrocities marked relations between the Vojvodina Serbs and the Hungarians during World War II. When the Hungarian government took steps to withdraw from the war, German troops occupied the region in March 1944. Soviet forces drove the Germans from Vojvodina between October 1944 and April 1945. The fighting devastated the fertile region, leaving many towns and cities in ruins.

Vojvodina, with its mixed propulation, was handed back to Yugoslavia in 1945. The new Yugoslav communist government, adhering to the Soviet model, granted limited autonomy in 1946. As constituted in 1946, Vojvodina consisted of three sections—the Srem in the southwest, which had formed part of Croatia-Slavonia before 1918; the Backa in the northwest, which was an integral part of Hungary; and the western part of the Banat of Temesvar.

During the years of the Cold War, Yugoslavia, although a communist state, tried to maintain an independent stance and opposed harsh Soviet rule in neighboring Hungary and other communist states in central and eastern Europe. The government of Josip Broz Tito allowed some local autonomy while retaining a strong central government. The Vojvodina recovered rapidly, more because of its natural resources than Yugoslavia's centralized command economy.

Under the Serbian Constitution of 1974, Vojvodina was guaranteed a high level of autonomy, enjoying almost all of the prerogatives of a sovereign state. Members of the national minorities were represented in the government and in almost all public institutions. The five largest national groups in the province—Serbs, Magyars, Romanians, Slovaks, and Carpatho-Rusyns*—were designated official nationalities. Nationalist stirrings in other consituent republics, particularly in neighboring Croatia, fueled the growth of a particular Vojvodine nationalism in the late 1970s and early 1980s. Vojvodine activists joined the region's Hungarians in demanding republican status for Vojvodina.

The collapse of communism in the Soviet Union and across eastern Europe also impacted on Yugoslavia. The Serbian Communist Party, in 1988, changed its name to the Serbian Socialist Party, and elected Slobodan Milosevic to be its president. The change in name lacked any substantive change in the hard-line communist and authoritarian platform of the party. A new Serbian Constitution was approved by referendum in July. It abolished the autonomous status of the Kosovo and Vojvodina provinces. Milosevic forced the Vojvodina government to resign and was able to exert significant influence over the reconstituted authorities. The Serbian media accused anti-Milosevic Vojvodines and Hungarians of being secessionist.

The success of the Serb Radical Party (SRS), with the support of the refugee Serb population, threatened the amicable relations between the Vojvodines and the Hungarians. Activists blamed the Serbian government and some local authorities for using the Serb refugees to exacerbate interethnic and social tensions and to change the ethnic composition of the Vojvodina population.

Following Tito's death in 1980, the multi-ethnic state became increasingly unstable. Croats and Slovenes prompted the disintegration of Yugoslavia when they declared independence in 1991–92. Their secession led to the break-up of the state as Bosnia and Hercegovina and Macedonia also voted for secession. Nationalists in Vojvodina, led by Dragan Veselinov and Nenad Canak, demanded a referendum on independence, but were blocked by Serbian troops of the Yugoslav army.

Many Vojvodines responded to the nationalist rhetoric of Slobodan Milosevich. Volunteers joined the Serb attacks on Slovenia, Croatia, and eventually Bosnia and Hercegovina. As the wars continued, and thousands were killed or injured, anti-war and anti-Belgrade sentiment became prominent. Increasing repression was Belgrade's response, further alienating many Vojvodines. Thousands of Hungarians chose to leave for Hungary or other parts of Europe. In 1992, the Security Council of the United Nations imposed economic sanctions on the remaining republics of Serbia and Montenegro. Seventeen political parties, associations, and organizations, known as the Vojvodina Coalition, signed a document in 1996 known as the Manifesto for Vojvodina Autonomy. The demands include changes to Serbia's and Yugoslavia's constitutions to enable Vojvodina to become an autonomous province and a modern European region in which all citizens would be equal irrespective of ethnicity, ancestry, or religion. In March 1997 the coalition, at a meeting in Novi Sad, openly demanded autonomy as part of a federal Serbia. Serb nationalists condemned the coalition for secessionist activities.

A military mobilization, called for by Milosevich, was prompted by increasing nationalism in the southern Serbian province of Kosovo in the late 1990s. Conscripts and reservists in Vojvodina rejected involvement in the growing ethnic conflict in Kosovo. Forced conscription began in 1998, further straining relations between the Vojvodines and Belgrade. In March 1999, a general mobilization was ordered in Vojvodina.

The Serbian government's policy of ethnic cleansing, the forced deportation of hundreds of thousands of Kosovars,* was opposed by the West. In 1999, the North Atlantic Treaty Organization (NATO) approved military action. NATO planes bombed strategic targets in Serbia, including the bridges and oil refinery at Novi Sad and other areas of Vojvodina. The Yugoslav army withdrew from Kosovo, but not before the majority of the Vojvodines had turned against the government.

Milosevich refused international help in clearing the wrecked bridges that blocked the Vojvodines important river trade. Many governments, including the United States, opposed any form of aid as long as Milosevich remained in power. The Vojvodines, having suffered thousands of casualties and four lost wars, looked to self-government and control of their lives and resources as a way of reasserting their independence. In May 2000, the opposition governor of Vojvodina was assassinated, reportedly on the orders of a Serbian strongman. The killing of the popular leader raised tensions between the Vojvodinans and Serbs of Belgrade.

In 2001, matters worsened when the provincial assembly dismissed one of Vojvodina's deputy prime ministers who belonged to Vojislav Kostunica's Democratic Party of Serbia. Kostunica and his nationalist supporters are reluctant to support Vojvodine autonomy or federalism in Serbia, which they see as the potential first step towards the break-up of Serbia.

Along with the dismissal of the deputy prime minister, the assembly voted to upgrade Novi Sad's status to that of Vojvodina's official capital rather than its previous lower status as the seat of the provincial administration.

Belgrade's decision to appoint a new director of Novi Sad's public service television brought renewed protests in 2001. The autonomists want Vojvodina's radio and television to be independent of Serbian government control. Vojvodina's assembly, roughly two thirds of which supports autonomy, discussed the controversary over the media in mid-November. The assembly voted to reject Belgrade's control.

The increasing separation of the Montenegrins and Kosovars has hardened Belgrade's attitude to Vojvodine aspirations for self-government, but has also stimulated a debate on the province's future. Many Vojvodines see the integrated European Union as their future rather than the continuing Balkan instability. A proposal for a sovereign federation of autonomous cantons on the Swiss model is supported by many Vojvodines, Hungarians, and other national groups.

One key consideration that favors the pro-sovereignty groups is the province's relative prosperity. As Yugoslavia's breadbasket and the producer of its modest output of oil, there's growing support for the goal of keeping more of Vojvodina's natural resources, and their tax revenues, from going to Belgrade. Activists claim that never in their long history have the Vojvodines enjoyed real autonomy, but have suffered exploitation, neglect of their interests, forced assimilation, and the forced changing of Vojvodina's national and ethnic composition. Nationalists believe that only autonomy or independence can protect, manage, and promote the material prosperity. Pro-European groups seek to return Vojvodina to where it used to be and where they feel it belongs, both geographically and culturally.

The Vojvodines, with their long ancestry in Vojvodina, who see their homeland as part of central Europe, as it was until 1918 under the Austro-Hungarian empire, are the most determined advocates of extensive autonomy or independence. Other Serbs, who moved to the prosperous province from poorer areas of the former Yugoslavia, especially those who came during the 1990s as refugees from Croatia, Bosnia, and Kosovo, mostly support Serb unity and fear loosing Vojvodina's ties to the rest of Serbia.

SELECTED BIBLIOGRAPHY:

Anzulovic, Branimir. *Heavenly Serbia: From Myth to Genocide.* 1998.

Gordy, Eric D. *The Culture of Power in Serbia: Nationalism and the Destruction of Alternatives.* 1999.

Malesevic, Sinisa. *Ideology, Legitimacy and the New State: Yugoslavia, Serbia and Croatia.* 2001.

West, Rebecca. *Black Lamb and Grey Falcon: A Journey Through Yugoslavia.* 1995.

Volga Germans

Russian Germans

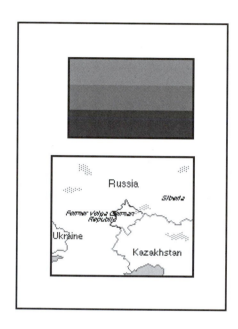

POPULATION: Approximately (2002e) 790,000 Volga Germans in the Russian Federation, most in the southern provinces of European Russia. Outside Russia there are an estimated 100,000 in Germany, and several hundred thousand in Central Asia, particularly Kazakhstan. The total German population of the Russian Federation and the other former Soviet republics is thought to exceed 1.5 million, including about 300,000 in Kazakhstan.

THE VOLGA GERMAN HOMELAND: The Volga German homeland, formerly called the German Volga Republic, occupies the rolling steppe lands in the valley of the middle Volga River on the arbitrary divide between Europe and Asia, along the international border with Kazakhstan. The Volga Germans, deported during World War II, now live scattered across the Russian Federation, from the Kaliningrad Oblast on the Baltic Sea, to Siberia and the Russian Far East. There are also Volga German colonies in most of the former Soviet republics. The Volga German homeland has no official status; it forms the eastern districts of Saratov Oblast. The Russian and German governments have agreed to the re-creation of an autonomous Volga German state in the region they occupied before 1941, but as yet nothing has been accomplished. *Proposed Volga German Region (Former Volga German Republic)*: 10,888 sq. mi.—28,200 sq. km, (2002e) 1,345,000—Russians 85%, Ukrainians 10%, Volga Germans 3%, Kazakhs and Tatars* 2%. In 1941 the region had a population 656,000—Volga Germans 67%, Russians 20%, Ukrainians 12%, others 1%. The major German cultural centers in Russia include Engels, (2002e)189,000, the former capital of the Volga German Autonomous Soviet Socialist Republic, and Moscow, the federation capital. The historic center is Marks, called Katrinenstadt, (2002e) 33,000.

FLAG: The Volga German flag, the flag of the republican movement, is a horizontal tricolor of red, pale blue, and black.

PEOPLE AND CULTURE: The Volga Germans originated with eighteenth-century colonists mostly from the southern German states. The Volga or Russian German culture is a mixture of both German and Slavic influences, incorporating traits and customs that have long since disappeared in Germany and borrowings from the Slavs they have lived among for over two centuries. Deported from their Volga and Black Sea homelands in 1941, the Germans have lived dispersed among the majority Russian population across a wide area of the Russian Federation, Kazakhstan, other parts of Central Asia, and areas of exile. Between 1950 and 1994 an estimated 1.4 million ethnic Germans from the region emigrated to Germany or the Americas. Other groups that have become part of the Volga Germans are the Siberian, Central Asian, Black Sea, Ukrainian, and Baltic Germans who shared the deportations and oppression of the 1940s and 1950s.

LANGUAGE AND RELIGION: The languages of the Volga Germans remain the Bavarian, Danubian, and Swabian dialects they brought with them from southern Germany in the late eighteenth century. In 1989 only 60% of the Russian Germans listed German as their first language; however, since the collapse of the Soviet Union and the reunification of Germany a rapid reculturation has taken hold in the German-populated areas with a revival of the German dialects. Few of the Russian Germans speak the standard modern German language, and those emigrating to Germany have difficulty with the language and culture.

The majority of the Volga Germans are Lutheran or Mennonite, often having emigrated from Germany to escape religious strife. Other groups are Roman Catholic or adhere to such Protestant denominations as the Baptists, Reformed, and Moravians. The religious traditions differ considerably, as their origins were in many states in eighteenth century Germany. Traditionally the churches are the center of cultural life, sustaining moral standards, languages, and ethnic identity.

NATIONAL HISTORY: Tsarina Catherine II of Russia, known as Catherine the Great, was born in the southern German state of Anhalt-Zerbst in 1729. To strengthen her empire and to exploit the rich southern agricultural lands newly won from the Turks and Tatars, the tsarina issued an invitation to the inhabitants of the German states to settle in the region. Peter I, early in the century, had done the same, especially for craftsmen such as shipbuilders. The inhabitants of the southern German states, suffering from overpopulation, crop failures, and religious conflicts, responded in large numbers. Catherine's manifesto, issued in 1763, guaranteed the colonists and their descendents free land, exemption from military service, freedom of religion, local autonomy, use of their own languages, local control of schools, and many other incentives designed to appeal to industrious German peasants.

Catherine's invitation provided a less costly alternative to emigration to

America. Between 1764 and 1768 thousands of German colonists settled the newly conquered frontier districts north and east of the Black Sea. Some 27,000 Germans moved farther east to establish over 100 farming communities along the middle course of the Volga River. Catherine's manifesto provided the settlers with a 30-year exemption from taxes as well as 10-year interest-free loans for homes and farm machinery.

The German colonists, isolated and self-sufficient, eventually prospered as farmers and merchants in close–knit communities having little to do with the neighboring Slav villages. Dialects, cultures, and traditions that gradually changed or disappeared in Germany continued in the region, eventually forming part of a distinctive Slav-influenced German culture. The German settlers, however, suffered great hardships as they spread out across the steppe lands of southern Russia and Ukraine. The lack of trees evolved a distinct type of dwelling, the sod house, similar to those later constructed on the plains of North America. The Russian government's determination that the region produce grains was embodied in a 1767 decree prohibiting the German settlers from engaging in any occupation other than farming. The decree violated Catherine's 1763 manifesto and reduced the German immigrants to serfs in all but name.

Poor output and frequent crop failures in the early years were worsened by the inability of the Russian government to deliver grain seed on time each spring. Often planting took place as late as May or June. The mixture of privation, government interference, and raids by Tatars and bandits took their toll on the settlers. Some returned to Germany, others fled to Russia's Baltic provinces, while many emigrated to North America, where they founded in the Great Plains region of the United States and Canada settlements that remained distinct from nearby German concentrations. The emigrants retained their distinct Slavic-German culture wherever they eventually settled. The German settlers that persevered had their first good harvest in 1775, and production thereafter improved markedly with the introduction of improved farm machinery imported from Germany.

Catherine's successors on the Russian throne progressively abolished the Germans' privileges. By 1870 all of Catherine's guarantees had disappeared. Over the next decade an official policy of assimilation and Russification closed German schools, publications, and institutions. The authorities introduced military conscription. Resistance to assimilation and conscription led to the growth of a German national sentiment in the 1880s and 1890s. The Volga German national movement evolved as a cultural campaign to preserve their language and culture, but it also became antigovernment. By 1890, land in the Volga region became scarce, and German colonists were diverted to the Altai region of Siberia. There were 1,790,439 Germans in the Russian Empire in 1897.

When war broke out in Europe in 1914, the Volga Germans were suspected of pro-German sentiment. The tsarist government imposed harsh new restrictions on the Germans and sought to curtail contacts outside the region. In 1916 the government issued a decree ordering the deportation of all Germans. The deportation order was to be implemented in April 1917. The decree, suspended when revolution swept Russia in February 1917, was finally rescinded, along with all other tsarist decrees, by the Bolsheviks who overthrew the Russian Provisional Government in October 1917.

The Bolshevik coup in October 1917 further divided the Russian Germans. In the western provinces the Germans generally supported the anti-Bolshevik Whites, but in the Volga region and Ukraine the German minority often supported the Reds, partly due to Bolshevik promises of land and self-government. When civil government collapsed local Volga German leaders took control of the region, some preparing to declare independence and to seek assistance from the German military units occupying Russian territory to the west. However, in late 1917 Bolshevik forces overran the region, and pro-Bolshevik Germans organized an autonomous administration, the first ethnic group to be organized under the Bolshevik's nationalities program. In 1919 the region was raised to the status of an autonomous republic within the new Soviet Russian Federation. Outside the Volga republic the Soviet authorities created 17 autonomous districts for the scattered German populations.

The Volga German homeland was created as a model showcase to encourage the spread of communism in Germany, but the Volga Germans suffered harsh repression when the post–World War I communist uprisings failed in Germany. As relations between the Soviet Union and Germany worsened during the late 1920s and early 1930s, the repression of the German population of Russia increased. Official repression eased only when the Soviet Union signed a nonaggression treaty with Nazi Germany in 1939. By 1940, more than 25% of the total German population of the Soviet Union lived in the German Volga Republic.

The German invasion of their Soviet ally in June 1941 ended the short period of leniency toward the Volga Germans. The Soviet leader, Joseph Stalin, accused all Soviet Germans of collaboration. In August 1941 the 440,000 Volga Germans and between 250,000 and 350,000 mostly Black Sea Germans were shipped east in closed cattle cars. The deportees, often without food or shelter, were dumped at rail sidings across Siberia and Central Asia under close control of the People's Committee of Internal Affairs, the NKVD. Another 350,000 Germans, living in areas overrun by the German armies, were evacuated by the German army to Germany. Over 200,000 of the evacuees, rounded up by Soviet troops in defeated Germany in 1945, were forcibly repatriated and sent directly to slave labor camps, where they remained until the survivors were granted amnesty after Stalin's death in 1953.

The postwar Soviet government began a radical denationalization program, whereby Germans were denied the opportunity to maintain their language and culture. The policy of forced assimilation, carried out with considerable force and brutality, was considered a success. Although the excesses of the program eased with Stalin's death in 1953, according to the 1959 Soviet census only 43% of the ethnic Germans in the Soviet Union stated that they spoke German in their daily lives.

The Volga Germans were not rehabilitated with the other deported Soviet peoples in 1956–57. The Germans were finally exonerated in 1964 but were not allowed to return to their homes in the Volga River basin or other areas of Russia. Their petitions and appeals constantly rebuffed, the German exiles developed a sense of grievance that stimulated the growth of nationalism in the 1970s. In 1975 a Volga German national movement formed to work for the reestablishment of an autonomous German homeland on the Volga. Improved relations between the Soviet Union and Germany in the late 1970s allowed a small number to emigrate, but the numbers were limited by Germany's inability to absorb all who wished to leave Russia.

The official reestablishment of an autonomous German republic within Russia was first raised by Premier Leonid Brezhnev in 1972. But each time the government issued a statement implying or clearly stating an intention to reestablish a German republic in the Volga region, it was met with demonstrations and strong opposition from the Russian population settled in the Volga region following the German deportation in 1941. The need for a German homeland in Russia was discussed in March 1991, during a meeting between President Mikhail Gorbachev and the German foreign minister, Hans–Dietrich Genser, but subsequent events, including the collapse of the Soviet Union, in August 1991, left the question of an autonomous homeland unsettled.

In July 1991 the Soviet government approved the formation of a German national county in the Altai Krai, comprising parts of the Slavgorod and Khabarovsk Raions (districts). The national *raion* was to be the first of several German national districts, but the plan was abandoned when the Soviet Union collapsed in August 1991.

Although cool to the idea of yet another minority nationalism, the Russian authorities were badly in need of Germany's political and financial assistance, and in a series of meetings with German officials they finally agreed to a Volga German autonomous homeland. The long delay in implementing the accord stimulated more militant groups and demands, and provoked the emigration of over a 100,000 a year to Germany in the 1990s. An estimated half of the ethnic Germans living in the Soviet Union in 1991 left for Germany, taking advantage of the German government's offer to return to their historical homeland. The majority of the returning Germans were descendents of the Volga Germans deported from the Volga in 1941. However, in the later 1990s, cultural and dialectical differences and Germany's reunification economic problems and high un-employment blunted the Russian Germans' welcome in Germany and again raised the question of a German-financed homeland on the Volga.

The continuing arrival of ethnic Germans from the former Soviet Union became increasingly sensitive in Germany. While Germans of Turkish origin, born in the country and speaking German as their first language, were denied citizenship, people of German descent, often Russian-speaking and culturally as distinct as the Turks, were automatically granted it. The Volga Germans, called *Aussiedler* (Outsettlers), whose German ancestors left Germany centuries ago, were the only immigrants whose presence was largely unquestioned by the German public, though most were farmers, with little to offer industrialized Germany.

A 1996 meeting of the initiative group uniting major cultural and nationalist organizations of Russia's ethnic Germans adopted a resolution on the Volga Germans' national-cultural autonomy, the first group of its kind on the territory of the Russian Federation. The participants in the meeting approved the membership of the organizing committee, which carried the Germans' case for autonomy to the various ministries, departments, and local administrations of the Russian Federation.

Germany's intake of Volga Germans began to be questioned by politicians in the late 1990s, mainly over the increased cost of supporting and training the new arrivals, which often included lessons in the German language. In 1999 there were demonstrations against the *Aussiedler* in Berlin, where, activists claimed, they immediately began to receive upon arrival welfare benefits at a cost of over two billion dollars a year. Opinion polls showed that around 70% of the Germans supported controls on Volga German immigration and changes to Germany's nationality laws, which considered blood over birthplace as a basis for citizenship. In late 1999 the German government ended the offer of free flights for ethnic Germans to come to Germany.

The German government, in an effort to persuade the Volga Germans to stay where they are, spent over $50 million supplying coal, flour, and medicines and promoting small businesses. But for many of the Volga Germans, the prospect of being unemployed in a rich country is still preferable to staying in poverty in the countries of the former Soviet Union. The number of Volga Germans that stay will partly depend on the political and economic conditions, including the crucial element—a self-governing homeland.

SELECTED BIBLIOGRAPHY:

Kloderdanz, Timothy J. *Thunder on the Steppe: Volga German Folklife in a Changing Russia.* 1994.

Koch, Frederick C. *The Volga Germans: In Russia and the Americas 1763 to the Present.* 1987.

Long, James W. *From Privileged to Dispossessed: The Volga Germans 1860–1917.* 1988.

Sinner, Peter. *Germans in the Land of the Volga.* 1989.

Vorarlbergers

Alemannis; Eastern Alemanis

POPULATION: Approximately (2002e) 326,000 Vorarlbergers in Austria, mostly concentrated in the Vorarlberg, but with substantial populations in Vienna and other parts of Austria, and in Switzerland and Germany.

THE VORARLBERGER HOMELAND: The Vorarlberger homeland lies in the extreme western portion of Austria. Called Vorarlberg, for the Arlberg Mountain, which lies on the border between Vorarlberg and Tyrol, the name means "Land before or beyond the Arlberg." The region is noted for its alpine scenery and for its cattle and dairy herds. Vorarlberg forms a state *(land)* of the Federal Republic of Austria. *State of Vorarlberg (Bundesland Vorarlberg)*: 1,004 sq. mi.—2,601 sq. km, (2002e) 355,000—Vorarlbergers 88%, Tyroleans* 8%, other Austrians 4%. The Vorarlberger capital and major cultural center is Bregenz, (2002e) 26,000. The other major cultural center is Dornbirn (2002e) 42,000. The Bregenz-Dornbirn metropolitan area has a population of 127,000.

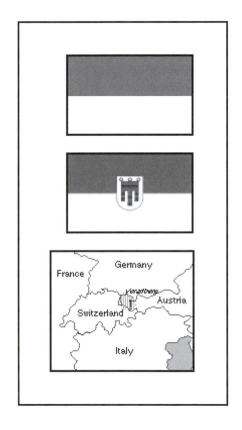

FLAGS: The Vorarlberger national flag, the official flag of the federal state, is a horizontal bicolor of red over white. Vorarlberger nationalists use the national flag with the addition of the arms of the region centered.

PEOPLE AND CULTURE: The Vorarlbergers are an Alemannic people historically and culturally more closely related to the Swiss-Germans and Swabians* than to the neighboring Tyroleans or Austrians. In the isolation of their mountain homeland they developed a distinctive alpine society that shaped their national character and culture. Even the baroque style, traditional in Austria, was not accepted in Vorarlberg, whose people developed a uniquely alpine style in rebellion against what they saw as Hapsburg extravagances. Although the most industrialized of the Austrian states outside Vienna, Vorarlberg remained isolated from the rest of Austria until modern times. The region's population is mostly urban and prosperous, and it retains close dialectical and cultural ties to the neighboring non-Austrian peoples of Switzerland.

LANGUAGE AND RELIGION: The Vorarlbergers are the only group in Austria to speak an Alemannic dialect, part of the group of dialects called High Alemannic, which includes the Swiss-German dialects spoken in neighboring Switzerland and the Swabian dialect of adjacent parts of Germany. The dialect, called Vorarlbergerdeutsch, Swabian in origin, is the language of daily life, although the majority of Vorarlbergers are bilingual and also speak standard Austrian German.

The Vorarlbergers, like the other Austrian nations, are primarily Roman Catholic; a Protestant minority lives mostly along the border with Switzerland. The isolation of the region helped the Roman Catholic church to retain considerable influence until World War II. Presently church holidays and festivals remain important cultural events, and religion remains an important part of Vorarlberger culture.

NATIONAL HISTORY: The highland region around Lake Constance has long been a European crossroads and early came under Roman rule, forming part of the province of Rhaetia. At the collapse of Roman power in the fifth century, tribal groups moved into the area, which was soon dominated by the Germanic Alemanni tribe. Part of the Frankish kingdom of Charlemagne in the eighth century, Vorarlberg later formed part of the eastern Frankish kingdom, the foundation of the modern Germanic peoples. In the thirteenth and fourteenth centuries, there was a migration from the present Swiss region of Valais, where the migrants formed the basis of the present Vorarlberg nation.

Vorarlberg was acquired by the counts of Montfort, until it was annexed, between the fourteenth and sixteenth centuries, piecemeal by the Hapsburgs. In 1523 Vorarlberg became a Hapsburg crownland administered by the neighboring Tyroleans. For centuries the Vorarlbergers formed a separate German-speaking nation in the multinational Austrian Empire controlled by the Hapsburgs.

During the Napoleonic Wars Bavarians* occupied Vorarlberg, a gift from Napoleon to his Bavarian ally. Along with Tyrol, Vorarlberg remained under Bavarian rule from 1805 to 1814. In 1809 the Vorarlbergers joined the Tyroleans in a revolt against the Bavarians and French. With Napoleon's eventual defeat the Vorarlbergers were again brought under Austrian rule. In 1861 a bishopric was established in Bregenz, the beginning of Vorarlberg's political separation from neighboring Tyrol.

The region industrialized in the late 1800s, utilizing the abundant hydroelectric power. Although the Vorarlbergers remained isolated from the rest of Austria until the construction of a tunnel under the Arlberg in 1884, their province was one of the most progressive in the empire. The Vorarlbergers had the first telephone, the first electric light, and the first hydroelectric turbine in the empire. A Vorarlberger was the first in the empire to drive an automobile. In some aspects, the region's schools were a century ahead of those in other parts of the empire. Industrialized, due to the abundant hydroelectric power, in the late nineteenth century, the region was one of the most advanced in the empire by the turn of the twentieth century. Proud of their achievements and of their unique culture, the Vorarlbergers, in the late nineteenth century developed a zealous local patriotism.

The Vorarlbergers supported the Austrians when the conflict swept across Europe in 1914. Their industries played an important part in the Austrian war effort. Insulated from the war by their mountains, the Vorarlbergers were unprepared for the defeat and collapse of the empire in November 1918. Amidst the chaos the Vorarlbergers proclaimed themselves a separate non-Austrian, Germanic people, and local leaders set up a separate administration as the civil government of the empire collapsed. They organized a plebiscite and voted for independence from Austria and an alliance with neutral Switzerland, with which they had economic, geographic, and linguistic ties. The independence of the Republic of Vorarlberg was declared on 3 November 1918, and the new nationalist government began to establish close ties to the neighboring Swiss Confederation. The secession of Vorarlberg from Austria was blocked by the allies and the new Austrian republican government.

Under strong economic and political pressure, the Vorarlbergers finally joined the new Austrian republic, becoming an autonomous *land*, or state, with a separate provincial assembly. The unstable Austrian government, dominated by anticlerical, socialist Vienna, was constantly at odds with the nationalistic Vorarlbergers. In April 1919, over 80% of the Vorarlbergers voted to secede from Austria and to attach themselves to Switzerland, but they were again blocked by allied opposition. The Austrian government feared that the loss of Vorarlberg would lead to the secession of Tyrol and other regions not closely tied to the Austrian heartland around Vienna.

The powerful provincial diet retained considerable autonomy, and another movement for secession, in 1921, was defeated only following allied intervention. Vorarlberg's autonomy was curtailed by the socialist government in Vienna, but political turbulence kept the nationalist movement active during the late 1920s and early 1930s. Opposition to rule from Vienna when the Vorarlbergers, who remained oriented to Zurich and the West, continued to fuel periodic unrest and strikes in the region.

In 1938 Austria was annexed by Nazi Germany, and the Vorarlbergers lost all their remaining autonomy. Initial enthusiasm for union with Germany waned following the bombing of the industrial cities in Vorarlberg in 1944. In 1945 French troops occupied the region, withdrawing only when the Allied occupation of Austria ended in 1955.

Standard German mostly replaced the Vorarlbergers' Alemannic dialect by the 1960s, but the region's unique alpine culture flourished with renewed vigor. Austria's state neutrality and prosperous postwar economy benefited industrial Vorarlberg during the 1970s and 1980s. Vorarlberg had the fastest-growing population in the Alpine region of Europe, growing 94% between 1923 and 1971. By the 1980s "guest workers" from southern Europe constituted about 20% of the workforce in the region, raising social tension with the closely knit Vorarlberger community.

In September 1979, an autonomist group, Pro-Vorarlberg, published an appeal in which it demanded a special statute for Vorarlberg within the Austrian republic. The appeal led to an initiative by the provincial diet to conduct with the government in Vienna negotiations on financial and fiscal autonomy, and increased control of local education, commerce, forestry, agriculture, and communications. The Vorarlbergers also demanded the right to conclude contracts with neighboring states, such as Germany, to which it sold substantial amounts of hydroelectric power. The autonomy initiative was approved by a provincial referendum on 23 June 1980 and was passed by almost 70% of the electorate, but it was opposed by the Austrian government and was never implemented. In the late 1990s the Vorarlbergers continued to claim that theirs was an independent nation, freely associated with the post–World War II Austrian republic.

Although the Vorarlbergers have close economic and historical ties to neighboring Switzerland and Liechtenstein, due to the rugged nature of their homeland and the struggle of its citizens to glean a livelihood from the meager resources, the Vorarlbergers have retained a very strong sense of their separate culture. Their national flag is flown more often than the Austrian national flag, and local heroes take precedence over Austrian heroes.

Economically the Vorarlbergers have attained considerable autonomy. Vorarlberg ranks second only to Vienna in industrialization, with more than half of its labor force engaged in industry and crafts. Although a rail tunnel was opened between Vorarlberg and Tyrol in the late nineteenth century, a car tunnel was completed only in 1979. The state's road and rail communications with neighboring foreign countries are far more extensive than those with neighboring Tyrol and the rest of Austria.

Austria's entry into the European Union (EU) on 1 January 1995 allowed for closer cross-border trade and cultural relations with German to the north. Closer ties between Switzerland and the EU also allowed a decrease in border controls between Vorarlberg and Switzerland. Economically oriented to the west and north, the Vorarlbergers have become among the most pro-European in Austria, supporting the opening of borders and close relations, both economically and culturally, with the neighboring non-Austrian peoples.

The increased contact with the neighboring regions of Germany as con-

tiguous parts of the European Union by 2002 had reoriented the Vorarlbergers to the west rather than to Vienna and central Austria to the east.
The introduction of the Euro, the common EU currency, on 1 January
2002 eliminated yet another difference between the Vorarlbergers and the
Swabians and Bavarians. Vorarlberger nationalists look to European integration to bring them the sovereignty they have long sought. Many Vorarlbergers, even those who oppose nationalist tendencies, see little sense
in maintaining another layer of government in Vienna to the east when
Brussels, to the west, is the center of integrated Europe.

SELECTED BIBLIOGRAPHY:

Jelavich, Barbara. *Modern Austria: Empire and Republic 1815–1986*. 1987.
Philpott, Don, et al. *Austria*. 1993.
Thaler, Peter. *The Ambivalence of Identity*. 2000.
Voegelin, Eric, ed. *The Authoritarian State: An Essay on the Problem of Austria*. 1999.

Votes

Vadjalaizit; Vadjalaizõt; Votians; Votics; Vatja; Vadjakko; Vaddalain; Maavätchi

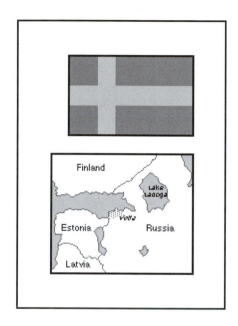

POPULATION: Approximately (2002e) 30,000 Votes in Russia, concentrated in the Votia region of Kingisepp district of St. Petersburg Oblast in northwestern Russia. Outside the region there are Vote communities in St. Petersburg, Ivangorod, Kingisepp, and in the Estonian border town of Narva. Because Votes hid their identity during most of the twentieth century, estimates of the total population are disputed, ranging from about 15, based on speakers of the Vote language, to over 100,000, based on the ethnic background of the regional population. Officially the Votes are counted as ethnic Russians.

THE VOTIC HOMELAND: The Votic homeland, called Votia, lies in northwestern Russia on the southern shore of the Gulf of Finland between St. Petersburg and the Estonian border. Most of the region is a broad, flat plain, with only slight variation in elevation. Once heavily forested, most of the territory is now farmland, particularly in the basin of the Luga River. The Vote homeland has no official status in Russia. Many Votes spend summers in the homeland but normally live in the nearby towns and cities, particularly St. Petersburg, Kingisepp, and Ivangorod/Narva. The Vote capital and major cultural center is Kotly, called Kattila in the Vote language, (2002e) 7,000. The major Vote-speaking village is Krakolye, called Jõgõperä in Votic. Ivangorod on the Estonian border opposite Narva, called Jaanilidna by the Votes, (2002e) 21,000, is becoming an important Vote cultural center.

FLAG: The Vote national flag, the flag of the national movement, is a blue field bearing a pale green cross known as the Cross of St. Peter.

PEOPLE AND CULTURE: The Votes are a Finnic people closely related to the neighboring Ingrians* and Estonians. They are considered the oldest indigenous group in the region. Every year on St. Peter's Day, the Votes hold their annual festival, where their revived singing and dancing forms are taught. The Votes in the western area are mostly fishermen; in the central and eastern parts, fishing is secondary to farming. Trades and crafts are an essential part of Votic life. Each Vote village traditionally had its blacksmith and shoemaker. The Votes were never a very numerous people, but they have survived wars, famine, pestilence, and suppression. Assimilation, both Estonianization and Russification, is far advanced, although a new interest in their culture and language may help to reverse the loss of their culture and language. The Votes have mostly lost their language; their ancient folk culture constitutes the mainstay of the Votic identity.

LANGUAGE AND RELIGION: The Votes are now overwhelmingly Russian speaking, although small numbers are able to speak Votic or Ingrian. The Votic language, called Vadja Tseeli or Vadyaa Cheeli, is a Western Finnic language of the Finnic group of Finno-Ugrian languages. The language was formerly spoken in four major dialects—Western, Eastern, Kurovtsy, and Krevin, in Estonia and Latvia. The dialects died out in the nineteenth and early twentieth centuries. The spoken language, the surviving Western dialect, is close to Ingrian and the northwestern dialects of Estonian. The dialects differed phonetically, and lexical peculiarities persisted, but the dialects were mutually intelligible. The Kurovtsy dialect was strongly influenced by Ingrian. The Eastern dialect became extinct in the 1960s. By 1989, there were still 62 Votes who spoke the language fluently. Votic has no official status in Russia. The language has been written only since the early 1990s, in translations by Estonian scholars, although some Votic texts were published together with translations into Finnish, Estonian, or Russian after 1935. Until the 1990s, no literature existed in Votic, except for two collections of Votic folklore published in 1908 and 1960. By 1997 only about 15 people were able to speak the language fluently, although younger Votes have now begun to learn the language. A grammar of the Votic language was published by Indiana University in 1968.

The Votes are mostly Orthodox Christians, although their traditional beliefs persist. The belief in water-related supernatural beings reflect the presence of bodies of water in the Vote homeland, both the Gulf of Finland and many lakes. Water spirits are still invoked by fishermen and farmers. The names of the water spirits are distinguished according to their location in sea, river, lake, stream, or spring, a manifestation of the belief that spirits inhabit every body of water. Traditionally the Votes devoted one day in the year to the goddess of the sea and rivers. Saints' days, particularly those of saints Peter, Elijah, and Florian, are traditional festival days on which to honor the traditional water spirits.

NATIONAL HISTORY: The Votes developed from early Finnic tribes that settled the region as early as 3000 B.C. The nomadic Finnic groups, originally from the Volga River basin, migrated to the shores of the Gulf of Finland before the Christian Era. They settled a huge area but were later pushed north and west by the Slav migrations of the sixth to eighth centuries. The Votes emerged during the first millennium from the Finnic tribes who had remained on the east side of the Narva River and Lake Peipus.

The comparatively small Votic tribes never formed a national unit or an administrative district. Their lands, located near the major commercial routes from the east to the west, included the Izhorian Plateau between Kingissepp and Gachina between the fourth and seventh centuries. The Slavic founding of Novgorod in 859 meant a foothold for the Slavs and tributes from the Votic tribes. In 1069, in an effort to free themselves from Slavic domination, the Votes revolted and attacked Novgorod but were defeated. As the rule of Novgorod expanded, their dependence on it increased. In written records, the Votes were first mentioned in the eleventh century in orders of Prince Yaroslav of Novgorod concerning roads and bridges in the region. The role of the Votes in the Novgorod state seems to have been significant. The Russian language, adopted by Votic noblemen and later by all prominent people, began to spread in Votia.

The southern and northwestern Votic groups, like all the Baltic-Finnic peoples, were called *chud*, or useless, by the Russians. The Votes were also mentioned in papal and Swedish records in the twelfth and thirteenth centuries. The written records of the Votes is directly linked to growing foreign interest in the Votic lands.

The Votes by the twelfth century had spread from the Narva River in to west to the Inger River in the east, and from the Gulf of Finland in the north to the present-day regions of Luga and Pskov. The Votes under the influence of the mercantile Russian republic of Novgorod in the eleventh and twelfth centuries were the most advanced of the Votic groups; their homeland was known as the Votic Fifth.

The fall of Novgorod to Moscow in 1478 began centuries of forced assimilation, dispersion, and repression. Assimilation, first into the larger Ingrian population, then into Russian society, gradually reduced the numbers identifying with the Vote culture and language. Votic resistance to Moscow's rule was broken by brutal deportations in 1484 and 1488 and by conversion to Russian Orthodoxy.

In the Middle Ages, following the German conquest of the Baltic region, the whole northwestern part of the Novgorod principality was called Watland or Voteland, and all the related Finnic peoples were called Votes. The name Watland (Votelandor Watlandia), covered a wide area south of the Gulf of Finland.

The Swedes took control of the region in 1558 but lost the region during the Northern War, which ended with the cession of the entire southern shore of the Gulf of Finland to Russia in 1721. Swedish influence included their Lutheran religion, which was adopted by the neighboring

Ingrians. To the present Ingrians are Protestants, while Votes and Izhors (Southern Ingrians) are Orthodox.

The region was officially designated the province of St. Petersburg in 1710, when Tsar Peter I decided to build a new capital on the Gulf of Finland. The influx of Slav workers, then the Russian government, pushed the Votes from the eastern districts, which became part of the Russian settlement area. The Votes, caught between the Russians to the east and the influence of the Baltic Germans and Estonians to the west, began to assimilate, their language and culture relegated to that of a folk culture. By the 1740s, serfdom was firmly established, and the majority of the Votes were treated as property of the Russian and Baltic German manors.

In the eighteenth century a Baltic German scholar from Narva, Friedrich Ludolph Trefurt, was the first to study the culture and language of the Votes. The Russian historian Feodor Tumanski studied the Votes in the St. Petersburg Guberniya (province) in the early 1790s. A 90-page Votic grammar, based on the Trefurt and Tumanski studies, was published by August Ahlgvist in 1856. The Finnish name for the Votes, Vadja or Vatja, is associated with the eastern county of Estonia, Vaiga. In 1848, 37 Votic villages were officially recorded in the region, with a population of over 30,000. The Votes, living as far south as the Latvian border in the mid-nineteenth century, were mostly trilingual, speaking Votic, Ingrian, and Russian. In 1850 about 50% of the Votes spoke Russian, and Church Slavonic, the language used in the Orthodox religion, could be understood by about 10%.

In the late nineteenth century, official Russian nationalism was strengthened in order to tie the outer provinces to the center. Alexander III, who came to the Russian throne in 1881, greatly reduced the feudal privileges of the landowners but also suppressed the activities of awakening Finnic identities. Russian was made the only language of government and education, censorship became very strict, and adherence to Russian Orthodoxy was enforced. The policy of Russification ended in 1897, allowing Vote activists to join the Estonians and Ingrians in supporting language and cultural events and studies.

The outbreak of World War I in 1914 brought new hardships, including conscription, the exchange of produce for useless government paper, and forced labor. The aspiration for cultural and political self-rule led to widespread Vote support for the revolution that overthrew the monarchy in February 1917. The creation of *soviets*, local revolutionary committees, ended the movement for an autonomous district following the Bolshevik coup that ended the democratic Russian revolutionary government in October 1917.

The government of breakaway Estonia laid claim to Votia in 1918, but fighting in Estonia and the spread of the Russian Civil War ended Estonian attempts to annex the region. By 1919 the region was under firm

Bolshevik control, with the new international border with Estonia established at the western edge of Votia.

Bolshevik rule, at first supportive of the small nationalities, became repressive under Joseph Stalin after 1924. The most industrious farmers and fishermen were deported, to force the remainder to give up their property and join the collectives. Physical violence was combined with national and religious persecution. Domestic handicrafts were forbidden, as was owning private fishing boats. Thousands of Votes were deported for refusing to register as ethnic Russians. Repression of the Votes resulted in the decline of the Votic population by over 90% between 1926 and 1959. Votes as far as possible concealed their Votic identity in the repressive Soviet era, pretending to be ethnic Russians. The Russians who lived in the Votia region were mostly unaware that the Votes had ever existed. From 1939 on the Votes were not recorded in Soviet censuses.

A Votic student at Estonia's Tartu University in 1924 compiled a 55-page grammar, but the textbook was never published, and the author met a tragic death. The Votes were the only minority in northwestern Russia for whom no written language was created. The Votic language was used briefly for primary education in the village of Pesky in the early 1930s, but most Votic children were taught Ingrian until Russian was enforced as the only language of teaching in the mid-1930s.

The Second World War again brought violence and destruction to the region. The Finns and Germans invaded the region, although the Finns refused to join the German siege of nearby Leningrad (St. Petersburg). Many Votes were forcibly conscripted into Estonian battalions by the German authorities. Some Votes succeeded in escaping to Finland when the Germans withdrew in 1944, but many were arrested and deported throughout the Soviet state, as far as Central Asia.

Stalin's death in 1953 resulted in numerous petitions being sent to Moscow. As a result, from 1956 on a number of Votes were allowed to return to their homeland in Votia. Their homes, already occupied by strangers, mostly Russians evacuated during the war, were never returned, and most Votes settled in villages or shantytowns around the larger cities.

Annual research expeditions, made up of teachers and students of Tartu University in Estonia, have been collecting linguistic materials in the Votia area since 1956. In the past Votic was mainly used in everyday family life, traditional industries, and folklore. The use of spoken Votic language has been encouraged by the annual summer expeditions of Estonian linguists and students, particularly following the collapse of Soviet power in 1991. The serious interest shown by outsiders in their language and culture raised the status of their native language in the eyes of the Votes and began the reversal of centuries of assimilation.

In 1992, nationalists, aided by Estonian activists, formed a cultural-regional movement called Vaddjalista. The activists of Vaddjalista, aided by the annual Estonian expedition, are collecting cultural and linguistic materials and supporting the rebirth of the Vote culture. Younger Votes, encouraged by Estonian aid and texts, have begun to learn and use the language as a matter of pride. In 1998 Vote leaders presented a plan for a cultural region to cover the Vote heartland in the Luga Valley.

SELECTED BIBLIOGRAPHY:

Ariste, Paul. *The Votian Ethnology*. 1977.
Levinson, David. *Ethnic Groups Worldwide*. 1998.
Mouritzen, Hans. *Bordering Russia: Theory and Prospects for Europe's Baltic Rim*. 1998.
Paasi, Anssi. *Territories, Boundaries and Consciousness: The Changing Geographies of the Finnish-Russian Boundary*. 1997.

Wa

Wah; Lawa; Lava; Lua; Lavu'a; Lowa; Va; Hkawa; Kawa; Kala

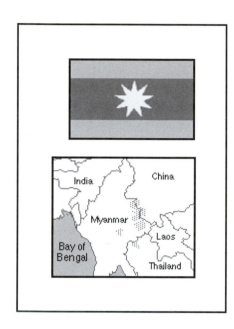

POPULATION: Approximately (2002e) 720,000 Wa in Southeast Asia, 615,000 concentrated in the Wa States region of Shan State in Myanmar, 85,000 in southern Yunnan in China, and 20,000 in northwestern Thailand. Outside the region there are Wa communities in other parts of Myanmar and Thailand. Wa nationalists claim a regional population of over 1.5 million, including 900,000 in Myanmar.

THE WA HOMELAND: The Wa homeland occupies the basin of the upper Salween River and the surrounding highlands of the Shan Plateau in northeastern Myanmar, the mountains and valleys of the Tanen Tanggyi Range that extend into China and Thailand. The Wa are primarily slash-and-burn agriculturalists, although settle rice farming is now becoming the predominant occupation. The Wa homeland has no official status. In Myanmar the former Wa States now form part of Shan State. *Wa States*: 3,332 sq. mi.—8,630 sq. km, (2002e) 714,000—Wa 80%, Shans* 20%, other Burmese. The Wa capital and major cultural center is Mong Yawng, called Maung Yawn in the Wa language, (2002e) 12,000. The other important cultural center is Kentung, called Kentun, the center of the Kentun Wa, (2002e) 67,000.

FLAG: The Wa national flag, the flag of the national movement, has horizontal stripes of pale blue, red, and pale blue, the red twice the width of the blue stripes and charged with a white nine-pointed star.

PEOPLE AND CULTURE: The Wa, popularly called Lawa in Thailand and Va in China, are believed to be the original inhabitants of the Shan Plateau region and form nine clan or tribal groups. A Mon-Khmer people, the Wa are ethnically and linguistically related to the Mons* and the Khmer of Cambodia. They are traditionally divided into the commoners and a small elite called the Kun. Until the early twentieth century, headhunting formed an integral part of the Wa culture and religion; the skulls were used to fertilize fields and were believed to ensure good crops and good health. Most are now cultivators of the rotational type and are skilled at making wet rice terraces in the foothills and uplands. Wa marriages are usually monogamous, and lineage is through the male line. In China the Western Wa are divided into two nationalities, the Blang and Va. The Lawa of Thailand are the smallest of the three major groups. Isolation has helped the Wa to retain their traditions.

LANGUAGE AND RELIGION: The Wa speak dialects of the Waic subbranch of the Palaung-Wa language of the Mon-Khmer language group. Wa is written in a Latin alphabet devised by missionaries. The language is spoken in six major dialects—Wa Lon, Wu, Kentun Wa, Son, En, and La. Although the Western Wa of China are closely related to the Wa of Myanmar and Thailand, there are few similarities in the dialects, although Kentung Wa can be understood. Illiteracy is a major problem, particularly among the Chinese Wa.

The majority of the Wa adhere to traditional beliefs; there are Buddhist and Christian minorities. Ancestor worship remains an important part of Wa beliefs, which are often combined with Buddhist customs and celebrations. The so-called wild, or pagan, Wa are concentrated in the isolated northern and central Wa States. The "tame" Wa have acculturated to neighboring peoples, sometimes marrying with them, and are now mostly Buddhists. Wa villagers believe in house spirits, local spirits, and spirits of the iron mines in the region. Many deities are regarded as the disembodied spirits of ancient heroes. In China about half the Wa claim to be Buddhists; however, they are still referred to as "Buddhist animists."

NATIONAL HISTORY: From their origins in eastern Tibet, the Mon-Khmer peoples migrated south along the Mekong and Salween Rivers. The Wa settled the mountains along the upper Salween, probably between the fifth and third centuries B.C. Some historians believe that the Wa are the original dwellers of the delta plain but were subsequently driven into the mountains by Thais, Shans, and Burmans who conquered the lowlands. According to Wa tradition they once inhabited the plateau lowlands, but stronger peoples drove them into the mountains. A primitive tribal people, the Wa, unlike most of the other peoples of the region, never came under the religious or cultural influences of India or China. Around 660 A.D. several Wa clans migrated into the Mae Ping Valley in present northern Thailand. They are believed to be the first settlers in northern Thailand and Myanmar.

The Shans, a Thai people, overran the Wa territory in the seventh century. The conquerors, from southeastern China, imposed their social order on the tribes, creating small Wa states ruled by an aristocratic elite. Allied to the Shans, the fierce Wa warriors helped to defeat a Mongol invasion in the thirteenth century. The Shan declined in the early nineteenth century, leaving the Wa States virtually independent as vassal states of the Burman king.

In the 1870s the Wa and Shan princes renounced their allegiance to the Burman king; the resulting chaos gave the British colonial authorities in India a pretext to intervene. Following the Third Anglo-Burman War in 1885–86, the Wa States, along with the Shan States, came under British rule. The British troops were often welcomed as liberators from oppressive Burman rule.

The colonial authorities established separate treaty relations with the Wa princes, the treaties formalizing their status as British protectorates not included in British Burma. Many Wa clans, particularly in the less developed northern states, resisted the imposition of British rule until 1889. British attempts to stamp out ritual head-hunting, an integral part of the Wa culture and religion, met fierce resistance. Although the states remained semi-independent under their traditional rulers, the British retained the right to confirm the succession of the rulers.

The colonial authorities consolidated the Wa and Shan states in 1922 to form the Federated Shan States. The federation, under the responsibility of a British commissioner, was structured to separate the Wa States as an administrative unit, with the British commissioner as adviser to the courts of the various Wa princes.

The European influence, particularly the impact of the missionaries who arrived in the Wa States in the 1920s, gradually ended the ancient practice of head-hunting. Missionary education, conducted in the Wa language using a Latin alphabet devised by missionaries for the purpose, introduced the Wa to the ideas and power of European nationalism and fostered a sense of unity among the various tribes and clans. In 1930, the first Wa national organization formed to promote and protect the Wa language and culture in the Wa States and the surrounding areas.

The Wa generally supported the British during World War II, acting as guides for Allied patrols and fighting the Burman, Shan, and Thai allies of the Japanese. The occupation of the region by the Japanese and their allies forced the Wa to retreat into the mountains, where they formed guerrilla groups that terrorized enemy patrols. In December 1943 the Japanese authorities placed the Wa States under the direct rule of their Burman allies, the first time in history that the Burmans were able to impose their rule directly on the fiercely independent Wa tribes. The Burmans, who switched to the Allied cause in 1944, maintained their control of the region following the Japanese defeat and the return of the British in 1945.

Preparations for the independence of Burma after the war stimulated Burman demands for the inclusion in the Burmese state of all the territories that had been tributary to the medieval Burman kings. In 1948, without their consent, the British included the Wa States in the territories ceded to the new Union of Burma.

In 1959 the government deposed the Wa princes, setting off a rebellion.

The Wa rebels, holding the strategic passes, formed alliances with insurgent Shans, who controlled the lowlands, and the Lahu,* in control of the mountain tops. The Wa insurgency spread to the formerly neutral Wa tribes following the takeover of the Burmese state by a brutal military regime in 1962.

Wa ties to the related tribes in China gave them a natural sanctuary and a conduit for military aid and arms, often provided by China's communist government. The Wa insurgents formed an alliance with the Chinese supported Burmese communist rebels active in the region. To finance the war, the Wa turned to the region's traditional crop, opium. In 1972, in the midst of a fierce rivalry with the Shan insurgents for control of the opium-producing eastern Shan Plateau, the Wa leaders for the first time openly espoused a separatist platform and independence in a federation of states to replace the Burmese military regime.

The crushing of the prodemocracy movement in Burma, in 1988, pushed the Wa to adopt a less doctrinaire and more openly nationalist ideology. In April 1989 the Wa tribesmen, accounting for 80% of the membership of the insurgent Communist Party of Burma (CAB), rebelled and drove the communist leaders across the border into China. The United Wa State Army (UWSA) signed a cease-fire deal with the Burmese junta, the first ethnic rebel group to do so. As part of the deal, the UWSA was allowed to continue its drug trade to finance over 20,000 combat soldiers.

The lucrative drug trade sparked a minor war with the Shan drug lord, Khun Shan, in 1990. The violent fighting for control of the drug trails along the Thai and Chinese border left hundreds dead. In April 1991 the fighting became so fierce that the Thai military intervened to drive both the Wa and Shan drug traffickers deeper into Myanmar and away from the sensitive Thai border.

The Wa insurgency in the early 1990s split between the groups fighting for autonomy or independence and those fighting to protect their contraband drug trade. Violence between the two groups seriously weakened the Wa national movement after 1992. Those Wa groups heavily involved in the drug trade increasingly cooperated with the Myanmar government against other ethnic insurgencies and rival drug traffickers. Fighting intensified in 1993–96 following government moves to allocate additional territories in Shan State to Wa settlers, which was vigorously resisted by the Shans.

The rebel groups began to experiment in methamphetamine production in 1995, making alliances with Thai producers and traffickers across the border. Members of the UWSA began to resettle its highland civilian population from the China-Myanmar border down to the southern districts along the Thai border. They and the Burmese government claimed that the resettlement was part of a campaign to wipe out opium cultivation in the Wa States by 2005. When the Shan army of Khun Sa signed a cease-fire agreement with the government in December 1995, the UWSA attempted to expand its control to cover the southern part of Shan State, leading to a government demand that the Wa pull back. The UWSA refused to comply with the ultimatum and then joined forces with the Shan rebels against the government troops in the region.

In January 1997, several Wa groups participated with representatives of 15 ethnic groups from across Myanmar to sign the Mae Tha Raw Hta agreement that calls for the establishment of a democratic federal union of Burma. At a subsequent meeting in November 1998, the Wa joined with Shans and other regional groups in a new alliance aimed at reducing the ethnic fighting that benefits Myanmar's military government.

In December 1998 government troops began a campaign against the forces of the Wa National Organization (WNO) but gave the Wa rebels of the UWSA until March 1999 to vacate their bases in southern Shan State. When their deadline was again ignored, Burmese troops were sent against all Wa groups operating in the region, including those formerly allied to the government.

Delegations from 15 ethnic groups met near the Thai border in April 1999 to consolidate their military actions against the Burmese government. The groups were under the umbrella of the Democratic Alliance of Burma. The government reacted with a new offensive, sending thousands of refugees, including many Wa, fleeing to refugee camps in Thailand. Representatives of the Wa National Organization and organizations of five other ethnic groups operating in the region met to set out conditions for reconciliation and peace in July 1999. Government efforts to depopulate rebel areas sent another flood of refugees into Thailand in 1999–2000.

The Wa have been fighting for autonomy for over five decades. Without a lasting resolution to the questions of local self-government and national power sharing, the Wa will continue to resist and will rely on drugs to finance their war against the government. Without peace, there is little chance of economic development that would reduce opium production and heroine trafficking in the impoverished Wa homeland.

Burma's ethnic Wa army, long accused of being involved in the nation's largest export industry, narcotics, is trying to shed its tainted image. Several Wa nationalist leaders, in 2001, announced that it was time for the Wa to move out of the drug trade that has sustained their poor nation, but that has harmed their drive for sovereignty. New industries, including pig farms and Myanmar's first vineyard, are being tried, but the Wa know that if they fail the only option is to return to the production of drugs to support themselves and their fight for self-determination.

SELECTED BIBLIOGRAPHY:

Diran, Richard K. *The Vanishing Tribes of Burma*. 1997.
Mirante, Edith. *Burmese Looking Glass: A Human Rights Adventure*. 1993.
Smith, Martin. *Ethnic Groups in Burma: Development, Democracy and Human Rights*. 1994.
Tucker, Shelby. *Among Insurgents: Walking through Burma*. 2000.

Waldensians

Waldenses; Valdese; Valdenses; Vaudois; Valdesi

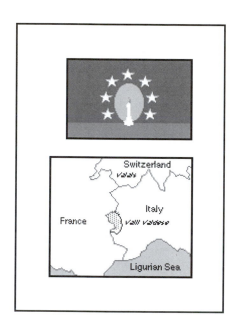

POPULATION: Approximately (2002e) 33,000 Waldensians in Italy, mostly in the Waldensian Valleys in northwestern Italy, but with some across the border in France. Outside Europe the largest Waldensian population, some 15,000, lives in the Rio Plate region of Argentina and Uruguay. Other Waldensian communities live in Missouri, Texas, Utah, and North Carolina in the United States, and in Canada.

THE WALDENSIAN HOMELAND: The Waldensian homeland, often called Waldensia, lies in the Cottian Alps, occupying seven valleys traversed by the Pellice and Germanesca Rivers, on the French border between Turin on the east and Grenoble on the west. The major valleys are the Pellice, Chisone, and the Germanasca. The region, mostly high valleys in the rugged Alps, remained one of Europe's most isolated until the 1950s, when new roads linked the region to the towns of Piedmont, particularly Turin. The Waldensian homeland has no official status; the region forms a historical area in the Italian region of Piedmont called the Waldensian Valleys. *Waldensian Valleys (Valli Valdesi/ Las Valadas):* 1,136 sq. mi.—2,943 sq. km, (2002e) 62,000—Waldensians 50%, Occitans* 32%, Italians and French 18%. The Waldensian capital and major cultural center is Torre Pellice, (2002e) 6,000, historically the nucleus of the Waldensian valleys, the center of the Waldensian Church, and the seat of the Waldensian Synod.

FLAG: The Waldensian flag is a blue field with a narrow red horizontal stripe at the bottom divided from the blue by a narrow white stripe. In the center is a white candle with an oval of yellow light around the flame surrounded by seven white stars.

PEOPLE AND CULTURE: The Waldensians are an ethnoreligious group, a division of the Occitan people who inhabit northwestern Italy and the Occitania region of southern France but are historically and religiously distinct as the oldest surviving Protestant nation in the world. The descendents the followers of the first Protestant religious dissidents in the twelfth and thirteenth centuries, the Waldensians became a nation through centuries of persecution, massacre, and isolation. The Waldensian culture, protected by self-imposed isolation, combines the original Occitan Latin culture with influences from the Piedmontese* and the Romands* in Switzerland. Today the Waldensians are governed by a seven-member board, called the Tavola (Table), elected annually by a general synod that convenes in Torre Pellice.

LANGUAGE AND RELIGION: The Waldensians speak an alpine dialect of Occitan that has been heavily influenced by Piedmontese, the predominant language of the region. The Waldensian dialect, belonging to the Northern group of Occitan dialects, is closely related to the dialects of the Occitans and Dauphinois,* who inhabit neighboring valleys, particularly the Queiràs dialect. The dialect, called Gavòt in Occitan, retains many forms and words that have disappeared in other areas. The majority of the Waldensians also speak standard Italian, and many also speak French.

The Waldensians represent the oldest Protestant nation, having adopted a reform religion in the eleventh and twelfth centuries. The followers of Pietro Waldo, the Waldensians were originally called the "Poor of Lyons." The earliest histories of the movement were commissioned by the Synod of Dauphiné in 1618, although some Waldensian documents date from as early as A.D. 1100. Considered forerunners of the Reformation, the Waldensians have retained their historical beliefs, which form an integral part of the Waldensian culture.

NATIONAL HISTORY: In the latter half of the twelfth century, in 1170, a wealthy merchant in Lyon, Pietro Waldo, also called Valdo or Valdesius, ceded his fortune to his family and took a vow of poverty. He began a life of religious devotion and poverty, vowing vengeance on the money he believed had reduced him to a form of slavery and made him more obedient to it than to God. He entreated people to place their hope in God and not in riches. Dedicating his life to meditation, he soon gained a following, known as the "Poor of Lyon." The ecclesiastical authorities were disturbed by Waldo's lack of theological training and his use of a non-Latin translation of the Bible.

Waldo and his followers questioned the existing religious doctrine and attempted to return Christianity to the simplicity and purity of the early Christian era. They demanded of the church hierarchy the freedom to worship in their regional Occitan vernacular, and to that end they published the Bible in the local dialect. Waldo advocated a return to the era when the church and the Bible dealt only with religious matters, and he rejected the papacy, purgatory, indulgences, and the opulence of the mass. Contrary to prevalent church teachings, Waldo laid great stress on gospel simplicity. To emphasize their return to the early values of Christianity, they spurned the elaborate clothing of the time and adopted simple costumes of dark cloth.

The early adherents saw themselves as Roman Catholics who were carrying the doctrines of Christianity farther than their weaker brethren. They even sent a delegation to the third Lateran Council in 1179 to obtain papal approval of their work. They presented to the pope a book written in the Occitan language. Their outspoken condemnation of the corruption and opulence of the Roman Catholic Church gained Waldo and his followers powerful enemies. It was the fact that they had translated the Scriptures, studied them, and "presumed" to preach what they believed, without reference to the clergy that was unacceptable.

Pope Alexander III forbade Waldo and his followers to preach. The dissidents' refusal to comply prompted the church to threaten to excommunicate them as heretics, but as they believed that they acted according to pure religious doctrine, they were not swayed by threats or the church's official condemnation. The Waldensians were driven from Lyon in 1182 for arguing that they could draw insight directly from the pages of their translated Bibles rather than through the Roman Catholic Church. At the Council of Verona, in 1184, they were condemned as heretics and excommunicated.

The Waldensians increasingly departed from the teachings of the Roman Catholic Church, rejecting some of the seven sacraments and the notion of Purgatory. Their views were based on a simplified Bible, moral rigor, and criticism of abuses in the contemporary church. Their movement, often joined or influenced by other dissident sects, spread rapidly to Spain, northern France, Flanders, Germany, and southern Italy. Some Waldensians even reached Poland and Hungary.

The Roman Church responded to the spread of the Waldensian heresy by turning from excommunication to active persecution. The first massacre began with the burning of more than 80 Waldensians as heretics at Strasbourg in 1211. In spite of persecution and the martyring of many adherents, the Waldensians gradually gained support. In 1215 the pope formally declared Waldo and his believers heretics, and the congregations were forcibly dispersed. The dissidents were separated, and Waldo himself fled to Bohemia, where he died in 1217. By the end of the thirteenth century persecution had virtually eliminated the sect in some areas. For their own security, the survivors abandoned their distinctive dress. Their simple pre-Reformation doctrines are set forth in the Waldensian Catechism, which was published around 1489.

In spite of church edicts that forbade Waldensian contact with Catholic believers, the movement continued to win followers. Many of the Waldensians suffered torture, burning, and exterminations by the church authorities. Many Waldensian communities in France and Italy were virtually wiped out. In 1487, at the instigation of Pope Innocent, most of the Waldensian colonies in Dauphiné, west of the Alps, were massacred. The Waldensian survivors fled to a seven-valley redoubt in the high Cottian Alps in Piedmont.

In the late fifteenth century the Waldensian valleys came under the authority of the Savoyards.* Pressed by the Inquisition, the duke of Savoy led the first systematic attempt to annihilate the Waldensians in 1494. The duke's troops overran many Waldensian towns, murdering and pillaging. Waldensian women threw themselves off high cliffs to escape the shame of rape by the rampaging soldiers. The Waldensians, although numerically fewer and more poorly armed, eventually repulsed the ducal troops and forced the duke to grant a peace treaty lasting 40 years.

A new era of the Waldensian history began when the French reformer Guillaume Farel introduced Reformation theology to the Waldensian ministers in 1526. The religious strife spreading through Europe caused by the Reformation again threatened the Waldensians. In 1532 the Waldensians joined the Protestant movement and thus reignited official church enmity. They paid for the publication in Switzerland of the first French Protestant version of the Bible in 1535. The Waldensians became openly Calvinist. In 1550 anti-Waldensian attacks reached a peak of ferocity and cruelty.

The persecution continued through the Thirty Years' War in the early seventeenth century. In 1685 the French king insisted that his cousin, the duke of Savoy, Victor Amadeus II, deal with the Waldensians as he had dealt with the Protestant Huguenots. The duke's Catholic soldiers swept through the Waldensian valleys killing thousands. Most of the captives were imprisoned in cruel, crowded conditions. Only 3,000 Waldensians survived the duke's bloody crusade. The survivors, after their release from the duke's prisons, migrated to Switzerland with the Waldensian leader Henri Arnaud, or to other parts of Protestant Europe. In 1689 Waldensians under the leadership of Arnaud left their homes near Geneva and, in what is called the "Glorious Return," fought their way back to their ancestral valleys against strong French and Savoyard resistance.

Their successful and vigorous mountain warfare so impressed Victor Amadeus of Savoy that he made peace with the Waldensians in June 1690 in exchange for their fighting with the Savoyards against the French during the War of the Grand Alliance. After Savoy made peace with France in 1696, the persecution of the Waldensians was renewed. In July 1698 over 3,000 were forced into exile in Württemberg. Between 1704 and 1706, during the War of the Spanish Succession, the Waldensians were again tolerated in Savoy in return for support against France, allowing the exiles to return to Piedmont.

The Waldensians finally defeated the forces sent against them and liberated their valleys, one after another. The Waldensian victory ended the wars and massacres, but not the persecution they suffered as church-labeled heretics. The recuperation of their beloved valleys began a long process of revival and renewal of the small Waldensian nation.

Genuine freedom for the Waldensians came only in 1848, when King Charles Albert of Sardinia granted them the full civil and religious rights they demanded. In spite of the official rehabilitation, the continuing hardships and hatred they faced drove many to emigrate. In the latter half of the nineteenth century many left for South America to begin anew. One group of Waldensians settled in the United States at Valdese, North Carolina, and others settled on Staten Island, New York, and in Missouri. In 1855 the Waldensians founded a school of theology in Torre Pellice, their modern headquarters. As late as the 1870s Roman Catholic historians were publishing material that denied the persecution of the Waldensians.

The Waldensians, before and during World War II, actively opposed Italy's Fascist government, with its enforced religious and national conformity so alien to their ideas of freedom. Many joined partisan units during the war, and their communities suffered official reprisals, particularly after the German occupation of northern Italy in 1943. Whole villages were destroyed in retaliation for the Waldensians' unbending opposition to Fascism.

The small Waldensian nation knew peace only after World War II. In 1979 the 130 congregations in Italy federated with the Methodist Church of Italy and moved to end their centuries of self–imposed isolation. The Waldensians began to participate in national and international religious affairs, and they began to organize their national life as a separate people.

In the 1990s, although not threatened by neighboring peoples, the Waldensians were threatened by unconstrained development, particularly alpine tourism. An active movement to win greater say over development projects in the 1980s evolved a more militant activism to save their unique culture and traditions from extinction. The Waldensians became one the latest part of Europe's ethnic and religious mosaic to emerge as a separate nation.

The small Waldensian nation, which survived as a religious and historical minority within a very strong Catholic tradition in Italy, in the 1990s experienced a cultural and religious revival that blended a strong Calvinist tradition and an alpine Occitan culture to sustain a unique national group. Increasingly ties are being reestablished between the European Waldensians and the diaspora Waldensians in the Americas.

At the end of the twentieth century, the Waldensians, faced with a decline of the traditional industries, such as mining, increasingly integrated into the industrial society of the towns of the Piedmont Plain. Mixed marriages between Waldensians and Catholics, modern problems such as drugs, and the end of the Waldensian isolation threatened the integrity of the small Waldensian nation.

The revitalized Waldensian movement of the late 1990s attempted to reestablish contact with other Waldensians in northwestern Italy, but also in other parts of Europe and the world. The reculturation of the Waldensians, focused on their unique history and culture, has begun to reverse decades of assimilation. The Waldensian movement, both cultural and religious, is based on their unique history and place in Europe.

SELECTED BIBLIOGRAPHY:

Audisio, Gabriel. *The Waldensian Dissent: Persecution and Survival, 1170–1570.* 1999.
Cameron, Euan. *The Waldenses: Rejections of the Holy Church in Medieval Europe.* 2000.
Tourn, Giorgio. *You Are My Witnesses: The Waldensians across Eight Hundred Years.* 1989.
Wylie, J.A. *History of the Waldenses.* 1997.

Wallisians and Futunans

Uveans; Wallisians; Wallis and Futuna Islanders; Uveans and Futunans

POPULATION: Approximately (2002e) 31,000 Wallisians in the South Pacific, concentrated in the Wallis and Futuna islands, with a sizable Wallisian community of about 16,000 in New Caledonia and smaller numbers in Vanuatu, Tahiti, and continental France.

THE WALLISIAN HOMELAND: The Wallisian homeland lies in the South Pacific, consisting of two small island groups in western Polynesia separated by an expanse of open ocean about two-thirds of the way from Hawaii to New Zealand. The volcanic islands include Uvea or Wallis, Futuna, and Alofi and 20 islets, traditionally divided into three kingdoms— Uvea or Wallis, and Sigave and Alo on Futuna. The three kingdoms or chieftaincies correspond to the three districts. There are no permanent settlements on Alofi or the islets because of a lack of natural fresh water. The islands form a self-governing overseas territory of the French Republic. *Territory of the Wallis and Futuna Islands (Territoire des Iles Wallis et Futuna)*: 106 sq. mi.—275 sq. km, (2002e) 15,500—Wallisians (including Futunans) 96%, French 2%, Vietnamese and Chinese 2%. The Wallisian capital and major cultural center is Mata-Utu on Uvea, (2002e) 1,600.

FLAG: The Wallisian national flag, the traditional flag of the islands, is a red field bearing a large white square centered and quartered by a red cross.

PEOPLE AND CULTURE: The Wallisians and Futunans, popularly known as Wallisians, are a Polynesian people related to the inhabitants of Samoa and other Polynesian islands. There are significant differences between the languages and cultures of the Wallisians and Futunans, resulting from different periods of settlement. The Wallisians are culturally and linguistically closer to the Tongans, while the Futunans share many cultural traits with Samoa. The Futunans number about 5,000. The majority of the islanders are subsistence farmers; about 80% of the labor force earn their livelihoods from raising coconuts and vegetables, livestock (mostly pigs), and fishing. About 4% of the Wallisians are employed by the territorial government. Slightly more than half of the total Wallisian nation lives in New Caledonia. Traditional culture remains strong in the islands.

LANGUAGE AND RELIGION: The Wallisian and Futunan languages belong to the Polynesian language group of the Austronesian languages. Wallisian, or Uvean, is related to Tongan and Futunan is closer to Samoan, the result of the early settlement patterns in the islands. Before the islands became an overseas territory, schools in the islands were operated tuition free by Roman Catholic missions. In 1961 the educational system came under the French Ministry of National Education. Elementary and lower-secondary schools remain free and obligatory in the territory, but higher levels of education must be pursued in New Caledonia or continental France. French is the official language of island administration.

The Wallisians are overwhelmingly Roman Catholic, the result of French missionary activity beginning in the 1830s. The Roman Catholic Church remains an important force in the politics of the islands. Protestants never had a presence in the islands, sparing the Wallisians the religious conflicts common elsewhere in the South Pacific. Christianity has tempered most customs and abolished some, such as polygyny, but many traditional customs remain important parts of island worship.

NATIONAL HISTORY: Historians believe that Uvea (Wallis) was settled about 3,000 years ago by people from the Asian mainland. The settlers were subsequently conquered by the Tongans, establishing historical, cultural, and linguistic ties between Tonga and Uvea. Local legends suggest that the Futunans had their origins in Samoa. Futuna was probably settled late in the first millennium B.C., and it may have been a center for Polynesian migrations to outlying islands in the western Pacific. As the populations of the islands increased, whole families left by boat to settle other islands farther south.

The islands were sighted in 1616 by the Dutch navigators Jakob Le Maire, and Willem Corneliszoon Schouten sighted the Futuna Islands. Le Maire named the islands for his home city of Hoorn in the Netherlands. Nearly 151 years passed before Capt. Samuel Wallis, sailing under the flag of France, encountered Uvea in 1767. The islands remained isolated and ignored for another 50 years, until the whaling industry reached the area. In the 1820s Europeans began to make regular calls at both of the large islands.

On both Uvea and Futuna there were persistent wars for supremacy between the various chiefs until early in the nineteenth century. The emergence of the three kingdoms of Uvea and Tua (Sigave) and Alo on Futuna brought relative peace; agreements over distribution of food and land ended the internecine fighting. The present kings are descendents of the rulers of these three kingdoms.

French Marist priests arrived as missionaries in 1837 under Father Balaillon. The Marists founded churches and schools on the main islands. They achieved considerable success within a decade, converting the majority of the population. Mission schools introduced Western-style education, and many chiefs' sons became the first to be educated in French. The missionaries remained the main European influence in the islands until the establishments of protectorates in the late nineteenth century. French priests often served as advisers to the island's rulers.

Threatened by "blackbirders" seeking slaves to sell to the plantations of Fiji, the island kings petitioned the French for protection in the 1840s. The French presence increased in the islands, but protectorate status was achieved for the Wallisians only in 1887 and the Futunans the following year. Over the next decades, the French administration became well entrenched and administered the small islands with a relatively firm hand, allowing little dissent or public participation in local government. Soon after the abdication of the king of Uvea in 1913, the French authorities annexed the kingdoms to create the colony of Wallis and Futuna, administratively a dependency of New Caledonia after 1917.

In 1942, during World War II, the Free French allowed the stationing of 6,000 American troops on Uvea. Within a short time the Americans built a system of roads, two landing strips, and facilities for anchoring ships in the lagoon. These developments, the first major infrastructure projects in the islands, remain the basis of the island's infrastructure to the present.

The islands remained neglected outposts of France, with minimum development and investment. Limited opportunities for the islanders forced many to migrate to New Caledonia or the New Hebrides, the nearest French territories with possibilities for employment.

The status of the islands remained unchanged until the decolonization period of the late 1950s. In late 1959, by an overwhelming majority, the islanders voted to change their political status from that of a protectorate to that of an overseas territory of the French Republic. Legislation passed in 1961 incorporated the traditional rulers into the new administrative arrangement and ended the protectorate status and the islands' ties to the administration of New Caledonia. In subsequent elections, the Wallisians and Futunans demonstrated a marked conservatism, opposing plans by socialist French governments and rejecting any proposal for change in their dependent status.

The Council of the Territory consists of the three island kings and three members appointed by the high administrator on the advice of the Territorial Assembly. The three traditional kings have limited powers. The Territorial Assembly consists of 20 members, 13 from Wallis and seven from Futuna, elected by universal suffrage. As an integral part of the French Republic, the Wallisians are represented in and elects a deputy and a senator to the French national parliament.

Island finances are dependent on French government subsidies, licensing of fishing rights to Japan and South Korea, import taxes, and remittances from the Wallisians living in New Caledonia. Exports are negligible, consisting mostly of breadfruit, yams, and taro root. Deforestation, largely as a result of the continued use of wood as the main fuel source, has become a serious problem. As a consequence, the mountainous terrain of Futuna is particularly prone to erosion.

Opportunities for employment in New Caledonia and limited options for work in the islands combined with growing population pressure in the 1960s and 1970s led to a large migration to the French territory of New Caledonia to work in the nickel mines. The expatriate Wallisian population sends funds back to families in the islands, making them a valuable asset as long as they remain abroad. They would place an intolerable burden on local resources if they were to return home.

In 1975 the Wallisians began talks with the French government to change the status of the islands from that of an overseas territory to that of an overseas department. Departmental status would give the islanders the same rights and financial subsidies enjoyed by the departments of metropolitan France. In spite of the denial of the change of status, island leaders in 1985 affirmed ties to the French government and announced that the islands would not seek independence in the near future.

The islands are the only French territory where local traditions supersede the French constitution. According to traditional laws, there are no written property agreements, and third parties can always claim land or other properties. This has deterred economic investment and has contributed to the poor economic situation in the islands.

The Futunans are reluctantly tied to the Wallisians, and in the late 1990s they expressed a desire to separate and to have separate territorial status. The Wallisians, should the Futunans separate from the joint territory, have discussed the possibility of seeking independence or other forms of self-government while retaining ties to France.

SELECTED BIBLIOGRAPHY:

Aldrich, Robert. *France and the South Pacific since 1940*. 1994.

Gantelet, Pascal. *Images of the Population of Wallis and Futuna: The Principal Results of the 1990 Census*. 1991.

Stone, William Standish. *Idylls of the South Seas*. 1995.

The Wallis and Futuna Research Group. *A Strategic Profile of Wallis and Futuna, 2000*. 2000.

Walloons

Walons; Wallons; Wallonians

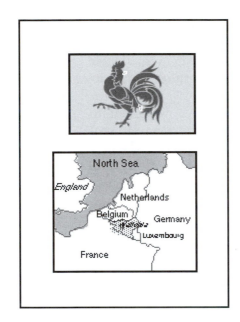

POPULATION: Approximately (2002e) 3,610,000 Walloons in Belgium and France, concentrated the Wallonia region in southern Belgium. Over 200,000 Walloons live in adjacent areas of France. Outside Europe there are Walloon communities in the United States, Canada, and South America.

THE WALLOON HOMELAND: The Walloon homeland, Wallonia, lies in southeastern Belgium, part of the north European Plain. The region occupies an area of low plains rising to wooded hills, the Ardennes, in the south. Most of Wallonia forms an autonomous region of the Kingdom of Belgium comprising the provinces of Liège, Namur, Walloon Brabant, Luxembourg, and Hainaut. The small southern region, lying within France, forms the Givet, Fourmies, and Maubeuge Districts in the northern part of the Department of Ardennes. *Region of Wallonia (Région Wallonne/Walonia)*: 6,504 sq. mi.—16,845 sq. km, (2002e) 3,347,000—Walloons 83%, Flemish* 9%, Germans 2%, other Belgians 6%. The Walloon capital is Namur, (2002e) 106,000, but the traditional capital and major cultural center is Liège, (2002e) 185,000, metropolitan area 904,000. The other important cultural center is Charleroi, (2002e) 201,000, metropolitan area 511,000. The major cultural center of the French Walloons is Maubeuge, called Mabuse in the local Walloon dialect, (2002e) 33,000, urban area 76,000. Brussels, which forms a separate autonomous region on the boundary between Walloon Brabant and Flemish Brabant, also has a sizable Walloon community and important Walloon cultural institutions.

FLAG: The Walloon national flag, the flag of the national movement and the official flag of the region, is a yellow field bearing a red rooster centered.

PEOPLE AND CULTURE: The Walloons are a Latin people, the most northerly of the Latin peoples in Europe. The descendents of Latinized Celts and Gauls pushed into the region when the Germanic peoples overran northern France, the Walloons tend to be shorter and darker than the Flemish of northern Belgium. A large Walloon population of about 200,000 inhabits the eastern part of France's Nord Department and has retained its separate culture, dialect, and ties to the Belgian Walloons. The culture of the region retains more Latin influences than that of the neighboring French. The Walloons are overwhelmingly Roman Catholic. Many Walloons also claim the city of Brussels, which is 80% French-speaking, but not necessarily Walloon.

LANGUAGE AND RELIGION: The Walloon language is actually a group of closely related dialects spoken in Belgium and France, and formerly in Luxembourg, where the language died out in the 1970s. The language is described as a Romance language with a Celtic substratum and Germanic influences. Walloon is spoken in two major dialects, Walloon and Picard (which is spoken from Tournai to Mons), and several minor dialects—Gaumais, Champenois, and Liègeois. The Walloon language has a substantial literature but no official status in Wallonia; it is not taught in the region's schools except as an elective subject. In the disputed city and suburbs of Brussels, both French and Dutch are officially recognized, although French speakers, mostly non-Walloons, are the larger group. French has replaced Walloon as the major language of the region; only about 15% use Walloon as their first language. The first writings in the vernacular date only from the twelfth century. The dialect only began to be used in literature and theater in the early seventeenth century.

The vast majority of the Walloons are Roman Catholic, the religion they share with the neighboring Flemish. The liturgical calendar formerly marked the year, and Walloon culture was constructed around church holidays and festivals, but in recent decades religion has declined, although it remains an integral part of the Walloon culture.

NATIONAL HISTORY: The region is first reported in Roman records as part of the large area known as Gaul. A Celtic tribe in the region north of the Ardennes, the Belgae, after fighting for seven years, fell to the Romans under Julius Caesar in 57 B.C. The Celtic inhabitants of the Roman province of Belgica, under Roman rule for over 400 years, became thoroughly Latinized and adopted the Latin culture and language.

Gradually the region was infiltrated by groups of Germans, until in the fourth century, traditionally in A.D. 358, Salic Franks moved down from the northeast pushing the Romanized peoples back on a line that approximates the present linguistic line between the Flemish and Walloons. Protected by the then dense forests of the Ardennes, the Latin population held their territories while the areas to the north and south of them were overrun and settled by the Germanic invaders. The pressure of the Germanic settlers began the tradition of self-defense and cultural protection that continues to the present. The northern Franks retained their Germanic language, which became modern Dutch and Flemish, whereas the

Franks moving south into Gaul gradually adopted the language of the culturally dominant Romanized Gauls, a language that would later develop as modern French. The language frontier between the Flemish and Walloons has remained virtually unchanged ever since.

The Walloon region split into a number of small independent states soon after Charlemagne's Frankish empire was divided by his heirs in 843. While Flanders became a dependency of France, Wallonia became part of the middle kingdom, Lotharingia, later called Lorraine. In 1226 the French imposed the Treaty of Mélun, which solidified Flemish subjugation to French culture.

Reunited in the fifteenth century under the Burgundians,* the Low Countries passed by marriage to the Hapsburgs in 1477. In the sixteenth century the Low Countries, then called the Netherlands, which included present Belgium, became a center of world commerce. Rule of the Walloon provinces passed from the Austrian Hapsburgs to the Spanish Hapsburgs in 1555. The southern districts of the Hapsburg province of Hainault, with a large Walloon population, came under French rule in 1678.

The French took the provinces from the Spanish in 1792, and Napoleon annexed Wallonia to the French state in 1801. French domination generated joint resistance by the Flemings and Walloons. The Congress of Vienna, convened in 1815 to reorganize Europe at the end of the Napoleonic Wars, added the Roman Catholic former Hapsburg provinces to the predominantly Protestant Dutch kingdom. A shared antipathy to Protestant rule united the Walloons and the Flemish in a revolt against Dutch rule in 1830. Supported by the United Kingdom and France, the Catholic provinces in Flanders and Wallonia united in a separate kingdom called Belgium in 1831. The Walloon dialect, often called Old French, remained the language of administration for the first three decades of Belgian independence, but standard French gradually took precedence in the 1860s.

The Romantic movement and Belgian independence stimulated Walloon literature and culture. In 1856 the Walloon Literary Society was established in Liège; it became a true regional academy, with a considerable influence on Walloon language and literature. The dialect spread from Liège to other cities, leading to a general cultural revival in the latter half of the nineteenth century. By the late nineteenth century Wallonia was experiencing a genuine literary revival.

Newly industrialized Wallonia dominated the kingdom in the nineteenth century, and the French language became the predominant dialect in Wallonia and Brussels and was the only official language of the kingdom. Prosperous and assured, the Walloons thrived in the 1870s and 1880s, easily dominating the rural, agricultural Flemish provinces.

The early twentieth century decline of religion in Belgian politics made language the center of Belgian disagreements. The standardization of the rules of spelling and grammar allowed the emergence of a true Walloon literary language. Although poetry remained the dominant form of Walloon expression, translations of international works into Walloon and the growth of a particular Walloon literature stimulated a Walloon cultural revival before and after World War I.

A new Flemish assertiveness after the chaos and destruction of the First World War challenged Walloon domination of the Belgian kingdom. United only by a common religion, the language issue emerged as the kingdom's primary preoccupation in the 1920s and 1930s. Amid growing cultural and linguistic tension, the Belgian government finally recognized Flemish as an official language for some uses in the late 1930s, ending over 400 years of Walloon domination.

The postwar history of Belgium consists of the struggle of the country's Flemish community to gain equal status for its language and to acquire its fair share of political influence and economic opportunity. The tension between the two peoples escalated after World War II, fanned by economic changes. Wallonia's outdated heavy industries declined rapidly, while new industries shifted to Flanders, nearer the Flemish port cities. The shift of economic and political power to Flanders fed a growing Flemish nationalist movement, stimulating Walloon nationalism in response.

In 1961 Walloon socialists demanded a new state structure, with local autonomy for the two Belgian nations. Demonstrations broke out in the Walloon cities in 1961–62, and serious nationalist clashes occurred in Brussels and the linguistic border regions. In 1963 a law was passed establishing three official languages within Belgium: Flemish was recognized as the official language in the north, French in the south, and German along the eastern border. Language rights spurred nationalism, and vacationing Walloons clashed violently with Flemish nationalists in Ostend in 1965.

Nationalist attitudes hardened in the 1970s as both the Walloons and the Flemish demanded greater political and economic autonomy. Teaching the Walloon language in regional schools was approved by the government in 1983. In August 1990 Wallonia and Flanders won major concessions in autonomy, opening a bitter debate over control of the Belgian capital, Brussels. The mainly French-speaking, but not Walloon, inhabitants of the capital evidenced little interest in the dispute, while the predominantly Flemish suburbs agitated for the metropolitan area's inclusion in Flanders.

The increasingly bitter communal dispute made Belgium all but ungovernable as administrations formed and fell on the linguistic and autonomy issues. In 1988 a dispute prevented agreement on the component parties of a coalition, leaving Belgium without a constitutional government for over four months. In 1989 the Brussels metropolitan area became a third Belgian autonomous region, a compromise reluctantly accepted by the Walloon and Flemish authorities. A serious constitutional crisis in late

1991 again left Belgium without an effective administration, bringing the dissolution of the kingdom ever closer.

Nationalists on both sides proposed that Brussels, the center of European integration, become a separate European capital district and that Wallonia and Flanders become separate independent states within a federal Europe. Nationalists claimed that the European option would formalize the division that had virtually turned Belgium into a geographic area occupied by two distinct nations.

The official devolution of additional powers to the regions in February 1993 effectively partitioned Belgium. Walloon authority, including control of the southern part of Brabant, called Barents, was augmented by the implementation of a federal state in mid-1993. The few powers left to the Belgian government, powers that will eventually become European responsibilities, are the only official ties left between Wallonia and Flanders. When the Belgian government surrenders the responsibilities to the European government, Belgium will effectively cease to exist, and Wallonia and Flanders could become separate states in a federal Europe. In parliamentary elections held in May 1995, the prodevolution coalition was returned to power; the election signaled the completion of the conversion to a more decentralized form of government.

The province of Brabant, which surrounds the Brussels metropolitan area, was formally divided between Flanders and Wallonia in 1995. The province was divided into Walloon Brabant and Flemish Brabant, north and south of Brussels. The region contains the Waterloo battlefield of 1815 in the northwest.

A six-party coalition took office in Belgium in July 1999, headed by a Flemish-speaking liberal. The new government improved economic output, but squabbling between the coalition partners and the various local governments continued to tear at the fabric of united Belgium. The federal government survives, but with a limited and still-declining range of powers. Three regional governments, Flanders, Wallonia, and Brussels, are increasingly taking over powers once reserved for the central government. In 2000 the regions took over responsibility for agricultural policy. The foreign service is being restructured so that it ceases to be a federal authority and becomes a coalition of regional, federal, and private-sector representatives.

In the late 1990s the conflicts between the Walloons and Flemish were noticeably fewer than they had been in the mid-1990s, but nationalism in both regions became more powerful. The Walloons increasingly resented Flemish domination of the Belgian state. Walloon leaders claimed that the Flemish had usurped political and economic power in Belgium, which they contended serves only one nation, Flanders, and marginalized the Walloons. Reacting to the rise of radical nationalism in Flanders, Walloon nationalist organizations, such as the Francophone Front, increasingly won support for their demands for a separate Walloon state within the European Union.

A new agreement, signed on 29 June 2001, the Lambermont Accord, gives even more autonomy to the two communities, while placating the Walloons with extra funds for French-language education systems. Economic disparities continue to sour relations while Flanders is booming, Wallonia is stagnant. Growing Flemish resentment of taxes used to support the large number of unemployed in Wallonia hit by the slow collapse of mining and steel continues to fuel Walloon nationalism.

SELECTED BIBLIOGRAPHY:

Deprez, Kas, and Louis Vos, eds. *Nationalism in Belgium: Shifting Identities 1780–1995*. 1998.

Fitzmaurice, John. *The Politics of Belgium: Crisis and Compromise in a Plural Society*. 1983.

Lijphart, Arend, ed. *Conflict and Coexistence in Belgium: The Dynamics of a Culturally Divided Society*. 1981.

Pateman, Robert. *Belgium*. 1996.

Welsh

Cymry; Cymraeg

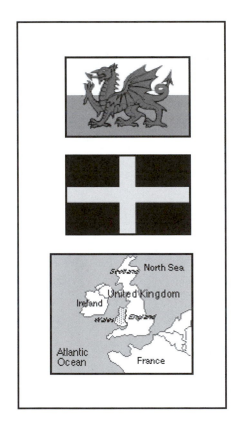

POPULATION: Approximately (2002e) 3,075,000 Welsh in the United Kingdom, concentrated in the Principality of Wales, with smaller communities in other parts of the United Kingdom. Outside Europe Welsh populations live in Australia, New Zealand, Canada, the United States, and Argentina.

THE WELSH HOMELAND: The Welsh homeland lies in the extreme west of the island of Great Britain, a large rectangular peninsula between the Irish Sea and the Atlantic Ocean, west of the border with England. Most of the region is uplands, known generally as the Cambrian Mountains, which includes the Snowdon Massif, the highest point in Wales. About two-thirds of Wales's population lives in the south. Wales forms a separate principality of the United Kingdom. *Principality of Wales (Cymru):* 8,016 sq. mi.—20,761 sq. km, (2002e) 2,937,000—Welsh 88%, English 11%, other British 1%. The Welsh capital and major cultural center is Cardiff, called Caerdydd in Welsh, (2002e) 281,000, metropolitan area 683,000. Other important cultural centers are Swansea, called Abertawe in Welsh, (2002e) 170,000, metropolitan area 302,000; and Newport, called Casnewyyd-ar-Wysg, (2002e) 115,000, metropolitan area 321,000.

FLAG: The Welsh national flag, the *Y Ddraig Goch*, is a horizontal bicolor of white over green, bearing the Welsh national symbol, a red dragon, centered. The other Welsh flag, often used by some nationalist movements, is the *Dewisant*, the Cross of St. David flag, a black field bearing a centered yellow cross.

PEOPLE AND CULTURE: The Welsh, calling themselves Cymry and their country Cymru, are a Celtic people with a vigorous and unique culture. Generally darker and shorter than the other British nations, the

Welsh have retained much of their historical appearance. The Welsh culture, highly developed before the eleventh-century Norman* conquest, is closely related to the cultures of the Cornish* and Bretons,* who inhabit the peninsulas to the south. About three-quarters of the Welsh population in Wales is concentrated in the large urban areas in the south. The reculturation of the Welsh in the latter half of the twentieth century, initially based on language use, has since extended to all parts of the culture. Support for Welsh cultural institutions, once mostly ignored, is now an integral part of most Welsh towns and cities.

LANGUAGE AND RELIGION: English is now the first language of Wales. Only 60,000 Welsh speak just the Welsh language, and only a quarter of the population is bilingual, although the numbers of speakers is increasing. The Welsh language, Cymraeg, belongs to the Brythonic branch of the Celtic languages, which also includes Breton and Cornish, and it has a long literary history. Essentially, the Welsh language is the language spoken throughout Celtic Britain and much of Europe in pre-Roman times. The language has been revived since World War II as part of the Welsh cultural resurgence. Welsh has borrowed words throughout history from Latin, Anglo-Saxon, Norman French, and extensively from English, but it still has a large native vocabulary of Celtic origin. Forty dialects have been identified in Wales. Standard Welsh has both a Northern and Southern variety. Welsh speakers are concentrated in the northern, western, and southern highland areas of the country. The coastal areas of southern and eastern Wales are heavily Anglicized. Much effort is being devoted to preserving the language and culture, with bilingual education, Welsh-language broadcasting, and attempts to maintain the long Welsh literary tradition.

The majority of the Welsh are Methodists, having adopted the Wesleyan doctrine. Traditionally the Welsh are predominantly nonconformist in religion, but secularism greatly limits church influence. Methodist ceremonies and church choirs have become an integral part of the Welsh culture.

NATIONAL HISTORY: The original inhabitants of the region are thought to be Iberians, the earliest settlers of most of the island of Great Britain. From the third millennium B.C., the region was settled by Mediterranean peoples, Iberians, immigrating by sea. The entry by sea was paralleled on the east by the immigration of peoples from the British lowlands and continental Europe. Celtic tribes, originally from the European mainland, populated the western mountains by the early Bronze Age. The Iberians and Celts often mixed, taking the general name of Cymry. The language brought to the area by the Celtic migrants from Europe formed the basis of the modern Celtic language.

Under nominal Roman rule from 55 B.C., the Cymry were only subjugated after a long struggle that was completed during the reign of the

Roman emperor Vespasian, A.D. 69–79. The highland tribes retained their culture and language, while the Celtic lowlands to the east and south became Latinized in culture and speech. Christianity, introduced to southeastern Wales, penetrated the region during the late Roman period.

The declining Roman Empire gradually abandoned Britannia in the early fifth century. In 410 the Romans withdrew their military garrisons leaving the island open to invasion. Overrun by Germanic tribes from northern Europe, the Celtic defenders fell back on the less accessible areas to the west, the peninsulas of Wales and Cornwall, and some eventually crossed the channel to Brittany. Other Celtic inhabitants of Britain, fleeing the wave of Anglo-Saxon invaders, took refuge in the Welsh mountains, where in time they merged with the Cymry and maintained their independence. The Anglo-Saxon invaders called the native Celts *waelisc*, meaning foreign, eventually corrupted to Welsh.

The Germanic invaders were unable to conquer the highland Celts, but their advance separated the Celtic populations north and south of the Bristol Channel. The Welsh defeated all attempts to invade their peninsular strongholds and raided the lowland communities. During the reign of Offa, king of Mercia in the eighth century, a defensive earthwork extending the length of the Welsh border was erected, which helped to isolate further the Welsh from the Anglo-Saxons. Irish settlers from across the narrow Irish Sea settled several coastal areas.

A number of kingdoms arose in Wales, including Gwynedd, Powys, Dyfed, and Gwent. Over the next centuries various rulers attempted unsuccessfully to unite them in one kingdom. In the sixth century the scattered bands united to form a viable nation. A Welsh king, Hywel Dda, in the tenth century, collected Welsh law and custom in a unified code for the kingdom but was forced to accept vassalage to the king of Wessex, in England.

The Normans from continental Europe conquered England in 1066, but fierce Welsh resistance halted their invasion at the Welsh border. The Norman leader, William the Conqueror, declared himself lord of Wales in 1071, though the Normans gained a foothold in south Wales only in 1093, a holding that was ruled as the March of Wales. Dissension in Norman England eased the military pressure on Wales in the twelfth century, the respite stimulating a great flowering of medieval Welsh culture. For over 200 years the Welsh repulsed sporadic attempts to conquer their homeland but ultimately failed to stop the English onslaught.

The three kingdoms of Gwynedd, Powys, and Deheubarth in northern and central Wales remained largely autonomous until they came under English rule in 1282. Edward I of England in 1301 named his eldest son and heir as prince of Wales. English settlers, particularly in the south, took control of much of the most productive lands.

The Anglo-Saxon and Anglo-Norman invasions from across the English border subsequently dominated the ethnic and linguistic evolution of Wales. Treated as a conquered nation and harshly treated by the English, and resentful of unjust laws and administration, the Welsh rebelled under the leadership of Owen Glyndwr (Glendower) in 1400. Initially successful, the Welsh rebels formed a government and created a representative parliament, one of the first in Europe. Defeated nine years later, the victorious English gradually curtailed the principality's rights.

In 1536 Wales was joined to England in a political union, reinforced by and act of 1543. The language of the conquerors, English, was made the official language of the principality, provoking fierce resistance. The Welsh were given seats in the English parliament, but all Welsh laws were replaced by English laws. In spite of forced assimilation, the Welsh struggled to retain their culture and language, which were threatened by Anglicization.

The Protestant Reformation, particularly the English version, also fueled Welsh opposition. In the late eighteenth century most of the Welsh finally accepted Protestantism, but not the Anglicanism England. The Welsh adopted the teachings of John Wesley, derisively called a "Methodist" for his methodical attention to study and religious duty. The Methodist creed became closely tied to the reviving Welsh culture over the next century.

The Welsh language was spoken by nearly all the inhabitants until the late eighteenth century and remained the language of the common people for another century after that. The language was also spoken in Merseyside and large areas of Shropshire in England. The industrialization of south Wales in the late nineteenth century brought an influx of English industrial workers. Industrial evils and rural poverty forced many Welsh to emigrate, while between 1870 and 1911 over 120,000 English settled the southern counties. At the time, a child overheard speaking Welsh in school playgrounds was caned by teachers and forced to wear around his or her neck the wooden letters "W.N.," standing for "Welsh Not."

The Welsh industrial expansion continued through World War I, but a serious decline began in 1918. The grave economic problems of the 1920s aroused Welsh nationalist sentiment. In 1925 nationalists formed Plaid Cymru, the Welsh National Party, as the party of Welsh economic and cultural grievances.

The spread of education, in English, after World War II and the spread of English-language radio and television decreased the number of Welsh able to speak their own language. The percentage of Welsh speakers declined by half during the 1950s. The decline of the language and culture stimulated the emergence in the 1950s of a modern nationalist movement, based on the effort to save the language and culture from extinction.

Historically the Welsh were dependent upon mining and heavy industry, the decline of which led to lower per capita incomes and higher levels of unemployment than in the rest of Britain. The coal mines of South Wales were first developed in the nineteenth century and became the premier source of British coal, but by the late twentieth century declining production had reduced coal to a minor factor in the economy.

An organized campaign to win some say in local administration spurred the growth of nationalism in the 1950s and 1960s. In 1964 the British government created a specific Welsh Affairs Office in London, with a separate government secretary for Wales. The nationalists denounced the offices as signs of continued colonialism. In 1966 Plaid Cymru advocating national status within a federal United Kingdom, elected its first member to Parliament.

European integration in the European Economic Community pushed the continent's Celtic nations to reestablish ancient ties. Annual congresses, folk festivals, and cultural exchanges increased and revitalized the Celtic cultures in the 1970s and 1980s. The renewed pan-Celtic ties gave the Welsh a reinforced determination to win self-rule and equal status for the Welsh language in education and administration.

Radical nationalist organizations formed in the 1960s and 1970s, developed close ties to other European groups, and received support from Libya and other states. A Libyan group, the Arab Social Union, visited Wales at the invitation of Plaid Cymru to discuss educational exchanges with Welsh nationalists. Other nationalist groups, such as the Welsh Socialist Republican Movement and Free Wales, turned to terrorism and attacked English targets.

A referendum on the devolution of administrative power to a Welsh parliament went down in defeat in 1979. The groups opposed to the devolution stressed British, as opposed to Welsh, nationalism. The large population in southern Wales of English origin mostly opposed devolution. Discontented with the result of the referendum, militant nationalists launched a campaign of arson, burning holiday homes and real estate offices dealing with the "foreigners" from across the English border who bought them.

Economic success in the 1980s and 1990s enhanced the Welsh confidence that their country no longer needed the monetary subsidies that had tied Wales to England for centuries. In January 1992 nearly three-quarters of the Welsh demonstrated support for devolution and a separate Welsh assembly. For the nationalists the vote represented a first step toward the goal of a separate Welsh state in an integrated Europe. The rising tide of Welsh nationalism won a concession on the language when in May 1992 the British government finally granted Welsh equal status with English in the principality.

On 18 September 1997, the Welsh voted on a devolution plan. Approval of the initiative set up a 60-seat legislature that will not have major financial responsibilities or even the power to make laws on the Welsh language;

however, the Welsh nation will have a form of self-government for the first time in over six centuries of English domination. Welsh nationalists approved the devolution of power, but continue to work for greater autonomous powers for the new Welsh legislature.

Voters in Wales elected members of their new regional legislature on 6 May 1999. The Welsh legislature was the first in Wales for almost 600 years, giving the Welsh powers that they lost in the 1500s. The British government, highly centralized in the 1980s, began to devolve powers to the constituent parts of the kingdom under the New Labour government, which campaigned for devolution in 1997. In September 1997 the Welsh voted by a slim majority, 50.3%, to the creation of a national assembly.

Welsh cultural autonomy has greater support than political autonomy. Their language is more widely spoken than any other non-English language in the kingdom, and the Welsh cultural distinctiveness remains strong. The large segment of the population that is of English origin is largely indifferent to the autonomy movement.

The Welsh Assembly has no fiscal sovereignty and no authority to pass what is called "primary legislation." It is empowered only to pass "secondary legislation," on a range of matters considerably more restricted than its Scottish counterpart. The areas of authority will essentially consist of health and education, economic development and regional planning, housing, transport, tourism, sports, and culture. The only groups calling for a rapid expansion of the new assembly's competence to cover primary legislation are the nationalist Plaid Cymru and other groups—who decided to set aside, for the period of the creation of the assembly, the question of complete national independence.

During the national census of 2000, nationalists stole thousands of census forms, which were carried around Wales in a coffin. The nationalists, supported by over 100,000 people who refused to fill out the forms, rejected the census because the Welsh, unlike the Scots* and Irish, were not allowed to tick a box stating clearly and unambiguously that they were Welsh. The nationalists demanded an apology from the Office of National Statistics for violating the human rights of the Welsh.

SELECTED BIBLIOGRAPHY:

Adamson, David L. *Class, Ideology and the Nation: A Theory of Welsh Nationalism.* 1991.

Davies, Charlotte Aull. *Welsh Nationalism in the Twentieth Century.* 1989.

Fevre, Ralph, and Andrew Thompson, eds. *Nation, Identity and Social Theory: Perspectives from Wales.* 2000.

Taylor, Bridget. *Scotland and Wales: Nations Again?* 1999.

West Papuans

West Irians; Papuans; Irianese

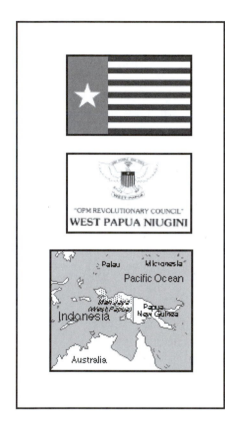

POPULATION: Approximately (2002e) 1,160,000 West Papuans in Indonesia and Papua New Guinea, concentrated in the Indonesian province of Irian Jaya (Papua), but with an estimated 200,000 living adjacent areas of Papua New Guinea, mostly in refugee camps along the border.

THE WEST PAPUAN HOMELAND: The West Papuan homeland occupies the western half of the large island of New Guinea. The region is mostly low, coastal plains surrounding high central mountains west of the international boundary with independent Papua New Guinea. The West Papuan population is spread over a vast and undeveloped terrain, mostly covered in dense tropical rain forests. The province includes a number of smaller offshore islands. West Papua, officially called Irian Jaya or, since 1999, Papua, forms a province of the Republic of Indonesia. Province of Irian Jaya (West Papua Niugini): 162,927 sq. mi.—421,981 sq. km, (2002e) 2,228,000—West Papuans 52%, Javanese and Balinese 21%, Madurese 16%, Ambonese* 5%, South Sulawesis* 4%, other Indonesians 2%. The West Papuan capital and major cultural center is Jayapura, known as Hollandia to the West Papuans, (2002) 136,000. Other important cultural centers are Sorong, (2002e) 100,000, Biak, (2002e) 47,000, Manokwari (2002e) 43,000, and Merauke, (2002e) 39,000.

FLAG: The West Papuan national flag, the "Morning Star" flag, has 13 horizontal stripes of blue and white bearing a wide, vertical red stripe at the hoist charged with a large white five-pointed star. The flag of the principal national organization, the Free Papua Movement, is a white field bearing the West Papuan coat of arms and the name of the organization and the country in blue.

PEOPLE AND CULTURE: The West Papuans, part of the island's Papuan population, are divided among 240 tribes and language groups. The largest tribal groups are the Dani, Asmat, Ekri, Moi, and Amungme. Considered some of the least developed of the world's peoples, the Papuans had little contact with the outside world until the twentieth century. There is a strong distinction between coastal and interior groups, with the coastal peoples having closer affinities to the Melanesians peoples to the east and south of the island. Many of the coastal peoples have mixed with other Indonesian peoples, while the peoples of the interior have long been isolated. Some of the interior groups, inhabiting nearly inaccessible areas, continue to avoid contact with the outside world. Their way of life has changed little in centuries. The interior peoples live in small clans, and their dialects, customs, and social structures display a degree of complexity that is not found among the indigenous coastal people. The majority of the West Papuans engage in agriculture.

LANGUAGE AND RELIGION: The West Papuans speak numerous local languages, perhaps as many as 250, some spoken by only a few people. Until the second half of the twentieth century, most Papuan languages were believed to be unrelated to each other. Modern research has since shown that many are related, although dialectal differences make them mutually unintelligible. Many of the languages of the region remain unknown, as they have never been studied. Most Papuan languages are of only regional importance, but a few have achieved some cultural significance outside their immediate areas due to their use as missionary languages. The majority of the Papuan languages are spoken by a few hundred to a few thousand.

The majority of the Papuans adhere to traditional beliefs; a minority, mostly in the urban areas, are Christian. A large Javanese population, settled in the province in government-sponsored migrations, are Muslims and form part of Indonesia's dominant Javanese ethnic group. The Christian minority forms the core of the West Papuan national movement.

NATIONAL HISTORY: Inhabited for at least 50,000 years, the island was early settled in autonomous villages. Never united under a central authority, each small tribe developed its own distinct culture and language. Through indirect contact with developments in Southeast Asia, the Papuans developed one of the earliest agricultural complexes in history, perhaps 9,000 years ago. The western half of the large island was known to Indonesian and Asian seafarers, who traded or took slaves in the coastal regions.

Portuguese navigators sighted the island of New Guinea in 1511, but no landings were made until 1527. The island was subsequently contacted by Spanish, Dutch, German, and English explorers. The Spanish named the island "Nueva Guinea" in 1546, due to the resemblance between the indigenous peoples and the people of Guinea in Africa. First visited by Dutch navigators in 1606, the island, without the economic incentives of the islands farther west, was generally ignored by the Dutch colonial authorities until the early years of the nineteenth century. The British made an attempt at colonization near Manokwari in 1793, but the colony was soon abandoned.

The Dutch, operating from their East Indies colony, laid claim to the southern coastal region west of the 141st meridian in 1828. In 1848 the Dutch extended their territorial claims to preclude claims by the British and Germans in possession of the eastern part of New Guinea. The three European powers formally divided the island in 1895. The first Dutch administrative posts were not set up in the region until 1898. The Dutch claim to the eastern 47% of the island's territory was confirmed by treaties with Germany and the United Kingdom.

The region was generally neglected in favor of the rich Indonesian islands, and only a few coastal trading bases represented Dutch authority. The bases, centers of Christian missionary activity, became the nucleus of a small, educated Papuan minority. The Christian-educated Papuans became the spokesmen in dealings with the colonial authorities and began to foster a sense of Papuan unity that gradually diminished the endemic feuds and tribal wars. Dutch administration and missionary activity slowly penetrated the interior of the island, although many Papuans would not see a European until well into the twentieth century.

Technically a part of the Dutch East Indies, Dutch New Guinea was set aside by the colonial administration as a restricted area, prohibiting migration to the island from the overcrowded Indonesian islands. Culturally, linguistically, and religiously separated from the other Dutch island possessions, the island effectively became a distinct Dutch possession. The only exception to the exclusion were political exiles. Haji Misbach, an Islamic communist, was exiled by the Dutch authorities to isolated New Guinea in 1924. Over 1,300 communists were rounded up on Java and exiled to the island following an abortive uprising in 1927.

The invading Japanese occupied the northern part of the territory in 1942. Seen by the Japanese as subhuman, thousands of Papuan tribesmen were killed or forced to work as slave laborers. The brutal Japanese occupation ended in 1944 but left the Papuans with an enduring hatred of all Asians. Thousands of Papuans cheered the return of the Dutch in 1945.

The Dutch administration, though forced to recognize Indonesian independence in 1949, rejected the Indonesian claim to Dutch New Guinea. In spite of Indonesian and international pressure to decolonize New Guinea, the Dutch refused to relinquish control as long as the Papuans wished them the stay. United Nations efforts to mediate an acceptable compromise failed. The Papuans adamantly refused inclusion in Indonesia, even with guarantees of autonomy. A Dutch plan for West Papuan independence, prepared in 1959–60, was blocked by Indonesia's communist and Third World supporters in the UN General Assembly.

In April 1961 the Dutch created a Papuan legislature and granted a degree of self–government. The Indonesians denounced the Dutch preparations for autonomy as yet another ploy to win separate independence for the Papuans and launched a surprise attack on the province, setting off heavy fighting. The West Papuans raised their new "Morning Star" flag and declared the independence of the Republic of West Papua on 1 December 1961. The West Papuans were able to enjoy partial self-government under UN auspices for just 18 months before they were betrayed.

The United States brokered a compromise that placed the territory under UN administration on 1 April 1962, with provision for a plebiscite to determine the wishes of the West Papuans. The UN administration, ignoring the plebiscite agreement and West Papuan protests, turned the territory over to Indonesia following a vote in the General Assembly in 1963, with provision that the Indonesian government hold the plebiscite before 1969. The West Papuan resistance movement mobilized following the creation of the Free Papua Movement (OPM) in 1965.

The Indonesian military occupied the major centers in the territory and set up a military government. In August 1969 the Indonesian government organized the UN-mandated referendum, but only 1,025 people, who had prospered under Indonesian rule, were allowed to participate. The UN General Assembly endorsed the referendum and the Indonesian occupation. Outraged by the United Nations betrayal and the excesses of the Indonesian military, Papuan nationalists led a widespread rebellion that pitted Stone Age warriors against the American-equipped Indonesian army. An estimated 60,000 Indonesian troops were deployed in the province during the height of the OPM insurrection between 1967 and 1972. The resulting violence reportedly caused between 30,000 and 100,000 West Papuan deaths.

The level of armed resistance diminished in the 1970s in the face of vastly superior force. The Indonesians, determined to hold the province and its newly discovered petroleum reserves, launched a campaign of brutal suppression. Indonesian troops attacked undefended Papuan villages and expelled Christian missionaries who denounced the measures. Pursued by helicopter gunships, thousands fled to mountain sanctuaries or crossed the border to refugee camps in Papua New Guinea. Papuan leaders appealed the United Nations but were ignored. On 9 December 1975 the leaders signed the Serui Declaration, a unilateral declaration of the independence of the Republic of West Papua. The proclamation stimulated renewed Indonesian suppression. In 1984, after a series of pro-independence demonstrations, thousands of villagers fled over the border into Papua New Guinea to escape the rampaging Indonesian army. By 1985 over 100,000 Papuans had died in the conflict, most of the dead innocent villagers killed in indiscriminate bombardments and mass executions.

The province's mineral resources, including petroleum, gold, uranium, and copper have been exploited for development projects in central Indonesia, with little benefit to the West Papuan people. Villages situated in areas marked for exploitation were summarily destroyed and their inhabitants driven into the jungle. Roads constructed by mining companies into the interior have been used by non-Papuan immigrants to penetrate formerly inaccessible areas. The migrants, often protected by the government and the mining companies, have taken control of thousands of acres of the best agricultural land.

The Indonesian government, with the financial assistance of several well-intentioned international aid agencies, has settled hundreds of thousands of ethnic Javanese and other from the central Indonesian islands in the province. The mass expulsion of the Papuan populations from the best and most productive lands preceded the implementation of the government-sponsored transmigration program. The *Transmigrasi* program has proved a human and ecological disaster for the region and threatens to obliterate the Papuan people. Most Indonesians feel superior to the Melanesian West Papuans, a fact that has steeled many nationalists against talk of compromise. By 1995 the transmigrants formed nearly half the population of the province.

Ignored by the world, the war in West Papua continued. Faced with genocide, a more radical generation of Papuan leaders vowed to pursue the war until their nation is either free or extinct. The West Papuan guerrillas, once dismissed as a "tee-shirt army" with few arms and little training, emerged in the late 1990s as a disciplined force, the only organization opposing the brutal, racist rule of the Indonesian military in the province.

The Indonesian military's enforcement of decisions to expand foreign-owned mining operations resulted in increased popular resistance to the military occupation. Fighting erupted in 1995–96 between the military and villagers being forcibly "relocated" to make way for mining company expansion.

The West Papuans have shown little desire or inclination to integrate into Indonesian society. Development of the province is beneficial mainly to the immigrant groups from the other Indonesian islands. Development projects focused on integrating the territory's oil and mineral resources into the state economy, generally ignoring the indigenous population. Communal tension between the immigrants and the West Papuans over land and other issues of resource competition led to periodic bloody confrontations.

The authoritarian Suharto regime ended in May 1998, after 32 years. The change of government in Indonesia opened a window of opportunity for the West Papuans. Thousands of students and activists demonstrated for autonomy in towns and villages but were met with a show of force.

Soldiers opened fire on several demonstrations, killing many West Papuans.

Abdurrahman Wahid, the first president of Indonesia not connected with the former regime announced in 1999 that he would allow the province to change its name from Irian Jaya (Victorious Irian) to the province of Papua. Many separatists took what had been intended only as a sign of good faith as a willingness to talk seriously about West Papuan independence.

Separatists in the Sorong district, in January 2000, raised the Morning Star flag beside the Indonesian flag, in defiance of the Indonesian military, in front of a crowd of over 3,000. The flag-raising was viewed by nationalists as the symbolic beginning of a new phase in the 35-year struggle for independence. The Indonesian government, as in East Timor, has given backing to "pro-integration" militias, leading to greater conflict with the local population.

A special congress called by nationalists in June 2000 issued a statement reasserting their claim to independence, as declared in 1961 and 1975. In spite of the difficulties of uniting the West Papuan communities (many of which are separated by forbidding mountains) and the political factions (which include pro-Indonesia, pro-autonomy, and pro-independence elements), a consensus was reached on the declaration of sovereignty. Much of the mobilization for independence was due to the determination of Theys Eluay, the unelected leader of the nationalist movement. The focus of the nationalist movement was the demand for a UN-supervised referendum, which would allow the West Papuans the vote on independence they were denied in 1969.

Two days before the planned protests on 1 December 2000, Indonesian troops arrested Theys Eluay but backed down during a confrontation, allowing the West Papuans to fly their separatist flag in Jayapura during a ceremony to mark 39 years since the 1961 declaration of independence. A heavy security presence discouraged West Papuan leaders from carrying out their threat to issue a formal declaration of independence.

In October 2001, the Indonesian government passed a new autonomy bill that changed the name of the province to Papua and permitted greater self-rule, but the West Papuan leaders claim that they were not consulted and most rejected the bill as too little and too late. After some many years and so many deaths, the majority of the West Papuans desire most of all to separate from the hated Indonesians.

Theys Eluay was found dead in November 2001, believed murdered for political reasons by Indonesian agents. About 10,000 supporters held a peaceful demonstration at his funeral, but the loss of their most respected leader enraged the West Papuans. While Eluay wanted a negotiated independence, the new leaders of the nationalist movement may not be so patient.

SELECTED BIBLIOGRAPHY:

Korva, Fred. *The Colony of West Papua*. 1983.
Lagerberg, Kees. *West Irian and Jakarta Imperialism*. 1981.
Muller, Kal, ed. *Irian Jaya*. 1991.
Osborne, Robin. *Indonesia's Secret War: The Struggle in Irian Jaya*. 1985.

Western Canadians

Westerners

POPULATION: Approximately (2002e) 7,920,000 Western Canadians in Canada, concentrated in the western provinces of British Columbia, Alberta, and Saskatchewan. Outside the region there are Western Canadian communities in other parts of Canada, particularly in the province of Manitoba and in the Northwest and Yukon Territories, and in the United States.

THE WESTERN CANADIAN HOMELAND: The Western Canadian homeland occupies a vast stretch of the Great Plains rising to the Rocky Mountains in Alberta and British Columbia. The region west of the Rockies is mostly forested, and the Coastal Mountains rise along the rugged coastline on the Pacific Ocean. Most nationalists claim the three heartland provinces of British Columbia, Alberta,

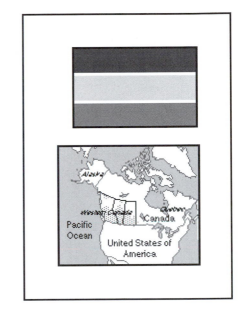

and Saskatchewan, but a minority would extend the region to include the Yukon, Northwest, and Nunavut Territories and the province of Manitoba, encompassing all of Canada west of Hudson's Bay. The three heartland provinces, as outlined by nationalists, form Western Canada. *Western Canada*: 811,206 sq. mi.—2,101,013 sq. km, (2002e) 8,365,000—Western Canadians 84%, indigenous peoples 9%, other Canadians 7%. The major centers of the region are Victoria, (2002e) 75,000, metropolitan area 257,000, and Vancouver in British Columbia, (2002e) 535,000, metropolitan area 1,936,000; Calgary, (2002e) 861,000, metropolitan area 908,000, and Edmonton, (2002e) 686,000, metropolitan area 924,000, in Alberta; and Saskatoon (2002e) 196,000, and Regina in Saskatchewan, (2002e), 183,000.

FLAG: The Western Canadian flag, the flag of the national movement, is a horizontal tricolor of blue, tan, and green, the stripes divided by narrow white stripes.

PEOPLE AND CULTURE: The Western Canadians are an English-speaking North American group whose culture, language, and heritage stems from the indigenous peoples, the early English settlers, and the later immigrants—mostly from Europe but increasingly from Asia and other parts of the world. Culturally, the Western Canadians generally reject the official biculturalism and bilingualism that has been enforced in an effort to persuade the Québecois* to remain within Canada. The Western Canadians are increasingly urbanized, the majority now living in the large urban areas around Vancouver, Calgary, and Edmonton although the traditional "cowboy" culture remains strong. People of British descent formerly formed a controlling elite, but since World War II ethnic diversity and immigration have changed the region's ethnic identity. The regional culture remains one of the most British in North America, but at the same time, particularly in British Columbia, it is one of the continent's most racially diverse. The population is concentrated in the more temperate zones in the south, and rural depopulation remains a serious problem.

LANGUAGE AND RELIGION: The Western Canadians speak the western North American dialect of English. The dialect, virtually indistinguishable from the dialects spoken in the United States, developed from the early English brought to the region by colonists, but since the early twentieth century the dialect has absorbed many words and phrases from other languages. Although Canada is officially bilingual in English and French, in the western provinces of Canada there are more people whose mother tongue is Cantonese than French.

European immigrants created a predominantly Christian society in the region, particularly Protestant. Most of the indigenous peoples were converted to Christianity after the settlers arrived. Protestants still predominate and remain influential in daily life and in attitudes throughout Western Canada. Religious conflicts over whether education should be denominational or nonsectarian never strongly influenced politics as they did elsewhere in Canada. The Protestant view that church and state must remain separate is fundamental to the regional culture. The region's Protestant identity is increasingly challenged by the growing ethnic diversity of the population.

NATIONAL HISTORY: At the time of the initial contacts with European explorers, indigenous peoples in the region numbered about 150,000, divided into the coastal peoples, such as the Haidas,* and the nomadic peoples of the Great Plains east of the Rockies, particularly the Sioux.* European ships sailed along the coast of British Columbia in the late eighteenth century, including that of Capt. James Cook, who was searching for the fabled Northwest Passage. Tuberculosis, diphtheria, smallpox, and other diseases brought to the region by the Europeans decimated the indigenous peoples.

British and American fur traders were the first to explore the area. The Hudson's Bay Company and the rival North West Company established vast networks of trading posts and contact points across the region. Furs traded by the indigenous peoples for manufactured goods brought enormous wealth to the fur traders. English, Scots, and Northern Irish played the major role in the establishment of the early settlements and remained a controlling elite until the mid-twentieth century.

The first Europeans appeared in the 1750s in the interior regions as the fur trade expanded across western North America. The Hudson's Bay Company and the North West Company began construction of trading posts in the last quarter of the eighteenth century along the major northern rivers. The two companies merged in 1821, leaving the Hudson's Bay Company to govern a huge, sparsely populated region of North America.

Away from the coastal settlements, fur traders, buffalo hunters, various indigenous tribes, Métis,* French and British explorers, and missionaries made up the bulk of the regions inhabitants until the mid-nineteenth century. In 1873 the Canadian government created the North West Mounted Police to maintain law and order in the vast region. In the 1880s the region was the scene of the Riel Rebellion, centered in the Métis* population in the northern districts.

The expansionist desire of the Canadians and the British desire to terminate its defense of inland Canada resulted in the movement for confederation in the mid-1800s. In 1867 the Dominion of Canada, comprising Nova Scotia, New Brunswick, Quebec, and Ontario, was created under the British North America Act. One aspect of the act important to the western territories was the sale of the Hudson's Bay Company's landholdings to the dominion government.

In 1849 Vancouver Island was made a crown colony. The mainland was proclaimed the colony of British Columbia in 1858. The inland region remained part of the territory ruled by the Hudson's Bay Company until 1870, when Alberta and Saskatchewan, as part of the Northwest Territories, were placed under federal control. The interior region was increasingly developed by homesteaders after the completion of the Canadian Pacific Railroad in 1886 and the extension of the line to Vancouver in 1887. Lumber and mining sustained the areas west of the Rockies, while farming overtook ranching as the major economic base of the prairie regions in about 1900. British Columbia joined the confederation in 1871, and in 1905 Alberta and Saskatchewan entered the Canadian confederation as full provinces. The federal government retained control of their natural resources, paying a subsidy in place of the revenues the resources might have yielded.

The prairie regions suffered the most from the Great Depression of the 1930s. Many abandoned farms in Alberta and Saskatchewan to move west to British Columbia, particularly the cities of Vancouver and Victoria, where jobs were available. By the 1940s British Columbia had become one of the most urbanized provinces of Canada. The Cooperative Commonwealth Federation established the first avowedly socialist government in

North America in Saskatchewan between the mid-1940s and mid-1960s. The "Salmon War" between Canada and the United States in the 1980s over fishing rights in the Pacific Ocean was just one episode in Western Canada's long alienation from the federal government.

A lawyer, Douglas Christie, began to advocate Western Canadian independence in 1974. He founded the Committee for Western Independence, which became the center of the growing Western Canadian separatist movement. He has been the leader of the movement for a new nation of Western Canada since the mid-1970s. Christie spent years touring the provinces, visiting service clubs, professional organization, schools and universities, conferences, and groups of private individuals. He is currently the leader of the major nationalist organization, the Western Canadian Concept, which is dedicated the creation of a new nation in Western Canada, with English as its sole official language.

The Reform Party, which emerged in the late 1980s as a protest movement, took majorities in the three provinces in 1997. The party was founded in 1987 by Preston Manning, an evangelical Christian from Alberta. The party sought to mobilize the Western Canadians who felt that the old-line Canadian political parties had let them down. It campaigned for a leaner government and questioned the constant attention that, it claimed, the federal government lavished on the Québecois. The party leaders claimed that there should be no "special status" for Quebec; instead, Canada should be maintained in its original model of 10 equal provinces.

The constant threat of Canadian breakup stimulated the growth of local nationalism in Western Canada in the mid-1980s. The deep discontent in the western provinces over the federal government's perceived favoritism toward Quebec led to demands for devolution of powers to all the provinces, even to the creation of an economic bloc of independent states similar to the European Economic Community. Ironically, Western Canadian hard-liners proved to be Quebec's allies by their demands for more decentralized power to the provinces.

The possibility of the separation of Quebec from Canada was again raised in 1994 with the election of a provincial government committed to independence. The event reverberated in Western Canada, where opposition to more concessions to keep Quebec in the federation was loudly voiced. Quebec's drive toward sovereignty brought to the surface a latent and potentially parallel independent streak among Western Canadians. In opinion polls taken between 1994 and 2000, an increasing number of Western Canadians agreed that the region could go it alone if the federation broke up. In the late 1990s, Western Canada underwent its own "Quiet Revolution," akin to movement that convulsed Quebec society in the 1960s and set the French-speaking province on its tortuous road to sovereignty.

The 1997 election gave the Reform Party a majority in the western provinces, making it the official opposition at a national level. The party appealed to the Western Canadians' belief that their interests in the federation were continually being subordinated to those of Ontario and Quebec. For the first time, a regional protest party had become Canada's official opposition party.

For more than 30 years Quebec brandished the threat of secession, and by the late 1990s, the Western Canadians were weary of it. They felt that more than enough had been done to placate Québecois nationalism—from official bilingualism to immigration. The nationalist backlash in Western Canada that began in the 1980s fueled local nationalism, with demands for the same rights to secession as Quebec. The region, the size of Western Europe, would suffer briefly, nationalists claim, but within three years would stabilize economically, and an independent Western Canada would take its place among the prosperous nations of North America.

Bilingualism is another source of western resentment. In January 1992, Alberta's premier, Don Getty, was accused of pandering to prejudices against French speakers when he called for an end to official bilingualism. Canadians, particularly in the heartland in Ontario, have feared French-speaking Québecois nationalism, but in 2000 a bigger challenge to their tranquility—or complacency—came from the West. In Alberta politicians promoted a robust, American-style agenda of less government, more individualism, and more private profit. They have succeeded to the extent that Calgary has replaced Montreal as Canada's largest financial and business center and that a regional political party, the Canadian Alliance, has emerged as the strongest party in the West, taking the place of the now defunct Reform Party. For years Alberta has been the largest net contributor to the federal government's revenues.

Successive Canadian governments have had their centers of power in the East, virtually ignoring the West except to exploit its natural resources. Ontario and Quebec together represent about two-thirds of the seats in the House of Commons, making it possible for the two provinces to elect the federal government. According to Western Canadian nationalists, this situation stems from the original confederation of 1867. Nationalists point out the lack of balance between the provinces, which gives the more populous eastern provinces virtual domination of the entire country.

The western provinces produce 52% of the gross national product in fisheries, forestry, and agriculture, and 90% of Canada's petroleum production. Nationalists point out that the West pays more in taxes than it receives from the federal government for all services, schools, roads, health care, and pensions. Alberta and British Columbia have lost hundreds of billions of dollars in equalization and intergovernmental transfers of funds, funds that nationalists would like to see supporting an autonomous government in the region. The three provinces are the only provinces in Canada that produce more foreign exports than imports.

In early 2000 the Reform Party, based in the western provinces, formed an alliance with the Progressive Conservatives, the official opposition party in Ontario, to form the Canadian Alliance. The Alliance participated in the 2000 elections but took seats only in the three Western Canadian provinces, as once again Canada's political territory split along regional lines. In December 2000, after the elections, Canadian prime minister Jean Chretien vowed to pay more attention the West, where his party won only 17 seats out of the 88 possible in the region. The failure of the western-based Alliance to break through in Ontario in the federal elections fueled regionalist sentiment against the seemingly impenetrable political wall at the Ontario border.

Canada is among the world's richest, most advanced societies, but it remains divided along linguistic, regional, and provincial lines. The West has traditionally been a resource-producing area, but in recent years there has been tremendous growth in other areas, including manufacturing, and with a particular emphasis on small business. The diversifying economy has given the Western Canadians new confidence to demand the same rights as those offered to Quebec, including control over resources, immigration, and fiscal policies. The more militant groups, including the Western Canadian nationalists, see the growing economy as the basis for a prosperous, independent Western Canada.

In November 2001, nationalists held their first congress in Alberta. The numbers that attended exceeded expectations, demonstrating the level of discontent in the western Canadian provinces.

SELECTED BIBLIOGRAPHY:

Brimelow, Peter. *The Patriot Game*. 1992.
Burgess, Phillip M., and Michael Kelly, eds. *Profile of Western North America*. 1995.
Kilgour, David. *Uneasy Patriots: Western Canadians in Confederation*. 1989.
Lamont, Lansing. *Breakup: The Coming End of Canada and the Stakes for America*. 1994.

Western Somalis

Ogadenis

POPULATION: Approximately (2002e) 4,075,000 Western Somalis in Ethiopia and Kenya, concentrated in the Somali Regional State of Ethiopia and adjacent areas of northeastern Kenya. Outside the region there are still thousands of Western Somalis living in refugee camps in various parts of neighboring Somalia in 2001–2.

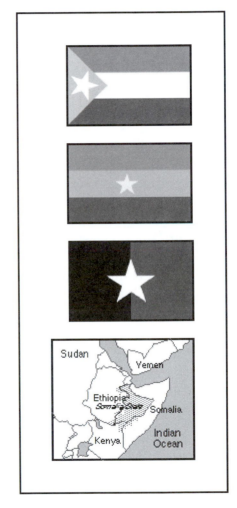

THE WESTERN SOMALI HOMELAND: The Western Somali homeland lies in eastern and southern Ethiopia, occupying the flat, semi-arid Ogaden Desert and the highlands of the Ahmar Mountains, which separate the region from central Ethiopia. Of the total region, 80% is *quola*, lowlands, 5% is *dega*, highlands, and 16% is *woyna dega*, or temperate zones. Many of the inhabitants of the region remain nomadic or seminomadic, moving across the vast region with their herds. The homeland, comprising nine administrative areas, forms the Somali Regional State of the Federal Democratic Republic of Ethiopia. *Somali Regional State (Ogadenia/Western Somalia)*: 106,612 sq. mi.—276,124 sq. km, (2002e) 4,269,000—Western Somalis 95%, Oromos* 3%, Amharas* 1%, other Ethiopians 1%. The Western Somali capital and major cultural center is Jijiga, (2002e) 38,000. Harar, called Hara in Somali, which forms a separate state in the Ethiopian federation, is also an important cultural center, (2002e) 95,000. Dire Dawa, (2002e) 207,000, also a separate state bordering Somali Regional State, is a traditional Somali cultural center.

FLAG: The Western Somali national flag, the flag of the national movement and of the Western Somali Liberation Front, is a horizontal tricolor of red, white, and green bearing a pale blue triangle at the hoist charged with a centered five-pointed white star. The flag of the other major nationalist organization, the Ogaden National Liberation Front, is a vertical tricolor of green, blue, and red bearing a centered five-pointed white star. The traditional flag of the Western Somalis is a vertical bicolor of black and red bearing a centered five-pointed white star.

PEOPLE AND CULTURE: The Western Somalis are of mixed Somali and Oromo background, encompassing the Western Somali clans, the Darod around Harar, the Dir around Dire Dawa, the Issa, Isaaks,* and Gadabursi in the north, the Ogadeni in the south and southwest, the Abo in the south, the Hawiye in the southwest, the Marahan in the southeast, and the Dolbahuna in the east. The Western Somalis share a common language, a single faith, and a cultural heritage that is an integral part of their nomadic lifestyle. Somali society is based on the nuclear family and the family herd of sheep, goats, and camels. The more camels a man has, the greater his prestige. The Somalis consider themselves a warrior people; women are often put in charge of the herds while the Western Somalis train to become fighters. As in other Somali areas, the Western Somalis are sharply divided among several rival clan groups.

LANGUAGE AND RELIGION: The clans speak the western dialects of Somali, a Cushitic language of the Hamitic language group. The Western Somali dialects, including the widespread dialects of Degodia and Ogaden, are written in the Ethiopian alphabet, not the Arabic alphabet used by the other Somali peoples. Somali is the working language of the regional state in Ethiopia. The total number of students enrolled in the area's schools is less than 75,000; females make up less than a third of the total.

The Western Somalis are a Muslim Somali people, with over 99% adhering to the Shai'ite rite of Islam. Numerous pagan beliefs and traditions have survived and have been intermingled with their Islamic practices. They achieve "ecstasy" by chanting or taking narcotics. Unlike most Muslims, Western Somali women have never worn veils. In the desert area they perform rain-making rituals. Belief in spirit possession is widespread, as is the belief that spirits live in trees, on hilltops, and in water sources.

NATIONAL HISTORY: Nomadic tribes have roamed the Ogaden Desert since ancient times. The tribes were never united but remained autonomous nomadic groups, often warring over water and grazing lands. In the fifteenth century Oromo tribes moved into the western part of the region, taking control of the best pasture lands. In the sixteenth century Somali tribes from the east began to migrate with their herds, displacing the Oromos from many areas.

Even though the clans spoke dialects the same Somali language, the desert peoples remained free of the coastal Somali states to the east. Islam, introduced to the Somali port cities by Arab traders, spread to the inland tribes in the seventh and eighth centuries. The new religion established a strong bond between the various clan and tribal groups. The clans united to defeat Oromo expansion from the west in the fifteenth and sixteenth centuries, the western Somali clans later mixing with the newly converted Muslim Oromo tribes.

The Muslim peoples, led by Ahmed Gran, waged holy war on the Christian Ethiopian kingdom in the highlands to the west from 1529 to 1542 but failed to take the Christians' mountain strongholds. With military support from the Portuguese, the Christians rallied and drove the Muslims back to the Ogaden. The war between the Muslims and Christians set off centuries of sporadic warfare in the region.

The Ethiopians conquered Harar, the traditional capital of the Western Somali clans, in 1887. The Ethiopians used the city as a base from which to extend Ethiopian rule in the Ogaden, as part of the colonization of the Somali lands. In 1896, having defeated the Italians, who also claimed the region, the Ethiopian emperor Menelik II forestalled Italian occupation by occupying the Ogaden. France, Italy, and the United Kingdom took control of the coastal Somali tribes. The Western Somali clans united in 1899 to launch a 21-year holy war against Christian Ethiopian rule. Ultimately defeated in 1920, the Ethiopian imperial government began a program to separate the western clans from their kin under European rule, including a ban on the traditional Arabic script used by the other Somali groups.

The Ethiopian government erected *ketemas*, garrison towns, to rule the Western Somali regions. Political authorities imposed the Amhara-Christian culture on the inhabitants of the towns and extracted resources from the region. The majority of the Western Somali clans remained nomadic, moving seasonally with their herds across the international borders established by Ethiopia and the European colonial powers.

The Italians, from their bases in coastal Somaliland, occupied the Walwal Oasis in the early 1930s and launched a full-scale invasion of the Ogaden in 1935. The next year, the Italians proclaimed Ethiopia, including the Ogaden, as part of Italian East Africa. During World War II the Italians also took control of British Somaliland. United under one government for the first time in their history, the Somali peoples evolved a pan–Somali nationalist movement dedicated to the creation of a "Greater Somalia" from the five colonial Somali territories. British troops moving north from Kenya drove the Italians from the Horn of Africa in 1941, taking control of the former British and Italian Somali territories and establishing a military government in the Ogaden following the liberation of Ethiopia. With the exception of French Somaliland, all the Somali territories were united under British military rule.

In April 1942 the Dir and Darod clans rebelled; the revolt marked the beginning of the modern Western Somali national movement. The British disarmed the Western Somali clans and restricted their movement but opened their lands and water resources to the still-armed Isaaks from neighboring British Somaliland. The Western Somali resentment of the coastal clans, which they perceived to be pampered by the British, accelerated the growth of Western Somali nationalism. Parts of the Ogaden and the Hawd were gradually returned to Ethiopian control.

The British authorities in 1946 proposed to the new United Nations a plan for a trusteeship to encompass British Somaliland, former Italian Somaliland, and the part of Ethiopian Somaliland under British military rule. The plan, blocked by the Ethiopian government, was discarded, although the disposition of the Somali territories continued to be debated by the General Assembly throughout the late 1940s. In 1948 Western Somali nationalists opposed to a return to Ethiopian authority led demonstrations and clashed with the British occupation troops.

In 1950 the United Nations recommended a return to the prewar borders, including the return of Western Somalia to the rule of the feudal Ethiopian state. The Italians returned to southern Somalia, given 10 years to prepare the region for independence under a UN trusteeship. The British retained former British Somalia as a distinct trusteeship. Vehemently opposed to Ethiopian rule, the Western Somali clan elders appealed to the British authorities. The British delayed the transfer of authority until 1954 but were ultimately obliged to relinquish control to the Ethiopians. In 1955 harsh Ethiopian restrictions provoked widespread violence in the region.

Independent Somalia, formed from British and Italian territories in 1960, agitated for the unification of all ethnic Somalis in an expanded "Greater Somalia." The Western Somali clans, never part of the coastal Somali states, felt little affinity with the Somali republic, although a majority supported a loose federation of Somali states. The national question divided the clans between those favoring Somalia, the advocates of separate independence, and the minority that had prospered under Ethiopian rule. By the end of 1963 a Western Somali uprising led by Muktal Dahir sparked border skirmishes between Ethiopian troops and forces of the Somalia government.

Independent Somalia also campaigned for unification of French Somaliland and the Somali-populated region of northern Kenya. In the spring of 1963 the Western Somali clans in northeastern Kenya failed in an attempt to separate and to join their territory to Somalia. The government of Somalia broke diplomatic relations with Britain, and a Western Somali guerrilla war broke out in northern Kenya, paralyzing the region until 1967.

The West provided military support to Ethiopia and Kenya, so the Somalia government turned to the Soviet Union for aid. Rebels of the Western Somali Liberation Front (WSLF), drawn from the northern clans and armed by Somalia and the Soviet Union, launched a separatist war against Ethiopian rule. The fighting intensified with the installation of a communist regime in Addis Ababa in 1974, following the overthrow of the feudal monarchy. The Soviet Union ended overt aid to Somalia and began to supply arms to the Ethiopians. In 1976 the Western Somali rebellion spread to the southern clans, seriously threatening Ethiopia's hold on the Ogaden.

In July 1977 the army of the Republic of Somalia invaded the Ogaden in support of the separatists. The 15,000 Western Somali rebels, backed by 35,000 Somali troops, nearly succeeded in separating the Ogaden from Ethiopia before intervention by the Soviet Union and Cuba bolstered the Ethiopians. In the spring of 1978 the Ethiopians, with Soviet equipment and Cuban soldiers, reconquered the Ogaden. In reprisal for the Western Somali uprising, government forces proceeded to bomb and strafe villages. The war and the harsh reprisals generated hundreds of thousands of refugees and exacerbated the instability of the Horn of Africa. By the early 1980s the number of refugees in Somalia from the Ogaden exceeded 1,500,000.

In 1981 a clan congress committed itself to the creation of an independent free state of Western Somalia. Civil war in Somalia in 1988 and the declaration of independence of the northern clans in Somaliland in 1991, administered the final blows to the long-held Somali dream of a "Greater Somalia."

In May 1991, a coalition of ethnic insurgent groups overthrew Ethiopia's communist government. In December 1991, the new coalition government created a federation of ethnically-based regions. The regions, allowing major autonomy, also created new conflicts. A Western Somali dispute with the Oromos over control of Dire Dawa and Harar erupted in serious fighting in 1992–93. Harar and Dire Dawa were separated from both the Somali and Oromo territories to form separate city-states within the new Ethiopian federation. Drought in 1992 led to famine, and over 4,000 people died of starvation.

The Western Somali national movement encompassed 12 separate nationalist groups supporting various autonomist and separatist views. Despite reservations, many of the nationalist groups, including the WSLF, signed the charter establishing the Somali state within Ethiopia and participated in regional elections in December 1992.

The Ethiopian government adopted in 1994 a new constitution that formally divided the country into regions based on ethnicity in an effort to ease ethnic tension by giving the largest national groups some control of their traditional territories. Some nationalist groups accepted the offer of autonomy, while eight others, including the Ogaden National Liberation Front, declared their intention to continue the fight for self-determination. The 10 groups that favored autonomy within Ethiopia formed the Ethnic Somali Democratic League, which won regional elections in 1995. Clan elders petitioned the Ethiopian government to grant amnesty in order to give rebels a chance to reconcile with the local population.

In the late 1990s, the Western Somali national movement was splintered among numerous groups and organizations, including an increasingly vocal Islamic fundamentalist movement led by al-Itihad al Islam. Islamic groups in Western Somalia joined similar Oromo and Afar groups in calling for the establishment of an Islamic state in Ethiopia in 1997. For the most part the Western Somalis have resisted the call to engage in holy war against the Ethiopian state.

Over 8,000 Western Somali refugees from Ethiopia were repatriated from Somalia in April 1998, and there were plans for repatriating 60,000 more. The refugees, many having fled the Ogaden in 1976–77, returned to a different region, an autonomous Somali state within the Ethiopian federation created in the 1990s.

The war with neighboring Eritrea in 1999–2000 contributed to a considerable worsening of the human rights and humanitarian situation in Ethiopia. An estimated 40,000 to 50,000 soldiers were believed to have been killed, wounded, or captured, including many drawn from the Somali state.

Unrest and antigovernment sentiment, put aside following the creation of the Somali state in Ethiopia, resurfaced during the Eritrean conflict and continues to spread as government neglect and underdevelopment continue. Increasingly the Western Somalis view the Ethiopian government as dominated by the Christian highlanders, the Tigreans* and the Amharas.

SELECTED BIBLIOGRAPHY:

Hodd, Michael. *East Africa Handbook: With Kenya, Tanzania, Uganda and Ethiopia.* 1998.

Legum, Bill Lee. *Conflict in the Horn of Africa.* 1978.

Nahum, Fasil. *Constitution for a Nation of Nations: The Ethiopian Prospect.* 1997.

Vestal, Theodore M. *Ethiopia: A Post-Cold War African State.* 1999.

Western Ukrainians

Galicians; Halychnyans

POPULATION: Approximately (2002e) 5,300,000 Western Ukrainians in Ukraine, concentrated in the western provinces of Ukraine, with smaller groups living in adjacent areas of central Ukraine, Romania, Poland, and Romania. Outside the region there are Western Ukrainian communities in the United States, Canada, Australia, and Brazil.

THE WESTERN UKRAINIAN HOME-LAND: The Western Ukrainian homeland occupies a flat plain, traversed by the Dniestr River and its tributaries, rising to the Carpathian Mountains in southwestern Ukraine. The region, including the northern slopes of the Carpathian Mountains and the valleys of Dniestr, Bug, Vistula, and Seret Rivers, forms the regions of Galicia, Volynia, and Bukovina. The Western Ukrainians remain more central European in appearance and culture than the inhabitants of the eastern provinces of Ukraine. Western Ukraine has no official status but forms the Ukrainian *oblasts* of Lviv, Chernivtsi, Ivano-Frankivs, Volyn (Volynia), Rivne, Ternopil, and Zakarpattya (Transcarpathia). *Western Ukraine (Galicia)*: 51,931 sq. mi.—134,501 sq. km, (2002e) 9,728,000—Western Ukrainians 54%, Poles 17%, Hungarians 3%, Moldovans 1.5%, other Ukrainians and Russians 24.5%. The Western Ukrainian capital and major cultural center is Lviv, (2002e) 782,000. Other important cultural centers are Chernivtsi, (2002e) 255,000, and Rivne, (2002e) 244,000.

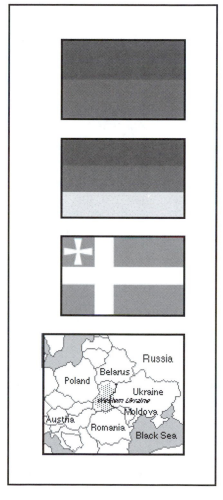

FLAG: The Western Ukrainian national flag, based on the historical flags of Galicia and Bukovina, is a horizontal bicolor of blue over red. The traditional flag of the region is a horizontal tricolor of blue, red, and yellow. The traditional flag of Volynia, the northern part of the region, is a red field bearing a white cross and charged with a small, white Volynian cross on the upper hoist.

PEOPLE AND CULTURE: The Western Ukrainians are an East Slav people, ethnically part of the Ukrainian nation, but historically, culturally, and religiously distinct. The Western Ukrainian culture, through centuries of Austrian and Polish rule, is a Central European culture and is notably free of the strong Russian influences in the culture of central and eastern Ukraine. The people and the region differ sharply from the rest of Ukraine, with a more Central European mindset and attitude. A cultural and linguistic revival, begun with Ukraine's independence in 1991, has won widespread support, making Western Ukraine the most nationalistic region of the Ukrainian republic. The Western Ukrainian cities, designed by Austrian architects, retain a definitely European appearance. Increasingly the Western Ukrainians call their region the old name of Galicia.

LANGUAGE AND RELIGION: The dialects spoken in the region, forming the Southwestern dialect group, contain borrowings from German, Polish, Romanian, and Hungarian and retain forms and words that are considered archaic by other Ukrainian language speakers. The Southwestern dialect of Ukrainian is quite different from the Russianized southeastern dialect spoken in Kiev and the eastern provinces. Forming part of the Eastern Slav language group, the Southwestern dialects are transitional dialects to the Western Slavic languages of Polish and Slovak.

The majority of the Western Ukrainians belong to the Byzantine-rite Uniate Catholic Church, with an Orthodox minority split between the Autocephalous Orthodox Church (an independent Ukrainian Orthodox sect banned in 1930), the official Ukrainian Orthodox Church, and the Russian Orthodox Church. Roman Catholics live mostly along the borders with Poland, Hungary, and Slovakia. There are several small but important Protestant denominations active in the region. The Uniates have long dominated the region, and their religion forms an integral part of the Western Ukrainian culture. About 20,000 Orthodox Ukrainians marched in Kiev in late June 2001 against the visit of the Pope. The Pope was greeted by tens of thousands of Western Ukrainians. His visit is seen as a much-needed support.

NATIONAL HISTORY: Slavs began to settle the river valleys in the sixth century, during the great Slav migrations. The Slavs of the upper Vistula and Dniestr Rivers early came under the influence of the non-Slavic peoples to the west. The region became part of the first great Slav state, Kievan Rus', in 1054. Within 50 years Kievan Rus' had fragmented into 12 principalities, the most southerly of which, Galicia, lay on the frontier between the Latins and the Byzantines.

The medieval principalities of Halicz and Lodomeria (Galicia and Volynia) emerged in the twelfth century and were united over the next century. Their independence was recognized by the pope in 1254. Separated from Russian territory by the Mongol invasion of the thirteenth century, Galicia eventually came under Tatar rule in 1324. The Poles liberated and annexed the region in 1349, and in 1386 Galicia became part of the merged Polish-Lithuanian state.

The Roman Catholic Poles, intent on converting the state's Orthodox subjects to Roman Catholicism, agreed to a compromise in 1596. The Orthodox Ukrainians formed a union with Rome and accepted the pope as their spiritual leader but retained the Byzantine religious rite and their own hierarchy, their priests preserving the right to marry.

Austria annexed Galicia, with its mixed population of Ukrainians and Poles, as a result of the first Polish partition in 1772. The southeastern area around Chernivtsi, the region of Bukovina, was added to Austrian Galicia three years later. Better educated and less restricted under the more lenient rule of the Austrians than the Ukrainians under Russian rule, the Western Ukrainians developed their culture and language separately, influenced by Vienna and Krakow, not Kiev or Moscow.

Officially called the Kingdom of Galicia and Lodomeria, the region retained a mixed population of Poles and Ukrainians under Austrian rule, united by their Roman Catholic religion and orientation toward the West. With access to Western ideas, the Western Ukrainians developed a distinctive history and culture, more European than that of the Ukrainian heartland, in the Russian Empire.

Serious unrest swept the region in 1848, marking the growth of Western Ukrainian nationalism in the Austrian Empire. Lviv became the center of Ukrainian nationalist activities in the Hapsburg territories. The Uniate Church, closely tied to Western Ukrainian culture, provided the focus of Western Ukrainian nationalism. In 1861 Galicia was granted a degree of autonomy and representation in the Austrian parliament. The Ukrainian nationalist movement, severely suppressed in Russian territory, continued to grow in Austrian Western Ukraine. The growth of nationalism in the region led to a parallel revival of the culture in the 1880s and 1890s.

A border region on the frontier with Russia, Galicia became a battleground when war began in 1914. As Austro-Hungarian defeat neared in October 1918, Western Ukrainian nationalists organized to oppose Polish and Romanian claims on the region. On 14 November 1918 nationalist leaders declared the independence of the Western Ukrainian Democratic Republic, claiming Galicia, Bukovina, Ruthenia, Volynia, Lemkia in present Poland, and the Presov region of Slovakia. Roman Catholic Western Ukrainians in the United States raised $140,000 in emergency aid for their kinsmen. Romanian troops invaded the new state to occupy the southeastern region of Bukovina, but a hastily organized national army repulsed a Polish invasion in 1919. The Poles, hoping to regain estates they held in the region under Austrian rule, continued to threaten from the north;

the independence of the Western Ukrainian state was also threatened by German, Bolshevik, and Ukrainian forces.

Threatened on all sides, the Western Ukrainians voted for union with newly independent Ukraine, despite vigorous opposition to the union on religious and cultural grounds. After the Soviet occupation of central and eastern Ukraine, Polish troops overran the region during a Polish-Soviet war in 1919. The Paris Peace Conference, convened after World War I, assigned most of Galicia to Poland, citing religious affinities, specifying that a plebiscite on continued union with Poland was to be held in 25 years, in 1944. Polish control of the region was confirmed in a treaty in 1923, with provisions for Ukrainian autonomy. Bukovina, in the south, was taken by neighboring Romania.

In 1922 the Polish government granted some autonomy, but anti-Polish agitation continued. Nationalist groups carried out campaigns of sabotage and assassinations of Polish officials. In 1932 the Polish government dissolved the Ukrainian Radical Party for advocating Western Ukrainian separatism. The Ukrainian problem in Poland was referred to the League of Nations, but without result. In 1937–39 periodic demonstrations swept the region, with demands for the autonomy promised in 1923. Nationalists formed the Ukrainian Military Organization, which aimed for the restoration of a Catholic Ukrainian state centered on Lviv.

The Soviets, as part of the secret Nazi-Soviet nonaggression pact signed in 1939, occupied the eastern provinces of Poland in November 1939, and in 1940 they took Bukovina from Romania. The Soviet government organized a plebiscite to show that the annexations were the choice of the people, but the only choice was in favor of annexation, voting was compulsory, and no secret ballots were allowed. The religious ties to Rome of the 3.5 million Uniate Catholics made them highly suspect. A campaign of severe repression was initiated, with over a million Western Ukrainians killed or deported, including all those with the smooth hands of the intellectual.

In June 1941 the Nazis launched an invasion of their Soviet ally, and as Soviet authority collapsed Western Ukrainian nationalists of the Organization of Ukrainian Nationalists emerged from hiding to take control of the region. On 30 June 1941 the nationalists declared Western Ukraine an independent state, but the Nazis ignored the proclamation and occupied it. The Germans suppressed the national government and sent the region's leaders to concentration camps. Separated from the eastern Ukraine and eventually promoted as allies in the Nazi's anticommunist campaign, many Western Ukrainians joined the Germans to fight the hated Soviets. The Uniates were favored by the German authorities and were less harshly treated than the Orthodox Ukrainians.

The Ukraine was retaken by the Red Army in 1944, and another 500,000 Western Ukrainians faced deportation or imprisonment between 1945 and

1949. Stalin accused the entire Uniate Catholic population, including the metropolitan of Lviv, of collaboration with the Nazis. Forced to renounce its ties to Rome, the Uniate Church was absorbed by the official Russian Orthodox Church. While Russian Orthodoxy received state subsidies, Ukrainian Uniate Catholic priests, nuns, and laymen filled Stalin's slave labor camps. The church, forced underground, became a center of clandestine Western Ukrainian nationalism.

The Soviet authorities treated Western Ukraine as a conquered, not liberated, zone. Government-sponsored immigration of reliable cadres to Lviv and other cities in the region produced a core of progovernment workers and government functionaries. As late as 1961 there were reports of armed nationalist groups in the region. In 1968–69 the government launched a massive crackdown in the western provinces of Ukraine, with mass arrests and detention of numerous priests and former nuns. The religious underground was closely tied to nationalist groups.

In the 1970s the Uniate Catholic provinces remained the most politically active in Ukraine, with periodic rioting and demonstrations. In 1973 a Uniate delegation from Lviv traveled to Moscow to hand in a petition, signed by thousands of people, asking for the reopening of at least one Uniate Catholic church. The Soviet authorities, claiming that the Uniate church was a front for nationalism, refused to receive the petition.

In 1986 reported sightings of the Virgin Mary drew crowds of up to 100,000 in Western Ukraine, giving the outlawed Uniate Church a new burst of energy. The church in the 1980s was the largest underground religious group in the Soviet Union. Unofficial estimates of the number of adherents of the unofficial church ranged from three to five million. An estimated 1,200 underground Uniate priests held day jobs and celebrated masses in private homes or in the woods. The underground network became known as the "forest churches."

The reforms initiated in the Soviet Union in the late 1980s allowed the expression of nationalist and religious beliefs. The Uniate church functioned openly after 1987 and received official sanction in 1988. The legalization of the church opened bitter disputes between the Uniates and Orthodox hierarchy over church properties confiscated in 1946; the controversy became part of the growing rift between the strongly nationalist western Ukraine and the traditionally pro-Russian central and eastern regions.

Ukrainian independence, enthusiastically supported in the western provinces and achieved during the disintegration of the Soviet Union in 1991, temporarily submerged the east-west rifts. In the 1990s, however, economic hardships exacerbated the split between the two halves of the country, the nationalists versus the unionists of eastern Ukraine, who were seeking renewed ties with Russia. In Ukrainian presidential elections in July 1994, the pro-Russian victor received less than 4% of the vote in the western region; the danger of civil war in Ukraine moved closer. Nationalist leaders reiterated their readiness to go it alone and suffer the initial hardships of independence.

A well-known aversion of the Western Ukrainians toward "Moskals"—a disparaging name for the inhabitants of Dnepropetrovsk and Donsk zones, where the men who dominate the Ukrainian government come from—has become part of the economic grievances. Nationalists in the western region, weary of Ukraine's corruption, political disarray, and the pro-Russian orientation of the eastern provinces, advocate a policy of orientation toward the West. A leaked report by the U.S. Central Intelligence Agency predicted civil war, as had occurred in Yugoslavia, should the two parts of the country continue to go their separate ways.

In a public opinion poll in 1996, only 21% of the Catholic Western Ukrainians—as opposed to the Orthodox Eastern Ukrainians, who traditionally have looked to Moscow—advocated closer cooperation with Russia. Other polls taken in 1997–98 showed striking and persistent differences between the populations of Eastern and Western Ukraine on cultural issues, although social and economic issues were less differentiated. One result showed that only 1.5% of Western Ukrainians thought that things were going well in the country and that Ukraine had a good chance of emerging from its present difficulties; only 7% thought that Ukraine was going in the right direction. Reviving the Ukrainian nation was considered a priority by 31% of Western Ukrainians, but only 7.5% of Eastern Ukrainians. However, the major difference was the stress in the west on national-patriotic values versus the economic preoccupations in the east.

The increasing possibility that neighboring Hungary and Poland will join the European Union (EU) and thereafter require visas for visiting Western Ukrainians stimulated a new debate on the region's status in 1999–2000. The region is dependent on border trade, and many work illegally across the borders, earning up to six times what they would get in the Ukraine for farm and construction work. The tight visa regime that the EU wants the Central European countries to impose on visitors from farther east before joining the Union would end the cross-border economic lifelines. Should a new "iron curtain," in the form of the EU boundaries, fall across Central Europe, the Western Ukrainians are sure they want to be west of the new divide. Talk of independence is increasing, although some nationalists claim this plays into the hands of pro-Russian groups in the east who want to ditch Galicia and unite with Russia. Most Western Ukrainians would settle for more autonomy in order to get closer to the EU and to neighboring Poland.

SELECTED BIBLIOGRAPHY:

Himka, John-Paul. *Religion and Nationality in Western Ukraine: The Greek Catholic Church and the Ruthenian National Movement in Galicia 1867–1900*. 1999.

Wanner, Catherine. *Burden of Dreams: History and Identity in Post-Soviet Ukraine.* 1998.

Wilson, Andrew. *Ukrainian Nationalism in the 1990s: A Minority Faith.* 1996.

Wolchik, Sharon, and Volodvymyr Zviglyanich, eds. *Ukraine: The Search for a National Identity.* 1999.

Yorubas

Yoobas; Yaribas; Ede-Yorubas

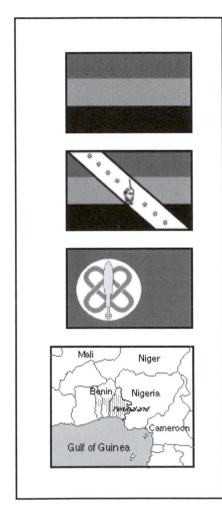

POPULATION: Approximately (2002e) 26,488,000 Yorubas in west-central Africa, concentrated in the region of Yorubaland, in southwestern Nigeria, and about 500,000 in adjacent Xou and Ouéme Provinces of Benin. Outside the region there are Yoruba communities in northern and eastern Nigeria, in other West African countries, in Europe (particularly the United Kingdom), in the United States, and in Brazil and the Caribbean.

THE YORUBA HOMELAND: The Yoruba homeland, Yoruba, lies in southwestern Nigeria, a region of rolling savanna and forest lands in the Plateau of Yorubaland, between the middle Niger River and the Bight of Benin. The population is highly urbanized, most living in cities with populations of more than 20,000. Formerly the Western Region of Nigeria, Yorubaland has no political status. Yorubaland in Nigeria forms the states of Kwara, Lagos, Ondo, Oshun, Ogun, Oyo, and the western districts of Kogi. *Yorubaland*: 43,502 sq. mi.— 112,670 sq. km, (2002e) 31,143,000—Yorubas 85%, Nupe 6%, Hausas* 4%, Ibos* 2%, Edos* 2%, other Nigerians 1%. The Yoruba capital and major cultural center is Lagos (2002e) 7,972,000, metropolitan area 10,769,000. Other important cultural centers are Ibadan, (2002e) 3,136,000, metropolitan area 3,756,000; Ogbomobsho (2002e) 739,000, metropolitan area 992,000; Oshogbo, (2002e) 428,000, metropolitan area 1,295,000; Oyo, (2002e) 632,000; Abeokuta (2002e) 533,000, metropolitan area 704,000; Ife, the spiritual capital, (2002e) 319,000.

FLAG: The Yoruba national flag, the flag of the national movement, is a horizontal tricolor of red, green, and black. The flag of Egbe Omo Yoruba is the same tricolor charged with a diagonal white stripe, upper hoist to lower fly, bearing an image of the mythical Yoruba ancestor and seven small stars representing the historical subdivisions of the nation, Oyo, Kabba, Ekiti, Egba, Ife, Ondo, and Ijebu. The traditional flag of the region, the official flag of the former Western Region, is a blue field bearing a large white disc offset toward the hoist charged with a yellow Yoruba sword backed by an ancient Yoruba design in green.

PEOPLE AND CULTURE: The name "Yoruba" is now applied to all persons who speak Yoruba dialects and share in the common Yoruba culture, but originally it designated only the inhabitants of the old Oyo kingdom; other related peoples were designated by the name of their respective kingdoms. There is much diversity in social and political organization among the Yoruba, but they share many basic features. The Yorubas in Benin are commonly called Nago or Nagot. Inheritance and succession are based on patrilineal descent. Members of the patrilineage live together under the authority of a headman, share certain family names, and have rights to lineage lands. The Yoruba are a people of mixed Hamitic and Bantu descent, claiming descent from ancient Egypt and the Nile Valley. The Yoruba have the only strong urban tradition found in sub-Saharan Africa; 65% of the Yorubas live in cities. The Yorubas' ancient culture is credited with one of the strongest artistic traditions in West Africa; they are the creators of the famous bronze sculptures of the Yoruba cities. The traditional Yoruba kingships still survive, though with only a shadow of their former political power. The Yoruba population has generally expanded to the west and southwest over the past several centuries.

LANGUAGE AND RELIGION: The Yorubas speak a language of the Yoruboid branch of the Kwa languages of the Niger-Congo language group. The language, divided into at least 20 mutually understandable dialects, has a long literary tradition, based on the Oyo dialect. The dialects are mostly regional and are based loosely on the former city–states. Speakers of the northern dialects have difficulty understanding the southern dialects, including the dialects of Lagos and Oyo. The Yoruba language is used for government and is taught in primary, secondary, and university education in the region. The Yorubas, who believe that education is the key to success and power, dominate the public and private sectors in many parts of Nigeria.

Religious pluralism is a Yoruba tradition that goes back to the midnineteenth century. Even though the Yorubas are mainly Christian in the south and Muslim in the north, religion is less important than clan and tribal ties. Christianity has been the dominant religion since the middle of the twentieth century; Anglican, Methodist, and American Southern Baptist denominations are the most widespread. Yoruba culture and religion have profoundly influenced the African diaspora in Brazil and the Caribbean, even among communities where the language has been lost. The traditional pantheon of Yoruba *orisha*, or spirits, is subservient to Olorun, the supreme being, too remote and important to be directly concerned with mortal matters. Although the majority of Yorubas are now Christian or Muslim, belief in their traditional elaborate hierarchy of the 401 deities continues.

NATIONAL HISTORY: The Yoruba tradition has all the Yoruba peoples descended from a common ancestor, Oduduwa, the first man, whom the supreme god Olódùmaré let down from heaven on a chain to create the Earth. With some soil, a cockerel, and a palm nut, he established the town of Ile Ife, which Yorubas regard as their spiritual home. The soil was thrown into water, the cockerel scratched it to become the land, and the palm kernel grew into a tree with 16 limbs, representing the original 16 Yoruba kingdoms.

Claiming descent from the ancient Egyptians and the Meroe civilization of the upper Nile, the Yoruba are believed to have settled their present homeland over 1,000 years ago. Little is known of the region's early history, although the system of divine kings is thought to have developed in the ninth century A.D. In the eleventh century the Yoruba began to coalesce in independent city-states. Ife, the oldest existing Yoruba city, dates from about 1300. All Yoruba chiefs trace their ancestry to Ife and consider the *oba* of Ife as their ritual superior.

Centuries of political contention among the distinct city-states and kingdoms divided the Yorubas among numerous tribal groups. The Yoruba kingdoms were essentially unstable; the central government had insufficient power to control chiefs in outlying areas.

Portuguese navigators visited the coastal cities in the late fifteenth century. Commercial relations developed, the Yoruba trading slaves and agricultural produce for European trade goods. The Portuguese were soon followed by English, French, Dutch, and Danish traders and explorers. The Yoruba coastal states satisfied the growing European demand for slaves by raiding the interior states and tribes.

The expanding power of the Oyo kingdom, aided by European firearms, superseded Ife in the seventeenth century. Over the next hundred years Oyo united the numerous Yoruba kingdoms in a powerful empire that ruled most of present Yorubaland but included non-Yoruba speakers as well. Muslim Fulani tribes invaded the empire in the early nineteenth century, overrunning the northern states, which mostly converted to Islam.

At the end of the eighteenth century, civil war devastated the Oyo empire. Muslim incursions and the slave trade finally destroyed Yoruba unity. Following invasions by the Fons of Dahomey and the Muslim Fulanis from the north, the Yoruba empire split into numerous smaller states farther south, many founded by refugees fleeing the Muslim conquest of the northern states in the 1820s and 1830s. The Yorubas of one of the new city-states, Ibadan, finally defeated the Muslim Fulani invaders in 1840.

The British gradually gained a predominant position in the Yoruba states. In 1807 the British navy attempted to end the slave trade, but the lucrative business continued for another seventy years. In 1861 the British annexed Lagos and began to intervene in the Yoruba wars in the 1880s. Over the next decade British authority extended to all of Yorubaland, partly by force, but often by the treaties that offered British protection. In the late 1880s, a British mediator compelled the various warring factions to sign a peace treaty.

Yorubaland became a British colony in 1901; it was ruled indirectly, through the traditional chiefs, an arrangement that mirrored the structure of Yoruba governance. The Yoruba states were divided between Lagos colony and the protectorates of Southern and Northern Nigeria. As early as 1908 Yoruba nationalists demanded a united Yoruba state in British Nigeria. In an attempt to promote unity and end inter-Yoruba conflicts, the region's leaders turned to the mythical common ancestor, Oduduwa. A Yoruba ethnic consciousness gradually developed, the resulting unity blurring differences in religion, history, and culture.

The Yoruba states, mostly included in the Western Region and Lagos Colony, were included in the united colony of Nigeria in 1914. The other regions, Northern and Eastern, were dominated by the Hausas and Ibos respectively. Legislative councils, authorized in 1922, were regarded as the first step toward autonomy from British rule.

Yoruba nationalism grew dramatically during World War II. In 1945 a group of Yoruba students in London formed Egbe Omo Oduduwa (Society of the Children of Oduduwa) to work for a united Yoruba state within the British Empire. From 1948 the movement gained substantial support, fanned by the increasing tension between Nigeria's three largest ethnic groups—the Yorubas, the Ibos in the southeast, and the Muslim Hausas in the north. Yoruba leaders again petitioned for an autonomous Yoruba region in British Nigeria in 1956.

In 1953 anti-Ibo rioting broke out in the Northern Region in protest of Ibo domination of social, political, business, and military institutions. The riots, leaving hundreds dead and injured, were mostly ignored by the Yorubas, who took no part in the Ibo-Hausa violence. Calls by Ibo leaders for southern, Christian solidarity were ignored, due to the traditional rivalry between Yorubas and Ibos.

A coalition of Hausa-Fulani and Ibo political parties blocked the Yoruba Action Group party from gaining any significant share of central authority in elections in December 1959. Nigeria became independent as a federation of three regions on 1 October 1960. The three largest ethnic groups immediately engaged in an acrimonious scramble for power. The northern Hausas often benefited from the deep distrust between the Yorubas and the Ibos in the south. The Yoruba-dominated Western Region was divided, and a new region, Midwest, was created in 1964.

Yoruba riots in protest against exclusion from the federal government spread in 1965. Federal troops, mostly from the Northern Region, intervened to restore calm. A continuing general breakdown of law and order in 1965–66, the product of the regional rivalries, aroused Yoruba secessionist sentiment. A military coup, involving many Ibo military officers, was seen as an Ibo plot to consolidate power and to overthrow the Hausa-dominated federal government. In July 1966 the Yorubas moved toward secession but were blocked by northern troops, loyal to the Muslim-dominated government, deployed to occupy Lagos and other important Yoruba cities.

In 1967 the Ibos of the southeast declared the independence of the Republic of Biafra; the secession prompted nationalist demands for the Yorubas to follow. Deterred by the Muslim occupation troops and the potential loss of the benefits of Biafra's oil wealth, the Yoruba ultimately rejected secession and supported the federal cause in the civil war of 1967–70. Many Yorubas fought for the idea of "One Nigeria," but most of their leaders fought for the oil wells and the wealth they represented. Military leaders were ordered to capture the oil fields in the southeast and to preserve the economic life of Nigeria.

Yoruba nationalism resurfaced in 1970 over a perceived conspiracy by the Muslims and the defeated Ibo to exclude the Yoruba from important government positions. Continued domination of the Nigerian government by the Muslim-controlled military fueled Yoruba nationalism in the 1980s. The political resistance was aggravated by severe economic problems. The standard of living in Yorubaland fell by 15% between 1980 and 1986.

The Muslim-dominated military government successfully applied for Nigerian inclusion in the Organization of Islamic Conference in 1986. This sparked widespread rioting in Yorubaland. Religious tension increased in 1987 when Muslims in the north called for the imposition of Islamic law and courts in Nigeria.

Dissident middle-ranking army officers, mostly Yorubas, attempted to overthrow the military government in April 1990. The mutineers' motives were reportedly religious and regional. Heavy fighting erupted in several areas, but the arrest of over 800 mutineers ended the coup attempt. In July 1990 the 42 leaders of the coup were executed, raising great resentment among the Yorubas. A number of others were executed later in the year.

The Muslim-dominated military government, pressed by international opinion, allowed free presidential elections in June 1993. The election, the first in 34 years of independence, was won by a Muslim Yoruba, Chief Mashood Abiola. The election was annulled by the military government of Maj. Gen. Ibrihim Babangida, effectively robbing the Yorubas of the victory and perpetuating the Hausa-Fulani hold on Nigeria. The dramatic increase of Yoruba national sentiment, particularly after Chief Abiola was put on trial for treason, raised separatist tension to the level of the 1960s.

In the early 1990s, many Yoruba leaders expressed regret over the part they had played in supporting the Hausas in their defeat of the Ibos during the Biafran war of 1967–70. Their former Hausa allies were increasingly turning on the Yorubas, while the Ibos, still weakened from their defeat in 1970, refused to join the Yorubas in a southern alliance. The process of regionalism, mirroring that of the late 1950s and early 1960s, raised the possibility of the splintering of Nigeria.

The Odua Peoples Congress (OPC) was founded in 1995 to campaign for autonomy for the Yorubas. The OPC and other militant organizations often acted as vigilante groups, lynching armed robbers and other "undesirables," often from rival ethnic groups. The groups are hugely popular as the defenders of the Yorubas in a country fed up with crime and government inaction.

Increasingly violent ethnic and religious disputes shook Nigeria following the return to democracy in 1999 under President Olusegun Obasanjo, the first Yoruba president of Nigeria. Although Obasanjo comes from the southwest, he got little support from the Yorubas, who see him as a tool of the Muslim-dominated military that has governed Nigeria for most of years since independence. In early 1999, the Odua Liberation Movement proclaimed its opposition to a federal system and support for the secession of the Yoruba homeland from Nigeria.

Ethnic conflicts between the Yorubas and the Hausa broke out in the Yoruba city of Sagamu in 1999 and left over 70 dead. The violence spread to the Muslim north where confrontations in Kano between Yorubas and Hausas left many dead and wounded. Thousands of Yorubas returned to Yorubaland to escape the spreading violence. In mid-2000 renewed fighting in the northern Yoruba city of Illorin killed over 100 and injured hundreds. In October the fighting spread to other Yoruba cities, particularly the Hausa neighborhoods of Lagos. Activists of the militant OPC clashed with police and with militants of mainly Hausa Muslim groups in several areas. Thousands of Hausas originally from northern Nigeria sought protection in military barracks as soldiers were deployed around Lagos. President Obasanjo proscribed the OPC and ordered the arrest of the organization's leaders. In October 2001 violence between Yorubas and Ibos erupted in Lagos, leaving five dead and many injured.

The violence is the outward sign of growing Yoruba nationalism. The OPC and other groups want the Nigerian government to restore the powerful regional governments of the early independence period. Although a majority of the Yorubas fear further balkanization of Nigeria, more militant groups see independence as the only way to end decades of economic, political, and cultural suppression, and the chaos they have experienced as part of a united Nigerian state.

SELECTED BIBLIOGRAPHY:

Apter, Andrew H. *Black Critics and Kings: The Hermeneutics of Power in Yoruba.* 1992.

Hallen, Barry. *The Good, the Bad, and the Beautiful: Discourse about Values in Yoruba Culture.* 2001.

Obafemi, Olu, ed. *Character Is Beauty: Redefining Yoruba Culture and Identity 1981–1996.* 2000.

Peel, J.D.Y. *Religious Encounter and the Making of Yoruba.* 2001.

Zanzibaris

Zanzibaris and Pembans

POPULATION: Approximately (2002e) 975,000 Zanzibaris in Tanzania, concentrated in the islands lying in the Indian Ocean just east of the East Africa mainland. There are also large Zanzibari communities on the mainland, particularly around Dar-es-Salaam, the Tanzanian capital.

THE ZANZIBARI HOMELAND: The Zanzibari homeland comprises two large islands, Unguja (Zanzibar) and Pemba, and a number of small islands in the Indian Ocean 22 miles (35 km) east of the coast of mainland East Africa. The low limestone islands are believed to have once formed part of the African continent. Pemba, the more fertile of the islands, is the world's leading producer of cloves. Zanzibar forms a semi-autonomous state of the United Republic of Tanzania. *Zanzibar (State of Unguja and Pemba)*: 640 sq. mi.—1,658 sq. km, (2002e) 1,013,000—Zanzibaris 92% (Shirazis 64%, black Africans 12%, Arabs 10%, Asians 6%), other Tanzanians 8%. The Zanzibari capital and major cultural center is Zanzibar, (2002e) 253,000. The other important centers are Chake Chake, the capital of Pemba, (2002e) 22,000, and Wete (2002e) 33,000, the center of northern Pemba.

FLAG: The Zanzibari national flag, the official flag of the autonomous state, is a horizontal tricolor of blue, black, and green bearing a narrow white vertical stripe at the hoist. The flag of the former sultanate, still used by a number of nationalist organizations, is a red field bearing a centered green disc charged with a golden stem bearing two cloves.

PEOPLE AND CULTURE: The Zanzibari nation comprises several distinct groups. The largest component is the Shirazi, named for early Persian traders from the city of Shiraz, claiming mixed black African and Persian descent. The major Shirazi groups are the Hadimu and Tumbatu of Zanzibar, and the Pemba of Pemba Island. The African population is mostly descended from former slaves, augmented by recent arrivals from the mainland. The Arabs, descendents of early colonists, formerly made up a ruling elite. Pakistanis, Indians, and Goans are the largest groups of the Asian population. The majority of the islanders, whether Arab or Shirazi, support greater cultural and economic autonomy. The Arabs refer to their ancestors as the "old" or "true" Arabs. Most Zanzibaris are fishermen or farmers; the only sizable urban population is in the islands' capital. Family remains extremely important to the islanders, providing security during times of economic hardship and in old age. The traditional island system has been weakened by younger Zanzibaris leaving their villages to find jobs in cities and towns.

LANGUAGE AND RELIGION: The primary language of the islands is Swahili, a hybrid language of mixed Arabic and Bantu influences spoken by most Zanzibaris, of all backgrounds. The classical dialect of Swahili spoken in the islands is Kiunguja. Arabic is also important as the language of religion, past Arab domination, and the large Arabic-speaking minority. The Arab minority speak the Arabiya or Coast Arabic dialect of Arabic. The Asian minority mostly speak Gujarati, Kutchi, and Hindi. English, widely taught in island schools, is often spoken as a second language and serves as a lingua franca.

The majority of the Zanzibaris are Sunni Muslim, with small but important Christian and Hindu minorities among the Asians. The mosque is the center of Islamic worship and an gathering place, which women rarely attend. Some Zanzibaris retain belief in spirits, particularly during times of crisis or sickness. Magic is often practiced to aid harvests, fishing, and business.

NATIONAL HISTORY: The history of the islands has been to a large extent shaped by the monsoon, the prevailing trade winds of the Indian Ocean, and by the islands' proximity to the continent. The islands were known for centuries to Arab and Indian navigators plying Indian Ocean trade routes. Persian and Indian traders established bases in the islands as early as the first century A.D. Merchants from the Persian city of Shiraz, attracted by the sheltered harbor, established a colony at Zanzibar, probably in the seventh century; the colony became the center of a large migration from southern Persia between the tenth and twelfth centuries. Africans, often brought to the island as slaves, began to settle in the islands around A.D. 1000. The Africans, living in small village groups, were gradually absorbed by the Persians, producing a people of mixed ancestry, the Shirazis.

Arabs traders from present Oman reached the islands from the eleventh century. They gradually expanded their operations from Zanzibar to the coastal regions of East Africa, founding a string of Arab trading towns and cities. Arab merchant adventurers penetrated far into the African interior, returning with slaves, ivory, and gold for sale in the Arab coastal cities and the famed markets of Zanzibar.

Portuguese explorer Vasco da Gama rounded the Cape of Good Hope in 1499, at the head of the first European expedition to penetrate the Indian Ocean. Da Gama returned to Europe to tell of an opulent island state, easy prey for the better-armed Europeans. A Portuguese squadron conquered Zanzibar and parts of the African mainland in 1509. The Portuguese later consolidated the conquered mainland settlements into the colony of Mozambique.

Omani Arabs, from the eastern Arabian Peninsula, ousted the Portuguese from Zanzibar in 1652. The islands became part of the Omani empire in 1698. An attempt to conquer the islands by mainland groups in 1753 failed, as the islanders remained loyal to the Omanis. The Omanis ruled the islands as a vassal state of the powerful Sultanate of Muscat, although the Arabs generally ignored the island province until the nineteenth century. Sultan Sayyid Zaid, recognizing the value of the fertile islands, introduced clove production from the Molucca Islands of the Dutch East Indies.

In 1832 Sultan Zaid transferred the capital of his possessions from Muscat in Arabia to the flourishing and economically more important Zanzibar. Zanzibar's resources, particularly spices, attracted ships from as far away as the United States. A U.S. consulate was established in Zanzibar in 1837. The early interest of the British was motivated by both commerce and the determination to end the slave trade.

A rigidly stratified society evolved, dominated by the Arab aristocracy and an Asian merchant class, which made up less than 20% of the island population. Local African populations were forcibly removed from the most productive land to make room for plantations. Vast clove plantations, worked by African slaves, supported an Arab-dominated culture famed for its wealth and extravagance. The importation of black African slaves from the mainland turned Zanzibar into one of the world's largest slave markets.

British pressure finally forced Zanzibar and Muscat to separate into two realms in 1861, bringing Zanzibar increasingly under British influence. The Zanzibari sultanate retained the islands and an extensive mainland coastal territory. Unable to resist European encroachments, the sultan closed the slave markets in 1873, and between 1887 and 1890 he sold or ceded the mainland territories to Germany and the United Kingdom. Agreements between Germany and the British, in 1886 and 1890, respectively, delineated the British and German spheres of influence in the interior of East Africa. The coastal strip claimed by the Omani sultan allowed the British to proclaim Zanzibar a protectorate.

History's shortest war broke out in Zanzibar in 1896. A British admiral anchored his fleet off Zanzibar so his men could watch a cricket match. The fleet so angered the sultan that he declared war and sent his only warship against the British fleet. The British promptly sank the Zanzibari ship and shelled the sultan's palace. The sultan sued for peace, ending the so-called Cricket War—which had lasted exactly 37 minutes and 23 seconds.

Considered an essentially Arab country, the British authorities maintained the islands' existing social order, effectively excluding the mixed-race Shirazi and the Africans from participation in the sultan's political life. The British separated Zanzibar from Kenya in 1925, and a legislative assembly, convened in 1926, reaffirmed the Arab domination of the island protectorate.

Political parties organized under British authority in the 1950s split along ethnic lines. Unrest in rural areas often arose in reaction to government efforts to establish multiracial district councils. The most important of the parties, the Arab- and Asian-supported Zanzibar National Party, soon had a powerful rival in the Afro-Shirazi Party, of the disadvantaged majority. Local elections in 1961 led to a further split between the Arab, Shirazi, and African populations. The election was followed by a week of rioting in which 68 Arabs were killed and several hundred injured. Supported by the Arab and Asian minority, the sultan declared Zanzibar independent on 10 December 1963.

A communist-inspired coup, led by a migrant worker from Kenya, John Okello, overthrew the sultanate government. Okello was immediately toppled by Shirazi Sheik Abeid Karume, who declared Zanzibar a people's republic on 12 January 1964. In a few days of savagery, between 5,000 and 15,000 Arabs and Asians were murdered, their women raped, and their estates and businesses looted and burned. The sultan fled into exile, accompanied by thousands of terrified refugees. Within a few weeks, a fifth of the Arab population, 17% of the population in 1964, was dead or had fled from the islands. Many others were imprisoned, and many Arab and Indian women were forced to marry Shirazi or African men.

A radical island government nationalized the clove industry and confiscated the remaining Arab and Asian properties. Fearing that the islands would be used as a revolutionary springboard into central Africa, Western governments supported a political union between Zanzibar and mainland Tanganyika. In April 1964, without the consent of the Zanzibaris, a treaty was signed by Abeid Karume and Tanganyika's president, Julius Nyerere, uniting the two independent states. In October 1964 Zanzibar merged with the mainland to form a united socialist republic.

Excesses by the Zanzibar Revolutionary Council and opposition to the merger with the mainland incited the formation of a Zanzibari national movement, which gained support as socialist experimentation impoverished the islands. In July 1965 Tanzania was declared a one-party state, and all opposition political organizations were outlawed.

The Tanzanian government, to avert a nationalist crisis, granted Zanzibar autonomy in 1979. The economic hardships and the widening rift between Zanzibar and the bankrupt mainland in the 1980s pushed even the former revolutionaries to reconcile their differences with exile and nationalist groups. In January 1984, increasing anti-union sentiment in the islands forced the resignation of President Aboud Jumbe and a radical reshuffling of the island government.

In 1990 a coalition of Zanzibar's ethnic and cultural groups demanded a referendum on independence, claiming that the merger with the mainland, based on a now dead ideology, had transformed Zanzibar from a bustling economic power to a poor, neglected colonial appendage. The state, which had once accounted for half the world's clove production, had seen its exports fall from 18,000 tons in 1967 to less than 2,000 tons in 1991. International aid agencies began distributing rice to 165,000 people in the islands in 1990.

In January 1992 the Tanzanian government approved multiparty democracy but outlawed political parties that were based on tribal or regional interests. The restriction, denounced by the Zanzibaris, opened new rifts with the mainland. Constitutional reforms and wrangling since October 1993, and a campaign by the mainly Christian mainlanders for a separate Tanganyika government, brought the breakup of the Tanzanian union ever closer. The Zanzibari government joined the Organization of Islamic Countries but later withdrew following protests from the union government and parliament.

A controversial election in October 1995 was won by the mainland-supported Chama Cha Mapinduz (CCM) amid widespread irregularities and reports by international observers that the Civic United Front (CUF), the main Zanzibari political party, supported by both Arabs and Shirazis, should have been declared the winner because of clear evidence of fraud. Unrest after the 1995 elections increased support for autonomy and greater local control. Intimidation, particularly on Pemba, where the vote was overwhelmingly for the CUF, also increased with reports of torture and arrests. Anti-Islamic sentiment, growing more vocal on the mainland, added to the secessionist feeling in the islands.

The death of Julius Nyerere in October 1999, united Tanzania's longtime president, loosened the mainland's hold on the islands. Zanzibaris, who increasingly identified with their trading partners in the Persian Gulf states and resented control by the mainlanders, initiated a six-month consultation in early 1999 that stopped just short of an official referendum on separation from mainland Tanganyika. Nyerere's death, for many Zanzibaris, opened the way for rethinking the union with the poorer, historically different mainland.

In 1997, after a by-election was won by CUF candidates, 18 activists were arrested for sedition at a pro-autonomy rally. For over a year they were paraded before a court every week, only to be repeatedly told that the state was not yet ready to prosecute. The European Union (EU) cut off aid to Zanzibar over the issue of the political prisoners, although aid to mainland Tanganyika continued.

The restive Zanzibaris, weary of political scandals and economic decline, fear that they are being absorbed by the much more numerous mainlanders. Moderates generally support separate governments for Zanzibar and Tanganyika, under a federal government. Nyerere had long opposed a federal structure, insisting that it would undermine the union. In mid-1999, the CUF and the ruling CCM signed an agreement to end political conflict. Zanzibar was to gain greater autonomy in exchange for recognizing and cooperating with the CCM government of Tanzania.

Parliamentary elections in Tanzania in October 2000 were preceded by months of police intimidation, torture, arbitrary arrests, and detentions in Zanzibar. The vote on Zanzibar, including the choice of regional president and parliament, was a shambles, leading to charges of vote rigging and intimidation. Demonstrations against the elections in January 2001 were met with a massive police response and tear gas. The government finally gave in to international protests and allowed a new vote in 16 of the 50 Zanzibari constituencies, but the chances of a fair vote are slim. The CUF and other opposition groups in the islands demanded that the entire election be held again and threatened to boycott any half measures. Attempts to manipulate elections are seen as yet another reason by Zanzibari activists for supporting the secession of the islands from its unhappy union with the mainland.

Continued confrontations between security forces and Zanzibaris in 2001 turned increasingly violent. Several hundred Zanzibaris fled the violence, crossing to mainland Kenya where they requested political asylum.

The Zanzibaris organized a de facto government of national unity following the signing in October 2001 of a peace agreement between the ruling CCM and the CUF. A timetable of implementation specifies when the various aspects of the peace accord must come into effect. There are those commitments that must be undertaken immediately by the Zanzibar government and by both parties, and others that must be completed by early 2002.

SELECTED BIBLIOGRAPHY:

Anany, Samuel G. *A History of Zanzibar: A Study in Constitutional Development, 1934–1964.* 1970.

Bailey, Martin. *Union of Tanganyika and Zanzibar: A Study in Political Integration.* 1973.

Jumbe, Aboud. *The Partnership: Tanganyika-Zanzibar Union, 30 Turbulent Years.* 1995.

Middleton, John, and Jane Campbell. *Zanzibar: Its Society and Politics.* 1985.

Zapotecs

Sapotekos; Be'ena'a; Dii'zh; Didxazá

POPULATION: Approximately (2002e) 605,000 Zapotecs in Mexico, concentrated in the southern state of Oaxaca. Outside the region there are Zapotec communities in Mexico City, in northern Mexico, particularly Baja California, and in the United States. The neighboring Mixtecs number about 500,000.

THE ZAPOTEC HOMELAND: The Zapotec homeland lies in the Tlacolula, Zimatlan, and Etla Valleys of the eastern and southern districts of the Mexican state of Oaxaca. The valleys lie in inaccessible mountains that rise in the south before dropping to the lowlands of the Isthmus of Tehuantepec. The terrain is divided into the large and fertile valleys, and innumerable smaller vales and dales, at various altitudes. The Zapotec population live throughout the central valleys, the eastern and southern mountain ranges, along the Pacific coast, and in the Isthmus of Tehuantepec. The Zapotec homeland has no official status. The Zapotec capital and major cultural center is Juchitán, called Xochitan by the Zapotecs, (2002e) 67,000. The other major cultural center is Oaxaca, the state capital, called Nduu'ah in the Zapotec language, (2002e) 258,000.

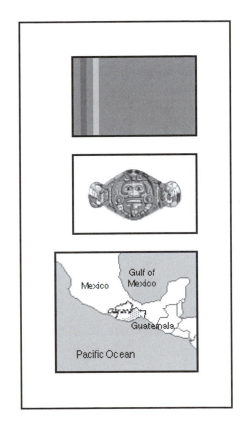

FLAG: The Zapotec national flag is a red field bearing two narrow vertical stripes of blue and yellow on the hoist. The flag of the Zapotec Cultural Center is a pale yellow field bearing a red mask and other traditional symbols.

PEOPLE AND CULTURE: The Zapotecs are an indigenous people of south-central Mexico. They call themselves some variant of the term "the People," or Be'ena'a. Zapotec society is oriented around villages or towns and remains agricultural. The Zapotec culture varies according to habitat—valley, mountain, or coastal—and according to economy. The culture combines traditional themes with later borrowings from the Spanish and Mexican cultures. The closely related Chatinos, numbering about 40,000, are often included as a Zapotec subgroup. The growth of cash crops, such as coffee, has resulted in abandonment of many traditional skills. The Zapotecs never mixed with the Spaniards and retain their original language and culture; for this reason they often suffer discrimination and oppression. Many Mexicans still scornfully refer to them as "Oaxacitas," or "little Oaxacans."

LANGUAGE AND RELIGION: The Zapotec language, a group of distinct dialects, belongs to the Zapotecan family of the Macro-Otomanguean language group. The language is spoken in many closely related, but mutually unintelligible, dialects, perhaps as many as 54. The dialects often vary from town to town. Ancient Zapotec writing, only partially deciphered, has helped archeologists and historians to chart the history of the Zapotec nation. The majority of the Zapotecs are bilingual, speaking their own dialects and Spanish. Many Zapotec women are monolingual, speaking only their respective dialect; illiteracy is three times as high among women as among men. General literacy, at 41%, is below the national average in Mexico.

The Zapotecs are nominally Roman Catholics, but belief in pagan spirits, rituals, and myths persist, often intermingle with Christian traditions. The *compardrazgo*, a system of ritual kinship established with godparents, remains very important. Portions of the Bible were translated into several of the Zapotec languages in the 1960s, mostly by evangelical sects that became active as missionaries in the region.

NATIONAL HISTORY: The ancestors of the Zapotecs, the Proto-Otomangues, probably settled in the region around 8,000 B.C. The Zapotecs began to emerge as a distinct nation between 800 and 400 B.C. in the Oaxaca Valley. By about 200 B.C., the major urban center at Monte Albán had a population of around 10,000; the ridge top where the town was located had been artificially flattened. The Zapotec civilization flourished between 400 B.C. and A.D. 600. The culture remained centered on the hilltop city of Monte Albán, possibly called the "Hill of One Jaguar." At its peak, between 100 and 600 A.D., Monte Albán had as many as 30,000 inhabitants and dominated an empire of former city-states that stretched over much of southern Mexico.

The sophisticated Zapotecs excelled in the arts, architecture, writing, and mathematics; they even devised an extremely accurate calendar. Their society was highly specialized and stratified, with a class of political leaders, a priesthood, and commoners. No intermarriage was allowed between the governing nobility and the common people. The commoners were mostly farmers and artisans, who paid tribute to the nobility, which in turn lived in magnificent ceremonial centers and managed the affairs of state, cultivated the knowledge of the sacred cycles of nature, communicated with their gods, and conducted warfare.

The Zapotecs rapidly declined after 700 for reasons that are not entirely clear. The city of Monte Albán was gradually abandoned, and regional states emerged. One theory is that the resources of wood and fertile, terraced slopes had been depleted. Between 1100 and 1350 Mixtecs arrived in the valleys and used old temples and tombs to bury their own dignitaries. Many Zapotecs moved east and south to escape conquest, but most remained autonomous until the Spanish conquest. The Zapotec and Mixtec cultures gradually fused, and at present the two populations are closely related in language and culture.

In 1486 the Aztecs penetrated the central valley of Oaxaca, bringing the Zapotecs into the Aztec empire. The Zapotecs and Mixtecs allied to fight the Aztecs, defeating the Aztec leader Ahuizotl in 1487. In 1496 Ahuizotl returned to avenge his earlier defeat by destroying the region's urban centers and dispersing the population. The Zapotec-Mixtec alliance again expelled the Aztecs from the valley and took control of the region of the Isthmus of Tehuantepec. In 1502 a truce brought peace.

The war resumed in 1519, when the Aztecs invaded, but fighting was interrupted by the news of the entrance of the Spaniards into the Aztec capital at Tenochtitlan. The Zapotecs sent emissaries to the Aztec capital to verify the reputed power of the invaders; the Zapotecs later surrendered to the Spanish forces without a fight. The Zapotec leaders were later baptized and took Spanish names. The Zapotec population at the time of the Spanish conquest is estimated to have been between 350,000 and 500,000.

The Zapotecs rebelled in 1531 but were quickly defeated by the European arms. The Zapotecs of the Villa Alta district again rebelled in 1544. Famine reduced the power of the Zapotecs following a severe drought and crop failure in 1563. Accused of idolatry, the last descendent of the Zapotec kings was executed in 1576. A European disease decimated the remaining Zapotec population in 1580. Another epidemic swept the Oaxaca Valley in 1660. The last serious Zapotec revolts, involving the Zapotecs of Villa Alta and Tehuantepec, were put down in 1691, 1700, and 1738. In 1739 yet another epidemic took a great toll among the indigenous Zapotecs. The Zapotecs by the early nineteenth century were mostly subsistence farmers living in small villages. Their former greatness had been mostly forgotten. Epidemics continued to decimate the population, particularly in 1805 and 1850–55.

The Zapotec homeland was never completely colonized by the Spaniards. The Zapotecs and the neighboring Mixtecs preserved much of their pre-Colombian languages and cultures, which set them apart from the Mexican mainstream, dominated by mixed-race Latinos. Demands for limited autonomy and an end to the domination by Latinos led to rebellions against state officials in Oaxaca, particularly the rebellion led by Che

Gomez in Juchitán in 1911. Another pro-autonomy rebellion was crushed by government troops in 1931.

In the 1960s thousands of Zapotecs left their ancestral villages, forced by poverty to seek jobs as migrant workers in northern Mexico or the United States. Mobilization of the poor, uneducated Zapotecs began in the 1980s among local syndicates and labor unions. The social movement gradually coalesced into a progressive power base, led by the Worker-Peasant-Student Coalition of the Isthmus of Tehuantepec (COCEI). Although Oaxaca was the most "Indian" state of modern Mexico, racism was widespread and markedly limited the health, quality of life, and potential of hundreds of thousands of Zapotecs, valued only for traditional menial work. By the late 1980s there were sizable Zapotec immigrant populations in Mexico City and in Los Angeles, California.

COCEI, functioning as a political party, won municipal elections in Juchitán in 1981. Two years later, disconcerted by demands for greater self-rule, the Mexican government impeached the city government and shut down its radio station, the first indigenous radio station to transmit independently in Mexico. The takeover of the city turned into a violent standoff between Zapotecs and the Mexican military; it lasted over five months. By December 1983, federal troops occupied the city and installed a local government of loyal members of the national political party. There were several serious street battles and demonstrations. The Zapotecs reorganized and again won municipal elections in 1992. COCEI extended its authority outside Juchitán and thereafter organized throughout the Zapotec homeland.

In 1990 it was estimated that between 60 and 70% of the immigrant farm workers in California's San Joaquin Valley were Zapotecs. Their remittances became the major economic asset of the Zapotec homeland. In September 1994, the Zapotecs and the neighboring Mixtecs joined forces to represent their peoples in California as well as in Oaxaca, calling their organization the Bi-National Indigenous Front of Oaxaca.

New skills and ideas spread to the homeland from the Zapotec diaspora, leading to a new militancy and cultural mobilization in the early 1990s. The small educated elite, many returned from northern Mexico or the United States, worked for Zapotec rights, organizing protests and strikes, and demanding cultural and economic reform in their homeland. In August 1995, state officials in Oaxaca agreed to allow indigenous communities to choose local leaders through traditional methods rather than party politics. In 1998 the state of Oaxaca changed its constitution to recognize the customs of its 16 indigenous groups, partly out of fear of a Chiapas-style uprising.

Zapotec activists of the Popular Revolutionary Army led a widespread insurgency, attacking police stations and military posts in late August 1996. Over 130 Zapotecs were arrested and accused of belonging to terrorist organizations. Government authorities detained 60 people in the Loxicha region, accusing them of supporting the rebellion. Reports of confessions extracted by torture led to increasing unrest in the southern Oaxaca. Relatives of the detainees suffered intimidation and harassment after the detentions, and many were forced to leave their homes. Others were arrested in March 2000 following a peaceful protest march in Oaxaca city to denounce human rights abuses in the Loxicha region. In July 2000, nine of the detainees were sentenced to 40 years imprisonment after what was perceived to be an unfair trial. In late 1999 a number of Zapotecs traveled to Seattle, Washington, to participate in protests held at the World Trade Organization annual meeting.

The Zapotecs remain among the most deprived in Mexico. Only about a third have access to health care; diabetes, alcoholism, and other diseases affect a large part of the population. Due to environmental factors, including mosquitoes along the coast, health standards in the Zapotec homeland are very low. Despite their organization and mobilization, educational and sanitation services are well below those of nonindigenous areas of Oaxaca state, and there are high rates of unemployment and poverty. In January 2001, the new Mexican government of Vicente Fox promised more autonomy and more cultural recognition to Mexico's indigenous peoples.

SELECTED BIBLIOGRAPHY:

Campbell, Howard, Leigh Binford, Miguel Bartolome, and Alicia Barabas, eds. *Zapotec Renaissance.* 1994.
———. *Zapotec Struggles.* 1993.
Flannery, Kent V., and Joyce Marcus, eds. *Zapotec Civilization: How Urban Society Evolved in Mexico's Oaxaca Valley.* 1996.
Whitecotton, Joseph. *The Zapotecs: Princes, Priests and Peasants.* 1977.

Zazas

Dimilis; Dersimis; Dersimlis; Zazakis; Kizilbashes; Kirmandz; Kirmanc; Zaza-Kilbashis; Kizilbach

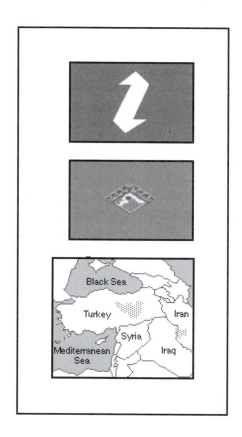

POPULATION: Approximately (2002e) 2,500,000 Zazas in Turkey and Iran, concentrated in the southeastern provinces of Elazig, Bingol, Diyarbakir, Tunceli, Sivas, Erzincan, Malatya, Mus, and Erizincan in Turkey, and the Bakhtaran and Kordestan provinces of northwestern Iran. Many Zazas live in *gecekondus*, shantytowns that have grown up around many Turkish cities. Outside Turkey there are about 400,000 in Germany and smaller communities in France, the United Kingdom, the United States, Canada, and Australia. The population figures can only be estimated, as the Zazas are not counted separately in Turkish census. Some nationalists estimate their number as high as four million.

THE ZAZA HOMELAND: The Zaza homeland, Zazaistan or Dersim, lies in southeastern Turkey and western Iran in the mountainous upper reaches of the Euphrates, Kizilirmaq, and Murat Rivers, forming a triangular area between the cities of Diyarbakir, Ezurum, and Sivas in eastern Anatolia. A smaller number live across the international border in eastern Iranian Kurdistan. Traditionally, Dersim, approximately the present province of Tunceli, is the cultural heartland of the Zazas. The Zaza homeland has no official status but is divided into a number of Turkish provinces. The Zaza capital and major cultural center is Tunceli, called Dersim by the Zazas, (2002e) 26,000. Other important cultural centers are Sivas, called Sewas, (2002e) 253,000, Erzurum, called Erzirom, (2002e) 328,000, and Erzincan, called Erzingan in Zaza, (2002) 113,000.

FLAG: The Zaza national flag is a red field bearing a traditional Zaza design resembling a large white Z centered. The flag of the Dersim Movement is a pale green field bearing a red diamond centered charged with a sun rising behind mountains.

PEOPLE AND CULTURE: The Zazas are an Indo-Iranian nation ethnically and historically related to the Kurds.* They are divided into 45 tribal groups, each directed by an important clan. The Zaza nation comprises three distinct groups—the Zazas, the Kizilbachs (numbering about 200,000), and the Goranis of Iran (with a population of about 150,000). The majority of the Zazas live in rural areas and are pastoralists or farmers. The origins of the Zazas are not fully clear. The most likely theory is that they are the descendents of the ancient Dailamites, who inhabited the mountainous southwestern region of the Caspian Sea coast known as Dailam. Zaza society remains tribal in organization, with a characteristic internal structure. The chiefs of the most important subtribes are both religious and secular clan leaders, and they exercise considerable influence. Unlike among their Muslim neighbors, divorce is strictly forbidden; also, the Zazas do not practice circumcision. The complex question of Zaza identity is still not settled; most now call themselves Zazas, while others use Alevi Kurds, Alevis, or Dimilis—meaning people from Dailam.

LANGUAGE AND RELIGION: The Zaza language, Zazaki, belongs to the Zaza-Gorani group of Northwestern Iranian languages. Long considered a dialect of Kurdish, which belongs to the Southwestern Iranian language group, Zazaki is now acknowledged as a separate language. The language is spoken in two major divisions—Dimli or Southern Zaza, and Kurmanjiki or Northern Zaza. Dimli is spoken in six major dialects—Sivereki, Kori, Hazzu, Moti (Motki), Shabak, and Dumbuli. Kurmanjiki (Kirmancki) is spoken in two major dialects, Tunceli and Varto. Many Zazas also speak Kurdish or Turkish as second and third languages. Hawrami or Gorani, spoken in adjacent areas of Iran, is closely related to Dimli. Turkish is often used for religious services and official purposes. In spite of decades of linguistic suppression, the Zazas have retained their language. In the late 1980s, the first Zaza journal was published, as an emphatically non-Kurdish publication.

The majority of the Zazas claim to be Muslims but Alevis; they see Ali, not Mohammed, as their religious head. Not recognized as Muslims by the Sunni majority in Turkey, they often face religious and cultural discrimination. A minority are Sunni Muslims, often the result of forced conversions in the past. "Alevi" is a blanket term for a large number of heterodox communities, whose actual beliefs and ritual practices differ greatly. Such Sunni Islamic practices as prayer (*namaz*), the Ramadan fast, the *zakat* tax, and the *hajj*, the pilgrimage to Mecca, are alien to the Zazas. Instead they have their own religious ceremonies, officiated by "holy men" belonging to a hereditary priestly caste. Many pre-Islamic elements of the Iranian and Turkish religions have been retained; pilgrimages to sacred springs and mountains are particularly important. The Alevis reject Islamic Shari'a law and profess obedience to a set of simple moral norms. Alevi women are free to participate in all religious ceremonies; they are not compelled to wear veils.

NATIONAL HISTORY: Zaza traditions tell of a migration of their ancestors from ancient Babylon to the regions around the southern shore of the Caspian Sea. The early origin of the Zazas is unknown, although a relation with the ancient Dailamites of the kingdom of Dailam, in present-day Gilan in northwestern Iran, has been established. They were mentioned by Ptolemy, as the "Delumïoï," in A.D. 2.

The Muslim invasion in the seventh century brought a reported 17 expeditions against the Dailamites by the invading Arabs. Although not conquered, the Dailamites gradually absorbed much of the Arabs' new religion. The power struggle that erupted in early Islam between two rival leaders, 'Ali Ibn Abi Talib and Abu Bakr, divided Muslims into two hostile camps. The first of the two contenders was initially defeated in his quest for the role of leader; his supporters were called Shi'a, or "partisans of 'Ali." A group of imams, supporters of Mohammed's cousin and son-in-law 'Ali, sought refuge in Dailam from persecution by the Sunnis. Over a long period of time the Dailamites combined elements of the Shi'a followers of 'Ali and their earlier religious practices.

The Shi'a Muslims rejected the Alevis, who split from Shi'ism by attributing divine powers to certain humans, heretical to both Shi'a and Sunni Muslims. From about 864, the imams who sheltered among the Dailamites helped to fortify Dailam against the Shi'a 'Abbasid dynasty of Persia and the Sunnis to the west. Sometime between 800 and 1000, Dailamites, fierce warriors in search of conquest, moved northwest into eastern Anatolia, where they settled in the broad river valleys.

In the early tenth century a local Dailamite ruler, Mardawij Ibn Ziyar, conquered most of western Iran. When he was killed in 937, his empire was inherited by a group of Dailamite mercenaries led by two brothers named Buwayhid. The Buwayhid (Buyid) dynasty controlled the Muslim caliphate in Baghdad for 109 years, relying heavily on Dailamite forces. A number of local dynasties, Dailamite and Kurdish, emerged around the empire's periphery.

The Turkish conquest further dispersed the Dailamites, and more tribal groups moved west into Anatolia. The Ottoman sultan launched a campaign of repression of the heretical Alevis in the late fifteenth century. In 1511, resentment of the Ottomans boiled over into a widespread uprising. A new sultan, Yunus Pasha, who ascended the throne in 1512 resolved to deal with the Alevi threat. He instigated an "inquisition" against the people the Turks called the "Kizilbach"—the Red Heads, for the red turbans they wore. Yunus Pasha led a campaign of widespread massacres and torture. Some reports tell of up to 41,000 dead, including those killed at the Battle of Chaldiran, where the Turks defeated the Alevis in 1514.

Kizilbach rebellions against Ottoman rule continued into the seventeenth century, although the Ottoman authorities mostly avoided the mountain fastness of Dersim. The tribes remained virtually independent, paying no taxes or tribute to the Ottomans, although some were forcibly Islamicized in the seventeenth century. Attempts to extend Ottoman authority to the region led to several serious revolts in the eighteenth and nineteenth centuries.

The Alevis of the Dersim region, calling themselves Zazas, were not subjugated, though the Ottoman government organized Dersim as a district in 1848. Determined to bring the Zazas under direct rule, the Turks sent a military expedition to Dersim in 1874–75. The Ottoman troops built a string of forts around the Zaza tribes but failed to subjugate them. It took a second expedition, in 1908, to bring the Zazas finally under direct Ottoman rule. Their villages were destroyed, their herds seized, and the majority were left in abject poverty.

During World War I, unrest spread across the Zaza homeland, caused by conscription, government requisitions in exchange for promises of future payment, and attacks by Sunni Muslims. In 1917 the Zazas rebelled against the tottering Ottoman government. They fought under red flags that they rolled up and wore on their heads as turbans. The rebellion was suppressed in 1919 by the newly organized Turkish national army at the end of World War I. Under the leadership of Ismail Aga, the Zazas again revolted in 1920–21. The revolt, seen as a threat to the integrity of the new Turkish republic, was suppressed with an estimated 20,000 deaths.

Western anthropologists and linguists working in the region in the early twentieth century tended to classify the Zazas as Dimli Kurds, Zaza Kurds, and Guruni Kurds, claiming that their language, Zazaki, represented several regional dialects and subdialects of Kurdish. Kurdish authorities, seeking greater autonomy for their nation, claimed the Zazas, to increase the size and importance of the Kurdish population within Turkey.

The secular Turkish republic of Kemal Ataturk adopted a constitution that guaranteed religious and linguistic freedom, which made the gradual emancipation of the Zazas possible, but the reality was continued discrimination and oppression. During the first great Kurdish rebellion in 1925, under Sunni leadership, the Zazas fought against the Kurdish rebels. Kocj Asireti led a renewed Zaza revolt in 1934 in the Dersim region; the revolt was renewed under Seyit Riza in 1937–38. The Zazas never joined the Sunni Kurds against the new Turkish state.

The Zazas began to leave their isolated mountain villages in the 1950s to settle in the towns and large cities. The Zazas' gradual integration into wider society after centuries of isolation brought them into close contact, and sometimes into direct competition, with the Sunni Muslim majority. This caused increased tension in the towns and in the ethnically and religiously mixed zones of Anatolia.

The political polarization that began in the 1970s exacerbated the situation. Increased discrimination also accompanied the spread of Muslim fundamentalism. Religious extremists fanned Sunni fear and hatred of the Alevi religious minority and provoked violent attacks and incidents. Anti-Zaza pogroms left many dead and wounded. Sunni attacks on Zazas because of their religion led to uprisings in Malatya in 1978, spreading to the city of Sivas in 1979 and Çorum in 1980. The Zaza revolt was brutally put down by the Turkish military government installed in 1980. Rebel leaders were arrested; many were executed or disappeared. Thousands of Zazas chose to emigrate, mostly to Western Europe, Germany, France, and the United Kingdom.

The Turkish police, which after the installation of a military government in 1980 were purged of left-wing elements, came to be dominated by conservative Sunnis and right-wing Turkish nationalists. The police participated in a number of murderous attacks on Alevis, causing a renewed alienation of the Zazas from the Turkish state.

The Zaza diaspora in Europe led a cultural and literary revival in the 1980s. The perception grew of the Zazas as a distinct ethnic group, a separate nation, that had to liberate itself from cultural domination by Kurds as well as the Turkish state. The birth of modern Zaza nationalism in the diaspora began as a marginal phenomenon, but gradually it began to influence the debate among the Zazas inside Turkey and Iran. A minority supported calls for a separate Zazaistan, distinct from Kurdistan, Turkey, or Iran, where the Zazas could develop their own culture and identity. The small separatist movement aimed to resurrect an independent state to be called Dersim.

The Turkish government, in a reversal of decades of assimilationist policy, repealed the ban on associations in 1989 and on languages other than Turkish in 1991. The end of the official bans stimulated a sudden resurgence of Zaza identity. The Zazas began to manifest themselves as yet another ethnic group, not a heterodox religious minority. Zaza cultural associations formed across the region and among the diaspora communities. Zaza intellectuals and community leaders set out to define Zaza identity, traditions, and history.

The Turkish government and the Kurdish national movement began to court the Zazas, and both did all they could to prevent the other from making inroads. Both, however, but especially the government, were handicapped by their dependence on Sunni majorities that had always been hostile to the Alevis.

The growth of Zaza ethnic consciousness prompted several scholars studying the Kurds in the 1990s to focus on the language and identity of the Zazas. The question of whether the Zazas are Kurds or an entirely different ethnic group opened new studies of their language, history, and religion. Several scholars concluded that the Kurdish language, Kurmanji, originated in southern Iran, while Zazaki originated in northern Iran. Between 1995 and 2000 Western scholars gradually became aware of the distinct identity of the Zazas of Anatolia. As research progressed, acceptance of the separate national identity of the Zazas became more widespread.

In July 1993, Sunni Muslim militants set fire to the Madimak Hotel in Sivas, during a festival in memory of an Alevi bard and spiritual leader. The fire killed 37 Zazas and began the process of Zaza mobilization. Until the arson attack—an event now called simply "Madimak"—the Zazas had attempted to assimilate and to be accepted; the arson attack marked a turning point in the growth of a separate Zaza identity.

Until the mid-1990s, Kurdish nationalism was the only movement in Turkey that openly defied the official doctrine that Turkey is a homogenous nation-state. The majority of the non-Turkish groups in the country, after centuries of oppression, were reluctant or afraid to define themselves as anything but ethnic Turks. Public support for the Zaza national movement as an alternative "ethnic" identity to the Kurds continued in the late 1990s.

The Kurdish identity thrust upon the Zazas by Kurdish nationalists in the 1970s and 1980s had been rejected, but Zaza national identity is still a new concept to many in the region. The revival of the Zaza ethnopolitical movement resulted from the conjunction of the radical political upsurge after the 1960s, the rise of peasant and working-class militancy, and a reborn sense of distinct identity. The three groups of the Zaza nation—the Zaza, Kizilbach, and Goranis—although historically distinct, share a culture, religion, and dialects that separate them from the surrounding Kurds, Turks, and Iranians.

SELECTED BIBLIOGRAPHY:

Andrews, Peter Alford, ed. *Ethnic Groups in the Republic of Turkey*. 1989.
Brunissen, Martin van. *Aga, Shaikh and State: The Social and Political Organization of Kurdistan*. 1992.
Kreyenbroek, Philip, and Christine Allison. *Kurdish Culture and Identity*. 1996.
Olsson, Tord, ed. *Alevi Identity: Cultural, Religious and Social Perspectives*. 1998.

Zomis

Zome; Zornis; Zo; Zou; Chins; Kuki-Chin

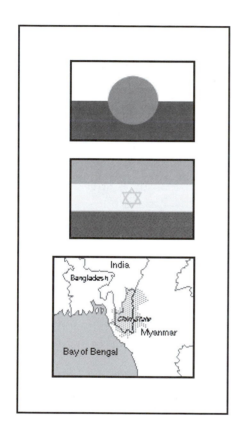

POPULATION: Approximately (2002e) 1,385,000 Zomis in South Asia, with 1,050,000 in Myanmar, and another 335,000 in adjacent areas of India and Bangladesh. An estimated 50,000 Zomi refugees from Myanmar are also in India—some in refugee camps, others living as nonregistered aliens. Some estimates of the Zomi population in the region puts the total population at over two million.

THE ZOMI HOMELAND: The Zomi homeland occupies part of the mountainous region separating Myanmar and India east of the Irrawaddy and Chindwin Rivers. The region is largely one of foothills and mountains that stretch northward from the Arakan Mountains to the Patkai Range. The Zomi hills, one of Myanmar's least developed regions, comprise a tangle of forested hill ranges that are traversed by deep, narrow gorges. The hills rise from the river lowlands to the highlands of the Chin, Pakokku, and Chindwin hills. Part of the homeland forms Chin State of the Federal Democratic Republic of Myanmar. *Chin State (Zoram)*: 13,907 sq. mi.—36,019 sq. km, (2002e) 562,000—Zomis 92%, Mizos* 3%, other Burmese 5%. The Zomi capital and major cultural center is Haka, (2002e) 15,000. The other important center is Falam, called Hpalam by the Zomis, (2002e) 22,000. The center of the lowland Zomis is Mawlaik, (2002e) 43,000.

FLAG: The Zomi national flag is a horizontal bicolor of white over pale blue bearing a large, centered red disc. The flag of the Zomi nationalist movement is a horizontal tricolor of red, white, and blue bearing a centered six-pointed gold star.

PEOPLE AND CULTURE: The Zomis, called Chins by the Burmans, are a group of tribal groups belonging to the southern Mongoloid racial group. The tribes are further divided into numerous paternal clans. Less than 60% of the Zomi inhabit the area designated Chin State; the remainder inhabit the mountains east of the state and in northern Arakan, and a sizable minority lives in the river lowlands, among a large ethnic Burman population. Traditionally Zomi villages are self-contained units, some ruled by councils of elders, other by headmen. There are also hereditary chiefs who formerly exercised considerable political control over large areas. Agriculture remains the basis of the Zomi economy. Land is cultivated in rotation; unused land is allowed to revert to forest. Status in life, and in the afterlife, is achieved by giving village feasts. The Zomis practice polygyny and trace their descent and heritage through the paternal line. Young people are expected to find mates outside the paternal clan. Outside influence in the region has remained limited to government officials and Christian missionaries, allowing the Zomis to retain their traditional identity and culture.

LANGUAGE AND RELIGION: The Zomis speak languages of the Kuki-Chin language family of the Tibeto–Burman language group. The Zomi languages are the only regional languages in Myanmar written in the Latin alphabet. The language, with 44 dialects, is closely to the languages spoken by the closely related Mizo and Kuki minorities in Myanmar and in neighboring areas of India. Each of the dialects or languages is further divided into regional subdialects. Many Zomis are bilingual in Burman. The Falam dialect is the basis of the Zomi literary language. The coastal dialects, influenced by other languages, differ considerably from the dialects of the mountainous Zomi heartland in the Arakan Mountains and the Chin Hills. The major dialects are Asho, spoken in the Arakan Yoma Mountains extending south into Magwe and Irrawaddy Divisions; Khumi, along the border with Bangladesh; and Tidim, spoken on both sides of the Myanmar-India border.

Traditional Zomi religion involves belief in numerous deities and spirits that have to be propitiated by offerings and sacrifices. The supreme god, Pathian, is revered as the most powerful of the pantheon. Christian missions in the region have made converts, but the Christians intermingle both Christian and traditional beliefs. Between 75 and 90% of the Zomis consider themselves Christian. Prowess in hunting has religious significance for the Zomis. The providers of game meat for feasts are believed to enjoy high status in the afterlife. In 1999 the government outlawed the practice of Zomi women tattooing their faces, part of their traditional religion.

NATIONAL HISTORY: The Zomis are thought to have originated in eastern Tibet in the eighth century. Pushed south by invasions of stronger peoples, the Zomi tribes moved south through the mountains and finally took refuge in the mountainous areas west of the Irrawaddy plains. Organized in autonomous tribes, the Zomi never evolved a state structure, the various tribes uniting only when faced with an outside threat.

Driven into the less accessible hills by larger tribal groups, the Zomis, called Chin by the Burmans and other lowland peoples, were often conquered but each time tenaciously defended their independence. They maintained a precarious degree of self-determination through most of their history.

Zomi history from the seventeenth century to the late nineteenth was a long sequence of tribal wars and clan feuds, complicated by sporadic involvement in the wars between the Burmans and the Assamese* and Meitheis.* At the same time the Zomi tribes came under pressure from the expanding Burman kingdom in the seventeenth century. The tribes often became involved in the wars between the Burmans and the states to the north of the Zomi homeland in present India. In the 1820s the tribes came under nominal Burman rule a tributary to the Burman kings, but aside from paying tribute and a nominal allegiance, the tribes remained effectively independent in their isolated hills.

On 1 January 1886, following the Third Anglo-Burmese War of 1885, the British laid formal claim to the region known as the Chin Hills. The first British expedition into the hills in 1889 effectively ended the Zomi raids on the peoples of the lowland plains. Ruled directly by a separate British administration, the Zomi territory remained a distinct political entity, not legally a part of British Burma.

Christian missionaries arrived in 1891, soon after the last tribes submitted to British authority. The Christians introduced European education and made important converts among the families of local chiefs. In the early twentieth century a Christian-educated minority began to take power in the region and to promote unity among the disparate tribes.

The fierce Zomi warriors, recruited by the British into their colonial forces, became the best soldiers in the colonial army. Young Zomis enthusiastically joined to fight their ancient enemies, the lowland Burmans. An elite Chin military unit, the Chin Rifles, maintained British authority in turbulent Burma, but they rebelled several times when the British attempted to assert colonial rights in the Zomi homeland.

The Christian leadership in the early 1920s began to reject traditional tribal authority and to stress Zomi unity. An emphasis on the shared culture and language, written in a Latin alphabet devised by missionaries, marked the beginning of the Zomi nationalist movement in the 1920s and 1930s. Several serious rebellions broke out against British authority, continuing the tradition of armed resistance to encroaching authority.

The Zomi territory, including the officially designated Chin Hills, remained isolated; the Zomis showed little interest in political relations with the lowland Burmans. They had more interest in the activities of their close relatives, the Mizos, in their conflict with the British authorities in India. The Zomis refused to recognize the colonial borders that divided their small nation, moving across the boundaries as they always had.

The outbreak of World War II divided the Zomis. Most remained allied to the British, while a minority joined the Burmans in supporting the Japanese, who promised autonomy and an end to colonial rule. The British were driven from the region, leaving the Zomis open to reprisals, particularly during the Japanese invasion of northeastern India, the Manipur campaign of 1942–43. The Zomis that had joined the anticolonial campaign were later abandoned by the Japanese to appease their Burman allies, who wanted a Burmese state that included all the British colonial territories in the region.

After World War II, the Zomis demanded separate independence as the British prepared India and Burma for independence. Arguing that their homeland had never formed part of British Burma, nationalists pressed for separation from the proposed Union of Burma but finally, under British pressure and Burman promises, settled for autonomy within the loose union. The Chin Special Division was created by the independence constitution adopted in 1947. The battle-hardened Chin soldiers formed the nucleus of the Burmese army, and they were largely responsible for saving Rangoon from the rebel Karens* in 1949.

Sentiment for independence emerged in the 1950s as the Burmese government became more authoritarian. Even though the government refused to fully implement the 1948 autonomy agreement, the Zomis were one of the few non-Burman ethnic groups not in rebellion against the state. Zomi soldiers continued to form the backbone of the Burmese military forces.

In 1961 the Burmese government passed a controversial law that made Buddhism the official state religion. The law deeply offended the Christian and animist Zomis, who had fought to preserve a secular state in Burma. Their demands for negotiations on the religious issue rebuffed, the Zomis rebelled. A national army, organized from Zomi units deserting the Burmese military, backed Zomi demands for political and religious freedom.

A Burmese military government, installed after a 1962 coup, dropped all pretense of federalism and attempted to impose military rule on the Chin Hills Special Division, the Zomi heartland. Fierce fighting erupted, but the Burmese soldiers failed to penetrate the Zomis' mountain strongholds. The Zomi leaders put aside their differences to demand the consolidation of the Zomi-populated areas of Chin Hills, Magwe, Sagaing, and Arakan in an independent Zomi state. In 1964 the remaining uncommitted Zomi tribes joined the growing separatist war. By the mid-1970s, for the first time in their history, the Zomi had united as a nation. In an effort to offset the growing nationalist movement, the Burmese government changed the status of the Zomi heartland to that of a state in 1974.

The military pressure on the Zomis eased in 1988, when many Burmese military units pulled back to Rangoon to combat massive popular demonstrations demanding democracy. Several Zomi organizations joined a 28-member coalition, the Democratic Alliance of Burma, in November

1988 to work for the replacement of the military junta with a federation of independent states.

The brutal crushing of the democracy movement in Rangoon, following the junta's refusal to accept the results of free elections, freed the military to resume its campaign against the ethnic insurgencies in the country. An offensive against the Zomis launched in 1989 led to the fiercest fighting of the separatist war in 1991–92. The Zomis, led by Michael Thangleimang, the secretary of the Chin National Front (CNF), fought the Burmese military to a standstill. In June 1991, several Zomi political parties participated in elections for the national parliament, but in 1992 they were among nine political groups abolished by the ruling junta, the State Law and Order Restoration Council.

In 1993, the government of the Indian state of Manipur requested help from the central government in fighting insurgent Kuki-Zomi forces. The insurgents, reportedly receiving military aid from the Myanmar government, included many Zomi nationalists driven out of Myanmar following several offensives by the Myanmar military.

Representatives of 15 ethnic groups met in Karen-held territory in January 1997 to sign an agreement for a proposed democratic, federal union in Myanmar. The new constitution drafted by the military junta was rejected as a "sham." The Zomi leadership, closely allied to the other insurgent groups in Myanmar and in neighboring Indian states, continued to advocate independence within a federation of sovereign states that would replace Myanmar's brutal military government. More militant nationalists contended that independence would be the first step to the consolidation of an expanded Zomi state, to include all the related peoples in Myanmar and India.

Zomi refugees in India, particularly in Mizoram, generally tolerated by the Indian government, mobilized to aid the insurgency in Myanmar in 1998–99. The mobilization was the result of increased detentions, interrogations, torture, and expulsions to Indian territory of persons associated with Zomi nationalist activities in Myanmar. Zomis fleeing the region reported widespread persecution of Christian groups. The government reportedly offered incentives and rewards to Buddhists who married Zomi women and weaned them away from the Christian churches, which are seen as the mainstay of the Zomi separatist movement.

The Myanmar military, beginning in September 1997, focused military recruitment in the region on military-type middle schools in which orphans and young children study. Zomi sources reported that most students completing the eighth standard were being forcibly conscripted. Families that attempted to hide their sons were severely punished.

The largest of the Zomi organizations, the CNF, rejected government preconditions for the opening of cease-fire talks in 1998. The preconditions included a surrender of arms and the exclusion of political issues from the negotiations. Government negotiators would be empowered to discuss only rural development. The Zomis countered by demanding that a national parliament, mandated by the 1990 elections, be convened. In August 1998, thousands of Zomis fled into India following renewed fighting. The military move new battalions into the area; in Chin State, in 2000, there were 10 battalions, as compared to just one before 1988.

The enhanced military presence has led to an increase in human rights abuses, forced labor, and intimidation and attacks on Zomi villagers. A number of development projects, including roads, irrigation canals, and dams, are being constructed almost exclusively by forced labor.

The Myanmar military government has used Buddhism, the state religion, to foster tension, suspicion, and resentment among the Zomi groups. The regime has reportedly instituted a system of "punishment and rewards" based on religious affiliation. Soldiers disrupt religious services and force Christians to build Buddhist monasteries and pagodas. Churches and graveyards have been desecrated by being used as army camps. In Sagaing Division, with its large Zomi population, the government has placed restrictions on attending Christian services and destroyed churches and religious symbols. Christian pastors are forced to obtain permission before they can perform their religious duties.

The CNF remains one of the few national organizations in Myanmar that has not reached a cease-fire agreement with the military junta. In June 1999, the CNF joined with groups from four other ethnic groups still fighting to form an alliance to coordinate their military and political campaigns against the Burmese military government.

Although some Zomi groups agreed to sign cease-fire agreements with the government, fighting between others and government troops resumed in 2001. The lack of unity among the Zomis is a serious problem. The fractured nationalist movement includes groups demanding independence for all Zomi-populated areas of Myanmar, others that claim only the highlands, while others would settle for real autonomy within a democratic Myanmar.

SELECTED BIBLIOGRAPHY:

Lintner, Bertil. *Land of Jade: A Journey through Insurgent Burma.* 1990.
Silverstein, Josef, ed. *Independent Burma at Forty Years.* 1989.
Smith, Martin. *Ethnic Groups in Burma: Development, Democracy and Human Rights.* 1994.
Tucker, Shelby. *Among Insurgents: Walking through Burma.* 2000.

Zulians

Marabinians

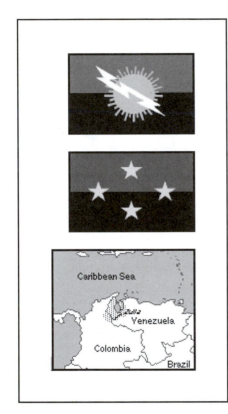

POPULATION: Approximately (2002e) 4,400,000, concentrated in the Zulia, Táchira, Mérida, and Trujillo states of Venezuela and the province of Norte de Santander in adjacent Colombia. Outside the region there are Zulian communities in other areas of Venezuela and Colombia, and in the United States, principally in the state of Florida.

THE ZULIAN HOMELAND: The Zulian homeland lies in northwestern South America in the region around Lake Maracaibo and the valley of the Zulia River just south of the Caribbean coast. The region rises to a spur of the Andes Mountains in the northwest, sloping down to the Zulian lowlands around Lake Maracaibo, the largest inland lake in South America. The region is one of the world's centers of oil production. The population is concentrated around the lake and in the marshy, fertile lowlands of the Zulia Basin to the southwest. Historical Zulia is divided; the heartland around Lake Maracaibo forms Zulia State of Venezuela. *State of Zulia*: 24,461 sq. mi.— 63,355 sq. km, (2002e) 3,187,000—Zulians 85%, Colombians (including Zulians) 10%, Guajiros 3%, other Venezuelans 2%. The Zulian capital and major cultural center is Maracaibo, (2002e) 1,372,000, metropolitan area 1,920,000. Other important cultural center are Cabimas, (2002e) 243,000, and San Cristóbal, (2002e) 286,000. The major center of the Colombian Zulians is Cucutá, (2002e) 656,000. The Cucutá-San Cristóbal metropolitan areas has a population of 1,133,000.

FLAG: The Zulian national flag, the official flag of Zulia state, is a horizontal bicolor of blue and black with a centered gold sun and a white bolt of lightning, called the "Catatumbo Ray," the Zulian guide to the future. The flag of Norte de Santander, the Zulian region in Colombia, is a horizontal bicolor of red over black bearing four gold five-pointed stars.

PEOPLE AND CULTURE: The Zulians are a Latin people, a mixture of early indigenous peoples, later Spanish colonists, African slaves, and other European migrants of the twentieth century. The conservative people of the Zulian lowlands share few values or perspectives with the citizens of the Venezuelan or Colombian capitals. The Zulians, isolated from both Caracas and Bogotá, have a long history of autonomy and self-support. Until the latter half of the twentieth century, their social structure was quite rigidly organized along class and racial lines. A small number of unmixed Caucasians continue to occupy the top rung of the social structure by virtue of their status as landlords and as self-styled inheritors of Spanish culture and customs. This heritage stresses the importance of the patriarchal extended family, disdain for manual labor, and a sharp distinction between the social roles of men and women. Traditionally, the lower class was rural, mostly poor peasants, usually of Indian or black descent. A growing middle class, made up of whites and some mestizos, urbanized and educated, have become the most aware of the Zulian identity.

LANGUAGE AND RELIGION: The language of the Zulians is Castilian Spanish, the Zulian dialects spoken around Lake Maracaibo predominating. The dialects, including borrowings from indigenous and African languages, and Dutch from the Antilles, differ considerably from the dialects spoken in the heartlands of Venezuela and Colombia. The Zulians also speak standard Spanish, the language of education, media, and government. The Zulian dialects is spoken throughout western Venezuela and in eastern Colombia. In the early colonial era, education by the Roman Catholic Church served a tiny, wealthy minority who sought schooling in the manner of Spanish aristocrats. The majority remained illiterate, speaking a Spanish patois that developed into the present Zulian dialect. Free education did not become available in Venezuela until 1870. The National University of Zulia, founded in 1891, was forcibly closed in 1904 and did not function again until 1946.

The Zulians are overwhelmingly Roman Catholic, although strict adherence to their religion has declined sharply since the mid-twentieth century. The church, formerly associated with the minority of wealthy landowners and the government in Caracas, remains strong, but competition from Protestant evangelical sects has grown rapidly since the 1980s. Although some 90% of Zulians were baptized in the Roman Catholic faith, most have little regular contact with the church. Adherence to traditional Roman Catholic beliefs is stronger in rural areas, especially in the highland areas.

NATIONAL HISTORY: The region around Lake Maracaibo was inhabited by indigenous peoples possibly as early as the second century B.C. The peoples of the region remained divided into small tribal groups, easy prey to stronger tribes moving into the region. The more advanced groups were ruled by chiefs, who supported a priesthood to serve local temples, whereas the more primitive lived as wandering hunters and gatherers.

The coast was sighted by Christopher Columbus in 1498 and was explored by other Spanish explorers the next year. Lake Maracaibo was first visited by Europeans on 24 August 1499. The initial Spanish colonization of the region began at Cumaná, far to the east, in 1520. The entire region, including the Lake Maracaibo territory, was granted to the Augsburg banking firm of Welser between 1528 and 1546. Maracaibo was founded as a trading post in 1571. Ethnic background served as an important criterion of status in colonial times; a small, Spanish elite controlled the land and economic resources of the region.

Slavery, disease, and violence decimated the indigenous peoples, who mostly disappeared from the coastal regions by the early seventeenth century. By the end of the first century of Spanish rule, some 20 tribes out of 40 or 50 in present-day Venezuela had become extinct. The early Spanish conquerors brought no European women with them, and many formed common-law relationships with indigenous women. Black African slaves were imported from other colonies to sustain the emerging agricultural economy. Racial mixing in the region was quite common.

Zulia was included in the Spanish viceroyalty of New Granada in 1718, which comprised the territory of present-day Venezuela, Colombia, Panama, and Ecuador. Venezuela was made a captaincy-general in 1731. Zulia remained part of the viceroyalty of Santa Fé de Bogotá until it was transferred to Venezuela in 1777. A Zulian leader, José Domingo de Rus, attempted to persuade the Spanish authorities to form a separate captaincy-general of Maracaibo, which would include parts of modern Venezuela and Colombia.

The independence of the United States to the north stimulated a strong campaign for an end of Spanish colonial rule in northern South America. The Republic of Venezuela was declared independent in 1811, but its independence was not assured until the Spanish were finally defeated at the Battle of Carabobo in 1821. Venezuelan nationalism did not subsume or overcome regional differences. Loyalty to the Zulian region remained far stronger than devotion to a country represented by the distant cities of Caracas and Bogotá. Regionalism was partly to blame for the protracted nature of the wars of independence in both Venezuela and Colombia.

The first attempt to form an independent Zulian republic began with a revolt against the Spanish authorities during the Venezuelan war of independence. On 28 January 1821, Zulian leaders in Maracaibo declared the region free and independent of the Spanish government and created a democratic, sovereign republic. The leader of the Zulians, Gen. Rafael Urdaneta, decided that the poor, backward region would prosper only as part of a larger political entity, the federation of New Granada, comprising present-day Venezuela and Colombia. Courted by both the governments of Colombia and Venezuela, Urdaneta opted for inclusion in the new Venezuelan state, which seceded from New Granada in 1830. Western Zulia, called Santander, was joined to the new Colombian state.

The Federal War, fought in Venezuela from 1858 to 1863, pitted centralizing forces against supporters of a loose state organization. At the end of the war, on 20 February 1863, Gov. Jorge Sutherland declared Zulia independent of highly centralized Venezuela. A provincial convention held on 2 March 1863 validated the secession. The provinces of Mérida, Táchira, and Trujillo voted to secede from Venezuela and to join the new Zulian state, with its capital in the city of Maracaibo. In 1868, President Jorge Sutherland of the sovereign State of Zulia signed an agreement for the integration of Zulia into the United States of Venezuela, as the Autonomy of Zulia. Zulia, including Mérida and Táchira, rejoined the Venezuelan union on 5 October 1868. The provisional state government resigned in November 1868, and Sutherland left the region. A popular assembly designated as the new president Gen. Venancio Pulgar, who broke relations with the Venezuelan government on 21 June 1869. Two days later, on 23 June 1869, the Zulian legislature reasserted the independence of the state under President Pulgar. Farther west, the inhabitants of the Santander region of Colombia, led by Gen. Vicente Herrera, also moved to incorporate the Santander districts into the Zulian state. Venezuelan troops invaded the region and quickly ended the secession.

The discovery of vast petroleum deposits in 1912–13 attracted international attention and foreign oil companies. Oil production, vital during World War I, expanded rapidly. Backed by the oil companies, the governor of Zulia, Vincencio Perez Soto, who took office in June 1916, prepared plans for the secession of Zulia from Venezuela. Archives later discovered in the Vatican included the proposed constitution and a prototype of the independence flag. The oil companies supported the secession bid, in an effort to manipulate or dominate the government and its oil reserves. The plan for secession was never implemented.

The idea of a separate Zulian nation in western Venezuela continued as an ideal throughout the turbulent 1920s and 1930s. The rapid development of the region's oil resources stimulated demands for greater control of the industry and a greater share of the revenue it generated. Successive Venezuelan governments squandered the oil wealth on prestige projects in Caracas and other areas outside Zulia, which remained one of the country's poorest and least developed territories. The threat of secession was often used to pressure the Venezuelan government to grant concessions and greater financial aid.

An American businessman, Guillermo Buckley, proposed in 1928 to separate Zulia from Venezuela as an independent state closely tied to the United States. The attraction of Zulia's oil was strong for the American government, but support for a separatist movement was lacking.

The case for independence, in both Zulia and in the adjacent areas of Colombia, emerged during times of economic or political unrest. Neglect by the governments in Caracas and Bogotá stimulated periodic demands for separation of the historical Zulia region and its natural resources. The centralism of the two governments in the 1940s and 1950s eliminated the historical autonomy of the provincial governments. Centralization of government functions in Bogotá and Caracas ended local autonomy while the imposition of tariffs and borders divided the natural trading and hinterland of Zulia that had functioned as a distinct region for nearly four centuries.

The Zulians began to urbanize in the 1950s, and by 1971 the Venezuelan census indicated that a larger percentage of the populations of Maracaibo and other cities had come from rural areas than from the cities where they lived. The government sought to encourage a reverse migration, but the results proved disappointing. The rural areas experiencing the most intense emigration were in the states of Táchira, Mérida, and Trujillo.

Decades of dictatorial rule in Venezuela finally gave way to democracy in 1958. The return of democratic freedoms, including the right to publish formerly banned ideas, opened the way for a modest reculturation of the Zulians. An increase in the arts, writing, and education spread the Zulian revival from Maracaibo to the area around Lake Maracaibo, and eventually to the more remote regions inhabited by Zulians in neighboring Venezuelan states and in the Zulian region of Norte de Santander province in Colombia.

The sense of separate identity, based on the region's history, began to reemerge in the 1970s. The process of self-discovery stimulated a new awareness of the region's distinct history and culture, and of its position between the two poles of Caracas and Bogotá. The opening of a historical research center and an institute of Zulian studies at the University of Zulia continued the process of the rediscovery of the Zulian national identity.

In the early 1990s, as the oil revenues dropped and poverty became widespread, unrest in the Zulia region became a serious threat to national security. Rioting in Maracaibo and other cities in 1994–95 resulted from the dramatic fall in the standard of living of the Zulians. The parallel growth of nationalism was stimulated by the economic and political crisis.

The creation of an autonomous region by left-wing rebels in southern Colombia in 1999, followed by renewed fighting, kidnappings, and bombings in Colombia, stimulated a renewed debate in Norte de Santander Province, in the western reaches of the Zulia River valley, over continued adhesion to the violence-ridden Colombian republic. The mayor of the region's principal city, Cúcuta, proposed the creation of a separate Republic of Zulia, which to him made more sense than concessions to leftist guerrilla groups that continued to terrorize the country. Zulian nationalists on both sides of the border supported the proposal, which would re-create a historical geopolitical region that had been artificially divided by colonial borders.

Nationalists in Zulia claim that Maracaibo is economically and culturally closer to Miami or New York than to Caracas. The long isolation of the region from the Venezuelan capital is a matter of historical record. Before the 1950s, Zulians wishing to visit Caracas had to travel with their passports, first by ship to Dutch Curaçao off the Venezuelan coast, then another ship to Puerto Cabello, and from there by train to Caracas.

Venezuela's president, Hugo Chávez, assuming increasingly dictatorial powers in the 1999–2000, needing more extensive control of Zulia's oil wealth in order to consolidate his power and rebuild the country's shattered economy, proposed to include Zulia state in a new, expanded Falcón state. As yet another humiliation for the Zulians, who generally opposed Chávez, the capital of the new state would not be Maracaibo but the small city of Capatárida. Chávez pushed for a new constitution, adopted in 1999, that give him near-dictatorial powers and eliminated the limited autonomy formerly enjoyed by the states.

Many Zulians support the idea of autonomy within Venezuela, with an autonomy statute modeled on that of the Catalans* of northeastern Spain. One point on which all Zulians agree is that they are not represented by a star on the Venezuelan flag, which has just seven stars, representing the states of the Venezuelan federation in 1811.

Francisco Arias Cardenas, the powerful governor of Zulia and a former supporter of Hugo Chávez and his campaign to root out corruption and self-serving politicians, in February 2000 issued a warning to Chávez of the serious consequences of reproducing the same vices they swore to end. The increasing corruption of the Chávez government has alienated many Zulians, who see the old pattern of their oil wealth being siphoned off for expensive and prestigious development projects outside the region, or to line the pockets of corrupt officials in Caracas. Many middle and upper class Zulians have left for the economic and social security of Miami.

President Chávez adopted a number of new laws affecting the economy and the Zulian oil production by proclamation in late November 2001. The Zulians, already opposed to the Chávez government, joined large demonstrations against the new laws. A general strike in early December brought the region to a stop.

The Zulians look to the prosperity of the Dutch island where most of their oil is refined which compares with the relative poverty of the oil-producing region around Lake Maracaibo. The small, but increasingly vocal, nationalist movement wants greater control of their natural resources, which would give the Zulians a standard of living among the highest in Latin America.

SELECTED BIBLIOGRAPHY:

Gott, Richard. *In the Shadow of the Liberator: The Impact of Hugo Chavez on Venezuela and Latin America*. 2000.

Karl, Terry Lynn. *The Paradox of Plenty: Oil Booms and Petro-States*. 1997.

Olivares, Haector Silva. *Zulian Autonomy in the Nineteenth Century*. 1977.

Yamarte, Gustavo Ocando. *The History of Zulia*. 1990.

Zulus

amaZulus; iziZulus; isiZulus

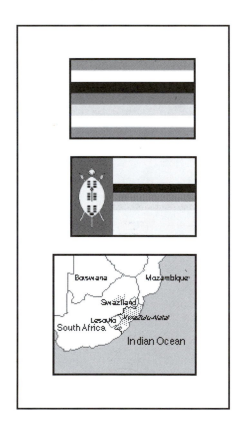

POPULATION: Approximately (2002e) 9,220,000 Zulus in South Africa, concentrated in the KwaZulu-Natal province in eastern South Africa. Outside the province there are sizable Zulu communities in Johannesburg and the industrial cities of the Gauteng, and in other parts of South Africa. Outside South Africa Zulus live in the Swaziland, Lesotho, Zimbabwe, and in Europe, particularly the United Kingdom.

THE ZULU HOMELAND: The Zulu homeland lies in eastern South Africa, a region of upland plains between the Indian Ocean and the Drakensburg Mountains, which divide the province from the rest of South Africa. The Zulus are spread across the province, although their heartland is in the northern KwaZulu region. The homeland forms the South African province of KwaZulu-Natal. *Province of KwaZulu-Natal (kwaZulu-eNatali)*: 35,591 sq. mi.—92,180 sq. km, (2002e) 9,326,000—Zulus 72%, Indians 9%, English South Africans, and Afrikaners* 8%, Coloreds 2%, Swazis 1%, other South Africans 8%. The Zulu capital and major cultural center is Durban, called Thekwini or eThekwini by the Zulus, (2002e) 2,369,000. The other important cultural centers are Pietermaritzburg, called eMgungundlovu by the Zulus, (2002e) 428,000, and Newcastle, called Madadeni, (2002e) 242,000. The traditional Zulu capital is Ulundi, (2002e) 22,000. There are also tens of thousands of Zulus in the metropolitan area of Johannesburg, called eGoli by the Zulus.

FLAG: The Zulu national flag, the flag of the largest political organization, the Inkatha Freedom Party, has equal horizontal stripes of red, white, black, green, yellow, white, and red. The flag of KwaZulu, the official flag of the Zulu homeland until April 1994, is a white field with three narrow, horizontal stripes of yellow, green, and black centered and bears a broad, vertical red stripe at the hoist charged with a Zulu shield.

PEOPLE AND CULTURE: The Zulus, South Africa's largest national group, are an Nguni nation encompassing over 100 separate tribes united by culture, history, language, and loyalty to the paramount chief, the Zulu king. They are a branch of the southern Bantu and have close ethnic, linguistic, and cultural ties to the Swazis and Xhosas, but they are separated by their distinct history. The Zulus are the single largest black national group in South Africa, although they remain divided politically and also over what it means to be Zulu. Since the 1970s a culture of violence based on the rural-urban division, and on tension between the traditional and modern, the young and old, has become deeply embedded. Fascination with the heroic Zulu past continues to be the focus of the Zulu cultural revival that began in the 1980s. Traditionally the Zulus lived in isolated patrilineal households rather than in villages. Cattle were central to the Zulu economy, which ranged from complete dependence on herds to mixed pastoralism and crop cultivation. Since the 1960s the Zulus have urbanized; over half lived in urban areas in 2000.

LANGUAGE AND RELIGION: The Zulu language, isiZulu, belongs to the Southeastern or Nguni subgroup of the Bantu group of the Benue-Congo branch of Niger-Congo languages. The Zulus speak dialects of their Nguni language along with English, the major European language spoken in the province. The language has many regional variants and dialects, many of which are mutually intelligible. Four of the dialects are recognized as the major dialects, Zulu of Zululand, Zulu of Natal, Lala, and Qwabe. The first Zulu-language newspaper was founded in Durban in 1903. There is a Zulu-based pidgin, known as Fanagalo, with a mixture of English, Afrikaans, Zulu, and other African languages, spoken as a lingua franca among industrial workers in several areas of South Africa. The Zulu language is written in the Latin alphabet.

The majority of the Zulu are Christians, both Roman Catholic and a variety of Protestant denominations. The traditional Zulu religion was based on ancestor worship and belief in a creator god (Nkulunkulu), witchcraft, and sorcerers. The Zulu king was responsible for all national magic and rain making. The Zulus believed it possible to appeal to the spirit world only by invoking the ancestors, the AmaDlozi, through divination. Many still believe that all bad things, including death, are the result of evil sorcery or offended spirits. Modern Zulu Christianity has been marked by the growth of independent or separatist churches under prophets, some of great influence and wealth.

NATIONAL HISTORY: European interest in the region began when Vasco da Gama sighted the coast on Christmas day 1497, naming the land Terra Natalis. Explorers of various European states sailed along the coast, but the fierce resistance of the local tribes to outsiders precluded the establishment of trading or supply posts.

Migrating tribal groups, believed to originate in great lakes region of central Africa, entered the territory from the north in successive waves of small family and clan groups to populate the plains east of the Drakensburg Mountains. Spreading across the region, the tribes established numerous small chiefdoms based on clan and family ties. Nguni political organization generally consisted of small groups, sometimes only a few hundred people, loyal to a local chief. Ancestors of the modern Zulus occupied most of the eastern coast by 1500.

One of the tribes, the Ama–Zulu, began to gain local power in 1799. The tribes, later called Zulus, expanded by incorporating or scattering neighboring tribes. Chief Dingiswayo in 1807 initiated the unique Zulu military system of disciplined regiments called *impis*. In 1818 civil war erupted between rival Zulu factions. Chaka (Shaka), a protégé of Dingiswayo, eventually emerged as the victor. Chaka refined the Zulu military system, making the *impis* the nucleus of a formidable army. The Zulus attacked one tribe after another, either destroying or absorbing the conquered tribes into the expanding Zulu empire. Many tribes fled, pushing others before them, creating what was known as the Time of Troubles.

Chaka fostered a new national identity by stressing the Zuluness of the empire. All subjects of the empire became Zulu and owed the king their personal allegiance. Zulu cultural traditions became the national traditions of the state. He developed a Zulu consciousness that transcended the original identities and lineages of the various peoples who became his subjects. Chaka, considered one of history's greatest military leaders, ruled a vast empire by 1826, but two years later he was murdered by his brother Dingaan. The Zulu empire weakened after Chaka's death and began to fragment, especially following defeats at the hands of the Afrikaners in 1838 and the British in 1879.

The British government claimed the coastal region south of Zululand, and the first English settlers to arrive shortened da Gama's name for the region to Natal in 1824. Afrikaners moving north to escape British rule in the Cape of Good Hope pushed into the interior in 1836, meeting fierce Zulu resistance. In 1838 the Zulus suffered a decisive defeat at the Battle of Blood River. The victorious Afrikaners created a new republic, Natalia, in the districts conquered from the Zulus. Conflicts between the Afrikaners and the British in the region ended with the British annexation of Natalia in 1843 and the creation of a united Natal in the districts south of Zulu territory as a separate British colony in 1856.

A Zulu prince, Cetewayo, succeeded his father to the Zulu throne in 1872 and immediately initiated a program to rebuild Zulu military power. A border incident in 1878 provoked war with the British. On 12 January 1879 a large British column crossed into Zululand and on 27 January suffered the most devastating defeat of a colonial force in British military history, the Battle of Isandhlwana. British reinforcements, rushed to Zululand, defeated the Zulus at Ulundi on 4 July. The defeat effectively ended Zulu military power and opened the way for the British military occupation of the Zulu homeland.

The British occupation of Zululand sparked a rebellion against British rule in 1882. The rebellion fizzled, and civil war over the succession to the throne threatened as Cetewayo neared death. Cetewayo's demise in February 1882 left the British in effective control of Zululand; the authorities proclaimed a protectorate in the region north of the Tugela River in 1887. Following renewed rebellion in the protectorate in 1897, the British annexed Zululand to Natal and exiled the king to the island of St. Helena in the Atlantic. The Zulus rebelled one last time in 1906, under the leadership of Chief Bambatha.

The Zulu homeland was included in the unified Union of South Africa in 1910. The Zulus' traditional economy was completely disrupted. Hunger and desperation forced thousands of Zulus to seek work in the mines and factories of white South Africa, particularly in the Witwatersrand, in the 1920s and 1930s. The united South African state proved as restrictive for Africans as the previous individual smaller states had been. All nonwhites were required to carry pass-books, internal passports. The first version of Inkatha was launched as a cultural organization in 1920. In 1931 a pass-burning campaign by Zulus in Durban led to serious violence.

The Zulu population remained fragmented during most of the twentieth century, although loyalty to the royal family continued to be strong in most areas. Leaders of Zulu cultural organizations and Zulu politicians preserved a sense of national identity through the symbolic recognition of the Zulus' heroic history and through local-level politics. Zulu identity and memories of the powerful independent kingdom became a unifying focus of cultural resistance.

The ascension to power in 1948 of the National Party (NP) meant the entrenchment of the apartheid system. Apartheid, separation of the races, restricted the movement, livelihood, and educational opportunities of the black population. Under apartheid all black ethnic groups were treated equally, but even during the black resistance to the system, competition for power and ideological disagreements continued to accentuate ethnic identities.

Successive NP governments pursued the "Homeland policy"—"self-governing homelands" for the country's various tribes. Several of the homelands were granted independence, although they were never acknowledged internationally. A Zulu homeland, KwaZulu, its territory fragmented among parcels of land separated by 13,000 white farms, was created in 1970 and was granted self-government in 1977. Chief Mangosuthu Buthelezi refused repeated government offers of homeland independence, preferring the self-governing status that allowed the four million residents of KwaZulu to remain citizens of South Africa.

Goodwill Zwelithini was installed as the eighth Zulu monarch in 1971. Zulu resistance to apartheid coalesced around the Zulu royal family and Chief Buthelezi, the nephew of Goodwill Zwelithini. Buthelezi became the KwaZulu head of government and the leader of the Zulu Inkatha national movement, later renamed the Inkatha Freedom Party (IFP), allied to the African National Congress (ANC). Zulu relations with the ANC deteriorated after 1980 over ideological differences and growing ethnic violence between Zulus and the Xhosas, the dominant tribe in the ANC.

In 1982 Chief Buthelezi set up the Buthelezi Commission in an effort to regulate Natal's ethnic relations. After eight months of talks between the three largest ethnic groups in the province, Zulu, white, and Indian leaders reached a consensus on integrating KwaZulu and Natal in a self–governing multi-ethnic state. In spite of broad support for the proposal in Natal and KwaZulu, and internationally, the South African government rejected the idea of multi-ethnic power sharing in November 1986.

Buthelezi and the IFP were accused of being allies of the apartheid regime, because high echelons within the IFP cooperated with the South African police and defense forces, for which the IFP received both financial and logistical assistance. Human rights abuses by both sides accompanied violence between the IFP and ANC followers in the province between 1990 and 1994. Many Zulu groups that had been conquered or resisted the Zulu expansion in the nineteenth century rejected the IFP and supported the rival ANC.

Zulu nationalism grew rapidly as South Africa moved toward black-majority rule. In January 1992 Chief Buthelezi raised the question of the secession of KwaZulu-Natal amid the expanding war that pitted his IFP supporters against the followers of the ANC. Both political parties sought to consolidate their influence in the province. Conflict occurred between youth and elders, the Zulu royal house and rival chiefs, and between the more sophisticated, urbanized organizations associated with the ANC and the rural-based Inkatha movement.

The end of South Africa's apartheid system and the emergence of a new multi–ethnic government mostly ended the severe ideological and ethnic violence that had left thousands of Zulus and Xhosas dead, but not Zulu demands for self-determination. In January 1994 Zulu leaders demanded guarantees for the KwaZulu-Natal and the monarchy before agreeing to participate in the first democratic South African elections. In February thousands demonstrated in Durban in support of immediate Zulu independence. In March 1994, King Goodwill Zwelithini declared KwaZulu-Natal a sovereign state, and in April the homeland of KwaZulu was officially dissolved and merged into the new province of KwaZulu-Natal.

The combined province had a large Zulu majority, which remains divided politically and ideologically to the present.

Buthelezi's drive to reestablish the precolonial Zulu kingdom became part of his fight for greater provincial autonomy. His aim of an autonomous Zulu kingdom within South Africa was backed by most of the 300 Zulu chiefs. The chiefs feared that their traditional authority would be challenged by elected district leaders. The promise of international mediation on a range of issues, accepted to get Inkatha to take part in local elections, included Zulu self-determination and provincial autonomy.

Allegations that local police were fomenting violence resurfaced in 1998, together with an upsurge in the ethnic and political conflict. In August 1998 troops were ordered into the province to try to quell the recurring violence. The police and security forces were accused by human rights organizations of mistreating suspects and prisoners in 1999. Amid the continuing violence in the province, local warlords managed to carve out small territories for themselves, over which the leadership of both the IFP and ANC seemed to have little or no control. Widespread violence returned to the province in the run-up to the 1999 national elections, though the IFP and ANC factions signed an electoral code of conduct in May 1999. By early 2000 tens of thousands of people had been killed in the political violence.

The objective of establishing a kingdom of KwaZulu as a federal unit within the South African republic seems to have been abandoned for the sake of establishing Zulu authority in KwaZulu-Natal, potentially one of the powerhouses of the new South Africa. Zulu leaders have called for international mediation to define a political role for the Zulu monarchy. The monarchy is closely allied to the traditional authority structures in the province.

The IFP won the elections in the province in June 1999 with 42% of the vote, against 39% for the ANC. The ANC wants to extend its power throughout South Africa, including KwaZulu-Natal, while the IFP wants to retain its power base in the province, which remains the focus of the ongoing violence. Municipal elections in November 2000 again brought the question of Zulu autonomy into local politics.

The question of Zulu separatism waned as the Zulus consolidated their power in KwaZulu-Natal. Their move into local government extended Zulu influence into areas outside the Zulu heartland in the north. In 2001, Zulu leaders reiterated their belief that the proud Zulus should form a sovereign state, but in the future when the Zulus were once again united.

SELECTED BIBLIOGRAPHY:

Lyndon, Glen. *The Zulus and Matabele: Warrior Nations*. 1998.
Military, Osprey, and Ian Knight. *The Zulus*. 1999.
Morris, Donald R. *The Washing of the Spears: The Rise and Fall of Zulu Nationalism*. 1986.
Nicholson, Robert. *The Zulus*. 1994.

Appendix A: Independence Declarations by Nation in Alphabetical Order

Abkhaz	8 March 1918	Republic of Abkhazia
Abkhaz	4 March 1920	Abkhaz Republic
Abkhaz	26 November 1994	Republic of Abkhazia
Acehnese	11 February 1950	State of Aceh
Acehnese	4 January 1977	Islamic Republic of Aceh
Acreaños	14 July 1899	Independent State of Acre
Ajars	18 April 1918	Southwestern Caucasian Republic
Ajars	12 February 1921	Ajarian Muslim Republic
Alawites	28 June 1939	Alawite Republic of Latakia
Altai	26 January 1918	Confederal Republic of Altai
Ambonese	25 April 1950	Republic of the South Moluccas
Anguillans	10 February 1969	Republic of Anguilla
Anjouanis	14 July 1997	State of Anjouan
Anyi	5 February 1960	Kingdom of Sanwi
Arabistanis	18 August 1923	Shaikdom of Arabistan
Asiris	3 August 1917	Emirate of Asir
Asturians	18 October 1934	Republic of Asturias
Avars	11 May 1918	Republic of North Caucasia
Basques	14 June 1931	Euzkadi Republic
Balkars	11 August 1942	State of Karachai-Balkaria
Baluch	15 August 1947	Khanate of Kalat
Baluch	20 June 1958	Khanate of Kalat
Bashkorts	29 November 1917	Bashkurd Republic

Basters	21 March 1991	Republic of Rehoboth
Bavarians	22 November 1918	Democratic and Socialist Republic of Bavaria
Bougainvillians	1 September 1975	Republic of the North Solomons
Bougainvillians	17 May 1990	Republic of Mekamui
Buryats	11 February 1919	Buryat Republic
Cabindans	1 August 1975	Republic of Cabinda
Californians	14 June 1846	Republic of California
Cambas	8 July 1921	Republic of Santa Cruz
Cambas	22 May 1935	Republic of Santa Cruz
Carpatho-Rusyns	1 November 1918	Republic of Carpatho-Ukraine
Carpatho-Rusyns	2 March 1939	Republic of Carpatho-Ukraine
Catalans	14 April 1931	Catalan Republic
Catalans	4 October 1934	Republic of Catalonia
Chams	19 February 1964	State of Champa
Chechens	2 December 1917	Emirate of Chechnya
Chechens	11 May 1918	Republic of North Caucasia
Chechens	27 October 1991	Republic of Chechnya
Chukots	28 October 1921	Free State of Chukotka
Crimean Tatars	16 May 1918	Crimean Democratic Republic
Dagestanis	20 October 1917	Terek-Dagestan Republic
Dagestanis	11 May 1918	Republic of North Caucasia
Dniestrians	2 September 1991	Dniestr Moldavian Republic
Don Cossacks	10 January 1918	Republic of the Don
East Timorese	28 November 1975	Democratic Republic of East Timor
Eastern Mongols	15 February 1928	Solon Republic
Eastern Mongols	15 January 1946	People's Republic of Eastern Mongolia
Edos	18 August 1967	Republic of Benin
Epirotes	17 February 1914	Republic of North Epirus
Faeroese	18 September 1946	Republic of the Faeroe Islands
Far Easterners	23 May 1918	Far Eastern Republic
Flemish	11 November 1917	Republic of Flanders
Flemish	29 November 1997	Republic of Flanders
Gagauz	18 January 1906	Gagauz Republic
Gagauz	11 August 1990	Gagauz Republic
Gandas	31 December 1960	Kingdom of Buganda
Gauchos	8 September 1892	Republic of Rio Grande do Sul
Gilakis	20 May 1920	Persian Soviet Socialist Republic of Gilan

Giulians	10 February 1947	Free Territory of Trieste
Hadhramis	30 November 1967	Democratic People's Republic of Yemen
Hadhramis	21 May 1994	Republic of South Yemen
Hawaiians	16 January 1994	Sovereign Nation State of Hawai'i
Hejazis	27 June 1916	Hashemite Kingdom of Hejaz
Huis	9 August 1953	Chinese Islamic Republic
Ibos	30 May 1967	Republic of Biafra
Ingrians	23 January 1920	Republic of North Ingermanland
Isaaks	26 June 1960	Republic of Somaliland
Isaaks	18 May 1991	Somaliland Republic
Kalmyks	12 June 1918	Kalmyk Republic
Kalmyks	7 August 1942	Kalmyk National Republic
Karachais	18 May 1918	Karachay Republic
Karachais	11 August 1942	Karachai-Balkar National Republic
Karels	21 April 1921	Republic of East Karelia
Karens	14 June 1949	Republic of Kawthoolei
Kasaians	9 August 1960	Mining State of South Kasai
Kashmiris	4 October 1947	Republic of Azad-Kashmir
Katangans	11 July 1960	Republic of Katanga
Kosovars	11 October 1991	Republic of Kosova
Kuban Cossacks	16 February 1918	Republic of the Kuban
Kunas	8 February 1925	Tule Republic
Kurds	22 January 1946	Kurdish People's Republic (Mahabad)
Lombards	15 September 1996	Federation of Padania
Malayalis	15 August 1947	State of Travancore
Manchus	8 February 1924	State of Manchuria
Manchus	9 March 1932	State of Manchukuo
Mayans	3 July 1924	Republic of Yucatan (Yukataan)
Mizos	6 July 1966	Republic of Mizoram
Montenegrins	13 July 1941	Kingdom of Montenegro
Nagas	14 August 1947	Republic of Nagaland
Northern Cypriots	15 November 1983	Turkish Republic of Northern Cyprus
Northern Tai	12 January 1927	Kwangsi Republic
Ossetians	12 December 1990	South Ossetian Democratic Republic
Palestinians	15 November 1988	State of Palestine
Pomaks	8 July 1913	Republic of Gumuldjina
Pushtuns	2 September 1947	State of Pushtunistan
Rhinelanders	1 June 1919	Rhenish Republic

Rhinelanders	22 October 1923	Rhineland Republic (Rheinische Republik)
Riffians	19 September 1921	Confederal Republic of the Tribes of the Rif
Ruwenzoris	13 February 1963	Republic of Ruwenzuru
Sahrawis	27 February 1976	Sahrawi Arab Democratic Republic
Sakhas	22 February 1918	Republic of Sakha Omuk defined
Sanussis	1 March 1949	Emirate of Cyrenaica
Saxons	19 November 1918	Soviet Republic of Saxony
Shans	3 October 1942	Federated Shan States
Siberians	4 July 1918	Republic of Siberia
Sicilians	10 July 1943	Republic of Sicily
Sikhs	30 April 1986	State of Khalistan
Sikkimese	15 August 1947	Kingdom of Sikkim
Sorbs	1 January 1919	Republic of Lusatia
South Sulawesis	16 February 1958	Celebes Republic
South Vietnamese	26 October 1955	Republic of Vietnam
South Yemenis	21 May 1994	Democratic Republic of Yemen
Southern Azeris	12 July 1945	Azerbaijan Democratic Republic
Southern Cameroonians	30 December 1999	Federal Republic of Southern Cameroons
Southern Mongols	23 April 1934	Mongolian Federation
Southern Mongols	8 December 1937	Federation of the Mongol Borderlands
Suvadivans	18 January 1959	United Suvadivan Republic
Szeklers	28 October 1918	Republic of Transylvania
Taiwanese	23 May 1895	Democratic Republic of Taiwan
Talysh	12 August 1993	Republic of Talysh-Murgan
Tannese	24 March 1974	Nation of Tanna
Tatars	30 September 1918	Idel-Ural Federation
Terek Cossacks	4 March 1918	Terek People's Republic
Texans	2 March 1836	Republic of Texas
Texans	1 February 1861	Republic of Texas
Tibetans	18 February 1912	State of Tibet
Tigreans	11 September 1943	Republic of Tigray
Tuvans	18 December 1911	Urjanchai Republic
Tuvans	14 August 1921	People's Republic of Tannu Tuva
Tyroleans	24 April 1919	Free State of Tyrol
Uighurs	23 January 1934	Islamic Republic of East Turkestan
Uighurs	31 January 1945	East Turkestan Democratic Republic

Vemeranans	27 December 1975	Na Griamel Federation
Vemeranans	25 May 1980	Republic of Vemerana
Vorarlbergers	3 November 1918	Republic of Vorarlberg
West Papuans	1 December 1961	Republic of West Papua
West Papuans	9 December 1975	Republic of West Papua
Western Ukrainians	14 November 1918	Western Ukrainian Democratic Republic
Western Ukrainians	30 June 1941	Republic of Western Ukrainia
Zanzibaris	10 December 1963	Sultanate of Zanzibar

Note that the names of states and the dates of independence are often a matter of confusion or dispute. The state names are subject to translation and interpretation, and the dates are subject to confusion between declarations of sovereignty or intent and the date the event was reported or the report received, and owing to differences in the calendars in use.

Appendix B: Geographic Distribution and National Organizations* Listed by Nation

*Note that a slash (/) between two groups denotes a close relationship such as a political organization and its armed wing.

SUB-SAHARAN AFRICA

Angola: Cabindans; Kasaians; Katangans; Kongos; Lozis

Benin: Ewes; Hausas; Yorubas

Botswana: Lozis; Ndebele

Burundi: Twa

Cameroon: Bamilekes; Kanuris; Southern Cameroonians

Chad: Kanuris; Logonese; Mabas; North Chadians

Comoros: Anjouanis

Congo: Kongos

Congo, Democratic Republic of: Bari; Kasaians; Katangans; Kongos; Ruwenzoris; Twa

Côte d'Ivoire: Anyi; Ashanti

Djibouti: Afars; Isaaks

Equatorial Guinea: Bubis

Eritrea: Afars; Tigreans

Ethiopia: Afars; Amhara; Isaaks; Oromos; Tigreans; Western Somalis

France: Mahoris; Réunionese

Ghana: Anyi; Ashantis; Ewes

Kenya: Maasai; Oromos; Western Somalis

Madagascar: Merina

Mali: Tuaregs

Mauritania: Kewris

Namibia: Afrikaners; Basters; Lozis

Niger: Hausas; Kanuris; Tuaregs

Nigeria: Edos; Ibibios; Ibos; Ijaws; Hausas; Kanuris; Ogonis; Tiv; Yorubas

Rwanda: Twa

Senegal: Casamançais; Kewris

Somalia: Isaaks; Majerteens

South Africa: Afrikaners; Ndebele; Zulus

Sudan: Bari; Fur; Mabas; Nuba; Southern Sudanese

Tanzania: Gandas; Maasai; Zanzibaris

Togo: Ewes

Uganda: Ankole; Bari; Gandas; Nyoros; Ruwenzoris; Toros; Twa

Zambia: Lozis

Zimbabwe: Ndebele

NATIONAL ORGANIZATIONS BY NATION: SUB-SAHARAN AFRICA

AFARS: Afar Liberation Front (ALF); Afar National Liberation Movement (ANLM); Afar-Saho Liberation Party; Afar Democratic Revolutionary Party (ARDU); Front for the Restoration of Unity and Democracy (Front pour la Restoration d'Unité et Démocratie (FRUD); Popular Front for Liberation (PFL); Popular Movement for the Liberation of Djibouti (MPLD); Front for the Restoration of Rights and Legality (AROD); Organisation des Masses Afars (OMA); Parti Populaire Djiboutien (PPD)

AFRIKANERS: Afrikaner People's Front (Afrikaner Volksfront); Monitor Action Group (Namibia); Boer Liberation Movement; Boer State Party (Boerestaat Party)/Boer Resistance Movement (Boere Weerstandsbeweging) (BWB); Orangia Unie; Afrikaner Resistance Movement (Afrikaner Weerstands Beweging) (AWB); White Liberation Movement; Boere-Republikeine; Freedom Front; White Protection Movement (Blanke Bevrydingsbeweging) (BBB); Conservative Party of South Africa (CP); Reconstituted National Party (Herstigte Nasionale Party) (HNP); Orange Workers (Oranjewerkers); Republic Unity Movement (RUM); Interim Council of the Boer People

AMHARA: All-Amhara People's Organization (AAPO); Amhara National Democratic Movement (ANDM); Ethiopian People's Revolutionary Party (EPRP);

Ethiopian Unity Front; Ethiopian Democratic Union (EDU); Medhin; Coalition of All-Ethiopia Socialist Movement (Meison)

ANJOUANIS: Mawana (Anjouan Nationalist Movement); Association of Anjouan and Moheli

ANKOLE: Nkore Cultural Trust (NCT); Banyankore Cultural Foundation (BCF); Ankole-Kigezi Association (AKA); Federal Democratic Movement; Kumayana Movement; People's Congress

ANYI: Front Populaire Ivoirien (FPI); Agni Students Association; Agni Union; Rassemblement des Forces National du Sanwi (RFNS); Sanwi Liberation Party (Parti pour la Libération de l'Sanwi) (PLS)

ASHANTIS: Ashanti Confederation; Ashanti United Party (AUP); Federal Party; Movement for Freedom and Justice (MFJ); National Liberation Movement (NLM); United Kotoko Society; Alliance for Change; Ashanti Union; Ashanti Congress; Asanteman Council; Kumasi Traditional Council (KTC)

BAMILEKES: Bamileke Independence Front (FIB); Kumaze; Union Bamileké (UB); Maquisards; Union of Cameroonian Peoples (Union des Populations du Cameroun) (UPC); Laakam; Revolutionary Committee (Comité Révolutionaire)

BARI: Lado Defense Forces (LDF); Lado Triangle National Movement (LTNM)

BASTERS: Rehoboth Baster Community; Federal Convention of Namibia (FCN); Rehoboth Assembly; Rehoboth Rate Payers Association (RRPA)

BUBIS: Front for the Liberation of Bioko (FIB); Eri Democratic Front (FDE); Bubi National Group April 1 (Grup Nacionalista Bubi 1 de Abril) (GNB); Movement Fernando Póo; Progressive Democratic Alliance (ADP)

CABINDANS: Government of the Republic of Cabinda (GRC); Front for the Liberation of the State of Cabinda (Frente para a Liberação do Estado de Cabinda) (FLEC); Popular Front for the Liberation of Cabinda (MPLC); National Union for the Liberation of Cabinda (UNLC); Movement for the Liberation of Cabinda (MOLICA); Armed Forces of Cabinda (Forças Armadas de Cabinda (FLEC-FAC); FLEC-Renovada (FLEC-R); Cabinda Democratic Front (Frente Democrática de Cabinda (FDC); National Liberation Movement of the Enclave of Cabinda (MLEC); Action Committee of the Cabindan National Union (CAUNC); National Alliance of the Mayombe (ALLIAMA); National Union for the Liberation of the Enclave of Cabinda (UNALEC): Comité Révolutionnaire Cabindais (Congo)

CASAMANÇAIS: Mouvement des Forces Démocratiques de Casamance (Movement of Democratic Forces of Casamance) (MFDC)/Atika; Casamance United National Movement (MNCU); Maquisards; Northern Front (Front Nord); Southern Front (Front Sud); Casamance Autonomy Movement (MAC); Parti de Regroupment Africain-Senegal (PRA-Senegal)

EDOS: Edo National Union (ENU); Otu Edo; Ogbomi Society; Great Benin Movement; Edo National Union; Benin Kingdom Association (BKA); Edo National Association (USA/Canada); Edo Democratic Front (EDF-Benin); Warriors of Edoland (Okaokulos of Edoland)

EWES: Togoland Congress (TC); National Liberation Movement of Western Togoland (NLMWT); Togolese Liberation Movement (TLM) (Ghana); All-Ewe Conference; Ewe Unionist Association; Ewe National Movement; National Movement of Mono-East Togoland (MNMTE) (Benin); Greater Togo Movement; Union of the Forces of Change (Togo); Comité d'Action pour le Renouveau (CAR) (Togo); Democratic Convention of African Peoples (CDPA) (Ghana); Ewe Unionist Association; Ewe Unification Movement (EUM) (Ghana)

FUR: Darfur Development Front (DDF); Fur National Movement (FNM); Sony Liberation Movement (SLM)

GANDAS: Buganda National Council (BNC); Democratic Party (DP); Federal Democratic Movement (MOFEDE); Kabaka Yeka Party (King Only Party) (KY); Remember Buganda; Democratic Party; National Democratic Alliance (NDA); Conservative Party (CP); Kumukamu; Ebika by'Abaganda; Ggwanga Mujje; Bulungi Bwa Nsi; Abaana ba Buganda; Uganda Federal Freedom Organization (UFFO); Federal Republican Movement (FRM)/Federal Republican Army (FRA); All-Uganda Kingdom Association

HAUSAS: Islamic Republican Movement; Muslem Brotherhood; Islamic Legion; Northern Elders; Islamic Movement; Northern People's Congress (NPC); Muslim National Council; Arewa Peoples Consultative Forum (APCF); Front al-Zakzaky; Arewa People's Congress (APC)

IBIBIOS: Brotherhood of the Cross and the Star; Ekpe Society (Leopard Society); Ibibio Union (Asan Ibibio); National Independence Party (NIP); Ekong Society; Akwa Ibom State Association (AISA); Oron Development Union (ODU)

IBOS: Adami Oha Society; Ibo Federal Union (IFU); Adami Oha Veterans Association; People's Party; Biafra; Eastern Mandate Union (EMU); Mmo Society; Keep Biafra Alive (KBA); United Coalition Against Tyranny (UNCAT); Movement for the Actualization of the Sovereign State of Biafra (MASSOB); Bakassi Boys; Eastern Mandate Union; Igbo National Council of Chiefs; Ohana-Eze; National Democratic Coalition (NADECO); Biafra Actualization Forum (BAF); People's Democratic Congress (PDC)

IJAWS: Ijaw National Congress (INC); Ijaw Resource Center; Council of Ijaw Associations Abroad (COIAA); Ijaw Protection Organization (IPO); Egbesu Boys of Bayelsa; Ijaw Youth Congress (IYC); Ekine Society; Movement for the Survival of the Ijaw Ethnic Nationality (MSIEN); Ijaw Council for Human Rights (ICHR); Niger Delta Human and Environmental Rescue Organization (ND–HERO); Niger Delta Women for Justice (NDWJ); Niger Delta Republic Movement (NDRM); Niger Delta Volunteer Force (NDVF); Federated Niger Delta Ijaw Communities; Chicoco Movement; Ijaw National Congress USA (INCUSA); Ijaw National Congress of the United Kingdom and Ireland; Ijaw People's Association (IPA); Movement for the Survival of the Ijaw Ethnic Nationality

ISAAKS: Somali National League (SNL); Somali National Movement (SNM); National Communities Conference; Northern Somali Alliance (NSA); Red Flag

KANURIS: Bornu Youth Movement (BYM); Kanem-Bornu; Kanowra People's Party (KPP); Islamic League; Movement for Kanembu Freedom (MLK); Pan-Kanuri Movement (MTK) (Chad/Cameroon); Movement for Democracy and Development (Mouvement pour la Démocratie et le Dévelopment) (MDD); Democrati Front for Renewal (FDR) (Chad/Nigeria)

KASAIANS: Front for the Liberation of Occupied South Kasai (FLKSO); Union of Federalists and Independent Republicans (UFERI); Federation of Kasai (Fedeka); Democratic National Movement of the Kasaian Peoples (MDNKP); Kasai Tiger Force (FTK); Conference for the Economic Development of Kasai; Civic Society Association

KATANGANS: National Resistance Council (CNR); Katanga Tigers; Front André Kisase; Sacred Union (Union Sacrée); Congo National Liberation Front (FLNC); Democratic Front; Congolese National Liberation Front (CLNC); Union for Democracy and National Social Progress; Union of Federalists and Independent Republicans (UFERI); Rebirth Katanga; Katanga Gendarmes; Confederation of Nationalists and Reformers; National Front for the Liberation of Katanga (FNLK); Confederation of Tribal Associations of Katanga (CONAKAT); Rally for Independence; Cokat (Katangan Confederation)

KEWRIS: African Liberation Forces of Mauritania (Forces de Libération Africaines de Mauritanie) (FLAM); National Front of Black Officers (Front National des Officiers Noirs) (FRON); Gorgol Democratic Block; Union of the Inhabitants of the River Valley; Coalition Africaine; Party for Liberty, Eqality and Justice (PLEJ); National Union for Democracy and Development (UNDD)

KONGOS: Association for the Maintenance, Unity, and Advancement of the Kikongo Language (ABAKO); Congolese National Movement (MNC); Kongo Popular Movement of Musikongo (MPKM); Matswa; Ngwizako-Ngwizani a Kongo; Union pour la Démocratie et le Progrès Social National (Congo); National Front for the Liberation of Angola (Frente Nacional para a Liberacão de Angola (FNLA) (Angola); Uniao das Populacoes do Norte de Angola (UPNA); Alliance for the Kongo People; Cocoyes; Ngwizako-Ngwizani a Kongo (NNK); Alliance of Bakongo (Alliance des Bakongo); Democratic Party for Progress-Angolan National Alliance (PDP-ANA) (Angola)

LOGONESE: Popular Democratic Front (FPD); Armed Forces for the Federal Republic/Victims of Aggression (Forces Armés pour la République Fédérale) (FARF/VA); Codos Rouge; Committee of National Revival for Peace and Democracy (Comité de Sursaut pour la Paix et la Démocratie) (CSNPD); National Council for Democracy and Revolution (CNDR); Union of Democratic Forces (Union des Forces Démocratiques) (UFD)

LOZIS: Movement for an Independent Barotseland (MIB); Itenge; Barotse Patriotic Front (BPF); National Party (NP); Llute Yeta (Zambia); Barotse Cultural Association (BCA); National Council of Barotseland; National Party (NP); Agenda for Zambia (AZ); Liseli Conservative Party (LCP); Barotse Royal Establishment; Kazanga Nkoya Cultural Association; Caprivi Liberation Movement (CLM)/Caprivi Liberation Army (CLA) (Namibia); Caprivi African National Union (CANU) (Namibia); Forum for the Restoration of Barotseland (FOREBA)

MAASAI: Maasai United Front (MUF); Maasai Warriors; Maasai Majimbo; Ilkerin Loite Poject; Maasai of Loita; Aang Serian (Tanzania); Indigenous Youth Forum

MAHORIS: Mahorais People's Party (PPM); Mahoran Popular Movement (MPM); Association for French Mayotte

MABAS: Maba-Wadai Liberation Front (FLMO); National Liberation Front of Central Wadai (FNLOC); Chad National Front (Front National du Tchad) (FNT)

MAJERTEENS: Puntland Movement; Majerteen National Organization; Majerteen Darod Association; Government of Puntland

MERINA: Active Forces (Hery Velona); Forces Vives Rasalama; Stone Ramification (Vy Vato Sakelika) (VVS); Merina Nation Movement (MNM); Democratic Movement for Malagasy Renewal) (MDRM); Congress Party for Independence (AKF); Feon'ny Merina (Voice of the Merina)

NDEBELES: Zimbabwe African People's Union 2000 (ZAPU 2000); Zimbabwe African People's Union (ZAPU)/Zimbabwe People's Revolutionary Army (ZIPRA); Democratic League; United National Federal Party (UNFP); Federal Party (FP); Committee for a Democratic Society (CODESO); Zimbabwe Active People's Unity Party; Matabele Autonomy Movement (MAM); Mthwakazi Action Group on Genocide and Ethnic Cleansing in Matabeleland and Midlands (MAGGEMM)

NORTH CHADIANS: Chad National Front (FNT); Chad Northern Army (ANT); Northern Armed Forces (FAN); Peoples' Armed Forces (Forces Armés Populaires (FAP); Volcan Army; Chad Liberation Front (Front de Libération du Tchad) (FLT); Western Armed Forces (FAO); Chad National Liberaton Front (Front de Libération de Tchad (FROLINAT); Front for the National Renewal of Chad (Front National du Tchad Renové (FNTR); Armed Forces for a Federal Republic (Forces Armées pour un République Féderale) (FARF)

NUBA: Group Yousif Kuwa Mekki; Nuba Mountains United Front (NMUF); Sudan People's Liberation Army/Nuba Mountains (SPLA/NM); Nuba Mountains Central Committee (NMCC); Nuba Mountains Solidarity Abroad (Europe); Sudan National Party (SNP); New Kush Battalion; People's Movement for the Liberation of the Nuba Mountains; Nuba Relief, Rehabilitation and Development Society (Kenya)

NYOROS: Ruhuga Society; Mubende Banyoro Party (MBP); Federal Kingdom Movement; Kitara Bunyoro Society; Bunyoro Kitara Empango

OGONIS: Movement for the Survival of the Ogoni People (MOSOP); Ogoni Community Association; Ogoni Oilwatch; Ken Saro Wiwa Campaign; Ogoni Assembly

OROMOS: Oromo Liberation Front (OLF); Islamic Front for the Liberation of Oromia (IFLO); Oromo People's Democratic Organization (OPDO); United Oromo People's Liberation Front (UOPLF); Oromo Abbo Liberation Front; Oromo People's Liberation Organization; Human Rights League; Oromo Relief Association; Oromo People's Liberation Front (OPLF)

RÉUNIONESE: Free-DOM Movement; National Front (Front Nationale) (FN); Understanding and Helping Hand Movement; Parti Communiste Réunionais (PCR); Movement for the Liberation of Réunion (Mouvement pour la Liberation de la Réunion) (MLR); Association for the Réunion Flag (Association pour le Drapeau de la Réunion) (APDR)/Alala Drapo La Renyon (ADR); Shri Anjaneya Sabha (SAS); Mouvement Entente et Coup de Main

RUWENZORIS: Ruwenzuru Movement; Bakonjo Life History Research Society (BLHRS); Bantu Solidarity Movement (BSM); Allied Democratic Forces (ADF); Harugali; National Army for the Liberation of Uganda (NALU)

SOUTHERN CAMEROONIANS: Social Democratic Front (SDF); All Anglophone Conference (AAC)/Anglophone National Council (ANC); Southern Cameroons People's Conference (SCPC)/Southern Cameroons National Council (SCNC); Cameroon Anglophone Movement (CAM); Southern Cameroons Youth League (SCYL); Free West Cameroon (FWC); Southern Cameroons Liberation Front (SCLF); People's Voice; Sons of the Soil; Liberal Democratic Alliance; Social Democratic Front (SDF); South West Elites Association (SWELA); North West Cultural and Development Association (NOCUDA); Southern Cameroons Advisory Council (SCAC); Southern Cameroons Restoration Movement (SCARM); Anglophone Patriotic Alliance

SOUTHERN SUDANESE: Southern People's Liberation Front (SPLF)/Southern People's Liberation Army (SPLA); Azania Liberation Front (ALF); Anyidi Movement; Sudan African Liberation Front (SALF); Forces of Unity; SPLA-Unity; Liberation Front for Southern Sudan; Sudan African National Union (SANU); South Sudan Defense Force (SSDF); New Sudan Brigade; National Democratic Alliance (NDA); South Sudan Independence Movement (SSIM)/Southern Sudan Independence Army (SSIA); Sudan People's Liberation Army-United (SPLA-U); Forces of Unity; Barh al-Ghazal Group; Resistance Movement of South Sudan (PRMSS); Federal Party; Union of Sudan African Parties (USAP); Equatoria Defense Force (EDF); United Democratic Salvation Force (SSDF); Nuer Youth Organization

TIGREANS: Tigray People's Liberation Front (TPLF); Tigray National Organization; Relief Society of Tigre (REST); United Independence Movement of Tigre; Renewal Association (Tehadiso Mehaber)

TIV: Tiv Progressive Union (TPU); Mutual Union of the Tiv (Mzough U Tiv); Middle Zone League (MZL); United Middle Belt Congress (MBC); Tiv Youth Movement (TYM); Taraba Relief Force (TRF); Mbatsav; Middle Belt Forum (MBF)

TOROS: Toro People's Organization (TPO); Federal Democratic Movement (FDM); Christian Democratic Party (CDP); Toro Kingdom Association; Bantu Solidarity Movement

TUAREGS: Democratic Revolutionary Front (Front Démocratique Révolutionnaire) (FDR); Tuareg Liberation Front; Popular Front for the Liberation of the Azawad (PFLA); Islamic Arab Front of Azawad; Amazigh World Congress (Agraw Amad'lan Amazigh) (AAA); Amazigh Cultural Movement; Front for the Liberation of Aïr and Azawagh (Front de Libération de l'Aïr et l'Azaouad) (FLAA); Front for the Liberation of Tamoust (FAT); Coordination of the Armed Resistance (CRA); Organization of the Armed Resistance (ORA); Revolutionary Army of the Liberation of Northern Niger (ARLN); Popular Front for the Liberation of the Sahara (FPLS); Union of Armed Resistance Fronts (UFRA); Azawad Popular Liberation Front (FPLA); Azawad Peoples' Movement (MPA); Front for the Liberation of Eastern Sahara (FLES); Azawad United Front (FUA); Revolutionary Movement of the Blue Men (Morehob); Front de Libération de Tamoust (FLT); Movements and Unified Fronts of Azawad (MFUA); Eirene Agadez (Niger)

TWA: Association for the Promotion of Batwa (Association pour le Promotion des Batwa) (APB); Community of Indigenous People of Rwanda (CAURWA); Twa Life Group; Batwa Organization of Burundi (OBB); Association for the Global Development of the Batwa in Rwanda (Association pour le Development Global des Batwa en Rwanda) (ADGBR)

WESTERN SOMALIS: Western Somali Liberation Front (WSLF); Ogaden National Liberation Front (ONLF); Islamic Union of Western Somalia; Somali People's Liberation Front; Al-Itihad; Islamic Union of Western Somalia (IUWS); al-Itihad; Oromi-Somali-Afar Liberation Alliance (OSALA); United Somali People's Liberation Front (USPL); Western Somali Democratic Party (WSDP); Somali People's Democratic Party (SPDP); Welfare Society of Ogaden; Ethnic Somali Democratic League (ESDL); Isa and Gurgura Liberation Front (IGLF); Gurgura Liberation Front (GLF); Eastern Gabdoye Democratic Organization (EGDO); Eastern Ethiopian Somali League; Horyal Democratic Front; Social Alliance Democratic Organization; Somali Abo Democratic Union; Shekoshe People's Democratic Movement; Ethiopian Somali Democratic Movement; Society of Western Somalis in Kenya (SWSK)

YORUBAS: Egbe Omo Oduduwa (EOD); Yoruba Action Party (YAP); Yoruba United Party (YUP); All–Yoruba National United Party (AYNUP); National Association of Yoruba Descendants (Egbe Omo Yoruba) (EOY); Afenifere; Yoruba Peoples Congress (YPC); Odua People's Congress (OPC); Afenifere; Alliance for Democracy; Action Group (AG); Unity Party of Nigeria (UPN); National Democratic Coalition (NADECO); Odua Liberation Movement (OLM); Revolutionary Council of Nigeria (RCN); Isokan Yoruba Ogene Ndigbo

ZANZIBARIS: Civic United Front (CUF); Zanzibar Democratic Alternative (ZADA); Bismillah Party; Maendelo Zanzibar; Movement for a Democratic Alternative (MDA); National Movement of Zanzibar (MNZ); Zanzibar National Party (ZNP); Zanzibar Voice; Pemba People's Party (PPP); Free Political Parties in Zanzibar (Karamhuru); Balukta; Zanzibar Arab Association (ZAA); Hamak

ZULUS: Inkatha Yenkululeko Yesikwe; Inkatha Freedom Party (IFP); Natal People's Conference; Natal Democratic Party; Amasinyora; KwaZulu Police (KZP); National Cultural Liberation Movement (Inkatha Yenkululeko Yesizwe); Self–Protection Unit (SPU)

THE AMERICAS AND OCEANIA

Antigua: Barbuda: Barbudans

Argentina: Mapuches

Australia: Aborigines

Belize: Garifunas; Mayas

Bolivia: Acreaños; Cambas; Quechua-Aymara

Brazil: Acreaños; Bahians; Gauchos

Canada: Acadians; Capers; Crees; Haidas and Tlingits; Innus; Inuits; Iroquois; Métis; Micmacs; Newfies; Ojibwe; Québecois; Western Canadians

Chile: Mapuches; Quechua-Aymara; Rapanui

Colombia: Antioquians; Zulians

Denmark: Greenlanders

Ecuador: Quechua-Aymara

France: Guadeloupeans; Guianese; Kanaks; Martinicans; Tahitians; Wallisians and Futunans

Guatemala: Garifunas; Mayans

Indonesia: West Papuans

Honduras: Garifunas; Mayans; Miskitos

Mexico: Mayans; Zapotecs

Netherlands: Antilleans; Arubans

New Zealand: Cook Islanders; Maoris

Nicaragua: Garifunas; Miskitos

Panama: Kunas

Papua New Guinea: Bougainvillians; West Papuans

Peru: Acreaños; Quechua-Aymara

Solomon Islands: Bougainvillians; Malaitans

St. Kitts and Nevis: Nevisians

Trinidad and Tobago: Tabagonians

United Kingdom: Anguillans; Belongers; Bermudians; Caymanians; Crucians

United States: Acadians; Alaskans; Apache; Cajuns; Californians; Chamorros; Cherokee; Crucians; Eastern Samoans; Haidas and Tlinglits; Hawaiians; Iroquois; Métis; Micmacs; Mormons; Navajo; New Englanders; Ojibwe; Pueblo; Puerto Ricans; Sioux; Southerners; Texans

Vanuatu: Tannese; Vemeranans

Venezuela: Zulians

NATIONAL ORGANIZATIONS BY NATION: THE AMERICAS AND OCEANIA

ABORIGINES: Aboriginal and Torres Strait Islander Commission (ATSIC); Aboriginal Land Council; Central Land Council; New South Wales Aboriginal Council; Northern Land Council; Council for Aboriginal Reconciliation; Indigenous Woman Aboriginal Corporation (IWAC); National Aboriginal and Islander Legal Service Secretariat (NAILSS); National Coalition of Aboriginal Organizations; Torrest Strait Regional Council

ACADIANS: Centre Acadien; Socitété de la Gaspésie; Société Historique du Madawaska (SHM) (United States); Assemblée des Francophones du Nord-Est (AFN); Federation des Communautes Francophones et Acadienne; Acadian Federation of Nova Scotia (Federation Acadienne de la Nouvelle-Ecosse); Acadian Society of New Brunswick

ACREAÑOS: Forest People's Alliance (APB); Chico Mendes Group; National Council; Worker's Party; National Council of Rubber Trappers (CNS); Union of the Indigenous Nations of Acre and the South of the Amazon; Center for Human Rights and Public Education (CDHEP); Amazonian Workers Center (CTA); Acre National Council (CNA)

ALASKANS: Alaskans for Independence (AFI); Alaskan Independence Party (AIP); Alaska Libertarian Party (ALP); Northern Forum

ANGUILLANS: Anguilla United Party (AUP); Anguillan Independence Movement (AIM)

ANTILLEANS: Antillean Restructuring Party (PAR); New Antilles Movement (Moveshon Antia Nobo) (MAN); Partido Nasonal de Pueblo (PNP) (Curaçao); Democratic Party (St Maarten); Jeugd Luchtvaart Brigade; Partido Laboral Krusada Popular (PLKP); Democratic Party of Bonaire (PDB); Patriotic Union of Bonaire (UPB) (Bonaire); Socialist Independent (SI); Nos Patria; Windward Islands People's Movement (WIPM); Saba Unity Party (Saba); Democratic Party of Sint Eustatius (DP-StE); National Progressive Party (NPP)

ANTIOQUIANS: Latino National Movement (MLN); Pro-Antioquia; Popular Militia; United Antioquia Movement (MAU); Antioquian Rebels; Free Antioquia Homeland (Patria Libre Antioquia) (PLA); Movimento Antioquia Soberana (MAS); Liberacíon Paisa; United Antioquian Federation (FAU)

APACHE: Apache Survival Coalition (ASC); Huh Whuli Nich

ARUBANS: Aruba People's Party (Arubaanse Volkspartij) (AVP); People's Electoral Movement (Movimiento Electoral di Pueblo) (MEP); Aruban Patriotic Party (Partido Patriótico Arubano) (PPA); Aruban Liberal Organization (Organisacion Liberal Arubiano) (OLA); National Democratic Action (Acción Democratico Nacional) (ACN)

BAHIANS: 2 July Movement; Regional Party of Bahia (Partido Regionalista do Bahia) (PRB); Sabinadas

BARBUDANS: Barbuda People's Movement (BPM); Barbuda Council; Barbuda Independence Movement (BIM)

BELONGERS: People's Democratic Movement (PDM); United Democratic Party (UDP); Progressive National Party (PNP)

BERMUDIANS: Progressive Labor Party (PLP); United Bermuda Party (UBP); Bermudians for Sovereignty

BOUGAINVILLIANS: Bougainville Revolutionary Government (BRG)/Bougainville Revolutionary Army (BRA); Independence Movement of the North Solomons; Melanesian Alliance; Bougainville Freedom Movement (BFM); Bougainville Interim Government (BIG); Bougainville People's Congress; Buka Liberation Front (BLF); Bougainville Resistance Force (BRF); Mekmui National Chief's Assembly; Mekamui Defense Force (MDF)

CAJUNS: Acadian Committee (Comité Acadien); Council for the Defense of French in Louisiana (CODOFIL); Congrés Mondial Acadien-Louisiane

CALIFORNIANS: Free the Bear; California Independence Movement (CIM); The California Republic; California Freedom Initiative; Native Sons; California Heritage Preservation Association (CHPA); Bear Flag Party (BFP)

CAMBAS: Conference of Campesino Unions; National Liberation Army (ELN); Santa Cruz National Party (PNSC); Santa Cruz National Confederation (CNSC); Acción Nacionalista (AN); Frente Patriótica de Santa Cruz Libre (FP); Front Che Guevarra; Santa Cruz-El Beni Association; East Bolivian Confederation (Confederacíon de Oriente de Bolivia) (COB)

CAPERS: Cape Breton Liberation Movement (CBLM)/Cape Breton Liberation Army (CBLA); Gaelic Heritage

CAYMANIANS: People's Democratic Movement (PDM); Progressive National Party (PNP)

CHAMORROS: Nasion Chamoru; Commission on Self-Determination; Republic and Unity Movement (RUM)

CHEROKEE: Cherokee Nation; Four Mothers Society; Five Nations Treaty Council; American Indian Movement (AIM); Sons of Sequoyah; Seven Clans Society; United Keetoowah Band of Cherokees; Keetoowah Society; Cherokee National Tribal Council

COOK ISLANDERS: Cook Islands Party (CIP); Democratic Party (DP); Democratic Alliance Party (DAP); Niue People's Party (NPP)

CREE: Grand Council of the Crees of Quebec (GCCQ) (Eeyou Istchee); Lubicon Cree; Lubicon Settlement Commission; Kitigan Zibi Anishinabeg

CRUCIANS: Virgin Islands Party (VIP); United Party (UP); Concerned Citizens Movement (CCM); Independent People's Movement (IPM) (British Virgin Islands); Crucian United Party (CUP); Independent Citizen's Movement (ICM)

EASTERN SAMOANS: Samoan National Party (SNP); Organization of the Peoples of Eastern Samoa (OPEA)

GARIFUNAS: Garifuna Awareness Movement (GAM); Organización Fraternal Negra Hondureña (Ofraneh) (Honduras); National Gafifuna Council (NGC); Lawanserun Garifuna Heritage (LGH); Loubavagu; Organizacion Negra Centroamericana (Oneca); Yurimein (St. Vincent)

GAUCHOS: Movement for the Independence of Pampa (Movimento pela Independência do Pampa) (MIP); Front of the Three (FT); Geralia Movement; Movement of the Democratic South (MSD); Republic of the Pampas (GRP); Party of National Construction (Partido de Construcão Nacional) (PCNG); Southern Party (PS); Movimento Nacional de Las Pampas (MNP); Partido Federalista (PF); Gaucho Liberation Movement (Movimento pela Liberación de Los Gauchos) (MLLG); Partido Republicano Rio-Grandense (PRR); Partido Liberal

GREENLANDERS: Greenland Home Rule Government; Inuit Circumpolar Conference (ICC); Siumut Party (Forward Party); Ataqatigiit (Inuit Brotherhood) (IA); Atassut Party (Solidarity Party); Akulliit Party; Issituup (Polar Party); Kattusseqatigiit (Candidate List)

GUADELOUPEANS: Revolutionary Alliance of the Caribbean; Popular Union for the Liberation of Guadeloupe (Union Populaire pour la Libération de la Guadeloupe) (UPLG); Groupement des Organisations Nationalistes Guadeloupénnes (GONG); Popular Movement for the Independence of Guadeloupe (Movement Populaire pour une Guadeloupe Indépendante) (MPGI); Guadeloupe Objective Party (POG); National Council of the Guadeloupean Resistance (Counseil National de la Resistance Guadeloupéine) (CNRG); Revolutionary Caribbean Alliance (ARC); Guadeloupe Liberation Army (GLA); Christian Movement for the Liberation of Guadeloupe (KLPG); General Federation of Guadeloupe Workers (CGT-G) General Union of Guadeloupe Workers (UGTG)

GUIANESE: Fo non Libéré Guyane; Action Démocratique Guayanaise (ADG); Guyane Democratic Forces (Forces Démocratique Guayanaise) (FDG); Mouvement pour la Décolonisation et l'Emancipation Sociale; Parti National Populaire Guyanais (PNPIG); Parti Socialiste Guyanais (PSG); Union de Travailleurs; Revolutionary Alliance of the Caribbean; Parti Socialiste Guyanais (PSG); Nationalist Popular Party of Guyane (Parti Nationaliste Popularire Guiana) (PNPG); Unité Guyanaise; National Liberation Front of Guyane (Front National Libéré de la Guyane) (FNLG); Walwari Committee

HAIDAS AND TLINGITS: Central Council of Tlingit and Haida; Council of the Haida Nation; Sgan Gwaii; Alaska Native Brotherhood (Alaska); Assembly of First Nations (Canada)

HAWAIIANS: Ka Lahui Hawai'i (Hawaiian Nation); Polynesian Sovereignty Movement; Lokahi aki paa (Unity); National Movement of the Hawaiian Peoples; National Homeland Movement; Hawai'i United for Liberation and Independence (HULI); Ohana Council; Hawaii Kanaka Maoli Tribunal Komike; Pro-Hawaiian Sovereignty Working Group; Institute for the Advancement of Hawaiian Affairs; Ha Hawai'i; Kaw Nation of Hawai'i; Nation of Hawai'i; Hawaiian Independence Movement (HIM); Aha Punano Leo (Language Nest); State Council of Hawaiian Homestead Associations; Hawaiian Sovereignty Election Councils; Hui Na'Na'auao; Ka Pakaukau

INNUS: Innu Nation (Mamit Innuat); Innu Campaign against the Militarization of Ntesian; Labrador Innu Association; Assembly of First Nations; Mamuitun (Quebec)

INUITS: Inuit Circumpolar Conference (ICC); Nunavut Constitutional Forum; Tungavik Federation of Nunavut; Inuit Tapirisat; Nunavut Government; Inuit Atagatiqüt; Inuit Movement

IROQUOIS: Haudenosaunee Council of Chiefs; Iroquois Confederation; American Indian Movement (AIM); Assembly of First Nations; Ganiekeh Movement; Mohawk Nation; Haudenosaunee Runners Society; Confederation of Treaty Six First Nations; Assembly of First Nations (Canada); Mohawk Nation Council of Chiefs; Oneida Indian Nation; Kahnawake Warrior Society; Six Nations Warrior Society

KANAKS: Kanak Socialist National Liberation Front (Front de Libération Nationale Kanake et Socialiste) (FLNKS); Ai'a Api (New Land Party); Progressive Melanesian Union (Union Progressiste Melanesienne) (UPM); Kanak Socialist Liberation Front (LKS); National Front (FN); Socialist Party of Kanaky (PSK); Kanak Liberation Party (PALIKA); Union to Construct Independence; Association for Information and Support of Rights for the Kanak People in New Caledonia (AISDPK); United Kanak Liberation Front (Front Uni de Libèration Kanak) (FULK); Radical Faction for the National Liberation of Kanaks (FRANILAK); Kanak Independence Organization (PTM); Union Nationale pour l'Independance (UNI); Federation des Comites de Coordination des Independantistes (FCCI); Groupe de l'Alliance Multiraciale (GAM); Independance et Progres; Loyalty Islands Development Front (FDIL)

KUNAS: Movimiento de la Juventud Kuna; Yar Burba (Espiritu de la Tierra); Anmar Burba (Nuestra Espiritu); Yuwipi; National Coordination of Indigenous Peoples of Panama

MALAITANS: Malaitan Eagle Force (MEF); Maasina Rule Malaita; National Party (NP)

MAORIS: Aotearoa Maori Te Taiwhenua o Heretaunga; Maori Congress - Aotearoa; Maori Whakapai; Maori Women's Organization; Taura Here o Te Whanganui Maori Kaumatuo Council; Peace Movement Aotearoa (PEA); Kia Whakataara; United Tribes of Aotearoa (UTA); Aotearoa Party; Maori Organization on Human Rights (MOOHR); Te Hokioi; Maori King Movement; Nga Tamatoa (Brown Power); Polynesian Panthers; Waitangi Action Committee (WAC); Maori People's Liberation Movement of Aotearoa (MPLMA); Ngaa Puna Waihanga; Mana Motuhake; Maori Independence Movement (Tino Rangatiratanga)

MAPUCHES: Mapuche People's Liberation Organization (AD-MAPU); Aukiñ Wall Mapu (Council for the Land); Central Cultural Mapuche; Party of the Land and Identity; Pelondugun Society; Mapuche Inter-Regional Council (Consejo Inter-Regional Mapuche) (CIM); Coordinacion de Organizaciones Mapuche; Mapuche Neuqina; Comite Exterior Mapuche; Mapuche Relmu; Organization Mapuche Pegun-Dugun; Folil-che Aflaiai (Eternal Indigenous People); Communal Association of the Mapuche; Council of All Lands (Aukin Wallmapu Nguklam); Nehuen Mapu; Choil Folilche; Cllfulican (Land and Identity); Lautaro I' Ailla Rehue; Guerrilla Army of the Poor (MIR); Kiñe Newentun; Organización Mapuche Urbana Meli Wixan Mapu; Consejo de Todas las Tierras Mapuches; Mapuche Aucan; Coordinación de Organizaciónes Mapuche (Argentina)

MARTINICIANS: Parti Progressiste Martiniquais; Martinique Patriots (PM); Martinique Independence Movement (Mouvement Indépendantiste Martiniquais) (MIM); Movement for a Liberated Martinique; Caribbean Revolutionary Alliance; Association for the Protection of Martinique's Heritage; League of Workers and Peasants; National Front for the Liberation of Martinique (Front National de Libération de la Martinique) (FNLM); Workers Party of Martinique (Parti des Travailleurs de Martinique) (PTM); National Council of Popular Committees (Conseil National des Comités Populaires) (CNCP); Armed Liberation Group of Martinique (ALGM); Mouvement des Democrates et des Ecologistes pour une Martinique independante

MAYANS: Army of the Poor; Mayan Language and Nation; Movement for Mayan Rights (MDM); Petenero Inde Front; Mayan Unity; National Heritage; Partido de Accion Nacional; Zapatista National Liberation Army (EZLN); Centro por la Vida y la Paz-Rigoberta Menchu Tum (Guatemala); Consejo de Organizaciones Mayas; Escuela Maya de Derechos Humanos; Liga Maya Internacional; Rujetay Nobal Tinamit Maya Kagchi Kel; Zapatista Front (Frente Zapatista de Liberación National) (FZLN); Democratic Assembly of the People of Chiapas; (Mexico); Acción Zapatista; Committed of Unified Countrypeople (CUC) (Guatemala); Maya-K'iche Organization (Guatemala); Mutual Support Groups (GAM) (Guatemala); National Widow's Coordinating Group of Guatemala (CONAVIGUA); National Guatemalan Council of Displaced Persons (CONDEG); Runujel Junam Council of Ethnic Communities (CERJ) (Guatemala); Communities of Peoples in Resistance (CPR) (Guat); Mayan Coordination of the New Awakening (Majawil Q'il) (Guat); National Front of Indigenous Integration (FIN) (Guatemala); Permanent Maya Assembly (Guatemala); Nukuj Akpop (Guatemala); Escuela Maya de Derechos Humanos (Ixim-Che); Guatemala National Revolutionary Unit (URNG)

MÉTIS: Métis National Council (MNC); Louis Riel Métis Council (LRMC); Confederacy of Métis Peoples (CMP); Métis Circle; Métis Federation; Métis Nation

MICMACS: Mi'kmaq Grand Council (Mi'kmaq Sante' Mawio'mi); Mi'kmaq Warrior Society (Mi'kmaq Sma'knis); Assembly of First Nations

MISKITOS: Moskito-Sumo-Rama Asala Takanka (MISURATA); Kisan Group; Misura; Yamata; Sukawala; Pana-Pana; Alliance for the Progress of Miskitos and Sumus (ALPROMISU); Descendants of Mother Earth (Yapti Masrika Nani) (YATAMA); Miskito Council of Elders

MORMONS: Church of Jesus Christ of Latter-day Saints; United Order of Enoch; National Society Daughters of Utah Pioneers

NAVAJO: Dine Bii Coalition (Coalition for Navajo Liberation) (DBC); Dine Land Movement; Dine Bikeyah (NAVAJO NATION)

NEVISIANS: Concerned Citizens Movement (CCM); Nevis Reformation Party (NRP)

NEW ENGLANDERS: New England Confederation (NEC); Coalition for New England's Future (CNEF); Free Vermont Organization (FVO); Vermont Republican Army (VRA); New England Home Rule Movement; Maine Republican Army

NEWFIES: Newfie Independence Movement (NIM); Party for an Independent Newfoundland; National Liberation Movement of Newfoundland (NLMN); Fishermen's Protective Union (FPU); Newfoundlanders for Lasting Democracy (NFLD)

OJIBWE: Great Lakes Intertribal Council; Ojibwemowin Zagaswe'idiwin (Ojibwe Language Society); Keewaytinook Okimakanak; First Ojibwe Forum

PUEBLO: All Indian Pueblo Council (AIPC); American Indian Movement (AIM); Hopi Tribal Council (HTC); Bataam-Corregidor Memorial Foundation of New Mexico

PUERTO RICANS: Puerto Rican Independence Party (Partido Independentista de Puerto Rico) (PIPR); Federación Universitaria Pro-Independencia (FUPI); Armed Forces of National Resistance (FALN); Armed Liberation Commandos (CAL); Armed Volunteers of the Puerto Rican Revolution; Boricua Popular Army-Los Macheteros; Partido Socialista Puertorriqueño (PSP); Partido Communista Puertorriqueño (PCP); Democratic Popular Party (PDP); Armed Forces of Popular Resistance; Hostosian National Congress (Congreso Nacional Hostosiano, CNH)

QUÉBECOIS: Parti Québecois (PQ); Quebec Liberation Front (FLQ); Bloc Québecois (BQ); Democratic Rally for Independence; Popular Liberation Front (FLP); Quebec Liberation Front (FLQ); Societé Saint-Jean Baptiste; Parti Action Québecois (PAQ); Action Démocratique de Québec; Free Quebec (Le Québecois Libre); National Liberation Movement of Quebec (Mouvement de Libération Nationale du Québec) (MLNQ); Front for the Liberation of Quebec (Front de Libération du Québec) (FLQ); Chevaliers de l'Indépendance (CDI); Mouvement Souveraineté Association (MSA); National Rally for Independence (Ralliement National pour L'Indépendance du Québec); Union Nationale

QUECHUA-AYMARA: Tuwantinsuyo Liberation Movement; Parlamento del Pueblo aymara (Aymara People's Parliament) (PPA); Chara–a Machaka Qurpa Marka; Consejo Indio de Sud América (Indian Council of South America) (CISA); Consejo Nacional Aymara (Chile); Movimiento Cultural Qullana; Movimiento Cultural Pre Americano; Yachay Wasi; Movimiento Indio Tupaq Katari (Mitka) (Bolivia); Federation International of Andean Communities and Indigenous Societies; Unión Nacional de Comunidades Aymaras (UNCA); Assembly for the Peoples Sovereignty (Asamblea por la Soberan'a de los Pueblos (ASP); Pachakuti Axis (Eje Pachakuti)

RAPANUI: Council of Elders; Easter Island Foundation; Reimiro Movement

SIOUX: United Sioux Tribes; Lakota Nation; Lakota Treaty Council; American Indian Movement (AIM); Paha Sapa Liberation Movement (PSLM); Plain Indians Cultural Survival; Black Hills Teton Sioux Nation; Alliance of Tribal Advocates: Yuwipi; Seven Council Fires (Oceti Sakowin); Dakota Tipi First Nation

SOUTHERNERS: Confederate Society of America; Southern Political Alliance (ASP); Southern Party (SP); League of the South (LS); United Daughters of the Confederacy (UDC); Confederate Society of America; Heritage Alliance; Heritage Preservation Association (HPA); Sons of Confederate Veterans (SCV); Southern American Heritage (SAH); Southern Cross Militant Knights; Southern Nation; Southern Independence Movement (SIM); Southern Caucus; Council of Conservative Citizens; Reform Party of Mississippi; Southern Preservation Association; Southern Phalange; Southern Traditionalists

TABAGONIANS: Fargo House Movement (FHM); National Alliance of Reconstruction (NAR); United National Congress (UNC)

TAHITIANS: Ai'a Api (New Fatherland Party); Free Tahiti Party (PTL); Front for Internal Autonomy (FAI); Te Nunaa Ia Ora; Pupu Here Ai'a; Tahitinui; Pupe Here Ai'a te Nunaa la Ora; Hiti Tau; Independent Front for the Liberation of Polynesia (Tavini Huiraatira/Tavini Party); Hau Tahiti; Polynesian Union; Te Tiarama; Pupu Here Ai'a; Independence Party (la Mana Te Nunaa); Te Aratia Ote Nunaa; Haere I Mua; Te e'a No Maohi Nui; Pupu Taina; Polynesian Liberation Front (FLP)

TANNESE: John Frum Movement (JFM); Four Corners Movement (FCM); Kapiel Alliance; Tafea Movement

TEXANS: Texas Independence Movement (TIM); Republic of Texas; Republic of Texas Provisional Government; Texas Veterans Association (TVA); Liberal Faction; Daughters of the Alamo; Texas Sons of Confederate Veterans

VEMERANANS: Na-Griamel Movement; Vemerana Autonomist Movement (VAM)

WALLISIANS AND FUTUNANS: Taumu'a Lelei; Lua kae tahi; Wallis Party (New Caledonia)

WEST PAPUANS: Free Papua Movement (Organisasi Papua Merdeka) (OPM); Melanesian Socialist Party; West Papuan Government-in-Exile; All-Papua Conference; West Papua Peoples Front (WPPF); Stichting Papua Volken; Papuan Taskforce (Satgas Papua); West Papuan Peoples' Front (WPVF); Papua Peoples Foundation (PAVO); Revolutionary Council of West Papua Niugini; Angganita

WESTERN CANADIANS: Western Canada Concept (WCC); Western Canadian Separatists; Western Independent Nation (WIN); Western National Association (WNA)

ZAPOTECS: Nahasthi Kandito Zapotec; Popular Revolutionary Army (Ejercito Popular Revolucionario) (EPR); Worker-Peasant-Student Coalition of the Isthmus of Tehuantepec (COCEI); Zapotec Cultural Center (CCZ); Bi-National Indigenous Front of Oaxaca; Union of Zapotec Indians

ZULIANS: País Zuliano; República de Zulia (RZ); Political Association of Zulia (APZ); Bandera Zuliana y Independencia; Frontier Liberation Force (Ejercito por la Liberacíon de la Frontera) (ELF)

ASIA

Afghanistan: Baluch; Hazaras; Pushtuns

Bangladesh: Arakanese; Bodos; Jummas; Khasis; Meitheis; Mizos; Rajbangsis; Tripuris; Zomis

Bhutan: Gorkhas; Sikkimese

Brunei: Ibans

Cambodia: Chams; Khmer Krom; Montagnards

China: Buryats; Eastern Mongols; Hmongs; Hui; Kachins; Lahu; Manchus; Northern Tai; Palaungs; Shans; Southern Mongols; Tai; Taiwanese; Tibetans; Uighurs; Wa

India: Ahmadis; Andhrans; Assamese; Balawaris; Bodos; Gorkhas; Jharkhandis; Kachins; Kashmiris; Khasis; Kodavas; Ladakhis; Malayalis; Masas; Meitheis; Mikirs; Mizos; Nagas; Rabhas; Rajbangsis; Santhals; Sikhs; Sikkimese; Tamils; Teleganas; Tibetans; Tripuris; Uttarakhandis; Zomis

Indonesia: Acehnese; Ambonese; East Timorese; Ibans; Melayus; South Sulawesis; West Papuans

Japan: Ainu; Okinawans

Korea: Jejuvians

Laos: Chams; Hmongs; Lahu; Shans; Tai

Malaysia: Dayaks; Ibans; Kadazans; Moros; Pattanis

Maldive Islands: Suvadivans

Myanmar: Arakanese; Kachins; Karennis; Karens; Lahu; Meitheis; Mizos; Mons; Nagas; Pa-O; Palaungs; Tavoyans; Wa; Zomis

Nepal: Gorkhas; Rajbangsis; Uttarakhandis

Pakistan: Ahmadis; Balawaris; Baluch; Hazaras; Kashmiris; Ladakhis; Mohajirs; Pushtuns; Sindhis

Philippines: Cordillerans; Moros

Sri Lanka: Tamils

Thailand: Hmongs; Karennis; Karens; Lahu; Northern Tai; Pa-O; Palaungs; Pattanis; Shans; Wa

United Kingdom: Chagossians

Vietnam: Chams; Hmongs; Khmer Krom; Montagnards; South Vietnamese; Tai

NATIONAL ORGANIZATIONS BY NATION: ASIA

ACEHNESE: Free Aceh Movement (Gerakan Aceh Merdeka) (GAM); Aceh National Liberation Front (ANLF); Aceh-Sumatra National Liberation Front (NLFAS); Hassan Tiro Group; Committee of Aceh Student Reform Action

AHMADIS: Ahmadiyya Jamaat; Ahmadiyya Movement; Qadiani Jamaat; Ahmadi General Council (AGC) (Nigeria); Ahmadiyya Mission

AINU: Untari; Ainu Association of Hokkaido (Hokkaido Utari Kyokai); Ho'aido; Ainu Way; Ainu Moshiri; David Suzuki Foundation; Ainu Nation (Ainu Minzoku); Ainu Liberation Movement of Ho'aido; Ainu Association of Hokkaido

AMBONESE: Ambonese Liberation Movement (ALM); Ambonese Union; Maluku Merdeka (Free Moluccas); South Moluccan Liberation Front (Front Siwa-Lima) (SMLF); Djangan Lupa Maluku (DLM); Republic of South Moluccas

(Republik Maluku Seletan) (RMS); Ambonese Protection League; Moluku Barduan (Moluccan Freedom Party) (BP); Ambonese Union (AU); Lashkar Jesus (Jesus Army); Homeland Mission 1950 Maluku; Human Rights on the Moluccas; Permuda Rms Maluku; Laskar Cristus (Christian Army); Maluku Sovereignty Front (FKM)

ANDHRAS: Andhra Nadu Party (ANP); Telugu Desam Party (Telugu Nation); Jai Andhra; Vandemataram; Swadeshi Movement; Andhra Mahasabha; Telugu Vani Charcha; Andra Nadu Party (ANP); Andhra Jana Sangh; Janmabhoomi Movement

ARAKANESE: Arakan Liberation Party (ALP)/Arakan Liberation Army (ALA); Arakan League for Democracy; Arakan Liberation Front (ALF); Arakan Rohingya Patriotic Front (ARIO); Rohingya Patriotic Front (RPF); National United Front of Arakan (NUFA); Mujahadin; Rohingya Solidarity Organization (RSO)/Rohingya Army; Arakan Rohingya Islamic Front (ARIF); Rakhine Democracy League; All-Burma Muslim Union (ABMU); Central Rohingya Jammatul Ulama; Ittehadul Mujahiddial; Rohingya Islamic Liberation Organization (RILO); Rohingya National Alliance (RNA); Muslim Liberation Organization; National United Party of Arakan (NUPA); Arakan Army (AA); Democratic Party Arakan/Arakan Peoples Army; Arakan Rohingya National Organization/Rohingya National Army

ASSAMESE: All-Assam Gana Sangram Parishad (AAGSP); Assam People's Front (APF); Free Assam; United Liberation Front of Assam (ULFA); All-Assam Students Union (AASU)/All-Assam Students Union Volunteer Force (AASUVF); Assam People's Assembly (Asom Gana Parishad) (AGP); Rashtriya Swayamsevak Sangh; Ahom Gana Sangram Parishad (AGSP); Independence (Swadhinatar); Assamese Movement; Naturn Assam Gana Parishad (NAGP); Asom Astitwa Surksha Manch; United People's Democratic Solidarity (UPDS); Asom Jatiyatabadi Yuva Chhatra Parishad (AJYCP); Assam Chah Mazdoor Sangha (ACMS)

BALAWARIS: Balawaristan National Front (BNF); Tehrik-i-Jaffaria Pakistan (TJP); Tanzeem-e-Millat; United Front; Baltistan Students Federation (BSF); Free Balawaristan Movement (FBM); Gilgit-Baltistan Jamhoori Mahaz; Karakoram Solidarity Movement; Gilgit Baltistan United Action Forum for Self-Rule; Karakoram National Movement (KNM); Al Jehad; Northern Areas Platform; Hunza-Nagar Movement; Gilgit-Baltistan National Alliance (GBNA)

BALUCH: Baluchistan Liberation Front (BLF); Baluch People's Liberation Front (BPLF); Baluchistan People's Democratic Organization (BPDO); World Baluch Organization; Popular Front for Armed Resistance (PFAR); Baluchistan National Front (BNF); Front of Nimruz (Afghanistan); Tehrik-i-Istiqalal; Jamboary Watan Party (JWP); Balochistan National Alliance; Baluchistan Liberation Front (BLF); Baluch Pesh Merga (Baluch Volunteer Force); Baloutche Warna (Baluch Warriors Organization); Baluch Islamic Liberation Struggle; Baluch National Alliance (BNA); Unity Movement; Baluch Student Movement; Baluch National Alliance; United Baluchistan Awam Alliance; Baluch National Council (Iran); Balochistan National Party (BNP); Pakistan Oppressed Nations Movement (PONM); Popular Movement; Baluch Student's Organization-Awami (BSO-A); Baluch Students Organisation (BSO)

BODOS: Bodoland State Movement Council (BSMC); People's Democratic Front (PDF); Bodo Security Force (BSF); All-Bodo Students Union (ABSU); Bodoland Liberation Tiger Force (BTLF); Bodoland People's Party (BPP); Bodoland Army; Bodo Security Force (BSF); National Democratic Front of Bodoland (NDFB); Bodoland State Movement Council (BSMC); Bodo People's Action Committee (BPAC); Bodoland National Front (BNF); Garo National Front (GNF); Achik National Volunteers Council (ANVC); Garo National Council (GNC); Bodo Autonomous Council (BAC); All Bodo Women's Welfare Federation (ABWWF); Bodo Sahitya Sabha (BSS); People's Democratic Front (PDF)

CHAGOSSIANS: Chagossian Social Committee (Comité Social des Chagossiens) (CSC); Chagos Refugees Group (Groupe Réfugiés Chagos) (GRC); Chagossian Forum (Forum Chagossien); Chagossian Social Committee (Comité Social des Chagossiens) (Seychelles); Swiss Committee in Favor of the Chagossians (Comité Suisse de Soutien aux Chagossiens) (CSSC) (Switzerland)

CHAMS: Cham Islamic Organization (OIC); Cham National Liberation Movement (MNLC) (Cambodia/Laos); Liberation Front of Highland Champa (Front de Libération des Hauts Plateaux du Champa) (FLHPC) (Vietnam); United Front for Struggle of Oppressed Races (FULRO) (Vietnam); Liberation Front of Champa (FLC) (Vietnam)

CORDILLERANS: Cordillera Peoples Alliance (CPA); Legal Assistance Center for Indigenous Filipinos (PANLIPI); Kalinga-Bontoc Peacepact Holders' Association; Front Abu-Anu; Federation of Indigenous Peoples of the Philippines (Kalipunan ng Katutubong Mamamayan ng Pilipinas) (KAMP); Cordillera Leaders Forum (CLF); Cordillera People's Democratic Front (CPDF)/Cordillera People's Liberation Army (CPLA); Igorot International Organization (IIO); BIMAK (Canada, Australia, United States)

DAYAKS: Free Dayak Republic (Republik Dayak Merdeka) (RDM); Institute of Dayakology (Indonesia); West Kalimantan Democratic Party (PDI); Ngaju Council

EAST TIMORESE: East Timor Liberation Movement (MLTE); East Timor Committee; Revolutionary Front of Independent East Timor (FRETILIN); National Council of Maubere Resistance (CNRM); East Timorese Democratic Union (UDT); Armed Forces for the Liberation of East Timor (FALINTIL); Student Solidarity Centre for East Timor (DSMTT); People's Front for East Timor (BRTT); National Council of East Timorese Resistance (Conselho Nacional de Resistência Timorense) (CNRT)

EASTERN MONGOLS: Eastern Mongol Leagues; Solon Democratic League; Pan-Mongol Democratic Union; United Herdsmen and Farmers Party; Independence Party; United Mongol Party of Eastern Mongolia; Believer's Party; Truth Party; Unification Party of the Hulun Buir Steppes

GORKHAS: Gorkhaland National Liberation Front (GNLF); Gorkhaland Independence Movement; Gorkhaland People's Party (GPP); Darjeeling Hill Development Council (DHDC); All-India Gorkha League (Akhil Bharatiya Gorkha) (ABG); Gurkha Ex-Servicemen's Organization (GESO); Gorkha Tiger

Force (GTF); Nepal Ex-Servicemen's Association; All Gorkha Students Union (AGSU); Gorkha Liberation Organization (GLO); Trinamool Congress; Bharatiya Gorkha Jana Shakti; Rashtriya Congress

HMONGS: Hmong People-Lao Human Rights Council; Chao Fah; Hmong Resistance League; United Lao National Liberation Organization

HUI: Chungkuo Islam Djemiyeti (Chinese Islamic Association); Gazavat; Islamic Democratic Party (IDP); Moslem Brotherhood; Akhawani; Wahhabi Movement; Qinghai Islamic Association; Hui Nationality Society

IBANS: Parti Bansa Dayak Sarawak (PBDS) (Malaysia); Sarawak Iban Assocation (SIA); Sarawak National Action Party (SNAP); Sarawak Dayak Iban Assocation (Gerempong Dayak Iban Sarawak) (Sadia); North Kalimantan Liberation Front (Tentara Nasional Kalimantan Utara) (TNKU); North Kalimantan People's Forces; Sarawak People's Guerrilla Forces; Sarawak Native People's Party; People's Justice Movement (ARAK); Sahabat Alam Malaysia Sarawak

JEJUVIANS: Self Defense Force (Ja-Wee-Dae); Independence Promotion Association; Cheju April 3rd 50th Anniversary Pan-National Committee; Jeju Sinbo; Jeju April 3rd Research Institute; Hanchonryon; Jejuan Island Defense Committee

JHARKHANDIS: Adivasi Liberation Front (AFL); Chota Nagpur Plateau Praja Parisad; Jharkhand Militia; Jharkhand Mukti Morcha (Jharkhand Liberation Front) (JMM); Jharkhand People's Party (JPP); Jharkhand Party (Naren); All-Jharkhand Students Union (AJSU); Koel Karo Jan Sangathan (Koel Karo Peoples' Organization); Jharkhand Area Autonomous Council; Jharkhandis Organization for Human Rights; Jharkhand Mazdoor Kisan Sangrami Parishad; Hul Jharkhand Kranti Dal; Left Democratic Action Committee for Jharkand (Vam Jamwadi Jharkhand Rajya Sangharsh Samiti); Jharkhand Unity Forum (Jharkhand Ekta Manch); Jharkhand Chhatra Morcha

JUMMAS: Jana Samity Samity (JSS)/Shanti Bahini (Force of Peace)/Parbatya Chattagram Jana Shanghati Samiti (PCJSS); Kaderia Bahini (Army of Free Kaderia); National Movement of Free Kaderia (NMFK); Kaptai Self-Defense Organization; Chittagong Hill Tracts Women's Federation; Jumma Nation; World Chakma Organisation; Chittagong Hill Tracts People's Association (CHTPA); Chittagong Hill Tracts Solidarity Party (CHTSP); Priti Kumar Chakma; Jumma People's Network (Manabadhikar Shomonay Parishad); Hill Students Council; Jana Samhati Samiti (JSS); Jumma Peoples Alliance (JPA); Hill Peoples Organization (HPO)/Hill Peoples Council (HPC); Pahari Chhatra Parisad; Pahari Gano Parishad; Hill Women's Federation; Jumma Peoples Alert

KACHINS: Kachin Independence Organization (KIO)/Kachin Independence Army (KIA); Kachin National Defense Organization (KNDO); Kachin State National Congress for Democracy; Kachin Defense Army (KDA); Kachin Independence Union (KIU); Kachin Democratic Army (KDA)

KADAZANS: Sabah United Party (Parti Beratsu Sabah) (PBS); Kadazan Dusun Cultural Association (KDCA); United Pasok-Momogun Kadazan Organization (UPKO); Kadazandusun Language Foundation (KLF); Sabah Kadazan Association (SKA); People's Justice Party (Ankatan Keadilan Rakyat Bersatu) (AKAR);

Kadazan-Dusun-Murut Task Force; Sabah Democratic Party (Parti Demokratik Sabah) (PDS)

KARENNIS: Kayah New Land Party (KNLP); Kayah State Nationalities League for Democracy; Democratic Organization for Kayah National Unity; Moslem Liberation Organization; Karenni States Independence Army (KSIA); Kayah State Nationalities League for Democracy; Karenni Revolutionary Army (KRA); Kayah State 2nd Division; Karenni Nationalities People's Liberation Front (KNPLF); Karenni National Peoples Liberation Forces; Karenni National Progressive Party/Karenni Army; Karenni National Democratic Front/Karenni National Democratic Army

KARENS: Karen Independence Movement (KIM); Karen National Liberation Front (KNLF); Karen National Union (KNU)/Karen National Defense Organization (KNDO); Karen People's Liberation Organization (KPLO); Karen State National Organization (KSNO); Karen National United Party (KNUP)/ Karen National Liberation Army (KNLA); God's Army; Karen Organization; Karen Liberation Army (KLA); Karen National Association (KNA); Kawthoolei Moslem Liberation Force (KMLF)

KASHMIRIS: Allah Tigers; All Pakistan Jammu and Kashmir Conference; Hizbul Mujaheddin; Jammu and Kashmir Liberation Front (JKLF); Jammu and Kashmir Plebiscite Front (JKPF); Kashmir Liberation Front (KLF); Muslim Jambaz Force; Muslim Liberation Front (MLF); Muslim United Front (MUF); People's League; World Kashmir Freedom Movement; Student's Liberation Front (SLF); Al-Umar Mujaheddin; Islamic Students League; Jaanbaz Force; Hezbollah; Friends of Kashmir; National Conference; All-Party Hurriyat Conference (APHC); Ikhwan-ul-Muslameen; Hizb-ul-Mujahideen; Harakatul Ansar; Jehad Force; Al Hadid; Jamaat-i-Islami; Al-Faran; Harakat-ul-Ansar; Farooq Ahmad Kanoon; Laskar-i-Toiba; Jammu Kashmir National Awami Party (JKNA) (Pak); Kashmir National Democratic Party (KNDP) (Pak); Jammu Kashmir National Liberation Front (JKNLF) (Pak); Jammu Kashmir National Student Federation (JKNSF) (Pak); Kashmir National Alliance (KNA) (Pak); United Kashmir People's National Party (UKPNP); Islami Harkat–ul-Mumneen

KHASIS: Hynniewtrep National Volunteer Council (NHVC); Hynniewtrep National Liberation Council (HNLC); Meghalaya United Liberation Army (MULA); Hill Peoples Union (HPU); Public Demand Implementation Council (PDIC); Hill State People's Democratic Party (HSPDP); United Democratic Party (UDP); Khasi Students Union (KSU); Hynniewtrep Achik Liberation Council; Federation of Khasi, Jayantia and Garo People; People's Liberation Front of Meghalaya (PLF-M)

KHMER KROM: Khmer Kampuchea-Krom Federation (KKF); Khmer Krom Youth Scholastic Association; Khmer Krom Buddhist Association; Khmer Kampuchea Krom Association for the Protection of Human Rights; Khmer Krom Millenium Committee (Cambodia); Khmer Krom Freedom Fighters

KODAVAS: Kodagu Rajya Mukthi Morcha (KRMM); Kodava Samaj; Akhila Kodava Samaj; Kodagu Youth Congress; Karnataka Rajya Raitha Sangha (KRRS); Jai Kodagu; Jai Cavuveramme

LADAKHIS: Ladakh Buddhist Association; Ladakh Youth Association (LYA); Movement for Culture and Education; People's Movement for Free Ladakh; Ladakh State Movement; Unity

LAHU: Lahu National Organization (LNO); Lahu Democratic Force (LDF)

MALAYALIS: Kerala Socialist Party (KSP); Kerala Christian Association; Moplah Association; Muslim League; Left Front; Revolutionary Socialist Party; Islamic Sevak Sangh; World Malayali Convention (WMC); World Malayali America Regional Convention; Left Democratic Front

MANCHUS: Kao Kang Memorial League; Northeastern Development Front; Manchu Heritage National Party; Manchu Development Front; Man-Northeastern Cultural Congress; Allied Committee of the Peoples of Eastern Turkestan, Inner Mongolia, Manchuria and Tibet

MASAS: Masa Sahitya Sabha; Dimasa Student's Union (DSU); Dima Halong Daogah (DHD); Autonomous State Demand Committee (ASDC); All-Masa Hill Students Association (AMHSA); North Cachar Hills Students Front (NCHSF); Dimasa Revival Demand Committee (DRDC); Dimasa National Volunteers (DNV); Masa National Security Force (MNSF); People's Guard; North Cachar Hills District Committee

MEITHEIS: Revolutionary Government of Manipur (RGM); Revolutionary People's Front (RPF); People's Liberation Army (PLA); Manipur People's Liberation Front (MPLF); Manipur People's Party (MPP); Manipur People's Revolutionary Front (Kangleipak); Kangleipak Liberation Organization; Meithei State Army (MSA); People's Revolutionary Party of Kangleipak (PRE-PAK)/People's Revolutionary Army of Kangleipak (RAK); Ireiba Kanba Lup; Islamic National Liberation Front; Revolutionary Government of Manipur (RGM); All-Manipur Students' Union (AMSU); United National Liberation Front (UNLF); People's Liberation Army (PLA); Kangleipak Communist Party (KCP); Manipur People's Liberation Front (MPLF)/Manipur Liberation Front Army (MLFA); Kanglei Yawol Kanna Lup; United Committee Manipur (UCM); Bof Meira Paibis (Meithei Women's Organisation); Kanglei Yawol Kunna Lup (KYKL); North East Minority Front (NEMF)

MELAYUS: Riau Mandate Party (PAR); Riau Independence Movement (MIR); Riau Historical Society; Melayu National Liberation Front of Riau (MNLFR)

MIKIRS: Karbi Students Association (KSA); Mikir Homeland Front (MHF); Karbi People's Front (KPF); Karbi National Volunteers (KNV); United People's Democratic Solidarity (UPDS); Karbi Anglong Party; People's Guard; Autonomous State Demand Committee (ASDC); Karbi Anglong-North Cachar Hills Autonomous State Demand Committee (KANCHASDCOM)

MIZOS: Mizo National Front (MNF)/Mizo National Army (MNA); Republic of Mizoram (ROM); Mizo Union (MU); Mizo People's Conference (Peoplesí Conference); Mizoram Zirlai Pawl (MZP); Young Mizo Organization; Mizo People's Convention (HPC); United People's Party (UPP)

MOHAJIRS: Mutahida Quami Party (MQP); Muttaheda Qaumi Movement (MQM); Muthiida National Movement (MNM); Mohajir Qaumi Movement-Alataf Group (MQM-A); Mohajir Qaumi Movement-Haqiqi Group (MQM-H);

National Solidarity Council (Milli Yekjehati) (MYC); All-Pakistan Muhajir Student Organization; Naim Sheri; Nadeem Commandos; Khidmat-e-Khalq Foundation (KKF)

MONS: Mon National Defense Organization (MNDO); Mon National Democratic Front; New Mon State Party (NMSP)/Mon National Liberation Army (MNLA); Mon People's Front (MPF); For a Democratic Honsawatoi (DH); Mon Unity League (MUL); Monland Restoration Council (MRC) (United States); Mon Community; Mon Naional Democratic Front (MNDF); Mon Freedom League (MFL); Mon United Front (MUF); National Council of Mon; Mon National Students Union (AMNSU); United Mon Patriotic Forces; Beik Mon Army (BMA)

MONTAGNARDS: The Montagnard Foundation; Dega Republic; The Montagnard/Dega International Human Rights Committee; Barajaka; Unified Front for the Struggle of Oppressed Races (Front Unifié de Lutte des Races Opreemées) (FULRO); Dega Highlands Liberation Front (Front de Liberation des Hauts-Plateaux Montagnard) (FLHPM); Human Rights Committee of the Dega Republic; Armed Forces of the Central Highlands; Dega Montagnard Association (DMA) (USA); Ethnic Minorities Solidarity Movement (EMSM); Vietnam Nationalities Cultural Association

MOROS: Moro National Liberation Front (MNLF)/Bangsa Moro Army (BMA); Moro Islamic Front (MILF); Bangska Moro Islamic Party; Bangska Moro National Liberation Front (BMNLF); Moro Autonomist Movement; Abu Sayyaf (Sword of the Father); Mindanao Independence Movement (MIM); Islamic Command Council; Union of Islamic Forces and Organizations (UIFO); Ansar el Islam; Moro National Liberation Front-Reformist Group (MNLF-Reformist Group); Muslim Reform Party; Islamic Missionary Movement; Confederation of Major Muslim Organizations of the Philippines; Maranao Islamic Brotherhood; Lumad Mindanaw Peoples Federation; Islamic Command Council

NAGAS: Naga Peoples Movement for Human Rights; National Socialist Council of Nagaland (NSCN); Nationalist Socialist Council of Nagaland-Isak-Muviah (NSCNIM); Naga National Council (NNC); National Socialist Council of Nagaland-Khaplang (NSCN–K); Naga Lim Army (NLA); People's Liberation Army; Naga Peoples' Convention (NPC); Nagaland Federal Government (NFG); Naga Nationalist Organization (NNO); United Front of Nagaland (UDF); Naga Students Federation; Naga Army; Angami Public Organization (APO); Chakhesang Public Organization (CPO); Sumi Hoho; Naga Tribal Council (Naga Hoho); United Naga Council of Manipur; All-Naga Students Association of Manipur; Naga Peoples Movement for Human Rights; Nagaland People's Council; Naga National Liberation Front (NNLF); Naga Hill Regional Progressive Party

NORTHERN TAI: Democratic United Front; Tai Zhuang Federation; United Nationalities Democratic Movement; Zhuang Strategic Alliance; Northern Tai National Organization (Thailand)

OKINAWANS: New State Organization; Okinawa Independence Party (OIP); Okinawa Independence League; Ryuku Islands Movement; Republican Movement of the Anami and Ryuku Islands (REMARI)

PA-O: Pa-O National Organization (PONO)/Pa-O National Army (PONA); Pao Shan Independence Party (PSIP); Union Paoh National Organization (UPNO); Paoh Nation Movement; Pa-O Women Union; Pa-O People's Liberation Organization (PPLO)

PALAUNGS: Palaung State Libration Party (PSLP); Palaung State Liberation Organization (PSLO)/Palaung State Liberation Army (PSLA)

PATTANIS: National Revolutionary Front (NRF); Islamic Republic of Pattani (IRP); Muslim Liberation Front; Pattani National Liberation Front (PNLF); Pattani United Liberation Organization (Pertubuhan Perbesan Patani Bersatu) (PULO); Patani National Youth Movement (Panyom); Hikayat Patani; Gerater Patani Malays' Movement (GEMPAR); National Revolutionary Front (Barisan Revolusi Nasional) (BRN); Muslim Commando Unit; Tantra Jihad Islam (TJI); Bersatu/National Patani Malay-Muslim Armed Forces (Tentera Nasional Melayu Patani) (TNMP)

PUSHTUNS: Mazdoor Kissan Party; National Democratic Party (NDP); Awami National Party (ANP); National Party of Pushtunistan (NPP); People's Democratic Party of Afghanistan (PDPA); Hizb-i-Watan (Homeland); Jehadi Shoora; Pakistan Oppressed Nations Movement (PONM); Afghanistan: Ittehad-i-Islami; Hizb-i-Islami; Taliban; Awami Action Committee; Khidai Khedmantgar (God's Servitors); Pakhtoon Khawa Milli Awanu Party; Pakhtoon wa Qaumi Party; Azad Pushtunistan; Khuda-i-Khidmatgar; Mazdoor Kissan Party; National Democratic Party; Pakhtun Front (PF); Pashtunkywa Milli Awami Party (PMAP) (Pakistan)

RABHAS: Rabha National Security Force (RNSF); Rabha Sahitya Sabha; Berek Rabha Kraurang (All Rabha Satiya Sabha); Rabha Sasong Surkhya Parishad (RHSP); Rabha People's Conference (RPC); Rabha Student's Union (RSU); Rabha Hasong Coordinating Committee (RHAC)

RAJBANGSIS: Koch Rajbangsi Sanmilani; Kamatapur State Movement; Kamatapur Peoples Party (KPP)/Kamatapur Liberation Organization (KLO); All Kamatapur Students' Union (AKSU); Kamatapur Women's Rights Front (KWRF); Koch Rajbangsi Protection Force (KRPF); Betna Mouza Koch Rajbangsi Sanmilani (BMKRS); Koch Rajbangsi Security Force (KRSF); All Assam Koch Rajbangsi Sanmilani; All Assam Yuba Chatra Sanmilani; Koch Liberation Force (KLF)

SANTHALS: Adivasi Cobra Force (ACF); Tea Tribes Liberation Front (TTLF); Adivasi Liberation Front (ALF); Santhal Militia; Adivasi Sewa Samity; All Adivasi Students' Association of Assam (AASAA); Johar Adivasi; All Santhal Cobra Force (ASCF); Adivasi Council of Assam; Bircha Commando Force (BCF); Adivasi Security Force (ASF); All Assam Adivasi Suraksha Samiti (AAASS); All Assam Tea Tribes Students' Association (AATTSA); Adivasi National Commando Force (ANCF); Adivasi Security Force (ASF); Santhal State Movement

SHANS: Shan State Progressive Party (SSPP)/Shan State Army (SSA); Shan United Revolutionary Army (SURA); Mongtai Revolutionary Army (MUA); Pao Shan Independence Party; Shan State Kokang Democratic Party; Shan Nationalities League for Democracy; Shan National Organization (SNO)/Shan

National Army (SNA); Shan State Army Eastern (SSAE); Shan State Restoration Council; Shan Democratic Union (SDU); Tai Revolutionary Council (TRC); Shan United Army (SUA); Shan Nationalities League for Democracy (SNLD); National Democratic Alliance Army (NDAA); Shan United Revolutionary Army (SURA); Shan State National Congress (SSNC); Mong Tai Army (MTA); Shan State National Army (SSNA); Shan States Organization (SSO); Eastern Shan State Army (ESSA); Shan Nationalities Peoples' Liberation Organization (SNPLO); Restoration Council of the Shan State

SIKHS: All-India Sikh Students Federation (AISSF); Babbar Khalsa International (BKI); Khalistan Liberation Army; Khalsa Dal; Sikh Youth Federation; Panthic Committee; Pure Tigers; Khalistan Liberation Front (KLF); Council of Khalistan; Eternal Party (Akali Dal); All-India Shiromani Akali Dal; Panthic Committee; Khalistan Commando Force (KCF); Bhindranwale Militant Group; Sikh International Organization (SIO); Shaheed Khalsa Force (SKF); Sikh Youth Federation (SYF); Bhinderanwala Tiger Force; Saheed Khalsa Force; Khalistan Liberation Tiger Force; Khalistan National Army (KNA); Saheed Khalsa Force; Azad Khalistan

SIKKIMESE: National Party of Sikkim (NPS); Sikkim Democratic Front (Sikkim Sangram Parishad) (SSP); Movement for the Restoration and Independence of Sikkim; Sikkim National Party; Sikkim Ekta Manch

SINDHIS: Jamaat-i-Islami; Jiya Sind (Free Sind Movement); Sind National Liberation Front; Sind National Liberation and Independence Movement; Sind People's Movement; Sindhi National Alliance; Sindu Desh (Sind Nation); Jumma Party of Sindu Desh; National Liberation Front (Quomi MNahaz-i-Azadi); Jiya Sindh Progressive Party; Jiya Sindh Student Federation; Sindh Ittehad Tehrik (SIT); Jeay Sindh Mahaz (SJM); Pakistan Oppressed Nations Movement (PONM); World Sindhi Institute (WSI); World Sindhi Congress (WSC); Sindhi Awami Tehrik (SAT); Sind People's Movement (Sind Swami Tehrik) (SST); Sindh Democrats Group

SOUTH SULAWESIS: South Sulawesi Coalition; Diang Parani National Front (DPNF); Muslim Student's Action Front; Muhammadiyah; United Sulawesi Development Party; Forum Informatika Komunikasi (FIK); Petta Puang; Sulawesi Merdeka Taena

SOUTH VIETNAMESE: Coalition of Vietnamese National Parties (Lien Dang Cach Mang Vietnam) (LDCMV); National Liberation Front of South Vietnam; Vietnam Anti-Communist League; Quoc Han (Black April); Vietnam Religious Alliance; Front for the Struggle of Oppressed Races (FULRO); Vietnamese Refugees Association; Free Viet Coalition; Association for the Restoration of the Nation of Viet-Nam; Democratic Alliance; Vietnamese Restoration Party (Phuc Viet Dan Toc Dang); Vietnamese Peoples' Block for National Restoration (Khoi Dan Toc Phuc Quoc); Vietnamese Populist Movement; South Vietnamese Resistance Force/Mekong Delta; Vietnamese Freedom Force/Saigon; Western Regional Resistance Force-4th Corp; Eastern Regional Resistance Force-3rd Corp; Student Association for Free Vietnam; Black Sail Group (Roman Catholics); Black Dragon Force; Yellow Crab Force (Cao Dai); White Tigers (Hoa Hao); Overseas Free Vietnam Association

SOUTHERN MONGOLS: Southern Mongolian Freedom Federation (SMFF); Free Inner Mongolia; Inner Mongolian People's Party (IMPP); Mongolian Democratic Alliance; Association of Mongols; Democratic Union; People's Revolutionary Party; Ulanfu Revolutionary Association; United Leagues of Mongolia; League of the Forty-Nine Banners; Southern Mongolian Independence Party; Association of Mongolian National Culture; Inner Mongolian League for Human Rights; Inner Mongolia Revival Movement; Inner Mongolian Youth Center; Allied Committee of the Peoples of Eastern Turkestan, Inner Mongolia, Manchuria and Tibet

TAI: Central Tai Committee; Overseas Tai Association of Vietnamese; National Cultural Movement of the Black Tai (Tay Dam)

TAIWANESE: Democratic Progressive Party (DPP); Formosa Independence Movement; New Nation Alliance; New Constitution Alliance; Organization for Taiwan Nation-Building; Taiwan Independence Movement; World United Formosans; Taiwan Democratic Party; Taiwan Independence Party (TAIP); World Formosans for Independence; People First Party (PFP); Taiwan Solidarity Union (TSU)

TAMILS: World Tamil Association (WTA); People's Front of the Liberation Tigers (PFLT)/Liberation Tigers of Tamil Eelam (LTTE); People's Liberation Organization of Tamil Eelam; Eelam People's Revolutionary Liberation Front (EPRLF); Tamil United Liberation Front (TULF); Eelam National Liberation Front (ENDLF); Ceylon Workers' Congress (CWC); All-India Ana Dravida Munnetra Kazhagam (AADMK) (India); World Tamil Movement (WTA); Dravidian Progressive Federation (Dravida Munnetra Kazhagam) (DMK) (India); Tamil Liberation of Front of Tamil Nadu (India); Free Tamil Movement (India); Dravidian Federation (Dravida Kazhagam) (India); Tamil National Forum; Tamil Nadu Liberation Front (TNLF)/Tamil Nadu Liberation Army (TNLA) (India); Marumalarchi Dravida Munnetra Kazhagam (MDMK) (India); Tamil Nadu Students Anti-Hindi Agitation Council; Tamil Maanila Congress (India); Tamilaga Janata (India); Ellalan Force; Free Tamil Nadu (FTN) (India)

TAVOYANS: Myeik-Dawei United Front (MDUF); Tavoyan Women's Union; Kalayanamitra Council; Myeik-Dawei Alliance Front; Myeik-Dawei District Unity Front; Tavoyan Human Rights Foundation

TELENGANAS: Jai Telengana Party (JTP); Telengana Mahasabha; Telengana Movement; Telengana People's Association (Telangang Praja Samithi) (TPS); Telengana Development Forum (TDF); Telengana Praja Party (TPP); Telangana Rashtra Samithi; Telangana Congress Legislators Forum; Telengana Nadu (Telengana Nation)

TIBETANS: National Democratic Party of Tibet (NDPT); Tibetan National Movement; Tibetan Government-in-Exile; World Tibetan Organization; Tibet Support Group; International Campaign for Tibet; Tibet Information Network (United Kingdom); Tibetan Government-in-Exile (India); Free Tibet Network; Allied Committee of the Peoples of East Turkestan, Inner Mongolia, Manchuria and Tibet; Tibetan Youth Congress (TYC); International Tibetan Independence Movement

TRIPURIS: National Liberation Front of Tripura (NLFT)/Borok Army; Tripura People's Liberation Front (TPLF); Tripura National Volunteers (TNV); Tripura Tribal National Volunteers (TTNV); Borok Nation of Twipra Kingdom; Tripura People's Democratic Front (TPDF); All-Tripura Tiger Force (ATTF); Tripura Liberation Organization Front (TLOF); Tripura Tribal Youth League (Tripura Upjati Juba Samiti) (TUJS); Youth Tribal Force of Tripura (YTFT); Tripura Tribal Volunteer Force (TTVF); All Tripura Volunteers Association (ATVA); Tripura Liberation Organization (TLO); Tripura Resurrection Army (TRA); National Militia Force (NMF); Tripura Tribal National Council (TTNC); Indigenous Peoples Front of Tripura (IPFT); Tripura Liberation Froce (TLF); Tripura Rajya Raksha Bahini (TRRB); National Liberation Front of Twipra (NLFT); Tripura Hill Peoples Party; National Militia Force (NMF); Indigenous People's Front of Tripura (IPFT); Tripura People's Democratic Front (TPDF); Tripura Pradesh Youth Congress

UIGHURS: Eastern Turkish National Revolutionary Front; Eastern Turkish Party; East Turkestan Cultural Association; Front for the Liberation of Uigherstan; Islamic Party of East Turkestan; National Liberation Front; Turki National Front; Joint National Liberation Front of East Turkestan; East Turkestani Union; Uighur Human Rights Coalition; Allied Committee of the Peoples of Eastern Turkestan, Inner Mongolia, Manchuria and Tibet; East Turkestan Refugee Committee; International Taklamakan Human Rights Association; Eastern Turkestan National Freedom Center; World Uighur Network; East Turkistan Center; Inter-Republican Uighur Association; Regional Uighur Association (Kazakhstan); Vijdan Avazi (Voice of Conscience) (Kyrgyzstan); United National Revolution Front of East Turkestan (Kazakhstan); Home of East Turkestan Youth

UTTARAKHANDIS: Uttarakhand Revolutionary Front (Uttarakhand Kranti Dal) (UKD); Uttarakhand United Struggle Association (Uttarakhand Chattra Sangharsh Samiti) (UCSS); Chipko Movement; Uttarakhand Joint Action Committee (Uttarakhand Sanyukta Sangarsh Samiti) (USSS); Uttaranchal Association of North America (UANA); Uttarakhand Environmental Education Center; Bahujan Samaj Party; Trinamul Congress; Uttaranchal Patrika; Uttarakhand Sarvodaya Mandal (USM); Dashauli Gram Swarajya Sangh (DGSS); Uttarakhand Jan Sangarsh Vahini (UJSV); Jai Uttarakhand; Sri Bhuvaneshwari Mahila Ashram (SBMA); Uttarakhand Jan Morcha (UJM)

WA: Wa National Organization (WNO)/Wa National Army (WNA); Wa States Independence Movement; Wa States Organization; Wah Democratic League; Wa National Development Party; United Wa Organization (UWO)/United Wa State Army (UWSA); Wa Army (WA); Wa Welfare Society (WWS); Wa People (Wa Pwi); Lawa Nationality Association (China)

ZOMIS: Chin National Front (CNF)/Chin National Army (CNA); Zomi National Front; Zomi National Congress; Chin National League for Democracy (CNLD); Chin Human Rights Organization (CHRO); Chin-Kuki Revolutionary Front (India); Zomi Revolutionary Volunteers (ZRV) (India); Zomi National Congress (ZNC); Revolutionary National Party (RNP); Hill Tribal Liberation Organization (HTLO) (India); Chin National Force (CNF); Chin Unity Movement; Zomi Revolutionary Army (ZRA); Kuki National Front (KNF)/Kuki National Army (KNA)

EUROPE

Albania: Aromanians; Epirotes; Roms

Austria: Tyroleans; Vorarlbergers

Belgium: Flemish; Walloons

Bosnia and Herzegovina: Montenegrins; Roms

Bulgaria: Aromanians; Pomaks; Roms; Rumelian Turks

Croatia: Istrians; Venetians; Vojvodines

Cyprus: Northern Cypriots

Czech Republic: Moravians; Roms

Denmark: Faeroese; Frisians; Scanians

Estonia: Ingrians; Livonians; Votes

Finland: Alanders; Ingrians; Karels; Samis

France: Alsatians; Basques; Bretons; Burgundians; Catalans; Corsicans; Dauphinois; Flemish; Ligurians; Normans; Occitans; Roms; Savoyards; Walloons

Germany: Bavarians; Frisians; Rhinelanders; Roms; Saxons; Sorbs; Swabians

Greece: Aromanians; Pomaks; Roms; Rumelian Turks

Hungary: Roms; Vojvodines

Italy: Emilians; Friulis; Giulians; Ladins; Lombards; Neapolitans; Occitans; Piedmontese; Roms; Sards; Savoyards; Seborgans; Sicilians; Tyroleans; Venetians; Waldensians

Latvia: Livonians

Lithuania: Karaims

Macedonia: Aromanians; Roms; Rumelian Turks

Moldova: Dniestrians; Gagauz

Netherlands: Frisians

Norway: Samis

Poland: Carpatho-Rusyns; Kashubians; Roms; Serbs

Portugal: Azoreans; Galicians; Leonese; Madeirans

Romania: Aromanians; Roms; Saxons; Szeklers

Slovakia: Carpatho-Rusyns; Roms

Slovenia: Istrians; Venetians

Spain: Andalusians; Aragonese; Asturians; Basques; Canarians; Cantabrians; Catalans; Galicians; Leonese; Occitans; Roms

Sweden: Alanders; Samis; Scanians

Switzerland: Jurassians; Lombards; Romands; Romansch; Savoyards

Transnational: Roms

Turkey: Pomaks; Roms; Rumelian Turks

Ukraine: Carpatho-Rusyns; Crimean Tatars; Gagauz; Jews; Karaims; Western Ukrainians

United Kingdom: Cornish; Gibraltarians; Guernseians; Jerseians; Manx; Northern Irish; Northumbrians; Orcadians; Roms; Scots; Shetlanders; Welsh

Yugoslavia (Serbia and Montenegro): Aromanians; Kosovars; Montenegrins; Roms; Sanjakis; Vojvodines

NATIONAL ORGANIZATIONS BY NATION: EUROPE

ALANDERS: Aaland Independence Party; Alänsk Center; Liberlerna på Aland; Stiftelsen Skånsk Framtid

ALSATIANS: Elsässiche Volksunion; Elsass-Lothringischer Volksbund; National Forum of Alsace-Lorraine (Nationalforum Elsass-Lothringer/Forum Nationaliste d'Alsace-Lorraine) (NEL); Alsatian People's Union (Union du Peuple Alsacien/Elsassische Volksunion) (UPE/EVU); Nationalist Forum (FN); Autonomist Front; Free Alsace; Home League (Heimatbund); Language and Culture; Black Wolves Alsatian Combat Group (Schwarzen Wölfe); Union pour L'Alsace (UPA); Association of Fidelity to the Alsatian Homeland

ANDALUSIANS: Andalusian Liberation Front (FLA); Andalusian Party (Partido Andalucista) (PA); Andalusian Nationalist Movement (MNA); Liberación Andaluza; Andalusian Nation (Nacíon Andaluza) (NA); Asamblea Andaluza; Revolucionarios de Andalucía (Andalusian Revolutionaries); Andalusian Left (Izquierda Andaluza)

ARAGONESE: Consello d'a Fabla Aragonesa (Counsel of the Aragonese Language); Ligallo de Fablans de l'Aragonés (Aragonese Speakers' League); Nogara (Asociación Cultural Autonomist); Dogana Aragonés; Aragonese Party (Partido Aragones) (PAR); Aragon Council (Chunta Aragonesista) (CHA)

AROMANIANS: Society Farsarotul (USA); Congress of Macedonian-Romanian Culture; Association of French Aromanians (France) (AFA); Trâ Armânami; Uniunea trâ Limba shi Cultura Armânâ (Germany); Armâneasca Sutsatâ de Culturâ (Australia); Sutsata Armânjlor Pitu Guli de Scopia (Macedonia); Comunitatea Armânjlor di Romania; Uniunea Mljearilor di Iutsudo (Romania); Sutsata Vlahilor di Elvetsia (Greece); Fundatsia Gramostea (USA); Fundatsia Cartea Armânâ di Custantsa/Dobrogea (Romania); Aromânii din Albania (Vlach Society) (Albania); League of Vlachs (Macedonia); Pan-Hellenic Vlach Society; Union for Arumanian Language and Culture (ULCA) (Germany); Sperantsa (Hope); Uniunea Mljearilor di Iutsudo (Romania); Panhellenic Union of Vlach Cultural Associations (Greece); International Association of Vlachs; Societatea Cultura Aromani; Communitatea Aromani din Romania (Romania)

ASTURIANS: Asturian Party (Partíu Asturianista) (PAS); Xunta pola Defensa de la Llingua (Association for the Defense of the Asturian Language); El Garrapiellu; Asturian Left (Andecha Astur/La Izquierda d'Asturies); Nationalist Left of Asturias (Izquierda Nacionaliega d'Asturies) (INA); Afayaivos n'Asturies; Puxa Asturies; La Izquierda d'Asturies; Asturian Nationalist Council (Conceyu Nacionalista Astur) (CNA); Autodetermin Asturies; Pais Astur; Asturies ye Nacion; Asturian Nacionalist Assembly (Ensame Nacionalista Astur) (ENA); Asturian Communist Movement (Movimiento Comunista Asturiano) (MCA); Asturian Nationalist Joint Assembly (Xunta Nacionalista Asturiana) (XNA)

AZOREANS: Azorean National Movement (MNA); Front for the Liberation of the Azores (Frente de Libertação dos Açores) (FLA); National Liberation Front (FNL); Social Democratic Party (PDC); Azorean Liberation Front (ALA); Democratic Party of the Atlantic (PDA)

BASQUES: Basque National Party (Partido Nationalists Vasco) (PNV); Basque Fatherland and Liberty (Euzkadi ta Azkaltazuna) (ETA); Euzkal Zizentasuna; Iparretarrak (Those of the North) (IK) (France); Iraultaz; Commandos de Iparreuskadi (Commandos of North Euzkadi) (France); Lurraldea; Euskadiko Eskerra; Iraultza; Elkarri; Basque Left (Euskadiko Ezkerra) (EA); Euskal Herritarok (EH); Hegoalde; Basque National Liberation Movement (MLNV); Getera Pro-Amnistia; Forward (Jarrai); Gazteriak (Youth) (France); Basque Solidarity (Eusko Alkartasuna); Kale Borroka (Urban Fight)

BAVARIANS: Bavarian Party (Bayernpartei); Christian Social Union (Christlich-Soziale Union) (CSU); European National Movement; Bavarian Catholic Alliance; Free Bavaria Movement (Freies Bayern); Bavarian Liberation Army (BLA)

BRETONS: Araok Breizh (Forward Brittany); Breton Liberation Front (BLF)/ Breton Liberation Army (BLA); Emgann; Breton Popular Aid; Front for Socialism and Liberation; Givenn Ha Du (Black and White); Republican Army; Front Breton; Breton Democratic Union (Union Démocratique Bertonne) (UDB); Party for the Organization of a Free Brittany (Parti pour l'Organisation d'une Bretagne Libre) (POBL); Comité Action Régionale de Bretagne: Kuzul ar Brezhoneg; Breton Republican Army (BRA); Breton Fight (Argaz Breizh); Breton Organization Movement (MOB); Breton Secret Army; National Breton Resistance Movement (MNRB); Liberation Front of Brittany for National Liberation and Socialism; Breton Revolutionary Army (ARB)

CANARIANS: Canary National Congress (CNC); Canary Nation; Movement for the Autonomy and Independence of the Canary Archipelago (Movimiento por la Autodeterminación y la Independencia de Archipiélago Canario) (MAIAC); Canary People's Union (UPC); Movement for the Independence of the Canary Islands (MIIC); Canary National Assembly (ACN); Asamblea Majorera (AM); Union Nacionalista de Izquerida (UNI); Coalición Canaria (CC); Free Canaries Movement (Canarian Libre) (CL); Popular Front for the Independence of the Canary Islands (Frepic-Awañak); Alternative Canaries (Canarias Alternativa); Canarian Nationalist Party (Partido Nacionalista Canario) (PNC); National Congress of the Canaries (Congreso Nacional de Canarias) (CNC), Progressive Union of the Canarian Islands (Unidad Progresista de Canarias) (UPCAN)

CANTABRIANS: United Cantabria Association (ATROPU); Labaru Cantabru; Association for the Defense of Cantabrian Interests (Asociación de Defensa de los Intereses de Cantabria) (ADIC); Partido Regionalista de Cantabria (PRC); Juventudes Regionalistas de Cantabria (JRC); Cantabrian Nationalist Council (Conceju Nacionaliegu Cántabru) (CNC)

CARPATHO-RUSYNS: Provisional Government of Subcarpathian Rus'; Ruska Bursa Association; Society of Carpatho-Rusyns (Obscestvo Karpatskych Rusynov) (Ukraine); Rusyn Renaissance Society (Rusinska Obroda) (Slovakia); Rusyn Matka Society (Yugoslavia); World Congress of Rusyns; Organization of Rusyns (Hungary); Institute of Rusyn Language and Culture (Slovakia); Sarkarpatske Ziganske Kulturno-Prosvitne Tovaristvo (SZKPT); Society of Friends of Subcarpathian Rus' (Spolecnost pratel Podkarpatske Rusi) (SPR) (Czech Republic); Democratic League of Nationalities of Transcarpathia; Duchnovych Society; Amaro Drom; Lemko Association (Stowarzyszenie Lemków) (Poland); Lemk Union (Poland); Lemk Citizen Circle (Poland)

CATALANS: Convergence and Union (CIU); Movement for the Defense of the Nation (Moviment de Defensa de la Terra) (MDT); La Crida a la Solidaritat (The Call to Solidarity); Republican Left of Catalonia (Esquerra Republicana de Catalunya) (ERC); Lluita; Catalan Liberation Front (FLC); Unió Valenciana (UV); Partit Valencià Nacionalista (PVN); Unió del Poble Valencià (UPV); Unió Mallorquin (UM); Terra Lliure (Free Land); Socialist Liberation Party; Catalunya Lliure; Patronat Català Pro Europa; Unitat Catalana (France); Plataforma per la Unitat d'Acció (PUA); Consell National Català; Bloc d'Estudiants Independentistes; Partit de els Països Catalans; Joves d'Esquerra Nacionalista; Catalan Liberation Front (Front de Alliberament Català) (France); Forward, Socialist Organization for National Liberation (Endavant, Organització Socialista d'Alliberament Nacional); Valencian Front (Front del País Valencià) (FPV); Nationalist Valencia Party (Partit Valencià Nacionalista) (PVN); Socialist National Liberation Party of the Catalan Countries (Partit Socialista d'Alliberament Nacional dels Països Catalans) (PSAN); PSM-Nationalist Entity (PSM-Entesa Nacionalista) (Balear Islands); Valencia Nationalist Bloc (Bloc Nacionalista Valencià) (Valencia); Valencian Left (Esquerra Valenciana) (EV); Valencian Nationalist Left (Esquerra Nacionalista Valenciana) (ENV) (Valencia)

CORNISH: Cornish National Movement (CNM); Cornish National Party (CNP); Stannary Court; Mebyon Kernow (Sons of Cornwall/Cornish National Party) (MK); Democratic Party of Cornwall; Celtic League; Cornish Language Board; Celtic Society; Cowethas Flamank; Cornish Solidarity

CORSICANS: Action for the Renaissance of Corsica; A Riscossa; Accolta Natiunali Corsa (ANC); Luta per l'Indipendenza; A Cuncolta; Corsican National Liberation Front (FLNC)/Corsican National Liberation Army (ALNC); Regional Action Committee; Union of the Corsican People (UPC); Muvimentu per l'Autodeterminazione (Movement for Self-Determination); Resistance (Resistenza); National Liberation Army of Corsica; Corsican Army (Armata Corsa); Scelta Nova; Corsican Liberation Army (ALC); Movement for Self-Determination (MPA); Corsican National Liberation Front Canal Historique (FLNCCH)/Cunculta Naziunalista (CN); Unione di u Populu Corsu; Corsican National Liberation Front-Historic Wing (FLNC-HW); Movement of the National Left (Muvimentu di a Manca Naziunale); Party for Independence (Partitu pa l'Indipendenza / Parti pour l'Indépendance) (PPI)

CRIMEAN TATARS: Crimean Tatar National Movement (Krimsko Tatskogo Natsyonalnogo Dvijenya) (OKND); Kirim Tatar Milli Meclisi (Milli Mejlis); Crimea; Crimean Tatar Youth Union; Committee for the Return of the Exiled Crimean Tatars; Incentive Group; Mili Firka; National Movement of Tatars; Organization of the Crimean Tatars National Movement; Republican Movement of Crimea (RDK); Rebirth of Crimea Foundation (RCF); Organization of the Crimean-Tatar Ethnic Movement; Crimean Tatar Congress (Kulturai); National Movement of the Crimean Tatars (Natsyonalynia Dvijenia Krimsky Tatar) (NDKT)

DAUPHINOIS: Ligue Dauphinoise; Critérium Dauphiné Libéré (CDL); Conseil des Vallées; Delphinal Council

DNIESTRIANS: National Unionist Movement; Dniestrian Republican Guard; Communist Party of Trans-Dniestria; Government of Cis-Dniestrian Moldova (GCM); Yedintsvo; Unity/Socialist Block

EMILIANS: Emilian League (Liga Emiliana); Libertà Emiliana; Nazione Emilia; Northern League (Lega Nord) (LN); Movimento per l'Autogoverno; Emilia e Libre; Terra Emiliana/Gruppo Culturale Terra Emiliana; Popol di' Emellia; Rivoluzione Emiliana; Free Europe Alliance (ALE); Agora Politic

EPIROTES: Panepirotic Federation; Student Movement for Epirus (ENVI); Democratic League of North Epirus; Democratic Union of the Greek Ethnic Minority in Albania (Omonia/Harmony); Struggle for North Epirus; North Ipiros Liberation Front (MAVI); Union for Human Rights Party; Initiative Committee for Northern Epirus; Epirotean Patriotic Organization; Government of Epirus in Exile (GEE)

FAEROESE: Home Rule Party (Sjálvstyrisflokkurin); Faeroese Independence Party/Republican Party (Tjóveldisflokurin); Socialist Independence Party

FLEMISH: Vlaamse Volksbeweging; Flemish Block (Vlaams Blok) (VB); Davidsfonds; Volksunie; Independence Organization of Flanders; Taal Aktie Komitee (TAK); Stop Euro-Brussels; Flemish Military Order; Flemish Union of France; Joris van Severn Group (France); Flemish Liberal Democratic Party (VLD); Flemish National Democrats (VND); Alliance for Freedom in Flanders (AFF); Flemish Republican Party (FRP); Flemish Freedom and Unity (FFU)

FRISIANS: Frisian National Organization; Fryske Kultuerried; In Fryske Akysjeploesch; Frisian Council; Foriining for Nationale Friiske (FNF) (Netherlands); Nordfriesischer Verein (Germany); Ried fan de Fryske Beweging; Frisian National Party (Frysk Nasjonale Partij) (FNP); Westfriese in den Niederlanden (WN); Foriining for Nationale Friiske (FNF)

FRIULIS: Moviment Friül (Friuli National Movement) (MF); Doxa; Union Furland (UF); Liga Friül (Friulian League); Famèe Furlane; Institute of the Friuli Culture (Institut de Culture Furlane) (ICF); The Ladin-Friulian Institute; Dumblis

GAGAUZ: Gagauz Khalki (Gagauz Nation) (GK); Gagauz Language Society; Republican Movement; Gagauze Republic; National Convention; Vatan Party; Gagauz People's Party; Communist Party of Gagauzia

GALICIANS: Union of the Galician People (Unión do Pobo Galego) (UPG); Galiza Ciebe (Free Galicia); Armed Galician League (Liga Armada Gallega) (LAG); Galician National Block (Bloque Nacionalista Galego) (BNG); Galician Popular Front (Frente Popular Galego) (FPG)/Guerrilla Army of the Free Galician People (Exército Guerrilleiro do Pobo Galego Ciebe) (EGPGC); Galician National Party; Movement for National Liberation (MLN); Asamblea do Povo Unido; Bloque Nationalista Gallego (BNG); Comissão pró-Autonomia do Nordeste Transmontano (Portugal); Alternative Revolutionary Left (Esquerda Revolucionaria Alternativa) (ERA); Popular Unity (Unidade Popular); Left of Galicia (Esquerda de Galicia) (EdeG); Nationalist Left (Esquerda Nacionalista) (EN)

GIBRALTARIANS: Association for the Advancement of Civil Rights (AACR); European Movement; Gibraltar National Party (GNP); Gibraltar Social Democrats (GSD); Gibraltar Socialist Labor Party (SGLP); British Party; Self-Determination for Gibraltar Group (SDGG)

GUERNSEIANS: L'Assembllaïe d'Guernesíais; National Organization of Guernsey (NOG)

GUILIANS: Julian League (Liga Giulia); Trieste List (Associazione per Trieste) Lega Triestina (Trieste League); Trieste Green Movement; Associazione per Trieste (Trieste Autonomy Movement); Umilo Movement (UM)

ISTRIANS: Istrian Union; Istrian Democratic Forum (IDF); Istrian People's Party (IPP); Asociata Culturale lu Istro-Rumeni; Istrian Democratic Assembly (Istarski Demokratski Sabor/Dieta Democratica Istriana) (IDA); Unione Istriana (UI) (Italy); Unione degli Italiani (UDI); United Istria Movement; Istrian Independence Party (IIP)

JERSEIANS: L'Assembliée d'Jèrriais; Pro-European Forum of Jersey

JURASSIANS: Juran Independence Movement (Mouvement Indépendantiste Jurassien) (MIJ); Assemblée Interjurassienne; Jura Regional Association (Association Régionale Jura) (ARJ); Rams Party (Bélier Groupe); Parti Socialiste du Jura Bernois; Jura Liberation Front (FLJ); Comité de Moutier; Rassemblement Jurassien; Women's Association for the Defense of the Jura; Avenir; Alliance Jurassienne

KARAIMS: Karaite Movement; Karaite Reformation Movement; Karaim Revival Movement; National Karaite Movement; Crimean Karaim Community Congress

KASHUBIANS: Kashubian-Pomeranian Association (Zrzeszenie Kaszubsko Pomorskie) (ZKP); Kashub Nation (Kaszubskiego); Kashubian Congress; Pomeranian Union; Kashubian Cross

KOSOVARS: Kosova Liberation Army (KLA); Democratic League of Kosova (LDK); Union of Kossovars (United States); Movement for the Liberation of Kosova (UCK); Democratic Party of Kosova; Albanikos; Council for the Defense of Human Rights in Kosovo (CPHRK); Kosovo National Liberation Movement; Lidhji Kosovare (Union of Kosovo); Parliamentary Party of Kosovo; Social Democratic Party

LADINS: General Union of Dolomite Ladins (Union Generela di Ladins d'la Dolomites); Patrje Ladine (Ladin Nation); Inant Adum; Ladin Union (Union de Ladins); Circolo Patriottico; Autonomia Integrale (FAR); Committee for National Liberation (Comitati de Liberazione Nazionale) (CLN)

LEONESE: Partido Regionalista del País Leonés (PREPL); Group Autonomista Leonés (GAL); Unión del Pueblo Leonés (UPL); Bierzo Party (Partido del Bierzo); Conceyu Xoven (Nationalist Youth of Leon); Dixebra (Independence); Autonomist Union of Leon (Unió Autónomista Lleónesa) (UAL)

LIGURIANS: Ligurian League (Lega Liguria) (LL); Northern League (Lega Nord) (LN); Autonomia Pro-Europa

LIVONIANS: Livonian Union; Livonian Cultural Society; Livonian Association (Estonia)

LOMBARDS: Lega Lombarda (Lombard League); Lega Nord (Northern League); Autonomous Lombard Unions; Alpine League; Armed Nucleus for Northern Separatism; Centro Filogical Milanesa; List for Milan; Padania Liberation Committee (CLP); Free European Federalist Entrepreneurs (LIFE); Consei Lumbaart per la Lengua; Forum Autonomista; Libertà Lombarda; Movimento Giovani Padani (Young Padanian Movement); Fronte Liberazione Armata Lombardia; Movimento Indipendentista Padano

MADEIRANS: Madeira Archipelago Liberation Front (Frente de Libertação do Arquipélago Madeirense) (FLAMA); Madeira Liberation Organization (OLM); Independence Movement of Madeira-Europe (MIME); Democratic Movement for the Liberation of Madeira (Movimento Democrático para a Liberação de Madeira) (MDLM)

MANX: Manx National Movement (MNM); Yu Trooar; Mec Vannin (Sons of Mannin); Celtic League; Alternative Policy Group (APG)

MONTENEGRINS: Alliance of Reform Forces; Democratic Coalition; National Party; Liberal Union; Democratic Party of Socialists; People's Party; Social Democratic Party; Liberal Alliance Party; Montenegrin Association; Alliance for Montenegrin Independence; Monarchist League; Peace and Democracy; Restoration

MORAVIANS: National Liberation Initiative for the Independence of Moravia-Silesia (Národnì Osvobozenecká Iniciativa za Nezávislost Moravy a Slezska) (NOI); Movement for Self-Government for Moravia and Silesia; Moravian National Movement; Moravian Democratic Party; Association for Moravia and Silesia (HSD-SMS); Moravian Civic Movement (MOH); Movement for Self-Governing Democracy-Association for Moravia and Silesia (HSD-SMS); Moravian National Party-Movement of Moravian-Silesian Unification (MNS-HSMS); Moravian Democratic Party (MDS); Moravian-Silesian Movement (MSK); Moravian Country Party (SMV); Hnutí samosprávné Moravy a Slezska (Movement for Self-government of Moravia and Silesia) (HSMS)

NEAPOLITANS: Nazione Napoletana-Due Sicilie (NNDS); Associazione Culturale Movimento Neoborbonico; Southern League (Lega Sud); Republic of Ausonia; Ausonia Movement (Mensile Meridionalista Independente) (MMI); Ausonia Liberia (Free Ausonia)

NORMANS: Flag and Country; Normandy United (Unité Normande) (UN); Norman Movement (Mouvement Normande) (MN); Normandy Youth Movement (Mouvement de la Jeunesse de Normandie) (MJN); Rouen Students' Federation (Fédération des Étudiantes de Rouen) (FER); Union for the Normandy Region (L'Union pour la Région Normande) (URN); Une-et-Une

NORTHERN CYPRIOTS: Government of the Turkish Republic of Northern Cyprus (TRNC); National Salvation Party; New Cyprus Party; Democratic Struggle Party; Free Democratic Party; Communal Liberation Party (TKP); National Identity Party; Social Democratic Party; New Dawn Party (YDP); Free Democratic Party; Republican Turkish Party (CTP); National Unity Party; Turkish Resistance Organization (TMT)

NORTHERN IRISH: Ulster Nation; Ulster Independence Party (UIP); Ulster National Congress (UNC); Ulster Independemce Movement (UIM); Ulster Volunteer Force (UVF); Ulster Defense Association (UDA); Ulster Union Party; Unionist Party of Northern Ireland; Orange Order; Ulster Nation; Third Way; Loyalist Volunteer Force (LVF); Red Hand Commandos; Ulster Freedom Fighters

NORTHUMBRIANS: Campaign Group; Council of the North; National Movement of the North (NMN); Northern Affairs Council; North-Eastern Constitutional Convention (NECC); Center for Northern Sovereignty; Geordie Nation (GN); Campaign for a Northern Assembly; Northumbrian Association; One NorthEast

OCCITANS: Occitan Party (Partit Occità/Parti Occitane); Farem Tot Petar; Félibriseñ Occitane Autonomy Movement; Regió Occitania; Occitània (Occitania Movement); Solidarité 13; Volem Viure al Pais (VVAP); Institut d'Estudis Occitans; Il Movimento Autonomista Occitano; Ousitano Vivo (Italy); Partit Nationalists Occitan (PNO); Päis Nòstre

ORCADIANS: Orkney Movement (OM); Orkneyjar (Orkney Heritage)

PIEDMONTESE: Piemonte Libera (Free Piedmont); Piedmont League (Lega Piemontèisa) (LP); Armed Nucleus for Northern Separatism; Our Roots (Nòste Rèis); Northern League (Lega Nord) (LN); Piedmontese Association (Associassion Piemontèisa) (AP); Free European Federalist Entrepreneurs (LIFE)

POMAKS: Initiative Committee for Recognition; Rodina Association; Democratic Party of Labor; Rodoljubie Organization

ROMANDS: Romandy Movement (Mouvement Romand) (MR); Coordinating Committee of Suisse Romande National Institutes; Pro-Europa (PE); National Movement of Romande Europe; Ligue Vaudoise (LV) (Switzerland); Mouvement de la Ranaissance Vaudoise (MRV) (Switzerland)

ROMANSCH: Lia Rumantscha (Romansch League/Ligia Romantscha) (LR); Grischa National Movement; Pro-Europa; Gray League

ROMS: European Roma Rights Center; Zentralrat Deutscher Sinti und Roma (Germany); Uniunea Românilor din Ungaria; Romániai Magyar Demokrata Szövetség; Roma Civil Rights Foundation (Hungary); Democratic Roma Union; Association Evro-Roma; Party for Democratic Development (Bulgaria); Romani Party of Croatia; Moskovskoye Tsyganskoye Kulturno-Prosvyetitelskoye Obshchestvo; Sektsiya Tsyganskoy Kultury pri Rossiyskom fonde Kultury (Russia); Democratic Union of Romani (Romania); Romani Democratic Political Party; Democratic Party of Gypsies (Yugoslavia); World Union of Romanies; Democratic Union of the Roms; International Romany Union; Rom International Committee; World Romani Congress; Eurom; Union of the Rom

RUMELIAN TURKS: Movement for Rights and Freedoms (DPS); Turkish Democratic Party; Committee for the Defense of Minority Rights (CDMR); Party for Democratic Change (Bulgaria); Guven (Greece); National Movement for Rights and Freedoms (NMRF)

SAMIS: Norsk Samers Riksforbund (Norway); Sami Lis'to; Sámiid Konfereanssas (Nordic Sámi Conference); Sami Komitet Severna; Svenska Samernas Riksförbund (Sweden); Sami Council (Samedikki); Sami Women's Organization (Sáráhkká); Kiruna Party; Swedish Saami National Union; Same-Atnam (RSA); Confederation of Swedish Saami (LSS) (Sweden); Association of Kola Saami (Russia); Sami Youth (Sami Nurash) (Russia); Skolt Village Assemblies (Siidsääbbar); Skolt Council (Säämmsudvõõzz); Saami Parliament (Finland); Confederation of Northern Reindeer Herders (NRL); Norwegian Saami Confederation (NSR); Saami Confederation (SLF) (Norway); Saami Public Organization (Russia)

SANJAKIS: Muslim National Council of Sanjak (Muslimansko Nacionalno Vijece Sanjakat) (MNVS); Helsinki Committee for Human Rights in Sandzak (HCHRS); Reformist Democratic Party of Sanjak/List for Sanjak; Rascia; Sandzacka Iskra; Muslim Cultural Society (Preporod); Party of Democratic Action of Sanjak (SDA); Helsinki Committee of Sanjak; Council of the National Liberation of Sandzak (AVNOS); Muslim Alliance Party; Merhamet; Muslim Democratic Union; Muslim Democratic Reform Party; Party of Democratic Action; Sanjak Equality Party; Democratic Coalition of Muslims; Sanjak Defense Forces

SARDS: Partito Sardo d'Azione (Sard Action Party) (PSA); Sard Party (Partidu Sardu) (PA); Sardigna Libertade; Sardigna Natzione; Sard Independence Party (Partidu Indipendentista Sardu) (PIS); Revolutionary Sardinian Army; Sardinian Party (PS); Sardinian Separatists; Free Europe Alliance; Sardinian Language and Culture (Limba e Cultura de sa Sardinia); Gruppi Consiliari Sardisti (GCS); Moimentu de su Populu Sardu (MPS); Sardinian Separatists; Sardinian Nation (Sardigna Natzione)

SAVOYARDS: Savoyan League (Ligue Savoisienne) (LS); Harpeitian Movement (Mouvement Harpeitanya) (MH); Uniti per Trinité; Autonomic Union; Free Zone Movement; Syndicat Autonome Valdotain (Italy); National Savoyard Front (FNS) (France); Progressive Democratic Party; Club des Savoyards de Savoie; Pour le Pays; Appel aux Jeunes Savoisiens (France); Union Valdotaine (Italy); Autonomisti (Italy); Rinnovamento/Renouvellement; Ensemble pour le Pays; Unis Pour Notre Pays/Uniti Per il Nostro Paese; Savoy Regional Movement (Mouvement Région Savoie) (MRS) (France); Pour la Vallée D'Aoste (Italy); Ligue Valaisien (LV) (Switzerland)

SAXONY: Nur fur Sachen; Saxon National Movement; Saxony United Movement; United Land Movement; Citizen's Movement for a Europe of Nations

SCANIANS: Befria Skåne (Free Scania); Scania United Left; Skånepartier (Scania Party); Pro Europe; Sjöbo Party; Föreningen Skånelands Ungdom; Skånsk Framtid (SSF); Skåneland Liberation Front

SCOTS: Common Cause; Constitutional Movement; Democracy for Scotland; Scotland United; Scottish Labor Action; Scottish Constitutional Convention; Siol nan Gaidheal (Seed of the Gael); Tartan Army (TA); Scottish National Party (SNP); Scottish Independence Party (SIP); Scottish Workers' Party (SWP); Scottish Phalange; Scotland United; Scottish Trades Union Congress (STUC); Settler Watch; Flame; Scottish Separatist Group (SSG); Scottish National Liberation Army (SNLA); Scottish Socialist Party (SSP); Scottish Republican Socialist Party (SRSP)

SEBORGANS: Knights of St. Bernard (CSB); Front for the Independence of Seborga (FIB); Associazione de Cooperazione per Principato di Seborga

SHETLANDERS: Zetland United; Island Liberation Front (ILF); Shetland Movement (SM)

SICILIANS: Movement for a Free Sicily (MSL); Republican Party of Sicily; Sicilian Independence Committee; Sons of Guiliano; La Rete (The Network); Sicilian Action Party (Partido Siciliano d'Azione) (PSA)

SORBS: Domowina (Nation); Lusatian League; Macica Serbska (MS); Sorb Democratic Union; Lusatian State Movement; New Forum; Swjazk Luziskich Serbow Domowina (Lusatian Sorb Society)

SWABIANS: Heimat; Swabian People's Party (Schwäbisch Volkspartei) (SVP); Association of Swabians in Bavaria

SZEKLERS: Home League of Eastern Transylvania; December 17 Association; Free Youth of Transylvania; Partidul Crestin Democrat; Hungarian Democratic Alliance of Romania (UDMR); Transylvanian World Federation; Women's League for Peace and Freedom; Hungarian Party (RMDSZ); Magyar Democratic Union of Romania (RMDS); All-Transylvanian National Union; Szekler Student Union; Pro-Europa; Transylvanian Association; Transylvanian Helicon (Erdély Helikon); Our War (Utunk)

TYROLEANS: Andreas Hoffer Bund; Ein Tirol (One Tyrol); Lega Trentina (Trent League); Alpine League; Trentino-Tyrol Autonomist Party of Trentino; Union für Süd Tirol (Italy); Tiroler Schützbund; Tirol; Südtirol Schützenbund (Italy); South Tyrol People's Party (Südtirol Volkspartei) (SVP) (Italy); Union for a United Tirol; Landesrat für Schule und Kultur Südtiroler; Südtiroler Volksgruppen (SV); Autonome Region Trentino-Südtirol (ARTS) (Italy); Autonome Provinz Bozen (Italy); Coordination Committee; Grünalternative Fraktion; Tyrolean Peoples' Party (Tiroler Heimatpartei); Soziale Fortschrittspartei; South Tyrol Social Democratic Party (Sozialdemokratische Partei Südtirols) (SPS); Wahlverband der Unabhängigen (WDU); South Tyrol Freedom Party (Freiheitliche Partei Südtirols) (FPS); Genischte Gruppe; Schutzen; Heimat Bund (Homeland League); South Tyrolean German Group; Trent National Alliance (Alleanza Nazionale de Trento) (ANT); Lista Civica; Popolari-Alto Adige Domani; Trentino Domani (TD); Civica-Margherita; Trentino-Tyrol Autonomist Party of Trento (PATT); Partito Nazionalista Trentino Tirolese (PNTT); Trentino-Welch Tirol

VENETIANS: Consorzio Venezia Nuova (New Venice Consortium) (CNV); Lega Veneta (Venetian League); Lega Nord (Northern League) (NL); Liste Venetes (Venetian Lists); Refundación Veneto; Union Veneto Livre; Armed Nucleus for Northern Separatism; Nathion Veneta; Veneta Liberarissima Repubblica; Fronte Marco Polo; Association of St Mark; Liga Veneta Repubblica; Veneto Serenissimo Governo

VOJVODINES: Vojvodina Resistance Movement (VRM); Vojvodina Coalition (Koalicija Vojvodina); League of Social Democrats (Liga Socijaldemokrata Vojvodine) (LSV); Republic of Vojvodina (ROV); Vojvodina Club; League of Social Democrats; Reformist Democratic Party of Vojvodina; Banat Forum; National Peasants' Party; Hungarians for the Fatherland; Democratic Community of Vojvodina Hungarians (DZVM); Association of Vojvodina Hungarians (SVM); Alliance of Democratic Parties

VORARLBERGERS: Association for Endangered Peoples; Amt der Vorarlberger; Vorarlberg Movement

WALDENSIANS: Waldensian Synod; Waldensian Church; Communita Montana Val Pellice; American Waldensian Society (AWS); Waldensian Movement

WALLOONS: Democratic Front of Wallonia (FDW); Francofone Democratic Front (FDF); Walonia Libre (Free Wallonia; Front National) (FN); Parti Wallon (PW); Walloon Rally (RW); Front Indépendantiste Wallon (FIW); Wallonia National Congress (CNW); Francophone Front (Front Francophonie) (FF)

WELSH: Welsh National Party (Plaid Cymru); Cadwyr Cymru (Keepers of Wales); Cefn; Free Wales; Meibion Glendwr (Sons of Glendower); Mudiad Amddiffyn Cymru (Free Welsh Army); Workers Party of the Welsh Republic; Welsh Language Society (WLS); Cymru Annibynnol (Welsh Independence Party); Red Wales (Cymru Goch, the Welsh Socialists)

WESTERN UKRAINIANS: Incentive Group of Western Ukrainia; Lion Society; Democratic Block; Galician Assembly; Ukrainian Catholic Defense Committee; Free Galician League; Ukrainian Helsinki Association; Ukrainian Popular Front (RUKH); Ukrainian Interparty Assembly; Ukrainian Conservative Republican Party; Galician Ukrainia; Organization of Ukrainian Nationalists (OUN); Ukrainian Insurgent Army (UPA)

NORTH AFRICA AND THE MIDDLE EAST

Afghanistan: Baluch; Hazaras; Pushtuns

Algeria: Kabyles; Sahrawis; Tuaregs

Egypt: Copts

Iran: Arabistanis; Assyrians; Bahais; Baluch; Gilakis; Kurds; Southern Azeris; Talysh; Turkomans; Zazas

Iraq: Arabistanis; Assyrians; Kurds; Southern Azeris; Turkomans

Israel: Druze; Palestinians

Jordan: Palestinians

Lebanon: Alawites; Assyrians; Druze; Kurds; Maronites; Palestinians

Libya: Sanussis

Morocco: Riffians; Sahrawis

Oman: Dhofaris

Saudi Arabia: Asiris; Hejazis

Spain: Andalusians; Riffians

Syria: Alawites; Assyrians; Druze; Kurds; Maronites; Palestinians; Turkomans

Turkey: Ajars; Alawites; Kurds; Northern Cypriots; Pomaks; Southern Azeris; Turkomans; Zazas

Yemen: Hadhramis

NATIONAL ORGANIGATIONS BY NATION: NORTH AFRICA AND THE MIDDLE EAST

ALAWITES: October Movement (Teshreen); National Progressive Front; Alawi Democratic Union; Alawiyah Movement; Red Knights

ARABISTANIS: Arab Front for the Liberation of Ahvaz (AFLA); Popular Front of Ahvaz (PFLA); People's Front for the Liberation of Arabistan (PLFA); Arab Political Cultural Organization (APCO); Ahwas Liberation Organization (ALO); Group of the Martrys; Chararshanbeh-e-Siah (Black Wednesday); Movement for the Liberation of Ahvaz (MLA); Movement for the Liberation of Arabistan; El Saadeh Party;

ASSYRIANS: Assyrian Democratic Union (Zowaa/ADM); Bet Nahrain Democratic Party (BNDP); International Confederation of the Assyrian Nation; Student Representative Council; Assyrian Quest; Assyrian Universal Alliance (AUA); Assyrian Patriotic Party (APP); Assyrian Academic Society; Assyrian American National Federation (AANF); Chaldean Federation; Assyrian Foundation of America; Assyrian Australian National Foundation; Syriac Universal Alliance (Lebanon); Assyrian Democratic Organization (Mtakasta); Mosul Vilayet Council; Assyrian Democratic Movement (ADM); Assyrian Student and Youth Union

BAHAI: National Spiritual Assemblies (NSA); Talisman; International Bahai Councils (IBC); Charles Mason Remey Society; Twenty-Seven Hands of the Cause; World Order of Baha'u'llah; Baha'i International Community

COPTS: Coptic Students' Association; International Coptic Federation; Birashty; American Coptic Union (ACU) (United States); Jubilee Campaign; Masarra; Coptic Pharaonic Movement

DHOFARIS: Popular Front for the Liberation of Oman and Dhofar (PFLOD); Dhofar Liberation Front (DLF); Popular Front for the Liberation of the Occupied Arabian Gulf (PFLOAG); Front for the Liberation of Oman and the Arab Gulf (FLOAG)

DRUZE: Druze National Unity; Juhal Movement; Progressive Socialist Party (PSP) (Lebanon); Sons of al-Atash; National Liberation Front of United Druzistan; Druze National Liberation Front (FNLD); Albakourat al-Druzeyat

GILAKIS: Gilaki National Movement; Hibz-i Jangali (Jungle Party); Djangali Movement; Jangli Mudajahedine; Front Kucik Khan; Azadikhahan; Gilanian Council (United States)

HADHRAMIS: Yemeni Socialist Party (YSP); League of the Sons of Yemen (LSY); Aden Socialist Action Party (ASAP); Democratic Forum; Hadrami Movement of National Liberation; Sons of Yemen League; Front for the Liberation of South Yemen (FLOSY); National Liberation Front (NLF); Socialist Party; Aden-Abyan Islamic Army

HAZARAS: Hazara Resistance Movement; Shura-yi Ittifaq (Unity Council); Nasr (Victory); Siqah Hazara (Hazara Guards); Harakat-i Islami (Islamic Movement); Hizb-i Wahdat (Unity Party); Wahdat al Islamiya (Islamic Coalition Council); Shuhada (Martyrs); Millat-e-Hazara (Hazara Nation); Shura-e Ittifaq (Solidarity Council).

HEJAZIS: Hashemite Movement; Hejaz Reform Movement; Hizbollah fil Hijaz (Hejaz Party of God); Hejaz-Red Sea Movement; Islamic Jihad in Hejaz

KABYLES: Socialist Forces Front (Front de Forces Socialistes) (FFS); Algerian Human Rights League (LADH); Union for Culture and Democracy (RDC) Sons of the Martyrs of the Revolution; Berber Cultural Movement (MCB); Rassemblement pour la Culture et la Démocratie (Rally for Culture and Democracy) (RCD); Association Nouvelle de la Culture et des Arts Populaires; Jeunesse Nationale Populaire; Armed Berber Movement (MAB); Worker's Party; Rally for Culture and Democracy (RCD); Amazigh World Congress (Congress Mondial Amazigh) (CMA); Berber Cultural Movement (Mouvement Cultural Berbère) (MCB); High Commission for Tamazight; Alliance for a Free Kabylie (AKAL)

KURDS: Kurdistan Democratic Party (KDP); Patriotic Union of Kurdistan (PUK) (Iraq); Front for the Liberation of Kurdistan (ERNK); Kurdish Worker's Party (Partiya Karkeren Kurdistan) (PKK) (Turkey); Pesh Merga; Kurdish Democratic Party of Iran (KDPI); Revolutionary Organization of the Toilers of Kurdistan (Komala); Socialist Party of Kurdistan (Partiya Sosyalist a Kurdistan) (PSK) (Turkey); National Liberation Front of Kurdistan (Eniya Rizgariya Netewa Kurdistan) (ERNK); People's Liberation Army of Kurdistan (Arteshen Rizgariya Gelli Kurdistan) (ARGK); Liberation Units of Kurdistan (HRK); Komkar (Komala Karjeren); People's Democratic Party (Tur); American Kurdish Network; Committee for the Defense of the Kurdish Nation; Revolutionary Leadership of the Kurdistan Democratic Party of Iran (RLKDPI); Free Kurdistan Campaign; Komalah Party; People's Party; Riz Qari; People's Labor Party

MARONITES: Christian Independence Movement; Lebanese Forces; National Liberal Party; Phalange (Kataeb)/Phalange Militia; National Independence Movement of the Enclave of Mount Lebanon (MNIEJL); Bloc National; Christian Social Democratic Party; Lebanese Front; Guardians of the Cedars; Social Democratic Party; Tiger Militia; Lebanese Forces (LF); Free National Current (FNC); Free Patriotic Movement; National Liberal Party

PALESTINIANS: Palestine Liberation Organization (PLO)/Palestine Liberation Army (PLA); Islamic Resistance Movement (HAMAS)/Ezzedin al Qassim; Fatah; Palestine Liberation Front (PLF); Palestine National Council (PNC); Popular Front for the Liberation of Palestine (PFLP); Islamic Jihad; Black September; Palestine Democratic Front (PDF); Hezbollah; Democratic Front for the Liberation of Palestine (DFLP); Palestinian Islamic Front; Fatah Revolutionary Council; Palestine Liberation Front (PLF); Palestinian Islamic Jihad (PIJ); Popular Front for the Liberation of Palestine-General Command (PFLP-GC); Popular Front for the Liberation of Palestine-Special Command (PFLP-SC); Popular Struggle Front (PSF); Abnaa elBalad; Sons of the Country; Hawari Group; Fatah Special Operations Group; Martyrs of Tal Al Za'atar; Amn Araissi

RIFFIANS: Rif Movement for Liberation and Liquidation (MRPLL); Popular Movement (MPR); Neapolis; Averroes; Democratic Union of the Peoples of the Rif (UDPR); Organisation Nacional del Rif (National Organization of the Rif); Liberation Committee of Er Rif (CLR); Popular National Movement (Nouvement Nationale Populaire) (MP); Popular Movement (Mouvement Populaire); Berber Cultural Society

SAHRAWIS: Government of the Sahrawi Arab Democratic Republic (SADR); Popular Front for the Liberation of Saguia al Hama and Rio de Oro (Frente Popular para la Liberación de Saguia El Hamra y Río de Oro) (POLISARIO-Polisario Front); Asociacíon por la tutela del Referendum de Autodeterminacíon Association of Families of Saharan Prisoners and Displaced; Union of Sahrawi Women

SANUSSIS: Sanusi Organization; Jihad; Sanussi Movement; National Liberation Movement of Green Mountain (Europe)

SOUTHERN AZERIS: Democratic Party of Azerbaijan; Tudeh Party; Mussavat; Assembly of Turkic Peoples; United Azerbaijan Association (UAM); National Liberation Movement of Southern Azerbaijan (NLMSA); Islam Partici; South Azerbaijani Women's Council; Great Nations Party; Council of South Azerbaijan Turks Freedom and Indpendence; South Azerbaijan National Council; Council to Protect the Rights of Azerbaijans of the World (CPRAW); Front for the National Independence of South Azerbaijan (FNISA); Azadikhahan; Voice of Southern Azerbaijan (VOSA); Front for the National Liberaton of South Azerbaijan (FNISA)

TALYSH: Talysh Popular Front (TPF); Talysh-Murgan Movement (Azerbaijan); Talysh Islamic Association of Iran; Avestan

TURKOMANS: Iraqi National Turkman Party (Irak Milli Turkman Partisi) (INTP); Turkman Congress; Turkman Brotherhood (Ocak); Turkman Independence Movement; Turkmeneli Co-operation and Cultural Foundation, Iraq Turks Cultural and Mutual Help Organization; Taza Kirkuk Supreme Council (SCIRI); Dawa Party; Turkomaneli Party (Turkmeneli Partisi); Turkman Islamic Union; Turkoman Independence Movement (Turkmen Bagimsizlar Hareketi) (TBH); Turkoman Brotherhood Association; Turkoman People's Party (Turkmen Halk Partisi) (THP); Iraqi Turks Cultural Assocaition (Iraq Turkleri Kultur ve Yardimlasma Dernegi); Turkoman Intellectual Brotherhood (Turkmen Aydinlari Kardeslik Dernegi); Turkoman Brotherhood Association (Turkmen Kardeslik Ocagi); Islamic Union of Iraqi Turkomans

ZAZAS: Dersim Movement; Cem Foundation; Dersim Genel Meclisi; Haji Bektash Federation; Pir Sultan Abdal Association; Zaza Kirmanc Dimili; Dersim Komünist Hareketi (DKH); Red Flag (Desala Sure); Australian Zaza Language and Cultural Group (AZLCG)

RUSSIA, THE CAUCASUS, AND CENTRAL ASIA

Armenia: Karabakhis; Kurds

Azerbaijan: Avars; Dagestanis; Karabakhis; Lezgins; Meskhtekians; Talysh

Georgia: Abkhaz; Ajars; Kurds; Meskhtekians; Ossetians

Kazakhstan: Altai; Chechens; Jews; Karakalpaks; Uighurs; Ural Cossacks; Uralians; Volga Germans

Kyrgyzstan: Uighurs; Volga Germans

Russia: Abaza; Adyge; Ainu; Altai; Avars; Balkars; Bashkorts; Buryats; Chavash; Chechens; Cherkess; Chukots; Dagestanis; Don Cossacks; Evenks; Far Easterners; Ingrians; Ingush; Jews; Kabards; Kalmyks; Karels; Khakass; Konigsberg Slavs; Koryaks; Kuban Cossacks; Kumyks; Kurds; Lezgins; Maris; Mordvins; Nenets; Nogais; Ob-Ugrians; Permyaks; Sakhas; Samis; Siberians; Tatars; Terek Cossacks; Tuvans; Udmurts; Ural Cossacks; Uralians; Veps; Volga Germans; Votes

Uzbekistan: Karakalpaks; Meskhtekians; Tatars; Uighurs

NATIONAL ORGANIZATIONS BY NATION: RUSSIA, THE CAUCASUS, AND CENTRAL ASIA

ABAZA: World Congress of Abkhazian-Abazian People; Abazashta Movement; Confederation of the Peoples of the Caucasus (KNK); Abaza Agylar (Abaza Unity)

ABKHAZ: World Congress of Abkhazian-Abazian People; Abkhaz National Council; Abkhazian People's Front; Aiglara (Unity); Adygylara Front; Apsua Movement; Confederation of Caucasian Highland Peoples; Government of the Republic of Abkhazia; Confederation of the Peoples of the Caucasus (KNK); Abkhaz Initiative Group

ADYGE: Adigha Shusha Khassa; Birlesik Kafkasya Dernegi (United Caucasian Association); International Association of Circassian Peoples; Adyge Khase (Adighe Khazbe); Union of Volunteers of Adygea

AJARS: Ajar Islamic Front; Revival Union (Revival Party); Ajar National Council (Showra)

ALTAI: Kurultai of the Altai People; Ene-Bayat; Association of the Shor People; Altai United Front; Confederal Nation of the Altai Tribes; Association of the Teleut (Ene-Bayat)

AVARS: People's Front Iman Shamil (Fond imeni Shamilia); Confederation of Caucasian Mountain Peoples; Avar People's Movement; Dzhamagat; Shamil

Movement; Islamic Revival Party; Tsoli; Avar Society (Azerbaijan); Islamic-Democratic Party of Dagestan

BALKARS: National Council of the Balkar People; Assembly of Turkic Peoples; Malkar Respublika

BASHKORTS: Party of Free Bashkortostan; Bashkort Popular Front (BPF); Bashrevkom; Republican Party; Assembly of Turkic Peoples; All-World Congress of Bashkorts; Fatherland Congress; Bashkort People's Front

BURYATS: Sinechiel (Renewal); Buryat Pan-Mongol Movement; Society of the Scepter of Indra; Buryat Mongol People's Party; All-Buryat People's Congress; People's Alliance; All–Buryat People's Parliament; All-Buryat Association for the Development of Culture (ABADC); Geser; Buryat Cultural Heritage Association; Ar Mongol; All-Buryat Congress; Siberian Accord; World Buryat Association of Cultural Development; Negedel (Movement for National Unity); Democratic Buryatia; Unity and Progress

CHAVASH: Chävash Jen; Chavash Popular Front; Tavas; Front for the Unification of Chavashistan; Chavash National Congress; Chuvash Public Cultural Center

CHECHENS: All-National Congress of the Chechen People; United Congress of Chechen People (UCCP); Chechen National Council; Confederation of Caucasian Highland Peoples; Muridic Brotherhood; Chechen National Movement; Khalkanaz; Islamic Renaissance Party; Nakh Congress; Vainakh National Organization; Chechen–Aikkin National Council (Dagestan); Vainakh (Dagestan)

CHERKESS: International Association of Circassian Peoples; United Caucasian Association (Birlesik Kafkasya Dernegi) (BKD); Yapeqhe Tcerqes (Forward Circassia); Circassian United Front; Islamic Revival Party; Confederation of Caucasian Highland Peoples; Cherkess National Congress; Adyge Khase; International Cherkess Association

CHUKOTS: Chukot National Movement; People's Movement of Northeast Asia; Association of Northern Minorities

DAGESTANIS: Dagestan People's Front; Islamic Revival Party; Confederation of Caucasian Mountain Peoples (CMPC); Tariqat; Democratic Party of United Dagestan; Tsadesh (Unity) (Dargins); Cultural Center for the Peoples of Dagestan; Kazi Kumukh (Laks); Tsubars (New Star) (Laks); Novolak Popular Movement (Laks); Union of Muslims of Russia; Central Front for the Liberation of the Caucasus and Dagestan; Fighting Squads of Jamaat Dagestan; Patriotc Forces of Dagestan

DON COSSACKS: Cossack Renaissance; Union of Cossacks; Supreme Circle of the Don; Great Brotherhood of Cossack Troops; Don Cossack Army (Voisko Donskoe); All-Russian Cossack Union; Cossack Union; Union of Cossack Republics of South Russia; Union of Cossack Hosts of Russia and Abroad (SKVRiZ); Community of Don-Kuban-Terek Citizens (URWJA); Union of the Cossack Hosts of Russia (SKVR); Free Cossackia; Edinstvo

EVENKS: Northern Forum; Association of the Numerically Small Peoples of the North (ARUN); Evenki Society; Association of Peoples of the North; Association of Indigenous Peoples of Krasnoyarsk Region; Yukte; Association of the Indigenous Peoples (Evenk) of the Chita Region; First Nations Siberians

FAR EASTERNERS: Far Eastern People's Front; Far East Forum; Republican Movement; Zemyak; Alliance of Pacific Peoples; Far East Independence Movement; Regional Association of the Far East

INGRIANS: National Movement of Ingrian Finns (Inkerin Liito); Inkeri Popular Front; Movement for Culture and Language; Ingrian Cultural Society (Estonia); Ingrian Society (Finland/Sweden)

INGUSH: National Galgai; Islamic Revival Party; Ingush Self-Defense Force; Ingush National Front; Federation of Caucasian Highland Peoples (KNK); Ingush People's Council; Zashchita

JEWS: Russian Jewish Congress; Jewish Agency of Russia; Jewish Confederation of Russia; Jewish Va'ad of Russia; Society for the Promotion of Culture among the Jews of Russia; Union of Councils for Soviet Jews (UCSJ)

KABARDS: Congress of the Kabardian People (CKP); Sons of Sausryko; Mountain People's Alliance; International Association of Circassian Peoples; Kafkas Dernegi; Omar Farouk Tamzouk; Adyge Khase

KALMYKS: Kalmyk Banner Organization (KBO); Kalmyk Buddhist Association; Kalmyk National Congress; Movement for an Independent Khal'mg Tangch; Institute for the Rebirth of the Kalmyk Language and Buddhism

KARABAKHIS: Karabakh Defense Forces; Republic of Artsakh (ROA); Dashnak Party (HHD); Hnchakian Party of Artsakh; Ramkavar Azatakan Party of Artsakh

KARACHAIS: National Council of the Karachai People; Volunteer Force of Free Karachaistan; Confederation of the Caucasian Highland Peoples; Congress of the Muslims of Karachay; Islamic Party of Rebirth

KARAKALPAKS: Kara-Kalpak United Front (Karakalpak League); Republican Movement of Karakalpakstan; People's National Party; Islamic Renaissance Party; Equality; Karakalpak National Organization to Save the Aral Sea

KARELS: Union of the Karelian People (Karjalan Rahvahan Liitto); Karelian People's Front; Party of Democratic Karelia; Karelian Association; National Movement of Eastern Karelia; United Karelia; Karel Federation of Finland; Social Democratic Party; All-Federation Society for Karelian Unification and Independence; Oma Mua (Our Land)

KHAKASS: Abakan; Tun Association of the Khakass People; Khakass Cultural Center; Congress of the Khakass People; Chas Khanat; Society for Traditional Khakass Religion; Khaidzhi; Center for Shamanic Culture; Khakass Council of Elders

KOMIS: Coordinating Council of Democratic Parties; Heritage; Permian People's Front; Komi People's National Organization; Party of Unity and Independence; Komi National Revival Committee; Komi Congress; Finno-Ugrik Peoples Consultative Committee; Committee for the Rebirth of the Komi People

KÖNIGSBERG SLAVS: Russo-German Society; Königsberg National Memorial Association; Königsberg Movement; Königsberg Free Zone Movement; Reconciliation; Movement for a Free Republic; Prusa; Balto-Slavic Relations Committee for the International Congress of Slavists

KORYAKS: Association of Northern Minorities; Chav' Chüv; Koryak Republican Movement; Association of the Peoples of North Kamchatka; Center of the Traditional Culture of People Itelmen (Kamchatka-Etnos); Narodovlastie (Peoples' Power); Association of the Peoples of the North; Association of Indigenous Peoples of the Koryak Autonomous Region; Tshsanom (Council for the Revival of the Itelmen People)

KUBAN COSSACKS: Black Sea Popular Front; Edinstvo; Kuban Citizen's Committee; Kuban Cossack Movement; Kuban Self-Help Organization; Union of Cossacks; Cossack Renaissance; Union of Cossacks; Kuban Cossacks Association; Kuban Cossack Voisko (Kuban Cossack Army); All Cossack Stanitza; Great Brotherhood of Cossack Troops; Community of Don-Kuban-Terek Citizens (URWJA); Union of Cossack Hosts of Russia and Abroad (SKVRiZ); Union of the Cossack Hosts of Russia (SKVR)

KUMYKS: Kumyk National Council; Tenglik (Equality); Assembly of Turkic Peoples; Kumuk Ish; Kumyk Peoples Movement; Kumyk National Movement

LEZGINS: Sadval (Unity); All-National Congress of Lezgins; Alpan; Chubaruk; Samur (Azerbaijan); Lezgian Democratic Party (Azerbaijan); National Council of the Lezgin People (Russia); Islamic Society

MARIS: Mari Popular Front; Kugu Sorta; Marii Civic Union; Mari People's Democratic Party; Social Party of Marii El; Mari Ushem (Mari National Movement); Mari Congress; Osh Mari Chi Mari

MESKHTEKIANS: Meskhtekian National Movement; Vakhtan (Motherland); Salvation; Society of Meskhtekian Turks in Azerbaijan (Meshet Turkleri Cemiyeti Azerbayanda); Provisional Organizations Committee; Deliverance (Khsna); Temporary Organizing Committee on Returning Home; Committee of the Meskhi Deportees of 1944

MORDVINS: Democracy and Independence; Mordva Front; Erzya National Cultural Association; Middle Volga National Movement

NENETS: Yasavei (Association of the Nenets); Hasava United Movement; Nenets National Movement; Association of Indigenous Peoples of the North; Nenet-Dolgan National Committee; Committee of Indigenous Peoples; Yamal for Future Generations (Association of Indigenous Peoples of the Yamal-Nenets Autonomous Region); Association of Indigenous Peoples of the Taimyr Autonomous Region

NOGAIS: Assembly of Turkic Peoples; Birlik (Unity); Association of Nogais of Dagestan

OB-UGRIANS: Khanty People; Association to Save Yugra; Society of Mansis of Sos'va; Yurga Restoration; Society for the Survival and Socio-Economic Development of the Mansi People; Association of Aboriginal Small Peoples of the North, Siberia and Far East of the Russian Federation

OSSETIANS: Adaemon Nejkhas (Ossetian Popular Front); Ossetian National Council; Adaemon Nejkhas (Ossetian Popular Front); South Ossetian Self-Defense Committee; Ossetian Republican Party; Iryston; South Ossetian Government; Alania Civic Organization; Congress of Ossetian Communities

PERMYAKS: Permyak National Center; Komi-Permyak Association of Perem

SAKHAS: Sakha Nation (Sakha Omuk); Association of Indigenous Peoples of the Republic of Sakha; Northern Forum; Yakut Union; Association of Peoples of the North; Sons of Dygyn

SIBERIANS: All-Siberian Democratic Union; Katchan; Siberian Republican Alliance; Siberskoye Zemlyachestvo (Autonomy Movement); Sibir; Free Siberia; Democratic Siberia; Siberian Agreement; Roar of the Taiga (Zov Taigi); Siberian Regional Organization (Siberskoye Zemlyachestvo)

TATARS: Harbi Shuro; Democratic Party of Tatarstan; Tatar National Council; Tangechebar; Party of Free Tatarstan; Assembly of Turkic Peoples Tatar Public Center (Tatar Ichtimagi Uzegi) (TIU); All-Tatar Social Center; National Independence Party (Ittifak Partisi); Freedom Committee (Azatlik Komiteti); Sovereignty Committee (Suvirenitet Komitesi); Merjani Association (Merjani Uyushmasi); Educational Committee (Magarif Komitesi); Homeland Association (Vatann Jemgiyeti); Assembly of the Turkic Peoples; Bulghar National Congress; Bulghar al-Jadid; Initiative Center of the People's Front of Tatarstan; Islamic Democratic Party; Republican Party of Tatatstan; All-Tatar People's Kurultay; Milli Meclis

TEREK COSSACKS: Free Cossackia; Ter Cossack Army; Terek Cossack Volunteer Movement; Union of Cossack Military; Edinstvo; Historic Land Association; National Liberation Movement of the Stavropole Plateau; Community of Don-Kuban-Terek Citizens (URWJA); Stavropol Self–Defense Force; Union of the Cossack Hosts of Russia (SKVR); Union of the Cossack Hosts of Russia and Abroad (SKVRiZ)

TUVANS: Tuvan People's Alliance; Uryanchai Banner League; Tuvinien People; Free Tuva Party (Tervetuloa Tuvan Tasavaltaan) (TTT); Association of the Indigenous Peoples of the Republic of Tyva

UDMURTS: Udmurt Kenesh (Udmurt Council); Republican National Party; Committee for the Defense of Udmurt Interests; Udmurt Language and Education Association; Odmort; Udmurt National Congress; Udmurt National Center

URAL COSSACKS: Union of Cossacks of the Volga and Ural; Commune of Ural Cossacks; Ural Cossack Army; Union of the Cossack Hosts of Russia (SKVR); Union of Cossack Hosts of Russia and Abroad (SKVRiZ)

URALIANS: Union of Ural Forces; Movement of Ural Sovereignty; Ural Republican Movement; Uralia Association; Regional Forces of the Southern Urals

VEPS: Vep Society (Vepsän Seuran); Veps Cultural Society

VOLGA GERMANS: Wiedergeburt (Rebirth); Heimat; Rat der Deutschen in Kasachstan (Kazakhstan); Volksrat der Detuschen Kyrgizstans (Kyrgyzstan); Union of Ethnic Germans in Russia (Internationaler Verband der Russlanddeutschen) (Russia); Zwischenstaatlicher Rat der Russlanddeutschen (Wieder-geburt) (Russia); American Historical Societ of Germans from Russia (AHSGR); Germans from Russia Historical Society (GRHS); Landsmannschaft der Deutschen aus Russland; Rebirth Movement; Congress of Kazakh Germans

VOTES: Vote National Movement (Vaddjalista)

INDEX

The page numbers set in **boldface** indicate the location of the main entry

Abashidze, Aslan, 67, 68

Abaza, **1–6**, 447; language, 2, 4; subgroups, 1–3; urbanization, 5

Abazashta, 1–6; Abaza, 1–6; Region of, 1

Abdirahman, Ahmed Ali, 809–10

Abdullah, Farooq, 959

Abdullah, Mohammed, 956

Abiola, Mashood, 2082–3

Abkhaz, 1–2, **7–12**; independence declared, 10; language, 8; Republic of Abkhazia, 7; subgroups, 8

Abkhaz National Council, 10, 11

Abkhazia, 2, 7–12; Abkhaz, 7–12; independence declared, 10; Mandadzhir Movement, 9; Republic of, 7; Shervashidze dynasty, 9; urbanization, 10

Abkhazo-Adygheian nations. *See* Abaza; Abkhaz; Adyge; Cherkess; Kabards

Aboriginal Land Rights Act, 16

Aborigines, **13–18**; Australia, 13; Dreaming, 14; land claims, 17–18; language, 14; right to vote (1962), 15; Tasmanian, 14; Torres Straight Islanders, 13; urbanization, 13

Abramovich, Roman, 461

Abu Sayyaf (Moros), 1326

Abyssinian Empire, 105

Abyssinians. *See* Amhara

Acadia, 19–24, 386

Acadiana, 355–59; Cajuns, 355–59; discovery of oil, 356, 358; Region of, 355. *See also* Acadians

Acadians, **19–24**, 356, 1251; education, 23; language, 20; Madawaska, 19; religion, 20. *See also* Cajuns

Aceh, 25–30; Acehnese, 25–30; independence declared, 27; Special Autonomous District of, 25, 27; Sultanate of, 26

Acehnese, **25–30**, 1228; language, 26; religion, 26; Special Autonomous District of Aceh, 25; uprising, 25–27

Acheampong, Ignatius, 190

Achiks. *See* Bodos

Achinese. *See* Acehnese

Acre, 31–35; Acreaños, 31–35; independence declared, 33; rubber boom, 32; State of, 31, 33

Acreaños, **31–35**; Acre State, 31; language, 32; rainforests, 33–34

Action Group (Yorubas), 2081

Adal, 43

Aden, 704; British colony, 704–5; independence declared, 705; Protectorate of, 704

Adenauer, Konrad, 1584–86

Adenis (Adeni Arabs), 702–3, 705

Adivasi Cobra Force (ACF), 1650

Adivasiland, 1648–53

Adivasis. *See* Santhals

Adrianople, Treaty of (1829), 38

Adyge, **36–40**, 444; Adyge Republic, 36; language, 37; religion, 37; World War I, 39

Adyge Khase, 36, 443

Adygea, 36–40; Adyge, 36–40; Republic of, 36, 1035

1576–80; Roms, 1604–10;
Savoyards, 1667–73; Tahitians, 1820–
24; Wallisians and Futunans, 2036–
39; Walloons, 2040–45

Franche-Comté, Region of, 90, 336–
40

Franco, Francisco, 112, 166, 214, 287,
383, 663, 1590; in the Canary
Islands, 377; Catalans, 403, 406–7;
Galicians, 640–41; Leonese, 1080,
1082

Franco-Chinese War (1884–85), 1410

Franco-Prussian War (1870–71), 299,
1671

Franconians. *See* Bavarians; Swabians

Francophone Front (Walloons), 2044

Franco's Legions, 407

frankincense, 528

Franklin, Benjamin, 802

Franks, 487, 517, 607–8, 614, 1512,
1669

Franque Ranque, Luis, 351

Fraternal Association of Emilia, 574

Fre-Dom Party (Réunionese), 1579

Free Aceh Movement 25, 28–29

Free Papua Movement, 2052, 2055

Free Tamil Movement, 1844

Free Tuva Party, 1939

Free Wales, 2050

Frémont, John C., 363

French, 488–90, 608–9, 695, 827,
1105; in Asia, 427, 740–41; in the
Caribbean, 651, 689; Catalonia, 402,
405; China, 1410–11; in East Africa,
43; Empire, 397, 690; Free French,
489, 547; in India, 1160; in the
Indian Ocean, 126; Indochina, 993,
1290; Indochina War (1946–54),
994, 1291; in the Middle East, 80,
82, 208, 546–47; in North Africa,
866, 975–76, 1131, 1590, 1925; in
North America, 356, 386, 451, 494,
791, 801–2, 1244–45, 1251; nuclear
tests in the Pacific, 465, 892, 1823–
24; opium, 741; in the Pacific, 1822–
23, 1983; Protestants, 518; in South
America, 699–702; in Southeast

Asia, 993–94, 1760, 1827–28; in
Southern Africa, 1141, 1233–34,
1577; Togoland, 592; Vichy, 518,
198, 993; in West Africa, 148–49,
263–64, 398, 591, 715, 898

French and Indian War, 801

French Equatorial Africa, 1105

French Polynesia, 465, 1820–24;
nuclear tests, 465; Tahitians, 1820–
24; Territory of, 1820

French Réunion Association, 1579

French Revolution, 87, 326, 1204,
1385, 1387, 1442, 1806

French West Africa, 1925

Friesland, 612–17; East, 612; Frisians,
612–17; North, 612; Province of,
612; West, 612

Frisia, 614

Frisian National Party, 615

Frisians, **612–17**; Friesland Region,
612; language, 613

Friuli, 618–23; Friulis, 618–23; Region
of, 618

Friuli League, 618

Friulis, **618–23**, 1599; Friuli Region,
618; language, 619

Friuli-Venezia Giulia, Region of, 618,
621, 672–73, 675

Frobisher Bay. *See* Iqaluit

Frobisher, Sir Martin, 796

Front for the Independence of South
Azerbaijan, 1771

Front for the Liberation of Québec
(FLQ), 1547

Front for the Liberation of South
Yemen (FLOSY), 705

Front for the Liberation of the Azores
(FLA), 223

Front for the Liberation of the
Enclave of Cabinda, 349–53;
Renovated FLEC, 349

Front for the Restoration of Unity
and Democracy (FRUD), 44–45

Frontier Congress (Pushtuns), 1539–
40

Fulanis, 396, 398, 714–15, 897, 1390;
Sokoto Caliphate, 715

About the Author

JAMES MINAHAN is a freelance writer and independent researcher living in Barcelona, Spain. His most recent books include *Miniature Empires: A Historical Dictionary of the Newly Independent States* (Greenwood, 1998) and *One Europe, Many Nations: A Historical Dictionary of European National Groups* (Greenwood, 2000).